*From Chivalry to Terrorism*

# Leo Braudy

## *From Chivalry to Terrorism*

Leo Braudy is University Professor and Bing Professor of English at the University of Southern California. He previously taught at Yale, Columbia, and Johns Hopkins. He has received a Guggenheim Fellowship as well as a Senior Scholar Fellowship from the National Endowment for the Humanities. He has been a fellow of the Rockefeller Foundation at the Villa Serbelloni in Bellagio, Italy, as well as a writer-in-residence at the American Academy in Rome. His book *Jean Renoir: The World of His Films* was a finalist for the National Book Award. Another of his books, *The Frenzy of Renown: Fame and Its History*, was a finalist for the National Book Critics Circle Award. He has written for *The New York Times, The Washington Post*, and *Harper's*. Mr. Braudy lives with his wife in Los Angeles.

Also by Leo Braudy

*The Frenzy of Renown: Fame and Its History*

*Native Informant: Essays on Film, Fiction, and Popular Culture*

*The World in a Frame: What We See in Films*

*Jean Renoir: The World of His Films*

*Narrative Form in History and Fiction: Hume, Fielding, and Gibbon*

*Norman Mailer* (editor)

*Shoot the Piano Player* (editor)

*Great Film Directors* (coeditor)

*Film Theory and Criticism* (coeditor)

# FROM CHIVALRY TO TERRORISM

*War and the Changing Nature of Masculinity*

LEO BRAUDY

*Vintage Books*

A DIVISION OF RANDOM HOUSE, INC.

NEW YORK

FIRST VINTAGE BOOKS EDITION, APRIL 2005


Published in the United States by Vintage Books, a division of Random House, Inc., New York, and simultaneously in Canada by Random House of Canada Limited, Toronto. Originally published in hardcover in the United States by Alfred A. Knopf, a division of Random House, Inc., New York, in 2004.

Vintage and colophon are registered trademarks of Random House, Inc.

Grateful acknowledgment is made to Warner Bros. Publications U.S. Inc. for permission to reprint excerpts from the song lyric "Remember My Forgotten Man" by Al Dubin and Harry Warren. Copyright © 1933 (Renewed) by Warner Bros. Inc. Excerpts from the song lyric "Strike Up the Band!," music and lyrics by George Gershwin and Ira Gershwin. Copyright © 1927 (Renewed) by WB Music Corp. All rights reserved. Reprinted by permission of Warner Bros. Publications U.S. Inc., Miami, FL 33014.

The Library of Congress has cataloged the Knopf edition as follows:
Braudy, Leo.
From chivalry to terrorism : war and the changing nature of masculinity / Leo Braudy.
p. cm.
Includes bibliographical references and index.
1. Men—Psychology. 2. Masculinity—History. 3. War—History. 4. War—Psychological aspects. 5. Chivalry. 6. Terrorism. I. Title.
HQ1090B7 2003
305.31—dc21 2003044600

Vintage ISBN: 0-679-76830-0

*Author photograph © Dorothy Braudy*
*Book design by Anthea Lingeman*

www.vintagebooks.com

Printed in the United States of America
10 9 8 7 6 5 4 3 2 1

*For Dorothy—*

*first reader, final*

*judge, constant support*

# Contents

## PART III. *From Armor to Personality*



## PART IV. *The Battle and the Sexes*



## PART V. *Heroes from Below*



## PART VI. *The Nineteenth Century: War and National Identity*

# *Introduction: Arms and Men*

As for the war,
That is for men. . . .
—Hector to Andromache, *The Iliad*

This book contains much about war and men at war, about wounds, weapons, and death, about soldiers and generals, strategy and tactics, the minute details of logistics and the fog of battlefield terror. But war is not its theme. Instead it is an effort to outline a history of the intertwined ideas of war and masculinity since the Middle Ages, especially, but not exclusively, focused on European and American history.

Near the end of the twentieth century the "crisis of masculinity" was seen in the chronic tunnel vision of the present as a phenomenon solely of our own time. On the one hand, boxing champion Mike Tyson was convicted of rape; on the other, newspapers reported drastically lowered sperm counts in various countries around the world. President George Bush promised to "kick Saddam Hussein's ass" for his aggression in Kuwait, while after the war the "Gulf War syndrome" became a national controversy: Were the crippling ailments of veterans caused by chemical and biological weapons, or were they the result of the psychological trauma of being in an unusual wartime situation? Were these soldiers, in other words, warriors injured by governmental deviousness or were they ultrasensitive products of an unmanly age? Male gym memberships were going up. Was it because an improved body image was the only available response to a menaced masculinity? Or because the birth control pill had deprived men of their natural function and all they could do was either hide their heads in shame or jump on the nearest treadmill? Into the new century, in discussions of subjects ranging from wars, natural disasters, and political controversies to tabloid stories like the severing of John Wayne Bobbit's penis by his aggrieved wife, a central national and even international drama was phrased invariably in terms of a dubious masculinity. At times modern masculinity was seen as ineffectual; at others, it was threatened and beset; at still others, aggressive and uncivilized.

Compared with the aroused national purpose in response to the terrorist attacks on New York and Washington in September 2001, many of these stories might seem to be the aimless trivia of a society looking for distraction. But that new threat highlighted the confrontation between one kind of war and another: a society of self-anointed holy warriors bent on preserving the exclusive purity of their culture versus a secular society of democratic inclusiveness committed to progress, technological change, and a world political system that was now finding a new set of heroes among policemen, firemen, and other civil servants.

Most of these stories came down to a solemnly familiar issue: What has happened to heroism? But all also invoke a challenge that lies behind that: What has happened to men? Questions of heroism shade imperceptibly into questions of masculinity, which in turn often point to a deep and ongoing confusion over where we are going as a society. Questions of femininity have been news since the advent of modern feminism in the 1960s and 1970s, but it is now also masculinity that attracts the attention of the national and international audience. Talk of the "glass ceiling" that looms for the aspiring female executive appears in the business section and stories about fairness issues for women appear throughout the paper. But they are now accompanied by other stories of the lost world of male privilege and new male roles in private and public life. That privilege certainly still exists, but many of its supposed beneficiaries nevertheless feel psychologically under siege, and from inside the castle at that. So when an otherwise anonymous young man dives into an icy river to rescue plane crash victims, or when policemen, firefighters, and ordinary citizens spring into action to save lives at the risk of their own, true masculinity appears to be momentarily reborn because men have acted immediately and instinctively to help others.

Some accounts ascribe this erosion in the traditional definition of masculinity to changes in the workplace that have undermined the importance of male labor; others to fear of feminism, feminization, and female power. Still other versions have targeted the effects of technology and mass production or the end of the Cold War.

The technological and cultural pressures on the boundaries and definitions of gender are unprecedented: surgery has been able to shape sexual characteristics in ways that were previously impossible; research into genetics, the mere idea of cloning, has opened up even more chasms in the idea of a stable personal identity. White-collar work and a service economy have expanded enormously, in many communities either replacing or surpassing the industrial and agricultural predominance of the past. At the same time, cultural dichotomies between masculine and feminine have also eroded. The anonymity of the Internet, along with the prevalence of morphing as a technological entertainment device, imply the unsettling possibility that age, gender, and ethnic masquerades that were previously only the fantasies of the scriptwriters of Jekyll-and-Hyde films may now be within the capacity of any eleven-year-old with a computer.

But these undeniably new forces that seem to have changed the nature of masculinity are not the whole story. Instead of considering this "crisis" as predominantly a question of this moment, I want to explore how modern assumptions about what constitutes masculinity, male behavior, and individual male identity have been gradually created over the last few centuries, and how understanding that development might allow us to step back and grasp more firmly what is happening now.

What is masculinity when it is much easier for the computer nerd to get a job and support a family than it is for a brawny factory worker? Who is the ideal man? Who is the common man? Is he muscular and physically powerful, or is he wily and able to map grand strategies? Does he wear a bulletproof vest or jogging clothes? Does he love women or other men or only himself? Is he a friend or a solitary hero? For a good part of the twentieth century, writers and thinkers have been interrogating anthropology, physiology, and primatology especially to answer such questions. Most of them look for some invariable root cause—in the chemical balance of brain circuits, in the activities of cavemen and anthropoid apes, or in unchanging "human nature" however defined—to explain the way we are *now*.

But throughout history the definitions of "man," "manly," and "masculine" have shifted in response to the prevailing social and cultural demands. Ideals, aspirations, and assumptions, conscious or not, are as much part of reality as physiology—and often the less understood they are, the stronger their influence. Instead of being a monolith, the mythical patriarchal society in which men enjoyed total power was a constantly mutating battleground, sometimes crisscrossed with sweeping charges and countercharges, sometimes dug into fixed positions with each square yard fought over ferociously. The medieval warriors in *The Song of Roland* can simultaneously slice an opponent entirely in half with one blow and weep copiously over a dying comrade in a manner that more tight-lipped definitions of masculinity reject. Similarly, the idea that male homosexuals make poor soldiers now seems "natural" to those who want to keep gays out of the military. Like previous efforts in the United States to keep out women, blacks, and, elsewhere, Jews, Gypsies, or other minority groups, the assumption is that they are "feminine." Because they lack the virile qualities necessary to engage the enemy, their mere presence will undermine camaraderie, loyalty, and the fighting will of the heterosexuals who stand in the trenches with them.

Yet many of these martial qualities believed to be so in need of protection are less natural or innate than they are based on ideas formulated in nineteenth- and twentieth-century Europe. The Sacred Band of Theban fighting men, made up entirely of homosexual lovers, were the pride of Greece in the fourth century B.C., until they were targeted and destroyed by the Macedonians under Philip in the Battle of Chaeroneia. Many other city-states similarly posted lovers to war together.* In the powerful armies of Alexander and later those of Rome, the ideal fighting man was often considered to be one of a loving pair who fought bravely for the eminently practical reason that, as Phaedrus argues in Plato's *Symposium,* he was fighting for the greatest glory, the admiration of his closest friend. Homoerotic and even homosexual relationships were a frequent aspect of warrior initiation and training in many military societies, including Sparta, Crete, and feudal Japan, as well as among spiritual warrior communities in monasteries. Even in the early fourteenth century, when the order of the Knights Templar was dissolved on charges of blasphemous and homosexual practices, no one suggested that their sins made them unfit or unable to be warriors. It was exactly their warrior prowess, together with their widespread banking interests, that made them such targets of persecution.

The historian Lynn Hunt, reviewing a history of women in western Europe, once remarked that "no one would write a such a book about 'the history of men' "—because "woman" is the anomalous historical category and men as such don't have to be explained. But neither masculinity nor femininity exists as a concept in itself. Each society has had its own specific definitions of manhood and what cultural values masculinity symbolizes. The fortitude to withstand pain, the ability to interpret a sacred text, the prowess with a special weapon, the willingness to seek revenge for a slight to family: each of these different local accents, often

* Elis and Boeotia were two of the other city-states that posted lovers (*erastes* and *eromenos*) as soldiers together. See Dover, *Greek Homosexuality* (192). The relation between Achilles and Patroklos is of course central to the *Iliad,* although their degree of physical relation has been often debated. Catharina Blomberg in *The Heart of the Warrior* says that homosexuality was "virtually the rule in feudal Japan."

stressed in special rituals, constitutes a particular culture's style of masculinity. Social anthropologists try to define those styles and political activists often seek to change them. Defining masculinity itself, in other words, must interweave with defining masculinity in relation to a multitude of factors, including the context of war, which for so much of human history and in the vast majority of human cultures has been the prime place to define oneself as a man.

Many contemporary psychologists and physiologists conclude that there is now little reason for men and women to behave differently solely because of their biological differences. But throughout the forty-thousand-odd years of human history, there has been a process of myth-making deriving from the imagined or real contrast between male and female. Defining "masculinity" and "femininity" as exemplary standards by which to measure normal human experience have thus been crucial ways for cultures to express their basic values. Masculinity particularly has occupied a position of special privilege because, in most such male-female distinctions, women are characterized as the victims of their biological nature as childbearers. Men, in supposed contrast, are free to escape from (or to express) biology, often in elaborate rituals of competition—for women, for possessions, for position. In this way, male violence, and the "masculinity" it suggests, is both regulated within a society and sanctioned against that society's enemies.

In what follows I will look at some crucial moments in this modern history of masculinity, especially as it has been redefined before, during, and in the aftermath of wrenching wars. Despite the millions of soldiers and civilians who have been wounded or died in war, still only a relative minority of human beings has actually experienced frontline battle. But war in all its protean forms—in news or in fiction, as propaganda or as history, fought by real people or by actors—has made its way inexorably into virtually every stage of learning, official and unofficial, permeating the conscious and unconscious minds of individuals, as well as the explicit and implicit values of whole cultures.

Just as ancient economies more often depended upon war than peace for their operation and expansion, wartime masculinity had an earlier evolution than its peacetime versions. But there is little reason to think that this connection between the history of masculinity and the history of violence, especially as expressed in war, is only something that happened in the primitive past and has now somehow stopped because we are more civilized or modern. The most appreciable difference between the past and the present may actually be the *greater* influence of cultural factors on the basic biology of clashing bodies because of the speed of events, along with their media presentation and representation—the interplay of artistic and literary representations of experience with experience itself. Who can think about World War II without the movies and novels set in it, or about the Gulf War without the way it played on television?

Men at war are on the front line of a more exacting and more one-sided definition of what it means to be a man than ever faces men at peace. By its emphasis on the physical prowess of men enhanced by their machines, by its distillation of national identity into the abrupt contrast between winning and losing, war enforces an extreme version of male behavior as the ideal model for all such behavior. Just as epic formulas focus on the hero with his undying fame, war focuses attention on certain ways of being a man and ignores or arouses suspicions about others. Wartime masculinity is a top-down and bottom-up effort to emphasize a code of masculine behavior more single-minded and more traditional than the wide array of circumstances and personal nature that influences the behavior of men in nonwar situations. With the end of a war—and perhaps with the ending of every war until women become an equal part of the military—an overriding and compelling story of friends and foes, violence and honor, often abruptly disintegrates or at least recedes into the background. The story of war, which until then has defined, tested, and guaranteed a specific form of masculinity, is gone, and other versions take the stage.

But the influence of war and its image of how men should be remains, however diminished. I was born in 1941, part of that generation called war babies, too young for the Korean War and too old, too married, or too antiwar for Vietnam. As a child, I went with my parents to camp on the battlefield at Gettysburg, where we slept under olive-drab shelter halves and dug latrines with army surplus foxhole spades. I was too young to feel the specific pressure of the battle, and the elaborate war memorials in the shape of triumphal arches made the scene seem even more sedate, but the name of Devil's Den still caused chills and roused my effort to imagine the sharpshooters amid the rocks. Nearby there was a tree with a perfectly semicircular curve in its trunk, where I was sure it had been grazed by a cannonball, and in a crevice between two boulders I found a shattered fragment of musket ball, itself only part of a perfect sphere.

That view of Gettysburg and that shattered piece of ancient ammunition were at least tangible evidence, even though half-obscured by the veil of history. But the less material shadow of war began early in my life as well, in the constant publicity of the Cold War, when I was collecting war cards from bubblegum packs, reading war comics, watching war movies, and in junior high school making elaborate lists of all the war novels I had read, carefully organized according to the war they were about and the branch of the service they focused on. When I was in the Boy Scouts, military drill and "policing the campsite" were part of our training. Later, in high school Latin, the words of war came early and often. *Pugno* was the model first-conjugation verb, *bellum* the model neuter noun, and Caesar's *Gallic War* the text we cut our teeth on. While in graduate school in the 1960s, I was against the Vietnam War but still preoccupied by it.

I therefore write simply as an ordinary modern man and citizen, steeped in a never-ending barrage of stories about men and war. It is the perceptions of war, how they trickle into the bloodstream of a culture and into the imaginations of individuals, that is my subject, the intertwined ideas and images that both set the scene for actual wars and later turn their meaning into precepts for how "real" men should live and be.

My prime interest here is not so much the necessities and the fatalities of masculinity and war as their contingencies and accidents. Both war and masculinity are ideas shaped by a long interwoven history. The usual way the question of which comes first is answered is to assume that masculinity is an essentially unchanging absolute and that war is a historical event: men are a certain way and therefore wars must occur. No matter how much we know of changes in masculine clothing, masculine attitudes, or masculine body types, there remains a sense of something invariable beneath the surface. Both nineteenth- and twentieth-century feminism frequently used this supposed bedrock masculinity as a backdrop for its own self-definition: women were made, not born; but men were always the same. Masculinity was thus often a stand-in for the power of patriarchy and other "unchanging" ideas. Or else, for the male supremacist, it was the stable standard in a corrupt world: as men are to women, so real men are to an effete and corrupt civilization.

These different and often contradictory uses to which masculinity has been put indicate something of its instability as a category of understanding. Even as both its partisans and its antagonists assert some immutable firmness, the shifting meanings of what it means to be a man seem more like a phantasmagoria of shapes that appear only to vanish. But these are contradictions only if one assumes some actual unity, some masculine purity from which the modern world has strayed. Part of the problem of dealing with two such general concepts as war and masculinity is the need to determine how to tell the story of their evolving meanings, both in themselves and in relation to each other.

To all appearances, the audience for war, or at least for the spectacle of war, is constantly expanding. Thousands of books have been written and are still being written about the techniques of warfare, as well as about the connection of warfare with politics and social change. Most are written to appeal to a general audience of war buffs and amateur historians who can fervently engage the enigmas of the past by digging into its details and second-guessing its generals. Increasingly in recent years, some members of this wide audience for war have also gone beyond armchair strategy to become participants. Weekend warriors are everywhere. Stockbrokers and plumbers fire multicolored paintballs at one another in war games, while elsewhere men dressed in period costumes and carrying highly polished replicas or authentic imitations of period armament refight some historical battle from the American Revolution or the Civil War—with just as much commitment as a scholarly researcher to discovering over which knoll at what time the original soldiers raised their now skeletal heads.

Wars not only end lives, revise political boundaries, and upset social values. They also require such a focus on one prime way of defining what a man is that the reaction against them is central to either the revision or the bolstering of traditional gender ideas. This result is less tangible and quantifiable than the destruction of lives, property, and institutions, but it is no less significant. Whenever war and competition occupy the national spotlight, the contours of masculinity are thrown into high relief. Usually the study of war's impact on social and political institutions tends to emphasize only one direction: something has been destroyed and now must be rebuilt or swept away. But considering these less material factors reveals the frequently ambiguous relation of historical causes and human effects between those who wish to continue wartime modes of manhood at any cost, and those who would like to see them vanish forever.

When I began this book I found myself reading deeply in the literature of war and warfare, until I could tell a hackbut from a howitzer, and then tramp over the battlefields at Marathon, Agincourt, the Little Big Horn, or the Somme, pointing out the fine points of both grand strategy and improvised tactics. But I soon discovered that most military history, with several distinguished exceptions, was not so much about men or war in general as about strategy and statistics, armament and uniforms. War was not the only place to hunt the most elusive ideas. It may be easier to visit battlefields and reconstruct strategy than it is to understand cultural attitudes, but both belong to history and both give a sense of how we have gotten to where we are now.

Although I came to be very interested in men at war, I was also more interested in the ways men at war had turned into men at peace, and what impact that change had on them *as men.* From its beginnings war has meant mobilization, not just materially but also culturally, not just to fight the enemy but also to define who the enemy is and what the enemy wants to take away. Modern war in particular is a total experience, for soldier and civilian alike, in which the variety and differences of normal life turn into a world in which everything fits together. In a war situation, all people—but especially men—are taken out of normal lives to face a wider world than they are used to. But at the same time, because a good portion of that world is called "the enemy," the expansion of perspective and geography turns into a constriction: your prime purpose is to kill. All questions, all ambiguities, all contradictions in what it means to be a man or a citizen are banished in the creation of the warrior.

Until comparatively recent times, war has been central to the writing of history. Of the two great Greek historians who stand at the fountainhead of Western history, Herodotus takes up a large proportion of his time with the Persian Wars and Thucydides writes entirely about the Peloponnesian War. In literature as well, the early poems of many Indo-European cultures are poems of warriors and war. The most familiar to Europeans and Americans are the two Greek poems of wartime and postwar return to domesticity, the *Iliad* and the *Odyssey.* The poems may have been composed in the eighth century B.C., and they refer to events that may have happened in some form in the thirteenth century B.C. But this is hardly the beginning of a tradition, for some seven hundred years before the presumed date of the Trojan War appeared the Mesopotamian epic of Gilgamesh, whose hero, the warrior king of the city of Uruk, meets in the forest his comrade and mirror self, the natural warrior Enkidu. So too, after the religious poetry of the Vedas (which were first written down c. 1500 B.C.), the early poetry of India also includes two war epics: the *Mahabharata* (c. 400 B.C.), seven times as long as the *Iliad* and the *Odyssey* combined, which tells the story of the warrior-hero Arjuna; and the *Ramayana,* which climaxes in a battle between Rama and Ravana.

At least in light of what texts have come down to us, the Asian tradition is somewhat different from the Indo-European. Unlike Indo-European literature, Chinese, Korean, and Japanese literature do not "begin" with stories of war, although the Confucian *Book of Odes*

(c. 1000–600 B.C.) does include some poems about the hardships of war, and one of the classic texts of military strategy is Sun Tzu's *The Art of War* (c. fifth century B.C.). Even in the Heian era in Japan (A.D. 794–1185) in which the *bushi* class of hired warriors rose to fight the court's battles, great literature is represented by Lady Murasaki's story of court intrigue, the *Tale of Genji*. Only later, at a time comparable to the European Middle Ages, under the warrior rule of the shoguns and their samurai retainers, does a warrior-oriented literature begin to develop.

The fortunes of Western epic heroism are thus particularly tied to war, sometimes in a grand defeat and sometimes in victory, but always triumphs that are inevitably connected to the way war destroys men but makes their memories last—Aeneas, Beowulf, Roland, the heroes of the Icelandic sagas, the warriors of the Celts and the Vikings. Down into the Renaissance, the military hero seems to reign virtually supreme, until John Milton in the seventeenth century condemns epic military heroism in *Paradise Lost* to praise a different kind of hero:

*Not sedulous by nature to indite*
*Wars, hitherto the only Argument*
*Heroic deem'd chief mastery to dissect*
*With long and tedious havoc fabl'd Knights*
*In Battles feign'd; the better fortitude*
*Of Patience and Heroic Martyrdom*
*Unsung.*

War still goes on, but *Paradise Lost* signals a significant eruption of other streams of thought and feeling, which will interact with military masculinity and inexorably change its shape.

Although I have been already using the word "history" freely, I want to open rather than close the question of whether masculinity can be said to have a history. Obviously, there is no clear and distinct delineation of stages by which the nature of masculinity has changed (or perhaps even "evolved") over the centuries. There are always revivals and revampings. New forms may exist simultaneously with older ones, and even ancient styles may still remain, caught in amber. The history of masculinity, like the history of many cultural attitudes as well as physiological responses, is a history of changes by which previously successful ways of engaging the world become increasingly irrelevant to new conditions. Nevertheless they often persist, even when their usefulness is gone, and masculine styles that had been beneficial to the larger community turn out to be destructive.

Much of the writing about war has focused almost exclusively on the search for causes. Carl von Clausewitz was a Prussian soldier who fought in the Napoleonic Wars and was deeply affected by their strategy, scale, and tactical confusion. His posthumously published *On War* had a tremendous impact on military strategy and attitudes toward war from the nineteenth to the twenty-first century. Even though he fully acknowledged the chaos of the battlefield itself, his most famous dictum—that war is political conflict continued through other means—assumes the prime importance of a political and military history in which the acts of monarchs, councils, parliaments, generals, and armies follow one another in a clear causal order.

I will look instead at the interplay of factors—the changing nature of the methods and goals of war, how the growth of the nation-state affects the identity of men as citizens in both war and peace, the advancing technology that undermines the individual honor to be gained in war, the changing relation between the sexes that by the twentieth century began to question the absolute division of male and female—to name only the most prominent. I have tried to paint on a broad canvas while still being mindful of detail and differences between nations, looking for similarities, while wanting to respect the often inchoate way changes occur, how even as we go forward we carry much of the past with us.

The relation between war and masculinity is such a vast subject that here I can only look to highlight a few themes and areas and to suggest however imperfectly and incompletely a variety of relationships without assuming any single causality. Depending on the shape of the argument, certain major issues, figures, and events may be treated breezily, while others require greater length. Those familiar with individual wars and historical periods may find my account of some of them sparse and lacking nuance, although I hope that the context in which they are placed will prove illuminating. Details are important and have their place in what follows, but it is also the larger patterns that interest me. Clearly, things happen at somewhat different times in different countries, whether it is the organization of an army based on regimental units or women receiving voting rights, and nothing moves forward evenly into the future without setbacks and diversions.

To consider war and masculinity historically involves some uncomfortable detachment, especially from those who suffered and died. But I hope that looking at longer movements of ideas and feelings beyond the lives of individuals will supply some fruitful perspective on dilemmas and confusions that are too often considered either matters of our own making or attitudes we have inherited from a generation or so before. I have therefore organized the book in a basically historical structure. After a consideration of seemingly ahistorical issues like biology (including testosterone) and anthropology (the tribal rituals of male initiation), I begin with the European Middle Ages and take the story through the events of September 11, 2001.

Although readers will, I trust, find much that is new to them here, this book adds little that is unfamiliar to professional historians working in these different periods. It is primarily meant for people like myself, curious amateurs who have had the relationship of war and masculinity dinned into them, and want to see to what extent the dynamics of that supposedly implacable duo may be more complicated than a matter of biology and supposedly innate behavior. In fact, the belief in the instinctual basis of aggression goes back to nineteenth-century assumptions about race and gender that in other ways have been totally outdated or at least heavily disputed. Then, the connection between visible racial difference and a whole array of other differences seemed obvious. Now, with the Human Genome Project, we are told that there is no genetic basis for the concept of race. How comparable might be our attitudes toward less visible differences between male and female? Obviously there is a biological basis for the concept of male/female sexual difference, but wherein do those differences lie, how directly do they affect the behavior of individuals, groups, and nations, how "necessary" are they?

I write not to settle such questions but to dig into them and try to unravel long-standing assumptions about the necessary relation between war and—not men, but masculinity. In that sense it is an amateur history: a book not of settled opinions but of exploration, a work of synthesis and analysis, and, I should admit immediately, the work of someone fascinated with the history of events and the details of everyday life, as well as the history of emotions and attitudes embodied in literature and the arts. Like my previous book, *The Frenzy of Renown,* which looked at the history of fame in Western culture, it deals with a topic that everyone has opinions about, but for a long time few investigated in any historical context, although that situation has changed in the last decade or so, as works with "masculinity" in their title began to appear with greater and greater frequency, each scouring an area of its own.

Without trying to cover this growing literature in any exhaustive way,

I seek here instead to sketch the outlines of a general history. Unlike the topographies of battlefields or the tactical reports of commanders, masculinity belongs at the intersection of a wide variety of evidence and phenomena, in particular the seemingly inalienable facts of biology and how it expresses itself in time, the difference between the feelings of individual men and groups of men, the immediate response to experience and the meditations and policy that go into making war. In simple terms, this is the tension between the hard facts of biology and weaponry and the less hard-edged, more fluid history of what it means to be a man through the centuries.

To explore this tension I try in what follows to juxtapose questions that are not usually connected: sexuality and technology, citizenship and racism, war making and the way men have defined themselves or been defined by others. Like gender and sexuality, military history has often suffered by being considered in isolation from social reality and cultural context—as if there were little connection between war and the rest of society. But in Europe and the Americas, especially from the Middle Ages through the theater of European war established in the seventeenth century and into the mass wars of the twentieth century, war and masculinity are two mutually dependent myths, merging the technological future, when men would become perfect, with the nostalgic past, when they already were. Perhaps the force of these myths is shifting once again in a world of both global economies and political terrorism that crosses national boundaries to create new opportunities and new dreads. But without understanding the historical and cultural pressures on the way men see themselves and are seen by others, without discerning how contrary masculine imperatives are shaped by individuals into the armatures of their own identities either in alliance with or in opposition to larger institutions, we will not be able to escape the fatal equation of war and masculinity to discern what is valuable and what is lacking in their interweaving. I am therefore very dubious about the claim that all masculinity is the same, either across history or in a particular era. I want to explore instead the moments where different kinds of history—political, economic, social—intersect, and masculinity becomes a land to explore rather than a foregone assumption.

Is the true soldier, for example, the stiff-upper-lip stoic, or is he the ranter who, like the ancient Anglo-Saxon or the nineteenth-century frontiersman, hurled elaborate insults before fighting? Is he Oliver Cromwell's plain buff-coated captain, whose language was as straightforward as his outfit, or is he a medal-bedecked dandy from the Napoleonic

Wars? Why, for example, has this "crisis of masculinity" occurred now, in the wake of an exhausted Cold War?

The distant solar system of the past throws off a variety of signals. Some, the heavily documented events and individuals, are strong, and their obvious signals may drown out the weak ones, whose sources and significance are harder to detect. But these less clear signals, in connection with other knowns and unknowns, are made stronger by their place in the array. Similarly, like every other significant aspect of culture, the idea of masculinity sends at times stronger and at times weaker signals. In some ages it may be a source of constant argument, in others assumed and ignored, and it is intriguing to wonder why the shift and why the change. Masculinity is a dynamic system rather than an invariable pattern, and it is more valuable to ask what is mutating and what is unchangeable in masculinity than to assume that it has always been as we now know it.

*Part I*

# MEN AND MASCULINITY

# REMEMBER MY NAME

Like the elephant sought by the six blind men, or the electron that changes position depending on when it is observed, masculinity must be mapped rather than merely discovered. Not only is it elusive, but there are also those with vested interests in keeping it monolithic and mysterious. Is masculinity, for example, entirely identifiable with patriarchy? That is, does masculinity in any age refer primarily to the power over groups considered to be weaker and more marginal to society—groups usually composed of women but also of men considered to be at best incomplete or imperfect, and at worst barely human? Certainly there have been many men, both in and out of public power, who believed and still believe this. But how was their own masculinity learned? Did it come directly from the experience of having the particular kind of male body their culture approved? Or are there a whole variety of preliminary and partial models, each with its own divergence from the grand norm and each with its contradiction of it?

One clue might be in the language of masculinity. Where do the words designating the male come from? What do they mean? In the West at least, this language has been heavily influenced by both the language of wartime masculinity (or fashioned in contrast to the language used to describe, say, the saint or the sage) and the language of social class. Man existed long before "masculine," a word that first appears in English in the Middle Ages as a French import used to designate not specific masculine characteristics so much as the general difference between male and female, whether in plants, animals, or human beings. Then, with the Norman conquest and the adoption of Norman-French as the standard for all educated discourse, "masculine" became a more frequent usage.*

"Man," as the older term, has a more tangled history. It goes back to an Indo-European root meaning "earth" that descends equally into "human" and "humus." There are two Latin words for man: *vir* and *homo. Homo,* related to the Greek word for "one" or "single," is the more general term—man in the abstract. It descends into the Romance languages fairly directly: *uomo* (Italian), *homme* (French), *hombre* (Spanish), and the impersonal pronoun in French, *on. Vir* in contrast refers to a man as defined by specific male qualities, and is the root of "virile" as well as "virtue," an association that prompted Plutarch in his biography of Coriolanus to complain that the Romans so valued military prowess that they made it stand for all human virtues, even though it refers to only one of them. *Arma virumque cano,* says Virgil at the beginning of the *Aeneid,* his epic poem of the founding of Rome: "I sing of arms and the man."

Unlike "masculine" and "feminine," which come from Latin, the immediate origin of "man" in English is Germanic. Like "masculine," "man" exists not as a concept in itself but amid an array of other possibilities: man as distinguished from boy, man as distinguished from woman, man as distinguished from beast, man as distinguished from demon, man as distinguished from gods and God. And perhaps the English embrace of the German *man* owes something to its similarity to the Latin *manus,* commonly "hand" but also a Roman legal term for the authority that a husband has over his wife.†

Much of human ritual and social organization, from the earliest tribes to contemporary societies, is preoccupied with reaffirming these

* "Masculine" comes from the Latin *masculinus,* which is itself a diminutive form of the adjective *mas,* meaning "male."

† To this list might be added man as distinguished from eunuch, to account for the Romanian word for man, *barbat* (bearded).

distinctions—perhaps suggesting a deep-rooted human (or masculine) fear that they are arbitrary enough to be constantly in danger of erosion or forfeit. Like all distinctions, they are especially clouded in times like war, when events have pushed people, families, tribes, kingdoms, and nations to the edge. In this sense, much social ritual—initiation, marriage, preparation for war—is exorcism: the casting out of what is feared and the affirmation of what is desired. At these moments, the normal fuzziness and uncertainty of boundaries, the lack of sharp differences between aspects of human nature, have to be policed and polarized for fear that otherwise they will collapse entirely.

Contrary to the argument that patriarchal society consistently values the masculine in any polarized distinction, "man" is not always the superior term in all groups. Latin writers often used *homo* to refer to a man who is somehow not free, whether socially subordinate or otherwise dependent—a meaning retained in the modern use of "homage," which originally referred to the feudal ceremony of allegiance of a vassal to his lord. Similarly, one of the earliest uses of *man* in Old English was to designate a subordinate, a vassal, even a servant, as in the phrase "my man," and the early frequency of a phrase like "free man" implies that perhaps men in general were not free. It took some time before all men were said to be created equal, and it is not until the eighteenth century that "man" was used to refer to some abstract idea of human nature in general. Until then, the positive connotations of "man" referred almost exclusively to the behavior (often military) of a man of rank, an aristocrat, as in the suggestive relation in German between *heer* (army) and the honorific *herr* (lord, master).

It may seem to be an occasion for obvious Freudian mockery that a frequent Anglo-Saxon word for male human beings as well as animals is *wæpned* (weaponed). But even though *wæpen* could also mean "penis," we should remember that only a particular class of men had the wealth and the social sanction to carry weapons, and so the interplay between the words for "man," the words for "man of high rank," and the words for "warrior" has a long history. Thus in the eighth-century heroic poem *Beowulf,* written in Anglo-Saxon but telling the story of a sixth-century hero of the Danes, *man* appears in such compounds as *feond mancynnes* (enemy of mankind), while what translators usually call "manly behavior" or "heroic prowess" is referred to as *eorlic ellen* (the power of an earl, or noble) while "manly deeds" are *eorlscipe efnde* (the doings of earlship). Similarly, in *The Song of Roland,* an eleventh-century poem written about events of the eighth century, when a knight of Charlemagne's host fights with particular bravery, he is described as being *en guise de baron,* a phrase usually translated as "valiantly" or "heroically," but which literally means "in the manner of a baron." Some centuries before, *baron* had been the French word that generally distinguished the male from the female. By the eleventh century, in a process similar to that undergone by the words for "knight," *baron* appears as an actual social title for those high-ranking warriors who (as in *The Song of Roland* ) support a higher-ranking lord or king. The title, of course, still remains in English, long since divested of its exclusively warlike implications. In Spanish it has gone back down the social scale to survive as *varón*—a man in general.*

Apart from the words themselves, much of the talk about what is "true" masculinity has also historically been tinged with, even steeped in, nostalgia for a lost masculinity. *Gilgamesh* begins by describing buildings of the past, "which no latter-day king, no man alive can equal." Even within the story of the *Iliad* itself, Nestor, the oldest of the Achaeans, frequently refers to the much greater warriors who walked the earth when he was younger, and he tries to instruct his not-so-heroic present-day comrades (heroic enough to Homer's audience and to us) in the fundamentals of battle tactics. With a similar longing after past greatness, Chaucer's Knight in *The Canterbury Tales,* who has come so quickly to the pilgrimage from war that his clothes are still smeared with the rust of his chain mail, tells a tale set in ancient Athens, when truly heroic knights fought for honor and the love of women.

One important component of masculinity thus embodies a myth of historical connection with past models and exemplars, while another looks to a future that will be different. As the Greek hero had to die young in the midst of battle in order to be considered a hero in song and legend, so one powerful form of masculinity is perpetually nostalgic in its judgments and standards. All the good men are already dead. That's how we know they're good. They may be dead, but their names and the masculinity they embodied live on to inspire future generations, and to ensure that other young, unmarried boys, who are not yet part of the settled social order, will go to war in the effort to be real men.

To a certain extent this is not entirely propaganda. From the impoverished medieval knight going to war to win estates and possessions by cap-

* As *baron* goes up the scale of social and cultural value, another early word for "man," the Old Norse *karl* (Old English *ceorl*) goes down, to become "churl" by Shakespeare's time. Compare the change from "villein" (a peasant serf ) to "villain."

turing enemy nobles for ransom, to the immigrant and ghetto-raised young men whose time in the army enables them to get an education and status that could almost never have been achieved outside, the military and especially wartime situations—with their immediate rewards for battlefield heroics and cunning tactics—have facilitated class change. In both hierarchic and democratic societies, the melting pot of war, defined by its total difference from peacetime stasis, has offered an outlet for otherwise stifled ambition. Periods of war thus often give rise to eras of social movement and change, and war's crucible of possibility has often engendered different ways of being a man, on and off the battlefield, even while it seeks to confirm the values of the past.

As the prime way of being a man, military masculinity thereby can assume the double aspect of both future goal and lost ideal, both for critics who are nostalgic for the past and for those who reject it entirely. Already in the late third century B.C. the Roman playwright Plautus, drawing on Aristophanes, had defined the stock type of the *miles gloriosus,* the blowhard old soldier constantly living in a fantasy of his past exploits. Shakespeare in his Henry plays splits such a character in two—the hot-blooded chivalric knight Harry Hotspur and the rollicking old campaigner Sir John Falstaff, both styles of military masculinity that are finally superseded, for better or worse, by the hard-edged pragmatism of Prince Hal, the future Henry V.

Whether as criticism or idealization, the presence of prior types of military masculinity in art and literature also implies a sense of generational change, especially when the wars in question are civil wars that divide families. The prewar and the postwar define a chasm that lasts long after the generations who actually participated are dead and gone. In the second half of the seventeenth century, both the French and the English looked back over the divide of their civil wars at the earlier part of the century as if it were an entirely different world.

A psychoanalytic perspective might call this conflict of male generations oedipal, and thereby a "natural" part of the male character. But such oedipal periods in culture are often brought into being by the experience of war. During war, personal honor comes at the expense of the enemy, but in times of peace it is the previous generation that often must pay. In the third of Shakespeare's *Henry VI* plays, which deal with the civil and foreign wars of fifteenth-century England, he dramatizes the inhumanity of the conflict specifically through an image of the clash of generations. In the midst of battle, Henry VI sits despairingly on a molehill and observes first, as the stage directions say, "a Son who hath Killed his father" and then "a Father that hath killed his son." Both enter bearing the bodies of people they thought were their enemies and then discover to be their kin. With less straightforward symbolism, the heroic plays of both England and France in the later seventeenth century, in the wake of the Thirty Years' War and the English Civil Wars, often feature conflicts between energetic sons and repressive fathers over questions of honor and duty. Likewise, after World War II, American westerns are shot through with conflicts between fathers and sons (and occasionally fathers and daughters). *Red River* (made in 1946–47 but not released until 1948), directed by Howard Hawks, for example, explicitly presents the conflict between father John Wayne and his adopted son Montgomery Clift as mediated by Clift's Civil War experience. Both are good with their guns, but Wayne's more brutal pioneering traits must be softened by war and history into Clift's more vulnerable, sympathetic—and successful—ones. Just as Hotspur in *Henry V* embodies an apolitical aggressiveness that must be superseded by Henry's new version of the warrior king, so in *Red River*, Wayne's outmoded, domineering, but still nostalgically treasured masculinity finally has to reach some accommodation with the ways of the new generation embodied by Clift.

# THE LANGUAGE OF THE BODY

(What do you see when you turn out the light?)
I can't tell you, but I know it's mine.

—John Lennon and Paul McCartney,
"I Get By with a Little Help from My Friends"

The prime reason many might think it unlikely that masculinity has changed over time is the seemingly irreducible fact of the male body. Until new weaponry and social change brought women into military ranks, war was generally fought by men, whose physical nature seemed especially suitable for its hardships. Male bodies are generally taller and more robust than female, with longer, thicker muscles, and larger lungs, heart, and limb-to-body ratios, as well as the inability to become pregnant and thereby sacrifice valuable fighting time. In a common metaphor of male-female difference, men are hard and women are soft: "matter too soft a lasting mark to bear," wrote Alexander Pope in "To a Lady," his poem on the characters of women. Pope himself was about four-foot-six and suffered for most of his life from numerous ailments, including tuberculosis of the spine. So the seemingly absolute distinction between male and female in his hands carries an ironic charge:

being soft, women were changeable and malleable, but also complex, while the hard, distinct male remained inflexibly the same.

But in less self-aware contexts this robust male hardness and imperviousness to change is itself unchangingly symbolized by the upright sword, the obelisk, and the column—all too easily accepted as figures for the aggressive and ever-ready penis, the most immediately obvious physiological difference between male and female, the most basic "fact" of all. In the imagery of the absolute biological distinction between male and female, affirmed by the popular use of Freudian formulas, the ritual phallus, the phallic symbol, and the actual penis are one and the same.*

Two contrasting views of masculinity therefore dominate the contemporary discussion. One emphasizes a strictly biological causality: men are men and women are women because of their physical traits and their genetic makeup. The other argues the almost exclusive "social construction" of masculinity and femininity: men are men and women are women because culture makes them that way. The first, "natural," explanation assumes Pope's formulation of the stable male and the changing female, but turns the moral weight of the distinction against men: throughout history, it is claimed, violence and brutality—whether individual, freelance, guerrilla, or organized—have remained the basic characteristics of the human race. The other view reverses this male dominance to argue that masculinity depends culturally upon femininity for self-definition. As the French scientist and philosopher Elisabeth Badinter writes, "when femininity changes—generally when women try to redefine their identity—masculinity is destabilized" (9). Yet even though this second kind of analysis emphasizes social forces in order to attack the history of a patriarchal society in which visible male power was assumed to be part of the natural order, it also often claims a biological basis: the ovum always has X chromosomes, while the sperm has X or Y. When it is X, the child will be XX, female; when it is Y, the child will be XY, male. The "natural" sex of all infants—or in computer language, the default sex—is female. Adapting this biological fact as metaphor (and it certainly is useful for making fun of the biblical story of Eve being fashioned from Adam's rib), theorists of gender difference have argued that maleness is therefore a kind of evolutionary afterthought, and the masculine urge to power a compensation for the fact of being biologically secondary. The

* In some cultures, columns, obelisks, and the earth-nurtured trees from which they spring were originally symbols of female power and authority.

female priority in the sexual development of the embryo becomes the metaphoric foundation for the assertion of female superiority, just as male physical superiority had in the patriarchal context been assumed to imply political, social, and intellectual superiority as well.

Actually, it turns out that the biological analysis itself is somewhat incomplete. With the recent discoveries of genes for the development of both male and female both sexual characteristics, it has been shown that the scientific basis for this metaphor of the female bent of all life (and the male aberration) needs some adjustment, or perhaps abandonment.

Even in the face of a more accurate scientific understanding of the processes of sexual differentiation, and widespread scientific criticism of the argument from chromosome makeup, however, there is still an overwhelming popular desire to believe that cultural and social distinctions between male and female have some simple biological root—particularly so that the problems of modern society (war, aggression, violence) can be attributed to something innate and permanent in male nature. Although it existed on a small scale before, this desire is part of a characteristic recent upending of the past celebrations of war and the epic hero. Because war is considered to be either an instinctual part of (male) human nature or a barbaric relic of the dim past, writers on both the political right and the political left have tried to find its immediate cause either in biology or in ancient psychological compulsions, for example, fear of predators. In the writings of Konrad Lorenz and Robert Ardrey that became popular after World War II, for example, the human race, i.e., men, was considered to be innately aggressive. It was a point of view suitable for the Cold War, stigmatizing any effort toward peace as, again, "unnatural." Even now the word "testosterone" still persistently appears in both learned discussions (outside of biochemistry) and comic monologues as an all-purpose explanation for any kind of masculine aggressiveness.

Many of those who search for the causes of war making entirely in either the shadowy necessities of primitive behavior or a hardwired male physiology tend to argue with grim fatality that war can never be eradicated. To them, any change in either masculine identity or weapons technology is merely the window dressing for an unchanging collection of ineradicable urges. But instead of focusing on how masculinity has necessarily given rise to war, I want to look at what war has done to the idea of masculinity, to treat masculinity not just as an invariable physiology but as a response to history as well.

The hormone testosterone was isolated just over sixty years ago, not long after estrogen. Its discovery was part of a scientific drive to determine the biochemical "essence" of male and female that in its wackier phase included therapies like the injection of dog urine or the grafting of monkey testicles to cure impotence. It is tempting to think that this scientific quest to explain complex social behaviors by a direct physical causality received added urgency from the just-ended World War I and the unsettled internal climate before World War II. It was a useful tool either to justify, and thereby explain away, the male tendency toward war and violence, or to furnish a scientific basis for those social scientists who sought ways to modify that behavior. Ever since, there have been popular writers and (fewer and fewer) scientists who have made much the same argument.

As recent studies have shown, however, the connection between testosterone and aggression is hardly straightforward. The vast majority of the scientific explorations of the biochemical basis of sexuality and sexual differentiation have documented the relative failure of biological determinism on the hormonal level to explain, predict, or modify immediate individual behavior (like attacking a rival), let alone more abstract social behavior (like waging war). Historically, counterexamples to the iron link between testosterone and aggression abound: Narses, the sixth-century Byzantine general, for example, was a eunuch from the royal household of Justinian who went on to defeat the Gothic tribes and regain control of Italy. Similarly, modern statistical studies have shown that castrating sex offenders is no guarantee against recidivism, and that soldiers in battle, as well as most aggressive thirteen-year-olds, actually have lower than average testosterone levels.

Testosterone alone, in other words, does not cause aggression, nor does its absence invariably imply a lack of manliness. In fact, some studies have concluded that testosterone *deficiency* is more often associated with aggression than is testosterone excess. When some men have had their testosterone lowered artificially or by castration, their aggression actually *increases.* Meanwhile, other studies indicate that it is not testosterone alone that needs to be investigated but its combination with serotonin levels in the brain, since the combination of high testosterone with low serotonin seems to be an indicator for aggression. Thus, to draw a social conclusion from biological data, it may even be a felt *lack* of masculinity that more often generates hypermasculine activity.

At the very least, if the relation between an individual's biochemistry and his behavior is neither clear nor direct, the general relation between biochemical fact and social event is an even greater leap. So far, we have remained inside the male body, but what then about the relation of these facts to human beings in interaction? Primate groups have been studied in an effort to associate biochemistry with group behavior. But the conclusions thus far seem to be that even among rats, spiders, and jellyfish there is an astonishing diversity of modes of sexual determination, and that the effect of sex hormones in any animal group with even a minimally complicated social structure is difficult to establish with any precision. To complicate the picture, it turns out that it is not the leaders of primate groups who have a combination of high testosterone and low serotonin, but the disgruntled followers. And there is no absolute division between testosterone for men and estrogen for women. Both sexes have both hormones, although in different amounts. Testosterone, in fact, is converted to estrogen in the brain, and some researchers have hypothesized that teenage aggressiveness, for example, which characterizes both sexes, may be "caused" by estrogen and testosterone in combination.

Biological difference, male and female, is consequently not directly equivalent to masculine and feminine, unless a lot of crucial details are left out. Sex, in other words, is not the same as gender. The causalities of the body, eagerly seized upon in a scientific age as ways to understand male and female, are scarcely so simple or direct. Biochemistry may initiate behavior, but environment reinforces it and keeps it going. There are other signals—a mother's smile, a ritual dance, or a heroic story—that encourage individual expressions of both male and female behavior. Communal life in all its aspects, the life of others, is as much a stimulant as are hormones. In the branch of recent developmental research that emphasizes upbringing, it appears that such factors as absentee parents and brutality actually have the potential of altering brain chemistry. The common computer metaphor of the hardware of genetic predisposition and the software of cultural setting (so similar to Marx's distinction between economics as base reality and culture as mere superstructure) needs to be dropped in favor of one that emphasizes a complex reciprocity.

Bodies may be grouped as male or female. But what constitutes that difference has been a varying assumption and argument for centuries. These formulations of the difference between male and female are more often attitudes than absolute facts, a series of variations on biological possibilities. There are biological structures that influence behavior, and there are cultural settings that modify biology. Christine de Pizan begins her fifteenth-century work in praise of great women, *The Book of the City of Ladies*, by admitting that there are differences between male and female size and strength that make it seem that women cannot be heroic. But she then goes on to show how many women have successfully challenged those ostensibly inflexible norms to become rulers and even warriors themselves.

Cultural evolution moves much more quickly than genetic evolution. Despite what the movies tell us, the bodies of the past aren't merely the bodies of the present wearing funny clothes. Important changes have occurred in perception, in feelings, and even in biological makeup. Both men and women are generally larger than they were in the past, and the age of first menstruation has varied with nutrition, climate, and perhaps cultural attitudes toward marriage. But we can see the resemblances amid the changes, just as the look and biochemistry of the adult retains—even as it has modified and transformed—the genetic inheritance of the child. The question is thus not whether testosterone or other male biological predispositions play any role in masculine behavior, but how much weight we should give to the seeming timelessness of human physical makeup and how much to the cranks and crotchets of human history.

Sociobiologists emphasize that our genes speak through our actions. But if so, the language they use is the language of our history, our surroundings, and our individual circumstances. Perhaps in terms of gene pool survival, it was a bad choice for some of the brightest minds of the Christian era, say, to choose to become celibate priests and monks. But it was often a choice rooted both in a complex cultural history and in particular events (for example, the youngest son of an impoverished family who could not inherit property or find any other family financial support). As the psychologist Leslie Brothers has argued, the brain interposes itself between the senses and the world and continually edits them in accordance with attitudes and ideas it has learned.

The brain is thus not an isolated perceiver of the world. It exists in and responds actively to a social context. On the level of sexuality, for example, it is obvious that what will stimulate arousal in men or women has tremendous cultural and individual variations, even within the same family. The physiology of the arousal may always be the same, yet no specific response to any of that multitude of stimuli can be called innate. Emphasizing the cultural and historical aspect of gender difference has the virtue of at least complicating that relationship, even though its definition of masculinity may imply men are passive vessels of history and culture, much as the biochemical view tends to make them slaves of their physical makeup.

. . .

Peace is often complex in its flowering of pacifist warriors, militant women, and other category-crossing character types. But wartime in human civilization has generally fostered an implicit and often explicit polemic about the difference between male and female, along with the similarly necessary single-mindedness of its view of men. In 1947, S. L. A. Marshall, the military journalist and chief historian of the European Theater of Operations, published *Men Against Fire: The Problem of Battle Command in Future War*, a book commissioned by the U.S. Army to assess the battlefield experience of World War II and to see what lessons had been learned for the training of future soldiers. In it he addressed what he called "the most complex topic in the military art—man himself as a figure on the field of combat," and emphasized the need for camaraderie and social connection on the battlefield, because "the belief in push-button war is fundamentally a fallacy" (26, 19). More than fifty years later, fed on a steady diet of movie special effects and computer war games, we may think his analysis is outmoded. But as the Gulf War and the war in Afghanistan showed, and acts of terrorism confirm, even in the technological age smart bombs have their limits, and war is still primarily a combat of bodies.

War thus emphasizes not only the presence of the human body, historically male, strained to its physical limits, but also a whole complex of expectations about how that body should act. Most of us are physiologically born male or female, but within those broad parameters we learn to act like a man or a woman from our family and community. The story of development within the womb differs from the story of what happens after birth. As soon as birth occurs, as Mary Douglas and other anthropologists have pointed out, the body is seen as a battleground for the social forces that produce it.

While *male* biology may, depending on the degree of scientific sophistication, be described in terms of seemingly quantifiable physical norms, *masculinity* is a more unstable concept and can rarely be defined once and forever. There are too many elements of performance (and performance anxiety) in its presentation. War may make masculinity more single-minded. But what constitutes male dress, let alone male behavior, shifts constantly throughout history, as do the rituals of becoming a man or going to the men's room. What a great change it must have been when the penis sheath or the loincloth was invented! Like the fig leaf in Eden, they allowed a man to conceal the crucial physiological change that might otherwise expose his robust show as an actual shrinking fear.

Immutable and all-determining biology may seem to be a more baseline truth than a social category like masculinity, but if we consider the varying balance of both "male" and "female" hormones in everyone, it seems clear that sexuality is not a polarized opposition but a continuum, a template with innumerable individual variants and possibilities. Biology, in other words, is not the opposite of culture; it has its own history. In any species, the variable number of eggs created and the need for the egg and the sperm to travel demonstrate that the neat atemporal account featured in textbooks only loosely reflects the complexities of real reproduction and growth, which are more like an adventure story, in which neither the steps along the way nor the end itself can be taken for granted.

The old terms of the argument over what created a person used to be nature versus nurture. In current thinking, it is the relation between the genotype, the genetic inheritance of an organism or group, and the phenotype, the observable physical or biochemical characteristics of a particular individual. Because the genotype is only a collection of possibilities, it is never totally expressed in the phenotype, although any future growth remains sensitive to the initial genetic makeup. Depending on the environment, latent, recessive, and inhibitive genes may never appear. Even on the genetic level, then, the expression of individuality must respond to environmental influences. Without that environment the preexisting gene pool has no means to come into existence. The expression of specific physical traits, such as stature or blood type, or the ability to leap tall buildings in a single bound, are based on a vital and individually unique interaction between genetic and environmental influences that change constantly. Otherwise, evolution is an empty concept, and we would all act, look, and be the same as our ancestors.*

* "Penetrants" is the technical word for the ability of genes to express themselves in the phenotype. The phenotype is also called the "morphotype," although some scientists reserve that word, with its root meaning of shape, for observable physical features, for example, speed at running.

# INITIATION: THE FIRST WOUND

Physiological and biochemical factors are therefore only the beginning of trying to define maleness, let alone masculinity. The physical body exists in a social context that shapes how it is perceived by both the person who possesses it and everyone else who experiences it. Much of the early social perception of what traits constitute a man is mediated by cultural rituals generally grouped under the name of initiation. Although such rituals purport to take place in the eternal present of the spirit, they are also grammars of belonging to a specific tribe or community. According to Arnold van Gennep, the early-twentieth-century anthropologist who first analyzed initiations across a variety of cultures, there are generally three stages in the ceremonies: a separation from former status, a liminal world of transition between stages, and a reassimilation into the group, when a new status is recognized. As the genetic inheritance must interact with environment and history in order to produce an individual, so the ongoing mythic definition of masculinity is in constant interaction with actual events and actual bodies. Through these rituals, an individual male's personal experience of biological change is transformed into a tribal and a cosmic experience as well. A man is described and in the process he is shaped.

Crucial changes that the male body undergoes are often connected to a particular rite of initiation, in which the passage to tribal membership is confirmed by a physical wound. Sometimes the wound, that payment in flesh, brings the infant male child into the tribe, as in the rite of circumcision shared by so many cultures (at varying ages), including the Jewish, the Turkish, and the Masai. This physical removal of part of the genitals is the moment of official entry, when the child receives a mutilation that links it with others of the same gender.

Female circumcision, with its explicit denial of sexual pleasure (even with an approved male), defines the woman as the property of her tribe, her family, and, later, her husband, without a history or autonomy of her own. Male circumcision in contrast identifies the young boy with the past, present, and future structures of tribal power and authority. Similarly, while female circumcision is an explicit and extensive wounding that removes the clitoris and often the labia as well, male circumcision usually limits the effect of its wounding to the less extreme and therefore more figurative snipping off of the foreskin. Both represent passages from one identity to another, but their results are virtually opposite: the male child is symbolically freed from his dependence upon his mother to become a man, with all the potential rights and privileges of that status, while the female child is defined as subject to male authority and deprived of an autonomous sexual power.

Circumcision generally, with some important exceptions, occurs in infancy, but more elaborate initiations occur to mark the point when the boy becomes a man. Such ceremonies carry the individual outside of himself and confirm his membership in a group of adult males. But the transition also hides a paradox: although designed to contrast with the rhythms of everyday life, and claiming a connection to the eternal, it cannot be tailored for every individual. Accordingly, the ceremony is often celebrated before most young boys are in fact sexually mature. As a result, male initiation (like circumcision itself), while it seems to commemorate the successful transition to manhood, may also instill a sense of inadequacy arising from the constant need to be tested. In many tribes the initiated may even return to the world of women until his biological or social time as a man has truly come. So, when the Trojan War loomed, Thetis, the mother of Achilles, dressed him as a girl and hid him among the women of Scyros, because she knew that manhood and battle would mean his death.

Ritual wounding sometimes precedes, sometimes accompanies, and sometimes even follows other rituals of change from childhood to adulthood, like the Vision Quest of the Plains Indians, the accession to arms in the ancient Germanic tribes, the initiation into the world of the book in the Jewish bar mitzvah, or the wearing of the toga by the Roman citizen. It may include as well extensive mutilations: the cutting of a deep groove in the underside of the penis (subincision) practiced by some African tribes, the perforated earlobes of Incan royal males, or the piercing of the chest, thighs, and biceps by long needles with weights attached to them that was part of the rituals of some Native American groups. In the vast variety of initiation rituals, the implicit question always seems to be "Can the candidate endure the pain?" To help him endure, elaborate preparations are made—incense is burned, potions are drunk—because the successful completion of the ceremony is a confirmation of the immortality of the tribe even more than it is the achievement of the individual. The initiation of the wound thus brings together spiritual life, warrior life, and political life. It presents the social world as a place whose rules must be known and whose rituals must be followed, in which the candidate must move from the unripened sexual identity of childhood into a world of adult gender difference, to ally with one gender and learn its ways, especially as they differ from those of the other. Subjective masculinity must give way to or at least merge with cultural masculinity. Being a man is thus a willful act, celebrated by the tribe, while being a woman is the default or natural state. Male initiation is complex and public, while menarche, even though young girls may also experience it as a wound, usually happens in private, whether there is any subsequent celebration or not.

The tribal rites of gender initiation described by ethnographers and anthropologists presage more "civilized" inductions into either all-male or male-dominated institutions such as sports and the military. They are more explicit versions of the assimilation to social norms in the nineteenth-century European novel when heroes and heroines marry, although there the price paid is usually more symbolic and the loss more spiritual, signaling the end of the freedom and self-development that made both the main character and the story itself interesting.

It may be hard to see a warrior being tested beneath the dark suit of the Victorian male embarking on marriage, but as a ritual it does signal an acceptance of the most valued norms of society. Modern industrial society, however, has few if any central rituals of initiation that all experience in any uniform way. Beyond the example of those sports teams and military units that bear the names of animals or primitive tribes, initiation in the modern world has little of the imaginative cachet of the primitive tribe or even of medieval and Renaissance forms of initiation. In fact, the implication is entirely opposite. From an expansion of the infant into identity with the adults of the tribe, initiation in adult male society has become instead a contraction of all that was inventive and vital in the childhood world: melodrama replaces myth. As this pattern of restriction developed in the nineteenth century, a countervailing effort appeared in the rise of anthropology itself (including the studies of van Gennep), which was fascinated with exactly those "primitive" but more exciting and seemingly more self-expanding forms of initiation that European society had left behind.

Instead of a central set of ceremonies, what principally remains are the cherished rituals of a wide variety of ethnic, religious, and social groups, which, in addition to less violent rites of passage, may often include the physical wounding of oneself or others: the saber-cut cheeks of German military cadets before World War I; the need to commit murder to be a "made man" in the Mafia and many street gangs; the torments of drunken fraternity hazing; the metal staples pounded into the chest of some American military cadets, to prove they can "take it"; and the tattoos and scarifications that in both primitive and modern cultures proclaim acceptance into the group after the price is paid in flesh.

# WARRIORS AND WOMEN

Throughout history, war has been one of the few social initiations that binds together this otherwise wide variety of masculine rites and traditions. Whatever the economic or political reasons for war, the elements of ritual cannot be ignored, especially when wars are waged for causes, to affirm national values, and to vindicate and celebrate the national past—pridefully making group and individual identity one. So many of the rituals of wounding and initiation are either primarily or exclusively for men because they do not just confirm that the candidate is a man. Especially in more primitive cultures, when war is endemic and every man is actually or potentially a warrior, they also emphasize that the candidate is expressly not a woman, and that manhood is eternal. Many also serve to legitimize a masculine line of social authority. As initiation separates the boy from both infancy and women, it creates the tendency to identify infancy with the world of women.

The next step occurs in those more complex societies that have evolved to a point that warriors have become a special subdivision of all men—the age of heroes (a designation that is obviously the product of a later world). Heroes were not just any men, but specifically warriors who defended the family, the tribe, and later even larger groups. The initiation ritual thus emphasized the central importance of the military model of masculinity to a culture, because in the ages when those ceremonies were evolving, this kind of man alone guaranteed social survival. In later ages, the same ritual that confirmed a specific class of men whose social function was to fight helped create and support a general conception of male responsibility for order of all sorts. In the Middle Ages, for example, when violence was often justified by feudal lords as a means to control worse violence, the fitness to rule and the capacity to use force to uphold legal command were virtually the same.

In the Greek myth of Ares, Aphrodite, and Hephaistos we find an intriguing suggestion of how the ancients wove together the concepts of war, sexuality, and wounding. According to Homer's account in the *Odyssey*, Aphrodite, the goddess of love, is married to Hephaistos, the blacksmith god of fire and craftsmanship, who is ugly, misshapen, and has a game leg—"the glorious cripple," as Homer calls him. For unspecified but perhaps clear enough reasons, Aphrodite is meanwhile having an affair with Ares, the god of war. One day, the suspicious Hephaistos traps them in the act by dropping a cunningly fashioned net of chains over their bed to hold them captive and make them ridiculous before the other gods.

This competition for the goddess of beauty between the powerful warrior god and the wily but lame god of making and manufacture suggests one way myth expresses the implications of different styles of masculinity. All stories of love triangles work out their romantic conflicts by expressing some ambivalence about the qualities of whatever gender is duplicated in the threesome, sometimes the woman, but usually the man. Aphrodite marries Hephaistos but has an affair with Ares, betraying the wounded creator with the mighty warrior man. Later, however, Ares turns out to be vulnerable to both the craft of Hephaistos and the derision of his fellow gods. Whose wounds then are the most crippling? Those of the lame Hephaistos, who believes Aphrodite has chosen his rival because of his own physical deficiencies, or those of the ensnared Ares, whose lust has made him feeble, imprudent, and the target of public ridicule?

As basic symbols of male and female, Ares and Aphrodite, Mars and Venus in their Roman guise, resemble Adam and Eve in the Bible. In addition, for the Greeks and Romans, they were also the names of two of the five known planets, the two in fact that flank our own Earth: Venus, the second planet, closer to the Sun's heat, and Mars, the fourth, between us and Jupiter. Later, in medieval science, their symbols continue to signify gender distinctions: the shield and sword of Mars (♂) alchemically representing iron; and the mirror of Venus (♀) representing copper, the "new" element of the Bronze Age, which allowed it to supersede the Iron Age. Thus, in the myth, even though the more "civilized" femininity of Venus may improve the archaic masculinity of Mars, it is Hephaistos (the Roman Vulcan), the blacksmith god and master shaper of both raw iron and copper, who traps them both. Wounded in his masculinity, he is yet more technologically advanced: without the weapons and armor he makes, Ares would be helpless.

In the myth of Ares, Aphrodite, and Hephaistos, man the warrior is placed in contrast with both female sexuality and man the maker. Such masculinity is thus the characteristic of a self-conscious group that is less an entity in itself than one defined by testing against either male enemies or the whole nonmale world. As war reflects or brings to completion the basic themes of male initiation, it is also historically a ritual of differentiation and distinction: who we are versus who we are not.

On the metopes of the north side of the Parthenon, for example, is a bas-relief rendering of one of the founding myths of Athens, in which Amazons from central Asia fight Greek warriors led by Theseus. Later, after the defeat of the Amazons, Theseus marries the warrior queen Hippolyta. The female warriors who have militarily threatened the male are thus co-opted into the world of their enemies, just as in many societies male blood feuds are cooled only by marriage. Difference thereby turns into relationship in a sequel to war reflected in works as different as Chaucer's "Knight's Tale" and Shakespeare's *Midsummer Night's Dream*. In both, Theseus and Hippolyta again preside over the marriages that close the stories. The Parthenon, we should remember here, was the temple celebrating the goddess for whom Athens is named: Athena, the virgin warrior usually depicted in helmet and breastplate.

Similarly, on the south side of the Parthenon, the metopes depict another founding myth, the battle between the Lapiths and the Centaurs. A Lapith wedding is in progress to which the Centaurs have been invited, but the unruly half men, half horses get drunk and start to fight.* As the

* The Centaurs are generally characterized in Greek mythology as drunkards and rapists, with the exception of the shaman and medicine man Chiron, whose skills reflect the positive side of their closeness to nature. As part horse, part man, they also indicate how archaic the horseman seemed to the Greeks as well as something of the devaluation of cavalry when horses became associated with chariots in warfare.

gods themselves had to defeat the more primitive giants who came before them, so too the civil state run by male warrior citizens defines itself at its origins against the two things that it is *not:* women and beast-men. Perhaps these are always the myths and stories that announce an effort to pull a culture out of disorder into order. In eleventh- and twelfth-century Europe, knightly tales take place in a chivalric world whose courtesy and decorum are in perpetual war against the darker, natural forces, like giants, but also against uncivilized urges within human society, especially greed and desire. Later in the Middle Ages, at a time when an embryonic preoccupation with national difference is exacerbated by war, the English will define themselves simultaneously against the "effeminate" French and the "beastly" Irish and Scots.

Such examples suggest that masculinity particularly defines itself in a polarized situation, and nowhere better than in war (and perhaps marriage) does that polarity seem so clear-cut and natural. Even when there is no specific enemy and no need to muster opinion through propaganda, the urge to define masculinity as a special way of being persists. The Cliff Dwellers of the American Southwest furnish an interesting example here. Living on the great mesas, they had a mixed economy: the women would generally farm on either the tops of the mesa or the canyon floors, while the men went forth to hunt. But this separated the men from the community, and so, over the centuries, the men evolved a purely masculine warrior religion whose home was not only within village precincts but also in a sunken area called the kiva, more natural, more connected to the earth than was the village itself.

The ethnographic distinction between hunter societies and planter societies is relevant here. Hunter societies are typically more involved in myths of initiation by ordeal, while the planter societies, which are generally larger (and more typically found in temperate climates), are often more matriarchal in their myths (as part of their connection to the earth) and emphasize ritual sacrifice. Planter societies, both horticultural and agricultural, also have a more elaborate task-oriented division of labor beyond the sexual division of hunter societies, and are generally more hierarchical. But the distinction between the two forms is hardly as absolute in history as it is in theory. The tension between a focus on the individual and a focus on the group underlies many stories from both mythic and historical sources, particularly in wartime, and it seems more useful to see a hunter versus planter interplay as characteristic of many cultures. The hero is celebrated for what he accomplishes in the name of the group, and the relation between his personal immortality and that of the group remains a delicate balance. Usually it is hard to decide which should have priority, and the conflict between the two furnishes the essence of stories of heroic prowess. Many medieval tales, for instance, tell of aspiring knights who were shepherds or cowherds or farmers before they decided to seek their fortune at Camelot, mirroring an actual world in which young men might dream of changing class solely by their strength in arms. As the historian Georges Duby has demonstrated, the peasant knight appears in medieval sociology as well as in medieval literature. In both fiction and reality, the young man leaves behind a former life for the incomparable goal of becoming a knight, alone on a quest but also partaking of the values and valor of other knights like himself.

Theoretically, planter societies may emphasize the group and hunter societies the individual, but the company of men into which the youthful candidate is initiated in hunter societies is at least equally important. As Emile Benveniste, the great scholar of Indo-European language and culture, has pointed out, even the word "self" historically derives from words meaning membership in a group. According to Tacitus in his ethnographic essay *Germania,* for example, warrior societies like the Germanic tribes of the early centuries A.D. were typified by scattered cohorts of young male warriors headed by a chieftain who shared food and booty with them. The solidarity among the members of these groups was so marked that it may have given rise to the Roman word for those regions, *Germania,* or, loosely, "the country of the brothers." Like the phratries of primitive Greece or the samurai of medieval Japan, these bands were brotherhoods that may have originated in family relations but in time transcended family and sometimes even tribal boundaries to constitute groups with rules and an ethos of their own. Individualism may have been one aspect of that ethos, but it would prove to be an individualism paradoxically dependent on group membership.

*Part II*

# ARMOR AND HONOR

# THE PURITY OF WAR

> A great flood of luxury and sloth which had submerged the land is receding and a new Britain is appearing. We can see for the first time the fundamental things that matter in life, and that have been obscured from our vision by the tropical growth of prosperity.
>
> —David Lloyd George, 1914

In any society where armies contain a large percentage of conscripted or volunteer citizens, as opposed to a small professional cadre, there is a potential for war to be interpreted as a type of social reinvigoration. Lloyd George's comment, made six weeks after the start of World War I (and thousands of British deaths), was hardly unique. Writers and politicians ranging from Henry James to Benito Mussolini explicitly supported the belief that the experience of war reveals the core of both individual and national character more truthfully and more naturally than does peace. Neither middle-class (and greedily commercial) nor feminine (and self-indulgent), war is a purifying crucible that melts away the false and corrupt manners of a bourgeois society to display the basic masculine mettle beneath the dross.*

* Others who expressed similar sentiments, often to their later regret, were Henri de Montherlant, José Ortega y Gasset, Rudyard Kipling, Rupert Brooke, and Ernst Jünger.

It is a point of view with a long history of both support and dissent. Classical scholars in particular have discussed the different degrees to which the various societies that considered themselves Greek thought that war was natural and therefore a good in itself. Heroic individuality was celebrated in their literature: the *Iliad*, in which the massed army of Greece sails to attack Troy in Asia Minor, features a multitude of single combats between heroes and even gods. In the later world of the Greek city-states, war was often right on the doorstep. The army was made up of citizen troops who were mobilized as circumstances dictated, organized and armed according to their tribal affiliation and wealth. But the norms of different city-states varied. The men of Sparta's upper class were trained for war from birth and did very little else, while Pericles in the oration included by Thucydides in *The Peloponnesian Wars* stresses that Athenian virtue depends on values other than those of war and the warlike. Nevertheless, both Athenians and Spartans agreed that participation in war was not only a continuing obligation for every male citizen but also a public stage on which masculine virtue could be stimulated, fostered, developed, and emulated.

Lloyd George's identification between personal character and the general character of political society in fact has a strong precedent (and perhaps even a direct source) in the Athenian argument over whether to launch an expedition against Sicily. The politician-general Nikias had argued against the expedition, accusing his rival Alcibiades of purely personal interest in promoting it. In response, Alcibiades does not deny his own desire for fame and conquest but instead intertwines it with the interest and the reputation of Athens:

> . . . by sinking into inaction, the city, like everything else, will wear itself out, and its skill in everything decay; while each fresh struggle will give it fresh experience, and make it more used to defend itself not in word but in deed. (350)

Alcibiades's identification between the individual male body and the body politic is plausible enough in those societies where only adult males were citizens. But, as the remarks of Lloyd George indicate, they are also sentiments that have been voiced in many eras as a way of inspiring men to better themselves *as men* by going to war, perhaps especially when the cause was dubious. Donald Kagan in *On the Origins of War and the Preservation of Peace* likens Alcibiades's speech to the views prevalent in Germany before World War I—*weltmacht oder niedergang*, world power or decline—and he quotes an intriguing statement by Honold von Ahlefeld, the director of the German imperial shipyards at Kiel, that presents the necessity of war in the terminology of nineteenth-century social Darwinism: "The 'struggle for survival' is raging between individuals, provinces, parties, states. . . . [T]here is nothing we can do about this, except to join in. He who doesn't will perish" (133).

Although the classical period of Greece and Rome, along with the European and Japanese medieval periods, were times of almost endemic warfare, the explicit belief that war is necessary for the full growth of human (i.e., male) nature becomes more widespread in the nineteenth and twentieth centuries. It has a special flowering in the time of Napoleon and later in Hitler's Germany and Mussolini's Italy. There the constantly emphasized presence of the great man as both political and military leader identifies the country he rules with his own nature; any divergence between individual desire and state imperatives is thereby erased and even outlawed.

Behind these different versions of the necessary conjunction of war and masculine survival runs an image not only of the group as an enlarged version of the individual, but also of the state as an organic growth like a human body that in crisis must be aggressive or else decline—the "fight or flight" dichotomy formulated by physiologists. Lloyd George's version of the argument may sound more optimistic (although moralistic) and von Ahlefeld's more pessimistic (although "scientific") about the ability of human will to express itself. But both basically still assume that there is no choice: the national struggle and the individual struggle are the same.

That analogy works best with what might be called immediate definitions of masculinity, such as desire, violence, power, and interest (or greed). Propaganda to the home audience of potential volunteers and draftees is all about the man and his country rising as one to combat the enemy. But the analogy is not very relevant to other traditional definitions such as endurance, stoicism, and asceticism. Fortitude and endurance are needed by soldiers at all times in all wars; as battles bog down and trenches have to be dug, those virtues will be spotlighted. When Alcibiades in Plato's *Symposium*, for example, praises the behavior of Socrates on the battlefield, he focuses first on the long-term elements of masculine character:

> His endurance was simply marvellous when, being cut off from our supplies, we were compelled to go without food—on

> such occasions, which often happen in time of war, he was superior not only to me but to everybody. . . . His fortitude in enduring cold was also surprising. . . . Socrates with his bare feet on the ice and in his ordinary dress marched better than the other soldiers who had shoes. . . . (61)

Later Alcibiades tells of Socrates's physical bravery in battle, but even that, to Alcibiades's amazement, is unaccompanied by the traditional warrior expectation that his exploits be widely known. Socrates wants no credit for rescuing the wounded Alcibiades and insists that the younger man take the day's prize for valor. In this world of physical combat and the quest for fame in battle, Socrates is the great puzzle, and Alcibiades anchors his praise in an anecdote of Socrates standing in one place from dawn one day to dawn the next, to the amazement of all onlookers—thinking.

A society in which military duty is incumbent on all men fosters a very different view of male solidarity than one in which being a soldier is only one of a variety of professions. The celebration of individual warriors in epic poems distinctly contrasts with the kind of war that the average Greek actually fought, usually in a tightly packed phalanx where his own life and the success of his army required an essential interdependence with his fellow citizen soldiers. In such battles, the hero is not the one who sallies forth in search of individual combat, but the one who stays unflappably in formation. As the Spartan poet-general Tyrtaeus wrote in the seventh century B.C.:

> *You young men, keep together, hold the line,*
> *do not start panic or disgraceful rout.*
> *Keep grand and valiant spirits in your heart,*
> *be not in love with life—the fight's with men! . . .*
> *You know that those who bravely hold the line*
> *and press toward engagement at the front*
> *die in less numbers, with the ranks behind*
> *protected; those who run, lose all esteem.* (West, 24–5)

Where necessity or tradition dictates that all male citizens fight against the common enemy, the image of masculinity is that of the warrior within, ready to emerge whenever the group requires it. One's ability to bring out that inner warrior when called for is therefore a good part of the measure of a man. Indeed, the word for cowardice in Greek is *anandreia*, literally "unmanliness." "Coward" in English, like *cobard* in Spanish and *codardo* in Italian, is akin to *cauda,* the Latin for "tail," evoking an image of a male animal scurrying off with its tail between its legs. In a purely functional way, the animal is protecting its testicles, and by analogy the gesture specifies what unmanly shape the coward has taken on—another Latin word for tail being *penis.**

Both Alcibiades, in Plato's *Symposium,* and the minor general Laches, in the Platonic dialogue that bears his name, thus praise Socrates not only for his philosophic view of the world but also for his character, as demonstrated by his courage and physical endurance on the battlefield. Similarly, most of our sources about the place of the Athenian military within the city polemically emphasize the direct connection of the hoplite, a citizen foot soldier who paid for his own equipment, with the essence of democracy itself (often in contrast with the despised cavalry, which was funded by the wealthy). Reflecting this emphasis on the virtues of endurance, courage, and stolidity over more sophisticated military skills, Plato's *Laches* prefers the amateurism of Socrates to the flash of the professional soldier, observing that those who do well in military shows rarely fight well in battle. The hoplite courage to stick to his post was superior to both the professional soldier's knowledge and the cavalryman's ability to move around.

The Greek ideal of the citizen soldier was imitated in the early centuries of the Roman republic, revived with the American and French Revolutions of the eighteenth century, and with a twentieth-century flourish in the mass mobilizations of World Wars I and II. Ernest Hemingway's post–World War I embodiment of real masculinity as a solitary soldier on the edge of extreme experience, against man and nature but respecting them, is influenced by it, as are the tales of outer space written in the wake of World War II by Robert A. Heinlein. In Heinlein's novel *Starship Troopers,* which was originally commissioned by the official Boy Scouts magazine *Boys' Life,* he imagines a world in which only soldiers, now both men and women, are real citizens and have the right to vote.

But however important the Greek model is, much of the language of war and the men who fight it owes a debt to Rome. As anyone who has taken introductory Latin will remember, the words for war (*bellum*), battle (*proelium*), and the verb to fight (*pugnare*) appear early on in simple rote sentences whose impact is hardly cancelled out by the stress on the

* "Coward" in Latin is *ignavus,* connected to words for laziness.

verb love (*amare*) in conjugation exercises. The frequency is comparable to that in Latin literature itself, especially that crucial work of early Latin study, Caesar's *Gallic War*, whereas the comparable Greek word for war (*polemos*) appears much less frequently and with nothing like the same pride of place.

Almost from the first, the Roman way of war was more premeditated than the Greek, in which, as one authority has written, beyond the phalanx formation the prime tactical device was the ambush. While even in Sparta, the most militarized of the Greek city-states, training for warfare was part of cultural initiation and development rather than a goal of public policy, Rome grew into a state constantly bent on warfare and conquest. Roman soldiers were organized into legions, and underwent military drill and training more elaborate than any that had existed before. The result was a highly trained army based in camps that became increasingly separated from the civilian world.

Like the Greeks, Roman armies had begun in a tradition of citizen soldiers seasonally obligated to a certain period of service. The story of Cincinnatus for a long time characterized this ideal of the citizen called away from his plow to fight who returns to his private life when the danger has passed. But even before Cicero began his career in the last century of the republic, the old requirement that a Roman had to serve in ten campaigns before he could stand for office had lapsed. Gradually the Roman army had begun to evolve into a largely professional organization, raised for the most part outside Italy during the later years of the republic. The primary allegiance to the state and the obligations of citizenship that still animated the early Roman army was gradually transformed into a force whose main allegiance was to the charismatic generals who had gathered it together. The rule of Augustus, the first emperor, established the permanent standing army, which required service (and no marriage) for twenty-five years. The military obligations of citizens were not abolished, but the army itself was composed principally of professionals, conscripts, and mercenaries, including some of the "barbarian" tribes against which Rome had previously fought. The old Greek and early Roman ideal of the inseparability of soldier from citizen, warrior from man, was effectively lost in the expansions of empire.

# THE WARRIOR AS BARBARIAN

While the Romans are credited with introducing a widespread discipline to warfare, the "barbarians" with whom they contended for centuries remained tribal and "heroic" in an older sense, more akin to the world of Greek epic. Polybius, a Greek historian of the third century B.C. who chronicled the rise of Roman power, argued that systematic military training actually made the Romans more flexible and individualistic than the Greeks could be in their rigid phalanxes. Others have sharply contrasted Roman warfare with the more personal fighting style that existed among the northern Celtic and Germanic tribes; contemporary Roman writers usually agreed.

Roman public myth stressed the subordination of individual glory to the needs of the group and the Roman *respublica,* the public thing. The tribal military emphasis, in contrast, was on the family and the clan. These warriors fought in individual combat rather than in elaborate group strategies, emphasizing the traditional Indo-European search for personal honor and fame after death, since fame itself originates in the belief that honor (and dishonor), especially in battle, lasts longer than life. But the Roman view of fame was more immediate, and to them the barbarians were both archaic and anarchic. Although in much of Roman literature the soldier is a comic or venal character, when he is contrasted with the warriors of the northern tribes, he becomes a model of proper military behavior. In Caesar's *Gallic War*, for instance, consonant with Caesar's emphasis on planning, tactics, and self-restraint, the Gallic tribes are condemned for their preoccupation with booty and individual boasting. Romans were certainly not immune to those temptations, but in Caesar's account, with its rhetoric of third-person detachment ("Caesar did . . ."), the Roman soldiers who succumb to such personal weaknesses are considered even worse than their rivals, for whom it is part of their culture. In one oft-told Roman story, Manlius Torquatus, a consul who himself had defeated a Celtic soldier in single combat, executes his own son for accepting against orders a virtually identical challenge.

Caesar's perception, if not his moral judgment, seems quite accurate. The Romans marched in formation and settled for the night in camps noted for their order and symmetry. According to Vegetius, whose fourth-century book on Roman military affairs is the only such work that survived intact through the Middle Ages, what distinguished the Roman conception of war and accounted in part for its success was the *ius armorum*, essentially, the rules of resource deployment. The legion must be cohesive no matter what, and each soldier had to be aware of the group effort into which his own must fit. But for what has been described as the gathering of mutually admiring heroic individuals who constituted the northern European fighting force of this period, a term like "army" is inadequate. The Old English word *host* seems more appropriate. It is a style of warrior masculinity very unlike the Roman, one that nevertheless survives long after the collapse of Rome. Even centuries later, there were few concerted military operations in the Icelandic sagas, or in the tales of the Nibelungs.

But whatever the political and social organization and its expectations, the needs of the group are not always the same as the needs of the individual warrior. Warriors are protectors of order who, to be effective, must have many of the traits of the enemies of order. Aristotle remarks that the hero is frequently not a good citizen, and Alexis de Tocqueville observed of early nineteenth-century America that the military in a democratic society was honored in war and shunned in peace. Like the movie action hero, the warrior embodies the incompatible traits of the disrupter and the defender of society—the criminal and the cop. Living on the boundary between the social and the antisocial, he is, in the words of the mythographer Georges Dumézil, an "integrated outcast," whose actions paradoxically both exemplify and seek to control the extremes of violence (*Destiny of the Warrior*, 116).

How does society encompass the violent man or the violent side of man? How does it decide when it needs him and when it does not? Not until the twentieth century was it widely questioned whether men could pass blithely from battle to peace and back again without psychological damage. In many earlier societies, whether they saw war as an occasional, consistent, or continual aspect of social behavior, there were rituals for assuring the smooth transition from bloody warrior to peaceful citizen. The participants in Plato's *Symposium* may reminisce about Socrates's soldierly stoicism on the battlefield just as fervently as they talk of the nature of love. But more usually, participation in the violence of war bestows a stain from which the fighters must be purified. Lawrence Keeley in *War Before Civilization* cites a number of different rituals used by tribal groups to cleanse the pollution caused by killing. In Rome, for instance, the victorious general had to ask a special dispensation before his army could enter the city. Ticker-tape parades were the favored mode in the United States for a long time—a halt in the business as usual of making money in order to celebrate the heroes. Perhaps part of the bitterness for so many Vietnam veterans was the lack of ritual welcome and purgation on their return—finally compensated, for some, by the Vietnam Veterans Memorial in Washington.

The citizen soldier is a modification and literally a civilizing of such a warrior, since after his period of sanctioned violence ceases, he can return to normal citizenship. But always in the background, as Aristotle's comment makes clear, is the dark possibility of the unassimilated warrior, whose character implies that violence is an innate part of human nature that can never be fully civilized. Thus the praise as well as the distrust or disapproval of the pure warrior persists through history. Plato in the *Laches* concludes that the professional soldier cannot really fight effectively because that requires moral qualities and a commitment to the community, while the professional primarily has, at best, a soulless technical skill and, at worst, a penchant for showing off. In action films, our own modern versions of the same cultural contradictions, we often find either a celebration of the triumph of the amateur inadvertently pulled into danger, or an investigation of the melancholy of the successful professional, whose life is empty without love or a cause.

One fascinating group of archaic warriors praised in some heroic stories and relegated to the shadows in others were the berserkers of northern Europe. The northern European gods, much more than the Greek or the Roman, were immersed in war. Even though Thor is specifically the warrior god, war fascinates Odin, the Teutonic high god, much more than it does Zeus in the *Iliad*. Odin is sometimes called a warrior himself, while the Teutonic afterlife, according to Snorri Sturluson, the thirteenth-century author of the *Prose Edda*, is overwhelmingly organized as a wonderland for warriors, a characteristic it shares with the afterlife in the Islamic, Shinto, and Aztec cultures, to name a few. In contrast with the Greek or Roman vision of the underworld, where warriors are sometimes present but rarely the whole show, Valhalla is a specifically military place, to which warriors are carried from battle by Valkyries to feast, romp, and tell tales of their valor. Unlike Mount Olympus, an exclusive citadel for those who are more than human, Valhalla is a place of eternal celebration for any man who distinguishes himself in battle, the reward for a life dedicated to war, a more dramatic and more tangible version of the glory after death in battle for which the Homeric warriors longed. In the *Iliad* Achilles is told by his mother that he has the choice of a short life, death in battle, and everlasting fame—or survival and a long life of anonymity. He chooses a short life and fame, but when Odysseus sees him in the underworld in the *Odyssey* he has changed his mind and says he would rather have lived an ignoble long life than be chief in the ranks of the dead. Somehow, for the Greek hero the values of peace and survival have come to overwhelm the brilliant heroics of war and death. No such second thoughts occur to the warrior dead of Valhalla.

In the midst of this war-oriented culture, the berserkers were a group of warriors whose behavior on the battlefield was so crazed and extreme that even their own side was appalled. In the few visual depictions we have, they are shown as coming into battle ferociously biting the edge of their shields, their faces and bodies sometimes painted red in an effort to make themselves invulnerable. Another figure in the primitive warfare of northern Europe is the specialist in flyting, the art of hurling insults before the physical battle begins, in the hope that words alone might shame the enemy into abandoning the field. By contrast, the berserker, either raving or coldly methodical in his warrior frenzy, is the quintessential man of violence for whom language has no meaning.

The name "berserker" comes from the words for "bear shirt." A similar group, the *ulfhedinn* ("wolf coats"), was also connected, like the

Plains Indians, to cults in which the warrior takes on the characteristics of a totemistic animal. Unlike "berserk," the name *ulfhedinn* has never received much currency in English, but its focus on of the beast-warrior appears in other ways in American and Continental traditions, through allied phenomena like the Navajo skin-walker, where aspects of the shaman and the warrior meet. In Roman mythology, the she-wolf was the favorite animal of the war god Mars, and of course she was present at the founding of Rome, as the foster mother of Romulus and Remus. The kind of warrior fury exemplified by the berserkers is thus connected to powerful wilderness and forest creatures like the bear, the wolf, and, on the shields of monarchs like Richard III, the boar. They represent a transitional stage between hunting and war that struck more orderly fighters from families, tribes, or communities as a solitary individualism they understood but had passed beyond.

In medieval Icelandic tales such as *Njal's Saga* and *Egil's Saga*, although there may be berserkers present, they rarely play major roles. The other characters accept them as a familiar but not quite normal part of the human scenery. Like the embattled community's need for the violent hero who, according to Aristotle, may be unsuited to be a citizen, the society that recognizes the archaic nature of the berserkers still needs their violence for its own ends. The berserkers are not always entirely invulnerable, especially when faced with a saga hero like Egil, who with his equal ability to break heads and compose poems is a synthesis of the man of violence and the man of language. Yet underlying their strange appearances is the implicit question of whether their extreme version of military masculinity—unadulterated force and violence—may be abnormal, inflexible, and deformed, more appropriate for beasts than for men, even when they happen to be on your side.*

This somewhat casual though quizzical acceptance of men who have a close relation to the animal world is explored further in a twelfth-century

* James E. Cathey connects the berserk warrior with "a larger tradition of totemistic identification, whereby the warrior would merge with his animal alter ego" (Strayer, 198). There may also be a psychophysiological basis for the berserker phenomenon. Peretz Lavie, a sleep researcher, has written about Kleine-Levin syndrome, usually a disease of young males, characterized by periods of prolonged sleepiness, sometimes accompanied by bouts of ravenous hunger, hyperactivity, and aberrant sexual and social behavior. Lavie doesn't give any information that would let us differentiate between national groups or nutritional histories (240–42). The elements of the syndrome intriguingly parallel the stories in which the furor-possessed warrior immediately falls into a deep sleep after decimating the battlefield. If there is a connection, it would be another example of the way in which what we call mad or aberrant behavior found a socially useful niche in some societies.

poem by Marie de France, "Bisclavret." Its hero appears to be a perfectly fine husband, loving and protective. But after his wife discovers that he needs to become a werewolf three days a week, she is frightened into unfaithfulness and plots with her lover to keep her husband in his beastly shape by stealing his clothes. As a wolf, he is violent but honorable, loyally obeying the lord of the area perfectly until he sees his unfaithful wife and immediately bites off her nose. The wife is tortured and questioned until she reveals the truth, the wolf is restored to his human shape, and the wife is banished.

Marie de France's story is written for a court society in which women had gained high status and importance. In it the Icelandic sagas' depictions of a shadowland of berserk maleness in which the line between man and beast can be crossed with ease becomes metaphoric. The clear implication is that masculinity itself may change its shape. The fault of the wife is that she fails to accept the necessary metamorphosis in her husband's nature from lover to warrior.

That the werewolf is a kind of warrior is a story that continues to wind its way through popular mythology, especially in periods when war or the prospect of war shadows the horizon. Dracula in Bram Stoker's 1897 novel is consistently presented as the debased or fallen version of a warrior tradition, who refers throughout to his illustrious past as "soldier, statesman, and alchemist." Early on, Jonathan Harker reports on Dracula's monologues about his descent from a race of "Besekers," whose fighting spirit was so inspired by Thor and "Wodin" that the peoples of Europe, Asia, and Africa "thought that the werewolves themselves had come." In modern times, however, all that Dracula can do is prey on those who come near him, while for sport or nostalgia he possesses the body of "Bersicker," a wolf at the London Zoo. Yet the shadow of his former greatness remains, and his susceptibility to the cross marks him particularly as part of a pagan warrior aristocracy, born in a pre-Christian world.

Similarly, the 1941 film *The Wolf Man,* written and directed by two German émigrés, Curt Siodmak and George Waggner, takes this basic werewolf/warrior story and turns it to generational and political themes. After Larry Talbot, a young American, is bitten by a wolf, his uncontrollable changes and awakened fury finally result in the death of his refined but tyrannical English father. The oedipal implications are obvious enough. But also, in the context of Hitler's often-expressed view that Americans were too weak and lazy to help England, the political point of the film and its fond portrayal of a reawakened (if for the moment misguided) warrior fury are apparent as well. Later, as the bombs were falling on Berlin, Hitler urged the German people to form a new underground organization to wage guerrilla warfare against the Allies. Its name, he said, would be Werewolf.

# 7

# THE SHAPE OF FURY

Some historians have said that the original berserkers were pre-cavalry shock troops and bodyguards for the royal and the elite. Others have argued that they were participants in mushroom or lycanthropy cults. But whatever their origin, they remain significant as a style of military masculinity that went too far, an edge over which the "normal" warrior would not go in war or in peacetime.

Now, aside from fictional berserkers like Rambo and the comic book *Sergeant Fury*, it is primarily military psychiatrists who discuss the enraged warrior. But in the past he was a more intriguing figure. Homer, for one, speaks of Agamemnon's "inhuman rage" in the *Iliad*. Similarly, the stories of the (supposedly first century B.C.) Irish hero Cú Chulainn further demonstrate the problematic quality of extreme, even if heroic, violence. Cú Chulainn is not specifically identified as a berserker. But he comes back after he heroically defeats the forces attacking Ulster and becomes a danger to the world he had been so ferociously defending. His warrior fury is so excessive and so little under his control that it threatens to tear Ulster apart and kill everyone in it, reminiscent of the murderous frenzies played out by some veterans in the wake of World War II. But in a clever plan, naked women are sent out to greet him. In modesty Cú Chulainn turns his head away, which gives the townspeople the chance to dowse him successively in three vats of cold water, making him normal again.

This story is, of course, part of Cú Chulainn's myth, but its basic elements appear historically as well. Tacitus's description of German tribal warriors similarly stresses the contrast between their frenzied activity in war and their inactivity in peace:

> When not engaged in warfare, they spend a certain amount of time in hunting, but much more in idleness, thinking of nothing else but sleeping and eating. For the boldest and most warlike men have no regular employment. . . . (114)

This torpor corresponds to the mythic image of the berserkers, who either were exhausted after battle or, like Cú Chulainn, had to be cooled down by stratagem so that they would no longer be a threat. It resembles as well the traits of monsters like Dracula, who are most vulnerable when they are asleep.

Georges Dumézil has traced the expression of this warrior fury back to the Indo-Europeans, who are the ancestors not only of the German tribes but also of the Greeks and the Romans as well as the tribes of India. Furor, argues Dumézil, expresses a warrior masculinity that draws so much energy from the animal and nonhuman world as to become antisocial, so individualist that it tears down its own side as readily as that of the enemy. Dumézil is especially interested in those occasions in the warrior myth when the furor that is crucial for winning battles becomes a liability in a new world of more orderly social and political forms. His basic contrast is between the Germanic tribes, where the older styles of warriorhood still exist, and the Roman "civilization" that disdains them. Certainly the Romans valued courage, just as the Germanic tribes could hardly neglect some aspects of strategy and tactics. But, says Dumézil, drawing upon Tacitus, they emphasized instead a personal bravery, *virtus* in Latin, "in forms that the civilized Roman considered to be monstrous" (*Horace et les curaces,* 13). As Tacitus remarks about the Germanic method for forecasting the outcome of wars:

> They contrive somehow to secure a captive from the nation with which they are at war and match him against a champion of their own, each being armed with his national weapons. The victory of one or the other is thought to forecast the issue of the war. (110)

With the maddened berserkers at one extreme and the disciplined Roman legion at the other, the model of the ordinary soldier across the centuries is a paradoxical interplay of individual fury and collective goals, rage against the loathed enemy and the cool discipline needed to defeat him, along with the belief, amply portrayed in modern action films, that righteous anger makes you impervious to pain (if not to wounds) and to terror (if not to reasonable fear and prudence). The need for only short-lived furor on the part of the normal soldier (in contrast with the berserker's perpetual mania) also serves as an exoneration for the violence and murder of war—a necessary concept if soldiers are to be able to return to normal society.

In the physical abilities of the heroic individual as exhibited in battle and conflict, in other words, the tribe discovers its destiny, even if in peacetime society those same abilities might be considered an offense to good order. To keep a safe distance from those dangerously unstable values, the events are often seen retrospectively, in a contemplation of the grand heroes of the past.

No epic poetry sings of current events, and one of its central themes is a meditation on the warrior sensibility and those male emotions particularly excited by conflict. But instead of merely celebrating those emotions and conflicts, the greatest works question them as well. War may be "part of human nature," but how it is carried on is a choice, and even in the bloodiest epics war is never treated as normal. Epic stories of battle and war in fact often focus on the points of stress and breakdown in a value system. The *Iliad* begins with what is usually translated as the "anger" of Achilles over his mistreatment by Agamemnon, who has taken away the woman Achilles believes to be his rightful battle prize. It is a conflict, in other words, of opposed views of honor: the honor of the leader Agamemnon, whose authority comes from the scepter handed to him by Zeus, and the primarily individual honor of the hero, Achilles. At first the conflict is breach of wartime customs, and the anger of Achilles is in response to Agamemnon's within the social sphere: he withdraws from the war entirely, his own injured honor more important than the battle against the Trojans. But by the end of the poem, Achilles moves beyond his earlier heroic pique and regains his heroic fury, driven not by loyalty to the Achaean forces so much as by the desire to revenge the death of his best friend, Patroklos, at the hands of Hector.

In search of a general Indo-European type behind warrior myths from India to Ireland, Dumézil identifies this fighting fury with a mystical force that embodies all that is essential in Achilles's warrior nature, which "carries a man outside himself, and puts him at a level of deeds that, normally, would be beyond him" (*Horace et les Curaces*, 23). He points out how similar the conflict between Agamemnon and Achilles is to that between Odin and Thor, Odin's own name (Wotan) being itself derived from *wut*, in Latin *furor*. But this is not the unalloyed and virtually involuntary furor of the berserkers, which pushes them to extremes beyond the human. Instead, it is the furor of the hero in battle, who yet has a human side. In the terms of the *Iliad*, it is an emotional state that must be reintegrated into a more flexible kind of heroism and masculinity.

The same values of individualism and recklessness praised in one side of the hero's story may therefore be questioned, if not rejected, by other aspects of that story, just as in the combat with the Giants the Greek gods battle an archaic version of themselves wearing the guise of a diverted or degenerate warrior. Like a berserker, the hero of Marie de France's "Bisclavret," when tamed, is potentially a sympathetic guard, but if rejected or left to solitude, may turn into a predator. Some of our own monsters have a similar genealogy: the warrior hero-king Vlad the Impaler turns into the solitary monster Dracula. And what of that aspiring knight of science Dr. Henry Jekyll, whose efforts to release and thereby purge his darker, more primitive self succeed only in letting loose the violent, antisocial Mr. Hyde?

As so many times in Western literature up until the Renaissance, the epic of war thus looks back on a more individualist warrior, whose self-regard threatens victory but whose self-sufficiency constitutes a continuing ideal. It is appropriate, then, that the Homeric poems should have been written down at the beginning of the sixth century B.C., when the armored phalanx of closely drilled and armed soldiers was replacing the more scattered battle tactics of the past, and when the collective army of citizen soldiers under elected generals was the norm, not the array of individual heroes each seeking single combat. In such a world of order, the old warrior furor represents an outmoded but nostalgically enticing masculine style, so that each phalanx member might nurture an Achilles behind his body-covering shield.

What transmutes the antisocial furor of Achilles into an acceptable form of masculinity is the influence of both society and religion. But the immediate needs of war and his comrades also play a significant role. In the Asian tradition, by contrast, the conflict between the individual honor of the hero and the needs of the group is not as significent an issue. Thus Sun Tzu in *The Art of War* emphasizes the need for an army to remain organized and coherent—"We can form a single unified body, while the enemy must split into fractions"—while two of the five faults he reckons most fatal to a general could be described as an oversensitivity to personal honor (59, 70). In the *Iliad,* by contrast, Achilles's transformation comes not from a new appreciation of the collective goals suitable to a general, but from a deeper sense of his own mortality. After the death of Hector and the funeral games of Patroklos, his rage now subsided, Achilles allows Hector's body to be taken back to Troy. The ruthless vaunting of the warrior hero who shows no mercy to his defeated enemy has been modified, if only partially, into a more just, and even more tender, kind of heroism. It is a change comparable to what classical historians have seen in Athens as the supersession of the warrior god Ares by the armed goddess Athena, whose care is not the individual but the entire city-state, in peace as well as war. To the extent that the *Iliad* looks back from a later age on the heroic warrior, its message is that the warrior himself must change.

Achilles achieves a new inwardness, discovering some identity beneath the armor and furious vaunting of battle. In *Njal's Saga,* written in the thirteenth century about events in tenth-century Iceland, the vehicle of change is the appearance of a warrior whose values are based not on the tribal conceptions of honor so much as on the dictates of religion. Here the religion is Christianity, although it is a northern warrior Christianity, more indebted to the Old Testament than to the New. In a revealing episode, Thangbrand, who had been sent by King Olaf Tryggvason to convert Iceland, is being feasted by Gest Oddleifsson, a local warlord. There are many at the feast who are apprehensive about the expected arrival of a berserker named Otrygg, of whom they are all afraid. Using the power of this fearsome warrior as the test, Thangbrand proposes that they light three fires, one to be blessed by the heathen priests, one by him, and one unhallowed. If the berserker fears the Christian fire but walks through the heathen, they must agree to accept Christianity. Otrygg the berserker arrives, marches fearlessly through the heathen fire, but pauses before the Christian blaze and complains of the heat. Raising his sword to attack the others, who are standing on benches, he catches it on a crossbeam. Like Van Helsing facing Dracula, Thangbrand then strikes the berserker with a crucifix. He drops his sword, whereupon Thangbrand stabs him, his companion cuts off his arm, and the others join in. Many religious conversions result, and the point is clear: Christianity is not a detriment to the warrior but an enhancement, replacing the pagan traditions of the ferocious animal cults with the new religious power of the present. What is positive in the warrior tradition will be embraced and sustained by the new religion, while what is excessive will be destroyed—but perhaps not entirely, since the old warrior remains as a figure of the shadows, monstrous but fascinating. Like Dracula, he and what he represents must be defeated again and again, or perhaps, as in twentieth-century fascism, he might be revived as a new source of energy.*

Some societies are more divided about their allegiances either to the warrior virtues of valor and furor or to the commander's virtues of strategy and control. Some freely discount the one in favor of the other. The Icelandic sagas, for example, with exceptions like the coming of Thangbrand with his warrior Christianity, rarely see any innate virtue in obedience to a monarch or other authority, even when he is on your side. In the same way, a faithful retainer like Roland refuses to call for the help of Charlemagne, his liege lord, until it is too late. The great military epic of Rome, Virgil's *Aeneid,* also features an ambivalent hero, who has sacrificed his personal desires and destiny to the historical fate of being a founder of Rome. In an image of this submission, Aeneas flees burning Troy carrying his father on his back and holding his son by the hand—inexorably bound to both past and future. Such, implies Virgil, are the limits of male valor in combat with the gods and time, especially when the issue is less personal fame than building the foundations of empire.

Such fatalism is often a prime characteristic of the warrior in older literature, as it is in history. It may be a relation to individual warrior gods and models or, as in *Beowulf* or Chaucer's "Knight's Tale," a relation to a god conceived specifically as destiny or fate. In Sun Tzu's pragmatic formulation, "It is only one who is thoroughly acquainted with the evils of war who can thoroughly understand the profitable way of carrying it on" (45). The greatest evil is, of course, the presence and constant threat of death. But to battle well means that one's name will outlast one's body and thereby conquer time, like the dead heroes Virgil tells to be proud that their names have been attached to a scrap of Italian geography.

* In the New Zealand film *Once Were Warriors* (1994), relearning the furor techniques of the tribe is presented as a crucial recapturing of Maori tradition otherwise lost or warped beyond recognition by the modern urban world.

Unlike the dead Achilles in the *Odyssey* who says he would rather be a poor farmer than chief of the heroic dead, Virgil's Aeneas must accept his role as the instrument of fate and subordinate his own life to history.

This supposedly cosmic truth usually underlies and validates a specific political hierarchy. Depending on the social situation of a culture, the eternal tension between will and fate, between men and the gods who can send them to death without being touched themselves, is similar to that between the warrior and the king. All are conflicts specific to social structures that emphasize a feudal lord/vassal or liege/warrior relation. These are worlds of essentially local loyalties and a local masculinity, displayed before small courts and small families, nowhere near the larger theater of the city or the nation. They are often cultures in which there is less choice about how to behave socially the higher up you are or want to go on the social ladder, cultures in which the structure of the universe depends on the honoring of an infinity of minute but unbreachable rules. Such hierarchic cultures, and their idea of masculinity, sharply contrast with democratic cultures that at least publicly celebrate the exercise of will and voluntary behavior. But the way these distinctions play themselves out is not always so obvious. Is it odd or appropriate that a fate-oriented society revels in tales of doomed heroic action (like *The Song of Roland*), while in a will-oriented society like our own, individuals feel victimized by social forces and stress personal satisfaction as their only salvation?

# THE SHIELD OF HONOR

The most lasting cultural mediator between the individual soldier and his social group, between violence and civility, between war and peace, is the concept of honor. Honor serves as a justification for the professional as well as for the conscript, for the warrior hero as much as for the ordinary soldier. Historically, it is the concept of honor that mediates between individual character and the pressure of outside forces, as well as between the body that wants to survive and the mind that seeks other goals, including a glorious death. In terms of masculinity, the invocation of personal honor—with its links to family, tribe, and nation—gives eternal justification to an act of immediate violence.

Thucydides said that the three causes of the Peloponnesian War were (as they are usually translated) fear, interest, and honor. In *On the Origins of War,* where Donald Kagan uses Thucydides as a lens through which to analyze the backdrop of more modern wars, he especially stresses those situations in which honor turns to interest. But one ambiguous aspect of all three of these motives is that they can be used to describe either individual or collective feelings, and that it is by no means clear whether one or another necessarily comes first—or what happens when they are at odds. In the triad, it is honor—for both the warrior and those who appreciate him—that metamorphoses individual fear and interest into something beyond a merely momentary response to events, and makes actions morally plausible. But does an injured sense of honor, on the level of an individual or a state, always set off the chain of causes? Small states may go to war for fear. Do big ones? In Thucydides's account, as Kagan notes, Alcibiades argues the need to strike at a superior first. Is there perhaps a hierarchy among the three causes, or a general historical way of proceeding through them, depending on which occurs first?

From a moral point of view, the three causes may even be analogous, differing only in their relation to time and resources. In fact, interest is the only motive that a collective institution like a state or a nation could really have. Fear is an emotion of individuals that only metaphorically is applicable to groups. Honor, too, is more individually rooted and only metaphorically a collective trait—although it is worth noting that when states and nations invoke a sense of injured honor requiring immediate action, that action is usually war.

Honor is therefore a crucial historical element of masculinity, mediating between the two enemies we have seen depicted on the Parthenon metopes: the struggle with men who are part beast and with women who challenge men. The solution to this struggle is the honor code, the organization and thereby the shaping of male physical violence into socially acceptable and even socially beneficial forms. In this way, violence is transformed into custom and tradition. Falstaff in *Henry IV: Part II* calls honor "a word," and by that he means a mere word. But words believed in and stuck to are essential to honor, especially in preliterate societies where an individual's word of honor guaranteed contracts and behavior of all sorts. By the time of Falstaff's world, however, both words and honor have become debased, and cynicism often thinly veils a nostalgia for the time when they meant something.

Although individual and family honor regularly reveal themselves in conflict, their codes differ from the rules of battle and military behavior, if only because warfare is a collective situation. Then the needs of personal and family honor may often have to give way—for a time—to the perspective of the larger group and its interests. Questions of honor are especially acute in egalitarian situations where there is little or no accepted hierarchy within the group, whether it be the street gang or the Olympian family in the *Iliad,* constantly at war over questions of precedence. In the Icelandic sagas, for example, as in the history of Iceland, battle and violence exist almost exclusively at the individual or family level, although the immediate desire for revenge to purify a tainted honor did coexist with an annual summer gathering, called the Althing (now the name of the Icelandic parliament), in which rivals who had not received satisfaction in the spring meeting of lower courts (*things*), or whose complaints crossed district lines, pleaded their cases.

But few of the societies of the Middle Ages had such a centralized and periodic way to resolve conflict. Even at the Althing many of the decisions were not final, since they depended on the goodwill of the participants, who might decide that the honor of obeying the jury's decision was less powerful than the honor of continuing the cycle of revenge. In other countries, with many different and scattered centers of power, with no sufficient centralized police authority, and often with an embryonic system of law, both violence and justice were the local monopoly of feudal lords. In effect, the realm of honor there was much larger than the realm of law. With the gradual growth of law and precedent as ways to control and modify social behavior, along with an emphasis on the continuities of lineage and family, individual honor either becomes weakened or has to seek some other justification. Whereas before it might have stood alone as the only shield against moral chaos, now it had to compete in a world of other versions of order and morality. But even by the twentieth century and beyond, despite a more elaborate and controlling system of law, personal revenge for injured honor still strikes a primitive chord.

Although, at least for the purposes of propaganda, modern wars cannot be entered for personal interest or out of fear, there is frequently a personal root in their professed causes and often an invocation of collective honor. Atrocities by the enemy may stir the blood and arouse the desire for vengeance. But they must be connected to wrongs done to the group or to a defense of national honor. The apocryphal Appalachian feud between the Hatfields and the McCoys, or the feuds that still go on in the Balkans, remain memorable in part because their cycle of revenge seems so unreasonable and so drawn out. But a frequent element in most stories of vengeance for besmirched honor is that the original occasion be lost or forgotten, whether a slight to a gang member or a battlefield defeat centuries before.

Much of the study of honor has been done by social anthropologists and ethnographers in terms of the codes of specific tribes and contemporary, primarily rural, social groups, as well as by historians focusing on the warrior codes of medieval Europe or Japan, for which our evidence is almost entirely literary. The goal of honorable behavior may be social (to attack an enemy, to defend a woman, to defend one's lord) or it may be rooted in a personal and internal sense of what is right. Often, as for the wandering lordless samurai in medieval Japan called *ronin*, personal honor may be almost totally submerged in general principles, even to the extent that its ultimate affirmation is suicide. But whatever the relation between the personal and the general codes, if one does not defend one's honor with action and usually with force, then one is not a man. Honor is thus the willingness to behave openly, immediately, and decisively on the basis of a moral belief that is felt internally as part of a general code. Thus there can be no honor that is ever untested. And no test is definitive, for honor must be proved again and again.

Honor thus always involves a policing of boundaries: personal, familial, national. At the level of the nation it seems to stop. No one talks about world honor or hemispheric honor, perhaps because by then the boundaries have gotten too large, and any clear opponent is missing, unless, of course, we are invaded from outer space. Then earthly or terran honor will definitely be at issue.

Was there an honor for the peasantry or the middle class in a world where honor was otherwise defined as a sense of self and community only available to the aristocratic? Certainly there were codes of behavior, and there are always local traditions. Anthropologists like J. Peristiany and Julian Pitt-Rivers who work in the area of contemporary Mediterranean culture have noted certain patterns in the idea of honor in those societies that seem relevant to northern Europe as well. But an important issue is which traditions get passed on and how, and which expand beyond provincial customs, working their way into literature and art to be taught to later, geographically far removed, generations as "natural."

The kind of society in which the constant testing dictated by the honor code occurs most often generally has an oversupply of young men with little expectation of status and success other than what can be accomplished by force of arms. Such societies are what J. K. Campbell, in a study of Greek shepherds from Epirus in northwestern Greece, describes as "without clearly delimited spheres of competence," whose daily uncertainties lead to a constant need for respect and the assertion likely to gain it (Peristiany, 188). Often, the more minor the offense, the more important the defense of honor in response to it, with the proviso that the offender be a worthy opponent, for there is no honor in defeating someone who has none. From a more "civilized" perspective, we might demean this prickly honor as a narcissism of small differences. But its fretful punctiliousness also underlines the fragility with which it is possessed. It must be defended at every turn because it is constantly under siege.

We frequently speak of gratuitous violence in terms of the callousness of drive-by shootings or the desire merely to kill. But in terms of the interplay between honor and violence, we may wonder whether violence is ever entirely gratuitous. When we look back on the honor praised in the past and mock its terms as outmoded and archaic, we ignore the need of all honor to be finicky. There's a tremendous legalism in male honor behavior, turning on fine points, at odds with the definitions of other groups, almost as if honor itself and its definition were a prime mode of differentiating *our* values, the values of truth and nature, from *their* values—the distortions of ignorance. In whatever warped or appropriate way, all violence can thus justify itself as being connected to some issue of male honor, just as every issue of honor is rooted in some question of individual and social identity.

Looking back on the centuries, we might also wonder if there is a principle of downward mobility defined by an honor based on tolerating not even the slightest offense. The individualist and tribal honor that brooks no resentment, however small, has now deteriorated into adolescent killers, with their peevish sense of "respect." The young men who kill strangers without compunction and the mothers who say "my boy was always good" claim like the "honorable" men of old to uphold family and tribal values against the impersonal equality of the law. But they also ignore the other side of the ancient honor equation: in order for honor to be truly satisfied, the opponent must be equally honorable, equally respected. Then, even though the enemy might be defeated and his body destroyed, his honor remains intact, as does that of the victor. The hero who fights a monster, like Beowulf against Grendel or innumerable heroes of horror films, gains honor from defending the weaker community. But to defeat someone who is not your equal, or to do it from ambush, is dishonorable because honor must be risked in order to be validated. When honor becomes separated from personal integrity, it becomes not an aspect of identity but a commodity. Like anything else in a commercial society, it is part of a world in which there is only a limited amount, and the only way to gain your own is take it away from someone else.*

Sociobiologists have argued that the pattern of violence is innate and the assertion of honor merely an excuse: men have always been aggressive; therefore aggressiveness is part of human nature, and honor at best a mere social channeling of instinctive aggressive impulses. It was a style of explanation popular in the 1960s for its unambiguous statement of the inevitability of war and violence, and it became popular once again in the 1990s.

But long before sociobiology, others, especially in the Middle Ages, argued for the relation between that particular style of honor called chivalry and the deepest spiritual impulses in human nature—a kind of innateness generally overlooked in sociobiological analyses. In its more elaborate and codified forms, personal honor in war took shape in the generally secular terms of European chivalry and Japanese Bushido, or in their religious equivalents: the promise of paradise for those who die on the battlefield in Germanic religion, in militant Christianity, in Islam, and in Shinto. Angels carry the souls of Roland and other warriors to heaven at the end of *The Song of Roland*, just as Archbishop Turpin, the priestly warrior in the epic, had promised. So, too, Shinto priests during World War II promoted kamikaze glory for Japanese suicide pilots, while nearer to the present some Muslim clerics promise paradise to suicide bombers. Religion thus helps transform personal into group honor through the sanction of eternity, creating a transcendent warrior masculinity from a maze of changing and contradictory shapes. Like the ritual of initiation, the code of honor anchors the personal impulse to a special group and set of values, restating and resolving the paradox of the need to be carried beyond your everyday self in order to become more authentically in touch with what is really you.

In wartime, especially, such a code ensures a belief in a purified, totemistic, and one-sided masculinity as a way of ensuring victory. The reversal of the process may be one way to understand the sense of emptiness, the feeling of being unappreciated and unknown that afflicts the veterans of so many wars: an externally validated sense of honor, an approved violence in the name of deeper and more central values, must

* Jonathan Shay in *Achilles in Vietnam* (103) considers this disrespect for the enemy, and the change from an honor society, to be the result of nineteenth-century racism and twentieth-century ideological wars. As a psychiatrist who has dealt extensively with traumatized Vietnam veterans, he says there is an actual clinical need to see the enemy as worthy before there can be any hope of a cure (115).

once again in the peacetime world become entirely internal and personal, even archaic, as the popularity of American westerns and samurai films in the United States, Japan, and Europe after World War II demonstrates. They summon up a lost world where individual honor and a male "code" were not only appreciated, but also necessary for survival.

In recognition of these lost intangible elements in the equation of honor, Peristiany and then Peristiany and Pitt-Rivers together published two collections of essays on honor in Mediterranean culture, almost thirty years apart. The first is called *Honour and Shame*, the second *Honour and Grace*. In the introduction to the latter they chastise their earlier effort for its almost exclusive emphasis on the social basis of honor and its material expression, while scanting the subject of the second volume: the relation of conceptions of honor to religion and ideas of the eternal. As Thucydides points out, politics may come into the equation, along with interest and fear. But there is also an honor that is more spiritual than political, like that of the Knights Templar of the Middle Ages, or the Jesuit "Soldiers of God." In the romantic visions of World War I, it becomes the brotherhood of honor and chivalry that transcended national boundaries, especially when fleeting aristocrats fought one another to the death in the pure realm of the air, high above the ordinary soldiers stuck in the blood and mire of the trenches.

# THE SPECTACLE OF KNIGHTHOOD

> No enemy can withstand a vision that is strange and, so to speak, diabolical; for in all battles the eyes are overcome first.
>
> —Tacitus, *Germania*

Throughout its history, masculinity stands at the crossroads of physiological type, individual psychology, and cultural definition. In *Men Against Fire,* S. L. A. Marshall concluded that the most important influence on the behavior of a soldier in World War II was not the chain of command or the quality of his equipment or his understanding of the situation, but what he believed to be the opinion of his immediate companions. In theory, honor is an internalized code of personal behavior, whose principles partake of spiritual truth. But it is armed combat that turns this individual honor into a social fact by its display in the presence of others, and it is preeminently in war that men make themselves men in the eyes of other men and in their own.

Paradoxically, then, what often plays out inside the warrior is the fantasy of acting honorably in front of an audience, where the possibility of shame must be avoided at all costs. The display of personal honor that overwhelms one's enemies, in other words, requires an audience, even an imagined one. This desire to be seen to act honorably necessarily highlights those aspects of identity that are the most theatrical while it also translates other, less overt traits into theatrical terms. In all the tales and histories of honor, in peace as well as in war, from the heroic period to the present, the presence of some spectator is crucial, to validate the behavior of the combatants and to carry their story both to those not present and to future generations. How would we know of honorable or courageous acts done if there were no one to observe them?

There is always a reciprocal relation between the products of a culture and the audience for those products; artists and writers propose and audiences process—accepting, rejecting, picking and choosing. Cultural evolution is thus dependent in part on cultural access. In one phase of that evolution, the literate classes or the classes that consume culture are the ones that change first. But in another it is the producers of culture—the writers and artists in particular—who are often the conduits by which other, less powerful, classes exert pressure for change. After World War I, a much wider literary as well as popular audience was exposed to war and its meanings. Blithely acknowledging and even embracing this vital ingredient of spectacle in war, the Allied command in World War II referred to "theaters" of operation. During and after that war films helped create for the first time a truly mass audience for the staging of both war and wartime masculinity.

If masculinity requires an audience, just any audience won't do. As there is no honor to be gleaned from defeating someone outside the honor system, there is no praise to be cherished from the wrong audience. Sometimes that audience might be in the present, sometimes in the past, sometimes in the future. As the great cities of the Roman Empire along with their armies decayed or vanished, a legendary line of inheritance linked the heroes of classical epic to the medieval knight and his cult of chivalry, with its romances of armor-clad heroes sallying forth to fight dragons and rescue fair maidens. In the Middle Ages, the prime audience for such stories was almost always either part of a royal court or a regional aristocratic stronghold, and much courtly chivalric literature strongly featured great deeds along with models of masculinity, both positive and cautionary. A large portion of the audience for these displays of literary knighthood and chivalry, in life as well as literature, were women. Some prosperous townsmen may have sat in the stands at tournaments or listened to the chivalric poems of writers like Chrétien de Troyes. But it was often primarily aristocratic women whose gaze directly inspired knights to great deeds and whose patronage supported the writers and artists who depicted them.

Despite the newly lavish panoply of the tournaments, however, the armor and weapons of the knights had not changed much since the Bronze Age. Until the crucial period from the end of the Middle Ages to the seventeenth century, in fact, the ways armies fought battles and sieges were similar to the methods of the past. The castles and equipment on the reliefs celebrating the eighth century B.C. victories of the Assyrian ruler Sargon II closely resemble those depicted on Trajan's second century A.D. column in the Roman Forum, while scenes on the Bayeux Tapestry chronicling William the Conqueror's invasion of England reflect those on Trajan's column nearly a thousand years before.

Whether the men who participated in those conflicts were the same is another matter. Part of the effect of new armament, strategy, and tactics was to suggest a much closer relation between the idea of masculinity and the evolution of war. The medieval literature of chivalry and masculine violence depicted battles and single combats with a particular attention to the psychology and ethics of knighthood—how men ought to behave. The turtlelike configuration of the Greek phalanx or the overarching shields of the Roman testudo transformed each soldier into a segment of an interdependent system. But the armored figure on horseback appeared as a grand individual hero. In the development of armor from the twelfth through the fifteenth centuries, first chain mail and then plate were the visible supports for a self-enclosed credo of knightly assertion. As in the encasing ritual familiar from dozens of films set in the Middle Ages, the medieval image of masculine force was built from the outside inward.

The first test of impenetrability was the tournament, where violence could be enacted before an audience that appreciated its rules and rituals, in much the same way that Romans applauded gladiators in the Colosseum or noncombatants tuned in to the Gulf War on television to be schooled by Pentagon spokesmen in the intricacies of smart bombs. The earliest tournaments were more physical than the stylized later ones. The most primitive were little more than a clash of arms between groups. Called *mêlées*, they are depicted in illuminated manuscripts as a tangled mass of armored men and horses. Such encounters had the practical function of honing fighting skills in the absence of actual war, and they would lapse when armies became more professional. But they also helped channel the otherwise aimless aggression characteristic of medieval life into codes of conduct and behavior that confirmed a close relation between male honor and physical violence. In essence, they were settings in which a young man could test his warrior skills as well as gain a reputation. And reputation often led to making money. The prime wealth of the Middle Ages was not in commerce but in land, and because there was a limited amount of land and resources over which to fight, there was also a limited amount of honor. "Valor" and "value" were as close together in fact as they are etymologically. Both were honorable, and the word "honor" itself could refer to either an intangible virtue or the material possessions of a feudal lord.

Chivalric lore and literature usually characterize the acts of battle and the defense of damsels in distress as selfless expressions of the code, unbesmirched with thought of personal gain. But in its early medieval form, warrior honor needed money, gifts, and booty to be validated. By the twelfth century, the growing importance of knightly display through elaborate armor, weapons, and decorations had collided head-on with the poverty of many wellborn men, especially younger sons of large families. In fact, there was a decidedly "freelance" side to medieval war, in which a man might enrich himself and raise his social status by amassing booty and ransom. In the tournament as well as in battle, to capture an enemy meant capturing his armor, his horse, and, as was true in the *Iliad* as well, a suitable ransom for his person. The squires and attendants who accompanied the knight not only took care of him and his equipment, they also helped collect the objects, animals, and people he captured as prizes while clerks toted up the haul.

Money was essential for achieving the ideal standards of aristocratic masculinity, but getting enough money to disdain it was the heart of the quest. This paradox persisted for enough centuries that it was sometimes hard to tell the difference between the knight and the mercenary, since neither especially wanted peace, with its lack of opportunity to amass a personal fortune.

The situation was similar when the combatants were fighting for dynastic or tribal ends. *Mêlées* and tournaments were hardly some armored form of the Olympic Games. They may have been pretend battles, but they still contained many of war's dangers. Killing opponents was generally frowned upon, though, and it was impractical as well, because it would mean no spoils or ransom, the prime way impecunious younger sons or members of noble but poor families could raise their status. Some, like the young William Marshal, later protector of England, would travel from tournament to tournament picking up forfeited horses and other equipment until they became wealthy indeed. William made his fortune in the late twelfth century, but the route he followed was even more possible in the later stages of the tournament tradition, when such specialized armor was used that, with its rigid visors and couched lances, it was much too expensive to risk in mere battle, but would bring a good price in the ransom market.*

Encased in the polished and hardened exterior of his armor, the warrior in battle epitomized what I would call a "bounded masculinity," focused on short-term and immediate advantage. For centuries it was the primary, if not the exclusive, masculine model in Europe, defining itself by a monolithic politics of order and hierarchy in contrast with both the spiritual world of religion and the domestic world of the feminine. This sense of self was bounded literally by the armored and adorned body that was the highest preparation for war. In the Middle Ages the hardened shell of armor resembled the more metaphysical prosthesis of knighthood itself—the projection of a grander and more terrifying figure than would be possible with the mere body inside.

In this long period of bounded masculinity that was the norm from antiquity to the Middle Ages, the underlying question is how much armor defends and how much it limits, as Homer implies in the story of Hector and his son Astyanax in the *Iliad*. Andromache, Hector's wife, holds up the baby to Hector and pleads with him not to return to battle. Hector replies that he must return or be thought a coward by those Trojan men and women who watch him from the parapets. If he dies and Troy is lost, he will still be remembered for his honor, as will she as his wife, even if she is carried into slavery by the Achaeans. "As he said this, Hector held out his arms/to take his baby. But the child squirmed round/on the nurse's bosom and began to wail,/terrified by his father's great war helm—/the flashing bronze, the crest with horsehair plume/tossed like a living thing at every nod" (156). Hector and Andromache laugh. Hector takes off his helmet, and prays that someday his son will be praised as better than he, returning from battle in "the bloodstained gear of some tall warrior slain—/making his mother proud." After Hector's death, Homer says nothing more of Astyanax. But in one non-Homeric version of what happens later, the child is thrown from the parapets of Troy by the son of Achilles, Neoptolemus, whose name means "young warrior."†

* Many social groups had their ransom prices, not just the upper classes, and making money from prisoners was a frequent mode of class movement. The medieval chronicler Froissart comments that English archers at Poitiers were taking four or more prisoners at a time.

† In another version, referred to in Euripides's *The Trojan Women*, Neoptolemus clubs King Priam of Troy to death with Astyanax's body.

The fear of Hector's son at the panoply of the warrior illustrates how much warfare, especially in the ages before firearms, emphasized the terrifying appearance of the warrior and his cohort. If battle is generally fought with weapons like swords, spears, and pikes that bring combatants into close contact, appearance has an important role to play, whether it is the painted faces and bodies of berserkers and Native American tribesmen, or the tall beaver or horsehair helmets of parading officers in the Napoleonic Wars. To Tacitus, writing about the Germanic tribes in the first century of the Roman Empire, this terrifying style presented a sharp contrast to the more orderly and disciplined impression of the inexorable Roman legion marching against its foes. Of a masquerading tribe called the Harii, he says, "They black their shields and dye their bodies, and choose pitch dark nights for their battles. The shadowy, awe-inspiring appearance of such a ghoulish army inspires mortal panic; for no enemy can endure a sight so strange and hellish" (137).* Similarly the males of the Suebi tribe tie their long hair into a topknot: "These are no love-locks to entice women to accept their advances. Their elaborate coiffure is intended to give them greater height, so as to look more terrifying to their foes when they are about to go into battle" (133). To the Romans, the tribes were *feritas* (like animals) and innately warlike in contrast with the civilized Romans, who, according to themselves, went to war only for cause. Similarly, the Romans referred to the most "barbarian" part of Gaul as Gallia Comata, hairy Gaul, while the more civilized areas were Gallia Togata, Gaul where they wear togas.

Classicists disagree about the extent to which Tacitus in passages such as this is either mocking the primitivism of the tribes or criticizing the military refinements of the Romans. But his attitude is characteristic of the way later generations often look back upon the military masculinity of the past with a mingled awe and disdain. Even when the heroic story or history (like the *Iliad* or *Beowulf* or *The Song of Roland*) is itself set in the past, it is frequently suffused with a nostalgia for a more heroic, and more distant, past, whose traditions are sometimes represented by ancient armor and weapons. As these Germanic tribes called on the forces of darkness for strength in battle, for instance, so the warriors of the *Iliad* depended on their helmets and shields to give them that mystic advantage. Odysseus, for example, borrows an archaic helmet outfitted with boar's teeth that has a long genealogy itself, and the enormous Ajax carries a "towering shield" whose ancient creation is also described at length.

* "Harii" is related to the Gothic *harjis* (army).

Like Nestor's remarks about the great warriors who used to be around, such objects of war invoke a tradition of heroism that would otherwise be lost.

The association of hairiness with an unalloyed masculinity is ancient in Indo-European cultures. As in the biblical example of Samson, the warrior's terrifying prowess is visually expressed by an abundance of head hair, either his own or that supplied by a shaggy helmet. The practice has an obvious connection to the practice of wearing animal skins in battle (as in Hercules's or Alexander the Great's lion headdress), and is socially confirmed by the Greek and Roman practice of having male slaves wear close-cropped hair. In both *The Song of Roland* and *The Poem of the Cid*, the beard serves as an emblem of prowess and authority; Charlemagne's in *Roland* overflows his armor and the Cid's is part of his grandeur after battle: "He rode, My Cid, on his fine horse,/his skullcap pushed back—God, how splendid his beard!—his mailed hood on his shoulders, his sword in his hand."

But when such an obvious contrast as long hair/short hair exists, it can be redefined. Caesar turns the distinction around at the battle of Pharsalia when he has his troops shave their beards so that they can't be gripped in hand-to-hand combat, while the more vain troops of Pompey wear their beards and long hair down to defeat. Henry V in the fifteenth century similarly popularizes short hair for the soldier, perhaps to emphasize by a monkish tonsure the religious sanction of his quest to become king of France. With the English Civil Wars of the seventeenth century, hairstyle supports an even more obvious ideological distinction, pitting the long-locked royalist Cavaliers against the close-shorn parliamentary Roundheads. The association of long hair with military prowess persists formally in the high beaver-fur helmets of nineteenth-century troops and informally in the long hair of irregulars like the bushwackers along the Kansas-Missouri border during the Civil War. In World War I, a plaintive assertion of a connection with the glorious past appears in the slang word for French ordinary soldiers, *poilus,* the hairy ones. By World War II, of course, the look of the soldier has once again become associated with short hair, and in the United States at least, the masculinity equation becomes reversed again in Vietnam, with the long hair of war protesters signifying an alternate to crew-cut military masculinity.

# THE BIRTH OF GENEALOGY: WHERE DID KNIGHTS COME FROM?

The significance of genealogy for warriors has come and gone in European history. To those reading the *Iliad* for the first time it often seems comic that the warriors proclaim who their fathers and grandfathers were before proceeding to split each other's helmets and dump their brains on the ground. It certainly is not battlefield etiquette now, nor perhaps ever was. But in the world of an aristocracy that defines masculinity in terms of its own physical valor, that genealogical vaunting is essential to the warrior's identity, whether it is in classical or medieval Europe or in medieval Japan. Most important, it ensures that one's immediate opponent is worthy and that true honor will result from the combat. But that immediate balance of honor is also rooted in a sense of history, particularly family history. The body exists in time and will validate its prowess in time, but, just as the frail body hopes to project itself through military fame into an eternal future, another crucial part of identity is connected genealogically to the past. Here is an important qualification of the individualism of the warrior hero: like the honor of the Mafia soldier or gang member, it is in its earliest phases tightly tied to family, the family of blood as well as the family of wartime camaraderie.

The invocation of a warrior tradition can be practical as well as nostalgic. The ancient Nestor, for example, is the only person in the *Iliad* who knows the proper chariot tactics for war. Chariot warfare had been widespread at the supposed time of the Trojan War. Because it required expensive equipment as well as a driver who took care of the horses while the warrior shot his arrows or threw his spear, owning a chariot was a class privilege, as chariot warfare was in early Egypt and China. But Homer, composing his epic in a period when the military function of chariots has been virtually forgotten, is himself often vague about how they are used. Instead of seeing them as part of charges, he frequently describes them as if they were glorified taxicabs that dropped off heroes on the battlefield for their single combats. Nestor, however, knows what chariots can do, and he celebrates the power of the past while criticizing the less mighty world of the present.

Knighthood, with its invocation of a lineage of heroism, also increasingly served very practical social and political purposes. Two issues are significant here. The first is the status of warriors themselves in medieval society, the second the effort of individual families to achieve that status. In the diffuse political world of the Middle Ages, when central authority, whether king or country, was weak or nonexistent, loyalty to a local lord was complemented by loyalty to family. Questions of genealogy—who actually was your father, and what was his family—became paramount, especially for those seeking to expand their own power and status, for those in the warrior and noble classes also believed that true honor was their sole possession.

In this complex period of several centuries, when style, standards, and codes of warrior masculinity varied greatly across Europe, there were yet some provocative trends in the changing role of the man of violence in the social order. Medieval theory generally viewed society as made up of three major groups or "estates": the *oratores,* the people who prayed, who were part of the Church; the *pugnatores* or *bellatores,* who were the war makers; and the *laboratores,* who were farmers and craftsmen. This tripartite arrangement bears some resemblance to classical efforts to describe the makeup of society, like Plato's division in *The Republic* between guardians (rulers), auxiliaries (warriors), and farmers and craftsmen. It is also similar to the three prime social functions that Georges Dumézil has ascribed to the Indo-European heritage: the priestly-judicial, the military, and the productive. These categories are very general, and they shift according to the specifics of social context. But they mark an explicit medieval effort to imagine the structure of society in terms of a differentiation of male social function.

That the warrior class became so dominant as to be acknowledged as the ruling class was surprising, since the priestly and judicial classes would seem to have that authority already well in hand. In Plato's *Republic*, for example, only those few auxiliaries who respond to philosophic training would ever become guardians. But in the Middle Ages, the masculinity of physical prowess is gradually equated with an exalted social status. Whether the context is a tournament or an epic poem, such men are highly praised and rewarded for acting out violence before an audience that both distances and enhances that violence. In our own time, it is akin to the high salaries given to entertainers and sports figures for being both physical and emotional weather vanes for the audience.

The language of epic also offers some clues here. The medievalist Joseph Dane has pointed out that it is the warrior function or estate that is particularly singular and straightforward, while the other two categories often have a variety of powers and spheres of influence, and so are less easily appreciated. As we have seen, the words for "manly" or "valiant" are often class-marked, like *eorlice* (earl-like) in *Beowulf*, the phrase *en guise de baron* in *The Song of Roland*, or *a guisa de varón* in *The Poem of the Cid*. In a society where show and ostentation are considered to be evidence of psychological and theological emptiness—like the antitheatrical English Puritans of the sixteenth and seventeenth centuries—such phrases have a negative connotation. But for a medieval world in which identity and reputation are united, it is praise indeed, implying not only that there is a direct correlation between degrees of manhood and degrees of social hierarchy, but also that a person who acts without an audience has not really done anything. As Chaucer says in a more ironic context, "Where as a man may have noon audience/Nought helpeth it to tellen his sentence." Without an audience, you may as well be silent.

This metaphoric analogy between high prowess and high social status lies behind the history of the medieval ascent of the knight to power and renown, a rise that could not have been predicted from its origins. Originally, the Latin word for knight, *miles*, legally meant a lower-level noble who had attached himself to the household of a feudal lord as a kind of employee or even a serf, a species of military henchman, sometimes also dressed and armed by the lord. Like the Mamluks of Egypt and the samurai of Japan, knights were originally low-ranked retainers to a noble class (*mamluk* means "slave"; *samurai* "military servant") whose rise to a ruling status of their own is marked by the mythification of their social position.

As the word for knight passed into the European languages, it took on different nuances. In French it is *chevalier,* like the Spanish *caballero,* coming almost directly from the common Latin synonym for *miles*—*caballerius.* Both invoke the horse and are words that, like the various Scandinavian versions of the Germanic *ritter,* can be traced back to the members of the Roman social class called the *equites,* who in the early republic were those not wellborn enough to be nobles and members of the Senate but who nevertheless had enough money to have their own horses, armor, and weapons. In English, however, the word "knight" contains a hint of its native and socially lower origins. Coming from the Old English *cniht* and connected to the German *knecht,* it originally meant a young boy who was an attendant or servant. Unlike the French and Spanish terms, which emphasize the horse as part of the equation, the English and German terms convey an atmosphere of youth on the verge of initiation into manhood. It is a transition also reflected in the term *enfances* for a knightly neophyte's first deeds of arms, and summed up as well in the archaic title *childe,* revived for Romantic and Victorian medievalism in Byron's poem *Childe Harold's Pilgrimage* and Browning's "Childe Roland to the Dark Tower Came."

From these unprepossessing beginnings comes the rise of a class that would define its ostentatious and public manhood as the moral core of society. An analogous process occurred in medieval Japan, when in the twelfth century the Taira clan was defeated by the Minamotos, who ushered in the shogunate, a government run by warriors that lasted some seven hundred years. Just as the samurai or *bushi* became a prime figure in Japan, so the knight focused for the Middle Ages an image of masculinity attractive to men from all rungs of the social ladder.

In classical times the gods and heroes represented a kind of trickle-down masculinity that could be admired and looked up to but rarely, if ever, achieved. But the status and prestige of the knight in the Middle Ages moved steadily upward. At first, the low social position of the medieval knight reflects that of the Roman *miles.* The vast majority came from the countryside and the peasantry, often the impecunious younger sons of families whose only chance for gaining anything from life was to attach themselves to the household of a local lord. There they might stay for the rest of their lives, or, if lucky, amass enough wealth from war or tournaments to set themselves up as minor lords, splitting their time between farming, their ancestral work, and the military service they owed to the lord above them.*

This independent knight, with his own small holdings, began to appear more widely in the eleventh and twelfth centuries. Between the twelfth and the fourteenth centuries especially, being a knight became socially significant, and literature began to focus much of its energy on his psychology and morality. In the battle scenes of the eleventh-century Bayeux Tapestry the Normans and their Saxon foes are not very individualized. The Normans may have mustaches and the Saxons close-cropped hair, but no one is, in the heraldic term, armigerous—identifiable by a shield or coat of arms. The confusion is great enough that historians have argued long and inconclusively over which figure in the section devoted to the Battle of Hastings represents King Harold. Similarly, an oft-told battle anecdote describes the moment when William has to take off his helmet to show his face to troops who believe he has been killed.

Not long after, however, in England as well as the Continent, previously indistinguishable warrior costumes started to sprout colors, emblems, and symbols, while heralds were employed to identify warriors on the battlefield by the bright signals of their devices. Arms—in the double meaning of weapons and the shield or escutcheon by which friends, foes, and heralds could identify a warrior on the field of battle—became synonymous with the most prestigious form of masculine identity. On the Continent, as Georges Duby points out, the word *miles,* previously inferior to *nobilis,* begins to loom more significantly in legal documents. By the late thirteenth century, it had become a title rather than a description, and "a nobleman who had not been knighted had to yield to knights who were not noble" (99). From a fighting class who served the nobility, knights had risen to a position that even nobles envied and coveted. Kings, too, were taking note. In 1166 Henry II asked for a list of the knights in his kingdom, that is, all those who possessed horses and war equipment, with an eye toward establishing their class cohesion even more explicitly.

A much-admired figure like William Marshal, who lived from 1146 to 1219, is thus central to the transformation of the knightly gang of rambunctious, relatively impoverished young men into the *mesnie,* the trained

* Emile Benveniste remarks that the warrior cohort was "always ready to follow and defend [the lord] and to win renown under his orders," but also only so long as he gave gifts and they got booty (64).

cohort. Beginning without either horse or armor, William was the very definition of a knight-errant, wandering from tournament to tournament in search of the fame and money to be earned by defeating richer men and holding them for ransom. Through his prowess in both England and Europe, he rose to great wealth, becoming earl of Pembroke and later regent of England. Like many knights who similarly consolidated their fortunes, because William had the experience of striving to make his mark (and gather his riches) he was more self-conscious about the panoply of knighthood and its obligations. After his death his family commissioned a poetic biography that emphasized his strength, his wisdom, and his piety. In 1241 Henry III, for whom William had served as regent, ordered all male subjects with sufficient property to become knights.

The medieval historian Jean Scammell argues that Henry III's order defined English knighthood as more explicitly economic than the genealogical and family-oriented knighthood characteristic of Europe. But in both the central similarity is the rise of knights as a self-conscious class with a particular public responsibility to defend society against its enemies. As a result, genealogy and inheritance became even more important as indicators of knightly worthiness to wield authority.

Heroic figures, of course, had always been ideals in martial societies. As the *Iliad* demonstrates, they helped preserve both a human tradition of heroic virtue as well as a relation to the gods who are their protectors. But when the past has little moral or exemplary influence, those genealogical links are flimsier. *Beowulf*, for example, is probably a product of the eighth century, two centuries or more before the general appearance of the genealogical self-consciousness I have been describing. Its basic unit is the warrior band, not the family. Consequently, Beowulf has a relation to God as embodied in Destiny or Fate, but little connection to any specific warrior gods or human models. *Beowulf* is concerned instead with the more immediate relation between lord and vassal or liege and warrior. Kinship is therefore more significant than genealogy as a spur to warrior virtue.*

The assumption that the right to rule is genetic also has a long history. Plato, for example, specifically says that the capacity to be a guardian, an auxiliary, or one of the farmer-craftsman class is innate. The tendency, he says, will be that members of those classes produce children who have the

* The Beowulf story is similar to that of Hercules, and both will stand behind the later redefinition of the warrior not as part of hereditary family, but as a dynamic individual.

same capacities, although he does leave the way open for those few children who show the traits of another group to be trained in the abilities suitable to that group.

For a good deal of the time between the fall of the Roman Empire and the Middle Ages, however, the concept of a continuous personal heritage, even the use of surnames, was fleeting at best. As Duby argues, the European idea that either the maternal or the paternal line ennobles its offspring is actually of comparatively recent vintage, coming into common usage about the year 1000 as part of the social passage from a more anarchic political situation to the relative orderliness of feudalism. A clear if not entirely accurate genealogy therefore became a crucial element in asserting the family's status, and by the twelfth century genealogical charts were being commissioned all over Europe to tie together noble status and family descent.

Directly connected to the effort to establish genealogies was a more general effort to link the embryonic nationalism of the later Middle Ages with the great tribes and heroes of the past, especially the Trojans and the Romans. Thus the French descended from the Franks and the greatness of Charlemagne, the Spanish from the Goths, the English from Brutus (the great-grandson of Aeneas), the Normans and Scandinavians from the Vikings, while Thor himself, according to the thirteenth-century *Prose Edda*, was a descendant of Priam, the king of Troy and father of Hector. Important objects also had a genealogy: Charlemagne's spear Joyeux in *The Song of Roland* boasts a spearhead from the lance that struck Jesus in the side. Meanwhile, for individual families, a (frequently mythical) founder who had established the family fame stood in the background.

Heroic figures, as portrayed in art and literature, thus remain personal ideals in martial societies, even when the individualism they represent may also threaten the social hierarchy, if it were ever truly revived. As eponymous progenitors of noble families, they also serve to furnish a distinguished genealogy for the men in their audience. In *The Song of Roland* as in the *Iliad*, there are lists of heroes who were there along with the central figures, including many who aren't themselves characters (and may have been inserted by later scribes). In such epics, the story of the hero and his particular battles serves as an epic vortex, sweeping into itself allusions to other conflicts, other revenges, and other feuds, to invite the members of the audience to connect the heroic myth with fancied events in their own genealogies, inheriting honor both physically and spiritually.

Pragmatically such a genealogy could establish arguments for rights to land and other possessions; psychologically it postulated a line of warriors whose code of family honor was validated by history. Fittingly, the authors of these chronicles were more often secular members of the family household than monks or other clerics. In the end, an elaborate warrior genealogy crucially validated military prowess in the present. By the sixteenth century in punctilious Germany—to which knighthood had come somewhat later than to France and England—an armored combatant had to trace his genealogy back four generations before he was allowed to participate in tournaments.

# KNIGHTHOOD, CHRISTIANITY, AND CHIVALRY: THE UNEASY TRUCE

> Let those . . . who are accustomed to wage private wars wastefully even against Believers go forth against the Infidels in a battle worthy to be undertaken now and to be finished in victory. Now, let those, who until recently existed as plunderers, be soldiers of Christ. . . . Let those, who recently were hired for a few pieces of silver, win their eternal reward.
>
> —Pope Urban II preaching the First Crusade, 1095

As the perception of masculinity developed in relation to war in the Middle Ages, "knight" was the bridge between the otherwise separable or even contradictory categories of "noble" and "warrior." Before the centralizing state and the international Church began to reorganize the medieval world, knighthood constituted the dominant masculine style. But as its power grew, both Church and state tried to tame the individualist traditions of the *pugnatores* and forge them into more amenable shapes. The evolving monarchies (especially in England and France) wanted more exclusive royal control of violence, and often supported the knightly class as a counterpoise to the power of local barons; the Church, in contrast, at first condemned violence per se, especially when it was directed against its priesthood. Throughout the period, war was continuously denounced by at least some Christian writers and theologians. By the tenth century, reforming monastic orders like those at Cluny in France had already defined the holy monk as a male ideal in contrast with the warrior. Yet because of political realities as well as doctrinal ambiguities, there quickly arose a series of ways in which the male domains of the priesthood and the military began to coalesce. This development distinctly resembles the evolution in India that George Dumézil describes in the shift from the polytheistic and warrior-oriented Aryan religion, with its many gods and heroes, to the single principle of good worshiped in early Zoroastrianism:

> Theologically, and probably socially, the most vigorous and difficult attack had to be carried out against the traditional warriors, human and divine . . . to redeploy them in the service of the good religion, that is, to preserve their force and valor while depriving them of their autonomy. (*Destiny*, 116)

This more ancient religious effort to retain warrior prowess while undermining warrior singularity is an intriguing forerunner to the transformation of knightly violence into chivalric Christianity sponsored by the medieval Church. It may even imply that the battle between warrior religion and monotheism lies at the heart of Indo-European ideas of masculinity—in later terms, an archetypal battle for the soul of man (and the definition of the masculine) between Satan and Christ.*

Especially after the Crusades had reconciled the Church to at least some forms of knightly violence, both Church and state could become patrons of tournaments, although not in England, where Henry II had banned them, forcing English knights seeking fame and money to travel to Europe, particularly Normandy, a part of his realm where they were still legal.† Early tournaments were in fact often considered to be provocative attacks against both religious and secular authority. Tournaments and the *mêlées* that preceded them had been in part designed to give hot-blooded young men a place to siphon off their energies in the lulls between wars. But because they emphasized personal prowess and local loyalties, they had a potentially subversive air that nurtured political unrest. Maurice Keen, a historian of chivalry, notes that earlier in the

* The anti- or non-Christian side of Western warrior culture is also reflected in the attack on Christianity made by the *bakufu* (military) governments in Japan until the nineteenth century, which included the *fumi-e*, a ceremony in which images of the crucified Christ and Virgin and child were trampled. In the militant Japan of the 1930s it took the form of a stress on Shinto and an opposition to Buddhism and Confucianism.

† Never one to bow so easily to Church influence, Henry II was upset when his sons Henry and Richard went on the Crusades.

century the assertions of individual rights against monarchical control that resulted in the Magna Carta (1215) began at tournaments, and in 1273, in what became known as the "little battle of Châlons," a French tournament turned into a pitched battle.

But whatever its allegiance to local lords, knighthood in its origin owed little to any larger political authority and even less to the Church. There had been exemplary warrior clerics, like the fictional Turpin of *The Song of Roland* and Don Jerome in *The Cid,* as well as the real-life Odo of Bayeux, William the Conqueror's half brother, who probably commissioned the tapestry and is depicted there in the Battle of Hastings. But the practice was technically against canon law. Indeed, to the extent that the warrior spirit emerged from any religious tradition, it was a pagan connection to the unsubdued individual and the earth, indebted to the warriors of the Norse sagas, the Greek and Roman heroes, and the Germanic tribes described by Tacitus. *Furor impius,* blasphemous furor, Virgil called it in the *Aeneid,* and in his first book he has Jupiter predict that such an irreligious frenzy will be purged by the peaceful reign of Augustus, whose own progenitor is Virgil's hero, *pius Aeneas,* rather than the furor-ridden native Italian warrior Turnus, whom Aeneas finally defeats.

Just as Virgil fashioned his *pius Aeneas* on the armature of the Trojan warrior, Christianity in the Middle Ages began to equip its own modification of the warrior ethic. Early efforts of the Church to diminish the random violence led to proclamations generally referred to as the Peace or Truce of God. Starting in France in the early eleventh century and gradually spreading to other areas of Europe, such edicts attempted to protect particular places and people (e.g., churches, pilgrims, widows, nuns) from violence and threatened with excommunication anyone who fought in a particular period of time, often from Thursday evening until Monday morning, tacitly accepting if not approving violence at other times.

The Crusades furnished a more complicated incentive for the Church to deal with the relation of war and violence to Christian spirituality, not by compartmentalizing them as did the Truce of God but by fusing them into a fight against a more appropriate enemy. First officially encouraged by Pope Urban II in 1095, the Crusades grew out of an earlier papal reform movement to exert its authority over more of secular life, chiefly by imbuing the laity, in particular those with armor and power, with a sense of sin that needed to be purged. Seizing upon the new social orthodoxy of the three estates of the *pugnatores, oratores,* and *laboratores* (itself a conception heavily influenced by Church philosophers), the propagandists and preachers of the Crusades assigned the *pugnatores* the specific task of freeing the sacred sites and Christian population of the Holy Land from the Islamic "infidel," who had in fact occupied them for several hundred years. Although there were ill-fated movements—like the People's Crusade in the eleventh century, led by Peter the Hermit and Walter the Penniless, and the Children's Crusade in the thirteenth century, inspired by the visions of a French peasant boy—that tried to spread the crusading urge to the whole population, Urban II and later popes specifically called upon the *milites,* the knights, to be the principal Crusaders. The result was to be what the French medieval historian Marc Bloch calls a new "double hierarchy" of the priestly *oratores* and the warrior *pugnatores*—to both of which the working *laboratores* were to be subject and beholden.

In this respect the Crusades foreshadow a new kind of war: war waged for a cause instigated by religion but waged independently of it. No longer just a possessor of armor, horse, and fighting skill, the knight became a figure whose violence was sanctioned by higher considerations than his personal prowess or lineage. Now it would be justified by a theological pedigree that went back to the last centuries of the Roman Empire, when the Emperor Constantine converted to Christianity after seeing a vision of the cross and the words *in hoc signo vinces* (by this sign you will conquer) before a decisive battle, and Saint Augustine developed a theory of just war to justify Christians fighting the barbarians attacking Rome. But with all these precedents, the preeminent validation was the Europe-wide effort to channel the violence of knightly power into the idealized code of personal conduct called chivalry. Chivalry, properly understood, would shape the behavior of the true knight and allow the condemnation of the false. Cloaked in its precepts, knights could no longer be accused of being bullies in armor, engaged in what Georges Duby in his biography of William Marshal calls "interminable discord." Instead they were now participants in a higher realm of morality and service.

Another significant result of the Crusades was a new phase in the professionalization of war in response to the logistic and administrative problems of sending out such long-range expeditions. Materially it was the time when fortifications of stone and brick began to replace those of wood and earthwork. Castles, towns, and private residences began to encircle themselves with grander and more secure enclosures based on new designs for walls, windows, foundations, moats, and drawbridges to facilitate protection and defense. At the same time, siege weapons like catapults and, by the fourteenth century, cannons became more effective, although the improvement and extensive use of handguns was still in the future and the preferred weapon for close combat remained the sword.

In origin the chivalric code may have been based on ethics more than religion. But when it was united with the crusading impulse, it gave the actions of the warrior a transcendent defense, combining military aggression with both divine favor and moral validation. As armor protected the fragile body, the code shored up the spirit, vindicating the show of power and turning self-promoting display into holy ritual. Despite the many fiascoes and the ultimate defeat of the waves of Crusaders by the Islamic world, both chivalry and crusade declared that spiritual approval is necessary for military victory, and military glory without spiritual sanction is vain. Dubbing, the ritual initiation in the status of knighthood, had previously been performed by lords and kings. Increasingly it was performed as well, or even exclusively, by Church officials, whose benedictions included rules for the ideal synthesis of military prowess and Christian piety—Constantine's vision reborn and codified into a system of knightly values.

To take up the Cross, to go on crusade, was to be the highest expression of knightly duties, and the Church sponsorship of the *miles christianus,* the Christian knight, defined a status well beyond that of the armored knight fighting off local enemies and foraging for booty. Not incidentally, along with the higher social standing, there were legal privileges that often came from crusading. But the most powerful lure crusading afforded was the indulgence for sins. Unlike the usual form of penitence for killing in battle, which required fasting and a symbolic stripping away of earthly identity, knights on crusade could do penance without taking off their armor. As a further inducement, if you died on the battlefield you would go immediately to heaven, perhaps, like Roland, carried by angels.

Church-sponsored initiatives such as the Truce of God had some chastening effect on brutal lords and nobles. But with the Crusades came an even more effective artistic and symbolic celebration of warrior saints to bridge the conflict between Christian peace and knightly war. In the Anglo-Saxon poem *The Dream of the Rood,* the narrator tells of his dream of the cross (*rood* in Old English) who speaks to him of its life, being cut down as a tree in the forest and used for the Crucifixion. In the poem Jesus rushes forward to climb the cross, much as secular poems would describe a young warrior plunging into battle:

*Then the young Hero (that was God almighty) took off his clothes.*
*Strong and resolute, he went up on high,*
*Mighty in the sight of many he would redeem mankind.*

(Dickins and Ross, 25)

*The Dream of the Rood* is usually dated to the eighth century (we know it in a tenth-century version), when Christianity is once again attempting to win over the British Isles, and the poem illustrates the effort to unite spiritual heroism with warrior tradition. The story of *The Song of Roland* was already well known in the eleventh century, when William the Conqueror supposedly had a minstrel draw upon it to inspire his soldiers before the Battle of Hastings. Reflecting the young warrior god of *The Dream of the Rood*, the feisty Archbishop Turpin in *The Song of Roland* and the combative bishop Don Jerome in *The Poem of the Cid* are spiritual warriors fighting the "heathen" Moors alongside the heroes. In visual art the effort to define the ideal warrior as a Christian knight appeared in a whole array of warrior saints, whose combination of armor with halos decorated altarpieces and stained-glass windows, often as part of a group of four saints, whose separate characteristics defined a limited world of masculine possibility, transfigured through martyrdom. This artistic celebration of the armored saint arrived at a moment in medieval art when painters were intent on depicting light, textures, and reflective surfaces. But it also corresponds to a cultural moment, when the warrior is no longer a potential danger to the Church but perhaps an ally—like Louis IX of France, who led two Crusades, brought the Crown of Thorns back to France, died in Tunisia, and was canonized a saint in 1297, only twenty years after his death.

At the head of the group of traditional military saints is usually Saint Michael, the leader of the hosts of heaven. But there are several others, some whose stories had long been part of Church folklore and some whose tales were either invented or enhanced: Santiago Matamoros (Saint James the Moor-Killer), the defender of Spain, whose shrine at Compostela was one of the most popular medieval pilgrimage spots; Saint George, the patron saint of England, Portugal, and Catalonia, a fourth-century Roman soldier martyred in Palestine, whose later legend included the defeat of a dragon after the threatened townspeople promised to convert to Christianity; Saint Eustache, a Roman general who was converted when while hunting he saw a cross between a stag's antlers; Saint Hubert, whose story is much the same as Saint Eustache's and who became the patron saint of hunters; and, somewhat later, Saint Sebastian, who appears on many Renaissance altarpieces as a young Roman soldier who has been stripped of his armor and pierced with arrows for his commitment to Christianity.

In common with many other historically compelling ideas, the concept of the Crusades constituted a field within which many seemingly opposed values could be fused: material gain and idealism, social hierarchy and social egalitarianism, spirituality and violence, local pride and allegiance to an international order. To dissolve such conflicts, the preaching of the Crusades emphasized the relation between military masculinity and the goals of Christianity. In some areas, the saint and the warrior were still at odds: Muslims, Jews, and other non-Christians obviously did not benefit from the new religious sanction, and the knightly attitude toward women would require more secular forms of persuasion. But a significant achievement of the Crusades was to bring a spiritual manhood—albeit in military guise—onto the stage of European culture. Instead of the warrior body, Christianity emphasized the soul as the essence of identity, first in conversion and later in its purification through penance. In the aristocratic and tribal view of honor, a man without honor was not a man. But in the Christian view a man not capable of honor (for class or other reasons) was still a man, although a somewhat different sort of man. He didn't need to continue to perform honorably in order to demonstrate his masculinity—he was already a man spiritually because of God's grace and Christ's sacrifice.

The awkwardness with which these two different definitions of the heart of masculinity attempted to find common cause is obvious. By the Second Crusade in 1146, a new institution had combined the military and spiritual into a kind of warrior monkhood. The earliest of many such organizations, the Knights Hospitaler, received papal approval in 1113, and the Knights Templar (named after the Temple of Solomon in Jerusalem, captured in the First Crusade) were recognized in 1128. Bernard of Clairvaux, who was to become the official preacher of the Second Crusade, praised the Templars as the "new soldiers" and helped write the rules of their order, which stressed their separation from ordinary knighthood and its frivolities (like hunting), prescribed various kinds of austerity, and emphasized the need for every brother knight to make a vow of obedience as severe as any samurai's to his lord. Significantly, in the face of the pagan tradition of warrior vaunting and self-celebration, there were also several injunctions that the order would not countenance any urge to personal distinction. Speaking of past exploits, military or sexual, was strictly forbidden, and "if any brother out of a feeling of pride or arrogance wishes to have as his due a better and finer habit, let him be given the worst" (Upton-Ward, 24).*

Like knighthood itself, the military orders drew their members chiefly from the landless younger sons who had no hope of inheritance because of the system of primogeniture. From their roots in the care of others—in hospitals, as custodians of religious places, and as protectors of pilgrims—they became a sort of private army. As the military orders grew, they were often used by rulers otherwise strapped for manpower as a political and military force to patrol boundaries and staff border castles against their enemies. Wherever they were in power, the government fundamentally amounted to a military theocracy. In the case of the Teutonic Knights, founded in 1190 during the Third Crusade and turned into a military order in 1198 during the Fourth, they even had their own country, Prussia, whose pagan inhabitants they either converted or exterminated. At the same time, they defended Catholicism from the Lithuanians, the last large pagan group in Europe—and one still worthy to be fought at the end of the fourteenth century by Chaucer's fictional Knight, by Harry (Hotspur) Percy, and twice by the future Henry IV.

Although the First Crusade had set enough of a pattern that its heroes, like Godfrey of Bouillon and Louis IX of France, continued to be invoked as models, most historians consider that the real onset of the direct connection between chivalry and crusading began with the Third Crusade (1189–92), which furnished heroes both real (Richard the Lion-Hearted) as well as fictional (Robin Hood). The Third Crusade was also the first to be called a "crusade" (although not in English until the eighteenth century), in no small measure because of the presence of the great Islamic general Saladin, the sultan of Egypt, who had decisively ended the Crusader occupation of the Holy Land after almost a century. It is also perhaps the influence of Saladin that decisively helped shift the meaning of jihad. Jihad, or holy war, is discussed in the Koran, although only one of its four elements decrees action against an infidel enemy; the rest focus on inner moral and ethical imperatives. But not many years after Saladin defeated the Crusader effort to recap-

* Lions were excluded from the prohibition against hunting because they were considered the embodiment of a particularly pagan evil.

ture Jerusalem the first Muslim comparisons between crusade and jihad appear, although which came first, crusade or aggressive jihad, is still debated by historians.

Individual figures like Saladin or Richard the Lion-Hearted could unite military prowess with divine sanction. But in France and, even more extensively, in England, it was particularly the figure of King Arthur who merged the warrior past with the Christianized present, the authority of a single ruler with the prowess of individual knights, and, not incidentally, the sanction of local pride with the universal claims of the Church. To the extent that there was an historical Arthur, his origins are shadowy. Recent archaeological evidence suggests that the sources of the Arthurian legend may be in Sarmatia near the Caspian Sea, to which many of the same names and stories have been traced. If so, Arthur is rooted in the same Indo-European idea of warriorship that also spawned the Teutonic and Scandinavian traditions.

In some of the earliest written sources, Arthur does appear as a Celtic or Welsh local hero leading the fight against the invading Anglo-Saxons. Later, Arthur begins more closely to resemble Charlemagne, especially the Charlemagne of *The Song of Roland*, the archetypal king and patron of knightly aspirants. His significance as the great native British monarch, whose Round Table included every great knight and whose seat at Camelot was the center of warrior honor, thereafter grew quickly, inspired by the political needs of the moment as well as by the cultural need for a charismatic leader figure whose authority could license the knightly urge to combat.

By the twelfth century, Arthur was definitely a ruler along the lines of the Norman kings, who had been invaders themselves, but were now beginning to think of their dynasty as in some way English. Completed in the late 1130s, Geoffrey of Monmouth's *Historia Regum Britanniae* was the first effort to establish a continuous political history of England as distinguished from the Romans. Geoffrey's Arthur is not entirely the Arthur of later legends, but his account does serve to help establish Arthur as a figure rooted in native traditions who is also the appropriate forerunner of the Norman kings, an epitome of chivalry to contrast with the heroes of the Celts and Saxons. In 1187, as if to confirm the lineage, Henry II named his grandson Arthur (as Henry VII would name his eldest son some three hundred years later). In 1191, with miraculous timing, the "bones" of Arthur and his Queen Guinevere were discovered and exhumed by monks at Glastonbury. It was a site well known for its mingled legends, identified as the Isle of Avalon of both Celtic and

Arthurian myth as well as the place where Joseph of Arimathea founded the first Christian church in Britain.*

As the story developed in the hands of British and French chroniclers and poets, Arthur became an ultimate judge of knightly accomplishment on earth, and Camelot the prime arena where knightly achievement—and knightly identity—could be validated. But by the early thirteenth century, the celebration of Arthur was almost entirely English and the parading of Arthurian sanction for both individual and national assertion well advanced. Jousts and tournaments often took the form of reenacting Arthurian stories, and knights would dress like, and even take the names of, characters from the legends. This process heated up considerably with what was later called the Hundred Years' War (1337–1453) between the English and various parts of the French ruling class. Near its beginning, Edward III of England, in a gesture stretching back to his great-great-great-grandfather Henry II's patronage of the discovery of Arthur's bones, vowed to reestablish the Round Table. In 1348 he went on to establish the Order of the Garter, a chivalric society that would enhance knightly prestige even further. A few years later John II established the Order of the Star, the first chivalric order in France.

* This impulse to bring together a contemporary ruler, a dead pagan hero, and the sanction of Christianity was hardly confined to Plantagenet England. It would be reflected not quite a hundred years later in Spain when Alfonso X of Castile composed epitaphs for the tombs of El Cid and his wife, Jimena, at Cardeña (1272). El Cid was an eleventh-century Spanish warrior and ruler. The poem celebrating his exploits dates from the twelfth century.

# CHIVALRY IN THEORY AND PRACTICE

For the medieval knight, with his mixed ancestry in pagan warriorship, Christian soldiery, and the dim memory of classical heroism, it was inevitable that conflicts would occur, especially when someone tried to harness this multiple heritage. Individual and group honor in particular were often at odds. Individual honor was fine when it fueled single combats and personal pique. But when it appeared in a war situation, it had the potential to undermine the common goal. In one of the sieges of the Hundred Years' War, Sir Hugh Calvely, assigned to be in charge of the English army's rear guard, refused because that represented to him a smirch on his honor. (Perhaps he hadn't read *The Song of Roland* on the glory of bringing up the rear.)

If physical violence as the ultimate test of personal honor were carried too far, it might finish off the family line that was supposedly the original justification for honor. This bizarrely self-destructive concept of personal honor defended at the expense of future heirs was notoriously characteristic of certain families. So many of the Lalaings of northern France died in battle that it seemed they preferred the afterlife of reputation to actually having any descendants. Carnage occurred in other warrior families as well, especially in time of civil war. Unless the family was extinguished altogether, it was often the female line that kept it alive.

The code of chivalry allowed such absurdities as Calvely's and the Lalaings' because it so emphasized personal behavior, regardless of the ways much larger institutions might try to align that behavior with their own ends. Stripped to its basics, chivalry means "the behavior of people who ride horses" (*chevaux*). But simply to have a horse trained for war was the specific attribute of a warrior class. Thus the code of chivalry, while seemingly only a set of moral precepts, emphasized social distinctions between the upper-class cavalry and the lower-class infantry and archers. All are involved in the violence of the battlefield, but knights could call upon lineage and caste to help them believe that war is a noble arena for male competition rather than just a bloody piece of work.

Of course "chivalry" as understood in the Middle Ages is a complex term that goes far beyond horses, and its meaning was as much in contention in the fourteenth century as it has been more recently among historians.* Our main sources for its definition are the books that themselves attempt to clarify into organized codes of behavior a vast array of different practices, and thereby create a tradition. None of these sources is earlier than the twelfth century. Briefly stated, the chivalric values they define are loyalty (to the knight's political superior); prowess (which includes both praise of the rash willingness to throw oneself into danger—*hardiesse*—and the skill to deal with that danger); *franchise,* or an openhanded largesse to one's fellows and followers; and courtesy to women, children, and the elderly. All of these words—including loyalty, prowess, and largesse, which have passed into English—are French in origin, and much of the codification of chivalric values and language, including the word "army" itself, comes from France. All have survived in some form in modern French and English, with the interesting exception of the particular courtesy due to women—*druerie* (which comes from a root adjective meaning "strong, vigorous"), even though the desire to exempt women from the harshness of war has been a characteristic of much warrior behavior, in cultures as disparate as the Xhosa of South Africa and the Confederate border raiders of William Clarke Quantrill.

* Johann Huizinga in *The Waning of the Middle Ages* began the modern debate by arguing that chivalry represented a noble attempt to escape the greed, violence, and cru-

This status for cavalry, and its particular connection to the military paraphernalia of the knightly class, is itself a growth of comparatively short duration in the history of warfare. Cavalry had been virtually unused as a tactic in the classical world except by Alexander the Great. Xenophon, for one, remarks on the low status of the horseman compared to the foot soldier, and considers it a dishonorable way to fight. Even though the Middle Ages saw an increasingly well trained infantry, armed with bows, pikes, and halberds (a pike with an ax head), the prestige of the knight and his almost symbiotic relation to his horse revised this classical disdain, marking one of many shifts between the moral superiority of the hoplite infantry—Socrates barefoot on the battlefield—to the chivalric and class-inflected code of the encased knight in armor. The French medieval historian Philippe Contamine has said that cavalry was in fact the real battlefield innovation of the Middle Ages. But the importance was as much cultural as it was practical. Until the Civil War and the post–Civil War battles between the U.S. Cavalry and pony-mounted Indians on the western plains redefined cavalry heroism, the belief in cavalry as a war tactic was historically connected in Europe directly to the belief in a warrior class, whose mounted presence will intimidate the enemy through sheer bravery. Destriers, huge horses bred to carry the weight of knights and their increasingly elaborate armor, were trained to charge despite the noise and tumult of battle. Because of the problem of regrouping, however, the charge needed to be immediately successful, and of course it wouldn't do for a knight to lose his horse. Richard III's cry at Bosworth Field—"My kingdom for a horse"—is as much a plea to regain status as it is for an essential piece of equipment.*

The image of the shining chivalric knight helps foster the vague impression that somehow past wars were more honorable and perhaps more humane than the grand slaughters of the twentieth century. But the difference is only superficial. By the outbreak of the Hundred Years' War, military masculinity had become a mixture of the most appalling slaughter in which men on horseback fought, chopped one another down in battle, stripped the armor from the dead, and often cut off their heads

---

elty of life through moral rituals of battle and piety, which became steadily emptier and more extravagant. More recently, Maurice Keen and others have maintained that the chivalric ideal indeed lasted into the late Middle Ages.

* Andrew Aytoun emphasizes that, although the term "destrier" is used generally for "warhorse" in many accounts of medieval warfare, they were so expensive they would only have been bought by a minority of knights. Perhaps the name "destrier" echoed in the head of pulp fiction writer Max Brand when he wrote a twentieth-century version of the quest for honor, *Destry Rides Again*.

(to ensure a proper tally)—with a deeply held belief that there was an overarching chivalric fellowship, underwritten and overseen by God. Within those high principles there were a multitude of distinctions. The code did not extend to the peasantry of the countryside and the bourgeois of the towns, who might be murdered and their property pillaged by all sides indiscriminately, and, whereas courtesy toward women might be part of an ideal chivalric code of honor, this behavior hardly existed in wartime practice, unless the lady was herself upper class.

Even among the warrior classes themselves, there were very different ways of translating chivalric precepts into military tactics. Particularly in England, the place of archers in the mix of cavalry and infantry was much more significant than in France, where for at least the first several decades of the Hundred Years' War the nobility and knighthood clung to an unswerving belief in the moral and physical superiority of the man on horseback. Cavalry had been central to some battles of the early Crusades. By the fourteenth century, in the often muddy landscape of France, its military usefulness was questionable. But the expense of cavalry ensured that knightly duties would continue to be dependent on wealth: an intricately woven mail shirt and a destrier cost about the same enormous amount.

In France war was thus still defined for the most part by the actions of the cavalry and how much money was spent on prestigious horses, armor, and weapons. In England, by contrast, while knighthood and knightly practices were encouraged, since the time of Edward I in the late thirteenth century every man in the country had been obligated by law to practice archery with the longbow every Sunday. The prowess of such mythic bowmen as Hercules and the Trojan War hero Philoctetes, as well as the presence of Sagittarius in the zodiac, implies the ancient prestige of archery. But in Greece and later in Rome, infantry was the backbone of the army. Archers were generally considered a minor aspect of battle strategy and were often recruited from outsiders; the Greeks, for example, hired Scythians. Even among the nomadic tribes, the bow was employed primarily to soften up their enemies for the direct power of the cavalry charge.

With the growing use of the crossbow and the even more efficient British longbow, however, the power of arrows to thwart a cavalry charge and pierce armor was enormously expanded. The disastrous defeat inflicted by English archers against numerically superior French forces at Agincourt has often been particularly celebrated as a defining moment for nascent British nationalism (as attested to by Shakespeare's *Henry V*).

Later, it also constituted evidence of the greater English commitment to battlefield democracy, as Arthur Conan Doyle characterizes the mix of cavalry, armored foot soldiers, and archers in his novel *The White Company.* Using the victory at Agincourt as a form of political self-congratulation is elaborated further by the film versions of *Henry V,* directed by Sir Laurence Olivier in the midst of World War II, and in 1989 by Kenneth Branagh, after the Falklands War brought a bellicose Britain both celebration and ridicule.

More than five hundred years later, after the mass armies of the modern world, the democratic implications of Agincourt may be more obvious. But at the time, Henry V was imitating a tactical innovation first used by his great-grandfather Edward III: ordering knights to dismount to buttress a line of archers and spearmen against an onrushing pack of armored enemy cavalry. The fighting at both Crécy (1346) and Agincourt (1415), where smaller English armies almost wiped out the opposing French, demonstrated for the moment at least the technological superiority of the longbow-driven arrow as a distance weapon versus the less accurate and shorter-range crossbow. More significantly, these battles also revealed the danger of adhering to a code of chivalric behavior that one's enemy may interpret very differently.

Military historian John Keegan has pointed out that knightly warfare was already a century out of date at Agincourt, and the very similar circumstances of the French defeat at Crécy several decades before Agincourt confirms his argument. Mounted French knights had also met an overwhelming defeat by Flemish foot soldiers at Coutrai in 1302, and dismounted ones met the same fate against the English at Poitiers in 1356. In fact, with the exception of Richard the Lion-Hearted's victory against Saladin at Arsouf in 1191, the Crusader cavalry, which was heavily French, had generally failed in their battles with the Arabs and Turks.

Somehow the triad of faith, chivalry, and aristocratic privilege (and subsequent defeats of the Flemish) nevertheless confirmed the French in their prejudice for cavalry as the ultimate weapon of chivalric warfare. The English meanwhile had learned other lessons. After Edward I defeated the Scots at Falkirk in 1298 with the first extensive use of the longbow, Edward II's cavalry was in turn defeated by Scottish foot soldiers led by Robert Bruce at Bannockburn in 1314, when the English archers could not be effectively deployed. But at Halidon Hill in 1333, Edward III decisively defeated the Scots with infantry and longbow tactics that would become the model for English success in the Hundred Years' War.

So there's more than a shred of truth in Conan Doyle's depiction of medieval English military democracy, at least on the level of their willingness to mix infantry with cavalry, and arrows with swords, while the French adherence to the individual knight was frequently self-defeating. At Crécy, for example, even after the French king had decided to wait until the next day for battle, the chivalric emphasis on boldness drove the French cavalry forward in a chaotic, disorganized mass, each with his helmet filled with dreams of personal glory, ripe for puncturing by English archers. As the chronicler Froissart describes the scene: "Each wanted to outshine his companions . . . with the disastrous consequences of which you shall shortly hear. Neither the King nor his Marshals could restrain them any longer, for there were too many great lords among them, all determined to show their power" (86). Similarly, at Poitiers many members of the recently founded Order of the Star died or were imprisoned because they adhered to the chivalric injunction not to leave the field of battle (for more than a specified and comparatively short distance). In fact, if we reserve "cavalry" as a term for an organized group, the clanking parade of French knights attacking at Crécy, Poitiers, and Agincourt should be called something else, perhaps "chevalry."

The rise of the English longbow was not the only success story of the Hundred Years' War. Cannons were improving and primitive handguns appeared. Chain mail gave way to the somewhat safer but much more expensive plate armor. Significantly, a great proportion of those who practiced the old-style chivalry wound up dead on the battlefield. But the inefficiency or inadequacy of a style of masculinity has never been a sufficient reason to dispense with it. Evolutionary biologists call "neoteny" the way traits characteristic of the childhood or youth of wild species are retained in the adult or domesticated phases, and dismissively dub them "atavistic" or "vestigial." Such terminology seems to exclude any interest in traits that do not directly contribute to the physical survival of an organism. But cultural change rarely follows a line straight enough that it is altogether clear what is useful and what is not. Individual will or group nostalgia plays no role in whether people will continue to be born with appendixes. But the willful summoning up of past styles of cultural behavior as a way of dealing with the present is always with us.

Cultures and individuals hang on to outmoded styles of masculinity in the same way that armies hang on to older technologies. In this sense there is a masculinity that is built on simple masculine myths: a bipolar difference between male and female; the decisive role of the body; male strength and male sexuality. And there is another masculinity that is defined by specific historical contexts. But the relation between the two is more an interplay than a hierarchy. Physiological masculinity never quite goes away, but historical masculinity often makes it unrecognizable. Just as individual behavioral difference and social context influence testosterone production more than the hormones shape behavior, so the social and historical setting of masculinity can either alter the simple masculine myths until they mean something quite different to a new audience, or confirm them despite, or because of, their obvious antiquity.

In discussing cultural change we therefore grope for words to describe the obstinate retention of cultural traits that are no longer useful and may even be counterproductive, or that sleep in their splendid caves until they are needed. Perhaps this is one way of saying that aggressiveness and violence, whether masculine or feminine, are potentials to be tapped when the occasion warrants. Depending on the situation, the invocation of those potentials can be either positive or negative or a mixture of both. History never moves all at once, and in every period behavior and thought that looks forward is often intertwined with more widespread urges to repeat compulsively an array of archaic gestures from the past. Often such revivals work, like the Japanese shogunate's decision in the seventeenth century to first control and then end gun production, and restore the sword as the crucial weapon of single combat. The ban lasted until the mid–nineteenth century, when new factors—including the arrival of Commodore Perry's fleet in 1853, which broke Japan's island isolation—made the decision obsolete.

For the votary of a knightly code, then, whether European chivalry or Japanese Bushido, the potential loss of the intangibles of prestige and self-definition is more significant than the immediate conflict. The English archers had as little trouble penetrating plate armor as chain mail, but it was more difficult to penetrate the French aristocracy's sense of itself and its status. Even when the French *Ordonnance* of 1445 established a standing army, the first in Europe since Rome, and shifted the balance from men-at-arms to archers, they appeared in the form of mounted heavy cavalry, only now furnished with bows and arrows.

One difficulty was the ambiguous connection between the abstract code and the physical weapons. Unlike the period after World War I, after Crécy or Agincourt there was no Charles de Gaulle or Billy Mitchell to mull over the defeat and then write a book demonstrating the superiority of some new technology—tank warfare or the airplane—and the need to at least consider it. Instead, it was easier to believe that some accident of weather or topography had caused the defeat rather than to blame the belief system itself. In the European chivalric ideal, if not in the battlefield reality, the emphasis was on the immediacy of personal prowess, which meant the sword, the ax, and other close-combat weapons. The greatest honor was to be gained in hand-to-hand battles.

In such circumstances, losing the day and watching your friends being slaughtered might just redouble your commitment to the cause. Viewed across a variety of warrior cultures, the adherence to a code of honor might mean more in defeat than in victory, asserting a superiority that transcends any immediate loss. The Mamluk rulers of Egypt, for example, who in the thirteenth century pushed the Christian armies out of the East, went down to defeat by Ottoman gunpowder in the sixteenth century because they thought it was ignoble to be trained in the use of firearms. As many in the South believed after the Civil War, honor is not lost but strengthened by being overwhelmed by a materially superior but thereby morally inferior force.

Some characters in the earliest books on both European chivalry and the Japanese samurai ethos already look back on a golden age of true honor to which the present can only weakly aspire, like Nestor in the *Iliad* contemplating the great heroes now gone. As the historian Ivan Morris has argued, an essential part of the Japanese warrior tradition also enshrines the noble failure, "tragic not as the result of mistakes or lack of stamina or ill luck, though all these may be involved, but because of the karma of a man who embraces a painful destiny" (14). Many of these figures lived long before there was an articulated code of samurai behavior, but their stories and their actions became absorbed into it, especially the moral stature to be gained from supporting to the death an obviously lost cause.

The European concept of knightly character celebrated loyalty neither to a superior nor to an ideal authority with as much single-mindedness as did the Japanese. Nor did it praise a self-containment and control of one's emotions extreme enough to encompass *seppuku,* ritual suicide, as the final mark of sincerity and integrity. Totally apart from the Christian prohibition on suicide, European ideals remained more individualistic. But they similarly invoked models of past behavior. Before the eyes of twelfth-century knights, for example, arose the giant images of the so-called Nine Worthies: the Old Testament triad (Joshua, David, Judah Maccabee), the classical (Hector, Alexander, Julius Caesar), and the medieval (Charlemagne, Arthur, Godfrey of Bouillon). In literature as well there were the cycles of Alexander romances, tales and histories of Charlemagne, and of course the stories of Arthur and the Knights of the

Round Table. Of these great models only one, Godfrey, lived within immediate memory, although there were always local candidates to be the Tenth Worthy: Robert Bruce for the Scots, Bertrand du Guesclin of France, the Black Prince in England, and Bayard, the great French military hero of the sixteenth century, the "*chevalier sans peur et sans reproche,*" the fearless and blameless knight.

Such rare greatness in the present only emphasized the fall from the past. Some historians have argued that by the fifteenth century chivalry was already decadent. Knights were less important on the battlefield, the rules for tournaments had gotten more intricate, and the chivalric code was as encrusted with quibbling irrelevancy as the armor of noble jousters was with jewels and embossed ornaments.

But there is always an aroma of decadence in the assertion of order and rules, for they inevitably invoke a prior time when proper behavior was instinctual. Even at its medieval peak, chivalry and the personal honor it supported had something of the atmosphere of a lost cause. In the world of such absolute honor, few lessons could be learned from either technological change or tangible superiority. But when the technological initiative was passed back and forth between rivals, honor had to adapt. At Crécy, Edward III used cannons frugally: they were expensive, hard to maneuver, and useful mainly for scaring the horses. The archers were clearly the more important tactical weapon. By the end of the Hundred Years' War, archery itself was giving way to percussion and gunpowder, and in the final desultory battles, French cannon overwhelmed English cavalry.

Nowhere in secular life, except perhaps in the law court, is any practice as marked out and determined by ritual and tradition as the waging of war. But there often seems to be an almost inverse relation between the prestige of an armament or element of strategy and its actual military usefulness. Cavalry, as we have seen, is the great example. It shared both a high status and a declining military usefulness with intricately chased armor and gaudy uniforms. All were emblems of an outsized and overpowering military masculinity, and all often still served to evoke traditional power as a way to ensure present success. No wonder that generals and priests so often make common cause: both attempt to organize the uncertain verge between life and death, chance and fate, through a mixture of ritual and immediacy.

Bear cults and berserkers might have vanished, but horse cults and cavalry persisted, although not always with a symbolism as overt as the erection proudly sported by William the Conqueror's horse in the

Bayeux Tapestry. In the seventeenth century, despite the widely discussed tactical innovations of the Swedish king Gustavus Adolphus during the Thirty Years' War, cavalry had become irrelevant to military strategy because of the growing importance of sieges and the ensuing advances in military architecture. Its glamorous possibilities as a vital part of warfare were revived during the campaigns of Napoleon, even though for the most part its actual use was confined to skirmishing, reconnoitering, delivering messages, and looking good, while the infantry did the bulk of the actual fighting. In the later nineteenth and early twentieth century, only in frontier situations demanding mobility—like the U.S. Civil War or T. E. Lawrence's operations in Arabia—did cavalry retain any real effectiveness.

Yet in the world of symbolism the cavalry, like the code of chivalry it invokes, remains alive and well. Even now, cavalry units like the French Guard of Honor, which parades primarily for show, sport helmets that resemble horse heads with a sprig of horse tail dangling down the back. Equestrian portraiture on the Roman model was revived in the early seventeenth century by artists such as Rubens and Velásquez as part of the heroic imagery of the ruler and military leader. From the seventeenth century to the eve of the Battle of the Somme, the man on horseback remained the prime embodiment of military and social authority. The Crusades themselves may have ended and the military orders been suppressed and dispersed, but the spirit lived on. In 1898 Kaiser Wilhelm on a visit to Jerusalem insisted on entering the city as a mounted Crusader. The propaganda posters that urged young men to enlist on both the German and the English side of World War I featured the image of an armored knight; both sides in the Spanish Civil War, on the eve of World War II, invoked the Crusader sanction for their politics; the best-selling book about World War II in the war's immediate aftermath was General Dwight D. Eisenhower's *Crusade in Europe;* and, in a complementary tribute to past chivalric greatness, both the Egyptian leader Gamal Abdel Nasser in the 1950s and Iraqi president Saddam Hussein identified themselves with Saladin.

# THE SOLITUDE OF THE WANDERING KNIGHT

Although the life of a knight and man-at-arms was typically in a group, as either a retainer amid a crowded household or a fighter struggling for life and victory on a crushingly crowded battlefield, he nonetheless became the legendary embodiment of male individualism and warrior prowess. The literary and artistic myth of his autonomy, the solitary knight on a quest to do what he believes is right, owes its genesis to the effort of Christianity and chivalry to reshape the warrior heritage into a new system of values. The difference is that the aloneness of the Christian knight is not the archaic autonomy of the hero whose unfocused prowess can destroy even his own community, but an aloneness with God and the chivalric code.

In this way, the competitive dangers of the violent male group were softened with an air of introspection and piety. It's a model that persists in the present, when the hero in westerns and action films is so often depicted as a bystander, a loner who doesn't want to become involved in the fray but finally must, because of personal relation and moral obligation. The artistic preoccupation in both Western and Japanese culture with the solitary adventurer, as well as the lure of aloneness in increasingly complex urban societies, owes a crucial debt to the chivalric model of the warrior, knight or samurai, whose primary function is not in fighting but in the quest for a truth that is both outside himself and within. So the western gunfighter Shane or the Eastern martial artist Bruce Lee is drawn to defend his weaker friends, and even Rambo (in *Rambo III*) is in a Buddhist monastery when he receives the call to action back in Vietnam.

No cultural movement proceeds in only one direction. Chivalry may have mutated into a religiously based affirmation of the ability of one class to defend society from its enemies. But its values had also confirmed a nongenetic bond between all those who believed in them. Thus, at the same time that the Crusades, the chivalric code, and the professionalization of armies led the knight to submit to an external authority, they also fostered an individual resistance to that submission. From a Marxist point of view that stresses the overriding claims of economic and social power, such resistance is merely a fantasy of individualism. It salves individual conscience by pretending that choices are personal even when they actually serve the interests of tradition and authority. Arthurian knighthood, in this account, was only a screen for submission to a royal authority interested in attaching knights to itself while undermining their allegiance to the authority of local barons. Yet those supposedly less individual and therefore less subjective interests were themselves fantasies wrought of symbols and stories. Cultural change often arises from a conflict of fantasies—with reality and with each other. Before we decide that individualist fantasies are somehow either more culpable or more empty than paternalistic fantasies—or merely equivalent to them—we need to examine more closely the symbols and stories themselves.

I have been stressing the movement from a knightly identity connected to family and force of arms to one that subordinates those genealogical and personal sources of identity to the needs of an embracing authority, whether Church or state. The lure of Crusade and the idea of a war waged at least ostensibly against a spiritual rather than an economic or political enemy owed some debt to the earlier Islamic idea of jihad as well as to biblical precedents. It proved to be tremendously compelling when transplanted to the medieval West. The original foe was, of course, in the East, blocking the way to Jerusalem. But in the shape of the Moors he could be close at hand in Spain, or in the pagans of the Baltics, or for that matter in the Christians of the Byzantine Empire. Along the way Jewish communities at home and abroad were also decimated in the name of the faith. Not much more than a hundred years after the First Crusade and in the wake of the Third, a crusade was promulgated by Pope Innocent III against the heretical Albigensians of southern France, even though they were supported by an impeccably Catholic ruler in Spain. Within another 150 years, popes and antipopes in Rome, Avignon, and Pisa were launching crusades against one another, against the marauding groups of freelance knights on leave from the Hundred Years' War, and against condottieri, soldiers of fortune hired by the Italian city-states to defend themselves from papal armies and from one another.

These companies of freebooting knights, for whom war was enough of a profession that they took the opportunity to hire themselves out to any crusade or conflict available, were a product of the first stages of the Hundred Years' War. They also owed at least an organizational debt to orders like the Templars and Hospitalers (even though the Templars had been disbanded in the early fourteenth century on charges of blasphemy and homosexuality). The Hundred Years' War did not last exactly a hundred years, nor was it continuously fought. Especially after the Treaty of Brétigny in 1360, there were hosts of fighters on both the English and French sides who had no other way to support themselves except to continue fighting for and against someone. Between the time of Edward III's efforts to expand English possessions in France in the mid–fourteenth century and Henry V's claim to the French throne in the early fifteenth century, an early English nationalism began to surface. But it did not prevent knights from banding together and hiring themselves out to the highest bidder, pagan or Christian. One of the most successful, Sir John Hawkwood, took on the defense of the city of Florence, among other commissions, and his equestrian portrait by Uccello hangs today in the Duomo as tribute from a grateful city.

Chaucer's Knight in *The Canterbury Tales* is another such freelance. Chaucer doesn't say if the Knight was a member of Hawkwood's White Company, the most famous of the knightly cohorts. But it is clear from his résumé that the Knight had been around:

*At Alisaundre he was whan it was wonne.*
*Ful ofte tyme he had the bord bigonne*
*Aboven alle nacions in Pruce;*
*In Lettow hadde he reysed [raided] and in Ruce,*
*No Cristen man so fote of his degree.*

In other words, the Knight was at the siege of Alexandria (1365), which Peter of Cyprus succeeded in capturing for all of a week. He also fought with the Teutonic Knights in Prussia (Pruce), in Lithuania (Lettow), and Russia (Ruce). Earlier he had been at the siege of Grenada and the subsequent capture of Algeciras (1343–44), along with battles in areas of Algeria and Morocco. About the time of the siege of Alexandria, he took part in other battles around the Mediterranean, in Armenia and Asia Minor, and had a stint helping one "hethen" against another in Turkey. Quite a career! Although perhaps more extensive than almost any real knight's would have been, most medievalists agree that it is what we might expect from Chaucer calling him "The Knight"—a fairly typical outline of a life's work in fighting.

But typical of what? The medievalist (and filmmaker) Terry Jones, for one, has argued that the Knight is in fact not an exemplum of true chivalry ("a verray, parfit gentil knyght" in Chaucer's phrase), but, in the subtitle of Jones's book, a "medieval mercenary." Far from admiring the Knight, says Jones, Chaucer sees him critically and the portrait in the "General Prologue" is not the respectful image it has usually been taken for but a satire of a crusading rationale that by the end of the fourteenth century was almost empty. In response, other historians have argued that even at the end of the fourteenth century, crusading "for oure feith" was not entirely cynical but still a vital part of knighthood, despite the fact that most English knights were now preoccupied with the Hundred Years' War and crusading itself would shortly lose what bloom it had left after the disastrous defeat by the Turks at Nicopolis (1396), a battle fought while *The Canterbury Tales* was being composed.

It seems to me that there is no real contradiction between what Jones and his critics say. First of all, Jones has definitely restored some balance to a formerly idealized picture by focusing on the dark side of late medieval knighthood. But even if the Knight believes wholeheartedly in his cause, and even if he is a totally moral and "a verray, parfit gentil knyght" himself, the tale that he tells depicts a world in which ideals are often empty forms that individuals follow mechanically beneath the gaze of a brooding and inhuman fate.

Fate (or *wyrd*, as the Anglo-Saxons called it) stood behind the pagan warrior's pessimism about the ability of human intelligence to explain the world or human will to change its ways. Fame in warfare was the only way to combat fate and have one's name live beyond death. By Chaucer's time, centuries of Christian theology in England had transformed that fate into God's providence, but it is clear from "The Knight's Tale" that

Christianity and organized chivalry had not succeeded in eradicating the belief that life is a meaningless battlefield in which only adherence to a personal code of behavior has any meaning.

Even before the Knight begins his tale, fate has made an appearance. Harry Bailly, the host of the Tabard Inn, proposes that all the pilgrims tell stories along the road to Canterbury. They agree, and draw lots to see who will go first; the Knight wins. So far at least, social status and fate seem to be in accord: the Knight is highest in rank among the pilgrims, and he wins in the world of chance as well.

Set in ancient Athens shortly after Theseus has defeated the Amazons and has taken Hippolyta, the queen of the Amazons, as his wife, his tale ostensibly aims to connect the mythic beginnings of chivalry to its present-day practitioners. In dress, action, and attitude, Theseus and all the other characters are from the fourteenth century.

As the tale begins, Theseus is riding home in triumph when he is accosted by a group of wailing women, whose husbands have been killed in a battle at Thebes against the tyrant Creon. Theseus and his retinue go to Thebes, defeat Creon, and restore the bodies of their husbands to the women. As pillagers go through the heaps of bodies on the battlefield to strip them of armor and clothing, they find two wounded cousin-knights from Thebes, Palamon and Arcite, who are put in perpetual imprisonment by Theseus. There the two young men hear Emelye, Hippolyta's younger sister, singing while walking in the palace garden. Both fall in love with her and argue over who is her true lover, even though she is totally unaware of their existence, let alone their love.

A kinsman of Arcite gets him out of jail, but he is upset because this means that Palamon can stay near Emelye and so he decides to return to Athens in disguise to be near her. Meanwhile, after seven years, Palamon escapes from the jail, vowing to make Emelye his. He sneaks back into the palace and overhears Arcite wandering in the garden, lamenting his love for Emelye, whereupon Palamon challenges him to a duel. As Palamon and Arcite fight, a hunting party, including Theseus, Hippolyta, and Emelye, comes upon them. Palamon and Arcite tell Theseus why they fight (this is the first time Emelye has even seen them). Theseus wants to execute them both, but the women of the court plead for mercy and he decrees that they should return in a year and compete properly for Emelye's hand in full tournament.

To put on the tournament in style, Theseus builds an enormous arena and hires painters and sculptors to create three temples—to Venus for Palamon, to Mars for Arcite, and to Diana for Emelye. The temple of

Venus is decorated with images of the misfortunes and delusions of love; the temple of Mars with gruesome images of the violence and treachery of war, murder, and desolation; and the temple of Diana with images of a vengeful and a militant chastity. The next day Palamon and Arcite battle strenuously, Arcite wins, and Theseus awards him the hand of Emelye. But as Arcite prances around the field in triumph, a "furie infernal" (a devil from hell or perhaps a small volcano) abruptly erupts from the ground. Arcite is thrown from his horse and dies from the fall. Years after his elaborate funeral, Palamon and Emelye are still mourning for Arcite when Theseus summons them and tells them they should "maken vertu of necessitee," cease mourning, and marry, which they do.

One of the most striking things about "The Knight's Tale" is Chaucer's fascination—like Shakespeare's in his Roman plays some two hundred years later—with the question of what the world would be like without Christianity. Although the Knight's characters behave in accord with recognizable versions of the contemporary dictates of chivalry and courtly romance, his story is set back in the beginnings of Western civilization, and it entirely lacks anything resembling a Christian system of values. Fate is at the heart of his tale, which purports to idealize courtly love and knightly friendship, but takes place in a world wracked by war and death. Its distant "First Mover" god, invoked by Theseus to persuade Palamon and Emelye to marry, comes straight out of Aristotle, and the gods who do appear are Venus, Mars, and Diana, who cause pain and death to human beings. As Theseus's father, Egeus, says after Arcite's absurd accidental death, "This world is nothing but a throughfare of woe,/And we be pilgrims passing to and fro." If there is any transcendent god, it is not god as love, or god as judge, or even god as nature, but god as fate. Death is the end of all things, and almost perpetual warfare is humanity's natural state.

Without the pious urge toward the conquest of Jerusalem and the defeat of the heathen enemy assumed in the Knight's portrait in the "General Prologue," "The Knight's Tale" is suffused with a sense of the dark fatality of human existence. He may "fight for oure feith," but his prowess and the chivalric code is all the Knight truly has for himself, and his tale celebrates them in one voice and mocks their deficiencies in another. Chaucer himself as a young man had been with the Black Prince during the invasion of France in 1359 and was captured and ransomed. Some twenty years later, as clerk of the king's works, he was in charge of constructing audience platforms for two tournaments sponsored by Richard II. By the evidence of "The Knight's Tale," he seems to have been familiar with the warrior outlook, while he retained a jaundiced view of the way in which war making itself can become the primary goal. In "The Tale of Melibee," one of the two in *The Canterbury Tales* told by the character actually named Chaucer, an old wise man counsels Melibee to deliberate before he embarks on a war of vengeance for the wrongs done to his wife and daughter: "There is ful many a man that crieth 'Werre! Werre!' that wot ful litel what werre amounteth" (Many men cry "War! War!" who know little what war means). But no one pays any attention to what the old wise man says, especially the young.

Fighting only in order to fight is the function of an established warrior class for whom peace affords neither profit nor honor. The Hundred Years' War, along with the disenchantment with crusading that sets in toward the end of the fourteenth century, marks a transition to more "rational" war characterized by the increasing use of gunpowder, as well as by the growing power of both the English and French states. Because of their island detachment (ignoring for the moment conflicts with the Welsh and the Scots), the English took advantage of the dissensions in France between the Burgundians and the Armagnacs in the Hundred Years' War to make great gains. But then they fell apart themselves in the family-honor conflicts of the Wars of the Roses and lost most of what they had won. In both countries it seemed that the centrifugal force of dissolution into regional enmities and the centripetal force of cohesion against an external enemy were locked in an unending cycle of alternating dominance.

But gradually the underlying movement of history began to favor political centralization. In their different ways both Henry V and Joan of Arc took the popular distinctions between "the French" and "the English" engendered by the Hundred Years' War, subdued (for a time) regional differences, and forged them into a more overarching distinction of France versus England, just as later in the same century the union of Ferdinand of Aragon and Isabella of Castile quieted local conflicts in the name of something called "Spain."

The local conflicts between independent barons, or between more assertive barons and kings who sought to centralize power, began to metamorphose into wars between often loosely defined geographic regions that were beginning to call themselves nations. A growing nationalism thus furnished individual warriors in Europe with an ideology of group coherence more long-lasting than the Crusades. Expanding beyond the constraints of chivalric individualism, the class with the prerogative of internal violence became the class charged with defending the country.

In contrast, say, with the thirteenth-century nobles who forced King John to confirm their rights in the Magna Carta, the rise of nationalism also encouraged a willingness to identify the country's interest with the king's. The fragmentary, breakaway independencies of earlier decentralized feudalism thus coalesced into nationalism when personal as well as group honor became focused on an individual—the king—who was at the top of the ladder of chivalry, the First Knight in the kingdom, redirecting knightly energies and rituals toward a budding national self-interest. During the Hundred Years' War, Henry V challenged the dauphin to single combat to decide the right of Henry's claims to French lands. In the sixteenth century, Francis I of France was similarly challenged—twice—by the Holy Roman Emperor Charles V. None of these challenges was accepted, but that they were made indicates how long single combat remained a nostalgic chivalric ideal by whose invocation rulers could assert their individual prestige in the name of sparing the lives of others.

Royal confirmation of knightly status, especially in England, thus allowed the king to undermine the potentially subversive authority of local lords. At the same time, the increasing professionalization of war was slowly beginning to undermine the assumption that it was exclusively an aristocratic undertaking. With the establishment in the mid–fifteenth century (1445–48) of a French standing army specifically employed by the king rather than raised by local magnates, the military also began to distinguish itself from a specific genealogical caste of male warriors on which it traditionally had drawn. Although until the nineteenth century social rank still had a significant role to play in the making of officers, the possibility had been raised that there was no necessarily direct translation from birth and social rank into military virtue.

After the death of Richard III and the victory of Henry VII at Bosworth Field in 1485, it was Henry VIII, together with his contemporaries Francis I of France and the Holy Roman Emperor Charles V, who were the most important sixteenth-century rulers to thrust forward the image of the monarch as First Knight so elaborately. As their careers make clear, the centralizing of the political state also centralized the power to make war, including a royal monopoly over certain weapons, like artillery. Henry in particular transferred the chivalric ethos into a support for national self-consciousness. Later, when England separated from Rome, he used knightly show to affirm opposition to international Catholicism in the name of secular rule, further justifying monarchical power by adding the divine blessing of being head of the church.

As the number of his suits of armor on display at the Tower of London imply, Henry had a more congenial relation to tournaments and military ceremonials than to actual warfare. Despite the declining importance of cavalry in siege warfare, he was also intensely preoccupied with breeding warhorses. In 1515, he set up a new royal armory to turn out more elaborate Continental-style armor, whose fancy-dress look, like the suits of armor being produced for royal and noble children, virtually proclaimed their irrelevance to actual fighting needs. But Henry was not all show, or at least his show needed the test of actual battle for authentication. At the same time that he was sponsoring tournaments and newly fashionable armor, he expanded the British navy and also personally led three military expeditions into Flanders and France, much as Francis I headed a cavalry charge at the Battle of Pavia in 1525, where he was wounded and captured by the forces of Charles V.

For the time, the role of the king in battle authenticated his ability to both fight and command. But the needs of a more complex royal bureaucracy were becoming more pressing. Henry was not the last English king to appear on the battlefield. That distinction belongs to George II, who in 1743, at the age of sixty, successfully led his troops against the French at the Battle of Dettingen. But through the long reign of Henry's daughter Elizabeth and the Stuarts after her, the English monarch wielded a scepter more often than a lance. Although Elizabeth declined to appear on the tournament field herself, she did have an official Queen's Champion, Sir Henry Lee, who tilted on her behalf on special occasions but particularly in the annual tournaments celebrating her accession day.

France was a somewhat different story. After the Italian wars of Francis I and the civil wars of Henry IV in the sixteenth century, Louis XIV took to the field until he was in his sixties, and Napoleon would later put his own turn on the close relation in French history between politics and warfare. With a few grand exceptions, however, like Gustavus Adolphus of Sweden during the early battles of the Thirty Years' War, Jan Sobieski of Poland's rescue of Vienna from the Turkish siege in 1683, William III of England in the 1690s, and the brief appearance of George II, the metamorphosis from the medieval to the modern state separated the king as political ruler from the king as war leader.

Yet, even though monarchs often adapted chivalry to their own purposes, part of its essential nature was in perpetual revolt against any centralized authority. The assimilation of chivalric knights into the service of growing states like England or France was therefore filled with problems. The successes, symbolic more than practical, of an outsider to the main warrior tradition, like Joan of Arc, illustrates what was changing in the concept of knighthood. Joan in particular stood outside the old categories: she was a warrior but she was also a woman. She was divinely inspired, but for the cause of the French nation rather than anything to do with international Church authority or hierarchy.

Robin Hood and his band were another set of outsiders with a nationalist tinge, challenging illegitimate authority to defend repressed native Britons. Robin himself was a chivalric figure who looked back to older myths, authorized by the land rather than by institutions, refreshing honor from its local roots. The longbow was his favorite weapon, and he himself had to demonstrate his authority and not always by winning, as the Friar Tuck and Little John stories show. Over the centuries, as the tales developed, Robin also became more upwardly mobile. Instead of the early forest outlaw stealing the king's deer, he turned into a declassed earl of Huntington, an enemy of the Sheriff of Nottingham and other royal representatives, and a supporter of Richard the Lion-Hearted, the true chivalric (but absent) king, against Richard's brother John, the false and oppressive king. Despite his absorption into later debates over political authority, Robin was a rural hero whose origins remain in the forest and in his decidedly nonaristocratic and nonknightly band, whose prowess and craftiness in every story easily defeated miscreants with shields and family escutcheons. Like Arthurian stories of knights who leave their plows and crops in search of a place at the Round Table, the evolution of Robin Hood's myth represents a trickle-up warrior masculinity, originally native and lower class, that is adopted by an upper class, refurbished with chivalric trappings and nobles in disguise, and then sent downward again—as will be the idea of knighthood itself, when it becomes necessary to animate the spirit of a democratic society for war.*

Robin Hood at first had to make his own way in the forest and gain the respect of those who would become his band. Similarly, many of the knightly tales of the Middle Ages deal with situations that combine

* According to J. C. Holt, the first references to Robin Hood appear in an early-fifteenth-century Scottish chronicle by Andrew de Wyntoun (1420), who sets Robin's career in the late thirteenth century (1283–85). But the version that has been more completely absorbed into the myth appears a hundred years later when John Major in the *History of Greater Britain* (1521) says that Robin flourished in the 1190s, just when Richard I was off on the Third Crusade and later imprisoned, Prince John, who ruled in his stead, was in his twenties, and the Glastonbury discovery of Arthur's bones was all the news. John Leland, Henry VIII's official antiquary, records seeing Robin's grave slab at Kirklees, and later historians and antiquarians confirmed the story. By the eighteenth century, it was illegible.

aspects of quest and initiation. A young knight appears at Arthur's court and is sent on a journey to prove himself. An older knight is faced with a problem that he too must solve by taking to the road. Almost always, the knight needs to be alone. In what seems to be an adult situation with adult characters, the structure is nevertheless a rite of passage from youth and ignorance to some kind of adult wisdom. In other words, honor in a military society is always being tested. You can't just assume you have it by lineage or divine fiat. Crusading is only one way of confirming its existence, and the sponsorship of the Crusades by an international Church may be the least significant aspect for the audience at home. Even in the quest for the Holy Grail, the elements of personal initiation are paramount. At a time of continual petty warfare and especially in the aftermath of major wars, despite the illusory "fairy" land of the Arthurian romance, a male listener is invited to identify with this continual physical, moral, and spiritual testing. The individual may be part of a group, even one as distinguished as Robin Hood's band or the Knights of the Round Table, but his identity is also forged and supported by the more solitary realm of the spirit.

The pious Joan of Arc and the raffish Robin Hood both represent an autonomous warrior spirit that, although it may be co-opted for purposes of nationalist propaganda, also evades them because they act not for any group so much as for the very idea of personal virtue. Even while Christianity supports the quest for knightly glory through violence in battle, it also has a similar potential to undermine the class and family aspect of honor by emphasizing the equality of all souls before God.

In a world of tournaments and ostentation, the solitary hero embodied a purer form of Christian heroism, willing to disappear from public sight and applause to act for virtue alone—the secular equivalent of the Christian idea of acting only for the audience of God. Yet, as the artistic celebration of the virtuous warrior implies, even though nominally alone, he still must be seen as, in the words of *The Dream of the Rood*, "mighty in the sight of many."

For the Middle Ages, literature particularly seems to take up the conflicts between varying chivalric imperatives, and a good deal of the medieval literature concerned with knightly activity dreams of the possibility of acting without an immediate audience. Even before chivalry itself is codified into a code of behavioral do's and don'ts, the chivalric tale is a way of instilling a self-regard that helps knights to regulate their own behavior. Knights look into mirrors and see themselves in the reflection of a window or the gleam of another's armor, but most often the standard of self-consciousness is the audience of one or more women, who are the object and support of their adventures. Often, too, the heroes are unknown. Their identities are disguised and they travel incognito. Like the women who are named only when they marry, the unnamed knights must undergo an adventure of initiation, only after which will they receive a name or have their own recognized.

It would be some time before a purely personal male honor emerged, one without indispensable connection to family, possessions, or social rank, and validated only by individual nature and character. The advent of an honor that did not just differ from but might even be opposed to national and group honor took even longer. But it was already beginning to appear at the end of the Middle Ages, when the direct connection between personal prestige and family began to fray in the face of new mercantile opportunities (and therefore new sources of wealth other than land) and expanding royal bureaucracies (and therefore new sources of political power other than genealogy). In *The Poem of the Cid,* for example, the Cid has his own sense of honor, which differs conspicuously from that of his often dishonorable rivals and includes even a strict loyalty to a king who has mistreated him. Victorious in battle, he is plotted against by nobles whose sons first marry and then beat and abandon his daughters, leaving them for dead. Trying to defend their mistreatment, "the heirs of Carrión" (their genealogy is their epithet) refer to the Cid as a lowborn merchant and miller. In the eyes of the poet, the lineage system may persist, but its representatives are corrupt. The men who have mistreated the Cid's daughters may be wellborn, but they are also cowards.

In great part, then, the future of warrior virtue advances by means of a myth of the past: the individual man of principle who triumphs over the entrenched forces of false honor to be recognized for who he really is. Whether the opponent is a morally bankrupt member of the nobility or a powerful but faceless state, the individual represents a spirit of reinvigoration and resurrection. The danger is always that that personal energy and honor itself might become rigid and codified, as one century's upstart turns into the next century's founding father. But the shift of imprimatur from family inheritance to individual bravery was also the necessary precondition for a world that would be fascinated by the rebellious imaginations of Dr. Faustus, Don Juan, and Don Quixote.

# THE INSPIRATION TO BATTLE AND THE LURE OF LOVE

With the Middle Ages, then, the grand institutions of Church and state compete for the allegiance of the knight. But what of the female audience for knightly behavior, those women who watched tournaments, listened to tales of knightly valor, and in other ways legitimized male combat and competition?

Even with women taking more part in the military today, it is difficult for many to accept that women should have anything to do with war and violence, other than to oppose them. In the contemporary stereotypes of male and female, the other side of the incantatory appeal to testosterone stresses that women are as innately against war and violence as men are innately drawn to them. But a central part of the literary tradition of war emphasizes that women are the guardians of family traditions and thereby the most sensitive to slights of honor. They may not be called upon to battle themselves, but they significantly affect the men who do.

One time-honored response for such women was to urge their men, especially their sons, forward. Christine de Pizan, daughter of the court astrologer of Charles V of France, lived from the end of the fourteenth to the beginning of the fifteenth century. Widowed in her late twenties, she turned to writing, at first poetry but then prose works, some defending women against the misogyny that was widespread in male writing, especially within the Church, and others exploring the nature of true knighthood. In one she retells an ancient story that has a distinctively modern psychological ring. After the fall of the Roman Empire, Theodoric, the king of the Ostrogoths, has invaded Italy and attacked the forces of Odoacer, Italy's first barbarian king. In the crucial battle before Ravenna, Theodoric's forces are doing poorly and he signals retreat. But before the order can be carried out, his mother, Lilia, rushes up to demand that he return to the fray.

> But as he did not pay much attention to words, the lady, overcome with great anger, lifted up the front of her dress and said to him, "Truly, dear son, you have nowhere to flee unless you return to the womb from which you came." Then Theodoric was so ashamed that he abandoned his flight, regrouped his troops, and returned to the battle in which, because of the incitement stemming from his shame at his mother's words, he fought so bravely that he defeated his enemies and killed Odoacer. (58)

From this story de Pizan draws the moral that the praise for Theodoric's victory should go to his mother rather than to him, because she cared about his honor while he ignored it. But the implication is also clear that his impulse to retreat is an act of cowardice whose shamefulness can be symbolized only by a retreat to a prenatal state: if a man behaves this way, it is better not to have been born.*

As in the story of Coriolanus, told by Plutarch in the second century A.D. and dramatized by Shakespeare some 1,300 years later, the crisis time for these soldiers came when their mothers were present. In the Theodoric story, his mother shames him into returning to battle; in the Coriolanus story, his mother stops him from attacking the Rome that had rejected him. But in each the sense of military honor is supported explicitly by the mother. Coriolanus, like Theodoric, embodies the soldier as mama's boy who needs her approval either to fight or desist from

* In historical fact, Theodoric killed Odoacer treacherously at a conciliatory banquet.

fighting. War may be for men, but women, especially mothers like these and the proverbial Greek mother who told her son to come home either carrying his shield or dead upon it, crucially encourage them. To these pagan tales, military Christianity will add a forceful new element: behind the wives and mothers who inspire to battle, and the fair maidens whom the code of chivalry enjoins knights to defend, is the great mother herself, the Virgin Mary, inspiration and indulgent protector of young knights.

One of these stories is set in the early Roman republic, the other in the waning empire; one is retold by a woman in the High Middle Ages and the other by a man in the Renaissance. In both the mother has the role of shaming her son back to the path of honor. Such a motif seems especially present in northern European works, which often feature willful women who ferociously hone the rage of their men in the cause of an honor the men may have forgotten or ignored. Shakespeare makes a late call upon this tradition as well when Macbeth tells the archgoader Lady Macbeth:

> *Bring forth men-children only;*
> *For thy undaunted mettle should compose*
> *Nothing but males. . . .*

But in the Icelandic sagas and Germanic epics like the *Nibelungenlied*, such women are martial themselves and often viciously berate the men for not plunging into battle, revenge, and feud more quickly and avidly. In *Njal's Saga*, for example, while the heroic Gunnar tries to keep his friendship with Njal despite the quarrel between their wives, his wife, Hallgard, calls him cowardly and unmanly and insistently mocks Njal as beardless. Similarly, in the *Nibelungenlied*, the Amazonian Brunhild sets in motion the events that will lead to the death of Siegfried by her belief that he is too lowborn to marry her husband Gunther's sister. Like the berserker, such women vent the hot-tempered substratum of warrior furor, proclaiming that honor through violence in these cultures is open to men and women alike. As Carol Clover points out, *drengr*, the most common Scandinavian word for honorable, bold, and valorous in battle, is class-rooted (it can also mean "wellborn") but not gender-specific and can be applied to both women (although rarely) and men as the highest form of compliment.

Christine de Pizan, who elsewhere argues that the true end of chivalry is the support of the monarch, begins *The Book of the City of Ladies* by telling how she weeps as she reads books by men that attack women and she wonders if women can ever be warriors. She goes on to argue that women become warriors particularly when men have been killed, as Semiramis took over Assyria after her husband's death. Women therefore have the capacity to be warriors in times of necessity, and she presents a long list of those who rose to the challenge when many men could not. But, she continues, women are also the great inventors and developers of the arts of domesticity, with their antiwar implications. The answer to such a division, decides Christine, is that, unlike the more single-minded male idea of heroism, women have a double tradition. One warlike and the other opposed to war, they resemble the two groups of iconic women that artists and writers created to parallel the masculine Nine Worthies—one of women warriors and another of women saints. Christine has an appreciation for both sorts but she also knows which is rarer, and her last poem hails the advent of Joan of Arc.

So much for the frequent equality of men and women as enthusiasts for war and honor. What of the private disruptions of the warrior temperament that women can represent? Like the spiritual quest, the lure of love, expressed through the twin enticements of the sexual and the domestic, has the tendency to erode the warrior ethic and expose the knight to potentially subversive forces. In one guise, women are thus the abettors and even instigators of knightly violence, while in another they can either threaten the self-containment of knightly manhood by their sexuality or represent the opportunity to demonstrate its highest virtues.

This more psychologically complex view of male and female also had its origins within the medieval culture of knighthood. In the twelfth-century *lais* of Marie de France, for example, the lobster carapace of the public knighthood is cracked to reveal a softer, more ambiguous, and perhaps more appealing interior. Three of her poems can give the flavor of her approach. In "Guigemar," a young knight is successful at war but has no idea of love. Shooting an arrow at a hermaphroditic deer with a female body and male antlers, Guigemar gives himself an appropriate wound in the thigh, which the dying deer says will not be cured until the knight finds a woman who will heal him through love. By the end of the poem, when he defeats a lord who refuses to give up Guigemar's beloved, he is still a warrior, but now one who also understands the wounds of love. In "Lanval," a young knight who is unappreciated at King Arthur's court finds love with the Faery Queen, who is invisible to everyone else. When

Queen Guinevere, irritated at his lack of interest in her, first accuses him of homosexuality and then of rape, the Faery Queen appears to clear him of the charges and they leave together for the magical island of Avalon. In "Yonec," the gender pattern of "Lanval" is reversed. A young wife, shut up in a tower by a possessive older husband, is visited by an ideal knight lover, who arrives in the form of a bird. Her jealous husband finds out and sets a trap that fatally wounds the bird. But the young wife is pregnant, and years later she, her husband, and son Yonec visit an abbey that contains a magnificent tomb. The tomb, of course, is that of the bird-knight. The mother tells her son the story and falls dead, whereupon the son slays his stepfather and becomes king.*

Derived from Celtic tales that originated in Brittany, Marie's stories often have a supernatural element that implies that this kind of ideal love cannot exist in the real world of arranged marriages and the legal power of husbands over wives. In both "Lanval" and "Yonec" it is the fantasy lover—appreciating the knight at a backbiting court and the wife cooped up by her jealous husband—who releases the beloved from dependence on the opinion of others. Fashioned for a world of eagerly listening knights and ladies in search of a spiritual honor either in place of or in addition to the honor of battle, ideal love in Marie's *lais* resembles ideal war because its rewards are not pleasure and satisfaction but death and transfiguration. Like the image of the magical unicorn who can only be controlled by a virgin, it is the medieval version of an otherwise impossible freedom.

In the late twelfth century as well, the same era when Marie de France wrote her *lais* and the supposed bones of Arthur and Guinevere were being unearthed at Glastonbury, Chrétien de Troyes, another poet about whose life we know little, wrote at the court of Marie of Champagne, the daughter of Eleanor of Aquitaine and half sister of Richard the Lion-Hearted. Unlike the epic perspective of poems like the *Iliad* and *The Song of Roland,* or the magical world of Marie de France, Chrétien's Arthurian stories focus closely on the personal side of warrior behavior, trying to discover a more practical balance between love and war, sex and jousting, women and men. Despite his name, Chrétien's knights live in a world where Christian rituals are taken for granted but priests or churches have

* The killing of a bird as an emblem of the thwarting of woman's freedom is a frequent literary image. It gets a special twist in Susan Glaspell's 1917 short story "A Jury of Her Peers," in which a beloved dead canary is the clue that tells a sheriff's wife that a woman has murdered her husband—a clue to which the men in the story are oblivious.

little impact. He does describe chivalric ceremonies and tournaments in intricate detail. But the real power of the stories comes from his interrogation of the warrior ethic in the light of love—as if the martial *Iliad* and the domestic *Odyssey* were combined, or as if Dido had persuaded Aeneas that staying with her in Carthage was a more satisfying destiny than founding Rome.

Chrétien never condemns the chivalric code outright, although his tales distinctly imply that love is the means by which women shape a harsh male world into something resembling civilization. In *Erec et Enide*, for example, Erec, an Arthurian knight, marries the beautiful but poor daughter of an inferior vassal. He is totally besotted with her, but she is upset with gossip from his fellow knights that because of love he doesn't care anymore either to bear arms or to participate in tournaments. Believing she has brought shame on Erec, Enide tells him what she has heard. Whereupon he vows that he will prove the gossips wrong by setting forth with her to find adventure without any escort or protection. In the many fights with criminal knights, evil counts, and grand champions that follow, Enide continually fears that Erec will be defeated but he always wins. Finally, after some years, Erec's royal father dies and he is crowned king.

Another of Chrétien's stories, *Yvain*, also explores how influenced the individual knight was by the opinion of his fellows—the young male gang for whom love with women means vulnerability as surely as Mars was trapped in the bedroom of Venus. In it, a young knight defeats and kills another knight whose task it was to defend a magic spring. Trapped in the knight's castle, he falls in love with the grieving widow, successfully woos her, and himself becomes the defender of the spring. But when his best friend, Gawain, arrives with other knights, they, like Erec's companions, mock him because he seems to have given up arms for marriage. Stung, Yvain gets permission from his wife to leave for a year to return to Arthur's court and the life of his knightly pals.

A year and a half goes by, and a messenger arrives to tell Yvain his wife never wants to see him again because he has broken his word. Yvain goes crazy and runs off to live like a savage in the forest. After his brain is cleared by a magic ointment, he saves a town from raiders and then rescues a lion, who in gratitude follows him like a dog. Finally arriving at Arthur's court, Yvain ferociously fights another knight—Gawain—in single combat, each defending an heiress claiming a father's estate. Encased in armor, at first they are both ignorant of each other's identity. When they find out, each wants to admit defeat and end the battle. Now aware of his identity, Yvain's wife again protests that he neither loves nor esteems her. Yvain tells her that it was madness that kept him away and they are reconciled.

Instead of the audience for the Homeric epics or the Icelandic sagas, listening to heroic tales of a grander past, the audience for Chrétien's stories is a court presided over by a woman, where knightly behavior is judged both in arms against other men and disarmed in a world of romance and lovemaking. Through his uncertain heroes Chrétien thus offers his readers and listeners a course in knightly etiquette—how to behave right now in this world, not just in battle. But underlying the recommendation of any particular behavior is the powerful suggestion that the knightly effort to keep the public warrior self and the private emotional self in separate compartments does not work, and may even turn out to be deadly and self-destructive.

On the road to a more complex identity, both Erec and Yvain frequently refuse to give their names either to those they fight or to those they defend. Medievalists call this the motif of the Bel Inconnu, the handsome unknown. Like the wandering solitary knight, they must lose the names known by an appreciative tournament audience in order to regain them from within. Chrétien's Arthurian tales thus help mark a crucial step in the development of the male image. From the vaunting warriors of classical epic parading their prowess along with their genealogy, the Anglo-Saxon flyters hurling insults at the enemy before battle, and the Icelandic berserkers chewing their shields, we have come to the stoic warrior who indicates his valor not by heat but by cool. In turn, they become the progenitors of the western movie drifters who come to town and combat evil only to leave again after it is defeated, or the wandering masterless samurai swordsman, who aims to lose his conventional social identity in the act of swordplay and thereby gain another, more rarefied sense of self.*

The difference in Chrétien's cosmos is that this transformation occurs not as a loss of self presided over by warrior religion but under the aegis of love. In the earlier epics, by contrast, there is a female audience for male prowess but not for male vulnerability, which usually must be quashed as soon as it appears. Thus the shaping of a masculinity that can distinguish itself from the demands of religion, genealogy, and the

* Intriguingly, although the figure of the drifter hero is common to both Japanese and American popular culture, the hero of such Japanese stories often dies, while in American tales he generally goes off into the sunset.

chivalric code owes an important debt to the presence of women. In the eyes of medieval male writers and artists, women validate masculinity by watching. But which masculinity? In the male warrior, identity is externalized most crucially in combat. Christianity and the chivalric code both attempt to give an interior to the warrior, spiritual or secular, but it is love that actually evokes what is within the individual. The presence of the beloved causes an ache and an emptiness in the lover, and thereby helps create his inner life. The relation between lovers thus begins with the sight of an exterior, but soon encompasses what lies behind and beyond it.

In one aspect, then, the chivalric romance motif of battle in disguise dramatizes the constant need to eradicate previous shame by reestablishing oneself in the world of male honor. But in Chrétien's tales it also invokes the question of through whose eyes honor is defined and validated. So Chrétien ruminates on what it means to be watched, and evolves a contrast between public seeing, in which women may participate but the action is defined by male panoply and show, and private seeing, which looks into the heart. Erec must take along his loving wife Enide on his adventures, even as he keeps telling her to shut up and not worry about him. The love of women separates men from the chivalric gang with its rashness and excess, although, as in both *Erec* and *Yvain*, not from the use of arms. In fact, Chrétien seems to imply that the male desire for rapture and love is the complement to the urge to go to war—a release from the chivalric shell that is always threatening to throttle the hero in a suffocating embrace of rules and limits. Unlike the inciting women of northern epic who whet their men as the men sharpen their swords, Chrétien's heroines foster beneath the warrior armor a self-conscious interior, so that a later Yvain need not go mad in order to realize he has made a mistake by unthinkingly assuming that marriage and warfare are incompatible.

The relation between men and women in Chrétien's Arthurian poems, as in the general European movement usually referred to as courtly love, thus becomes as important as arms to knightly reputation. Until the twelfth century in Europe, the time of Marie de France and Chrétien de Troyes, literary depictions of a sympathetic male vulnerability characterize it as existing primarily between men. Achilles may leave the battle for Troy in the *Iliad* because Agamemnon has taken the slave girl Briseis for himself, but he returns because Hector has slain Patroklos, his sworn companion. Such male camaraderie hardly disappears from war. But the works of Chrétien mark the literary dawn of the possibility of receiving similar support and emotional nourishment from women as well.

Hidden not very deeply in Chrétien's presentation of the conflicts within the chivalric assumptions about masculine and feminine identity (and even more explicit in the works of Andreas Capellanus, thought to be another member of Marie de Champagne's court) is the distinction between a nobility of birth, verified by the externals of knightly and noble show, and a nobility of virtue, validated by individual nature. In the midst of the Hundred Years' War, some three hundred years after Chrétien, Chaucer revisits the Arthurian romance in "The Wife of Bath's Tale" and dramatizes for a war-weary audience the submerged implications of what happens when women and their perspective are allowed into the chivalric world.

After a long prologue in which the Wife of Bath recounts her life, tells of her five husbands, and attacks the efforts of medieval misogynistic literature to regulate women's behavior, she surprisingly tells a tale set not in a contemporary realistic world but in an Arthurian fairyland that existed "many hundred years ago." At first the Wife of Bath is nostalgic about this world, particularly because it lacked the wandering friars who use their place in the Christian hierarchy to prey upon women. But even in this ideal world there is brutality. A knight from Arthur's court, "a lusty bacheler," sees a young woman walking by the river and rapes her. By law, he is to be beheaded. But the queen and the ladies of the court ask that he be given to them for judgment, and Arthur agrees. The queen then tells the knight he will be spared if within a year he can find out what it is that women most desire.

Fruitlessly, the knight searches for the answer, since no one he talks to agrees with anyone else, until, the year almost gone, he comes upon a woman in the forest who says she will give him the answer if he promises to marry her. Even though she is "foul, and old, and poor," the knight agrees. She tells him that women most desire "sovereignty" and "mastery" over their husbands. They return to court where the queen and her ladies accept this answer and free the knight from his death sentence. However, when the old woman claims her recompense of marriage, he balks: "Take all my good [possessions] and let my body go." But a promise is a promise, she says, and he is forced to marry her.

Almost everyone in the medieval social hierarchy, but especially the upper classes, needed permission from some authority to marry and especially to marry off a daughter. Like military action, the exercise of legal sexuality and procreation was increasingly in the hands of a lord or king. In this mingled knightly and noble context, where marriages were made principally to link families genealogically and economically, impecunious young knights imagined displaying their prowess in tournaments in order to catch an heiress. Why then should adultery and illicit sexuality be so often at the heart of the Arthurian tales and their influence? One answer may lie in the interplay between male violence and male sexuality in the chivalric code, on the one hand enforcing a cult of womanhood akin to the spiritual service owed to the Virgin Mary, while on the other encouraging an almost berserk warrior fury. Faced with a real woman, the knightly rapist of "The Wife of Bath's Tale" is as uncontrollable in sexual desire as he has been taught to be in war.

As the story then unfolds, it focuses on the confrontation between a sexually immature but aggressive male knight and a sexually unattractive but wise lower-class woman, a confrontation that illustrates how the relation between the sexes taught by chivalric literature fosters emotions that may at first intensify a relationship but then too quickly lead to its destruction. Even though his new wife has saved his life, the knight in "The Wife of Bath's Tale" feels that all his social and sexual prestige have vanished with his marriage. But now the tale takes another turn, as they lie in bed and talk, the knight bemoaning that he has married someone so ugly, old, and socially beneath him. In response the woman questions all the knight's assumptions about the way the world should be, especially his definition of what constitutes social prestige. The word she uses is *gentilesse,* but not in its usual meaning of high social position. True *gentilesse,* she says, has nothing to do with family or wealth or position, but comes from God alone. It is a personal characteristic, not a social one, validated by deeds, not by ancestors or possessions. Choose then, she says. Would you rather have me ugly, old, and faithful to you, or would you rather have me be young, beautiful, and wellborn and take your chances with the trouble that might bring? "I put me in your wise governance," he answers. Well, she responds, since you have given me the mastery, I will be both beautiful and true.

In the context of *The Canterbury Tales,* "The Wife of Bath's Tale" is a story of wish fulfillment by which the Wife, who has railed against misogynist doctrine in her prologue, constructs an ideal relation between husband and wife. In it, she counters the institutional Christianity that licenses the hatred of women with another Christianity that emphasizes the equality of all—male and female, high and low, ugly and fair—and reverses the knightly value system of judging primarily by grand appearances and ostentatious victories. The underbelly of knighthood that justifies any male aggression must be qualified by an idea of masculinity that, even in a stumbling way and under duress, struggles toward empathy.

The early stages of this crucial shift in the nature of military masculinity might be explained by saying that Marie de France was a woman and Chrétien de Troyes wrote for a court ruled by a woman. But in a larger context, it came at a time when a significant proportion of male deaths were the result of natural causes rather than violence. War was no longer perpetual but intermittent. Moreover, female life expectancy, which had been much lower than male, increased throughout the Middle Ages, due in part to the softening influence of Christianity as well as to the rise of towns and the increase in access to health care.* Complex, too, is the relationship between a warrior culture and institutional misogyny, especially in medieval Europe when, as the Wife of Bath amply demonstrates, that misogyny is mainly promulgated by churchmen. But "The Wife of Bath's Tale" focuses on the retrievable young knight rather than on the venal churchmen who insult and dishonor women. The only character with a name in "The Wife of Bath's Tale" is Arthur; the queen has a title, but the other characters, like the Bel Inconnus of Chrétien, must define themselves. The knight, whose only way of relating to women is either to rape or to venerate them, is transformed into a husband who can appreciate the knowledge and insight of his wife as an individual. The woman, whose relation to marriage is otherwise as a commodity to be bought, sold, and traded for genealogical and political benefit, becomes instead the source of a new way of looking at the world.

This potential for an identity unindebted to either the social or the gender hierarchy had always been present in Christian doctrine, but it is only in the fourteenth century that it becomes an explicit criticism. In the fifteenth century, even the chivalric courts are penetrated by the Wife's argument that inner *gentilesse* constitutes true nobility and that personal virtue must anchor social honor and external show. At the beginning of the fifteenth century, not long after Chaucer created the Wife of Bath and Christine de Pizan wrote of women's capacity to fight and rule, Joan of

* The significance of this change varies with the political system. Generally, in democratic societies women tend to have unofficial power when there are few of them, and official power when they are numerous. But in more authoritarian societies, absolute numbers may not make as much difference. Some demographers have correlated a high male/female ratio with institutionalized war cultures: When there are more disposable men than women, war becomes a good investment. But when men are few, war is not as attractive as domesticity and peace. Of course, which comes first—the high ratio of men to women or the tendency to war—is itself a chicken-and-egg issue.

Arc managed to combine all these threads of inner spiritual conviction, national self-consciousness, and warrior zeal—in the form of a woman. Leading troops while dressed in battlefield armor, she defends the idea of "France" sung to her by saintly voices. At her trial for blasphemy one of the primary charges against her was that she had illegitimately disguised herself as a man, to the disgust of God and nature. But, like those knights of chivalric romance who learned of love, it is precisely this crossing of a previously impermeable boundary that helped create her legend.

If a clue to the dreams of a culture can be found in the quality of its escapes, we now seem to be living in a debased if modern chivalric world, still fascinated by the solitary knight sallying forth to cure the evils of the world. Something of the medieval obsession with the knight in armor returned especially in the 1980s and 1990s with the simultaneous minting of two popular images: the buffed and muscular human body as a rugged container from within which to meet the challenges of life; and, in science fiction and action films, the image of the armor-plated cyborg or robotic hero, like Robocop or Lieutenant Ripley in *Aliens,* climbing inside a full-body prosthesis to combat the monster. Superman is no longer a being of special power from another planet; with the right technology, he can be created right here on earth. The films of Arnold Schwarzenegger, Sylvester Stallone, and Jean-Claude Van Damme, for example, combine the two images: the omnicompetent body complete with the paraphernalia of advanced technological weaponry. In part, such characters hark back to a more personal style of medieval warfare in the face of the dehumanization of modern war. Perhaps in an unknowing tribute to Joan of Arc, this neomedieval body is also not always masculine—as Ripley and other heroines like her indicate—nor must it always be in armor to be armored in effect. Yet it remains almost the sole way of dramatizing heroism, for men and women alike.

*Part III*

# FROM ARMOR TO PERSONALITY

# UNIFORMS AND THE ECLIPSE OF ARMOR

Manliness died when firearms were invented.
—Turkish saying

The figure of the knight on a solitary quest carries forward into later centuries an influential vision of masculine self-containment and personal prowess. In Albrecht Dürer's popular engraving *Knight, Death, and the Devil* (1513), for instance, he is allegorized into the ideal Christian warrior, clad in elaborate parade armor, who moves sternly and inexorably on his journey past the grotesque and demonic forces arrayed against him. But just when the lone knight who creates his masculine identity in tests of love and war was becoming a powerful mythic figure, his dream of spiritual independence was being inexorably eroded by the rapid growth in the size of armies and the sophistication of armaments that by the seventeenth century would make Europe the center of world military and political power. The new gunpowder technology, though at first less efficient than the older methods, gradually began to replace them. Standing armies were organized to support centralized governments, and a professionalized and hierarchic officer corps was brought into being to run the show.

Most of the histories that try to take an overview of the history of warfare seem awfully thin for the first few thousand years. The obligatory paragraphs on the chariot, the phalanx, and the legion, the arguments over whether the introduction of the stirrup into medieval Europe did or did not make a difference in the use of cavalry (it provided a more secure seat for fighting on horseback) don't take up much space. But as soon as gunpowder is adapted for military use, interest picks up, details abound, and battle strategies and tactics become more elaborate and thereby more alluring for authors and readers alike.

Part of this quickening interest reflects a tangible change in the history of war itself. Even after the decisive use of archery by the English longbowmen in the Hundred Years' War, battle in Europe was still generally immediate and hand-to-hand, leading some historians to view the victories at Crécy and Agincourt as isolated cases. It is only with the ability to engage at a distance, allowed by the development of the cannon and the gun, that the nature of warfare changed decisively from the direct encounter of shock tactics. Also changing was the conception of what battle was for and how men participated in it. Waving his banner and brandishing his escutcheon, the knight entered the *mêlée* of Agincourt or Crécy under a clear sky, and the archer notched his arrow with the general expectation that he could see his target. For both knight and archer, there was a physical sense of the engagement of the whole body. But with the gun came an odd detachment. The era of the grand individual gesture was submerged in volleys of gunfire—a new technique devised to compensate for slow musket reloading time (about two minutes)—and salvos of siege artillery, bringing an all-suffusing and smoke-filled uncertainty to the battlefield, in which death now often came from far away.*

The alchemist Roger Bacon has been credited with formulating a gunpowder mixture in the thirteenth century. By the fourteenth century, cannons were in sparse use to terrify, if not to kill, and by the fifteenth a primitive hand cannon called the culverin was available. At about the same time Sir Thomas Malory wrote his elegaic collection of Arthurian stories, *Le Morte d'Arthur,* in which betrayal takes up more imaginative

* Both "salvo" and "volley" are late-sixteenth-century words, imported into English from Italian and French.

space than love, cowardice and treachery more than chivalric values and the glee of knightly adventure.*

But it was not until the sixteenth century that guns in any number appeared on the battlefield. The Spanish in particular were innovators in small arms, and the first extensive use of them in England was by Spanish mercenaries hired by the English to battle the Scots at Pinkie Cleugh (1547). The weapon used by the Spanish there was the harquebus, a long gun heavy enough that it usually needed an attached tripod to steady its aim.† The basic principle was simple enough: a metal tube, a bullet, and a way to ignite it. Except for the firing mechanism, it changed little until the nineteenth-century invention of the percussion cap and the easy-to-reload minié bullet. Otherwise, muskets, pistols, harquebuses, and other such hand weapons were the major competitors of the sword in Europe and America for some 250 years. A primitive rifle was invented early on as well, with an inner grooved barrel that made firing more accurate. But the rifle, like the other guns, was a single-shot weapon and even harder to reload. Other than in hunting, where aim was more important than speed, it was not used extensively until the mid-nineteenth-century development of breech-loading ammunition and magazine clips. Even then, in the American West, the most common long weapon remained the unrifled shotgun.

Before such modern improvements could appear, even more basic changes had to occur. The Battle of Lepanto, which was fought between the Ottoman Turks and a Christian coalition off the coast of Greece in 1571, is usually considered the first major battle in which gunpowder was decisive; more romantically, it is the last gasp of chivalric warfare. The Christians, heavily supplied by the Spanish, had the guns, the Turks had mainly bows and arrows, and the Christians won overwhelmingly. But tradition still maintained a strong hold over the mechanisms of warfare. The English especially were slow to accept gunpowder-driven small arms, and it was already 1595 before the longbow was considered outmoded enough for it to be explicitly banned as a basic weapon. With the example of the impressive pikework of the Swiss before them as well, the

* Malory's work is the first full-length version of the Round Table story in English, and his view of the Camelot world is both jaundiced and suffused with nostalgia.

† The harquebus, which used a matchlock firing mechanism, was invented in the fifteenth century and the name was used in the sixteenth century to refer to virtually all handguns.

musket did not replace the pike as the primary weapon of the English infantry until the seventeenth century.

Historians differ over the social and psychological significance of the rise of the gun and the eclipse of the sword. Perhaps lowborn musket bearers could draw a bead on and kill a panoplied knight. But the crossbow and the longbow had already made possible that undermining of social hierarchy. The difference was that with guns such slaughter occurred with greater and greater frequency. The longbow was only as good as the person pulling it, but the gun could kill regardless of the physical strength of the person at the trigger. There was no need for knightly training and little even for the target practice of the yeoman archer. An awareness of how often the low could bring down the high with guns, along with a greater commitment (by a long-entrenched military government) to preserving the relationship between status, political power, and warrior prowess, was behind the gradual Tokugawa outlawing of guns in Japan in the sixteenth and seventeenth century. Without the homogeneous culture of the Japanese, this was hardly a European option, although Europe did continue to maintain a double track for weapons: guns and cannons to win, swords for prestige.*

With firearms becoming more efficient and more prevalent, armor itself began to disappear from war, although into the seventeenth century it still reigned over the tournament and the show ground as a ceremonial reminder of the glorious past. But in a world of steadily improving guns, it made little sense for individuals, and especially rulers, to go to the enormous expense of armoring their soldiers. Accordingly, both armor and iron helmets would be generally discarded as equipment by the end of the Thirty Years' War (1618–48).

At the same time, the war dress of the upper classes also became less distinctive. The armored medieval knight who waded into battle on his similarly armored horse was clearly no barefoot Socrates but a visual advertisement for his own status and wealth. Similarly, the bright signaling of heraldic devices on shields and armor, the plumes and saddlecloths on horses, were the chief way of showing who was who on the medieval battlefield, not as "English" or "French" but as a person of particular genealogy and family allegiances.

Political factors were at work as well. The crucial issue in a society constantly in arms is who has the control over violence. In England, William the

* This restriction of guns in Japan has frequently been cited as an important historical reason why the Japanese still prohibit personal possession of handguns and severely restrict ownership of other arms.

Conqueror, twenty years after the Battle of Hastings, exacted the Oath of Salisbury (1086) from the nobility of England, in which they swore a loyalty to the king that was superior to any loyalty to a feudal lord. As the Wars of the Roses indicate, titled and untitled Englishmen still periodically fought one another for prestige and power. But the Oath of Salisbury did help create a hierarchy at the top of which was a monarch whose ability to wage war could be modified and even somewhat controlled by other groups with political and social power, but never quite destroyed. The fluid hierarchy of physical prowess, in which there could always be a new challenge, was being transformed into a permanent hierarchy of politics.

With the rise of the centralized monarchies and the increasing sense of national difference, both the makeup and the look of armies changed. Mustering too few men for too short a time, the feudal levy of local warriors was unsuited for the new style of sieges and longer wars. Accordingly, armies evolved first into a mixture of mercenary knights, pikemen, and archers, then later to standing armies, with the regiment beginning to appear as a distinct unit. These soldiers were paid, fed, and, increasingly, clothed in uniforms that identified them not as part of a local knight's or noble's cohort, but as subjects (or, in the case of mercenaries, hirelings) of a nation. The personal banners of the past, the scarves, ribbons, and random pieces of symbolic vegetation that signified who you were and what side you were on (like the Welsh leek attached to Fluellen's helmet in *Henry V*) gave way to the first modern appearance of uniforms. Even though there was still an incredible array of clothing on the battlefield, national and regimental colors begin to be codified to replace the heraldic escutcheons and local liveries of old.* The emblems of units also superseded the patterns derived from social hierarchy—although the colors were often the same. The new hierarchy was the army itself, and stories about the idiosyncrasies and strategic skill of generals replaced tales of the prowess of knights. As the nineteenth-century military theorist Antoine-Henri Jomini says, in addition to prayer before battle and a judicious amount of drinking, the greatest inspiration for the soldier in battle was the presence of the famous.

None of this new panoply was unprecedented. Geoffrey Parker points out that the terra-cotta warriors in the tombs at Xian, China, are dressed in uniforms that include a regimental color coding and have individualized features. In Europe, gaudy knights may have been on the way out,

* The persistence of heraldry is still apparent in the colors of sports uniforms, university marching bands, and the international marine signaling code, which uses some of the same devices for visibility at sea that were designed for the medieval battlefield.

but until the invention of smokeless powder in the late nineteenth century, the theater of war was crowded with ostentatious and even garish uniforms. Like the red paint on the faces and bodies of berserkers or the blue woad favored by the Picts, few of these sartorial styles had any direct military point beyond the desire to intimidate (especially evident in enormous helmets) that went back to the Germanic tribes described by Tacitus. But their bright colors did have one preeminently practical purpose. Commanders, who had only runners for communication, relied on the visibility of uniforms and flags to see broad differences between their own troops and those of the enemy. Nevertheless, there were many examples of firing on friendly troops, especially when minute variations of the basic military palette of red, blue, and white confused the matter of who was on which side.

Even in an age before mass-produced cloth, war and its bodily adornment had become a central influence on general male fashion. Unlike the stolid statues of the Xian tombs, the intricacies of the uniform (along with whatever might be the fashionable haircut and beard) in seventeenth- and eighteenth-century Europe indicate a new self-consciousness about both the paraphernalia of war and war's place in the definition of masculinity. Just as printing helped diffuse military tactics, allowing training methods and weapons (like the bayonet from Bayonne) to spread across Europe, so armies also copied the look of other armies, often in a kind of sympathetic magic, as the weaker imitated the uniforms that adorned the more triumphant.

Developing at about the same time as dynastic emblems slowly began to give way to national flags, uniforms and colors functioned as the soldier's badge of connection to entities larger than himself, not to his feudal lord but to his unit and his country—or to his employer. Visitors to Buckingham Palace, for instance, who watch the marching and horseback riding of the regimental groups in their sumptuous uniforms, are watching an essentially seventeenth-century display: the Coldstream Guards, established in 1650 as a parliamentary regiment, who became Household Troops in 1661 after the restoration of Charles II; the Life Guards, established in 1659, who were with Charles II in Flanders; the Grenadier Guards, established in 1656 to protect Charles II; the Scots Guards, established in 1642, re-formed in 1660, who became part of the English army in 1686; and many more now primarily ceremonial regiments.

For the next few centuries, then, European war became an odd spectacle of men dressed in fancy clothes trying to kill one another. Although in the later Middle Ages much tournament armor—with, say, narrow-peephole helmets suitable only for fighting in lists—could never have been used on the battlefield, it still generally did have a defensive as well as a decorative point. The leather greatcoats of the English Civil Wars similarly helped deflect short swords in close fighting. The red coat faced with blue that the Civil Wars also introduced, along with the red uniforms later favored by the Danish and Hanoverian armies, may have had some justification as a morale-enhancing disguise for wounds. But what was the point of, say, the brilliant white uniforms of the Austrian and Bavarian armies, which so easily showed dirt and blood?

There is an intriguing interplay between uniforms and weapons that belongs more to the later history of men and war than it does to the cusp between the Middle Ages and the Renaissance. Instead of being enveloped in unyielding metal, the lavishly uniformed European soldier until the early nineteenth century wore battle dress that had little or no defensive use, with the possible exception of his helmet. Until the spreading use of khaki undermined their flamboyance, uniforms still conveyed some of the same romance of war that armor once did. The shift from bright, virtually peacock-hued clothing to the khaki and camouflage garb of the modern army reflects innovations in war technology as well as in attitudes toward war and the kind of masculine presentation it requires. In a world of smokeless powder, for instance, flashy uniforms, once meant to be seen through smoke, became suicidal. But the uniform retains its allure. As the great French filmmaker Jean Renoir said about *La Grande Illusion,* he wanted to make an antiwar film that was yet in love with uniforms.

# NATIONAL IDENTITY AND THE CAUSE OF RELIGION

> Battells do not now decide national quarrels, and expose countries to the pillage of the conquerors, as formerly. For we make war more like foxes, than like lyons; and you will have twenty sieges for one battell.
>
> —Roger Boyle, *A Treatise on the Art of War* (1677)

The increased technologizing and professionalizing of war that marks the modern period was well under way by the seventeenth century. Printing made guides to tactics, as well as books about war and its theory, more easily available to anyone who wanted to learn. War and politics would continue to be the business of governments and aristocracies, but because wars began to cost more and more, public opinion had to be courted as well. News of glorious victories and diatribes against the atrocities of the enemy rubbed shoulders on the shelves with more accurate maps, manuals of training methods, and the newly translated precepts of Greek and Roman military theorists.

As Roger Boyle points out, the warfare of the sixteenth and especially the seventeenth century tended to focus on fortresses, with many more sieges than actual pitched battles. The high-walled, moat-encircled medieval castle, designed to resist lengthy sieges, continues to look impressive to tourists. But in the sixteenth century it was also becoming obsolete in the face of new, long-range cannons and more efficient, more powerful, and (in the earlier innovations of the Hussite armies) more mobile artillery. The new guardians of borders and frontiers were (on the Continent, not in England) angled bastions elaborately surrounded by ditches and escarpments designed to allow artillery and cannons to rake an enemy from a variety of angles. And such intricately baffled defenses were not limited to the defenders, for when the siege went on long enough, the besiegers built their own fortifications to protect themselves from relief armies.

On the seas as well, cannon-bearing warships replaced the older-style rowed galleys, which had been the norm in naval warfare since before the Persians and the Athenians. In Japan, the poor quality of cannons made sieges difficult to mount, and in 1615 the Shogun Tokugawa Ieyasu prohibited castle building as a hostile provocation to war. But in Europe a new science of fortifications (to which artists such as Dürer and Leonardo da Vinci lent their talents) grew up in response to the advances in artillery, ensuring that long sieges again became more prevalent than pitched battles. It was a period of sustained innovation in weapons and defenses that would not be substantially improved upon until the end of the eighteenth century, when France introduced more mobile artillery; the British pioneered the fragmenting shell, named after its inventor Henry Shrapnel; and Eli Whitney in America turned his attention from the cotton gin to the musket as the product with which to demonstrate how mass production could be achieved using interchangeable parts.

While sixteenth-century presses were turning out treatises that aimed to define and regulate a vast variety of information, military theorists argued for greater standardization in equipment. Gun calibers and mechanisms, previously custom-made by artisans in the same way that swords or armor had been, were becoming more standardized. But the interchangeable parts of weapons and the mass armies of disposable soldiers that were each other's appropriate metaphor still lay in the future. On the sixteenth-century battlefield, the medieval legacy mixed uncertainly with the new technology. There were so many different kinds of weapons—pikes, halberds, harquebuses, swords—that the Spanish, again innovating, began to organize armies into units to better exploit their special qualities in support of one another.

In light of a growing military population and much larger armies than ever before, the haphazard medieval authority of the ruler or his representatives on the battlefield had to be transformed into a firmer chain of command for soldiers who often lacked even the rudimentary sense of class and local cohesion that marked medieval knights and archers. The massed medieval formations that recalled the classical phalanxes were giving way to longer, thinner lines of battle. Every study of military effectiveness has stressed the importance of camaraderie between men as a crucial element in morale. But battle lines that stretched for miles, no matter how useful they were for siege warfare, presented a comparatively fragile command structure in a world without field telephones. There needed to be a more efficient way for officers to synchronize action. Otherwise there was little hierarchy in combat below the king, general, or commander—and little difference of function beyond the separation of cavalry and infantry.

Despite the defeat of mounted knights by archers and dismounted knights at such battles as Agincourt and Crécy, cavalry continued to be the most prestigious branch of armies. But losses like that of the French at the Battle of Pavia made commanders reconsider the usefulness of horses of the old heavy destrier kind. When horses were useful in battle, it tended to be not as chargers, but either as skirmishers or as part of the stately German caracole movement, in which each rank rode forward, shot, and then wheeled to make way for the next.

The gradual introduction of firearms and the battle success of Swiss mercenary troops had begun to demonstrate that, with order and precision, infantry was often tactically more effective than cavalry. Hiring themselves out across Europe but particularly to the French, the Swiss had reintroduced to warfare something like the classical phalanx, along with the training and discipline necessary to keep it coherent. Their main weapon was a twenty-one-foot pike, which survived as the weapon of choice until guns become efficient enough to destroy their boxlike formations. But there's something about military show that dearly loves uniforms and weapons that the battlefield has long since consigned to mothballs, the junk heap, or the museum. The picturesque descendants of what four hundred years ago was the most feared infantry in Europe, dressed in traditional red-blue-and-yellow-striped uniforms, now more modestly brandish a seven-foot halberd before the gates of the Vatican—the legacy of Pope Julius II's early sixteenth-century admiration for their prowess, relic of a time when the halberd was already becoming obsolete as a military weapon.*

* As William H. McNeill points out in *Keeping Together in Time: Dance and Drill in Human History*, the Swiss also revived the classical habit of music accompanying troops into battle.

Contemplating the decrease of pitched battles along with the success of the tightly organized Swiss military unit, Maurice of Nassau, the captain general of Holland, initiated at the end of the sixteenth century a group of innovations in military discipline and structure. As the defender of the Protestant Netherlands against its Catholic Spanish overlords, Maurice also emphasized that he wanted to train citizens rather than hire professionals, and an essential part of Maurice's answer to the problem of a wider war, which required the services of many more participants than could be drawn from the hereditary war-making classes, was drill. Accordingly, instructional books were published showing appropriate postures for the use of different weapons as well as explaining the commands of the new system. This emphasis on practice and premeditation in warfare, although drawn freely from the military texts of the Romans, went in tandem with the new importance of firearms. Years of training might go into the creation of a knight who could ride a horse and swing a broadsword, or an archer who could fire accurately and swiftly. But firing a gun required hardly any physical prowess at all, and the weapon's general imprecision made simultaneous firing more important than aim.

Drill also had social implications, and William H. McNeill makes great claims for its effectiveness in forming a new cohesiveness among Maurice's soldiers:

> Prolonged drill allowed soldiers, recruited from the fringes of an increasingly commercialized society—individuals for whom the cunning and constraint of the marketplace were repugnant and unworkable—to create a new, artificial primary community among themselves. . . . (131)

Drill was also the physical equivalent of a greater uniformity and codification in military tactics and strategy after the relatively looser and more freelance Middle Ages. Military theorists of the time like the Italian Niccolò Machiavelli and the Flemish Justus Lipsius claimed that training in military drill could implant a stoic virtue in soldiers who otherwise knew nothing of military traditions.

For many of these writers, looking for answers in Roman precedents reflected the general Renaissance disdain for most of what went on in the Middle Ages: there were no lessons to be learned from the wars of the previous several centuries. Now that war was no longer a normal upper-class vocation, chivalry, knighthood, and the whole medieval perspective on male behavior and beliefs could be looked back on, criticized, and rejected, as well as become the stuff of nostalgia. Machiavelli, who lived in an Italy where cities were constantly attacking one another, particularly asserted the need for an almost perpetual readiness, so that every citizen might be immediately transformable into a soldier when conflict threatened. Many of the Italian city-states, especially Machiavelli's Florence, were heavily involved in commerce and banking and therefore delegated the military role. But Machiavelli in *The Art of War* (1521) attacked their practice of hiring the mercenary condottieri (from *condotta*, contract) and mocked what they got for their money: a showy reliance on cavalry spectacle and relaxed battle order that he saw only as a way of draining more money from city coffers. The crucial difference for Machiavelli was between a soldier who had a stake in the continuity of the country for which he was fighting and one who did not. Instead, he promoted a part-time version of the Roman legionary model complete with what he considered to be its traditions of civic pride and commitment to the common good.

Although it has been argued that Machiavelli underestimated the importance of guns, his ideas found fertile ground in a time when the concept of a military service "owed" as part of feudal obligation by men who were otherwise farmers and landowners began to break down as wars became more elaborate. The modern nation-state was at different stages of development across Europe, and all monarchs had to face the issue of where to find manpower. Many were forced to contract with military entrepreneurs who supplied troops for a fee. But others took the route of Machiavelli and his Roman precedents: make citizens into soldiers. This was a particularly appealing solution when the issue was itself one of national renewal. Thus, part of Maurice of Nassau's rejuvenation of the Dutch for the war against their Spanish overlords went beyond drill and methodical fighting procedures to include the goal of a national army (with as few mercenaries as possible), long-term enlistments, and regular pay.

To a certain extent, Machiavelli's ideas reflected the widespread medieval assumption that warfare was a temporary activity. In ancient times the soldier was no different from any man of the tribe, ready to fight when necessary and to return to his plow when it was over. But the impulse to tie the structure of the army more closely to the political structure and values of the state—for Machiavelli, the city-state of Florence—illustrates the way war and nationalist aims were becoming identified with each other in the sixteenth and seventeenth centuries.

Our soldier/civilian distinction—with its implication that there are two separate spheres of civic life and that war is the affair of soldiers, not civilians—arrives with the early modern period. In monarchies and republics alike, the new model of a permanent male soldiering establishment presupposed ongoing international conflicts. With the Renaissance, the dynastic impulses of the recent past, in which wars arose primarily from issues of inheritance and ruling family honor, were being transformed into a nascent national self-consciousness. The explicit propaganda was increasingly that of national interests, usually expressed as the need to acquire land and expand boundaries into neighboring territory. Sweden, for example, after a century of efforts to separate itself from the political sway of Norway and Denmark, took the center of the European stage in the Thirty Years' War under the rule of Gustavus Adolphus. It became, if only briefly, one of the dominant military forces in Europe until the expenditure of money and soldiers, along with Gustavus's death in a ditch at the Battle of Lützen, forced it to the sidelines. Sweden rose again as a military power in the early eighteenth century under Charles XII, also feted as a hero throughout Europe. This time the fiscal ruin was complete. Like the Swiss in the sixteenth century, the Swedes in the seventeenth and eighteenth centuries were celebrated as a warrior culture with a warrior leader. But their aggression lacked clear political goals as well as money. The Swiss, as we have seen, became one of the prime sources of European mercenaries; the Swedes became the pacific nation we know today, and both sat out the wars of the twentieth century as neutrals.

Just as the medieval Church allayed its prohibitions against bloodshed when it was a question of crusade, religion also played its part in helping to energize the thrust toward national self-consciousnesses of the sixteenth and seventeenth centuries. The principle of *cuius regio, eius religio* (whose region, his religion) gave a proselytizing gloss to conquest. Religion was thus part of the strife between Spain and Holland, as well as between Sweden and the Holy Roman Empire. Sweden was a monarchy led by one of the few warrior kings in a world where monarchs increasingly spent more time in court than on the battlefield. But the rule of Gustavus Adolphus was also Lutheran in religion, and the combination of a militant Protestantism and a small country that had broken away from its larger and more powerful neighbors marks the nationalism, often asserted in the name of religion, that was one of the most significant political results of the Thirty Years' War.

Religious cause was always invoked during the Crusades, of course, but in the conflicts that followed the beginnings of Protestantism, the infidel enemy was much closer, and the threat to the homeland and the threat to its religion were intertwined. John Foxe's *Book of Martyrs*, with its attacks on the persecutions of the reign of "Bloody Mary" of England; Dutch propaganda about the Spanish; French Protestant prints depicting Catholic atrocities (and Catholic prints depicting those by Protestants)—these are only a few of the publications that helped define the combined national and religious enemy in the sixteenth and seventeenth centuries. The state and its interests were not yet identified in the patriotic motive we call nationalism. But at a time when nations were beginning to emerge, war supplied more acutely than any other means a validation of both national difference and national superiority. It is perhaps no accident that the first major break with the medieval Church comes from England, the most advanced in bureaucratic centralization of all the European countries and not incidentally an island unto itself.

Machiavelli in *The Art of War* recommended religion and religious rituals as one of the ways to inspire the loyalty of soldiers, and he especially praised what he considered to be Charles VII of France's very sly pretense of consulting with Joan of Arc in all military matters. But although his book appeared in the year of Martin Luther's excommunication, Machiavelli recommended religion only as a support to primarily civic virtue, in the same spirit that he recommends the harangues of generals and the fear of death as inspirations to military triumph. Justification by faith alone, let alone the consequences of religious conflict for the shape of politics, was not in his vision, nor did he foresee the importance of the ability of the new medium of printing to convey words and images to an audience of unprecedented size.

Yet the greatest importance of religion in warfare from the mid–sixteenth century onward was its contribution to the embryonic idea that war should be fought for an abstract "cause." By the Thirty Years' War, religion is firmly in place as an aspect of both personal and national identity. During the English Civil Wars, shortly after the battle of Edge Hill (1642), Oliver Cromwell wrote to a friend that for the Parliamentarians to win against the Royalists, men of honor had to be conquered by men of religion. "Godly, precious men," Cromwell called them, men who, as one contemporary historian remarked, had joined the Parliamentary side in the Civil Wars "upon a matter of conscience" and were therefore "well armed within" as well as without (Abbott, I, 204).

Cromwell was a great military tactician who helped reform the Parliamentary cavalry in the light of the theories of Maurice of Nassau and the cavalry tactics of Gustavus Adolphus. Although Cromwell's New Model

Army also included preachers attached to every regiment, he himself was hardly relying on godliness alone to win battles. But he did see the infusion of the element of belief into the soldier's attitude toward warfare as an improvement, spiritually and politically as well as militarily. In Cromwell's view, the changes in the nature of warfare meant that the army was a democratizing force that could be swung like an avenging hammer against an oppressive oligarchy.

In time, military prestige would invigorate the old hierarchies of rank with a new rationale of service in the name of the state. In future moments, such as the shift of the army's support from the monarchy to the republic in revolutionary France, or from the tsar to the Bolsheviks in revolutionary Russia, Cromwell's belief in the democratic potential of opening up military service would be justified. On many other occasions, of course, it would be the army that enforced repression and supported tyranny.

# MONEY, NATIONALISM, AND THE "MILITARY REVOLUTION"

The military model of masculinity becomes overpowering in an age of war. In the sixteenth and seventeenth centuries, more men were on the march in Europe than at any time since the fall of the Roman Empire. In addition to at least rudimentary training, these masses of men and matériel, which were needed for sieges that involved new fortification techniques, had to be fed as well as paid. To a great extent in the sixteenth century, this was the business of independent contractors who had financial resources, access to credit, and an organized supply of manpower that most governments could not yet mobilize. To fill the breach, entrepreneurs such as General Albrecht Wallenstein were a mixture of the military hero and the businessman. A Catholic convert who built his fortune by confiscating the estates of Protestants in Bohemia, Wallenstein raised thousands of troops and often tried to negotiate with other countries as if he were head of a sovereign state himself. This kind of imperious behavior brought about his downfall and later murder. But his image as a great warrior ill served by the ruler who depends on him (similar to the eleventh-century story of the Cid) was still being celebrated 150 years later in the age of Frederick the Great and Napoleon.

Alongside these military entrepreneurs, incipient national bureaucracies were starting both to arm and provide for soldiers and sailors, if only for practical reasons. Not only were hired generals like Wallenstein often politically unreliable, but with the changes in scale and hardware, it was also primarily monarchs—and fairly rich ones at that—who could afford war at all. It is generally accepted that the cost of putting a soldier on the battlefield increased some 500 percent between 1530 and 1630. The social rituals of violence that had taken up so much of medieval masculine life were therefore to be focused instead on violence in the name of the state. At the same time, the actions of the man of violence, whose personal inclination as well as class compulsion was to fight, would be justified not only by a chivalric code but also by a nascent sense of national identity.

Early forms of nationalism had followed in the wake of the Crusades as edifying alternatives to internecine war. Diplomacy, its international twin, was developed as the way to ameliorate and to some extent organize external war. Certainly, there had always been intermediaries between hostile groups to help oversee battles and settle their conclusions. The medieval heralds, who knew everyone's livery and could identify them on the battlefield, served some of these functions, but they were rarely charged with the power to negotiate. More often than not, the monarch or local sovereign leader was on the battlefield himself, with all his retinue. So what need was there for a surrogate?

But as issues became less local and national interest more pressing, officials appeared who might reasonably be expected to further the larger goals of bloodletting. The most important change occurred in the mid–sixteenth century when ambassadors, who had earlier been charged with specific tasks, took on a more permanent role in the correspondence between heads of state, even to the extent of establishing residence in national capitals. Venice was one of the earliest powers in Europe to have such standing representatives, but by the end of the seventeenth century, they were widespread in Europe.

What brought about the realization that war requires a system of generally accepted rules, and that differing national interests require negotiation to redirect war energies into more fruitful areas? Practical necessity is often a spur to both the innovations of politics and the abstractions of political theory. The increased use of ambassadors in the sixteenth century was in part an effort by less bellicose or less financially able states to counterbalance the attempt of the Habsburg-ruled Holy Roman Empire to conquer all of Europe, just as new diplomatic alliances would be formed to counter Louis XIV's similar efforts in the seventeenth century. Similarly, the long struggle of the Netherlands to free itself from the control of Spain, as well as the early stages of the Thirty Years' War, stands behind the appearance in 1625 of *De Jure Belli ac Pacis* (*On the Law of War and Peace*) by the Dutch jurist Hugo Grotius.

*On the Law of War and Peace* is the first work exclusively devoted to the establishment of international law. In his rudimentary effort to bring war within the sphere of "civilization," Grotius seeks to hold down abuses by drawing boundaries within which warrior fury and warrior honor would be equally unwelcome—if they refused to give way to the goals of the group. The French political philosopher Jean Bodin had argued in the midst of France's tumultuous wars of religion that only a powerful monarch could bring order out of such chaos. Just as the monarch and his central government would be the sole authorized source of group violence, they also began to claim for themselves the bestowing of all honor, which, in the tradition of the Garter, the Rose, and the other chivalric orders, was itself defined by either actual service in war or its equivalent.

Grotius's ideas similarly broadened chivalric injunctions to organize haphazard personal violence into a code of honor with the monarch at the top. But while the chivalric code focused on questions of moral behavior, diplomatic theory and the theory of the sovereign state that went along with it subsumed individual violence as well as individual morality into a system of national goals and international assumptions about their limits. The class issues of who belongs and who does not, never far below the surface of chivalry, will reemerge especially in the makeup of the officer corps. But on the international level a crucial shift of emphasis has been made in the issue of how states and their armed representatives ought to behave.

Ever since Michael Roberts first proposed the term "military revolution" some thirty years ago, historians have been arguing over whether or not there was one in the period from the middle of the sixteenth century to the middle of the seventeenth. Although different writers alter dates, locations, and emphasis, there is not much argument over the basic elements: new gunpowder armaments, new styles of fortification, larger armies. But these substantial changes in the waging of war are only part of the argument, since significant political transformations also occurred in response to the administrative and logistic needs of the new shape of war, and war transforms itself in relation to new social ideas and civic institutions. A more bureaucratically organized national government that gradually assumes all police powers is central to the emergence of royal absolutism, and later to the undermining of that absolutism in the name of the modern industrial state. But what is of special interest here, as much as the tangible changes in the modes, materials, and structures of war making, are the psychic bonds and constant interchange between war and nationalism that help shape masculine identity in this period.

National stereotypes in particular gather strength from wars and foment new wars in return—especially when the propaganda of war needs to justify a conflict with the Antichrist, the Infidel, or just the Other. The issue is not only "Who is the enemy?" but also "Who are we?" And the answer is often "We are men, and they are not." Just as popes and antipopes learned to preach and war against each other from the Crusades, the incessant exhortations to destroy the infidel stand like a grim shadow behind the nationalist antagonisms, both internal and external, of the next several centuries. From the expulsion of the Jews from Spain in 1492, to the burning of Mayan books by the Spanish conquistadors in the early sixteenth century, to the English selling of rebel Scots and Irish as slaves in the late sixteenth and mid–seventeenth centuries, to the policies of Louis XIV that provoked so many Huguenots to leave France after 1685—the urge toward national "purity" is often predicated on seeing the enemy as less than human, opposing his culture and eradicating his life. With such a perspective, economic arguments (Do these people strengthen rather than enfeeble the nation?) are irrelevant. Like the knight in armor, the pure nation is the encased nation, making itself ready for warfare by purging whatever races and peoples it deems not to correspond to its idea of itself.

Nations are often ideas about cohesion and community before they become infrastructures or royal bureaucracies. We have seen, for example, how the Hundred Years' War helped sharpen the urge of both the French and the English to insult each other's national character (and along the way to figure out what their own might be). At the beginning of the war the aristocracies of both countries were speaking Anglo-Norman French; by the end of it the English were speaking English. This is the world in which Chaucer's works appeared, and he generally used "English" to refer solely to the language and rarely refers to "England" as a geographic place. Even two hundred years later in Shakespeare's plays (which were written during the reign of monarchs little inclined to military adventuring), only Henry V and Elizabeth were addressed as "England," to acknowledge the identification of monarch and nation. Within a hundred years after Shakespeare's death, Sir John Arbuthnot, Queen Anne's physician and a friend of Pope and Swift, created "John Bull," an early nonroyal symbol of the country, as part of a series of pamphlets calling for England's withdrawal from the war with France. Even though the Tory and monarchist Arbuthnot meant the character as satire, it marked the beginning of the possibility of seeing the quintessence of England not as the monarch but as the ordinary middle-class citizen writ large.

These shifts in political symbolism, however small they may be at first, reflect changes in national self-image. Up through the eighteenth century, as so often in English history until the defeat of Napoleon, it is typically still the French who help engender the idea of "England," not least in mid-eighteenth-century anthems such as "Rule Britannia" and "God Save the King." "The Marseillaise" in its turn rejects the circle of enemies around revolutionary France whose "impure blood" will never be allowed to pollute the national heredity—a national self-concept that has become the battle cry of ethnic cleansers down to the present—while the nineteenth-century "Deutschland über Alles" announces its vision of national superiority in its title. By contrast, the peculiarly self-involved quality of American nationalism might be gauged first by "The Star-Spangled Banner," which recounts how the flag still waves after a battle with an invisible (and unspecified) enemy, and then by "America the Beautiful," which focuses on the physical beauty and plenty of the country, along with God's special care for it. This hardly means that America is immune to national stereotypes, just that its songs and symbols do not support them so obviously.

The creation of national flags, national symbols, and national music marks the need to turn inhabitants into citizens, to persuade them that they owe some debt to the nation (to be discharged by taxes and soldiering), and to induce a Yorkshireman to accept that some part of his identity is "British" or an Occitanian that he is "French." For all the new military hierarchies, one effect of the larger armies, the new weapons, and the codification of training was to allow a wider cross section of men to become soldiers.

The nobility's importance as the source of warriors, as well as the belief that war experience is the finishing school of aristocratic life, varies considerably from country to country. But the general trend, for the moment, is downward. Lawrence Stone, in *The Crisis of the Aristocracy*, estimates that for England in the mid–sixteenth century 75 percent of male aristocrats had been at war, while in the mid–seventeenth century (just before the English Civil Wars), the total was only 20 percent. In some instances, the decline is more dramatic. France during the youth of Louis XIV (from 1648 to 1653) was ruled by his mother, Anne of Austria, and Cardinal Mazarin. Trying to break Mazarin's control and the growing power of the monarchy, a group of nobles tried a last-ditch revival of the politics of aristocratic chivalry. This revolt, referred to in French history as the Fronde, ended with the victory of the Crown and the effective finale for any militarily independent nobility in France. When Louis assumed personal power, he made sure that the nobility was financially dependent upon him. The war making that had been an exclusive aristocratic preserve was now to be carried on in the name of the state.

The cavalry especially was still associated with the aristocracy, but as the century evolved, what constituted an aristocrat was itself in flux. (While "aristocracy" dates from the late Middle Ages, "aristocrat" only appears with the French Revolution.) At opposite ends of the military hierarchy, then, and within the same army, an ancestral heritage and a carefully honed skill faced a rabble of socially undesirable and perfunctorily trained cannon fodder. Their tradition was that of the young men in need who formed the cohort of knights in the lord's household and whose greatest examples, like William Marshal, could climb with their prowess to the highest levels in the kingdom. But in the new world of mass armies, that status was driven down the social scale by the sheer numbers of youngest sons, orphans, the disinherited, the urban and rural poor, and even criminals who were impressed into or joined armies for their own gain.

The hostility to these made-rather-than-born soldiers was extreme, and in the view of many noble and professional officers justified. By the late sixteenth century, there had been a growing and respectable body of opinion that stressed the ingloriousness of war and the actual dishonor of the soldier. Some of it, like that in Thomas More's *Utopia,* arose from the same kind of theological concerns that prompted the medieval Church to declare the Peace of God. But other writers, such as Rabelais and Montaigne, were reacting directly to the bloody wars of sixteenth-century France. By the early seventeenth century in France, the army was seen as a kind of prison, in which ordinary soldiers were kept by threats and punishments. They were the dregs of the social system, who improved civil society by leaving it. Jonathan Swift characterizes soldiers as barely civilized yahoos in *Gulliver's Travels;* Sir John Fortescue, author of an early history of the British army, writes that the eighteenth-century army was made up of the "scum of the nation"; and one nineteenth-century French military historian remarked that "the army is basically like a stream into which all the impurities of the social body are emptied" (Delbrück, IV, 229).*

As these remarks about "scum" and "dregs" indicate, the image of the soldier had changed, especially for those classes (and officers) who longed for the noble army of yore. But the disdain for the ordinary soldier could spread to encompass the greater warrior and even to war itself. On the whole, in fact, despite such ambiguous plays as *Henry V*, Elizabethan theater seems more preoccupied with grand military failures than with national triumphs. Christopher Marlowe, in plays like *Tamburlaine the Great*, *The Jew of Malta*, and *Doctor Faustus*, shows his fascination with outsized characters who try to go beyond human confines but also necessarily fail, defeated by their own ambitions for grandeur. The tribal world of *Macbeth* (so handily adaptable into the samurai terms of Kurosawa's *Throne of Blood* or the African warriors of *Zulu Macbeth*), the Roman posturings of *Coriolanus* and *Antony and Cleopatra*, Hamlet's admiration for the uncomplicated warrior sensibility of Fortinbras, the jealous passions of Othello—so many of Shakespeare's plays are populated by warriors either undone by warrior pride, unable to bend it to the needs of love and relationship, or trapped within its assumptions. In *Hamlet* and *Othello* he asks what is a soldier without a war, in *King Lear* what is a king without a state. The most striking of Shakespeare's images of the warrior appears late in *Troilus and Cressida*. After the play has exposed the vices of both the Greeks and the Trojan heroes, Hector in the midst of battle spies a Greek with a fine suit of armor and chases him offstage to strip it for booty. But as Hector discovers, the dazzling surface hides a corruption within: "Most putrified core, so fair without, / Thy goodly armor thus hath cost thy life. / Now is my day's work done; I'll take my breath. / Rest, sword; thou hast thy fill of blood and death" (1015).

Even beyond this "putrified core," with its grossly explicit mockery of the emptiness of chivalry, Shakespearian tragedy seems almost detached and ethnographic in its view of warrior culture. It was an attitude that

* In a kind of gallows humor, common soldiers, like other oppressed and despised groups, frequently turned these contemptuous names into badges of honor. The *poilu* of World War I evoked the berserk warrior of the past, and the German soldiers of the trenches called themselves *frontschwein*.

became more widespread during the Thirty Years' War. Although the old medieval vision of the independent warrior fighting for good had been adopted by the new nation-states, in the ferocious religious and national partisanship of that war, both the heroic knight and the war blessed by God often gave way to the decidedly unglamorous clash of arms and the brutal, predatory fighter. In works like Hans Jacob von Grimmelshausen's soldier-picaresque novel *Simplicissimus*, as well as in inexpensive popular engravings by Jacques Callot and others, there was a new awareness of the indiscriminate slaughter and brutality bred by the armies that foraged freely across an already blasted countryside. Descriptions of central France during the Hundred Years' War of the fourteenth and fifteenth centuries seem equally grim. But before the advent of printing, such articulate representations of war's horrors were not so widely available.

But at the same time that the war-making classes showed contempt for the ordinary soldier, they continued to propagandize the older heroic view of battle for themselves. Naval warfare, where an officer class sailed on a little island of privilege and had absolute authority over the ordinary sailor, retained more of an aristocratic gloss than land soldiery. On land as well, despite the presence of "scum," to go to war remained the highest form of ambition, even, as Jonathan Dewald has remarked of French aristocrats, "for those who stayed home" (45). With more men of varied backgrounds becoming soldiers, aristocratic officers in many countries moved to rigidify the new military hierarchy. Maurice of Nassau may have wanted to make soldiers from citizens in the model of classical Greece and Rome, but in France as well as Prussia, nobles hung on to all officer ranks.

Despite the shrinking percentage of aristocrats in uniform, military service, especially in the navy, did retain an ample portion of class honor along with something of its older possibility of being an avenue by which the well born but impoverished could find social and financial advancement. The nobility may have monopolized most of the officer class and its scorn for the soldier may have been a commonplace. But in the beginnings of national states, war was becoming what to a great extent in many countries it still is: one of the few ways of breaking out of an inherited social hierarchy, through which members of disadvantaged and immigrant groups could make their names—or die in the process.

Just as soldiering itself was becoming both an occupation for the many and a profession for the few, so the ability to make money from war was no longer restricted to the destitute younger sons of the nobility. By the seventeenth century, the Latin word for soldier (*miles*) was reserved for ceremonial occasions, while "soldier" became current as the word for an experienced, skilled land fighter, without quite shedding its origins in the Old French *sou* (from the Latin *solidarius*). A soldier, in other words, was someone who was not feudally obliged to fight but was paid to do it, and that pay came in different forms. The expensive initial outlay on armor and horse was no longer necessary in the world of prolonged sieges and lighter equipment. But, as in the past, towns would be sacked and booty collected. Ransom for captured officers was also still a generally accepted way for military men to come home more flush than they departed.

The governments who mustered, conscripted, hired, or impressed these soldiers had a somewhat more difficult time assembling their financial nut. The Thirty Years' War was the first of a series of Europe-wide convulsions that would not end, it seems, until World War II and the Cold War passed into history some three hundred years later. Neither the Hundred Years' War of the fourteenth and fifteenth centuries nor the dynastic entanglements of the sixteenth century were any match for its scale and devastation. Fueled by a "burn the crops of your enemy" strategy that reflected the earliest days of warfare, the Thirty Years' War expanded to vast areas of Europe, drawing on the manpower and money of so many countries that it readily falls into phases whose ends correspond to the exhaustion of resources. As Frank Tallett has remarked, "The history of war is also the history of debt" (175). Across Europe, new systems of taxation were introduced, monopolies in new products were sold by rulers and governments, public offices were on the block and knighthoods available to the highest bidder—all to raise money for treasuries depleted by war. In the monarchical urge for glory and power, the selling of honors had become the prime way to finance what had traditionally been the only source of male honor.

This happened even in England, which generally stayed out of direct involvement in the Thirty Years' War. But England was also a country where monarchs had to go hat in hand to Parliament for any extra funds, especially those for war and foreign policy. With such considerations in mind, James I created 906 new knights in the first few months of his reign and in 1611 authorized the title of baronet, which was awarded to anyone who could come up with £1,095—a figure determined by the cost of supplying thirty soldiers for three years. Although baronets were entitled to be called "Sir," they remained commoners and the title lapsed with their deaths. Knighthood was ceasing to imply a military role and starting to signify primarily a social position and title.

James's creation of the baronetcy indicates that some distance had been covered since the time in England when aristocrats mustered and paid for their own troops in support of the king's quarrels. Shakespeare in his English history plays makes much fun of the incompetence of many of the men pressed into service by their feudal lords and local captains. But with the beginning of the seventeenth century, the king was offering higher status to virtually anyone who could put up enough money for the monarchy to hire soldiers either at home or abroad.

This intrusion of money in a world that nostalgically considered itself to be preoccupied exclusively with military honor was not confined to those who paid. It also involved those who wished to be paid. In the early sixteenth century, the same era when Martin Luther was posting his Ninety-five Theses and Henry VIII of England and Francis I of France were competing for chivalric honors, the word "mercenary," came into use to mean specifically someone who fights for a foreign power.

Fighting on behalf of a country and a country's religion may seem to make the act of hiring or being a mercenary unpatriotic or even immoral. Yet because mercenaries were such a large part of early modern armies, and because some smaller and less bellicose societies took pride and profit in exporting their soldiers, the word for a long time was only rarely negative. During the late seventeenth century, for example, after the bloodless Glorious Revolution of 1689 brought William and Mary to the throne of England, "English" battles were fought between William, whose army was largely Dutch, and the deposed James II, whose army was largely French, until James's defeat at the Battle of the Boyne. Similarly, when in 1715 James's son continued the battle in favor of the Jacobite succession to the throne of Great Britain, his army, which was predominantly raised in Spain, fought that of George I, whose troops were from George's native Hanover and other parts of Germany.

It would be a long century or more before reliance on mercenaries in war became less common than reliance on citizens. Even in the early eighteenth century, Frederick William I of Prussia considered that it was an almost impossible goal to field an army that was only two-thirds foreign and one-third native. Similarly, throughout the Thirty Years' War, it was common for prisoners of war to be impressed, willingly or not, into the army of their captors. Side switching also occurred with some frequency, and not just among mercenaries. But the development of national loyalty had begun to fortify the soldier's emotional identification with not just his leaders but also his country.

A more nationalistic wind was blowing. One of the most tangible results of the Thirty Years' War was to confirm in the Netherlands the establishment of the first republican state in Europe by the final withdrawal of the troops and political control of Spain, perhaps the most feudal and authoritarian of European monarchies. The English Civil Wars were also fought largely over what constituted "England": the Royalist idea that there was a single national creator (William the Conqueror) whose descendant was the monarch, or the Parliamentary idea that England was a multiple creation whose authority stretched back to the witenagemot ("meeting of wise men") of the Anglo-Saxon parliament. The contempt with which the Hessian mercenaries of George III were viewed by the colonists in the American Revolution similarly springs from the difference perceived between fighting for money and fighting for a national "cause." It is an idea of comparatively recent birth. Even in an era like the Cold War, when soldiers of fortune fought for pay around the world, Hollywood movies told uplifting heroic stories in which the outlaw, the pirate, or the mercenary and his band were won over by the simple truth of a cause—usually when they had originally been hired by the other side.

# *DON QUIXOTE* AND THE FICTION OF MALE INDIVIDUALITY

"Sancho, my friend," he said, "you may know that I was born, by Heaven's will, in this our age of iron, to revive what is known as the Golden Age. I am he for whom are reserved the perils, the great exploits, the valiant deeds. I am—I say it again—he who is to revive the Knights of the Round Table, the Twelve Peers of France, and the Nine Worthies."

"To tell the truth, [said Sancho,] your Grace is the very devil himself, and there's nothing you don't know."

"In the profession I follow," replied Don Quixote, "one needs to know everything."

—*Don Quixote*, Part I (1605)

Two kindred transformations in the European idea of war and masculinity were occurring at the beginning of the seventeenth century. In the dawn of military professionalization, marked by Maurice of Nassau's introduction of drill and some (abortive) efforts to found military academies, contemporary captains were looking more avidly for instruction in war than for inspiration in being a warrior. Books on tactics were beginning to replace books on chivalry on the professional soldier's narrow camp shelf. Meanwhile, Spain, considered by all of Europe to be the heartland of feudal and Crusader culture—where personal honor came before everything and men wore the longest swords—gave birth to a very different sort of masculinity in the form of Miguel de Cervantes's great character Don Quixote. In 1571 Cervantes had lost the use of his left hand at the Battle of Lepanto, that swan song of chivalric warfare, and *Don Quixote*, published thirty-some years later, embodies a half-mocking, half-serious nostalgia for the age of the knight.

Its hero is a man who hankers not for the military status and manly prowess of the present, but for a long lost knightly honor that seeks glory not in war but in individual encounters.

The popularity of the figure of Don Quixote indicates that, even though moribund on the battlefield and disdained in the military textbooks, the ideal of the knight-errant had a portability beyond the medieval world in which it was born. At a time when monarchs in England, France, and Spain were replacing local honors with their own forms of validation, this solitary warrior, with his trusty squire, Sancho Panza, quests for a personal honor outside the social system, validated only by the books he has read. Accompanying him in fiction are two other characters—Doctor Faustus and Don Juan—who in their different ways reflect the deindividualizing of warfare through larger armies, more powerful guns, and more obsessive dynastic and national interests. This moment at the end of the sixteenth century and the beginning of the seventeenth marks the appearance of what Ian Watt has called "myths of modern individualism," new characters on the world stage who foretell the future development of a European sense of self. But the break with the past is not so clear or so complete. "Chivalry is a religion and these are sainted knights in glory," says Don Quixote. But despite these Christian metaphors, the don's knightly code is not validated through religion and divine will; it harkens back to an older, more pagan, sense of warrior honor, the kind depicted in the romances of Chrétien de Troyes, crystallized in individual honor and love.

Unlike the religious nationalism that was animating rulers and armies across Europe, this new kind of personal identity often paid lip service to, ignored, or was in actual combat with God. At the end of both the Faustus story and the Don Juan story, the main characters go to hell as a judgment on their sins of pride. But the message of their characters—and why they have lasted well beyond the literary works that gave them birth—is not their punishment but their aspiration: Faustus's desire for power and Don Juan's for an unbridled freedom. The stories seem to end with a puncturing of the balloon of self-assertion. But the audience remembers only the glorious struggle.

Although there is some evidence that the real-life origin of many tales was a wandering magician named George Faust, the literary figure of Faust first appears in the *Faustbuch* (1587), the source of many of the Faust stories later drawn upon by Christopher Marlowe and Goethe. Don Juan and Don Quixote arrive not much later (*Don Quixote*, Part I, 1605; Part II, 1615; first production of Tirso de Molina's Don Juan play, *El*

*Burlador de Sevilla,* 1630). Of this group, Faustus, the German scholar-magician, is the least directly indebted to the chivalric tradition, although perhaps only because he is its diametric opposite. He is a product of the Germany whose nobility, coming a century after France and England to chivalric display, elaborated its spectacle well beyond its predecessors, while Quixote and Juan are sons of Spain, the country with the most highly organized group of chivalric military organizations.

Dürer's lonely knight outfaced the world, the flesh, and the devil, but Faustus embraces them all. Although the historical George Faustus was attacked by Renaissance humanists as well as by Martin Luther for his magical fakery, the literary Johann Faustus, in his conceited conviction of his own universal knowledge, also resembles a wayward Renaissance humanist for whom learning is no longer enough. Like Don Juan, his solipsistic pride believes it can surmount even a combat with the forces of death and the underworld. For Faustus it is his famous pact with the Devil, which is still the prime mark of the antisocial sinner; for Don Juan it is the willingness to sup with the ghost of the commendatore, whom he has killed in a duel after seducing his daughter.

Next to these obvious though grand sinners, Don Quixote makes an uneasy third. Faustus and Don Juan are in fact both characterized as tricksters, Faustus wasting his powers on trivial party gags like turning the pope's meal to sawdust, while Don Juan is called a trickster (*burlador*) in the title of Tirso's play. As Watt argues, their final punishments constitute an attack, perhaps inspired by the Counter-Reformation, against the new, Protestant-accented individualism they otherwise embody.

But at the end of his adventures, Don Quixote gets no such comeuppance. He is no trickster, playing on and manipulating the weaknesses of others, but virtually a force of nature, whose quest has the power to entice even the most skeptical of those he meets. When he awakens from his dreams of knight-errantry, instead of being punished, he reassumes the ordinary identity of Alonso Quijano, a dying old man. More clearly than the stories of Faustus and Don Juan, which dramatize what happens when unbridled desires are set free, the story of Don Quixote is a celebration of the individual imagination, taking its own path and never compromising with the brute reality that keeps trying to contradict it.

A central influence on the idea that an inner self exists, an individual nature that differs from one's social role, is the Christian idea of the soul. But in the vision of theologians like Saint Augustine, the soul is not a personal characteristic; it is a connection to the community of believers. In contrast, Faustian ambition, or the rampant self-centeredness of a Don

Juan, defines early modern individualism as what happens to that sense of inwardness and personal justification when God is absent. Both Faustus and Don Juan restlessly move around the world with no goal in mind but self-aggrandizement. Don Quixote is restless, too, but Cervantes roots his quest in a knightly and chivalric aloneness, which Don Quixote for one believes belongs to a mythic past: "It grieves my soul that I should have taken up the profession of knight-errant in an age so detestable as this one in which we now live." Personal identity in *Don Quixote* is presented as an explicit problem, complete with willful name changes, an awareness of the fictionality of social roles, and an acute sense of the difference between the glorious past and the corrupted present, as well as the difference between how you explain yourself and how others explain you.

I'll have something to say shortly about the specifically male quality of this problematic self-definition in all three of these new mythic figures, as well as some comments about the role women and sexuality do or do not play in their stories. But for now I want to stress some of the differences. Don Juan's murder of his father-in-law the commendatore is intertwined with the latter's position as the quintessence of Spanish chivalry, the leader of Spain's primary chivalric organization, the Order of Caltrava. Thus, as Julio Caro Baroja has emphasized, Don Juan's seductions as well as his duels are in essence an attack upon and a triumph over family honor; Don Quixote, by contrast, leaves his family behind to go on his quest alone. Don Juan attacks the institution of chivalry through his murder of his father-in-law; Don Quixote defends the profession of arms as the ideal path for the man of the present to follow because it includes all other professions, including that of letters.

The relation between letters and arms appears frequently in sixteenth-century literature. The fervor with which it is argued implies the extent of the effort to transform the chivalric image and topple the military aristocracy from its position of exclusive privilege. At the same time, however, there was also an urge to preserve some of those virtues in the service of a distinction between the ordinary solder, who merely fought, and the true soldier, who understood the traditions of warfare and their role in shaping a masculine ideal. In Japan as well in this period, *bun* (learning) and *bu* (military arts) were considered to be the two defining accomplishments of the samurai. Baldassar Castiglione, a mid-sixteenth-century Italian soldier and diplomat, similarly tries to synthesize the man of letters and the man of arms into the figure of the ideal courtier, whose ability to draw upon both talents makes him the appropriate successor to the knight of old. Like a good courtier himself, Castiglione wants to assert a chivalric genealogy for his position. But another trait of the courtier, like that of the samurai, is his ability to fit into court society and his deference toward his prince.

Neither of these traits characterizes Don Quixote, whose desire to be recognized as a famous knight never compromises his readiness to follow his own whim wherever it leads. In *Don Quixote*'s substitution of a psychological and secular idea of an imagined self for the Christian idea of the soul as the key to inner nature, the villains are usually those who try to bring the don back to "reality," which usually means a restrictive social order in which everyone must be who they were born to be. Although there is some religious language in *Don Quixote,* there is no metaphysical presence, either of angels or devils. Faustus and Don Juan, in contrast, directly spit in the face of social and religious conventions and so they must face the retribution of a Christian social order, symbolized by the avenging figure of Satan.

The figure of Satan or the Devil is so important to the stories of Faustus and Don Juan that we might ask where it came from. Like any human idea, Satan has a history, and his growing importance in sixteenth- and seventeenth-century Christianity furnishes an intriguing counterpoint to these issues of masculine individualism and self-assertion I am tracing. In the tale of Faust's contract with the Devil in the 1580s, the combat of Satan with God in Milton's *Paradise Lost* in the 1660s, and the Salem witchcraft trials of the 1690s, Satan seems to be the eternal principle of evil. But, in fact, he is virtually missing from the Old Testament, as he is from early Christian thought, which, following the lead of theologians like Augustine, defined evil not as the *opposite* of good but as its absence. The Book of Job is one of the few places in the Old Testament where Satan makes an extended appearance, and even there he is still a member of God's court, albeit one with a special interest in putting human beings to the test, and he discusses Job's torments with God like a fellow symposium member.

From these ambiguous origins, as Jeffrey Burton Russell has argued, Satan increasingly becomes a dualistic principle in what is otherwise a nominally monotheistic religion—the tempter, accuser, and punisher of human weakness. In a common theological formula, *sine diabolo nullus Dominus*—without the Devil there is no God—they depend on each other. Protestantism's condemnation of the intercessory power of the

Catholic priesthood to protect the believer from evil therefore places the individual soul precariously between the Devil and Christ in a combat distantly presided over by that holy umpire, the Supreme Being.

Along with a personality and a theological role to play, Satan in the late Middle Ages also gains a home. Although even in the New Testament there is not very much detail about hell, the modern image of the diabolical underworld is pieced together, as in Dante's *Inferno,* from fragments of the classical underworld with its exemplary punishments and of the Old Testament Gehenna with its fire and brimstone.

To the list of Faust, Don Juan, and Don Quixote, we might therefore add Satan as a prime type of the masculine assertion, self-absorbed egotism, and manipulativeness contemplated by Europeans in the seventeenth century. Dante's Satan sat immobilized at the frozen center of hell, chewing on the three great betrayers: Judas, Brutus, and Cassius. But the seventeenth-century Satan, like the various characters who either embody or try to combat his characteristics, speeds around the world, looking to stir up human discord and conflict as part of his own battle with God. He is preeminently a figure of worldliness and society, embodying all the lures that turn men away from God. Satan is the consummate role-player and shape-shifter, not like the berserk warrior whose totemistic animal nature shone through in battle, but a manipulative warrior-courtier—Castiglione's ideal turned hypocrite. When he leaves hell in *Paradise Lost* to seek revenge on God by corrupting man, Satan disguises himself as "a stripling Cherub," the emblem of innocence, and so is able to fool the angels detailed to keep the devils in hell: "For neither Man nor Angel can discern/Hypocrisy, the only evil that walks/Invisible, except to God alone. . . ." Satan as the First Hypocrite thus stands behind the obsessive seventeenth-century theatrical interest in hypocrisy—the self-conscious wearing of a mask, the psychological descendant of the knightly visor, to disguise one's real ends and real nature.

Milton, in fact, makes a direct identification of the satanic with the chivalric and the military. Satan, who first appears in *Paradise Lost* after his defeat by God in the war in heaven, is above all a military man, described with reference to Achilles, Aeneas, Roland, Arthur, and the whole panoply of mythic military heroes whose model of human nature Milton seeks to reject. As the consummate warrior, Milton's Satan has two chief traits: in his view of the world, he judges everything by matter and the standards of physicality with no understanding of the world of the spirit; and in his psychology he stays trapped within an obsessive combat with God and Christ. Like the other archindividualists, he has no resources for standing back from himself. Yet at the same time, Milton does not deny our human affinity with the satanic, or the enticing side of Satan's willingness to fight with God. After all, we are fallen as well, and the problem that *Paradise Lost* poses to the reader is how to be fallen—individual, restless, and adrift—without becoming satanic.

As a crucial part of his answer, Milton associates the epic hero's vaunting desire for military triumph and physical defeat of his enemies with Satan's fatally flawed self-sufficiency. Like Faust, Satan knows much but to little effect, and, unlike Castiglione's courtier or Don Quixote, no immersion in letters or learning will make his military prowess any more substantial: "Deep verst in Books and shallow in himself." Milton thus links the epic military hero with the individualist ego of the present and contrasts Satan's eternal manipulations with the spiritual ability to leave behind all social definitions of identity and, for that matter, masculinity. Despite his power and allure, Milton's Satan remains inveterately superficial, whether he is covered with glistening armor in his guise as Lucifer or trapped in the serpent's shimmering skin. Gathering his troops for the war in heaven, he assesses God's power by numbers and equipment only and, among other innovations, invents the cannon, which Don Quixote cursed as the destroyer of honor in battle: "a device by means of which an infamous and cowardly arm may take the life of a valiant knight, without his knowing how or from where the blow fell." Although their superiority is spiritual, not material, the army of heaven at first fights on Satan's terms but make no headway until the moment when they remove their own protection: "Thir arms away they threw." Then, "light as the Lightning glimpse they ran, they flew" and, pulling out chunks of hills and trees, they drop them on the devils. Although set in heaven, it is a scene like a medieval battle, Agincourt perhaps, where the armored and caparisoned flower of chivalry is crushed by a lightly armed infantry:

*Thir armor help'd thir harm, crush't in and bruis'd*
*Into their substance pent, which wrought them pain*
*Implacable and many a dolorous groan. . . .*

# TESTS OF THE BODY: TRIAL BY COMBAT, SINGLE COMBAT, AND THE DUEL

Two basic changes in seventeenth-century warfare—larger armies and more sieges than battles—thus provide metaphors for the new images of war: the individual soldier desperately trying not to be lost in the masses of his fellows; and the enclosed fortress, situated both geographically and psychologically on a border or a frontier. In the transition from medieval to early modern warfare the roles of the single fighter and the government are rebalanced, with the weight going toward the latter. Instead of a body submerged in the panoply of armor, the individual uniformed soldier becomes part of an army on the move. One pole of the new masculine identity is thus an awakening national identity shaped behind the fortress wall. The other is an intensified awareness of the physical body and its frailty without armored protection. Caught between Milton's image of Satan's troops defeated by their own defenses and Saint Sebastian pierced with arrows yet looking to heaven, the soldier on the battlefield invokes the spiritual mantle of both his religion and his nation to protect his vulnerable body.

As usual in history and human affairs, nothing moves in a straight line with a clean demarcation of eras, suitable to chapters in a book. Things may change in a manner that seems to look forward to what happens later, but at the same there are revivals of the past and a frequent unwillingness to let older traditions disappear.

Throughout human history, innocence and guilt have often been proved or inflicted upon the body. By being inspected (as for the supposed marks of a witch), by being tortured, wounded, dismembered, or killed, the body bears witness to the law. So, too, throughout the Middle Ages, in the Arthurian romances of Chrétien de Troyes, as well as in the laws of many countries, men of the war-making classes had the option of proving their innocence or settling legal conflicts by risking death or defeat in judicial duels. There was little precedent for this in Greek or Roman law. But its prevalence in the Middle Ages shows how the conception of order was often so local that the gods or God had to be called upon to witness the rightness and probity of the accused. With that divine sanction, the body—particularly the male body—would either prove guilt by physical punishment or innocence by physical prowess.

By the sixteenth century, the social context for the trial by combat was changing along with the conditions of war itself. With God standing less on the side of any individual combatant than behind the overarching power of the state, the operation of law began to shed its warlike methods of proof. Judicial combat was banned in France, although it remained on the books in England until 1819, when one Abraham Thornton claimed the privilege and was refused. What then happened to the upper classes, who were used to having their feuds and lawsuits settled in a style that reflected their conviction of personal honor?

Male monarchs and upper-class men in general were obviously more caught up in the remnants of the tradition of medieval honor, but other men were looking for their share. *Don Quixote,* written in the early seventeenth century, is again a central document of the change I am describing, both for its embrace of the importance of the imagination in a hero's creation of himself and for its satire of the honor-inflamed young men infesting the Spanish countryside. Although duels were fought in many countries, it was Spain particularly that viewed itself and was viewed by others as the country of the *pundonor,* the punctilious refinement of honor, where the most trivial slight would be occasion for a bloody contest, just as in the late twentieth century Spanish is the source of "macho," our own generalized word for hypermasculine assertiveness. The characterization is, of course, a stereotype, but like many stereotypes it reflects both internal and external perceptions of a national trait. In the early decades of the seventeenth century, the count-duke of Olivares, the chief Spanish statesman and military leader, repeatedly invoked the need to restore and strengthen the national reputation and honor of Spain—especially the Spanish monarchy. As he wrote to the twenty-year-old Philip IV in 1625, "I have always been deeply anxious to see Your Majesty enjoying throughout the world *opinión* and *reputación* equal to your greatness and parts" (Elliott, 82). These were sufficient reasons for Olivares to pursue policies of aggression, even though incessant wars on several fronts were succeeding only in depleting the country financially, inspiring Portugal's breakaway from Spain, and guaranteeing that by the end of the seventeenth century Spain would be a second-class European power. This was the darker, unreflective side of Don Quixote's quest for knightly honor: not the fertile imaginative reshaping of the world by an individual, but the willful blindness of national policy. No wonder that other countries caricatured the Spanish as blind adherents to an unrealistic conception of their honor.

Even though monarchs could with some justification declare the confluence of personal and national honor in their own military actions, the equation of personal prestige with the violent defense of honor presents a problem for anyone less exalted. When state warfare becomes more pervasive, and the approval of violence rests increasingly in the hands of a centralized monarchy, the leeway for individual warfare shrinks. Similarly, when the state moves to monopolize the bestowal of honor, there is a resurgence of earlier modes of prestige, separated from their tribal roots and deployed as emblems of a new individualism. Olivares was also a great supporter of the arts; he was a patron of Rubens and Velázquez, among others. Accordingly, in an effort to invoke the sanction of the classical past for reputation in the present, Philip IV and his portrait painters took the example of the recently discovered equestrian statue of Marcus Aurelius in Rome to pioneer a revival of this image of the monarch whose military prowess was epitomized by his seat on a rearing horse.

But what happens, for instance, when personal honor demands a satisfaction that is not in the state's interest? The single combat that was asserted as a quintessential chivalric battle between monarchs or champions had its private equivalent in the personal duel for reasons of sullied honor. Although the impulse to dueling would last and duels would be fought in some countries, as well as in some families and professions, for many years to come, the violent defense of individual honor was a "right" that was by the seventeenth century rapidly being superseded by and transferred to the state. Previously, the judicial duel had often been part of the legal code. But in the new world of increased state control over law and violence, it was now outside the law, to be fought for offenses that the legal code either ignored or, in the opinion of the combatants, for which it was insufficient. In the late Middle Ages, these more personal duels had been defined by the Church as a revolt against God because they forced divine justice to intervene in a private dispute. By the late sixteenth century, in France particularly, dueling became a crime against the state as well, because the combatants were undermining the power of the monarch to dispense justice.

The outlawing of duels by the growing judicial and executive power of a centralized monarchical state thus signaled a steady narrowing of the legal sphere within which male, usually aristocratic, honor was able to authenticate its own system of values. But, instead of disappearing, the cultural importance of the duel expanded. Reaching into the medieval past to claim a pedigree in the knightly combat, its modern form became intricately codified, even while it began to be proscribed both legally and militarily. Like Don Quixote's sallying forth to right the wrongs of the world based on his reading of chivalric romances, the investment in the duel by the aristocracy (and by anyone who wanted to be thought to have an aristocratic sense of personal honor) was a fantasy of armor and individuality, similar to the military's own attachment to cavalry—a case of believing propaganda about the life of honor that it had manufactured itself.

Honor, always in danger of needing validation by an audience, was decisively turning into reputation. For individuals, therefore, it had to be defended in duels, for duels need to be known and talked about to have any meaning. As much as the secular monarch defined an aggressive masculinity identifiable with his nation, the ethic of dueling justified that aggressiveness as a sign of personal style and individualism. Artists like Caravaggio were notorious for their short tempers and duels, while Benvenuto Cellini, the sculptor, metalworker, and writer, spends at least as much time on his duels and quarrels in his *Autobiography* as he does on his artwork and his patrons. The seemingly more cerebral René Descartes both dueled and, in addition to his works of philosophy, collected notes for a treatise on fencing. It was an ability that marked a kind of upper-class or aspiring manhood, and, depending on the country, could indicate that he who did not possess it was socially and even sexually less of a man.

For organized governments and legal systems, dueling was thus a threateningly individualistic act, but it also remained fascinating for its continuity with chivalric traditions of single combat. Similarly, in early-seventeenth-century Japan, when the Tokugawa shogunate was in the throes of trying to fashion centralized political institutions from a competing group of local feudal authorities, laws were passed forbidding private disputes and vendettas. Although the state was beginning to take over all decisions about public honor in both war and peace, the duel continued to thrive because it furnished a way for men of a certain class to assert their membership in that class and their consequent personal honor *as men*. Whether or not you ever used it, the ability to wear a sword at your hip signaled a masculinity more socially sanctioned than our own superficial Freudian designation of the sword as phallic symbol implies.

With the growth of centralized monarchies, the self-contained image of the knight as solitary defender of values is thus explicitly outlawed even as the new states try to absorb some of the same glory for their own ends. In Japan, as in Europe, there was always a grudging respect for dueling along with the urge to punish, especially from that mega-individual the monarch or the shogun, whose own stature had such strong chivalric underpinnings. Dueling reached its height in seventeenth-century Europe but managed to exist as a cultural event for much longer—and in some cases, especially for politicians and soldiers, even into the late twentieth century. While in actuality the feudal rituals that confirmed male identity were being replaced by national allegiances and individual warfare was being absorbed into state warfare, the celebration of personal heroic combat was increasing as well.

In this new world, the monarch occupied an ambiguous place as both supreme individual and supporter of the abstract idea of the nation. The desire of the duelist to ignore the law paradoxically mingled with obeisance to the ruler, not as guarantor of law but as epitome of honor. In France, for example, dueling was explicitly outlawed in the coronation oath, and jurists assailed the practice as a mistaken diversion of the noble and military role to private ends. Accordingly, duelists were caught, convicted, and executed, often after they had proclaimed their loyalty to a system their acts seemed to ignore but actually ennobled. François Billaçois cites for example the case of the Chevalier d'Andrieu, who was executed in 1638, having killed seventy-two men in duels before he reached the age of thirty. This "arsonist, necrophile, rapist and blasphemer" nevertheless made his last words a blazon of his loyalty to Louis XIV (98). Likewise, the forty-seven *ronin* retainers who avenged the death of their lord in Japan in 1704 committed *seppuku* for the insult to the government their vendetta represented, but not long after were celebrated in the play *Chushingura* as the exemplars of true honor. Similarly, the distinction between the *noblesse d'épee* (the warrior nobility) and the *noblesse de robe* (the political nobility) remained a seventeenth-century French commonplace. Both are required to preserve the nation.

These parallels between Europe and Japan at a historical moment of transition between feudal and centralized government are striking. But the intriguing European difference is again the way in which the warrior imperatives, the religious imperatives, and the political imperatives continue to conflict. In Japan, both the lack of an individualist ethos in the system of samurai honor and the overwhelming loyalty to the lord implied a deep support for the political and social order even as their actions seemed on the surface to invalidate state authority. French edicts of the seventeenth century, in contrast, characterize dueling as pagan and libertine, or free-thinking, while the apologists for dueling invoke the biblically sanctioned model of David and Goliath.*

Even though European duelists might employ a Christian language of God's validation and justice, the morality of the duel and the needs it satisfied were considered by both supporters and critics to spring not from religion but from a revitalized warrior masculinity, whose relation to the ends of the state was at best ambiguous. It is hardly any wonder then that duels remained one of the most obvious examples of a tenacious style of male honor that could not quite be eradicated in the name of kingly power. The *gloire de France* that Louis XIV so often invoked as the reason for his military adventures defined the state and its interests as the true embodiment of the dreams of the military noble class—and every other Frenchman, into which all desire for personal glory ought to be submerged. Personal honor must give way to a larger sense of duty. In the heroic tragedies of the period written by Pierre Corneille (*Horace, Le Cid*) and Jean Racine (*Bajazet, Phèdre*), the hero is faced with an irresolvable dilemma—between love and honor, or friendship and honor, or

* The absent figure of Saul in the David and Goliath story also allowed the apologists to say that dueling might be in the king's service as his champion rather than an insult to his justice.

family and honor—but in death his lonely grandeur helps serve the state's dearest self-image.

The masculinity whose emblem is single combat hence remains ready for revival as both support and criticism at any time that national honor seems lacking. To say, along with the anthropologist Julian Pitt-Rivers, that the assertion of honor always carries with it the threat of physical violence assumes a much too general view of both honor and violence, and glosses over their particular relation to the world in which they appear. In his study of duels in seventeenth-century France, Billaçois remarks on the way in which these often adolescent duelers show aggression without hostility—a characteristic that is an explicit part of the ethic of the Japanese warrior avenging his honor.

The paradoxical place of dueling in the early modern state also resembles the politically ambiguous figure of the cowboy in American westerns. The western movie duel on a dusty main street in full view of the townspeople draws deeply upon the chivalric underlay of modern masculinity. Professing motives of personal revenge and honor, it appears to be beyond politics, yet it has political implications. But the cowboy's ambiguity also mirrors that of the duelist. Depending on your assumptions about male honor, the cowboy hero's individuality, his code, and his sense of honor can be understood as either right-wing or left-wing, conservative or radical, his self-assertion as either an attack against general order or the expression of that order's deepest values.

Like the duelist, the movie avenger of private wrong acts beyond the law. The difference in the twentieth-century versions of these conflicts is that the hero involved is rarely wellborn. These are men without family names, who have only themselves. Rambo, whose name plays on that of the rebellious French poet, must engage in single combat because institutions—and the honor they claim to represent—have failed him. The only way to restore that honor is by personal action, even though he is thwarted constantly by the government he continues to defend. It may seem that the cowboy and the action hero going it alone against villains are modern fantasy compensations for the anonymity of mass, technological war. But they are also figures who invoke contradictions present at the creation of the modern state, when war became a matter of policy and logistics, and individuals were usually lost in the shuffle.

Thus the very instability of the relation between man, soldier, and hero became part of the European history of masculinity. The submergence of the now-uniformed soldier in the ranks of others who looked much like him was accompanied by a growing fascination with the individual warrior and his flamboyant characteristics. This development was too gradual to be called a "crisis." But it constituted a crucial revaluation of traditional ideas of masculinity in the growing light of a style of warfare that little resembled what was practiced by Cú Chulainn and Henry V, or even Henry VIII and Francis I.

# PIRATES AND HIGHWAYMEN

In terms of their attitudes toward the society and the political state in which they lived, we might sketch a rough continuum of these styles of heroic action, from ideal insiders to contentious outsiders. On one end would be the theories of heroism, plays about heroism, and celebration of such leaders as Wallenstein and Gustavus Adolphus that proliferated in England, France, and Germany after the middle of the seventeenth century. There the hero's military prowess exemplifies a manly virtue at the service of society that confirms its sense of proper order, shedding, as Thomas Hobbes says, "a lustre and influence upon the rest of men resembling that of the Heavens" (II, 224). As we might expect, such a hero often, as in Hobbes's formulation, resembles the monarch; in other versions, like Andrew Marvell's view of Oliver Cromwell, he is a more egalitarian figure:

*He seems a king by long succession born,*
*And yet the same to be a king does scorn.*
*Abroad a king he seems, and something more,*
*At home a subject on the equal floor.* (136)

But whether monarchist or republican, his personal masculinity is the guarantee of his country's prowess, sometimes subtly and sometimes more overtly, as in "An Horatian Ode" (1650), when Marvell says that Cromwell's valor causes the Scots to "shrink beneath the plaid" while his own sword is triumphantly erect.

In the middle of this hypothetical masculine continuum are the duelists who both flout the laws of society and pay homage to their monarch, so intent are they on proving that their defense of their personal honor ought to be a public concern of the world in which they live. At the other end are those whose aggression opposes the societies that exist, forming little seagoing or hideout utopias of their own.

These were the highwaymen and pirates whose ranks were often swelled with men—and a few women—in the wake of peace treaties and demobilizations that made their skills redundant for ordinary purposes. One benefit from the use of mercenaries was that a nation's own population wouldn't be taken away from productive nonmilitary work. Another was that, after they were mustered out, they would generally return to their own countries rather than, like natives, take their war-honed skills into highway robbery or piracy. Robin Hood, for example, begins in legend as a local rebel, but his story soon expanded to make him a returning veteran of the Crusades disgruntled with what had happened to his country during the reign of King John. More immediately, in the Middle Ages, tournaments not only were preparation for wars but also expanded after wars to drain off some otherwise disruptive energies. The White Company of freelance knights in the late Middle Ages was similarly spawned by a peace treaty during the Hundred Years' War, and the glow of their chivalric reputation spread in the late seventeenth and early eighteenth centuries to envelop pirates and highwaymen as well.

But it was also their unruly antisocial behavior that made such men fascinating. Any number of books have tried to debunk the romance of piracy as an invention of nineteenth-century writers like Robert Louis Stevenson and Captain Frederick Marryat, helped along by the even more garish demands of Hollywood adventure films. But the deeper question is how such outlaw masculine individualism, characterized by bloodshed and violence, first gained a foothold in both reality and the Western imagination during the great national and military expansions of this period. Pirates did increase in numbers after the peace treaty between England and Spain at the beginning of the seventeenth century as well as after the Treaty of Utrecht in 1713, the prelude to the last great age of piracy in the Caribbean. Similarly, after the English Civil Wars, highwaymen, often from the losing Cavalier side, took to the road and did not go straight after the restoration of Charles II.

Both the highwayman and the pirate represent a freedom from conventional identity, possible for every man in wartime, but impossible in peace. With such a sense of asserted freedom in mind, Eric Hobsbawm in *Primitive Rebels* labels pirates and gang members of the early modern period as "social bandits," whose criminal acts should be interpreted as protests against the early growth of capitalism. But I think that it is the hostile response to official order of all sorts, particularly the expanding military organization of the modern state, that is more pervasive. Just as the story of Robin Hood and his Merry Men became increasingly interpreted as an attack from the natural world against a court-bound monarchy, piracy struck a blow against the state's claim to a monopoly over both violence and the accumulation of wealth, especially as European navies were pillaging the rest of the world.

For Plutarch, writing in the second century, pirates were extravagant and gross, and Roman comments about piracy, like Cicero's description of the Mediterranean depredations of the son of Pompey, tended to stigmatize them as unworthy opponents for proper members of society to have any truck with, as well as general problems against which all countries should band together. In the sixteenth and seventeenth centuries, however, English and French pirates were at first sanctioned by the state as privateers licensed to get back some of the wealth of the Americas that the papacy had reserved for the Spanish. Then, as England under Cromwell became a great sea power itself, the need for such extralegal marauders declined and the Royal Navy itself in the 1720s was given the task of cleansing the Caribbean of their presence.

The eradication of the pirates only helped enhance their allure. The actual social makeup of the late-seventeenth-century pirate ship or the highway bandit gang may have included a percentage of disgruntled aristocrats, social radicals upset at the restoration of Charles II, freed slaves, and inveterate warriors for whom the state of war was the only natural way to be. Thieves and highwaymen are noted in legend for their special sense of honor, the members of the early Mafia have been mythologized in films like *The Godfather* for their loyalty, and the ghetto gangsta ethic stresses the gang as a better family in a world where normal society scarcely cares about you at all. Despite the popular image of the autocratic pirate leader, pirates in fact often considered themselves more egalitarian and internally cohesive than the official world that looked down on them and tried to wipe them out. Like the mountain men of eighteenth- and nineteenth-century America, who held annual conclaves before they would take off for the wilderness again, pirates also met in periodic rendezvous, virtually declaring their status as an alternate society. On the practical level as well, pirates represented a contrast to the societies that hunted them. As recent studies have shown, many pirate ships elected their captains, drew up their own rules of incorporation and behavior, and shared in the booty according to their contribution to the victory.

B. R. Burg has argued that the pirate ship was often a sexual utopia as well, specifically homosexual, in which the new national state's growing desire to regulate personal sexual mores was denied, like a floating version of the warrior homosexuality insisted upon by some military cultures and demolished by the Church in the attack against the Knights Templar. But whether homosexual, heterosexual, bisexual, or just omnisexual, the colorful dress and outrageous look of pirates specifically evoke both archaic and exaggerated forms of masculinity. As Hobsbawm points out, male bandits in this period characteristically dressed up in some personalized version of aristocratic dress, while woman gang members dressed as men. With such masquerade, pirate mockers of normal social order seem to question the way men appear in public itself. In the wake of a much later war, Cole Porter, himself a homosexual who married and lived a public life as a heterosexual, parodied the tradition in *The Pirate* (1948), with his song about the marauding Macoco, "Mack the Black," who "throughout the Caribbean and its vicinity" blazes "a flaming trail of masculinity." As the story turns out, the real pirate, who has settled into respectability as the mayor of a small island town, is finally defeated and exposed by a traveling performer who has pretended to be Macoco for romantic reasons. Says the fake-pirate actor (Gene Kelly) to the ranting real-pirate mayor (Walter Slezak): "Next time, underplay. It's very effective." The line is a purely modern twist. In the same way that the seventeenth- and eighteenth-century pirate had in his person and his actions mocked proper society, the metamorphic performer now taunts the pirate who has decided that respectability suits him fine.

# THE RITES OF "MAN"

Of Man's First Disobedience, and the Fruit
Of that Forbidden tree, whose mortal taste
Brought Death into the World, and all our woe,
With loss of *Eden,* till one greater Man
Restore us, and regain the blissful Seat . . .
—John Milton, *Paradise Lost* (1667)

Know then thyself, presume not God to scan;
The proper study of Mankind is Man.
—Alexander Pope, *An Essay on Man* (1733)

But what of other men, who did not decide to become pirates or highwaymen, career sailors or soldiers? Was there a different kind of man emerging from the new wars and warfare of the seventeenth century? How do changes in the story of war—what it is, how it is conducted—connect with changes in the story of masculinity? The revival of classical learning in the Renaissance created as well a growing sense of history. In the seventeenth century, the word "feudal" was coined to describe the conventions of a world that had clearly passed. The medieval chivalry established through genealogy and girded with armor was slowly giving way to a world of men literally without shields, fearfully venturing into new territory. Instead of automatically behaving like men in accordance with tradition, they were beginning to sense the arbitrary side of masculinity: Must a man always behave in the old ways? What and who is a man here and now?

I have frequently referred to the "individual" in these pages, as though this were an agreed-upon concept, though of course it shifts from generation to generation, from age to age, from class to class, and from culture to culture. One preoccupation of social historians for many years has, in fact, been the effort to find the abstract "roots" of individualism by asking what makes someone individual. Is it in the idea of the soul, and the relation to God? Is it in economic and financial self-sufficiency? Is it the political ability to be autonomous, not a mere subject? Is it determined by thought and self-awareness?

Outlaw masculinity of the pirate or highwayman type in particular sprang up in the shadow of a general European realignment of philosophical thought about the place of human nature in the world. Many thinkers and scientists contributed to this change. René Descartes in France and Francis Bacon in England, for example, are usually given joint credit for formulating the precepts of the move toward experimental science that marks the seventeenth century's growing separation from medieval habits of mind. As part of that effort to disencumber science from the weight of inherited religious authority, which had assigned causality exclusively to God, both Descartes and Bacon emphasized the individual as the source of all accurate knowledge of the world.*

The Thirty Years' War, the English Civil Wars, and the expansionist policies of Louis XIV may have taken center stage in the political history of the period, but to keep the picture of seventeenth-century masculinity in balance, it should be noted that many compound words in English that begin with "self-" first made their appearance in the same period: "self-interest," "self-denial," "self-love," "self-esteem," "self-deception," "self-respect," "self-conscious," and "self-sufficient," as well as the indispensable "selfish." The era in which Descartes emphasized the individual basis of perception and formulated his noted maxim of personal existence—"I think, therefore I am"—is the same in which national states and collective identity were first being formulated. When Louis XIV said *"L'état, c'est moi,"* he underlined the French state's intimate relation to his own heroic masculinity, just as Descartes not long before him had emphasized thinking and speaking as the traits that decisively distinguish human consciousness from both the unknowable mind of God above and what he considered to be mechanical animal instinct below.

* Perhaps appropriately enough, one of the first intellectual innovations of the early Renaissance had been a fascination with perspective and point of view, particularly as it helped to explain the geometry of missile paths made possible by more powerful artillery.

Following Descartes and Bacon, in the later half of the seventeenth century, Thomas Hobbes and then John Locke revised the religiously based definition of human nature by embedding their philosophy in the question of man in society and how civilization began. Their answers depended on whether they thought society was created to be an improvement over the past or a fall from it, and whether its goal was to suppress the evils of human nature or to enhance the good. In Hobbes's view, the world before society was filled with a perpetual violence he called "the war of all against all." In such a world the main goal of individuals was survival, and so men were forced to band together for self-protection. Locke, in contrast, saw the world before society as a kind of paradise, a "state of nature," whose benevolent individualism society turned to the general benefit.

Hobbes, who had been Bacon's secretary, published his great philosophic work *Leviathan* in 1651, but the route he took to his ideas can be seen in part in his translation of Thucydides's history of the Peloponnesian war, which appeared in 1628. Like Thucydides contemplating the breakdown of Athenian society, Hobbes worries especially that the end of feudalism and its rituals of male relationship has brought about a world of "masterless men" whose only security lies in constant conflict, an intimidating world outside "normal" social order that resembles the highwayman gangs or the alternate society of the pirate ships.* To remedy this situation required a national self-consciousness and a state built on a single principle of authority, exemplified for Hobbes in a monarchy justified not by its connection to God but by its embodiment of the nation. Controversial during his lifetime, Hobbes's views nevertheless helped set the stage for the secularization of political life, especially the denial of the divine right of monarchs to rule, that will furnish part of the philosophic background of the French and American Revolutions.

The genesis of the modern theory of man in the state is thus inextricably interwoven with the theory of man in himself, how he lives and what he aspires to. The social self and its preoccupation with reputation—so important a theme in seventeenth-century drama—is inseparable from the search for personal survival that helps create society. For Hobbes in particular the context of such meditations was the disruptive world of the Civil Wars with their conflict between king and Parliament over who truly represented England. But for Locke as well, as for Descartes and

* This time of "masterless men" in England is also the time of the masterless *ronin* in Japan.

Bacon, the basic shift was from God as the ground of all inquiry to the nature of man.

Or perhaps I should say "man" in quotation marks, for the speculations of these philosophers mark the entry of that collective concept into European thought. The "man" whose mythic forebears created society, as well as the "man" whose perception would be the basis for the new science, will shortly be followed by many other kinds of "man"—social man, economic man, postmodern man—meant to stand for the entire human race. The early feminist polemic against the use of "man" as an all-inclusive noun was often pushed to extremes, but its critics were being historically disingenuous when they responded that this usage was nothing more than a grammatical convention. Just as the growth of the idea of the individual and the state were mutually reinforcing, so both display the inherent maleness of their formulation.

The seventeenth- and eighteenth-century meditation on the nature of "man" initiates a scrutiny that will not be directed so intensely at women until the nineteenth century. The English word "conscience," for example, which in its earliest appearances in Middle English had specifically referred to questions of religious conviction, came to be used as the general term for that internal aspect of the self that was to be consulted about all public action. Shakespeare, for one, tended to use it in the religious sense earlier in his career and in the general sense later. In *Titus Andronicus,* for example, one character says sarcastically to another, "[F]or I know thou art religious/And hast a thing within thee called conscience." Of the nonreligious uses, the most familiar is Hamlet's line "Thus conscience does make cowards of us all." There, in the "To be or not to be" soliloquy, Hamlet links conscience and self-consciousness to depict how thinking about death and its mysteries undermines willpower: "And thus the native hue of resolution/Is sicklied o'er with the pale cast of thought. . . ."

This emphasis on individual will, even to the point of suicide, like the samurai's act of *seppuku,* snatching personal honor from the ashes of a hopelessly lost cause, has more than a tinge of the older warrior's view of life. In the monarchical and institutional view, the state was the individual writ large and all proper identity should ultimately flow from compliance with the political order. The alternative was that individual identity should define itself in opposition to social categories. Caught in the intrigues of court, Hamlet throughout the play hankers after the warrior decisiveness of Fortinbras, whose army keeps skirting the boundaries of Denmark and who will deliver Hamlet's epitaph at the end.

A third possibility was to look for the nature of man in neither the political state nor the warrior character, but in values opposed to both. Milton in *Paradise Lost* places man between hell and heaven and identifies him with Jesus, the divine made human. Nor is woman left out in Milton's account. Although generations of literary critics have argued just what the relation between Adam and Eve is—how equal and how subordinate—Milton's vision of Adam as man relies upon it as part of an identity conceived privately and domestically, rather than through any public social role. Instead of Hobbes's postulation of the beginning of society as a response to the "war of all against all," *Paradise Lost* tells a tale of beginnings, with the expulsion from paradise part of God's plan to start the human race on its precarious journey toward growing up. As Milton says at the end of the poem:

> *The World was all before them, where to choose*
> *Thir place of rest, and Providence thir guide:*
> *They hand in hand with wand'ring steps and slow,*
> *Through* Eden *took thir solitary way.*

In contrast to the companionship of Adam and Eve, Satan, the warrior and epic hero, remains alone.

Milton's idealization of how the domestic sincerity and sociability of Adam and Eve triumph over Satan not only reflects the seventeenth-century preoccupation with the schemer in drama and politics, but also prophesies the establishment of the nuclear family as a stay against the Hobbesian world that aggressive ego creates. It indicates how much individuals in that time felt caught in the difficult necessities of making one's way in a more crowded social world, with more enigmatic people in it. On one side was the Scylla of unleashed aggression, only tenuously controlled by the duel and the honor system; on the other was the Charybdis of a bland but more sinister manipulation and hypocrisy.

Suitably enough for a time in which male social roles were being brought into question, the seventeenth century was also a period of lavishly and explicitly expressed paeans to the pleasures of male camaraderie. The Three Musketeers, Alexandre Dumas's nineteenth-century creation, with their motto of "all for one, and one for all," accurately mirrored a great age of male friendship. Exemplary friendship was certainly nothing new in Western culture. It appears centrally in Virgil's *Aeneid* (Nisus and Euryalus), as well as the *The Song of Roland* (Roland and Oliver), and we have seen how in Chrétien de Troyes's *Yvain* the hero's emotions are torn between marriage and his loyalty to his cohort of male knights. All of these paradigms of friendship from the past, even the biblical pair of David and Jonathan, forged their friendship in war, and often the strength of those relationships was in contrast to peacetime relationships mediated by family and church. But seventeenth-century France, England, and the German states in particular transformed these legendary tales of battlefield comradeship into a virtual cult of male friendship in peacetime as well. Like the seconds at duels, or the men who would fight at any affront to a friend, they evoked that passionate wartime solidarity against all threats. Just as the war economy was penetrating peacetime life with its increasing demands on resources, the cult of friendship brought war psychology home as well.

Throughout the period people were also fascinated with both new and traditional types of individual nature, overwhelmingly but not exclusively male. So Andrew Marvell in "An Horatian Ode" at first likens Cromwell's extraordinary success as leader of the Parliamentary armies to a force of nature like a whirlwind or a lightning bolt. But then Marvell anchors that outsized grandeur in Cromwell's personal nature: "And, if we would speak true,/Much to the man is due." Once again, the focus is the *man,* whose nature is more enigmatic and secret than that of Cromwell's counterpart in the poem, Charles I, heroically but fatally caught in his overpowering role as king. Mirroring this wide interest in the intricacy of personal behavior and the problems of interpreting it correctly, the *Characters* of Theophrastus, who followed Plato and Aristotle as the chief philosopher of Athens, was widely translated, as were those of his contemporary imitators, especially Jean de La Bruyère. The lure of trying to assess and sum up another was also a feature of social life during the period. A common diversion at parties in England, for example, was for the guests to write character sketches and have the others guess who they were.

Like the heightened perception of hypocrisy, the lure of character interlaced with an emphasis on the social context of individual nature. Through what the social historian Norbert Elias has called "the civilizing process," the seventeenth-century French court of Louis XIV in particular sought to control the ruder side of the honor system in the name of its own superior claim to authority over aggressive behavior, primarily by creating violence-free public spaces like the court itself. The fountainhead of intricate courtly manners and ceremonies, Louis XIV also made the French military establishment permanent and instigated the most aggressive military adventures and the goriest wars of the century, all designed to make himself and France the central power on the Continent. Louis XIV's court dancing master, teaching the elaborate steps of the new quadrille, is the comrade in arms of Jean Martinet, his now-proverbial inspector general of the infantry. The "civilizing" ceremony of his court, its perpetuation of elaborate costumes and customs, was to a great extent a premeditated compensation for the bloody battles outside its gates: the First Gentleman was also to be the First Warrior—until, that is, the other European states evolved politically into a balance of power that could oppose him.

Whatever the changes in the standards of aristocratic behavior in Louis's court, however, the military profession retained its allure as part of a long-standing French tradition that even the effort to create a veneer of manners and proper behavior could not quite eradicate. Montaigne had noted as much in the late 1570s:

> It is worth considering . . . that our nation gives valor the highest rank among the virtues, as its name shows, which comes from *value;* and that according to our usage, when we say *a very valuable man*, or *a worthy man*, in the language of our court and our nobility, we are saying nothing else than *a valiant man*, as in the Roman fashion; for the Romans took the general term *virtue* from their word for *strength*. The proper, the only, the essential, form of nobility in France is the military profession. . . . (277)

But as the assumed equation of warrior and aristocrat declined with the increasing size of armies and the lack of opportunity in siege warfare for heroic deeds, the need to distinguish between the knight and the mere soldier had become more socially and culturally pressing.

In the older typology, the blunt warrior and the suave courtier were also often contrasted, not always to the benefit of either. Castiglione had proposed a warrior-courtier who could both fight and appreciate the arts, and Don Quixote affirms the inseparability of arms and letters. But there were new character types that at first overlapped the older aristocratic models, and then became rivals to them. On one end of the continuum of new male models was the almost anarchic individualism of a Don Juan; on the other was the ideal character that seventeenth-century France called the *honnête homme*, whose literal English equivalent—the honest man—conveys little of the original's implications of decorum and discretion, naturalness and *politesse*. Both Don Juan and the *honnête homme* were originally upper-class possibilities, but many of the most notable real-life examples of either type did not come from the aristocracy. Like Don Juan and Don Quixote, they carried the banners of a chivalric aloneness and personal prowess now fallen into a modern world of guns, sieges, and mass armies.

The *honnête homme* cared little for personal show and actively countered the flamboyant dress of the fop and the sumptuousness of the courtier. His standard was *négligence*, a disregard for fashion that was the seventeenth-century version of what Castiglione had called *sprezzatura*, the ability to do a difficult thing casually. The maxims of La Rochefoucauld, distilled from his experience in French aristocratic life, give a keen flavor of the way such inwardness becomes paradoxically public. "To be a truly honest man," he writes, "is to wish to be always exposed to the view of honest people" (206). But at the same time "Perfect valor is to do without witnesses what one would be capable of doing before the entire world" (216). Self-awareness, in other words, is essential, even to the extent of acting as if one were not self-aware.

In a variety of ways, then, European masculinity in the seventeenth century draws upon precedents such as the spiritual sanction of Christianity (outside any institutional church) as well as the new human-centered sciences to help create masculine models free from a primary dependence upon war and violence. Obligatory nationalist allegiance, ideas of "human nature," meditations on the origin of society and their political implications—all are part of this transmutation of military masculinity.

This shifting process of male definition in the seventeenth century might be described as the transition from armor to personality. In essence, the seventeenth century invented the postwar world, as a place and a time from which the world of war and the world before war can be explicitly contemplated. It is energized by a fresh self-consciousness about how war shapes male identity, which gathers force over the centuries down to our own: the wartime reduction of acceptable types of male behavior followed by the peacetime opening—either to carry a straitened wartime masculinity into peace as the only acceptable style, or else to react against it in favor of a more expansive view. *Paradise Lost* sums it up in its title: the world that has been lost and the need to go forward.

Thus it should come as no surprise that simultaneously with the development of a more "civilized," less militarily defined man like the *honnête homme*, there was also a fascination with the individualist hero, infused by "nature," who at least tried to behave as if there were no society or institutions that could hamper his self-expression. Even though noble skills in the newly "civilized" world of court-centered nationalism were being redefined to include dancing and an all-embracing decorum, a virtually compensatory bias toward the natural appears as another answer to the issue of inherited versus personal character. In one guise such characters are aristocratic duelists or pirate captains; in another, the doomed heroes and heroines of the tragedies of Corneille and Racine, fatally entangled in irresolvable conflicts between love and duty; in still another, nobly born young men brought up by shepherds who come to court to find their destiny.

In essence, the change from the newly minted mythic figures of the late sixteenth and early seventeenth century—Faustus, Don Juan, Don Quixote—to those of the late seventeenth and early eighteenth century—Christian (*Pilgrim's Progress*, 1678), Crusoe (*Robinson Crusoe*, 1719), Gulliver (*Gulliver's Travels*, 1726)—is a metamorphosis from a social rebellion in the name of the individual to a personal quest that to a great extent ignores all social values except what can be pulled out of and validated by oneself. Similarly, the mythic individuals of the first phase react against institutional authority, while those of the second absent themselves from the past and paternal succession entirely: Christian leaves his family and friends behind; Crusoe rejects his father's advice and sails the world instead; Gulliver decides to live only with horses—in a parody of the embrace of the natural.

Even monarchs are not excluded from the general pattern. Kings may have divine dynastic rights, but they must also justify God's mantle by their individual natures. As Dryden writes in celebration of the restoration of Charles II to the throne of England, "Recov'ring hardly what he lost before/His right endears it much, his purchase more." Such a monarch, justified by both genealogy and nature, might then rule over a natural society, like that Gonzalo had described in Shakespeare's *Tempest:*

> *All things in common nature should produce*
> *Without sweat or endeavour: treason, felony,*
> *Sword, pike, knife, gun, or need of any engine*
> *Would I not have; but nature should bring forth,*
> *Of its own kind, all foison, all abundance,*
> *To feed my innocent people.* (II, i, 155–60)

In this identification of the natural with the free, the most conspicuous figure, derived in part from the stage Don Juan, was the libertine, whose very name invokes the idea of freedom. The English libertine often defined his freedom as a general hostility to institutions, especially the monarchy. But for the European libertine, there was a particularly close relation between his signature sexual licentiousness (both heterosexual and homosexual) and the religious skepticism that reflected the emphasis seventeenth-century science was placing on the evidence of the senses, the direct perception of the world of immediacy, in contrast to the contemplation of eternity.

In part, the libertine's celebration of personal freedom was, like the *honnête homme*'s emphasis on self-possession, an effort of certain sections of the aristocracy, particularly in France, to recoup the "natural" for itself. The courtier and the fop were as one in their commitment to a world of rules and rituals, the fop especially indulging in the most extreme artifice of costume and behavior. In contrast, both the libertine and the *honnête homme* rejected the conventional standards of male behavior to stress instead the inward justification of their actions and beliefs: for the libertine a call upon nature as the sanction and standard for every human activity; for the *honnête homme* an inner integrity that resembled the English appeal to conscience and something of Chaucer's *gentilesse*, but now shaped and carried out with self-conscious purpose.

For all his detachment, however, the *honnête homme* still remained part of society, while the libertine's invocation of nature was an explicit challenge to the artifice of social roles and codes. But it was an impossible task to create a reputation not in the possession of other people, like creating a language in which there is only one speaker, and misanthropy was often the result. In one poem, for example, John Wilmot, the earl of Rochester, describes the preoccupation with dress and gossip that marks the unnaturalness of human behavior in the fashionable resort of Tunbridge Wells, and then concludes:

*Bless me! thought I, what a thing is man, that thus*
*In all his shapes, he is ridiculous?*
*Ourselves with noise of reason we do please*
*In vain: humanity's our worst disease.*
*Thrice happy beasts are, who, because they be*
*Of reason void, are so of foppery.*
*Faith, I was so ashamed that with remorse*
*I used the insolence to mount my horse;*

*For he, doing only things fit for his nature,*
*Did seem to me by much the wiser creature.*

It would not take long for the libertine style to itself become frozen, as self-enclosed as the fashionableness of the fops—even with the efforts of such late-eighteenth-century figures as Casanova and the Marquis de Sade to resurrect it personally and philosophically. Sigmund Freud in the twentieth century dubbed Don Juan a repressed homosexual repeatedly trying to demonstrate a flimsy heterosexuality. But the historical roots of what the French called *libertinage* in a dream of personal freedom should not be minimized, along with its effort to free the individual from the opinions of others. In the ferment of seventeenth-century ideas of masculine identity, it succeeded in establishing a style of individualism based on sexual conquest and adventure that conferred another sort of aristocracy. As Rochester remarked, there's "something noble in mere lust."

*Part IV*

# THE BATTLE AND THE SEXES

# WAR AND PORNOGRAPHY

> People are right to notice the unruly liberty of this member, obtruding so importunately when we have no use for it, and failing so importunately when we have the most use for it, and struggling for mastery so imperiously with our will, refusing with so much pride and obstinacy our solicitations, both mental and manual.
>
> —Montaigne, "Of the Power of the Imagination"

I have been tracing the symbiotic relation of images of male individualism to the developing centralization and bureaucratization of governments, the increasing size of armies, and tactics that in the seventeenth century made for fewer battles and more sieges of fortified strongholds. These are the public forces that bear on the issue of the development of masculine identity—codes of honor, armor and uniforms, national self-consciousness (at least in certain classes), and adherence to Catholicism or Protestantism as both a religious and a political faith. But what of more basic biological definitions of maleness, sexuality, and the body itself?

While we have long been used to histories of wars, politics, philosophy, the arts, sciences, and law, the history of the body has only in the last decade or so become a subject for serious study. But even this study often defines its central issues by postulating what Michel Foucault called *mentalités*, the thought patterns of an age. It is a paradox akin to the crude assumption that matters of the body, particularly sexual matters, are at once the most basic of human issues and yet must be controlled and given shape by analysis and language. Similarly, when many critics and cultural historians look back on the bodies of yesteryear, they glide imperceptibly into blaming the past for attitudes that the enlightened present knows are "wrong," as if somehow our ancestors could consciously have behaved differently, but perversely chose not to.

Historians of sexuality like Foucault have argued that before the nineteenth century, there were sexual acts but not sexual identities, sex without self-awareness, bodies without an attitude toward them. Sex, in other words, was connected to personal identity, without being the sole or primary basis of it. But it is in the seventeenth century that the interplay between the actual male body and the cultural idea of masculinity becomes an explicit presence—coordinate with the new forces of nationalism, the decline of the old chivalric warrior ideal, and the growing distinction between public and private life.

It is difficult to talk historically about such a change, because social mores and historical events often seem to exist in a separate compartment from personal emotions and the seemingly invariable processes of the body. But masculinity is a historical concept; it not only describes some physical traits but also shapes them, and is in its turn shaped by the myriad perceptions of individuals. Culture is thus not just a matter of language and naming. It is the medium by which individual perceptions and emotions find public voices, and the way those public voices shape the attitude of individuals toward themselves. In other words, we have two bodies: one that is our own, and another that belongs to the world in which we live. They aren't two halves of the same coin, but interpenetrating aspects of each other, like a tangelo or some other hybrid fruit.

The misperception of the body we attribute to either past eras or past individuals may therefore have been an authentic perception of a body that did exist then, but does no longer. Certainly bodily processes have always been there, but cultural contexts modify them and they in their turn modify the culture. We are familiar enough with how some meanings of the body have changed—how it should be dressed, what kind of body is considered sexually attractive—in accord with the mind-sets of different eras. But the physical body also changes, along with its meaning. Depending on the historical moment, the line between the body we have and the body the culture tells us we ought to have continues to fluctuate. Ideals, aspirations, and assumptions are as much a part of physical reality as biology—and can influence it. Of course, we make choices—to dress, to fall in love, to resist the culture's demands—but they are choices within the comparatively narrow compass of our own times.

The images that have come down to us show how much the classical ideal of battle was vested in the male body, weaponed but often only scantily protected. In that alternative to war, the Olympic Games, the participants competed naked. In fact, despite all that we know archaeologically of the development of armor among the Greeks, the Homeric heroes depicted on pottery often look like only a helmet and a shield, from which extend powerful legs and arms. The "man-covering shield," Homer called it, behind which the hero would not hide for long. And this so-called epic nakedness was of course what made him the hero, in contrast to the citizen soldiers listening to the stories of his adventures, whose battlefield experience was more likely to be behind the shields of the phalanx. Even the Romans, who fashioned the first great European war machine, were fascinated by the Gallic warrior, who always went into battle naked, with just a necklacelike torque around his throat. They celebrated him as a worthy opponent and as an evocation of their own more barbaric past in the sculptural figure known as the "dying Gaul." Contemporary hero figures like Rambo or various characters played by Arnold Schwarzenegger have their place in this lineage as well: stripped to the waist, their muscles pumped up and glistening, they assert physical vulnerability along with indomitable prowess.

The difference in our modern action heroes is how infrequently they are wounded. In fact, it is quite remarkable how often the early literature of war refuses to mask its horrors and even may exaggerate them in order better to celebrate the hero. In actual war the threat to the sexual self-definition was direct, as hoplites in their phalanxes held their spears low, aiming to thrust below the shields and into the groins of their enemies. But even in literary wars, identification of the male body with the triumphantly armored body is balanced by an awareness of the fallibility of that body beneath its metallic coat. Antiwar literature and film have no monopoly on depictions of war's bloodiness. The gory details of battle death—heads split in two, chests and groins pierced with spears—suffuse much of the *Iliad:*

> *Peneleos drove his spearhead*
> *into the eye-socket underneath the brow,*
> *thrusting the eyeball out. The spearhead ran*
> *straight through the socket and the skull behind,*
> *and throwing out both hands he sat down backward.*

> *Peneleos, drawing his long sword, chopped through*
> *the nape and set the severed helmeted head*
> *and trunk apart upon the field.* (345)

The gore appears as well in the even less restrained heroics of *The Song of Roland:*

> *Slashing his helmet where the bright rubies gleam,*
> *[Roland] slices his hood and downward through his hair,*
> *Between the eyes he cuts his face in two,*
> *Through the bright hauberk, of tightly-woven mail,*
> *And all his body down to the groin is split.* (104)

The most detailed Anglo-Saxon poem of war, *The Battle of Maldon*, not only describes the violence of the battle itself, but also includes the women who come to the battlefield later to strip the dead and the birds who come to peck out their eyes and feast on their bodies.

Similar passages can be found in many poems of war up through the Renaissance and into the time of Grimmelshausen's tales of Simplicissimus in the Thirty Years' War. In Thomas Nashe's 1594 picaresque novel, *The Unfortunate Traveller*, for example, Jack Wilton tells of his adventures as a soldier at the siege of Milan:

> In one place might you behold a heape of dead murthered men overwhelmed with a falling Steede, in stead of a toombe stone: in another place, a bundell of bodies fettered together in their owne bowells . . . the French King [Francis I] himselfe in this Conflict was much distressed, the braines of his owne men sprinkled in his face. . . . (283–84)

Such a description is not antiwar so much as grimly matter-of-fact about what happens to bodies in battle. The duke of York, like many noble warriors before and after, brought in his luggage to Agincourt a huge cauldron in which to boil his bones in case he was killed and his body had to be transported to England for burial. As late as the Third Crusade, and in Japan until the nineteenth century, the heads of the defeated were collected as a means of quantifying victory, while into the seventeenth century the fingers of archers and the hands of harquebusiers were cut off to prevent them from fighting again.

Beginning with the rise to social power of a class of military knights in the tenth and eleventh centuries, the male body was defined by its genealogy, its armored container, its codes of honor and behavior, and, somewhat later, its national identity and its ethic of individualism. But the Thirty Years' War and its aftermath disseminate a more acute general sense of the body's vulnerability both in war and in peace that falls on newly fertile ground. A relaxation of a centuries-old prohibition against the dissection of corpses, together with the invention of the printing press, led in the fifteenth and sixteenth centuries to advances in the understanding of human anatomy that went far beyond a received wisdom that had hardly changed since Galen in the second century (who gained his knowledge primarily from animal dissections). The most remarkable of these works came out of Italy and France, from practicing surgeons like Andreas Vesalius and Ambroise Paré. But they had a strong influence on surgical practice all over Europe, particularly in Germany, where surgeons were often less learned (because of the lack of medical schools) but had a wide experience with war wounds. Not even the largest cities and towns could furnish the variety and quantity of cases that appeared every hour at the field hospital during battles and sieges. Paré in particular spent a large part of his working career as a war surgeon. In the history of surgery generally, in fact, it is hard to underestimate the importance of war in advancing surgical knowledge, tools, and techniques. As guns and gunpowder became more widespread, new methods had to evolve as well, especially to handle issues of blood poisoning.

The male body in war is thus wounded, torn apart, and otherwise destroyed with a grim certainty that even the most heroic literature does not leave out. But what of the male sexual body, in itself and as it exists beneath the armor?

Sexuality is a special test of the relative importance of mind and body in the definition of character and personal identity because it is both shaped by social forms and dictated by biological needs. Consider, for example, the relative importance of the penis and the testicles. Our culture is used to considering the large penis to be the emblem of a quintessential male sexuality, which marks its possessor as a "real man." In the eighteenth century, sexually explicit works such as *Fanny Hill* and *Memoirs of an Oxford Scholar* feature penises whose enormous size is praised by active and eager sexual accomplices. In the nineteenth and twentieth centuries, both heterosexual and homosexual pornography feature well-endowed characters (and "well-endowed" itself implies a significant masculine inheritance). As in *ukiyo-e* prints in eighteenth-century Japan, the penis size represents male power and potency, although it is not really until the nineteenth century that quacks and manufacturers of patent medicines started to advertise nostrums "guaranteed" to enlarge the penis.

But for many centuries in the West, the large penis denoted the animal and the witless. In nude Greek male sculpture and art, it is the small penis that is considered attractive, as it is again when those standards of beauty are revived in the Renaissance. The Greek Old Comedy chorus of men who appear onstage with immense artificial phalluses, for example, is meant to be laughed at, not admired. It is a common joke that also underlies the comic novel *The Golden Ass*, Apuleius's second-century tale of his transformation into an ass, a notoriously well-hung creature. In another manifestation, adorning the figure of the minor Roman god Priapus, as many visitors to Pompeii can attest, the large penis also stands as an emblem of the fertility of the domestic garden. But the stronger association is between the large penis and "asinine" behavior, testified to by the cognate forms of "ass" that appear in almost all European languages.

So far as masculinity is concerned, then, for many centuries it was less the large penis than the testicles that determined the man. Arjuna, the hero of the *Mahabharata*, has one thousand balls, and the Celtic hero Cú Chulainn has at least seven. The testicles stood for (and in their Latin etymology *witnessed*) courage, even if that courage was the prime possession of one social class: "He had a crotch as large, and a stature as striking, as only a gentleman could have," writes the author of the biography of William Marshal. It's a meaning that is still preserved when we say someone has balls—nowadays this could be a man or a woman—and we mean nerve, courage, or, in yet other bodily metaphors, "heart" and "guts." So then, the modern emphasis on the length of the penis rather than the size of the testicles may signify a swing of masculine mythology away from the primarily military and toward the erotic.

By the sixteenth and seventeenth centuries a considerable shift occurs from the older preoccupation with the male body in war and its peacetime twin, the male body in athletics, as the only specialized physiological types of masculinity. The medieval Christian postulation of priestly chastity and the perfection of both male and female virginity succeeded primarily in establishing only an antitype—the spiritual and desexualized male body. But a figure like Don Juan, along with the philosophy of the libertine, which emphasizes sexuality in masculine identity, indicates how the traditional male hypersensitivity to matters of honor acquired an increasing sexual component as the seventeenth century continued.

Another significant strand in this new awareness of the vulnerable male body is the appearance of visual and verbal manuals of pornography, in Japan as well as in Europe, often with instructions on how to approach and woo a courtesan as detailed as those that marked the drill manuals of Maurice of Nassau. Such works register the self-conscious jump start male/female sexual relations needed after what Renaissance thinkers believed was the repressive austerity of the Middle Ages. As scholars have often observed, there is virtually no pornography in Europe from Petronius in the second century to Pietro Aretino in the sixteenth, and visual representation of sexual acts is equally sparse. (Pornography literally means "writing about prostitutes," although when it was coined in the mid–nineteenth century, it was almost immediately applied to any sexually stimulating literature or visual art.) The newly explicit lessons in female sexual anatomy, the discussion of sexual techniques and varieties of sexual pleasure, imply that just as the literature of courtly love aimed to teach the social skills of male/female relations to young knights otherwise trained by and accustomed to the company of men, so pornography focused on their inadequate heterosexual skills in the physiological arena.

To fashion this new era of Christian sexuality, writers and artists looked to pagan Rome and anointed the classic poet Ovid as their pope, cementing an almost exclusive Renaissance connection between erotic writing and visual art with Italy. One popular format was the dialogue, in which a seasoned prostitute counsels a beginner about the nature of pleasure, the variety of sexual positions, and, along the way, the differences between male and female sexual pleasure. Pornographic engravings also made their appearance. One well-known collection, called *I Modi* (*The Postures*), was based on drawings by Giulio Romano, and appeared in multiple editions, each engraving allied with a poem by Pietro Aretino.

Instead of the sociosexual maneuvering that fascinated Ovid, these dialogues deal preeminently with the act itself, with the sexual parts that perform it, and especially with sexual adeptness as a sign of masculinity. Such pornographic instruction implied that women, or at least some women, were specialists in this new arena of the male body, exposing male inexperience and possible sexual weakness. Nor are the women who speak and participate in these dialogues, poems, and scenes the misogynistically depicted temptresses of old, sexual raptors associated with diabolical forces. Instead they are possessors of sexual knowledge, which they aim to put at the service of both male and (some) female readers so that they might master, or at least become aware of, the sexual possibilities of the male and female bodies. For men in particular these early pornographic works seem designed as a way to get to know the Other, not the national Other and potential enemy but the sexual Other and potential ally, at least in pleasure. Now, with that knowledge, manliness could expand into the domestic and sexual sphere as well and, as John Donne writes, "make of one room an everywhere."

At the same time that there were new possibilities, the message of rediscovering the male body beneath the armor was nevertheless also very mixed, because the knowledge of the women in pornography, as well as their explicit requests and directions for sexual satisfaction, posed a danger to the armored integrity of the warrior body. Appropriately enough, *I Modi* includes at least one scene that invokes the Mars and Venus story: the warrior lies naked in bed, his armor and sword forgotten in the corner. Such women, in other words, must be approached cautiously, even when they seem to be telling their secrets. Like the witch, so persecuted in the seventeenth century, or the femme fatale in film noir after World War II, their sexuality threatens male control because they can invoke a power to which men have little direct access.

The need for instruction in sexuality attested to by the manuals of pornography implies that at least some (book-buying) men considered intercourse, even the paying of what Protestant theologians called "the conjugal debt," to be a risk for masculinity rather than a reward for maleness. Stephen Orgel has described the Elizabethan and Jacobean periods as a time when "the love of men for men . . . appears less threatening than the love of men for women: it had fewer consequences, it was easier to de-sexualize, it figured and reinforced the patronage system." He goes on to note the physical similarity between the ideal woman's look in Elizabethan England and the bodies of boys: "What we would call boyish they called womanly: slim-hipped and flat-chested" (70). In this context, it is intriguing that *I Modi*, that sine qua non of seventeenth- and eighteenth-century salaciousness, characterizes anal sex as aristocratic and vaginal sex as plebeian because there is no fear of pregnancy in the former; its only goal is pleasure.

War and the persistence of the warrior image also plays a part here. In some wartime and postwar periods, the boyish-looking girl, the tomboy, is thus a characteristic figure, along with the ethereally beautiful male. So Ovid describes Atalanta, the only woman in the party at the legendary Calydonian boar hunt, whose face was "maidenly for a boy or boyish for a maiden," like the flapper of the 1920s. The boyish female and the maidenly male belongs to the "Why can't a woman be like a man?" side of the sexual question, while the breast fixation of much of Europe and the United States in the 1950s emphasized the motherly and nurturing as truly erotic—the "I want a girl just like the girl who married dear old dad" option.*

The anal/aristocratic, vaginal/plebeian contrast in *I Modi*, however, even more distinctly implies that erotic relations with women depend on either the absence or repression of any possibility of children. That is, in an era of uncertain birth control, the highest (most aristocratic) form of heterosexual relations involved anal sex, while vaginal sex was relegated to the lower classes or reserved for producing children and expanding families. Through the influence of the new view of marriage and heterosexuality polemicized by the Reformation, a male-dominated social system in which procreative heterosexuality was a choice among competing homosocial choices (like warriorhood and clerical celibacy) was gradually being transformed into one in which procreative heterosexuality would be the dominant choice.

Just as the propagandistic assertion of the divine right of kings may signal that fewer subjects than before actually believe it, so the instruction for men in sexual prowess necessarily raises the issue of male inadequacy. As all the early pornographic works imply, women know and men have to learn, and they may not turn out to be very adept students. The unprecedented sexual predatoriness that marks the Don Juan character is thus as much a cause of anxiety as of inspiration in his male audience. His success with women, like that of other stage libertines, is a counterpoise to the power of women, even while it confirms their sexual sway.

Aretino and others used the sexual situation in their dialogues to introduce elements of social satire as well, pivoting on the current etymology that tied satire to the horny satyr of classical mythology. As satire developed in seventeenth-century Europe, it similarly drew upon the Roman equation of sexual corruption with political malfeasance. Sexual reference was meant to humiliate, to say that the butt of satire was without honor and, often, unmasculine. So pornography began by letting its readers into secret sexual knowledge, then became through satire a blast at backstage depravity, the corruption behind the mask.

Some feminist writers have argued that because women are penetrated, the sexual act is inherently humiliating to them. Certainly for the war-defined male body, physical prowess is central to self-image and self-definition. But, as sexually oriented satire implies, and as pornography

* In contrast, like the comically large penises of Greek and Latin theater, the big breasts that in the 1950s signified sexiness would in this period at best have evoked the anti-erotic image of wet nurses.

tries to remedy, male humiliation is also an inherent potential of heterosexuality. The problem in reducing masculinity to the penis as the mark of power is that it can easily become the mark of impotence. Thus the need for pornography to teach—the original urge of its earliest examples—and the reason why, until the advent of videotape allowed solitary viewing, pornographic films were traditionally shown at stag parties as a part-comic, part-serious initiation for soon-to-be-married men. The feminist argument that men in the past were not writing about real women but about a male idea of women is certainly persuasive, as far as it goes. But to stop there enshrines a very vague notion of the power of one sex over the other that neglects significant historical differences between male images of women as passive objects of desire, as receptive audiences for male sexual performance, but also as exacting judges of it.

# PERFORMANCE ANXIETY

Two late-seventeenth-century English poems about premature ejaculation, one by Sir George Etherege and the other by John Wilmot, earl of Rochester, nicely illustrate the tension between male inadequacy and male power. In their focus on sexual failure, they explore the humiliating potential of the sexual act itself, along with an explicit militarizing of sexuality (and sexualizing of war?) in direct analogy to male/female relations. Both poems bear the title "The Imperfect Enjoyment." Our phrase "premature ejaculation," now commonly used to describe their subject, derives from the psychoanalytic term *ejaculatio praecox*, which describes male failure to measure up to some standard of proper physiopsychological behavior.

But a few hundred years before the medical and psychological terminology of the twentieth century, the situation was well known enough that it could be the subject of poetry. It's hard to know exactly when these poems were written because for many years they were circulated in manuscript—private poems about the behavior of private parts. But it's probable that they come from the early 1670s, some twenty years after the end of the English Civil Wars and more than a decade after the restoration of Charles II, at a time when Rochester was in his mid-twenties and Etherege ten or so years older.

The hallmark of both poems is the sense of immediacy. In each the poet tries to make the experience of the sexual situation parallel the unfolding of the poem itself. This is no emotion recollected in tranquillity, but an effort to mimic the effect of being in the moment. Yet the "moments" of Etherege and Rochester are quite different. Like the production of a civilized *honnête homme* faced with his body's rebellion, Etherege's poem is suffused with politeness and aesthetic balance: "After a pretty amorous discourse," he begins,

> *She does resist my love with pleasing force,*
> *Moved not with anger but with modesty:*
> *Against her will she is my enemy.*

Every effort to resist, he says, turns into acquiescence:

> *Her eyes the rudeness of her arms excuse,*
> *Those do accept what these seem to refuse. . . .*
> *Then with her lovely hands she does conceal*
> *Those wonders chance so kindly did reveal. . . .*
> *Guarding her breasts, they do her lips expose.*

But at the critical moment of entrance, when her arms "seem" to welcome him, "my zeal does my devotion quite destroy." He has failed to perform.

He has failed physically, that is, for his poeticizing continues undaunted, spinning out comparisons between himself as worshiper and the woman as holy site, followed by a potentially more hostile set of analogies between man as soldier and woman as besieged town: "When, overjoyed with victory, I fall/Dead at the foot of the surrendered wall."

Even though it is he who has fallen "dead," Etherege assumes that both he and his partner have completed the physiological act of ejaculation. Yet something is still missing—the need for sexual intercourse to be in some way mutual: "The action which we should have jointly done,/Each has unluckily performed alone." Their passion, in other words, has risen so high that it has extinguished their pleasure, their love annihilating their lust, the union of souls preventing the union of bodies.

So far the man has spoken—and this woman is no emissary from Aretino's *I Modi* poems, issuing sexual orders and giving directions. But she has her standards nevertheless. When she is, however slightly, allowed to respond, she does seem surprised that it's all over so quickly: "She blushed and frowned, perceiving we had done/The sport she thought we had not yet begun." To which the poet replies with more equivocal compliments. Her own beauty, he says, has paradoxically resulted in his inability to perform the pagan rites of love and war: "You'd been more happy had you been less fair." In other words, Etherege may have failed to penetrate her physically, but he "wins" nevertheless. His verbal wit makes up for his physical failure, his poetic performance compensates for his sexual inadequacy. There is no catastrophe, no tears. All blame is hers, because of her beauty and the power of her eyes. Focusing on a moment of sexual failure, when the masculine desire to conquer by penetrating the "mystery" of Woman undermines itself, Etherege's poem recoups his self-sufficiency by identifying it with a mastery of language, imprisoning his disappointed lover in a net of eloquence.

Etherege's self-image in his poem is that of a courtly lover whose command of language and poetry is more than appropriate for even the most potentially depressing of all male situations. In contrast, the younger Rochester, who never fought in a war but whose father had been ennobled on the battlefield, reveals without apology the wound to the male ego given by sexual failure, along with the inadequacy of the soldier as an image of male power. Unlike Etherege's prettily "poetic" beginning, Rochester's poem immediately plunges into the physical situation:

*Naked she lay, clasped in my longing arms,*
*I filled with love, and she all over charms;*
*Both equally inspired with eager fire,*
*Melting through kindness, flaming in desire.*
*With arms, legs, lips close clinging to embrace,*
*She clips me to her breast, and sucks me to her face.*

Etherege's lovers are dressed in metaphors appropriate to their roles—worshiper and saint, soldier and besieged town—with just enough gaps for the unmentioned parts to meet. Rochester's lovers are clearly naked, with all the vulnerability that implies for both male and female, bereft of the clothing that assigned both a fixed social status. From the perspective of our world of bathing suits, seductive advertisements, and doctor's offices, it is difficult to really understand what nakedness meant in the past. Yet still there is a gender contrast: female nakedness retains some of the power of an insoluble mystery, while male nakedness more often than not undermines male assertion and makes men look foolish, because the gap between the mystique of the penis and its actual size is so immense.

Rochester's subject is just that disparity between the mythic phallus and the physical penis. In contrast with Etherege's urbane recouping of his sexual self-esteem, Rochester refuses to ennoble either poetry or the poetic sensibility as a source of identity. There is nothing transcendent or permanent in Rochester; there are only bodies. This is not the all-sufficient male body of later pornography, but one in which Rochester believes he is more trapped than any woman would be in her own.

At first, his tone is bravado, as her tongue in his mouth "orders" him "to throw/The all-dissolving thunderbolt below." It is an ambiguous image: in the myth, the mortal Semele asked that her divine lover Zeus appear to her not as a man but as a god, whereupon he impregnated her (with the future Dionysos) and in the process blew her apart—the perfect image of male huffing and puffing about sexual prowess. But just as the assertion of male physical authority is more extreme than in Etherege's polite lines, the loss of potency is more abrupt, and godlike phallic power is suddenly reduced to an undependable scrap of anatomy:

*But whilst her busy hand would guide that part*
*Which should convey my soul up to her heart,*
*In liquid raptures I dissolve all o'er,*
*Melt into sperm, and spend at every pore.*
*A touch from any part of her had done't:*
*Her hands, her foot, her very look's a cunt.*

"Spend" was the usual term for ejaculation in English until the late nineteenth century. "Come," its successor, would not be appropriate here; the issue is not arrival, but loss. The self-aggrandizing classical invocation of the "all-dissolving thunderbolt" has turned inside out. Thrown by an imploding Zeus, it has dissolved itself.

Rochester's lapse of nature cannot be recuperated through a mastery of language like Etherege's balm of pretty military-religious compliments. The basic words of the physical—sperm and cunt—brutally disrupt the traditional rhythm, order, and "amorous discourse" of the poetry. Instead of Etherege's brief setback, Rochester's defeat is more shattering. His partner's nonchalant command of her own sexuality has triumphed over his braggadocio. In attempting to possess her, he has dispossessed a sexual identity invested entirely in his prick—which has failed—while her sexual identity is diffused throughout her entire body. But his unity and power is now in fragments, while her multiplicity remains calm and secure.

How singular is the power of "cunt" as a word in English! Although any account of its etymological origins comes up with bland cognates like "corner" and equivalents like "triangle," it has an impact far beyond them. "Cunt" cuts through history and society alike, unlike the class and national associations of the male organ: the knightly "prick," the stubby Germanic "dick," the strutting barnyard "cock" or haughty "pecker" (evoking the Chaucerian Middle Ages or a gaggle of men watching two roosters slash it out), the comical Yiddish insults of "schmuck" and "putz," the Scandinavian solidity of "dork."

Is the cunt silly or stupid (as is *conne* in French)—or, like the prostitutes and courtesans of early pornography, does it signify a hidden knowledge, a wise innocence (cognate with "cunning" in English) unknown to the world of masculine control? Perhaps it is "cunt" that writing really seeks to be, like "cuneiform," the wedge-shaped written language of the Babylonians. In any case, to see the word in Rochester's poem, after the propriety and measure of Etherege's, is like opening a trapdoor to a darker world beneath the social surface. Like an *honnête homme,* for whom the aesthetic of life is more important than the reality, or a libertine, whose self-containment rests on an ability to ignore the reality of others, the social savoir faire of Etherege's response to his failure to perform sexually contrasts absolutely with Rochester's total upset about his inability to order his body around.

Rochester's partner also responds more directly than Etherege's. First, she wipes away "the clammy joys" and then asks if his "love and rapture" is all there is—"Must we not pay a debt to pleasure too?"—that is, her pleasure as well. Female appreciation is still the main goal of male performance, sexual or poetic. But the "imperfect" in imperfect enjoyment, like the "premature" in premature ejaculation, implies a growing awareness of the need for female sexual pleasure in intercourse, a word whose own sexual implications of reciprocity do not appear in English until the late eighteenth century. The myth of the shattered Semele, with its celebration of male sexual autonomy and blithe unconcern for female pleasure, must give way to a newer myth that female pleasure is itself not autonomous, but depends upon male action and attention. The Rochester in the poem does try again. But first desire, then shame, and finally "rage at last confirms me impotent." Despite his partner's willingness to help out with "her fair hand," nevertheless "a wishing, weak, unmoving lump I lie."

If this were Etherege's poem, it would now be time to turn his failure into a pretty compliment to the woman, whose excessive charms have caused her lover to turn from lust to love and thereby lose normal masculine control. Rochester's response is first to mingle sorrow for the flaccid present with a bragging nostalgia for the potent past. Then, male and female were equally defenseless in the path of his "dart of love," equally its victims, but now it has failed, "shrunk up and sapless like a withered flower." The only way to be exonerated from that failure is to separate the sexual part from him. Before he had praised his penis for its grandeur and sought to hover godlike above it, directing its progress. Now that he has lost control, it must be totally condemned as "false to my passion, fatal to my fame."

Here I think we are witnessing one of the earliest modern examples of that ambiguous relation between the male sexual body and the male sense of personal identity that will become one of the main themes of writing in Western literature. While the high-minded poet wants to love, penetrate, surmount, and (perhaps) give pleasure, the detested prick only wants to come. Passion, it seems, speeds ejaculation too soon on its way. Only disdain and contempt are assurances of retention and therefore of prowess:

*What oyster-cinder-beggar-common whore*
*Didst thou e'er fail in all thy life before?*

Like Oliver Goldsmith's hero in *She Stoops to Conquer* a century or so later, the speaker has no trouble with control and self-restraint when it comes to wooing lower-class women. But when it comes to someone he actually might love, all his defenses fail him.

The last third of Rochester's poem thus becomes an attack on his sexual part as another being, separate from himself, his enemy—because before he had so identified with it in a fantasy of his sexual prowess. Such a fantasy runs deep in male literature from the seventeenth century onward: the sexual, the obscene, and the unsayable have turned into the basic armature of the personality, repressed so long that in revenge it takes over the daylight self.

Visibility always risks the threat of judgment. If the penis is not erect and ready, then the man assumes that no woman could possibly be interested in his body. As I suggested in the Introduction, perhaps the first steps forward in "civilization," and the movement away from the physical and toward the metaphoric, came with the covering of the penis in public. The lack of visible evidence effectively quashed any efforts by the audience of power to equate authority with size or to note degrees of fealty from observing who shriveled in front of whom. But after the well-padded courtly codpieces of the Renaissance, Rochester reintroduces or focuses for the first time on the member itself, in all its frailty.

This frailty, which Etherege jovially likened to a soldier falling at the wall of a battlemented town, Rochester then compares to a soldier of another sort, "a rude, roaring hector in the streets/Who scuffles, cuffs, and justles all he meets," but then hides when war is at hand. Rochester here has begun to presage a modern male sense of being unmanned rather than empowered by sexuality. And an essential part of that unmanning is to experience the penis as a separate being, a "hector," a military braggart, who hides shrinking cowardice under his bluster. Beginning with a romanticizing of male sexual power and his own penis as "the dart of love" and "the all-dissolving thunderbolt," Rochester's poem concludes by attacking it as the "worst part of me, and henceforth hated most," and condemning it to a whole array of venereal diseases along with the humiliation of watching "ten thousand abler [although not specifically larger] pricks" accomplish with his lover what he has been unable to.

As the bully violence of the "hector" arises from an unwillingness to face real combat, the failure of the "thunderbolt" reveals an inner sense of actual impotence before women—the shiftiness and instability of masculinity as a category, even though war and the warrior pose make it seemingly more single-minded. The "hector" also parodies an heroic poetry in which masculinity is defined almost entirely by military prowess. Writing in a century marked by more ferocious wars than had ever existed before, and long before Freudian interpretation made it a commonplace, Rochester exposes and mocks the crucial element of sexual adventuring in military aggression, the insight that "rape" in "rape and pillage" was not incidental but integral to the whole show, and that fucking someone else's motherland was an appropriate acknowledgment of who was really on top.

What does it mean to make a poem from the experience of premature ejaculation? There is a long poetic tradition of praise for women, in which the poet confesses his inability to praise them enough. Both Etherege and Rochester play on this tradition, and both take a step toward noticing that "love" may involve women's pleasure as well as men's. Etherege pays witty tribute to this pleasure, but Rochester more intensely associates the inability to know women sexually with the inability to connect with his own sexuality.

To call premature ejaculation "impotence" is already to assume an identification of sexuality with control. For Etherege the control of wit and language make up for the fallibility of the male body; even when "unmanned," he has no anxiety about who he is. But the language of Rochester's poem arises from a male body that is the site of an elusive, fallible sexuality. Ridiculing past models of male assertion, Rochester cannot stay so distant, because he is also dramatizing the way in which men become dupes of their own traditions of masculinity.

Let us therefore consider the possibility that the male orgasm itself is a cultural formation as much as a physical fact, and that the awareness of orgasm is part of the same historical era that witnessed so many other changes in the evolution of masculine identity and self-definition. The word "orgasm" first appears in English in the late seventeenth century. (The first reference in the *OED* is 1684.) In the 1970s, when feminists were championing the clitoral orgasm, a parody article appeared entitled "The Myth of the Male Orgasm," as if there could be any question about something so obvious. If, however, we distinguish orgasm, a change of personal consciousness, from ejaculation, a physiological event, the evidence becomes much more ambiguous. Perhaps male ejaculation is necessary, but is male orgasm? When early-seventeenth-century French poets, for example, speak of *la petite morte* and English poets of "dying" on the breast of their mistresses, were they in some sense registering the impact of a human experience that was occurring, if not for the first time absolutely, then for the first time in such language?*

The connection between the history of art and the history of human emotion is hard to pin down. Art may run ahead, behind, or be simultane-

* Usually the two states are collapsed together, even by experts. Melvin Konner, a physician who has written books on human nature with a sociobiological bent, makes a typical slide from orgasm to ejaculation: "Female orgasm is a phenomenon that seems puzzling from an evolutionary point of view. The potential for orgasmic response in women is much greater than it is in men. Yet on the surface, it seems to have little evolutionary value—unlike male ejaculation, female sexual satisfaction isn't necessary for reproduction" (12).

ous with the emotions of its creator and its audience. It may reflect or help fashion our feelings. It is difficult to know when it is doing what. Surely, it seems, we are able to have emotions, feelings, and attitudes before we have the vocabulary to name and distinguish them. But are emotions once named the same as they were when unnamed? Or does language somehow intervene in their creation, focusing and shaping the previously inarticulate experience, and in turn being influenced by them?

Such questions are difficult enough to determine when we're talking about politics or social mores. But sexuality is even more on the linguistic as well as emotional border between what can and cannot be said. Are descriptions of sex in literature, for example, a mirror of what people are actually doing? a fantasy about what they might do? a prediction of what they will or ought to do? Do they describe the typical or the unusual?

When the poetry of earlier ages addresses the feeling of human love, it tends to use images of suffusion akin to those either of pain or exaltation, the wound, or the religious experience. But these late Renaissance images of orgasm as a kind of death refer specifically to the extinction of consciousness, the loss of control, the momentary obliteration of public identity. In much of sixteenth-century literature, say, love may be a problem but male sexual performance is not. In English, one euphemism for the penis was "will," and Shakespeare's Sonnet 135 runs punning circles with it, including one on his own name:

> *So thou, being rich in Will, add to thy Will*
> *One will of mine to make thy large Will more.*
> *Let no unkind, no fair beseechers kill;*
> *Think all but one, and me in that one Will.*

But in the seventeenth century that virtually unquestioned sexual will often turns into images of the loss of both will and consciousness.

Two impulses seem to fuel this reorientation. First, as we have seen, there is sexual curiosity itself as a metaphor for exploring a whole new world of sense experience. The feminine New World, for example, penetrated and thereby brought into civilization by masculine colonists, is a commonplace image. As John Donne writes of his mistress in the midst of a poem of sexual engagement,

> *O my America! my new-found-land,*
> *My kingdome, safeliest when with one man man'd,*

*My Myne of precious stones, My Emperie [empire]*
*How blest am I in this discovering thee!* (96)

The other impulse, which arises when fear overwhelms curiosity, is toward a reimposition of male power. It appears predominantly in images of war, particularly when the absence of actual war becomes the occasion for carrying its psychology into sexual and romantic life.

Male orgasm and premature ejaculation had certainly happened before. But until poems like "The Imperfect Enjoyment" they were not self-conscious cultural events; whatever meaning they may have held for an individual had not yet interlocked with concepts of gender difference, masculine self-definition, and sexual "performance." Other poems of sexual seduction, for example, such as the carpe diem poems of the seventeenth century (for example, Marvell's "If we had world enough and time,/This coyness, lady, were no crime"), featured a self-assured male speaker who argued that because age would waste a woman's beauty, they should make the most of it now. At the other end of the seduction scenario, poems of postcoital disgust (for example, Shakespeare's "Th' expense of spirit in a waste of shame/Is lust in action") similarly assumed that the ability to judge sexual rights and wrongs was the sole possession of men.

Rochester's "Imperfect Enjoyment" thus stands at the threshold of a realization that male orgasm entails a loss of control, an inability to perform sexually, at a cultural moment when the norms of sexual behavior were in flux. While older forms of misogyny were left to the politically and theologically conservative, other men of the time paid ambiguous tribute to a new awareness of female sexual power. Both Etherege's and Rochester's poems specifically relate maleness to male sexual anatomy. The test of sexual congress is not siring an heir but gratifying a woman's desire for pleasure. The threat of unmanhood is depicted not as the laying aside of the warrior social role (as Ares takes off his armor to bed Aphrodite), but as the failure both to penetrate and to satisfy. In Rochester's poem, it becomes the central loss of honor, to which the false honor of the military hector is a mere analogy.

A mature masculine sexual identity, implies "The Imperfect Enjoyment," is something that needs to be achieved rather than just assumed. A century or so later, in the time of the Romantic poets, the fear of ego annihilation in sexual intercourse—the little death—is transformed into an aspiration toward that void, redefined as transcendence. Like many other aspects of human nature that we consider timeless, masculinity is instead a history of changes in which previously successful attitudes become irrelevant to the present conditions. In this history Rochester's poem is a nodal moment, when what was previously at least one class's assumed or "natural" masculine norm becomes threatened because it clearly has become an empty performance whose only goal is to allow the performer to boast equally of military triumph and sexual conquest.

Denied power and control by the old male ways, the Rochesterian male's natural ally would seem to be woman, but he cannot measure up to her either. "The Imperfect Enjoyment," instead of treating the incident as atypical, implies that every male sexual encounter with a woman is a test that the man must necessarily fail because of his deep-rooted fear that women don't really need men. In another, more mocking poem called "Signior Dildo," Rochester sketches the history of the "noble Italian" with the "leather coat" who has won the hearts of the ladies of the court. As a penis substitute, the celebrity of Signior Dildo thus eliminates the need for men while it ridicules the only part of them women find useful:

*Our dainty fine duchesses have got a trick*
*To dote on a fool for the sake of his prick:*
*The fops were undone, did their Graces but know*
*The discretion and vigor of Signior Dildo.*

Signior Dildo is finally attacked by an outraged "rabble of pricks" who would have chased him out of town if their balls hadn't slowed them down. The moral is clear: given the choice, women are perfectly satisfied with the signior. Like the many medieval and Renaissance stories of men who test the fidelity of their wives (such as Chaucer's "Man of Law's Tale," Shakespeare's *A Winter's Tale,* and the story of the "One Who Was Too Curious for His Own Good" in *Don Quixote*), "Signior Dildo" is about the male fear that women either lack or do not need sexual commitment. The crucial difference is that instead of one man fearful of the sexual allure of other men, "Signior Dildo" more apocalyptically trumpets the lack of need for any men at all.

This sense of a growing gender war in which personal as well as public power are equated with—and then diminished by—sexual performance is not just a crotchet of one late-seventeenth-century English poet, although Rochester's formulation is among the most vivid. Charles II's whole style of governing, along with the well-publicized profligacy of the court of the "merry monarch" and his many mistresses, emphasized the direct relation between actual power and its performance, and often the substitution of one for the other.

We have seen how questions of masculine identity—particularly the identity of warrior—wind their way through the literature of different centuries. In many Arthurian stories premeditated or inadvertent disguise plays a central role: the anonymous knight who turns out to be lowborn, the battle fought between helmeted friends who don't recognize each other. There, the implicit issue is one of the passage from an untried boyhood to acceptance as a man, i.e., a knight. But the potentially uncertain line between male and female and the self-conscious artifice of gender roles took center stage in the seventeenth century, particularly on the stage. Transvestite plots become frequent in French and Spanish drama, although it is only English drama that contains the added fillip of an all-male cast and boys playing female characters (who may be disguised as men). In the 1620s there were both attacks on and defenses of transvestite fashions in which even such an august personage as James I condemned women who dressed in male attire, while women responded that if men were not so unmasculine, *they* wouldn't have to restore the balance.

During the Civil Wars, such issues became more politicized through pamphlets in which Parliamentary pamphleteers attacked Royalist supporters, many of whom had fled to France, for the effeminacy of their long hair, and promised that while they were abroad their wives would be sexually serviced by potent Roundheads who had the proper political point of view. Similarly, throughout the century, one of the stock figures in comedy was the cuckold, the foolish lover or husband who is punished by the hero and mocked by the audience for letting down the masculine side. In the 1670s, William Wycherley's play *The Country Wife* turns the joke around by featuring a hero who succeeds in sexually scoring with a variety of wellborn women by having rumors spread of his impotence (from venereal disease) so that their husbands trust him to be alone with them.

In the same decade, a perhaps even more intriguing concatenation of sex and politics occurred in two pamphlets called "The Womens Petition Against Coffee" and "The Mens Answer." Arguments about coffee and coffeehouses would seem to be an odd place to find evidence of large movements in cultural attitudes. But coffeehouses, like teahouses and chocolate houses, were a new phenomenon and ripe to be blamed. "The Womens Petition" basically argues that coffeehouses have destroyed the sexual potency of men who "were justly esteemed the *Ablest Performers* in

Christendom." Coffee has so dried up their juices that—like Rochester's hector/penis—they "are not able to *stand* to it, and in the very First Charge fall down *flat* before us. . . . [S]o unfit they are for Action, that like young Train-band-men [civilian militia] when called upon Duty, their *Ammunition* is wanting" and they have no fire, "but Flash in the Pan" (*Old English Coffee Houses,* 11–2). "The Mens Answer" aims at "vindicating their own Performances" by, for one, arguing that coffee is Turkish and "no part of the world can boast more able or eager performers." Far from drying up masculine essences, coffee

> makes the erection more vigorous, the Ejaculation more full, adds a spiritualescency to the Sperme, and renders it more firm and suitable to the Gusto of the womb, and proportionate to the arduous and expectation too, of the female Paramour. (22)

In fact, Charles II's government for years had been trying to curtail the expansion of coffeehouses because it feared that they would become centers of sedition or what we would call opposition politics. The "Womens Petition," however, rejects any such fears. The men in coffeehouses are not "dangerous to Government" because they have been made "too tame and too talkative," i.e., too much like women, to be a threat. In 1675 Charles II finally did suppress coffeehouses, but the outcry was so extreme that the order was rescinded in eleven days. Accusations of impotence and effeminacy were, in other words, part of the cultural and political atmosphere, and partisans on all sides could use them as they liked. By the second half of the seventeenth century, they came readily to hand as part of the polemics between rival political factions.*

Yet with all this discussion of the newly pressing question of male impotence and inadequate sexual performance, we should not forget the question Rochester's lover asks in "The Imperfect Enjoyment": "Must we not pay a debt to pleasure too?" In other words, is the relation between the sexes a combat on the military model, or is it a collusion in the name of pleasure, enjoyment, or what the French called *jouissance*—a sexual love beyond the merely physical? The preoccupation with the natural that undergirds the libertine's sexual philosophy in effect dis-

* Fears worked both sides of the street—excessive masculinity on one hand, lack of it on the other. One of the rationales floated by a government pamphleteer to limit the number of available stagecoaches (which gave individuals too much mobility) was that "they effeminate his Majesty's subjects."

places man from the center of the universe and emphasizes his affinity with other beings, including women. In *Paradise Lost* Milton's Adam makes an analogous point when the angel Raphael tries to dampen his physical love for Eve by comparing it to "the same voutsaf't/To cattle and each Beast"—a mere pleasuring of the sense of touch. Adam is unconvinced because, as he says, the physical feeling he has for Eve is intertwined with his emotional and spiritual "harmony" with her. In any case, he presses Raphael, "Love not the heav'nly Spirits, and how thir Love/Express they?" To which Raphael blushingly answers that touch is not in question with angels because they mix entirely: "Easier than Air with Air . . . Union of Pure with Pure/Desiring."

Whereupon Raphael bids a hasty farewell. The difference between humans and angels is clear. Angels are spiritual beings cut from the same ethereal cloth. But human nature depends on bridging the gaps of separateness over the barriers of flesh and bone to create through pleasure, love, and harmony one soul from two bodies.

# THE OPPOSITE SEX

Love . . . turns a man into a woman.
—Robert Burton, *Anatomy of Melancholy* (1621)

All generalizations are opposed to sexuality.
—John Berger, *G.* (1972)

This seventeenth-century male body, which pornography and satire often subjects to a derision virtually unknown in the centuries of the armed knight, is not entirely a creature of literature and art. Thomas Laqueur has documented at length that there is also a physiological component to the changes in male identity I have been discussing on the social and cultural level. In *Making Sex*, Laqueur describes how a single-sex model of male and female is superseded by a double-sex model sometime in the eighteenth century. His examples are drawn almost entirely from the writings of anatomists, physicians, and biologists, although he also sketches briefly the way in which writers and philosophers draw many of their conclusions about human nature from these physiological assumptions. The single-sex model, he argues, was the standard view from classical antiquity to the end of the seventeenth century. It considers female sexual anatomy to be a homologous but inverted version of the male body. Until the ovaries, for example, got a name of their own in the nineteenth century, they were called "female testicles"; the vagina, also unnamed for many centuries, was considered to be an inside-out penis. Even when the fallopian tubes were discovered in the sixteenth century by a scientist appropriately named Renaldus Columbus, he still thought they produced an ejaculate like that of the male.

Unlike the one-sex biological model, which reflects the view that imperfect woman is subordinate to perfect man, the two-sex model postulates a maleness and a femaleness that definitely differ from each other. But no matter how much more accurately it described bodily structures and processes, the two-sex model was not necessarily a cultural improvement. Sexual desire—what Freud would later call libido—in the one-sex version did not differ in kind; both men and women had the capacity for desire, and the pleasure both sexes had in the sexual act was identified with the ability to create a child in the active mingling of male and female fluids. But with the two-sex model the hierarchy of male and female was replaced with what Laqueur calls the "incommensurable difference" between them. In our own time, this shift from subordination to divergence might be viewed as a move in the right direction, but as Laqueur points out, difference had its problems as well. One effect that particularly interests him is the disappearance of the female orgasm into the assumption that women had generally low levels of sexual desire. This change helped create the mythical "angel in the house" of the nineteenth century, who embodied spiritual values and had little interest in, and much disgust for, the carnality that so preoccupied men. What a turnaround that was from the classical and medieval idea of the sexually devouring woman in pursuit of the unflappably rational and/or spiritual man!

Tracing the extent to which the understanding of physiological differences between men and women has been conditioned by the mind-set that anatomists and physicians bring to their study, Laqueur correctly says that it is not so much a question of the two-sex model replacing the one-sex model as it is their new coexistence. Although the general weight of cultural assumptions—along with scientific attitudes—may have shifted, which interpretation of male and female is brought into play still depends on factors other than the physiological. In present-day arguments over abortion, for example, the age-old preformative theory (the character of the individual is totally present from the first) faces the more recent epigenetic theory (the fetus develops through stages of gender identification and consciousness).

As part, then, of our consideration of the interlacing of changes in the ideas and practice of warfare with changes in male self-definition, I again want to suggest here something of the reciprocity between anatomy and culture, and the way in which other social factors—like the growth of the state, nationalism, and the changing nature of warfare—contribute to our understanding. Books on anatomy may still have assumed the validity of Laqueur's single-sex model, but with the Renaissance and the seventeenth century, sexual difference became a much more explicit category of interpretation in everyday life. Words such as "masculine," "manly," "feminine," and "effeminate" appeared in a variety of contexts to imply a bifurcation of the world into two genders of experience. So, for example, Inigo Jones referred to the Palladian-style Queen's House he built at Greenwich as "solid proporsionable according to the rulles, masculine and unaffected."

In the misogynist literature of the early Church fathers and their medieval heirs, "man" as distinguished from God was interwoven with "man" as distinguished from woman. But it is in seventeenth-century Europe that "man" and "masculine" first became explicit concepts rather than natural and assumed categories. Whereas in the past clerical celibacy and military camaraderie might find common cause, by the seventeenth century, in Protestant countries especially, where priests could marry, it was more difficult to discuss masculinity without emphasizing, even polemically associating, some aspect of masculinity with heterosexuality. How was a man created from a boy? What were his attributes? What was the difference between a man and a woman? In tribal and even feudal warfare, these were relatively simple questions. But in the seventeenth century they were pressed more openly, and it is here that we can see, sometimes dimly but sometimes with clarity, how issues of gender development and distinction that still vex us were first formulated. Baldly stated, then, when did the practice of heterosexuality (sometimes, although not always, distinguished from homosexuality) become an explicit part of male self-definition? How did both the relation between male and female develop into what each side since the eighteenth century has called "the opposite sex"?

One reason is the inescapable fact that we are a species marked, like most on this planet, by bilateral symmetry. But culture also often maintains itself through either/or stereotypes, even though the stereotypes of one era might be entirely the reverse of another. Changes in social organization also have an intimate connection with changes in the relation of the sexes, especially in those societies in which the equation of man and warrior is closest. For the patriarchal society premised on war has no necessary view of what men or women are, only that man is the independent and woman the dependent variable. And it is in the nature of what is perceived as a two-part contrast—like right and left, male and female, black and white—that whenever one shifts meaning, the other shifts as well, usually ignoring the immense landscape that lies between the two poles. In such a world the oppositeness of the opposite sex becomes an integral part of the reconstitution of the warrior as an appropriate male model.

When sexuality enters the discussion, it may seem that we have strayed far from the role of such grand issues as war, honor, and nationalism in the shaping of masculinity. But in the seventeenth-century reorientation of masculinity, all of these elements interlaced with one another. Like dueling and piracy on the one hand and fears of effeminacy and emasculation on the other, the preoccupation with *both* male sexual potency and male sexual inadequacy was a private reaction against a world in which male public roles were becoming increasingly uncertain. Our contemporary tendency to see sexuality as the key to character owes a great debt to the influence of Freudian psychology. But historically it owes even more to these seventeenth- and eighteenth-century efforts, first to recognize a private nature, and then to heal the split between it and the older public self. This "self" that is making its earliest explicit appearance on the European stage, the "man" who is the new subject of a secular political philosophy, is a contradictory compound of all these elements, single but collective, private but public.

The seventeenth century thus resumes an old tension between the urges toward military definitions of masculinity and the urges against it. There were precedents from the classical past, especially in the alternatives to the Roman soldier-emperor posed by writers like Ovid and theologians like Saint Augustine. But the particular stage in the evolution of warfare and national self-consciousness that marked the early modern period powerfully metamorphosed and reinvigorated those cultural attitudes. The ancient tribal imperative that defined a man's honor as composed of both honor in warfare and protection of his family's sexual purity in peace became a prelude to a newly reinforced belief that women were a threat to male control. This confession of frailty was a striking change from earlier assurances that male sexuality was still the human standard, although its composure and integrity might be threatened by female. In the sixteenth century, for instance, Castiglione in *The Courtier* approvingly cites Aristotle's view that women naturally love the first man they have sex with, while men naturally detest their first woman, because women are perfected by men while men are made imperfect by women.

At the same time, the crucial difference between male and female honor was beginning to erode. In the traditional honor code, female chastity must be physically defended by male relatives to ensure the continuity of the family and the purity of its blood. Women's honor, in other words, is essentially sexual, and in a very definite sense is not theirs so much as it is the possession of the male members of their families. While men can both lose and gain honor, for women honor is either retained or lost. In Montaigne's satiric formulation, just as a man is defined by his military valor,

> just so our passion, combined with the feverish solicitude that we have for the chastity of women, brings it about that *a good woman, a worthy woman, a woman of honor and virtue,* means in effect nothing else to us than *a chaste woman;* as if, to obligate them to that duty, we were indifferent to all the rest, and gave them free rein for any other fault provided they abandon this one. (277)

The more set apart women are from men in a society, the more physical strength and military prowess are the main criteria of masculinity. A macho culture, in other words, is a separatist culture. The belief, then, that women are the weakness of men—either because they induce sexual inadequacy by causing the "little death" of orgasm or because their own sexual lapses must be revenged by male family blood—persists when there is no alternative, no middle ground between the sexes.

In an early moment of the story of war told in the eleventh century by the Bayeux Tapestry, an enigmatic scene occurs. After being captured in Normandy by a local lord named Guy of Ponthieu, Harold has been rescued by William of Normandy (not yet the Conqueror) and brought to his palace. Soon he will accompany William on a military expedition against Conan, a rebellious vassal. But before that public military event the tapestry's stitched and usually explicit captions cryptically tell us only "Where a clerk and Aelfgyva." There is no explanatory verb; it almost seems to have been bleeped from the tapestry's high-minded recounting of the events of the Norman Conquest. But still the scene itself is included. In it, a woman in a long, hooded dress, with only her face and hands and the tips of her shoes visible, stands between two columns topped by horned beasts with protruding tongues. Next to her a cloaked man with a tonsure touches, caresses, or slaps her face. Next to him is an elaborate building, perhaps a church, distinctly phallic in shape. Meanwhile, below Aelfgyva's feet, in the lower border of the tapestry, a naked man crouches, his right arm akimbo, his left extended, while to his left another naked man seems to be taking an ax from a box.

What is happening here? It may be a reference to some sexual scandal, but we have no external source. There are a few clues. In the tapestry, not too long before the Aelfgyva scene, while the main story depicts Guy bringing Harold to William, in the lower border a man with an erection holds his arms out to a naked woman. Until the Battle of Hastings, these are the only scenes of nakedness in the tapestry, and in the battle, instead of the nakedness of sexuality, it is the naked bodies of dead soldiers, stripped of their armor and even dismembered. Just as the bare and vulnerable bodies of the dead appear pointedly beneath the account of the events of the battle, so too the sexuality that the Aelfgyva scene may allude to appears in the lower margin, the realm, it seems, of the unclothed and thereby unsocial body. What is the point of the Aelfgyva scene in a story that otherwise focuses on the politics and ethics of the medieval honor system? Does it refer to the disruptive force of male desire for women, and how that, along with other breaches of honor, leads to what the Normans consider to be William's justified war against Harold? Perhaps. But what is certain is the enigmatic juxtaposition of images of the unprotected bodies of the male war dead with the unclothed bodies of men who have been sexually compromised in some way.

Even in its ambiguity, the Aelfgyva scene in the Bayeux Tapestry, like the myth of Ares trapped in his love for Aphrodite, underlines the difficult relation that has long existed between men at war and men at love. Traditionally, the code of honor emphasizes the integrity and autonomy of the warrior, physically underlined by the suit or armor or the uniform. But the Western view of sexuality, as Aristophanes elaborates the myth in Plato's *Symposium*, emphasizes the essential incompleteness of every individual. Zeus has split the original wholeness of human beings into halves constantly in search of each other, no matter what their gender or sexual preference. The presence of sexual desire, then, is an indication of the loss of integrity and autonomy and thereby a threat to the Indo-European warrior value system, and Christianity adds to the myth of sexual incompleteness the spiritual incompleteness of man before God.*

By the seventeenth century, for some European cultures at least, the exclusivity of military masculinity was being challenged by cultural changes that made it more possible and even more acceptable for a man to invest at least something of his emotional life in a relationship with a woman. The real change in the discussion of male sexuality in the seventeenth century was thus that biological maleness, especially male sexuality, instead of being merely assumed, becomes a more discussable aspect of social identity, and therefore more open to debate. The biological treatises cited by Thomas Laqueur obviously add to that discussion, but they are only a part of a sea change in the standards by which masculinity is defined and judged. Rochester's poetry similarly helps single out a historical moment in which masculinity was becoming not the God-given portion of every male but an aspect of character primarily defined by sexual accomplishment and performance, constantly needing to be reattained—floating, intangible, and emasculated without the feminine harbor that it simultaneously longs for and fears.

By comparing his derelict penis to a strutting hector, Rochester's poem reveals the inadequacy of an old-style warrior masculinity to the new challenges. The honor a soldier gained for the willingness and ability to fight is empty, and sexual weakness gives the lie to its braggart assertions. Women and the sexual response they can evoke thus represent all that is problematic for men in their own masculinity. We use "effeminate" pejoratively to refer to certain traits of male behavior. But for the Elizabethans, in a usage that lasted through the seventeenth century and beyond, an effeminate man was one who was too interested in women. "Love," writes Robert Burton in the early seventeenth century, "turns a man into a woman," and Burton's *Anatomy of Melancholy* traces in elaborate and mocking detail the ways in which love and longing create all sorts of mental illnesses tending to the enfeeblement of men.

It was an attitude that went back to classical precedents as well. Cicero, for one, denounced as effeminate the desire to have sexual pleasure, either in marriage or elsewhere. The specific words he uses for a man who has such desires are *mollis et enervata,* soft and weakened. As one of Rochester's songs has it, "Love a woman? You're an ass!/'Tis a most insipid passion/To choose out for your happiness/The silliest part of

* Compare the remarks of Simon Leys: "The view that human beings, as sexual creatures, are essentially incomplete, belongs to Western culture; the Chinese view is that every individual contains in himself both yin and yang elements and therefore should be able to achieve his own perfection in isolation" (29). Peter Brown points out that early ascetic Christianity supersedes sexual incompleteness with religious completeness and asserts that virginity is a completeness of its own.

God's creation." Leave women to porters and grooms and other lower-class lovers, he continues, I will sit and drink with my male friends, and then concludes: "Then give me health, wealth, mirth, and wine,/And, if busy love entrenches,/There's a sweet, soft page of mine/Does the trick worth forty wenches." Rochester's own attitude is unclear: is he approving this attitude or mocking it? But the connection between a manly disgust with women and the satisfaction of lust with someone of the same sex reflects an ancient tradition. To engage in homosexual activities, especially if you are the penetrator or the person in power (lord to page), hardly reflects on your own sexuality; it may even enhance your sexual reputation. In the same period, to be "manly" was to be frank and straightforward, even a bit antisocial, telling it like it is. To the extent that it was physical, it implied a certain stature and musculature, and was hardly automatically heterosexual, although Alexander Pope in his "Epistle to Dr. Arbuthnot" compares his own "manly ways" to the fawning unctuousness of the bisexual court poet Lord Hervey.

What exactly is wrong with effeminacy of this sort? Why is a masculinity that speaks with only one voice required for social order? Once again, the answer lies in the assumption of the armored masculinity of the soldier in battle, and the fear that any chink in that armor, especially an opening to pleasure, is potentially deadly. As in every war film, when a soldier opens his wallet to show a picture of his wife or girlfriend, we know that he is doomed. Even the libertine's utopian view of sexual freedom was not immune to these fears. In one aspect a sexual predator, in another a man who was truly interested in and attracted to women, the libertine also wielded his often callous promiscuity as a shield against the effeminacy of excessive attachment to individuals.

In the public world of war, the new gunpowder and siege technology begun in the sixteenth century had by the aftermath of the Thirty Years' War fueled an expanding controversy over whether the old models of military epic and heroic action in war were still valid. After Habsburg expansionism had been stymied by the Thirty Years' War, it was Louis XIV's territorial ambitions that took center stage in Europe, and helped feed French and French-influenced English theories of the importance of military heroics.

Roughly speaking, the aristocratic perspective, in both France and England, insisted that the military hero was still the prime sort of man, while the bourgeois and Parliamentary perspective responded that the class-oriented heroism of the past was no longer relevant: honor must give way to virtue. The aristocratic view has more than a touch of anxiety about it, reflecting the dilemma of a class that has lost its implicit justification and needs to find a more explicit one to go along with its self-important public gestures. The days of the disguised knight who must prove himself before revealing his name were over, if they ever existed. Military heroism, in other words, with the aid of writers and publicists, had to become more theatricalized and explicit. The English writer Sir William Davenant, for example, reflected aristocratic opinion in both France and England when he strongly argued in midcentury that heroic poetry was necessary because it helped reform the upper classes, who were the only audience suited to understand it.

But just as literature and theater can be vehicles of aristocratic self-preservation and self-presentation, they can also undermine such assertions by the mere fact that actors can impersonate those qualities. If an actor can pretend to be a hero, what about heroism isn't pretense? Davenant, for example, was caught between his suspicion of the monarchical state and his inability to conceive of any another social validation for the poet and playwright. A member of a younger generation, like Andrew Marvell, in contrast, could depict Oliver Cromwell in "An Horatian Ode" as both a rampaging force of nature and a private man who came to war from his garden, with none of the trappings of class or family authority. Similarly, as Rochester in "The Imperfect Enjoyment" dramatizes the outrage and psychic disintegration of the male who has sexually failed, so in a more philosophical poem like "A Satyr Against Reason and Mankind" he also mocks the chivalric emphasis on the honor to be gained on the battlefield: "Merely for safety, after fame we thirst,/For all men would be cowards if they durst." Just as the authentic male sexuality recognizes the possibility of failure, the authentic male courage recognizes the possibility of running away.

Rochester's poems, with their remarkable hostility to warrior assumptions, illustrate the degree to which England in the late seventeenth century was in transition from a court-oriented warrior society to a city-oriented bourgeois society. The seventeenth-century impasse of male sexual license faced with male sexual impotence thus most immediately mirrored the gyrations of an aristocracy whose military justification was being taken over by centralized monarchical governments. At the same time the ancient misogynist view of women's demanding sexual nature began to allow for the possibility that it is male failure rather than female avidity that is the crucial issue. Rochester had a discontent like

Satan's with the portion patriarchal authority had given him. But he also understood how the new world had undermined some of the basic assumptions of aristocratic male sexual privilege.

The effort to recoup military masculinity therefore aimed to identify it with sexual potency rather than to contrast war and sexuality. In one version of a story about the duke of Marlborough, the enormously successful commander of the English armies against France in the late seventeenth and early eighteenth centuries, he arrives home from battle in a fit of hearty desire, causing the duchess to write in her diary, "His Grace returned from the wars today and pleasured me twice in his topboots."

Other versions of this story have different details. Sometimes the pleasuring is increased to seven times or more, and sometimes a difference between pleasuring in general and pleasuring in top boots is introduced. Richard Dawkins in *The Selfish Gene* approvingly cites a student of his who likens Marlborough's lustiness (and by extension all similar male behavior) to that of a male cricket who is "more likely to court females if he has recently won a fight against another male." Dawkins calls this the "Duke of Marlborough Effect."

In a book that argues the overwhelming and perpetual importance of genes and genetic inheritance in influencing behavior, it may be an appropriate tale to tell. But even apart from any questions about the ease in making such direct analogies between male human and male cricket behavior, the truth may be somewhat more timebound. I have searched through Sarah Churchill's diaries and letters, as well as books about her and her husband the duke, and found no trace of this quotation or any reference to the incident. I am therefore inclined to think of it either as a folk myth that seeks to unite in one story (and one superhuman person) military heroism and sexual prowess, or as part of the anti-Marlborough invective of the time that explained his rise to power by his liaisons. Otherwise, it seems out of keeping with Marlborough's lifetime, when the theme of the soldier unmanned by love is so much more widespread. The only source I could find is in fact not a history but Ford Madox Ford's post–World War I novel *No More Parades,* in which an unfaithful wife trying to visit her husband at the front remembers it as part of a letter from the duchess to Queen Anne. All in all, the anecdote seems to be a more characteristic nineteenth-century equation (as in the slang word "swordsman") between victory in battle and lustiness in private, and in accord with, say, Stendhal's remark in the post-Napoleonic *De l'amour* (1822) that the lover is a general plotting maneuvers. In the story, a triumphant courage and an aroused sexuality are connected rather than opposed, making a bridge between military and sexual macho.

Whatever its actual origin, what an intriguing contrast the Marlborough story makes with either the legend of King Conchobar's deflection of the hero Cú Chulainn's attack by sending out women with bare breasts to confront him and then cold water to douse him, or the capture of the war god Ares by Hephaistos, after he had been sexually diverted by Aphrodite. Those are the more traditional views of the opposition between war and sexuality, in which womanly wiles paralyze the soldier's ability to fight. In many tribal societies men were ritually barred from warfare while their wives were menstruating and barred from intercourse for some time before and after battle, usually for much the same reason: the contact with female sexuality would reduce their prowess.*

This contrast between war and sexuality did not die out but, like the one-sex and two-sex theories, coexisted with the idea of the soldier as lusty lover, defeating the unmanning sexuality of women by conquering them. Frederick the Great, the most celebrated war maker of the eighteenth century, writes in his poem on the art of war that "the hussar was supposed to seek his happiness by the saber . . . and not by the sheath" (*vagina* in Latin). In early modern warfare, ordinary soldiers were often forbidden to marry. Perhaps this was done as an unconscious shadow of the old ritual decrees, but Isabel Hull points out a more practical economic reason: by enforcing the marriage prohibition, rulers and governments could "escape pension costs and demands for higher pay and to increase mobility" (109), a motivation similar to those inspiring many seventeenth-century army prohibitions against camp followers.

Frederick William I, the father of Frederick the Great, in fact considered his son and heir to be effeminate and much too devoted to the arts, especially as practiced in France. Perhaps to teach him the proper soldierly stoicism, he had Frederick's best friend beheaded for treason and forced the eighteen-year-old Frederick, also under a sentence of death, to watch. Frederick most probably was homosexual himself. After a marriage forced upon him by his father, he moved into a palace from which all women were forbidden. And, as his comments on the need for saber and not the sheath imply, he certainly believed that undue heterosexuality and success on the battlefield did not go together. But even in

* Incan rituals connect fertility and the battlefield through the medium of blood. Among the Kikuyu of Africa, men at war were separated ritually from women, but this prohibition was breached, for example, during the long Mau Mau struggle.

Frederick William's bullying contempt there is little sense of any problematic relation of homosexuality in general to soldiering, only its effeminate version. Frederick himself frequently called troops who were hesitant to fight effeminate—i.e., not good—soldiers. The exclusive equation of effeminacy and homosexuality (if effeminate, then homosexual; or if homosexual, then effeminate) does not become a general cultural assumption until the second half of the nineteenth century.*

In fact, as we have seen, homosexual or homoerotic relations have, in different cultures, historically been easily compatible with wartime prowess. But these and any other strategies of continuing male authority must also be juxtaposed, as they are in "The Imperfect Enjoyment," with the increasing presence of female power and, as in the Middle Ages, with women as the audience of masculine performance. Faced with the presence of female sexuality, armor and weapons fail, and strength shrinks beneath the uniform. The testimony of traditional epic poetry is very clear about this. In the *Iliad* the seizure of Helen by Paris is, of course, the immediate cause of the war, and in the *Aeneid* Dido unsuccessfully tries to keep Aeneas in Carthage, safe from war and his heroic destiny. In *The Song of Roland*, by contrast, there are no women at all. In *The Poem of the Cid*, the hero is married and has two daughters but they exist in a sphere separate from his war making until they have been insulted by the men whom they were to marry. In *The Nibelungenlied* and the Icelandic sagas, women either sexually weaken and erode the will to war, or else urge their men on to even greater bloodthirstiness. Not until the twentieth century was it widely argued that women are somehow innately opposed to war, and such sentiments as "I Didn't Raise My Son to Be a Soldier Boy" during World War I—let alone the 1960s antiwar slogan "Girls Say Yes to Boys Who Say No"—became widespread.

Ares thwarted in his affair with Aphrodite is only the mythic version of a contradiction between the plain speaking of the soldier and the love rhetoric of the courtier or courtly lover that persisted for centuries. Castiglione and Don Quixote in their different ways may try to break down that distinction, but into the Renaissance the clash remains, if only as convenient apology. Shakespeare's somewhat cynical view of the military lover offers some intriguing examples. *Henry V* ends not with Agin

* Frederick's physician J. G. Zimmerman later defended him against the charge of homosexuality by saying that his diffidence before women was due to an "emasculation" that occurred when he was treated for gonorrhea. He then makes the somewhat implausible argument that Frederick "was fond of being charged with a vicious failing of so many Grecians and Romans, of which he never was guilty," so that no one would suspect he was otherwise injured (Snyder, 136).

court but with Henry's wooing of Katharine, the French princess, and his battlefield eloquence lurches precipitately into the mumblings of a tongue-tied lover. Theseus in *A Midsummer Night's Dream* says of his future wife, Hippolyta, whose Amazons he has defeated in battle, "I wooed her with my sword"—not the most propitious way to begin married life in Shakespeare, as Othello's seductive telling of his military victories to Desdemona also confirms.

Restoration comedy in late-seventeenth-century England, like the comedy of Molière, to which it often paid a debt, frequently dealt with an explicit war between the sexes (the phrase seems to have been coined in this period) with men and women plotting against each other as if they were from different planets, or at least warring countries. It is thus tempting to reinterpret this "war" as reflecting a realization that there are in fact real differences between the sexes.

Part of that awareness, in works written by both men and women toward the end of the century, is a frequent polarization into "men are/women are" formulations. At the extreme ends of the comic spectrum in many plays, for example, are male characters who would rather be with other men, drinking and carousing, and women who would rather be with other women, sometimes reading uplifting works, sometimes gossiping and plotting. So in a typical dialogue from Congreve's *The Way of the World* (1700), we read:

> MRS. FAINALL
> Dost thou hate those vipers, men?
> MRS. MARWOOD
> I have done hating 'em, and am now come to despise 'em;
> the next thing I have to do, is eternally forget 'em.
> MRS. FAINALL
> There spoke the spirit of an Amazon, a Penthesilea.
> MRS. MARWOOD
> And yet I am thinking, sometimes, to carry my aversion
> further.
> MRS. FAINALL
> How?
> MRS. MARWOOD
> Faith, by marrying. . . .*

* "Mrs." is a title that does not necessarily mean that a woman is married. Here, Mrs. Fainall is married (to a husband she hates) and Mrs. Marwood is not (but is having an affair with Mrs. Fainall's husband).

Attitudes toward this rift between the sexes varied. Molière in *The Learned Ladies* (1672) mocks the cabal of women who decide that the way to be free of bestial men is to embrace "womanly" reason. Mary Astell, writing in England in the last decade of the same century, argues that marriage was out of the question for women, because they needed to be celibate to realize their full power. Astell envisions instead a nunnery-like college where women would become truly learned, but her idea of celibacy as the condition for female power once again presages the nineteenth-century "angel in the house" whose moral stature was predicated on either her inability to feel or her lack of interest in sexual passion. Not only Rochester in "The Imperfect Enjoyment" identified love and passion with loss of control.

As we might expect in such a society, the great sexual failing, perhaps more important even than premature ejaculation, was masturbation, which received more attention from moralists than did prostitution, homosexuality, or venereal disease. Masturbation was not only a physical act, it was a threat to social order because it symbolized the opulence, luxury, and self-indulgence of the commercial civilization that was gradually replacing the warrior world of the past. As Isabel Hull remarks about Germany in the seventeenth and eighteenth century, "Masturbation was everywhere, a kind of original sin of the privacy wrought by civil society" (275). In 1711 Richard Steele wrote in the *Spectator,* one of the early organs of public opinion that helped transform British politics, "The great Foundation of civil Virtue is Self-Denial" (Addison, II, 462). Accordingly, masturbation not very long after was first termed "self-abuse," and the historian Lawrence Stone has referred to a virtual "masturbation panic" in early-eighteenth-century England. Tracts against masturbation flourished and would remain popular among both quacks and medical practitioners for the next few centuries. Masturbation emphasized self-involved as opposed to socially useful pleasure. It "wasted" seed that ought to be put to work in creating the continuity of family blood, and it confused sexual distinctions, creating effeminate men and masculinized women. One of the earliest large-scale English attacks on the new sin was the anonymous *Onania, or the Heinous Sin of Self-Pollution* (1700–10). Later in the century, a Swiss doctor named Simon André Tissot argued in *L'Onanisme* that masturbation was the root of all disease. These examples of male sexual insecurity and sexual conflicts between men and women in the later seventeenth century had a significant social dimension as well. For the fearful, the combination of female power assailed the foundations of family authority, watering down genealogy and making men politically if not also sexually impotent. French tragic drama at the same time was also preoccupied with generational conflict and competition, what Jonathan Dewald has called "the psychology of lineage," just as many of John Dryden's heroic dramas featured older rulers competing with younger warriors, often their own sons, for the same woman.

As such efforts to confirm proper boundaries for male and female indicate, what male and female represent often doesn't matter as much as their opposition to each other. Contrary to twentieth-century polarities that cast women in the essential role of defenders of nature, for example, while men are the creators of society, in the seventeenth century women—upper-class women in particular—were either celebrated or excoriated for their social and behind-the-scenes political power, while men, as in libertine theory, were the sources of a sometimes antisocial natural energy and potential social regeneration. Thus the shift in physiological understanding from a one-sex premise to a two-sex premise documented by Laqueur was also accompanied, even foretold, by a cultural shift to a polar relation of the sexes in which oppositeness is an explicit category.

In Louis XIV's France, as much as in Charles II's England, women were perceived as having a significant hand in the running of the court, while the former warriors of the aristocracy, compelled to dance attendance on all court activities, were now, as Norbert Elias comments, "bereft of the knightly function" (*Court Society*, 194). Later in the eighteenth century, in the midst of his critiques of monarchical political life, Jean-Jacques Rousseau argued that it was women's sexual power over men that had led to social degeneration, and only an enforced modesty could help restore social and political vigor. Rochester states the connection between sexual and social power somewhat more directly in a satiric poem about Charles II and his mistresses: "His scepter and his prick are of a length;/And she may sway the one who plays with the other." But Rochester's point is less that Charles's politics are at the service of his pliable masculinity than that politics and war are intertwined with masculinity, whether it is aggressive or passive. At first in the poem, Charles's more sybaritic rule is contrasted with the military adventures of Louis XIV: "the French fool, that wanders up and down/Starving his people, hazarding his crown." By the end of the poem, however, both alternatives seem ridiculous: "All monarchs I hate, and the thrones they sit on,/From the hector of France to the cully of Britain." Louis XIV may be a hector, like the bully-penis of "The Imperfect Enjoyment," and

Charles may be an ass and a fool; neither represents an authority to be admired or a masculinity to be emulated.

In addition to being a vehicle for making war, the modern state was slowly but expressly taking on a moral mission as well, preoccupied with regulating private sexuality as it tried to regulate private honor. Marriage was becoming a legal term as much as, if not more than, a religious one, and illicit sexuality would be a threat to it and to the state stability that stood behind it. Whatever authority might have been lost to women by individual men would be remedied by the law. But a very few years after the licentious court of Charles II that Rochester so mocked came the new court of the first English dual monarchy, William and Mary, a married couple intent on stopping Louis XIV's march across Europe as well as reforming manners in their own kingdom in order to "discourage profaneness and immorality."

*Part V*

# HEROES FROM BELOW

# WAR AND ANTIWAR

History can only take things in the gross;
But could we know them in detail, perchance
In balancing the profit and the loss,
War's merit it by no means might enhance,
To waste so much gold for a little dross,
As hath been done, mere conquest to advance.
The drying up a single tear has more
Of honest fame, than shedding seas of gore.
—Byron, *Don Juan* (1819)

Near the beginning of Shakespeare's *Henry IV: Part I,* Harry Hotspur, whose name proclaims his warrior enthusiasm, speaks with contempt of a "popinjay" lord he has met after a battle "when I was dry with rage and extreme toil,/Breathless and faint, leaning on my sword," who demands Hotspur's prisoners in the name of the king. Hotspur refuses.

*. . . he made me mad*
*To see him shine so brisk, and smell so sweet,*
*And talk so like a waiting gentlewoman*
*Of guns and drums and wounds—God save the mark!—*
*And telling me that the sovereignest thing on earth*
*Was parmacity [sperm-whale ointment] for an inward bruise,*
*And that it was great pity, so it was,*
*This villainous saltpetre should be digged*

*Out of the bowels of the harmless earth,*
*Which many a good tall fellow had destroyed*
*So cowardly, and but for these vile guns,*
*He would himself have been a soldier.*

So Shakespeare confronts the begrimed soldier with the perfumed courtier as two extremes of mutually uncomprehending masculinity. However excessive the knee-jerk aggression of Hotspur, the lord's distaste for guns and cannons is a feeble and, as Hotspur emphasizes, effeminate excuse for not being engaged in war.

Byron's more explicit condemnation of war and its goals lies some two hundred years in the future. But by the middle of the seventeenth century the courts and salons of Europe were publicly debating what constitutes heroic action and character. In one form this skepticism appears in parodies of heroic poems like the *Aeneid*, in another in stories told from the point of view of the common soldier, as in Grimmelshausen's picaresque account of the Thirty Years' War, *Simplicissimus*. More politically, it was embodied in a still developing attack on bellicosity as an unreflective policy undertaken not for national goals but for the self-aggrandizement of monarchs and the nobility.

Just as there was a strong Christian tradition favoring resistance to the demands of the state (Rome in particular) to make war, there were individual writers in the Middle Ages who took antiwar positions, usually for religious reasons. John Wyclif, who in the fourteenth century first translated the Bible into English, in *De Officio Regis (On the Office of the King)* denounced all war as an illegitimate usurpation by the state of the individual body's relation to God, just as the priesthood disrupted the relation of his soul. The refusal to bear arms was also a tenet of such fifteenth- and sixteenth-century sects in Germany as the Hussites and the Anabaptists, who reemphasized the pacifistic elements in Christian doctrine that had somehow been laid aside in the enthusiasm over the Crusades. Seventeenth-century pacifist groups like the Quakers in England similarly founded their antiwar position not only on an unwillingness to take life (as in Eastern religions like Buddhism) but also on a refusal to go along with the political demands of the new nation-state.

In the seventeenth century, political theorists like Hugo Grotius, by speaking of a just war, assumed war's inevitability in human affairs, but also stressed the need for international relations and diplomacy not just as happenstance agreements between nations but as an articulated code of conduct. Thomas Hobbes in *Leviathan* was perhaps the first to argue at length that society itself is specifically created by the fear of war, in an attempt to contain and channel for the good of the group the inherent male disposition to fight. Once again, when "man" is at issue, misanthropy comes in its wake. In "A Satyr Against Reason and Mankind," Rochester expands Hobbes's argument to indict the inherent viciousness of men: "Pressed by necessity," animals may feed on their fellows, but only "Man undoes man to do himself no good":

> *For hunger or for love they fight and tear*
> *Whilst wretched man is still in arms for fear.*
> *For fear he arms, and is of arms afraid;*
> *By fear to fear successively betrayed;*
> *Base fear, that source whence his best passions came:*
> *His boasted honor, and his dear-bought fame. . . .*
> *The good he acts, the ill he does endure,*
> *'Tis all from fear, to make himself secure.*

As he did somewhat differently in "The Imperfect Enjoyment," Rochester here focuses almost exclusively on the subjective experience of war rather than the grand God's-eye view from which heroes are celebrated. In military history the perception that fear is a normal part of war is usually dated to the middle of the nineteenth century. Of course, there is fear and horror in the *Iliad* as well, although it tends to be the emotions of the victims of the great heroes rather than those of the heroes themselves. What marks these seventeenth-century discussions is the dawning possibility that fear is in the very nature of war rather than an anomaly experienced by the cowardly and the treasonous. Here are the seedbeds of a vision of war, like Byron's, that stresses confusion and darkness and the human inability to control events rather than the heroic domination of them.

A surprisingly concise and complicated statement of the conflict between traditional views of war and the new awareness appeared in the political and poetic controversy over an Anglo-Dutch sea battle in the late 1660s. Marxist interpretations of war are often antiheroic because they emphasize the economic basis of conflict: the Trojan War was not about the abduction of Helen and the rivalry between Hector and Achilles but about trade routes to the Middle East. But what happens when that awareness, instead of being just our own ex post facto perspective, is an explicit part of what people at the time thought they were doing? This Second Anglo-Dutch War, which lasted from 1665 to 1667, was the middle of what would be three wars between the English and Dutch that had no dynastic or religious justifications but were admittedly over foreign markets and trade. To the more rarefied speculations about the nature of heroism in a postchivalric and postepic world, then, they added the question of what heroism could possibly be in war carried on for overtly commercial reasons.

In 1663, shortly after the restoration of Charles II to the throne, the English provoked the Dutch by attacking their ships in Africa and seizing New Amsterdam in America. Then, on June 3, 1665, the English fleet decisively defeated the Dutch at Lowestoft, just off the English coast, but failed to pursue their advantage. In 1667 the Dutch would return the favor with a humiliating defeat of the English fleet at the very mouth of the Thames. This was in the future, however, and at the time the victory of Lowestoft was celebrated everywhere. The duke of York, who led the fleet, had pictures of each of his senior officers painted by Sir Peter Lely, the court painter. (Many are still on display at the National Maritime Museum in the Queen's House, Greenwich.) On the literary side, Edmund Waller, a favorite court poet who had been in exile with Charles II in France, wrote a poem called "Instructions to a Painter." The poem was modeled on a very trendy Italian format whose conceit was that the poet was directing an imaginary painter to depict the grand naval triumph in the appropriate heroic style.

Waller's poem is nakedly celebratory: the painter easily follows the poet's instructions, every moment of the battle is seen clearly, and the heroes step forward to take their bows. Here, for example, is Waller's account of a moment in the battle when the British flagship, commanded by the duke of York, is shelled and three noblemen are killed:

*From whence a fatal volley we received:*
*It missed the duke, but his great heart it grieved;*
*Three worthy persons from his side it tore*
*And dyed his garment with their scattered gore.*
*Happy! to whom this glorious death arrives,*
*More to be valued than a thousand lives!*
*On such a theatre as this to die,*
*For such a cause, and such a witness by!*

The world of battle is not chaos but an order created by the duke's vision of the deaths of his companions. That he saw it happen was enough to make them heroes as well.

Almost immediately, the political opposition in England, until then fairly scattered, seized on this victory and this poem as a way of uniting against their opponents. Instead of the triumph and victory of heroic war, the opposition turned Lowestoft into politics, mocking the pretensions of war and revealing the self-interest behind the urge to glory, tearing the veil of triumph away from the battle to show it in a much more corrupt light: What is the Dutch war for? How does it help England? What is the foreign policy of the king's government? Are his ministers capable of carrying it out? Who is responsible?

The first response, "The Second Advice to a Painter," which may have been written in whole or in part by Andrew Marvell, has a very different view of the battle. Unlike Waller's uniformly sunlit heroic world and his above-it-all perspective, things here, like the political motives behind the battle, are seen from a point of view more enmeshed in real life and therefore more confused:

*The noise, the smoke, the sweat, the fire, the blood,*
*Are not to be expressed nor understood.*

Similarly, the death of one of the three noblemen has also lost its heroic gloss, although, unlike Waller, Marvell at least names him:

*The Duke himself (though Penn did not forget)*
*Yet was not out of danger's random set.*
*Falmouth was there (I know not what to act—*
*Some say 'twas to grow duke, too, by contact);*
*An untaught bullet in its wanton scope*
*Quashes him to pieces and his hope.*
*Such as his rise such was his fall, unpraised;*
*A chance shot sooner took than chance him raise.*
*His shattered head the fearless duke distains*
*And gave the last-first proof that he had brains.* *

Heads had certainly been broken and brains spilled before in both war and war literature. But the head splitting and bone cracking is usually in the general context of the glory or at least the inevitability of war and battle, where male bodies participate in a transcendent and transfiguring violence. Unlike previous satires of war and the warlike, "The Second

* The Penn mentioned here is the Quaker William Penn's father.

Advice to a Painter" highlights recognizes the possibility of inglorious death and mocks the heroic transcendence that Falmouth—and by extension all men at war, especially aristocrats—seeks. Violence here deflates aspiration of all sorts, and no one, even of high rank, is spared.

These so-called Painter poems are thus part of a self-consciousness about not only the heroics of war but also the assumptions about war making that characterized a good proportion of European opinion after the Thirty Years' War, even while Louis XIV was intent on gobbling up more territory. Only a small minority took up the critical view, and it hardly signals any great change in the connection between warfare and national interests. The eighteenth century was in fact an age that institutionalized the military and embraced war as a primary form of foreign policy. But at the same time, "The Second Advice" presciently marks how the next century would also nurture a growing skeptical attitude toward war in general, as both an arena of personal honor and an instrument of national identity.

It is not only the unthinking poetic celebration of war that Marvell's satire attacked, but also the audience that complacently read such poems and viewed such paintings without a thought for the gruesome deaths and shattered bodies they necessarily entail. The lure of war as spectacle has a long history. Louis XIV's court went out on excursions to watch nearby battles, Washington society climbed into their carriages to visit the Battle of Bull Run, and every American with a television set tuned in to CNN during the Gulf War. The upper classes may have monopolized the spectatorship of war before the advent of mass media, but the rest of us can now easily join in.

By contrast, aboard the duke of York's flagship in "The Second Advice," the exalted spectacle that many would like war to be abruptly explodes in their faces, splattering the duke with the gore of his less fortunate companions. Waller's poem ultimately generates more advice to painters to paint what really happened, instead of what the royal war makers want the public to think happened. Like "The Second Advice," these later poems both satirize Waller's bland celebration by stressing that the concept of military heroism ennobles for individuals what is collectively a bloody slaughter, even for the winners. It is a lesson that the Napoleonic Wars, the American Civil War, and World War I will make even more obvious.

The only fighter unambiguously celebrated in all these antiheroic poems is a certain Captain Douglas, referred to in "The Last Instructions to a Painter" as "the loyal Scot," who dies on his burning ship:

*Like a glad lover, the fierce flames he meets,*
*And tries his first embraces in their sheets. . . .*
*And, as on angels' heads their glories shine,*
*His burning locks adorn his face divine.*
*But when in his immortal mind he felt*
*His altering form and soldered limbs to melt,*
*Down on the deck he laid himself and died,*
*With his dear sword reposing by his side. . . .*

In the immediate political context, Douglas's purity was directly contrary to the corrupt machinations of the supposedly patriotic British court. But in contrast to the traditional hirsute and muscled stereotype of the warriors celebrated as "British heroes," Douglas also seems unmanly, even effeminate. Although the historical Douglas had a wife and children, what the poet stresses is a sexual purity almost on the verge of androgyny: "modest beauty yet his sex did veil,/While envious virgins hope he is a male." Instead of sex, it is war that is his beloved, and death in war the consummation he seeks. The clear implication is that because of the corruption of war and war making, the military assumptions about what constitutes manliness have themselves become questionable. In this dawn of the tightening connection between male individualism, sexual self-definition, and national identity, Douglas represents a prophetic and paradoxical effort to regain male stature in a very different way. He is neither the ferocious soldier nor the self-aggrandizing aristocrat, but another kind of warrior, more akin to what the revived Arthurian Galahad will be for nineteenth-century England: the warrior as purifier of the warrior tradition itself, without sexuality, without competitiveness, with only personal pride and the zeal for self-sacrifice.

# THE FIELD OF BATTLE: MONARCH'S EYE

When the equation of man and soldier is in question, as it is in the poems of Rochester or in the character of Douglas, then male sexuality and the relative meaning of male and female are in question as well. The eighteenth century was an age of belief in man's ability to penetrate and control nature through intellect, an age enamored of the idea of progress, an inexorable movement forward like that already apparent in such scientific discoveries as gravity (Isaac Newton), calculus (G. W. Leibniz), properties of gases (Robert Boyle), and oxygen (Antoine Lavoisier and Joseph Priestley), among many others. But cultural change rarely moves forward with the same obvious improvement of today over yesterday and tomorrow over today that seems to exist in science. Often styles of being long outdated are resurrected as possible ways of meeting a new world. So at the end of the eighteenth century Don Juan and Faustus were revived by Mozart and

Goethe—two hundred years or more after their first vogue—to express something of the search for images of masculinity at the time of the American and French Revolutions.

In a world where the monarch had run foreign policy alone, wars were slowly beginning to be debated, although political animosities were hard to tell from principled dissent. In early-eighteenth-century England, for example, Tory hostility to the bellicosity with which Robert Walpole and the ruling Whig party conducted foreign policy resulted in a negative view of war generally. Thus Jonathan Swift, a notable anti-Whig and critic of the military heroics of Marlborough, in *Gulliver's Travels* has the king of Brobdingnag severely question Gulliver's bland celebration of English politics:

> He wondered to hear me talk of such chargeable and extensive wars; that certainly we must be a quarrelsome people, or live among very bad neighbours, and that our generals must needs be richer than our kings. He asked what business we had out of our own islands, unless upon the score of trade or treaty, or to defend the coasts with our fleet. Above all, he was amazed to hear me talk of a mercenary standing army in the midst of peace, and among a free people. (105)

Gulliver is taken aback at the king's lack of understanding and tries to change his mind by describing the conduct of wars, especially the invention of the cannon, which Gulliver offers to duplicate for his host. The king, of course, is even more horrified:

> He was amazed how so impotent and groveling an insect as I (these were his expressions) could entertain such inhuman ideas, and in so familiar a manner as to appear wholly unmoved at all the scenes of blood and desolation, which I had painted as the common effects of those destructive machines, whereof he said, some evil genius, enemy to mankind, must have been their first contriver. (109)

Swift's portrayal of the magnanimity of the king, in contrast with the unthinking bloodthirstiness and greed of Gulliver, underlines his nostalgia for a truly humane monarchical society rather than the budding parliamentary democracy in which he found himself. But standing armies were a common fact of European life in the eighteenth century, and, as warfare took its place in national identity and pride, the soldier became a more familiar element of peacetime society. Even in England, where opposition to a standing army had been the rallying cry against royal tyranny, the military man and the military hero joined the pantheon of popular figures. As playwrights and novelists from George Farquhar (at the time of the War of the Spanish Succession) to Jane Austen (during the Napoleonic Wars) attest, the military character as well as the military influence on male character again became interesting to writers, more so than at any time since the plays of Shakespeare. Battles were experienced, recounted, or (as in Henry Fielding's *Tom Jones*) avoided, and soldiers appeared not just as caricatured types but also as part of a complex social fabric. Increasingly, being in the military was a lifetime career. Both armies and navies had become permanent arms of the state, and the plain-spoken, sometimes uncivilized, often brutal soldier characters of the seventeenth century were socialized into peacetime heroes and lovers.*

In the European eighteenth century, two prime perspectives on war can be distinguished. The first, rooted in the rise of monarchy and the state organized for war, emphasized a top-down authority in which the soldier was a tool on the battlefield, not an individual but an object like a toy soldier, to be moved back and forth at the whim of his commanders. Closely connected to this view was a growing nationalism in which the individual combatant easily identified with his monarch and thereby with his country. The other perspective comes at the same experiences, but from the focus of the confused and uncertain individual.

This soldier's-eye view of battle, the heroic inspiration faced with the bloody actuality, would have more and more spokesmen as the centuries wore on. But for most of the seventeenth and eighteenth centuries, the God's-eye view of the monarch was more pervasive. It characterizes, for example, both the political strategy and the battlefield tactics of Louis XIV. Like the symmetrically idealized palaces and gardens at Versailles and Vaux-le-Vicomte, all that exists is seen best from only one point of view, the overpowering monarchical perspective. It may be too appropriate a detail, but it is certainly satisfying to know that the young Louis was given a set of silver toy soldiers and artillery. Vauban, the great builder of fortresses and fortifications, had supervised its manufacture.

* As a lieutenant in the Grenadiers, Farquhar often put soldiers in his plays, whereas Austen's sympathetic military men are exclusively from the navy, the more respectable branch of the services.

But the ironies of Louis XIV's miniaturized war hardly end there. As Antonia Fraser has noted, "It is probable that this splendid army was eventually melted down to pay for [his] highly expensive campaigns" (86).*

In the course of eighteenth-century war and politics, Louis XIV's view from above became even more intricate and detailed. Frederick the Great, king of Prussia from 1740 to 1786, set the style of eighteenth-century war that every military man of ambition wanted to emulate: the thinking soldier who also happened to be an absolute monarch, sending his generals a constant stream of his own rules for drill, battle, and campaign, along with lengthy translations of the extracted wisdom of other writers on military affairs, classical and contemporary. In particular, the Seven Years' War, which Frederick fought against a coalition including Austria, Russia, and France, marks an epoch in the writing of military manuals, the appearance of books on strategy and tactics, the scientific and engineering analysis of weaponry, the logistics of troop movement, along with, at midcentury, the founding of military schools and academies in France, Austria, and elsewhere—all bent on rationalizing the operations of war and the behavior of officers and soldiers. Across Europe, fueled by Frederick's example, there arose a widening competitiveness not only in the theory and practice of warfare, but even in its uniforms, parades, and general display. Frederick's influence as a model stretched far beyond the actual leaders of men who might put what they considered to be his precepts into practice. Fraser in her *History of Toys* remarks that the most widespread manufacture of soldier toys in the eighteenth century, when they became playthings outside the aristocracy and royal court, was in the congeries of states called Germany. In short, war had become both an object of study for soldiers and its intricacies a source of entertainment for children.

Yet in some basic way, Frederick's reputation was also a throwback to the military monarchs of the seventeenth century like Gustavus Adolphus of Sweden and Louis XIV in France; it only very slightly reflected the new attitudes toward war that were beginning to affect the popular imagination. His preparations for battle harked back to the innovations of Maurice of Nassau in the early seventeenth century, emphasizing rigorous drillwork that allowed his armies a speed of maneuver and movement that dazzled opposing generals. After the long, thin lines of the seventeenth century, Frederick also brought back column warfare, in which the

* Vauban also introduced the socket bayonet, which replaced the pike and allowed common soldiers on both sides to be brought more directly into the face of the enemy.

individual soldier was part of a virtual military machine, firing volleys that, at least in theory, were meant to overpower the enemy.

But unlike such forerunners as Sun Tzu, who stressed being able to outwit and outmaneuver the enemy by appearing in the least expected place, Frederick had to deal with a large and unwieldy mass of soldiers. Consequently, he frequently advised a manipulation of appearances. Look weak when you're actually strong, he writes, and strong when you are about to collapse: "An army must always put up a good front, and when it is on the verge of withdrawing, it should give the enemy the impression it intends to fight" (Luvaas, 325). In the Seven Years' War, such tactics brought enough victories, as well as enough narrow escapes from defeat, to put Prussia firmly into the ranks of major European powers, even though little actual territory was won.

Perhaps because of his reliance on military theater, the widespread imitation of Frederick's military style (not always with his successes) helped for a time to reestablish the monarch not just as ruler but preeminently as First Soldier. It was a style of rule that had ample precedent in the earlier part of the century through such figures as Charles XII of Sweden (who died in 1718), Peter the Great of Russia (1725), and Frederick's own father, Frederick William I of Prussia (1740). Peter in particular had remade an inherited army and navy that were inefficiently managed and indifferently equipped. In stark contrast, Frederick the Great commanded an army that had been built first by his grandfather and later by his father, Frederick William, who had made it perhaps the largest in Europe, famously creating a personal troop of excessively tall soldiers on horses to intimidate his enemies—an eighteenth-century equivalent of the Scandinavian berserkers.

But Frederick the Great did all that and more, developing both strategy and tactics that could be admired, argued over, and replayed by professionals and amateurs alike. For a time, France, Spain, Austria, and Russia danced to his tune. Joseph II of Austria, for example, against the wishes of his chancellor insisted on personally commanding his army against the invading Turks in 1788, and even Catherine the Great reviewed her army in military attire (although perhaps not so sveltely fitted into her jodphurs as Marlene Dietrich would be playing her in *Scarlet Empress*).

In terms of the increasing publicity of monarchy, the period just before the American and French Revolutions emphasized a "greatness" that was defined specifically in terms of how much a ruler, or his generals, marched his country toward military victory. In eighteenth-century

Prussia, Russia, and Austria particularly, the army became the center of the state in a way that prophesied the later rise of Napoleon in France, whose troops would bring those previously triumphant states to their knees. Wars were started and stopped at the impetus of sovereigns who had taken total command of foreign policy, and foreign policy meant primarily war or the threat of war. In some countries, principally England, there was a growing public opinion (and a parliamentary control over the monarch's purse strings) strong enough to assert the demands of domestic policy as well. But for the most part, war was the center of all political policy—the normal state of things—and to maintain its position in Europe, the Americas, and around the world, England was constantly in arms as well.

In the Europe where war was the prime instrument of national assertion, military figures were the men admired, the ideals and examples for male behavior in everyday life. At the same time, however, both war and politics had become the concerns of an increasingly wide audience; they were no longer the private preserve of the ruling dynasty. Thus the same leaders who were celebrated by some might be mocked, along with war itself, by their political and cultural rivals. Marlborough's many victories were scorned by English Tories as Whiggish warmongering and self-aggrandizement, while writers such as Lessing attacked Frederick the Great's visions of Prussian military power as integrally related to his adoration of France and his total distaste for German culture.

In terms of the "great men" of war, then, the seventeenth and eighteenth centuries mark a decided shift away from the most celebrated names being either the monarch, who ruled by inherited authority, or the military entrepreneur, who mustered armies through their money and bureaucratic sway over their mercenary troops (like Wallenstein during the Thirty Years' War). Frederick was in fact an idiosyncratic exception to the new heroes, who were cast in a more explicitly nationalist mold, sometimes monarchs like the energetic Charles XII of Sweden or Peter the Great of Russia, but more often such political generals as Marlborough and George Washington, a genealogy of talent rather than birth whose most notable issue would be Napoleon.

Napoleon certainly agreed with Rochester (and Hobbes before him) about the primacy of fear and self-interest in human motivation, especially of men on the battlefield. But instead of Frederick's constant maneuverings and wars of attrition that exploited small advantages, Napoleon in his heyday pressed forward to decisive battles that would bring absolute victory. As a former artillery officer, he emphasized massive bombardments before and during battle along with immediate engagements of his troops in direct shock tactics. Unlike the seventeenth-century wars in which slow attrition determined who would remain victorious after the last *sou* was spent, decisive battle emphasized not just defeating but destroying the enemy, and preferably right away.

In such an environment, the state's military power and its monarch-general, figurehead or leader, also defined the core of a growing nationalism. In England, in the early part of the century, the symbol of John Bull had suggested the possibility of a nationalism unrelated to the current dynasty. But in most of Europe sovereigns ruled subjects who owed them personal allegiance, and rulers tried to consolidate political power on the basis of an officer class. A century after the traditional aristocratic role in warfare had been undermined by gunpowder and entrepreneurial captains who could muster enough soldiers to fill the ranks of newly expanded armies, the nobility was making a comeback as the foundation of the officer classes, not this time as the antagonists of the monarch but as his handmaidens. In Frederick the Great's Prussia, for example, even though citizens were protected from high-handed treatment by soldiers, there was no doubt who was closer to the real life of the state. Unusually hospitable to foreigners who could help the economy, Prussia was still a garrison society founded on military hierarchy, in which the monarch had decreed that a soldier should fear his officers more than the enemy—a precept that lasted at least down to the U.S. Marine Corps drill instructors after World War II.

In part, this reinvestment of the aristocracy with military privilege was practical. Especially in those states, for the most part in Eastern Europe, that were bellicose by tradition but without the tax or fiscal system to support their ambitions, the expense of being an officer, who might have to clothe and feed his own unit, limited who could do it. No longer knights except in propaganda, aristocrats had instead become officers. In France, for example, the higher realms of war were still aspired to as a class privilege. Shortly before the revolution, in the face of those rich upstarts who were buying their commissions, the Ordinance Ségur (1781) decreed that an officer had to have four noble ancestors—a number reminiscent of that decreed centuries before as the precondition for participation in prestigious tournaments.

In the absence of a national cause other than the sovereign's will, military hierarchy and military tradition themselves were extolled. For many of the countries of Europe in the eighteenth and nineteenth centuries, as Alfred Vagts points out, "*esprit de corps* was considered by the officer

Column of Marcus Aurelius

Like its second-century a.d. predecessor, Trajan's column, this one celebrates military victories—in this case over the Germanic tribes—through a soaring cylindrical shaft topped by a statue of the emperor. Spiraling up its side is a bas-relief narrative of the wars.

Bayeux Tapestry

This eleventh-century embroidery presents the Norman Conquest from the Norman point of view: William the Conqueror was compelled to invade England because Harold, whom he had saved from death and who had sworn fealty to him, had nevertheless assumed the throne. In this late scene, the Battle of Hastings (1066) has been won by the death of Harold—*Hic Harold Rex interfectus est* (Here King Harold is killed)—who is shot in the eye with an arrow. Both sides wear mail armor. The French are on horseback while the English stand, holding spears and battle axes. Archery had a low tactical priority at this time. Below the scene, the dead are being stripped of their armor.

The Duke of Anhalt in a Mêlée

Before individual knights tilted against each other in stately single combats, the usual style of tournament fighting was similar to that of the battlefield, with a swarm of armed knights slashing at one another in a confined space, as depicted in this medieval scene, while an audience of women watches, making enigmatic hand gestures.

Trench Warfare, World War I

Before an attack, British soldiers look out into no-man's-land, the space between opposing trenches, where enemy troops have waited, virtually without significant movement, for months and years. The primitive gas masks, cloth moistened with a chemical solution, date this photograph to 1915, probably during the battle of Ypres.

MARS AND VENUS

In this first-century A.D. detail for the House of the Punishment of Cupid in Pompeii, Cupid hovers in the background while a helmeted Mars rests his spear and fondles Venus's breast. Venus looks less like a goddess than like a Roman matron, perhaps to emphasize the seductiveness of the warrior for respectable women.

BAYEUX TAPESTRY

In the midst of an otherwise political and military narrative appears this enigmatic scene, in which a tonsured cleric (*clericus*), standing next to a remarkably phallic tower, looks as though he is angrily striking a woman (Aelfgyva), but nothing tells us why. Below, a naked man may be offering some clue to the situation.

VENUS AND MARS SURPRISED BY VULCAN

(Hendrick Goltzius, 1585) The other Olympian gods watch as the liaison of Mars and Venus is revealed. In the background the cuckolded Vulcan prepares an iron net to imprison them. On the floor in front, Mars's discarded shield and sword testify to his vulnerability.

Venus and Mars Surprised by Vulcan

(François Boucher, 1754) In this detail, the main reference to the mythological story is in the title and the net being held by Vulcan. Otherwise, the image could be of any husband or lover coming on an illicit scene.

The Romantic Side of Knighthood

Knightly deference to women wasn't just an invention of Hollywood films. Here, Ulrich von Liechtenstein, a famous knight of the thirteenth century, wears his "Lady Venus" helmet. Ulrich wrote a poem about his adventures going from tournament to tournament in this disguise. Later, he took on a similar tournament-to-tournament quest, challenging all comers in the name of King Arthur.

THE ARMED SAINT

Saint Demetrius, portrayed in this Byzantine ivory icon from the second half of the tenth century, was supposedly a converted Roman soldier who was martyred in Thessalonica. Along with Saint George he was a patron saint of Crusaders.

SAINT MICHAEL ENTHRONED BETWEEN SAINT ANTHONY THE ABBOT AND SAINT JOHN THE BAPTIST

(Angelo Puccinelli) This late-fourteenth-century Sienese altarpiece depicts Michael as captain of the heavenly hosts in the fight against Satan, his breastplate in place and his sword at the ready.

Saint Sebastian

(Antonio and Piero del Pollaiuolo, 1475) Saint Sebastian was supposedly a captain in Emperor Diocletian's Praetorian guard and a protector of Christians; he was executed when his own Christianity became known. In a few early images he is old and bearded. But in the fifteenth century the image of a young man pierced with arrows became immensely popular.

Knight, Death, and the Devil

(Albrecht Dürer, 1521) Perhaps basing his engraving on Erasmus's conception of the Christian knight, Dürer, at the dawn of the Reformation, created a symbolic figure pursuing his quest while outfacing or ignoring the forces of darkness.

PORTRAIT OF A HALBERDIER

(Giacomo Pontormo, 1529–30) This young man was part of the civil guard of Florence at a time of intense civil war between factions supporting and opposing the Medici family. With his smooth features and his foppish dress, his look contrasts sharply with both the stern knight of the Middle Ages and the unshaven dogface of World War II.

CAPTAIN THOMAS LEE

(Marcus Gheeraerts the Younger, 1594) There are mixed messages here: Lee is dressed down with the bare legs and feet of an Irish kern or foot soldier, but he also wears a fancy shirt and carries an expensive helmet indicative of his social rank. The portrait resembles those the Dutch called *tronie,* in which the sitter wears armor that is decidedly antique and nostalgic. Lee's symbolic connection here is with the poor, "barbaric" soldiers who conquer by their fighting spirit as much as by their weapons.

JIM BRIDGER IN A SUIT OF ENGLISH ARMOR

(Alfred Jacob Miller, 1837) Miller made this wash drawing while accompanying Sir William Drummond Stewart, a veteran of Waterloo, on a trip from the Missouri frontier to western Wyoming. Stewart so admired Bridger, the famous trapper and mountain man, that he gave him a full suit of armor, which Bridger wore on special occasions.

BRITAIN NEEDS YOU AT ONCE

Saint George kills the dragon once again, this time in 1915 on behalf of the Parliamentary Recruiting Committee.

PRINCE ALBERT AT AGE TWENTY-FOUR

(Robert Thorburn, 1843) As a young man, Albert liked to play chivalric games and was an enthusiastic supporter of the revival of Arthurian imagery in British art and politics. This miniature shows him in archaic armor, reflecting his commitment to a combination of social virtue and personal honor that he and many others associated with medieval knighthood.

nobility as militarily superior to nationalism" (86). I have pointed to the development of a self-conscious "science" of war in the eighteenth century as an indication of the growing need for professionalization as armies grew larger and weapons more complex. But the favoring of officers whose only qualification was their birth hardly died out, nor did the new textbooks eliminate (sometimes they even fostered) a rote-driven incompetence. Loyalty to military tradition, as embodied in the regiment or the drill manual or some combination of both, often overpowered the urge to win. To disdain the specifics of terrain in order to maintain a close-order formation possible only on the parade ground, to refuse to dull the metal of armaments so that they couldn't catch the sun and reveal a position, to consider battle as a gigantic canvas on which personal and unit honor were the main goals—all these and more were exemplified in eighteenth- and nineteenth-century warfare, down to such fiascoes as the notorious Charge of the Light Brigade in the Crimean War, or the first years of trench warfare on the Somme and the Marne.

For some rulers, however, the social stability gained by restoring the aristocracy as the military officer class threatened to be at the expense of military effectiveness, and in many countries, officers in the eighteenth-century army could no longer rely solely on aristocratic birth as a sufficient qualification for warfare. Instead of manipulating toy soldiers, more and more officers were being forced to learn how to see war as a complicated problem that needed analysis and study. In the Austrian army under Maria Theresa, for example, the older system of nobles who virtually owned their own troops was being replaced by what Jeremy Black has described as "a military establishment financed by regular taxation and commanded by loyal professionals" (130). To focus the wavering attention of young men on a military career, Maria Theresa decreed that becoming a professional officer could raise a man to the nobility. It was a policy that went back to the roots of knighthood in the Middle Ages, when landless knights were given land and status in exchange for military service. Instead of just assuming the nobility's role as the hereditary warrior class, in other words, Maria Theresa's policy explicitly acknowledged that this was a specific social route by which warriors could become hereditary nobility.

But there was no sure way to balance the claims of hereditary privilege and the needs of modern war. The Ordinance Ségur in France was not simply a rearguard action by nobles wanting to preserve their ancient privileges; it was aimed specifically against the growing practice of buying one's way into an officership. In contrast, in England the duke of

Marlborough had championed the sale of military offices both to evade parliamentary control and to prevent aristocrats with no ability at all from expecting a position as their class due. The ordinance did allow a small safety valve to the nonnoble classes by allowing those without adequate pedigree to apply for lower positions, or to go through military college—the route taken by the son of an impoverished family of the provincial nobility, Napoleon Bonaparte.

In the formulation of the ideal officer there thus came to be a conflict between justification by birth and justification by training. The aristocrat was a career soldier by class but often without any specific war-making ability, part of a system of entrenched privilege that would be shaken up by Napoleon's defeats of the old monarchies. But even Napoleon, for all his talk of "careers open to talents," sought legitimation under the old banners, not just the Roman revivals of the titles of consul and emperor, but also the reestablishment of an aristocratic hierarchy in which he himself was the center. Similarly, the cavalry, which had been declining in military importance almost as long as the middle class had been rising in economic importance, revived in tandem with its aristocratic sponsors. Frederick's war of movement indicated how wars had shifted away from siege warfare and its primary reliance on infantry. Often in seventeenth- and eighteenth-century battles, cavalry and infantry attacked together. But as deployed by Napoleon, for instance, cavalry reassumed some of its psychologically intimidating aspect. Infantry and artillery softened up the enemy line while cavalry stood in readiness to make the decisive blast through—a tactic that was still in the armory of the European military until World War I, when it gradually became clear it was totally unfitted for trench warfare.

# THE FIELD OF BATTLE: SOLDIER'S EYE

The history of a soldier's wound beguiles the pain of it.
—Laurence Sterne, *Tristram Shandy* (1760)

The literary roots of the soldier's-eye view are in those solitary adventurers, like Nashe's Jack Wilton or Cervantes's Don Quixote, who inhabit works usually referred to as picaresque, that is, stories structured by one person's adventures. From the *Odyssey* onward, the picaresque is a kind of literature that flourishes particularly in the aftermath of wars, when the collective vision of battle gives way to the individual's effort to make sense of what has happened. Wilton bears witness to the grimness of sixteenth-century battle while Don Quixote strives to restore a golden age of knight-errantry and chivalric honor. But neither condemns the motivations of either war or warriors. It will be in the nineteenth and twentieth centuries that writers take that next step in figures like Byron's Don Juan at the Battle of Ismail (1790), Stendhal's Fabrizio del Dongo in *The Charterhouse of Parma*, and Tolstoy's Pierre in *War and Peace* at the Battle of Borodino (1812)—soldiers who wander their battlefields with hardly a clue about what's going on in the "big picture."

From the perspective of the common soldier or lowly officer participant, war was not the road to glory or the game of kings, but a deadly testing ground for the uncertain willingness to sacrifice personal nature to national goals. At Ismail, says Byron, Juan and his friend Johnson

> *. . . fought away with might and main, not knowing*
> *The way which they had never trod before,*
> *And still less guessing where they might be going;*
> *But on they marched, dead bodies trampling o'er,*
> *Firing, and thrusting, slashing, sweating, glowing,*
> *But fighting thoughtlessly enough to win,*
> *To their two selves, one whole bright bulletin.* (250)

Only the promise of glory, their names in a report of heroism in battle—the "bright bulletin"—lights their way through the havoc and chaos. Otherwise, for Juan,

> *He knew not where he was, nor greatly cared,*
> *For he was dizzy, busy, and his veins*
> *Filled as with lightning—for his spirit shared*
> *The hour, as is the case with lively brains. . . .* (253)

In the words of "The Second Advice to a Painter," more than a century and a half before, when it comes to the experience of war, the celebratory clarity of painting is a sham: "The noise, the smoke, the sweat, the fire, the blood,/Are not to be expressed or understood." This may seem to be a poetic vision, mixed with a helping of polemical politics. But for the individual soldier, it was also realistic. After a very few eighteenth- and early-nineteenth-century volleys, smoke was everywhere and little could be seen even in the immediate area. Intent on reloading as quickly as possible (estimates vary from one to five shots a minute), the soldier was lost in a confusing swirl of his own and his comrades' making. As Clausewitz said in *On War,* his post-Napoleonic meditation on the new face of warfare, while the ideal ends of war dreamed by generals and politicians might be rational, the natural state of the battlefield is confusion.

To characterize war as confusion was a particularly nineteenth-century perception, in great part because the Napoleonic Wars were the first in which enough officers and common soldiers had both the literacy and the interest to write letters about their experience and even to publish their memoirs. The bewildered Don Juan does nothing to discern, let alone make sense of, what is happening around him; only the strophes of Byron's poem and his witty rhymes offer any sense of order. One of Juan's most intriguing eighteenth-century forerunners, however, like an Enlightenment philosopher dedicated to the power of his own reason, desperately wants his experience to make sense. This character is Uncle Toby Shandy in Laurence Sterne's *Tristram Shandy.* Sterne's novel began appearing in 1759, but Toby's war experiences are in the armies of the duke of Marlborough in the late seventeenth century. There, among the defensive walls of the town of Namur—which would be one of the first in Belgium to fall to the Germans in World War I—Toby was wounded in the groin.

Unlike Swift's (and Gulliver's) more general argument about war, Uncle Toby's concerns are very personal. He shows no explicit philosophic or political distaste for war, and in many ways is an embodiment of the stock figure of the garrulous and obsessive old soldier, sweeping the dinner table clean and refighting his battles with saltshakers and pepper mills. But Toby also wants to ask the unanswerable question: Why was I wounded? In search of an answer, he and his fellow casualty Corporal Trim are in the process of first mapping and then reconstructing the battle of Namur on the Shandy bowling green. Once every detail of the fortifications and the weaponry is mapped, and the place where he was wounded precisely determined, then and then only will Toby be able to explain his wound to himself. In the absence of rituals that justify the wound, to specify it by time and place and detail is to regain power over the wounding.

The swaggering soldier-penis of Rochester's "Imperfect Enjoyment" reveals this traditional figure of sexual license and bravado as actually a hollow shell, but one still oblivious to his emptiness. Toby's greater awareness creates the model of Namur with its trenches and fortifications in a comic but pathetic effort to surround himself and his wound with an impregnable explanation that will hold off all besiegers. Like a parody of the new strategists of the eighteenth century, hovering over tables of toy soldiers, founding military academies, and writing manuals of arms, Toby wants certainty. His search for an unequivocal answer is endless because it tries to make the events of battle logical and explainable rather than haphazard and irrational.

Toby's urge to heal his sexual wound by explaining its precise place in the Battle of Namur is only one of the most elaborate set pieces in *Tristram Shandy,* a novel filled with male characters who are trying to order and explain the vagaries of both history and human experience. Tristram's father, Walter, for example, consults reams of authoritative texts in order to choose what he considers the best name for his new son, Trismegisthus (with its connotations of magical power). But by an accident of miscommunication, the boy is dubbed the worst name, Tristram (with its connotations of the fatal wounds of love). As Toby's story also makes clear, the need to construct such systems of explanation is an effort to control the world of chance and accident, and finally to compensate in some way for a direct wound to the seat of masculinity. Like "the loyal Scot" Douglas mating with his burning ship, Toby's effort to reconstruct the battle—what Sterne calls his "hobbyhorse"—is his true love. Yet the cycle of wounding is endless, and in order to salve his own sexual wound, Toby inadvertently becomes the cause of others. In one instance he steals the sash weights from a window to be used in a mock cannon. When Susannah the maid raises the window and places the five-year-old Tristram in the window seat to urinate out the window, the window falls and circumcises him. As the older Tristram dryly remarks, "*Susannah* did not consider that nothing was well hung in our family." War, whether in reality or in replica, is simultaneously the quintessence of masculinity and the greatest threat to it.

As Toby's example shows, the lot of the individual soldier in eighteenth-century war was often "unmanned if you do and unmanned if you don't." A similarly divided view can be found in the attitudes of an even more archetypal eighteenth-century Englishman than the fictional Uncle Toby: Samuel Johnson, shortly after the beginning of the American rebellion. In one mood, Johnson believes that the urge to be a soldier is part of general masculine character: "Every man thinks meanly of himself for not having been a soldier, or not having been at sea" (Boswell, 926). The word "meanly" is striking here, with its invocation of a form of guilt, as are the words "every man." Although the male aristocrat had lived by the premise that not being engaged in war was a blot on his honor, it is relatively new to presume that such an urge to war, and the feeling of guilt if one does not go to war, exists for the generality of men.

When Johnson uttered this sentiment, however, it was predicated on a very specific sense of the call of national duty that would hardly have been there for the nonnoble in the Middle Ages, or the nonprofessional thereafter. At another time, and in a somewhat different mood, Johnson says that patriotism is "the last refuge of a scoundrel." Worried that Johnson will be misunderstood, Boswell rushes forward to assure us that Johnson's statement does not refer to "a real and generous love of our country, but that pretended patriotism which so many, in all ages and countries, have made a cloak of self-interest" (615). For one who has said that military service is an essential element, even the armature, of male identity, the potentially corrupt patriotism of even the most blameless politician is implicitly contrasted with the purer motives of the soldier. The fervent commitment to Napoleon as the embodiment of France that helped the legendary Nicolas Chauvin give his name to the extreme nationalistic attitude we call chauvinism waits in the future. But Johnson's remarks, in their milder way, similarly emphasize how revulsion with politics and politicians can inspire the political urge to turn governments over to the leadership of soldiers.

Yet at the same time that Johnson voices some universal male anxiety about missing military service, he also considers the lives of both soldier and sailor to be horrible. In his view, they are dignified only by the ability to overcome fear, which happens, he says, principally because of the presence of a collective venture: "Soldiers consider themselves only as parts of a great machine." Although Johnson also remarked, "A soldier's time is passed in distress and danger, or in idleness and corruption," he much preferred the soldier's life to that of the sailor, which he described as "such crowding, such filth, such stench!" (927).

How to explain the longing so intertwined with the distaste? One political reason that Johnson can say such things may be that the English were virtually unique in Europe in having some civilian control over the military (although not so much that the Declaration of Independence wouldn't make unreasonable military authority over civilian affairs one of its prime complaints). Gulliver makes fun of the Brobdingnagians for having an army whose soldiers were only the tradesmen of the town and country people, led by nobles without pay—in other words, not a professional standing army, but a militia or, as they were then called, armed bands. Although to Gulliver this seems the opposite of the true heroics of war, the antipathy to standing armies helped ensure that even when its armies were used to put down popular rebellions England never imitated the military states and courts of Prussia and Austria.

But there is as well an emotional root to Johnson's remarks, a sense of the coalescence of individual and national identity that is reflected by his *Dictionary of the English Language*, with its codification of English culture as an emanation of the written language, hostile to both aristocratic influence and patronage. Finally, it is the great soldier who is Johnson's idea of the prime sort of man:

> Were Socrates and Charles Twelfth of Sweden both present in any company, and Socrates to say, "Follow me, and hear a lecture on philosophy"; and Charles, laying a hand on his sword, to say, "Follow me, and dethrone the Czar"; a man would be ashamed to follow Socrates. (926–27)

This is Socrates the philosopher, of course, not Socrates the citizen soldier, and, although Charles was a king, it is more important that he was a hero. Charles XII had died in 1718 and Voltaire had written a biography detailing his reckless military adventures, his brilliant headlong successes in battle, and his defeat after taking his army to the gates of Moscow, bringing glory to himself even as he effectively destroyed his country as both a military and political power. But despite Voltaire's bitter criticisms, Johnson's comments attest that Charles was still igniting heroic spirits some seventy years after his death, at much the same time that Voltaire himself was flattering Frederick the Great as a philosopher king.

The Enlightenment sense of the power of individual reason thus plays an odd counterpoint to the continuation of dynastic wars, as well as to the admiration of the *encyclopédistes* and philosophes for the prime architect of and standard-bearer for the new self-consciousness about war—Frederick the Great. Like Voltaire, many of the writers of the French Enlightenment were generally antiwar, although they often had a soft spot for so-called benevolent despots like Frederick or Catherine, who showed their heroic individualism by embracing French culture. Such rulers, along with Maria Theresa and Joseph II in Austria, on the eve of the democratic revolutions in America and France, continued to represent the ideal combination of national and dynastic destiny in an era of larger and larger armies, complete, thanks to the new technology of prepackaged cartridges and lighter cannons, with a more rapid and deadly rate of musket and artillery fire.*

In military affairs, the eighteenth century marked a renewed expansion of the size, equipment, and organization of armies and the deindividualizing of the role of the single soldier. In the realm of ideas and literature, it was characterized by an emphasis on the archetypal individual and first-

* Cast-iron cannons had by this time replaced the heavily ornamented brass of the previous century.

person perspective. European Christianity was becoming a religion rather than what it had been before (and still is for fundamentalists): a way of understanding all experience. Religious categories gave way to a secular meditation on the essence of the individual. The *honnête homme,* the libertine, and the noble savage of the seventeenth century had been particular social (and antisocial) styles of behavior. Instead, the eighteenth-century Enlightenment sought to ponder rationally the central aspects of man's nature. Waiting in the wings were the "political man" of Montesquieu, Voltaire, and the philosophes, the "economic man" of Adam Smith, the "moral man" of Immanuel Kant, and other such "men"—industrial man, revolutionary man, natural man, good-natured man—all efforts to see the general case in the individual example. In attendance as well were the numerous eighteenth-century novels whose structure was basically that of the picaresque, following the adventures of a single person: *Robinson Crusoe, Moll Flanders, Tom Jones, Manon Lescaut, The Sorrows of Young Werther.*

But this interest in a new approach to the nature of man, unmediated by religion, was hardly all rational. The works listed above themselves attest to the change from the beginning of the century to the end, from Crusoe's piece-by-piece reconstruction of English civilization on his island, to Werther's suicidal passion for a married woman in the heady atmosphere of the Alps. Even more extreme versions of the first-person sensibility, as in the poetry of Byron or the tale of *Frankenstein,* emphasize the man alone, the melancholic giant striding the crags, fatally caught in a combat with God.

The atmosphere of this individualist Romanticism also helped revive the spirit of national cultures, giving an autonomous soul to what was otherwise a history of dynasties and wars. The idea of the national past became not a top-down celebration of the elite, but a bottom-up view from custom and folklore. Not long after Frederick the Great burst onto the European scene in the Seven Years' War, and in the face perhaps of his notable contempt for German literature and language, the Sturm und Drang movement in Germany celebrated the ancient myths along with such writers as Shakespeare and Homer, forerunners of genius, who had tapped the roots of human feeling. In part, Sturm und Drang seems to have been a reaction in the name of the individual voice against the militarization of social life. To the extent that war is at all praised either in German or English Romanticism, it is only in the nostalgic terms of the individual hero.

# THE UNIFORMED NATION

> It may be worth remarking, among the *minutiae* of my collection, that Johnson was once drawn to serve in the militia. . . . It may be believed that he did not serve in person; but the idea, with all its circumstances is certainly laughable. He upon that occasion provided himself with a musket, and with a sword and belt, which I have seen hanging in his closet.
>
> —James Boswell, *Life of Samuel Johnson* (1791)

The militia uniform hanging expectantly in Samuel Johnson's closet was one small example of how central uniforms were to the new identification of the soldier with the state. As armies grew larger in the seventeenth century, brightly colored uniforms helped fulfill the need to distinguish friend from foe as well as to establish a visible hierarchy loyal to the commander and thereby to the monarch. The individual soldier in uniform may have been more like his fellows than the caparisoned knight had been, but he was still noticeably different from the rest of society and from other men.

These visible distinctions of rank added an intricate set of gradations to the order of the medieval estate of the *pugnatores* that went far beyond the older distinctions of family and genealogy. As early as the 1720s, a British diplomat visiting Prussia was moved to remark on the "very odd" fact that almost all men he met were in uniform. In Russia under Peter the Great and Austria under Maria Theresa and Joseph II, as well as France during the Napoleonic empire, the military uniform became the preferred and sometimes the exclusive court dress. It represented a virtually exclusive emphasis on the ruler in his military role that extended far into the nineteenth century—by midcentury even the Ottoman sultan had shed his traditional garb to wear a uniform at court—and would be revived by the totalitarian dictatorships of the twentieth. When Louis Philippe of France, who ruled from 1830 to 1848, explicitly rejected martial paraphernalia, he was still reacting against the norm of the uniform, whether royalist or Bonapartist, and the umbrella he habitually carried (the bourgeois version of the sword?) was caricatured as a symbol of the impotence of his reign.

Just at a time, then, when secular society was in the process of dropping signifying clothing that identified men by caste, class, and profession, uniforms made soldiers more identifiable, not just on the smoke-filled battlefield but in civil society as well. As in most such cultural metamorphoses, the different rates of change are often as striking as the similarities: Louis XIV was approving uniforms for his troops in the 1670s; in contrast, there was no official uniform for British naval officers until 1748 (and none for ordinary seamen until 1857). But generally, along with the resurgent military masculinity of the early modern period came a decided helping of foppery to buttress the new regimental and national loyalty. Such flashy dress also helped to reduce the large number of friendly-fire incidents that occurred on the eighteenth-century battlefield, when detailed maps were not yet in ample supply, officers were often reduced to asking the occasional civilian passerby just where they were, and firepower had outdistanced eyesight.

By the early nineteenth century, military uniforms had reached an intricate grandiosity that historians have called the most lavish in history, and the names of many nineteenth-century generals, with the possible exception of Wellington and his boot, have been remembered longer for the clothing styles they inspired than for their battles: the Blücher shoe, the Cardigan jacket, the Raglan sleeve. The English word "uniform," which as a noun referring to military attire appears in the mid–eighteenth century (and as a verbal adjective—"a uniformed regiment"—in the early nineteenth), carries with it an atmosphere of similarity and repetition that hardly accords with the peacock prodigality of eighteenth- and nineteenth-century battle dress. It is reflected in other European languages as well, although the French alternative *tenue* (*de campagne*, or "battle dress") connects more to words meaning deportment and bearing, as the Italian *tenuta* does to words for estate or personal holding, while the German *dienstkleidung* (literally "service clothes") emphasizes the aspect of subordination. Only gradually did the distinction between fighting dress and parade dress arise. For the most part, until at least midcentury, going to war in what we would consider to be parade dress was the norm, just as British soldiers were sent around the empire wearing virtually the same uniform they would in European conflicts. Only much later, too, was there a distinction made between summer and winter uniforms. For centuries winter had meant a total cessation of hostilities, and Napoleon's *Grande Armée* trekked to Moscow and back through the deep Russian snows wearing virtually the same clothes they would have worn at the height of a summer campaign.*

The rise of the khaki uniform (together with the smokeless-powder cartridge that made excessive visibility on the battlefield a real liability) awaits in the second half of the nineteenth century. But for a time near the end of the eighteenth century the uniforms of both the French and American Revolutions attempted to reflect a democratic fashion ethos in revolt against the popinjay aristocrats that so bothered Shakespeare's Hotspur. Before 1776, the American army, disdaining the "lobsterback" gaudiness of the British troops, often fought in haphazard civilian, rural buckskin, or Indian dress. But with official war and rebellion, a national military costume was quickly established, along with a host of other national symbols like the eagle and the Stars and Stripes.†

In France, the royal fleur-de-lis disappeared and loose, striped trousers at first replaced the close-fitting knee breeches of aristocratic officers. With Napoleon's establishment of the empire and the eruption of French armies across Europe, however, uniforms once again became more elaborate, rising to ever-increasing heights of national differentiation and display. Napoleon himself for some time keeps his corporal's garb, even while his marshals embellished themselves with more and more gold braid and medals. It was an early self-conscious gesture of connection to the common soldier that would be reflected at midcentury in America by U. S. Grant, who, unlike his more elegantly bedecked rival, Robert E. Lee, always wore a private's uniform. Of course, military clothes that could

* Similarly, the uniforms worn by American soldiers in World War II were found to be impractical for Korea.

† The first official uniform color was brown (1775), which later was replaced with blue, complete with four different facings that corresponded to the states in different regions. Despite the effort of both Washington and the Continental Congress to put a uniformly dressed army in the field, fighting clothes still varied a great deal from group to group and state to state. Blue remained the most familiar, but there was much brown and red as well.

be considered democratic in contrast to an elite fastidiousness might also signal the noblesse oblige of the absolute monarch who didn't need to prove anything by an elaborate show. Frederick the Great, whose personal habits were often described as unbelievably slovenly, often led his troops in a ratty private's uniform. Unlike later, more charismatic leaders, Frederick in his unkempt uniform had little interest in the accolades of Prussian citizens for his accomplishments and no need for them to sanction his goals.

One cause for this conflict of military styles lay in the effort of the American and French Revolutions to define the nation apart from any particular ruling dynasty. For the bleary-eyed student attempting to keep straight the multitude of large and small wars that marked the eighteenth century, their names indicate how often, before the American and French Revolutions, the motive for war was dynastic expansion. In the War of the Spanish Succession, the War of the Austrian Succession, the Seven Years' War of Frederick the Great to expand Prussia into Silesia, and all the others, combatants attempted to expand power on the pretext of lines of inheritance and marriage. Such wars were still fought by countries that were in effect owned by individuals, called kings or princes, much as battle groups had once been owned by the entrepreneurial captains who raised them.

But the democratic revolutions of the late eighteenth century transformed the question into one of whether the cohesion a monarch supplies could be found in the country itself. "State," the word that had come to the fore in seventeenth-century political discussions of monarchical power, comes most directly into English from the Old French *estat,* which in turn is rooted in the Latin *status:* rank, order. When Louis XIV made his famous pronunciamento, *"L'état, c'est moi"*—I am the state—he was also saying that as monarch he encompassed the separate political estates of the realm as well: the aristocracy, the clergy, and that more amorphous third estate, composed of lesser landowners, professional men, merchants, and artisans, that during the French Revolution came to hold the balance of political power.

But "nation," sometimes used interchangeably with "state," actually carries with it, encoded in its etymology (*natus,* born), a potential disengagement from the traditional orders of social and political power, and a sense that participation in the *meaning* of the nation/country/state is the birthright of those born there. *"Je reveille pour la Nation"* crows the rooster of the revolution—"I wake up the nation." And the nation evoked by such symbols is decidedly a potential to be aroused. *"Allons, enfants de la patrie,/Le jour de gloire est arrivé*" begins the "Marseillaise"—"Let's go, children of the fatherland,/the day of glory is here." Similarly, "The Star-Spangled Banner" is not a third-person celebration like "Rule, Britannia" or "Deutschland über alles" but a direct address: "O, say can *you* see."

As new nations, both the United States and revolutionary France dug deeply within Western culture, particularly the Roman past, to come up with symbols that would connect them with a world that existed long before the advent of the medieval monarchies and dynasties. Such a nation is also more appropriately represented by the individual citizen, or a national symbol, or by a ruler, like Napoleon, who at least presumes to style himself First Citizen, than it is by any hereditary monarch. On the frontispiece of Hobbes's *Leviathan* in the mid–seventeenth century appears an image of a king (looking much like Charles I) as a giant individual whose body is made up of his multitude of tiny subjects; by the mid–eighteenth century John Bull and Britannia appear in this emblematic role much more frequently, just as Columbia and later Uncle Sam came to represent the United States, and the bare-breasted female warrior Marianne, France and the French Revolution.

Impelled by an urge to cleanse the past of political mystification and religious prejudice, writers such as David Hume in England and Voltaire in France had already created histories of their countries that could be read by any literate citizen who had the money to buy or rent them from the circulating library. Such histories helped detach the idea of "England" or "France" from being exclusively owned by a particular person or classes. They made an increasingly sharp distinction between the authority of a dynasty (along with its tendency to aggrandize its territory) and the sanction of the country itself and its traditions.

To the crucial late-eighteenth-century question of what defines a citizen and what *his* rights are, Hume, Voltaire, and others answered that it was the consciousness of history, especially national history. The philosophers of the Enlightenment were simultaneously preoccupied with the nature of *man* and with the differences between national characters, one of the most popular theories of which was Montesquieu's belief that it all came down to differences in climate. Perhaps in tribute to Montesquieu, one of the earliest acts of the French Revolution was therefore to rename the months with seasonal names like Floréal and Brumaire, as well as to change the traditional family names of regions into departments differentiated by geography. The heart of the nation was emerging, no longer warped by the incrustations of dynasty.

These fresh symbols for the newly founded or refounded nation often drew upon female imagery to emphasize a change from the male and dynastic past, an investment of spiritual energies in natural religious beliefs like deism in place of official Christianity, and a connection to the fecundity of the land rather than to the panoply of the court. They also recall foundational myths that emphasized the domestication of powerful forces—the transformation at Athens of the vengeful female Erinyes into the benevolent Eumenides; the nurturing in Rome of Romulus and Remus by the she-wolf Lupa Genetrix. I despair of making some clean generalization to account for why some countries are typically called "motherland" and others "fatherland." But it is clear that with the popular revolutions of the late eighteenth century, the family metaphor, severed from any particular dynastic genealogy, became pervasive in civil society, even in countries whose political systems were yet unaffected by revolutionary fervor. And in that family the soldier took a central role.

# CITIZENS INTO SOLDIERS, SOLDIERS INTO CITIZENS

*Aux armes, citoyens!*
*Formez vos bataillons. . . .*

—"La Marseillaise" (1792)*

Just as action in war helped identify the prime form of masculine identity and authority from the primitive tribe down into premodern Europe, it is the propaganda of men at war that has in large part defined masculine possibilities since the seventeenth and eighteenth centuries. When wars became increasingly expensive, requiring more taxation and an elaborate bureaucracy to support them, justification by national interest became more pressing than that of either dynasty or class. The interdependence of the army and the political state, the growing expense of military preparedness, have their cultural corollaries in the focus on military service as the prime form of masculine citizenship. The degree to which this occurs varies from state to state, but the overall pattern helps characterize the last few centuries in Europe as a coherent

* "To arms, citizens!/Form your battalions. . . ." "La Marseillaise" was originally titled "Chant de guerre de l'armée du Rhin."

period that may have ended or at least reached a significant moment in the 1980s with the military and political enfeeblement of Russia, until then the last intact survivor of the old balance of power.

What, then, might military service have meant to masculine identity when it was not mustered or impressed by captains, or called into being by dynastic ambitions, but defined as patriotic service for the nation? The medieval battlefield was described (by those who could write, for those who could read or be read to) primarily as a noble space, where the military aristocracy strove for glory in a competition generally closed to other classes, whatever their prowess. Traditional heroic literature makes clear that war until the age of the democratic revolutions was essentially a stage for the great in combat with enemies, whose name and status had to be known before a true battle of honor could be risked. Certainly there were instances of young men ennobled on the battlefield for their courage and valor, and many noble houses dated their founding to such acts. But it was only when the idea of the "nation" became pervasive that individual behavior in battle began to separate from both class origins and professional training and to connect more closely to conceptions of national character.

At the dawn of modern warfare, Machiavelli had declared that men will fight desperately only if they either have confidence in themselves and their past victories or esteem their general:

> Such esteem is a result of the opinion they have of his *virtù*, rather than of any particular favor they have received from him; or it is a result of their love of country, which is natural to all men. (129)

Accordingly, even before the American and French Revolutions, rulers like Louis XIV and Frederick William I (Frederick the Great's father) were moving toward the concept of a subject's obligation to do military service, an updated version of the obligations of military service and corvée labor owed to the local lord in the Middle Ages.

But obligation did not necessarily imply loyalty, patriotism, military competence, or even compliance. The need to keep troops in some kind of order and discipline naturally increased with the size of the army. As in the previous century, much of the large eighteenth-century armies were made up of the least productive members procurable from either the native country or other countries—released convicts, vagabonds, young men with no other prospects. The growing practice of impressment (seizing men off the street and packing them off to involuntary military service) merely expanded the number of reluctant soldiers looking for any easy way out once they were in uniform. Punishment and drill were two of the ways commanders kept them in. Frederick's elaborate volumes of instructions to his generals include at their heart a well-calculated fourteen rules aimed to prevent desertion. Professional soldiers below the officer class were hardly any more loyal. About one-third of Frederick's army of 160,000 were mercenaries, and he had to assume that in battle about half of those would try to run off as soon as possible. Some absolute monarchs considered hiring mercenaries to be more politically reliable than arming their own countrymen, but mercenaries were also more likely to take the money and run. Even when they fought, victory (with its spoils and booty) could be as much an inducement to decamp as defeat.

In the new mass armies of Europe, the need for organization and order was therefore a pressing issue. Although the French had begun to experiment with the division by the middle of the eighteenth century, and Napoleon would later stress the somewhat larger corps, Frederick the Great's army, like that of the Austrians, was not yet divided into smaller tactical units. Its structure was triangular, with the monarch at the top and the officer corps and a mass of soldiers below him. The drawback to creating a more complex command structure was the autonomy and independence it potentially gave to the units. As for many commanders in the seventeenth and eighteenth centuries, a pervasive element in Frederick's battle strategy was thus to minimize the possibility of desertion and focus the troops on killing the enemy.

Machiavelli's stress on "love of country" was thus easy enough to say and perhaps to manage in the context of the small city-states of sixteenth-century Italy. But the enormous dynastic armies of the eighteenth century—frequently with only the most rudimentary hierarchy of command below the level of general, organized by tabletop strategy and incessant drill, and characterized as machines when they were working well—were usually put in the field with little attention paid to what actually animates a fighting spirit. If the army, like the land itself, is the possession of the dynastic ruler, what need is there to make the individual soldier *believe* in the war? England once again somehow managed to avoid for a time some of these more egregious problems of states like Prussia or France before its revolution by gathering both its monarch and its citizens together in the name of an abstract "Britannia." But it is the

American and French revolutionary concepts of the nation in arms that most directly addressed the new reality: how to infuse individual soldiers with an emotional connection to the "cause." The role of the common soldier had to be more personalized and individualized, not as fighter per se so much as embattled citizen and defender of freedom.

The million and more soldiers of the French revolutionary army presented quite different logistic challenges than did the mobilization of Athens that brought Alcibiades and Socrates together at the Battle of Mantineia. But the mercenary army and the professional army, which had replaced the chivalric army, were now themselves being modified, if not replaced, by the cause-driven army. There was an element in its fervor that recalled the Protestant-Catholic battles of the Reformation and the Thirty Years' War. But those wars had themselves often been fought by large companies of mercenaries brought together by subcontracting entrepreneur-generals who charged rulers a fat fee for their service. Now the cause was not religion so much as the ideology of the nation-state.

In essence, then, the later eighteenth century in France and America saw a revival of a style of citizen soldiery that loudly invoked the Greek city-states and republican Rome. There may still have been mercenaries, even among the French revolutionary cockades. But revolutionary propaganda stressed that the cohesive spirit of the army was in the name of national unity, invigorated by an attachment to the "genius of the people" that in the same era sponsored the late-eighteenth-century revival of folktales and folk songs, along with the exploitation of themes of nature and the countryside in both poetry and painting.

The machine armies of Frederick the Great were superseded by the even larger armies of the French Revolution, but his column tactics helped revolutionary officers keep in line their unseasoned but enthusiastic troops, much as did the city-state phalanx of the classical period. To stir the imaginations of those who served, as well as the many in whose name they fought, stories of civilian sacrifice and preparedness—in the United States the Minutemen and Paul Revere's ride—formed a vital part of the national mythology and set the stage for more total wars that followed. It was a confluence of forces that, for a time at least, transformed the image of the cruel and rapacious soldier of the Thirty Years' War, as well as that of the eighteenth-century riffraff, into an agent of liberation.

By the end of the nineteenth century, the soldier in European armies would once again fall out of social favor and be called "scum" by officers and civilians alike, drawn from the bottom layers of society, drifters and the unemployable well below the working class. Only with World Wars I and II would the soldier be freshly romanticized as the apotheosis of the common man. But for the eighteenth century it was popular revolution especially that restored the gloss to the stories of men in arms. Instead of a mercenary and hireling, an involuntary draftee of press-gangs, or a land pirate out for plunder, the soldier of the French Revolution was one of the people he was defending. The specific class element of the old knightly image was gone, but the sense of spiritual commitment and chivalric individualism had revived. Only now its object was the nation rather than religion. In both the United States and France, the army was the living symbol of the revolution, and the citizen soldier the ideal citizen.

This new soldier hero had his recent precedents as well. There had been popular revolutions in the eighteenth century before the American and French. Some were against an oppressive foreign power, like the revolt of the Genoese against the Austrians in 1745. There had also been quasi–civil wars in favor of one dynasty against another, like the Jacobite Rebellions of 1715 and 1745 in England. Among these, the most publicity was gathered by the 1768 revolt of the Corsicans against the French, which made the Corsican leader Pasquale Paoli a famous figure in Europe and impelled fans like James Boswell to don a liberty cap to show their support. But it was the American Revolution that decisively changed the picture of politics. In its wake, the French Revolution overthrew its monarchy and defended itself against its foreign attackers, sallying forth against the rest of Europe in a war that explicitly combined battle and propaganda.

The myth of national (as contrasted with class- or officer-corps-based) heroism had a strong appeal in an era when mass armies drew upon the entire male population. Nationalism presented itself as a new form of group identity for individuals willing to take up the patriotic cause. In the American Revolution particularly, this citizen soldier arose from men often without either much land or any genealogy. Total conscription, as pioneered by revolutionary France, similarly sought to imply the equality of all men in the country as citizens and warriors. The prime document of the French Revolution was the Declaration of the Rights of Man and of the Citizen: "*Aux armes, citoyens,*" sang "The Marseillaise." It was not that the Bourbon dynasty or their underlings sought more land and wealth but that, as French revolutionary journals and pamphlets kept emphasizing, *la patrie* needed to be defended. Before Louis XVI faced the guillotine, his title had been changed by the revolutionaries from "King of France" to "King of the French."

This late-eighteenth-century shift to a broader sense of national self-definition is also a shift to a war-based definition of masculinity even more explicit than when war was the business of a particular class in a hierarchic society. Honor itself was redefined as less exclusively individual or the possession of a single class than as an allegiance to the state and its goals. No matter how ferociously you might fight and how lustily you bellowed "The Marseillaise," you were still part of an enormous group of men doing much the same thing. But those soldiers whose lives were committed to a war for national values had a different aura than the *miles gloriosus* of the classical past. Instead of stereotypical braggarts, they were men of the people who fought the people's fight. The hallmark of such an ideal soldier might be exuberance, as in the armies of the French Revolution, or self-containment. The requirements of drill and continuous volley firing were linked, for example, to stolid bravery and the stiff upper lip—a phrase that seems to date from the end of the Napoleonic Wars. Although it had some affinity with the self-contained restraint so admired in Frederick the Great's troops, the English expression emphasized much more the individual soldier as exemplary stoic—a model for all men.

The lesson bequeathed by the American and French Revolutions to the propagandists of nineteenth- and twentieth-century Europe was thus that military masculinity could become a pervasive ethic in modern citizen-soldier societies, even though it directly affected only a relatively small portion of the male population. So, too, arose the continuing paradox of Western warfare that the invocation of honorable behavior in warfare went hand in glove with both an advancing technology and a political propaganda that focused on victory above all for the group, whatever happened to the individual. The more technologically advanced and the more widespread war became, the less individual its combat could pretend to be, and the less plausibly battlefield action was a source of traditional military honor and masculine identity. Battle had long since ceased to be single combat writ large, except in the minds of the fervid seeker for military fame. In great part, the democratizing of honor thus paralleled the deheroicizing of war. The focus instead fell on the psychological affinity with the charismatic leader, whether Napoleon or John Wayne.

Unlike the seventeenth-century Japanese shoguns, for example, who gradually gave up the gun and returned to the sword as the more honorable weapon of battle, war in the West rarely took a technological look backward. Hardly five years after the 1793 *levée en masse* conscripted virtually the entire male population in France to the defense of political revolution, Eli Whitney revolutionized what was still essentially a cottage industry by introducing a system of musket manufacture not of individually handcrafted weapons but of factory-made interchangeable parts. Eighteenth-century war pressed forward industrial advance in a variety of ways. Machine-made cloth was the first stage of the Industrial Revolution in the 1740s, and both the metallurgy and woolens industry had been established in the Russia of Peter the Great to respond to the needs of the army. Some fifty years later, the advent of cheaper, quicker, and more efficient methods of gun manufacture signaled how decisive industrial and technological change would be in future national and international conflict.

As had happened since the introduction of the longbow and the cannon, those who claimed to want to keep war "honorable" protested the prepackaged percussion cap, the breech-loading rifle, and every advance in military technology. In the U.S. Civil War, General Grant deplored the exploding musket balls used by the South as "barbarous" and General Sherman became enraged at an early form of land mine ("This was not war, but murder"), but those weapons were not exactly dropped from the growing armory. Similarly, during World War I, the English first condemned the German use of poison gas in April 1915 and then by September had adopted the practice themselves. Perhaps in compensation, then, for the advancing specialization of war weapons, there arose a deep-seated need to reassert battle as the space in which the highest form of masculine honor could be achieved.

With war becoming more and more an ideological operation of the entire state rather than the function of one class, medieval metaphors of the body politic took on a new life. Soldier-man-citizen was the implied equation, military service a growing obligation of citizenship, and the virtuous citizen the manly warrior. So for a morally depleted citizenry, war could be a tonic. As Oliver Goldsmith wrote:

> The exercise of war for a short time may be useful to society, which grows putrid by a long stagnation. Vices spring up in a long continued peace from too great an admiration for com-

> merce, and too great a contempt for arms; war corrects these abuses, if of but a short continuance. But when prolonged beyond that useful period, it is apt to involve society in every distress. (III, 21)

It was a sentiment that would be repeated frequently in the centuries that followed, usually without the final caveat. In France, the Committee of Public Safety that ruled during the early years of the revolution repeatedly emphasized how the revolutionary genius of people was best expressed in the shock tactics of hand-to-hand fighting, the use of the bayonet, and even the pike, which had been discarded early in the century but now carried with it the benevolent political aura of Swiss independence. Even though historians have pointed out that a good proportion of the revolutionary battles were fought with techniques of the ancien régime, this symbolic equation of military tactics, national honor, and individual prowess clearly galvanized the spirits of French soldiers as well as those of the populace that supported them. But such ideas were very portable as well, and it would not be long before the assertion of a distinctive national war spirit would similarly stir France's enemies. Textbook tacticians, previously inspired by Frederick the Great, slowly began to realize that they needed to wage cultural warfare as well, whether the model was the guerrillas in Spain defending their own land against the dubious new freedoms promised by the *Grande Armée*, or the Prussian army reformers, who after their disastrous defeat at Jena in 1806 advocated the abolition of serfdom and the opening of the officer class as necessary moves in the war with Napoleon, which led to their own *levée en masse* in 1813.

Historians have argued over to what extent Napoleon's strategy and tactics were a product of the revolutionary changes and to what extent he used changes in the nature of citizenship and nationalism to expand already existing approaches to war. Once again, it seems unnecessary to choose between one explanation and the other. As an aristocratic enclave, the army was seismically disrupted by revolutionary change, losing almost 90 percent of its chain of command to emigration or the guillotine. Especially in Napoleon's early years, when he headed armies made up of a large proportion of draftees, inexperienced officers, and enthusiasts with little training, his speedy and immediate encounters with the enemy avoided the problem of demoralization. In a parallel development, one of the greatest expenses in seventeenth- and eighteenth-century war was the construction and maintenance of a system of supply depots and magazines for food and especially for forage to support the cavalry. But when the revolution expanded to Europe and the *Grande Armée* pursued a policy of living off the land—that is, exploiting the countries they marched through—decisive battle was the best use of scarce resources.

Napoleon's grand vision for war engendered often unprecedented problems of strategy, tactics, and logistics, as did the equally complex mobilizations required to defeat him. ("Strategy" itself is an early-nineteenth-century word; before that some version of "campaign plans" was thought sufficient.) But nevertheless the question of personal honor and individual battlefield glory persisted and grew to be an even more significant part of the ways men were persuaded to go to war. Like the merging of the foppish and the uniform in military dress, this underlying cultural collision between the individual soldier and the mass army, the solitary hero and the interchangeable mechanical part, may have been one of the more intangible psychological causes behind the heavy increase in dueling in the Napoleonic army, as well as across Europe (although there was still hostility toward it in England). In the midst of the first truly mass wars of the modern period, individual military pride needed a recharging that only the violent focus on delicate points of honor seemed to give.

The solitary warrior virtue celebrated by the Middle Ages had been translated by the Renaissance and the seventeenth century into fighting for a sovereign or, in Machiavelli's formulation, a combination of ruler and city—an embryonic species of public service. As Machiavelli argued, the show of medieval knighthood, embodied for him in the chivalric display of the condottieri, was empty next to the true knighthood that was in the gift of the Prince. The adherence to a national or civic cause thus at first seemed to renovate the place of individual honor in battle. Napoleon's frequent use of skirmishers, for instance—troops, often cavalry, whose individual aiming and nonstandard forms of attack helped demoralize the enemy before a pitched battle—underlined the different degree of will and responsibility accorded to soldiers in the new national armies. Frederick the Great had also sometimes used skirmishers and so-called free battalions. But he referred to them with great contempt and always set their actions in the context of a precise plan of strategic order in which they were the easily sacrificed first combatants. By contrast, Napoleon's willingness to trust to the occasion and to prepare his troops for improvisation implied a more flexible view of both order and armies. As Clausewitz concluded in *On War*, strategy is the ability to work effectively in the midst of muddle and disarray. The audience for war, he writes, believes that generals know exactly what they are doing, whereas in fact commanders do not need foresight and premeditation so much as boldness—that is, tactics, not strategy. Their real talent is the ability to convey that there is order in what is otherwise chaos.

# VOLLEYS OR AIMING, REGULAR ARMY OR MILITIA?

> Whoever has form can be defined, and whoever can be defined can be overcome.
>
> —Sun Tzu II, *The New Art of War*

Both the rights of man and the rites of manhood had been given the benediction of the state. But although the propaganda of military masculinity might have changed, its application to actual men continued to lag behind. Issues of national military style, available weapons technology, and cultural ideas of who a man is and what he does in battle intersected intriguingly in the argument over the relative merits of volley firing and close order on one hand, and skirmishing, aiming, and loose order on the other. Aiming is now as normal a part of military training as saluting. Cowboy heroes are renowned for their aim, and most war movies have obligatory scenes on the firing range and plot turns involving snipers. In part the reasons are aesthetic rather than military. Like shock tactics in which individuals directly confront one another, aiming is more photogenic, more dramatic, and more engaging than firepower at a distance. The defeat of the solitary sniper thus probably takes up a disproportionate amount of space in war films because he distills into an individual story the struggle against the otherwise faceless enemy.

But the military decision to develop aim through target practice required both a gun capable of such precision and a command structure and a tactical style that encouraged some form of individual initiative. Volley firing in the seventeenth and eighteenth centuries was necessary because smooth-bore muskets were so slow to load and so inaccurate. Rifles were even slower to load; the bullet had to be jammed forcefully down into the rifling. Their relatively greater accuracy, therefore, did not become an issue until much later, and even then some theorists, as well as officers, considered aiming to be murder, not war. Firing drill, in other words, sought to remedy lack of troop coordination rather than hand-weapon accuracy, since, whether you were Maurice of Nassau or Frederick the Great, accuracy was hardly the point next to massed relentlessness and steadfastness.

By the eighteenth century some strategists had begun to advocate that individual soldiers should aim their weapons at specific targets, and in the political upheavals of the end of the eighteenth century, it didn't require much imagination to give that tactic a polemical edge. Like the celebration of the bayonet by the French revolutionaries, both skirmishing and aiming make a conspicuous political point. According to what I was taught in high school, the distinction between the rigidity of drill and the individuality of aiming was the essence of the difference between the Old World and the New. Specifically, it was the lesson to be drawn from the defeat of the British general William Braddock in 1755 at Fort Duquesne—the "green hell," my ninth-grade American history textbook called it—where the foolish, hidebound British, against the advice of their American allies, marched in strict file through the forest only to be mowed down from behind trees by Indian sharpshooters who were supporting the French.

In fact, according to many writers, frontier marksmanship actually had less effect in battle than in sniper situations. But the man with the rifle (which was first used as a hunting gun and not generally adopted by European armies until much later) is crucial to the myth of the American warrior. It helped cement a basic contrast between the organized army of the encroaching, oppressive state and the individual battles of from-the-soil partisans, between those who respected the differences in terrain and those who were oblivious to it, as potent a weapon of propaganda in Napoleonic Spain as it would become during the resistance to the Nazi occupation of France.

Not that regular army officers, even in democratic cultures, were overpowered by the symbolism. Consider two observations by successful Civil War generals writing about events some fifty or more years after Napoleon's defeat at Waterloo. In the first, William Tecumseh Sherman supports the Old World/New World distinction:

> Very few of the battles in which I have participated were fought as described in European text-books, viz., in great masses, in perfect order, manoeuvring by corps, divisions, and brigades. (885)

Because of the heavily wooded countryside, says Sherman, "strong skirmish lines" were needed, not precise formations. In the eye of U. S. Grant, however, skirmishing was still not quite war in any proper sense:

> The battle of Champion's Hill lasted about four hours, hard fighting, preceded by two or three hours of skirmishing, some of which almost rose to the dignity of battle. (346)

Even closer to the revolutionary atmosphere, however, no less an officer than George Washington had even more extreme doubts about individual initiative in battle. Unlike many other American soldiers, then and later, Washington, who was a twenty-three-year-old colonel under Braddock at Fort Duquesne, never criticized his superior's tactics. During the revolution, his professional commitment to the discipline and even the tactical rigidity of a European-style army generated doubts that focused particularly on the use of local militias. Symbolic figures like the Minuteman, fighting for his own soil, have enshrined the militia in American folklore. Supporters of free access to guns still invoke the Second Amendment to the Constitution, with its reference to the need for "a well-regulated militia," as a license to oppose most forms of gun control, and antifederalists use the name "militia" to label their own idiosyncratic forms of local self-protection.

But all of Washington's biographers point out his contempt for the frequently poor training and discipline of the local militias. Instead, Washington wanted to create a regular army that would bridge local antagonisms and loyalties to become a source of coherent national identity at home, while at the same time projecting an image of responsible nationhood on the stage of international politics. Historians of the American Revolution have noted with some puzzlement the abrupt shift from the popular pamphlets praising the militia in 1774 to the adoption by the Continental Congress of a standing army in 1775, with the militia-disdaining Washington at its head. But the change hardly seems so paradoxical, just the natural corollary of whether the revolution was facing outward or inward, creating an external image of professionalism or an internal myth of revolutionary immediacy and spirit. In other moods, Washington, in many ways a self-taught soldier himself, eagerly identified with the individual fighter, Cincinnatus dropping his plow and picking up his gun.

As an institution, the actual militia at the time of the American Revolution may have been generally moribund, and local versions as motley and ill-prepared for war as the unprepossessing group of Mouldy, Shadow, Wart, Feeble, and Bullcalf mustered for Falstaff in *Henry IV: Part II.* But the idea of the militia had a longer shadow. Like the French revolutionaries, who wanted the monarch—if he was to be kept at all—to be "King of the French," Washington and other Founding Fathers aimed to weld the disparate colonists into a cohesive group called "Americans." When publicists of the American Revolution emphasized the militia as its backbone, they were highlighting the individual, the small group, and the intense localism that Washington needed to galvanize in order to succeed in fighting an enemy who was both far from home, yet seeking to find local roots.

Like those of the United States in Vietnam, British supply lines had to stretch across thousands of miles of ocean. If a British soldier deserted or was killed, his replacement had to come from abroad. The only alternative was to foster a loyalist militia. In the hundreds of small towns of eighteenth-century America, the revolutionary militias were their strongest competition. Whereas the British army had, at least in theory, to pacify and even garrison every American town, native groups could spring up like dragon's teeth from the soil itself. Whatever the problems with the training, experience, and equipment of American soldiers, they were already in place. The widespread laws in the colonies (except for Pennsylvania) that required all men from sixteen to sixty to be expert in arms aimed to reproduce something like a Greek city-state's readiness to defend the native land.

Washington's regular army encouraged supplies from the French government and attracted help from like-minded soldiers, generals, and drillmasters like Lafayette, Kosciusko, and von Steuben, all of whom arrived in 1777 and 1778. But in the early phases of the revolution, when some 30 percent of the population still supported England, the local militia was the symbol, if not the reality, that gave the nascent nation its identity. The clear message was that these soldiers were not the medieval peasantry who watched armored knights tilt against each other, nor were they part of a later peasantry dragooned into the battles of dynasty. They weren't peasants at all in the European sense, but farmers and townsmen fighting for their land and liberty. It was a contrast between American and European armies that was clear to many American commentators at the time. As U. S. Grant wrote in his memoirs, summarizing a by then century-long tradition:

> The armies of Europe are machines: the men are brave and the officers capable; but the majority of the soldiers in most of the nations of Europe are taken from a class of people who are not very intelligent and who have little interest in the context in which they are called upon to take part. Our armies were composed of men who were able to read, men who knew what they were fighting for, and could not be induced to serve as soldiers, except in an emergency when the safety of the nation was involved, and so necessarily must have been more than equal to men who fought merely because they were brave and because they were thoroughly drilled and inured to hardships. (766)

Just as the *levée en masse*, the bayonet, and shock tactics helped symbolize and solidify the individual Frenchman's commitment to revolutionary equality, the celebration of the American militia emphasized that the soldier was pledged to the values for which the war was being fought, while it created a set of ritual actions and objects to enhance that commitment. The word "morale" itself, often used by Napoleon to refer to the common values and inner feelings that bind together a group, had migrated into English by the mid–nineteenth century, retaining its French pronunciation.*

Nevertheless, beneath the sharp contrasts that Grant makes between the unthinking European soldier and the thinking American soldier is a basic similarity: at the dawn of both American and French democracy, as much as in any European dynasty, the army was identified with the state,

* The differentiation in French is between *moral,* which can refer to the spirit and values of a group, and *morale,* which refers to ethics. In English the connotations are reversed.

and military masculinity with state power. The celebration of the militia in the early stages of the American Revolution is thus also a reminder of the constant need in military history to invoke a nostalgia for past heroes, past modes of heroism, and past styles of battle, even—or especially—in the midst of the most acute technological and political change.

Just at the point, then, when the advance of technology and the consolidation of nation-states through balance-of-power politics were further minimizing the role of the individual soldier, national propaganda was aimed in two complementary directions: maximizing the impression of individuality on posters, paintings, and, later, photographs; and venerating the great leader, the hero in history, as Thomas Carlyle called him. The result was a keener and even more paradoxical relationship between the image of the warrior and the actuality of the battlefield—a sense of masculine identity irredeemably split between the fallible body and the indomitable spirit.

Individual aiming had particular political significance, for it implied a willingness on the part of commanders to trust soldiers to fight outside the unitary order and mass volley firing that was characteristic of an eighteenth-century army command intent on keeping its troops under an iron hand. Instead of the hierarchic model of an army led by a monarch-general, individual aiming assumed a more participatory model, dependent upon camaraderie and lateral communication as much as top-down command. Like skirmishing, individual aiming, to be truly effective, required the cheap, rapid-firing rifles that first began appearing in the mid–nineteenth century. But its increasing use as a tactic in the late eighteenth century in the context of a nondynastic nationalism presaged the importance of smaller-unit action in later wars, down to the World War II literary and film emphasis on the patrol, with its members of varied social and ethnic backgrounds, as well as the rapid-response brigades of the contemporary United States Army.

*Part VI*

# THE NINETEENTH CENTURY: WAR AND NATIONAL IDENTITY

# TECHNOLOGICAL PROGRESS AND THE LOST CAUSE

> I doubt whether the history of war can furnish more examples of skill and bravery than attended the defense of the railroad from Nashville to Atlanta during the year 1864.
>
> —William Tecumseh Sherman, *Memoirs*

The degree to which national identity—the willingness to describe oneself as a "Frenchman" or a "Russian"—is experienced as either an imposed or an inherent part of personal nature depends on a country's political system, an individual's temperament (and class), and his level of cultural self-consciousness. Until the late eighteenth century in Europe, that willingness, when it existed, resembled the allegiance of the feudal subject to a local lord more than it did any modern sense of national citizenship. But it was the ideal of the democratic revolutions that, when individual choice was engaged through elections and other forms of public opinion, state and individual would become more closely identified. Unlike the older dynasties, which needed mercenaries to fill the armies that ordinary citizens often felt no obligation to join, this new national identity would inspire citizen soldiers eager to defend ideals they all presumably shared. But not many years after citizen soldiers became the ideological core of the democratic revolutions, technology and the battlefield would change more than they had since the advent of gunpowder and cannons. As they changed, the gap between the myth of the indomitable citizen soldier and the reality of modern war grew even wider.

Advancing technology shifted the question of war from who would prevail in the present to who would own the future. By the late nineteenth century, a highly publicized arms race between the major European powers led with seeming inevitability to World War I. No longer only the occupation or preoccupation of dynasts, military aristocrats, and professional soldiers—or the backdrop for heroic fictions—war had become a subject of general public interest. Even though actual war was often far distant, competitiveness made the warlike personality, often complete with its tribal roots, central to national identity.

Visible changes in military technology fed the age's fascination with new inventions and scientific progress in other spheres. The scientific revolution of the seventeenth century for the most part took place in an atmosphere of international intellectual interplay, symbolized by the fact that most such works were written in Latin. But political, cultural, and economic competition in the nineteenth century also spawned a cult of the inventor, whose works were evidence of national superiority and reason for national pride. Virtually every scientific advance invited immediate speculation about how useful it might be for warfare: heavier and more rapid guns, new kinds of ammunition, faster and more thickly armor-plated warships. Newspapers and magazines constantly displayed new armaments. Pictorial magazines in England, France, and Germany connected images of uniforms and weapons to the heroics of empire. Dime novels in the United States documented westward expansion with tales of bloody conflicts between settlers and Indians, vigilantes and cattle rustlers, miners and cowpokes on a Saturday night—with a heavy emphasis on the paraphernalia of new guns and rifles.

Certainly, there were also inventions that had some impact on the domestic world, creating more comfort and leisure, like the electric light and the phonograph, as well as advances in medicine and sanitation. But weighed against the advances either in the technology of war (like weapons) or advanced by war needs (like the steam and internal combustion engines), these were comparatively few. Looking back on the century, William James, in his 1910 essay "The Moral Equivalent of War," quotes H. G. Wells (from *First and Last Things*) on the disparity:

> The house-appliances of today for example, are little better than they were fifty years ago. . . . Houses a couple of hundred

> years old are still satisfactory places of residence, so little have our standards risen. But the rifle or battleship of fifty years ago was beyond all comparison inferior to those we possess; in power, in speed, in convenience alike. (18)

By the 1890s houses across Europe were still poorly built, and even the very rich often lacked the heat, water supply, and toilet facilities we now take for granted. But inventions with military applications and, more enticing, the prospect of actual use in combat won more direct government financial support, while those that might have been appropriate for civilian use were pressed into more rapid development because of war. Some were prosaic but still crucial. The Napoleonic army, for example, like many before it, depended on foraging in the countryside for its food. By the 1840s advances in the techniques and speed of canning made it much easier to carry provisions.

Like the inventor, who pushed forward the frontiers of practical knowledge, the engineer and mathematician were central figures in nineteenth-century armies, *armes savantes* whose talents, especially at artillery and with other new forms of weaponry, had more lasting impact on warfare than the grand design strategies of the officers who led from a distance. It was a question that would arise again after World War II and the atom bomb: if something has been invented, will it not therefore be used? But for the nineteenth century, innocent of "weapons of mass destruction," the even more overwhelming public issues were "Are we ahead?" and "Can we catch up?"

We are still enmeshed in the period of extraordinary technological and scientific change that began in the nineteenth century, and it hardly looks as though the pace will slacken in the future, although much of the international political activity after World War II has been the effort to modulate or limit the use, if not the invention, of weapons and military technology. Less than a hundred years separate the dropping of the atomic bomb on Hiroshima and Nagasaki from the first significant appearance of a prophetic new military technology in 1855 during the Crimean War, when France and England moved their troops by steamship to the shores of the Black Sea to fight Russia on behalf of Turkey. There the first ironclad warships appeared, early forms of both poison gas and tanks were proposed, and, perhaps for the first time, in the French siege of the Russian stronghold of Malakhov, watches were synchronized before an attack.*

* To be able to do so was the privilege of an officer class, since watches cheap enough to be bought by soldiers were a product of the twentieth century.

But it is really the U.S. Civil War that deserves to be called the first modern war. It marks the beginning of technological advances in infantry weapons and almost every other area of warfare that made all subsequent wars more like one another than like the wars that had been fought since the introduction of gunpowder three hundred or so years before. Rifles had been around for centuries, but it was only with the appearance of Capt. Claude Minié's self-expanding bullets in the late 1840s that they became practical for warfare, instead of only hunting. The percussion caps that had appeared earlier in the century made the whole business of loading and reloading much quicker, by replacing the delayed action of the matchlocks and flintlocks with an instantaneous effect that has been called the greatest single innovation in the history of firearms: you pulled the trigger and the bullet was fired. Psychologically, the direct effect of percussion made the firearm into an extension of the hand and eye, more so than the cumbersome apparatus of the past, which was likely to become fouled and misfire after a few shots. Four hundred years after Agincourt, the gun had finally superseded the bow and arrow.

Somewhat later, it was the self-contained metal cartridge that brought the previously separate powder, bullet, and means of ignition together in one unit, allowing rifles greater distance, accuracy, and, above all, speed. The smoothbore musket of the Napoleonic Wars could fire fifty yards with some precision. The rifle of the Franco-Prussian War a half century later increased that to some 1,200 yards. That same Napoleonic gun, according to which expert you read, could fire between one and three rounds a minute. By contrast, the machine gun developed by Hiram Maxim in the 1880s could fire eleven bullets a second.

The new cartridges were also essential for the development of effective breech-loading rifles, into which a magazine of bullets could be inserted. Breechloaders had also been around for a while: Henry VIII had one, and the British used them experimentally in the American Revolution. Newer models like the Prussian needle gun, which was first developed in the 1840s, had at first been criticized for inaccuracy. As Sherman points out in his *Memoirs*, only one infantry brigade toward the end of the Civil War carried them, although the cavalry were more generously supplied. Not only could the needle gun and its cousins (when perfected) be reloaded faster and fire five shots a minute, there was also no need to bite open the greased paper cartridge casing when reloading. This disastrous necessity had in 1857 set off what the British called the Sepoy Mutiny and the Indians the First War of Independence, when already discontented Indian troops under British control believed, with some reason, that the grease was made from the fat of cows and pigs, forcing them to break both Hindu and Islamic taboos.

Not that everything in the Civil War was so immediately up to date. For all the changes in armament and tactics that were first exemplified there, it was still largely a civilian war, with all the haphazard outfitting that implies. "Standard" was a word more honored in the breach. We may think of "the Blue and the Gray" as a clear distinction between the Union and the Confederacy, but uniforms in fact varied from regiment to regiment, and many adopted exotic foreign military dress as well; the Zouaves modeled theirs on the Algerians in the French army. Similarly, ammunition may also have improved with the minié bullet, but it has been estimated that there were more than a hundred different calibers of rifles being used at various times during the war, especially in the Union army, since the Confederates with their blockade-runners could bring in more standardized weapons from England.

None of these changes happened quickly or in a straightforward developmental line. In many countries the military's resistance to new weapons grew even while a flood of inventors were trying to devise better ways to obliterate the enemy. Effective repeating rifles appeared only after the Civil War, with the 1866 and 1873 Winchesters. Even then the army did not adopt them as standard issue, and Custer's troops at Little Big Horn in 1876 did not have repeaters, while the warriors of Sitting Bull and Crazy Horse did (Custer himself always carried his favorite breech-loading Spencer). The Gatling gun met similar resistance by the quartermaster powers: it could fire some three hundred bullets a minute, was demonstrated to Union officers during the war, but was not adopted until after Appomattox.

Other crucial areas of technological change besides weaponry were communications and the ability to transport troops quickly to the field of battle. Many other inventors had experimented with an electrical telegraph before Samuel F. B. Morse's first message was sent in 1844, and by 1861 the first telegram had been sent from New York to San Francisco, effectively ending the glamorous but brief reign of the Pony Express, and making a potentially greater knowledge of the whereabouts of armies more immediately available to military strategists. During the Civil War, telegraph systems were much more advanced in the North than in the South, and Grant several times in his *Memoirs* pays tribute to the importance of telegraphed messages between commanders as the key to battlefield success. In 1865 the Atlantic cable was laid, linking Europe and America, and by the 1870s the British controlled much of world communications. Military procurement and supply stretched worldwide: in the late 1870s a British supply officer found himself in Texas buying mules to ship to Africa for the British war with Cetewayo and his Zulus.

Often to the dismay of the military, this early communications net brought not only the news of war but also the news about war, along with analysis of strategy, evaluation of officers, and whatever other interpretation and shading the reporters could squeeze in. Such reporting obviously varied from country to country depending on the relative freedom of the press. But even in the most open societies, war was tied to national interest, and criticisms were usually about how to wage it best rather than whether it should be done at all. With telegraphs, the transatlantic cable, steel engravings, and then photography, the war came home much more immediately. Grant in his memoirs frequently pauses to complain that the Union newspapers felt free to criticize anything the army did, while the Southern newspapers maintained the solid front of what he calls "an armed camp."

This shaping of public opinion had begun in earnest with British war correspondents in the Crimea who, along with exposing the blundering charge of the Light Brigade, stirred up readers at home with their stories of diseases that caused four times more deaths in the allied armies of England, France, Turkey, and Sardinia than did the Russians. Such reports about the poor medical care for common soldiers helped bring down the ministry in Britain and enticed Florence Nightingale to the hospitals of Scutari.

The reporting of the Crimean War began to tap newly available modes of communication to turn war into a spectacle, both gruesome and uplifting, for the home-front public, criticizing political and military strategy but also creating popular support for military ventures, jingoistic and otherwise, in the name of national honor. Later in the century, both the European and the American press also helped whip up the public desire to be first—a national preeminence that would be clearly ratified only by winning a war. Technologically, the access to this newly malleable public opinion was helped along by the introduction in the 1860s of cheaper ground-wood-pulp (rather than more expensive rag-based) newsprint. With their scare headlines and hyped reporting, William Randolph Hearst in the United States and the Harmsworth brothers (later Viscounts Northcliffe and Rothermere) in England helped fashion for this wider audience an atmosphere of imminent crisis and testing for the national will, invariably expressed in images of wounded honor and metaphors of besieged masculinity. In the 1890s, Hearst's *New York Morning Journal* notoriously fomented war with Spain over Cuba, while congratulating itself constantly: "An American Newspaper Accomplishes at a Single Stroke What the Red Tape of Diplomacy Failed to Bring About in Many Months" ran one headline. When the artist Frederic Remington, sent to Cuba to record Spanish atrocities, telegraphed that all was quiet and no war was in the offing, Hearst supposedly shot back: "You furnish the pictures and I'll furnish the war." Only slightly less blatantly, William Le Queux, one of Alfred Harmsworth's top reporters, ferreted out supposed anti-British conspiracies across Europe and in England's own backyard. Not coincidentally, he was also the author of the immensely popular preparedness thrillers *The Great War in England in 1897* (1893) and *The Invasion of 1910* (1906), as well as the purportedly more factual *Spies of the Kaiser Plotting the Downfall of England* (1909) and *German Atrocities: A Record of Shameless Deeds* (1915).

Explicitly imaginative literature also took a hand in the instigation of war hopes and fears. The last decades of the nineteenth century were a fertile time for literary utopias and dystopias, some hostile to technology, like Samuel Butler's *Erewhon* (1872), in which machinery is prohibited, Edward Bellamy's *Looking Backward* (1888), in which machines enable a socialist paradise, and William Morris's *News from Nowhere* (1890), in which machines are once again rejected, this time in favor of a return to a more personal medieval craft tradition. Other tales were fueled by technological romance. In 1871, a year after the German victory in the war against France and a year after Jules Verne in *Twenty Thousand Leagues Under the Sea* told the tale of Captain Nemo and his marvelous submarine, George Chesney published an early science fiction story of the "it can happen here" variety. Called *The Battle of Dorking* and detailing the history of a German invasion of Britain, it spawned numerous fantasies of future European war, German and French as well as British, that would cease only when World War I brought those fears into reality. Often written by professional soldiers like Chesney, which gave a patina of authenticity to their imaginings, such stories aimed both to influence specific military policy (who is the enemy, and what new weapons do we need to deal with him?) and to inspire the public to demand government intervention. Hardly five years after the Wright brothers launched at Kitty Hawk, H. G. Wells published *The War in the Air* (1908) detailing the effect of German bombers on a poorly prepared England.

The future war in these pre–World War I technofantasies was generally fought with one or another of the European powers. After World War II, the enemy was usually no longer of this earth but extraterrestrial, although the domed forehead and inhuman shape of the aliens were often a thin veil for the apparatchiks of the Soviet Union. It was a transformation foretold by H. G. Wells in his 1898 novel *The War of the Worlds*, which upped the ante beyond mere European enemies by imagining an invasion by an immensely superior civilization before which humans were powerless. Managing to satirize the self-satisfied moral assumptions of imperialism along with the call of the future-war writers for technological superiority, the novel concluded that no man-made weapons could be sufficient to defeat the aliens, only the lowly and inadvertent microbe. Mark Twain a decade earlier had done something similar in the reverse direction, by having Hank Morgan, the hero of *A Connecticut Yankee in King Arthur's Court* (1889), introduce modern industrial methods to sixth-century England, only to have his dream of a New England–inspired golden age collapse into an apocalyptic war:

> I touched a button, and shook the bones of England loose from her spine!
>
> In that explosion all our noble civilization-factories went up in the air and disappeared from the earth. It was a pity, but it was necessary. We could not afford to let the enemy turn our own weapons against us. (249)

The journalists of the Crimean War thus stood on the eve of a world in which the publicity of current wars and the imagining of future wars would become an essential part of the public diet of information and fear. But Florence Nightingale's presence there marked another new awareness in the history of war, one that tended in a somewhat different direction. Disease had always been a crucial factor in warfare. Thucydides's description of the plague in Athens during the Peloponnesian War is only one of many examples of epidemics in wartime. Surgeons, too, had long been present on the battlefield, and Napoleon for one helped foster field hospitals that would take care of wounded soldiers, and also made it common practice to inoculate new soldiers against smallpox with a vaccine developed by Edward Jenner at the end of the eighteenth century. But the great move forward in the control of battlefield disease would not occur until the turn of the twentieth century, pioneered by the Japanese effort in the Russo-Japanese war to check typhoid and smallpox. In that war, for the first time, the ratio of deaths from disease to deaths from war wounds was less than ten to one. In World War I, again for the first time, British deaths from battlefield casualties exceeded those from disease. But the widespread realization that disease killed more in war than did weapons had already gained a human face from Nightingale, Clara Barton in the Civil War, and Jean-Henri Dunant, a businessman whose horrified witnessing of the Battle of Solferino in 1859 inspired him to found the Red Cross. In the same years Francis Lieber's *Instructions for the Government of Armies in the United States in the Field* stressed care for soldiers on the battlefield, and his precepts were made Union army standard procedure by Abraham Lincoln in 1863.

Nightingale herself did not believe that germs caused infection; after all, she reasoned, she had tended the sick and never gotten cholera. But from a slightly less personal point of view, the midcentury germ theory of Louis Pasteur, the antiseptic procedures pioneered by Joseph Lister, and Robert Koch's isolation of the organism that causes cholera ironically made war more winnable than any tactics of Napoleon and even more acceptable than the meditations of Clausewitz. In short, although advancing weapons technology produced more ghastly injuries, better medical care for soldiers had the paradoxical result of "civilizing" war. By the twentieth century the virtually absolute distinction between death and life on the battlefield, where wounds quickly turned gangrenous and amputations were a matter of course, gave way to a world where many medical procedures could be carried out quickly and effectively. Previously fatal fevers vanished in a matter of days, and men who would otherwise be dead or invalided out could return to the front lines.

Conceived as a humane activity in response to a new awareness of war's horrors, the intervention of the healing professions thus put soldiers back on the line much more quickly. As Charles Bowles, an American delegate to the first Geneva Convention (1864), commented, "To reconcile humanity with the exigencies of war, or inhumanity under another name, is a task of almost insurmountable difficulty" (Moorehead, 46). Later Geneva Conventions made some progress in policing the more extreme weapons. Soft-nosed bullets, for example, had begun to be used for battle in the 1850s. Manufactured in Dum Dum, a suburb of Calcutta, they had originally been used for big-game hunting because they expanded on impact, causing extensive damage. The South had used them in the Civil War, much to Grant's scorn, "because they produce increased suffering without any corresponding advantage to those using them." Dumdums were prohibited by the Geneva Convention of 1899, and various governments began to sign on, like Great Britain in 1905.

After the extensive use of gas in World War I, in 1925 it too was prohibited. But once again the convention was only advisory and needed each individual government to agree separately.

From the 1860s onward, the movement of troops speeded up along with everything else. Railroads, or rather their absence, had been a factor in the Crimean War because Anglo-French troops could get to the Crimea by ship much more efficiently and quickly than their Russian foes could come overland. But with the Civil War, as Sherman notes, railroads became crucial in getting soldiers to battle. In 1861, for example, Joseph E. Johnston's army evaded their Union foes in the Shenandoah Valley and hopped the train in time to reinforce P. G. T. Beauregard and achieve a Confederate victory at the first battle of Bull Run (Manassas).

It was principally Helmuth von Moltke, chief of the German general staff after 1858, who exploited the lessons of the U.S. Civil War and his own experience as a shareholder on the board of a Hamburg-Berlin railroad in the 1830s to use railroad mobilization as a decisive factor in the Austro-Prussian War of 1866. Fully aware that railroads could create dependency and an actual lack of mobility if ancillary logistics were not in place, Moltke tried to avoid the problem of railhead crowding and undistributed supplies by using the network of German railroads to advance on a wide front. Other new technologies were in place as well. At the Battle of Königgratz, despite a telegraph failure that kept Moltke's orders from getting through, the improved Prussian breech-loading rifles were decisively superior to the Austrian muzzle-loaders, not least because breechloaders could be reloaded while the soldier was lying down, while muzzle-loaders had to be reloaded while standing up. A few years later, in the Franco-Prussian War, Moltke confirmed his insight into the uses of advanced technology in warfare by quickly and easily defeating the troops of Napoleon III, who had entered the war thinking that the French army was unbeatable. Despite this imperial conviction, France lost by a combination of poor tactics and an inability to muster the resources of a small and often privately owned French rail system, even though the breech-loading Chassepot rifle used by the French was in some ways superior to the needle gun.

The rapid transformation of warfare from the 1870s forward was largely due to technological advances in many areas: telegraph, railroads, armored steamships, copper hulls for sailing ships, breech-loading rifles, machine guns and other magazine weapons, and (somewhat later) smokeless powder and the precision screw that made the construction of weapons (and machines generally) more refined, as well as the low-tech but militarily crucial barbed wire, which would become central to trench warfare defense. Unlike the more haphazard development of weapons in earlier centuries, with the 1870s rapid causal links were made between newly refined techniques, new materials, and new inventions. The result, incited by larger armies and colonial wars that required more and more weapons, was that entrepreneurs and engineers competed to supply new and more efficient products. This embryonic arms race, born in Britain's upset over the ease with which Prussia defeated the French, was to reach full-blown political as well as military importance in the late-nineteenth- and early-twentieth-century rivalry between England and Germany to build the best battleships. This focus on naval armament reflected the way submarines and steamships began much of the European advance to technology and empire in the nineteenth century, as well as the immense popularity of works like Alfred Thayer Mahan's *The Influence of Sea Power upon History* (1890): if you wanted to tip the balance of power in your favor, you needed the best navy.

To many this onrushing technological development actually seemed more humane than war as usual, and even a way of making wars more limited—and therefore more honorable—once again. Sherman was only one of a long line of military and political men in the nineteenth century and later who argued that advanced weaponry would lead to shorter and more decisive battles. In fact, a frequent nineteenth-century view was that the more devastatingly effective the technology, the greater inducement for peace. Who would benefit from that peace was more uncertain. In the general pattern of technological development after 1870, brief spurts of superiority were quickly imitated and often improved by the other side.

The most elaborate argument for a constantly advancing military technology would later entail the belief that nuclear weapons needed to be developed because they would make war impossible. This lay a scant hundred years in the future, but its roots were in the nineteenth-century assumption that only respectable nation-states would be the combatants (not terrorists or "rogue states"). Like the seventeenth-century military academies set up to bring some more rational order to gunpowder war, the nineteenth-century military curriculum also stressed scholarly studies. The German general staff in particular became a virtual publishing company by instituting the writing of official war histories in order to make strategy more "scientific." Both war and technology would be the product of reason. But by the last third of the century technological advance was running far ahead of what was being taught in the military schools that had been founded in the early 1800s to help professionalize the modern army: Sandhurst in England, 1802; West Point in the United States, 1802; St. Cyr in France, 1808; the Prussian Kriegsakademie, 1810.

Moltke was, in fact, one of the few strategists who could actually bend the new technology to his own purposes. War may have created the environment for pressing earlier inventions into practical use, but just as often the response of regular army officers to advanced weapons was resistance. The new technology often demanded a tactical flexibility not always present in armies that were still following Napoleonic models of success in decisive battles. At the same time, the renewed strength of a hereditary officer class in several countries raised its own questions: if better weapons allowed greater flexibility, then more power would be put in the hands of junior officers leading smaller groups—an insult to military hierarchy.

In the clash between what was needed to defeat the enemy and the needs of social order, the latter was often the victor. The new military academies of the early nineteenth century may have taught the rudiments of engineering and mathematics necessary for effective use of artillery and some of the new military technology, but their curricula were also to a great extent still imbued with concepts of "honorable" behavior in war along with the strategy and tactics that came from that assumption. The urge to maintain the honor of war was not born solely of concern for the individual soldier. In large part it grew from the need to guarantee a peacetime social system, which in many countries was predicated on the assumption that the military embodied national history and values more perfectly than the general public ever could. As Moltke once remarked, the army was the central social institution because it guaranteed the existence of all the rest. In Moltke's Prussia, then, military victories strengthened a tradition of autonomy from civilian control reminiscent of the world of Frederick the Great, and until 1912 the war ministry prevented army expansion for fear that more middle-class officers would dilute its control. Foreign wars had the added advantage of supplying a handy supply of images of national unity that allowed internal conflicts to be ignored or glossed over in the name of national honor. It was a process of enforcing social and political harmony by execrating the enemy, and it differed in intensity and premeditation from country to country. But its importance in the nineteenth century cannot be underestimated, especially when those enemies were in far-off parts of the world and little resembled the home folk.

. . .

So was the essence of war honor, or was it technology? To the observer of the vagaries of military masculinity, underneath the propaganda of national pride that fostered the arms race was the growing belief that technology and supply were more important than men and honor, personal bravery, leadership, and even group discipline in winning battles. Some observers speculated that they could easily coexist. Optimistic about the more brisk wars of the future, Sherman thought that rifles, especially the breechloaders that were beginning to be used at the end of the U.S. Civil War, would heighten individual initiative. Modern weapons, in other words, might depersonalize the act of killing, but they democratized the soldier's role on the battlefield. As the firepower improved, Sherman argued, the soldier—who in Sherman's time had been less well trained and more dispersed over the battlefield—had to focus and improve as well: "A higher order of intelligence and courage on the part of the individual soldier will be an element of strength" (886).

But for those less democratically inclined, technology was a leveler of those heroic and chivalric traits that ought to be the essence of the warrior. It was an argument that went back in European warfare to the time of the English longbowmen: how could this be true warfare if any well-muscled peasant could strike down a noble knight in armor? In other words, technology, instead of being a way to enhance male power in warfare, actually undermined any moral claims the warrior might have, because he was not fighting as his own pure self. Once again, the mythic relation of Ares, Aphrodite, and Hephaistos seems relevant, especially the contrast between the powerful warrior and the wounded but technologically more advanced blacksmith god.

One of the prime reasons for resistance to new weapons was the belief that war fought with them would not be honorable. For Grant, who considered the exploding musket bullet to be "barbarous"—or for the generals in various armies who refused to adopt the rifle or the machine gun or, after World War I, the airplane—honor came, above all, from man-to-man combat. The French revolutionary emphasis on the bayonet was paid special obeisance in the brief war between Austria and France over the Piedmont (1859), when Napoleon III called it "the terrible arm of the French infantry" (Griffith, 59). The cynical might say that this was propaganda to cover up the inadequacy of French rifles. But such shock tactics did work well for the French because of the Austrians' lack of training, and their low supply of bullets. Later, the Austrian emperor

Francis Joseph I came over to the bayonet side as well, just in time to be defeated by Prussian needle guns in the Austro-Prussian War (1866), where in four days at the Battle of Königgratz the Austrians lost 30,000 men.

The European officer classes on the eve of, and well into, World War I thus clung to what they believed was an ideal of military honor and often refused to look directly into the bloody face of war. Mass communication from the Crimean War and U.S. Civil War onward may have begun to make that bloodiness and death painfully obvious, but those same newspapers were also in the forefront of convincing both the public and the individual soldier that the latter was a gallant knight in a just cause. In this view, money and technology were both corrupters of honor, and so the inexorable progress of science and technology was qualified and opposed by a mythically invoked genealogy of heroes, codified in the curricula of military academies by the study of old battles and great generals.

In the twentieth century, honor and technology came together momentarily in the popular World War I imagery that emphasized the chivalric relation of pilots fighting their battles high above the trenches. (The air war, after all, was the only sphere in which the old ideal of single combat could be even vaguely replicated.) But military hierarchies, even in the United States, remained suspicious of airplanes as instruments of warfare, despite General Billy Mitchell's post–World War I argument that air forces and strategic bombing were the key to winning future wars. Mitchell was court-martialed in 1925 for his aggressive advocacy of an independent air force and his attacks on the other branches of the armed service, but his ideas had staying power and many were adopted for World War II.

Nevertheless, the suspicions of technology remain. The cyberspace atmosphere of the Gulf War with its smart bombs may have implied that future wars would be entirely fought by technicians in bunkers far behind the lines. But the contrary argument was that it would only and always be men on the ground that counted for true victory. Without them, as S. L. A. Marshall argued in *Men Against Fire*, his analysis of the U.S. Army in World War II, the decisive capture of territory and defeat of an enemy army was impossible. The recriminations against President George Bush after the Gulf War and his inability or unwillingness to pursue Saddam Hussein into Iraq reflected this basic split between the supporters of new technology (often associated with the air force) and the resisters (often associated with the army). Even at the end of the twentieth century, during the American interventions in the Balkans, voices inside and outside the military called for ground troops because somehow aerial bombing "was not really war." Later wars in Afghanistan and Iraq struck an uneasy compromise.

Those who search for the causes of war either in the shadowy necessities of primitive behavior or in a hardwired male physiology tend to argue with grim fatality that war making can never end. To them, any changes in masculine identity or weapons technology are merely the window dressing for an unchanging collection of ineradicable urges. But the idea of what it means to be a man, military or otherwise, is in an endless interchange with the social facts of civilization as well as with the advancing material culture of science and invention. With the nineteenth century it became clear that to postulate an advancing or developing, let alone an evolving, masculinity would be to accept the parallel with highly visible progress in the technology of armament and to ignore the nostalgia, backsliding, and slow changes in masculine identity that are also an essential part of the story. The surface permanence of physical details—size, shape, and, later, biochemistry—masks their shifting nature, just as the seemingly rigid paraphernalia of the military role—the uniforms, the medals, the salutes, and the stiff upper lip—drape uneasily over an unstable, irregular human core. Whether the immediate purpose is bragging or sorrow, over triumph or defeat, each war, has fallen from the perfect honor and warriorhood of the past, and can only struggle to regain a semblance of that perfection. The social and cultural changes that shape masculine identity thus always collide or must make peace with a strong countertide of honor and nostalgia. As with the slow growth of industrial economies out of agricultural ones, there will still be local cottage industries of masculinity, each laced with its own memories of underdevelopment. Focusing primarily on the history of technology, with its impatient rush ahead, thus risks ignoring or minimizing the irrational and the emotional in all human ideas—the desire not to go forward, the longing for the past rather than the eager embrace of the future.

The inability to live up to the standards of the past became a prime fissure in nineteenth-century masculine identity. Technology might be the ornament of the present and the beacon of the future, and popular war the promise of a new age, but honor almost always belongs to the past. Which past that is and who defines it is another question. For the nineteenth century, the most pervasive image of honor in warfare was a resurgent cavalry, connecting honor with social status and allowing the aristocratic officer class to ignore the watershed of the French Revolution and breathe instead the more congenial air of the ancien régime. It helped matters tangibly that cavalry units were useful in outposts of imperial expansion like the American West and the African desert, where conflicts stressed skirmishing and surprise attacks. Yet, so far as national psychology and propaganda were concerned, there was nothing more honorable than a useless cavalry charge against an enemy with greater firepower.*

As in many army-oriented American westerns after World War II, the cavalry, whether they won or not, stood ready to rearray themselves in the military honor forfeited by the supporters of the new technology. At a time when people were becoming more and more aware that their lives were being shaped by impersonal forces like business cycles, cavalry nobility represented a disdain for this new mercantile and commercial world and a belief that it was only through military honor that war could be fittingly carried on. Appropriately enough for a war in which Moltke's adroit use of technology forecast much of the strategy that would be in place by the start of World War I, the Franco-Prussian War also marked what Michael Howard has called "perhaps the last successful cavalry charge in Western European warfare," at Vionville, near Verdun (Howard, 8; Friedrich, 165). In the same area, some forty years later, British and French generals would still be waiting for infantry to surge from trenches and break the German lines so that the cavalry could pour through.†

As war either directly or indirectly becomes part of the experience of more of the male population, it highlights a fall from the ideal past at the same time that it furnishes the only contemporary stage on which that past can be restored. The English may have been the first modern nation to suffer this loss, with their widespread sense that the mid-seventeenth-century Civil Wars represented a fall from the Edenic world of Elizabethan England. After the American Civil War, the antebellum South, although gone with the wind, had something of that same paradisiacal aura, just as after World War I, many looked back fondly to the giddy atmosphere of the summer of 1914 before the guns of August boomed.

But what of those who did not actually fight but, as European war began to spread over the earth, had their lives shaped by those events?

* Guerrilla warfare, like that of the Spanish against the Napoleonic occupation (where the word "guerrilla" originates), also stresses bravery as much as, if not more than, foresight, and the British in the Boer War were often undone, in battle as much as in propaganda, by frontal attacks that were not by the book but succeeded anyhow.

† The last official French cavalry charge was that of two dozen Moroccan tribesmen, led by Jean Ballarin of the Free French forces, against an Italian army encampment in Eritrea in January 1941.

One change in masculine identity that might be loosely put into the column of "progress" is the area of work. Through an expanding industrial economy, the older and relatively simpler ways by which individuals were defined in relation to the order of society (and often the ways by which they defined themselves) were exfoliating into the multiple professions and occupations of modern industrial society. For many, this vision of a new world of work is profoundly mercantile and commercial, with each man identifying himself primarily as a seller of services. But within industry *itself* the effect was often to reduce identity to those body parts that did the work. Charles Dickens in *Hard Times* (1854) has Mr. Gradgrind constantly refer to the men who work in his factory as his "Hands," kin to the oppressed ordinary sailors of the eighteenth-century British navy. Here is yet another way that advancing technology, in seeming to expand the scope of male action, actually reduced it, undermining the myth of masculinity as a bodily sufficiency for all occasions. Marshall McLuhan's twentieth-century formulation that technology had created "extensions" of man puts an optimistic gloss on what historically has been a more mixed blessing.

Yet, as the increasing complexity of European society engendered masculine vocations, behaviors, and character types that immensely complicated the medieval division of *pugnatores*, *oratores*, and *laboratores*, the core assumption that associated masculinity exclusively with military prowess began to erode. It was a process already begun with the professionalization of armies and the accompanying implication that war making is a profession or occupation among others, and it would become more complicated when the mobilizations required by World War I reached deep into the population of male citizens who otherwise would never have thought to be soldiers.

Is then the soldier in the nineteenth century a figure that signified manhood, contradicted it, was irrelevant to it, or was just one way among many of being a man? One approach to answering such a question is to investigate how each country tied its sense of nationalism—national identity and national destiny—to military action. In a Europe that knew relative peace for almost one hundred years, politicians might boast of the national wealth brought by industry and invention, while writers like Baudelaire treated these new possibilities for masculine identity as trivial and fragmentary next to the purer masculinity of the past:

> There are only three beings worthy of respect: the priest, the warrior, the poet. To know, to kill, and to create. Other men

> can be taxed or forced to labor. They are made for the stable, that is to say, to pursue what are called *professions.* (684)

Baudelaire's sardonic maxims, like the knightly disdain for the lowborn medieval archer, indicate an underlying awareness that, whereas the army in time of revolution might be the embodiment of the nation, for the most part its hierarchy was the greatest bulwark of the class system—a very different way to define the nation. From the eighteenth century onward, especially in authoritarian states, but in more democratic ones as well, armies often functioned internally to reinforce the centralized state's monopoly of violence as peacetime police and labor forces—suppressing rebellions, building roads, even collecting taxes. To a certain extent, the founding of actual civil police forces in England and France in the early nineteenth century helped improve the army's bad reputation at home as the enforcers of state decrees by letting them focus their attention on external enemies. But still the specter of a national army being used against its own citizens, especially liberal reformers and the working class, was continually resurrected. In 1819 British cavalry charged a meeting of working-class reformers in Manchester. When the dust cleared, eleven were dead and some five hundred injured in what became known as the Peterloo Massacre, with its obvious echo of Waterloo. Similarly, national armies were heavily involved against their own citizenry in the repression of the nationalist revolutions in 1848 as well as in the violent clashes with the growing labor movement in the late-nineteenth- and early-twentieth-century United States.

But in the publicity of nineteenth-century national honor, war was romantically viewed as a transcendent experience, conditioned by a growing identification of the male citizen with the state, and helped along immeasurably by a literary and artistic revival of the warrior past. Thus the devastation of the Napoleonic Wars, and the frequency with which war and its aftermath were more often experienced by ordinary people as loss rather than gain, was countered with a sense that war was the source not only of individual and national honor but also of political and cultural regeneration, a source of camaraderie and fellowship that would build a bridge to a new world and a new society. In response to the French Revolution and Napoleon's effort to expand French power throughout Europe and into Africa and Asia, many of the dynastic states tried to energize their inhabitants with a sense of national identity. Often it was to their later regret, as the events of 1848–89 showed, when popular agitation in France, Italy, Austria, and several of the German states demanded a liberalization of dynastic control, constitutional change, and political autonomy for ethnic and linguistic groups. After 1848 all of these threatened dynasties reasserted their power, largely because the newly awakened local nationalisms did not yet have much backing within their armies. But for some, like the Habsburg empire, an unwieldy double monarchy split between Austria and Hungary but centralized in Vienna, the centrifugal force of popular nationalism was only delayed until World War I, which began when a Serb student assassinated the Austrian crown prince in Sarajevo.

This fantasy of war as the purer, more intense place (even as tales of war profiteers continued to mount) defined the real villain not as the military enemy so much as the peacetime commercial world that made men soft and society corrupt, ripe for purgation and regeneration. The nationalism evoked by the French mass army was complemented and strengthened by the nostalgia for the ancient military heroes displayed in folktale and folk poem as well as in high culture in England, Germany, and across Europe. The military leader, wrote Thomas Carlyle in *On Heroes, Hero-Worship, and the Heroic in History* (1841), was the greatest of great men, and such greatness could never be achieved in peace.

War was thus not only the touchstone of all that was best in masculine nature, but also a concerted effort to repair a pervasive sense of loss. The injury to Uncle Toby's groin in Sterne's *Tristram Shandy* is direct and physical; his effort to understand how it happened has little to do with an abstract national sense of honor and all to do with his personal past. But the cause-oriented wars of the American and French Revolutions redefined honor as well. In 1804 Benjamin West, an American painter transplanted to England, painted Achilles mourning over the dead Patroklos as an image of the lost promise of the American Revolution.

The chivalric code had emphasized the vulnerable female body as an object for which men were ready to fight as part of their defense of civilized virtue. Edgar Allan Poe would write in the 1840s, far enough from both the revolution that preceded and the civil war that came later, that the prime subject of poetry was the death of a beautiful woman. But during and immediately after wars, as the nineteenth century particularly established, it is the death of a beautiful young man and the display of the vulnerable male body that is so overwhelming: wounded, bleeding, lying dead in piles from the Crimea to Gettysburg to battlefields in Africa and on the Khyber frontier. Perhaps appropriately enough, in West's painting, Patroklos looks androgynous enough to be both male and female.

In such an atmosphere of longing the celebration of the deaths of young men symbolized the waste of innocence and potential, and the feeling in the postwar world that we have inherited only the ashes of past glory. During the Gilded Age, the camaraderie of the Civil War was invoked as the counter to a society built on greed. So, too, the bloody wastelands of World War I retained during the hedonism of the Jazz Age an ambience of purer relations between men, a time when friendship meant something. In the aftermath of World War II, the dark American musical film *It's Always Fair Weather* (1955) perfectly encapsulated this fall into a degraded commercial world through its story of three pals who pledge after the war to help and support one another, and then return ten years later to realize how completely they have gone their own ways, pursuing their own selfish interests.

Often the mourning for vanished honor and camaraderie was even greater when the war or the battle was lost. The profound tactical ignorance, arrogance, and general malfeasance that brought about the charge of the Light Brigade in the Battle of Balaclava during the Crimean War were trivial in the balance against Tennyson's poem written a few weeks later—"Theirs not to reason why,/Theirs but to do or die"—which celebrated the charge as the epitome of military honor, even though "someone had blunder'd." As a French observer notoriously remarked, *"C'est magnifique, mais ce n'est pas la guerre."* Increasingly throughout the nineteenth century, the demands of ideal honor and the demands of actual war were fatally in conflict, and courage (however pointless) counted more than tactical sense in the realms of true heroism.

Here in a nutshell is the poetry and imagery of the Lost Cause. War was serious business, and if there was transcendence to be gained, it was often less gleefully triumphal than somber and death-filled, with an aura of noble failure that deflected the curse of ambition and assertion. Of the centuries since the fall of Rome, it was the nineteenth that preeminently promoted in brick and mortar and metal the cult of the heroic dead, the triumphal arches, the bronze statues, and the grand mausoleums filled with bones. In new or aspiring nations from the Thames to the Danube and beyond, fiction and poetry contributed a lion's share to this celebration of past heroes, especially when they had lost. In 1814 Sir Walter Scott, who as a young man had been much impressed with the German folktales of past heroes, published *Waverley*, set during the Jacobite rebellion of 1745, in which the English defeated the Scots under Bonnie Prince Charlie. Scott himself was richly ambivalent about the historical passage from the traditional and heroic world of the clans to the more hardheaded authority and power of England. But *Waverley* was the first of an immensely popular series of novels whose romantic view of past conflicts helped create a nostalgic nationalism that was not content merely to memorialize but often sought to take revenge as well against those who had triumphed. This was the era in which repressed nationalisms of many sorts dredged up the battle losses of the past and took them as a cue for ethnic resurgence in what Eric Hobsbawm and Terence Ranger have called "the invention of tradition." Victors and vanquished alike could take the seeds of honor from their often fictionalized pasts and plant them in the present. German nationalists invoked the spirit of Arminius (Herman), who defeated the Roman legions of Varus in A.D. 9, and Lord Byron took up the cause of the Greek War for Independence from the Ottoman Turks (and designed uniforms for the troops he had helped muster) as a tribute to the lost ideals of the classical world.

In eastern Europe, at virtually the same time, it was the era of Pan-Slavism, the idea generated by poets and intellectuals that the southern Slavs shared an ancient heritage that made them a unity within, and opposed to, the domination of the Habsburg empire. As it was for the ballad collectors of the late eighteenth century and as it would be for Richard Wagner in the series of operas he began writing in the 1840s, the material evidence of this unity was in folk songs, folktales, and epic. In the wake of the French Revolution and the Napoleonic Wars, such otherwise erudite explorations of literary roots became the polemic springboard for an awakening nationalism in works like Adam Mickiewicz's epic poem *Pan Tadeusz*, published in Paris in 1834, which celebrates the chivalric world of the Polish gentry.

The figure of Napoleon foreshadowed the twentieth-century politics of nations symbolized by a single individual who was not the monarch, but who was in effect the embodiment of popular will. To English cartoonists and caricaturists like James Gillray, as France was "Boney," so England was John Bull. Sometimes such a figure was fictional, like Uncle Sam in the United States, but often the role was taken by someone real, who purportedly acted in the interests of the people in ways they might never have articulated themselves. Although his name quickly became allied to any extreme sort of nationalism, Chauvin's particular chauvinism was to believe in Napoleon as the embodiment of the French state and French character.

With the heaven-sent Great Leader as its model, the nation could thus appear on the world stage as an outsized version of the romantic individual, in search of challenges to match his ambitions. In one sense, then, the American and French Revolutions represented a break with the monarchic world and an opening to democracy as well as the participation of citizens in the governance of the state. In another, however, they fostered an even closer identification between the country and the individual.

A central part of the new leader's charisma, or prestige, as Napoleon called it, was to embody the national past. As Napoleon took Joan of Arc as his forebear and the French later invoked the concept of *revanche*, or revenge for past slights and defeats, as a reason for war, so nationalist Serbs of the twentieth century invoked their defeat by the Ottoman Turks in the Battle of Kosovo (1389) as justification for their war against the Bosnian Moslems—even though it had been almost entirely forgotten before it was celebrated by the early-nineteenth-century Pan-Slavists. Paradoxically enough, then, in a century much of whose public rhetoric was devoted to the glorification of progress, the psychic energy given form by these lost causes was in a very conspicuous degree opposed to the march of technology. Technology implied commerce, money, and the future, while the lost cause summoned up the values of a now-obliterated past whose all-infusing honor, like the ancient ideal of military fame, was more surely affirmed by death and loss than by any trivial victory. During the American Civil War, for example, the South cast the conflict with the North as a duel between a male society built on honor—their own—and a debased commercial society, in which honor was impossible. When the South lost, it came as a shock, since clearly those with the most honor should be the winners.

But the loss was also metaphorically inevitable because of the contrast between the industrialized North and the mainly agricultural South. Before the war it was common in the South to believe, as Napoleon had of the British, that commerce and industry had enfeebled the North's warrior honor so much that they would not even fight. Even after the Southern defeat, the attitude persisted. Commentators in the late nineteenth century, in language that is still a staple of neo-Confederate Civil War interpretation today, ascribed Union victory to the greater numbers, money, and more advanced technology of the North—everything but the ability to wage a better war, which was considered to be the sole possession of the South and its culture of honor. As James McPherson points out, such an interpretation must minimize the actual military technology deployed by the South—including more standardized ammunition than was available in the North—just as those who labored to supply the Confederate troops were ignored when the palms of battlefield honor were handed out.*

Another cultural stream that fed this antitechnological attitude was the virtual mania in England, France, and Germany for things medieval. Across Europe, people read the stories of Walter Scott, Alexandre Dumas, and Victor Hugo, along with the powerfully nostalgic essays of John Ruskin and William Morris; they collected armor and artifacts, restored ancient buildings in what was considered to be a medieval style, and generally paid homage to the Middle Ages as a time when real values and real men flourished. If you were on the right, those centuries were a time when the aristocracy rightfully ruled; if you were on the left, they were a time before handicraft had been replaced by machines and communal activities could flourish. For the nostalgics of both the left and the right, the enemy was commercialism, industrialization, and the supine loss of individual autonomy they seemed to bring. Just as the French Revolution had reached back over the medieval world to find its roots in the Roman republic, the Middle Ages represented for nineteenth-century Europe a world of chivalry and honor that might successfully compete with the mercantile and industrial corruption of the present. In the midst of a century that often loudly prided itself on being modern, the cult of the medieval was a direct attack on or solace for the industrial and capitalist reduction of male worth to money and labor. Not incidentally, it also clothed in heroic legend an image of the monarchy as the center of authority and high civilization, stressing a sense of civic duty and subordination well suited for the secular nationalism that might often be linked to Christianity but was just as often independent of it.

An intriguing variable in the history of armies is in fact the extent to which they support, are indifferent to, or oppose the state religion. Fascism in Franco's Spain, for example, depended crucially on the interrelation of church, state, and army; in Nazi Germany there was active hostility to the church, while in the United States, which is without a state religion, the armed forces have no official religious role. One substantial element of the heritage of the medieval European knight was his embodiment of a personal morality potentially or actually unbeholden to religion, and the shadow of the Crusades and the Church's effort to refashion this often nonreligious warrior heritage hangs over all these possibilities. But the variations are there in Islamic countries as well.

* McPherson in *Battle Cry of Freedom* cites the boast of Senator James Chesnut of South Carolina, who was so convinced of Northern cowardice that he vowed to drink all the blood shed due to secession, believing it would hardly amount to a thimbleful (238).

Some armies still, like that in Turkey, often function on the side of secularism, while others, like the Taliban in Afghanistan, enforced strict religious doctrines.

At the end of the eighteenth century, the new revolutionary states in both France and America, with their assertion of a nationalism hostile to dynasty and its supposed divine rights, had to a large extent been competing with Christianity's claim to define human identity. In this combat, the separation of church and state mandated by the American Constitution was much more lasting than Robespierre's Festival of the Supreme Being (1793), which may have been spectacle enough to divert Parisians for a few days, but hardly succeeded in replacing Christianity with a new state religion based on reason.

Chivalric nostalgia had at first partaken of the same nonreligious character, resting its defense of monarchy on national traditions rather than on religion. Scott, for example, in his preface to *Quentin Durward* (1823), asserted that the essence of chivalry was "generosity and self-denial." But with the expansion of European empires into "pagan" lands, the need for extranational justification brought Christianity back onto the side of military adventure in a more concerted (and more widely propagandized) way than it had been since the Crusades. Under the banners of the Round Table, Christian evangelism and English imperialism could stride the world together, no doubt singing "Onward! Christian Soldiers," based on a poem written by Sabine Baring-Gould in 1864 and set to music by Arthur Sullivan in 1871.

In *The German Ideology* (written in 1845–46 but not published in full until 1932) Karl Marx and Friedrich Engels took aim at romantic nationalism and argued that such ideologies masked contemporary contradictions by conjuring up a manufactured account of misty origins. But such an account makes the whole process of mythmaking too premeditated and self-consciously deceptive. Certainly there was some explicit effort to create a propaganda that would solidify the nation behind its leaders. But what of the more inchoate desire that chivalry could be relevant to the present, and that its code of honor was the only way to sort out what it meant to live in a Europe that from about 1790 to 1815 was in almost perpetual conflict? The Tudor and Stuart monarchs had used Arthurian imagery to buttress the legitimacy of their reigns, while in the seventeenth century much of the debunking of the legends was, like John Milton's in his *History of Britain*, motivated by antiroyalist politics, and the Arthurian model went into eclipse.

But the resurrection of Arthurian legends in the nineteenth century allowed men living in a world of imperialist expansion to believe that they were engaged more in a spiritual quest than in a materialistic conquest. At the same time that British, German, and French power was spreading across the world, such tales also enshrined the warrior vitality of northern Europe at the expense of Roman imperial decadence. This was not a faceless, valueless empire; this was Beowulf, Siegfried, Arthur.

The medieval "matter" of the Arthurian tales was geographically focused on England and France. But in Germany it was connected to the *Nibelungenlied* and therefore part of German national traditions as well, and would be revived again in the Nazi idealization of the German past and its cult of Wagner's operas. But long before, in less explicitly politicized times, Prince Albert of Saxe-Coburg-Gotha played at chivalry as a child in Germany complete with boy-sized suits of armor. Later, as the consort of Queen Victoria, he was instrumental in fostering the artistic depiction of Arthurian legend, including William Dyce's extensive frescoes for the Queen's Robing Room, begun in 1848, only a few years after Tennyson began writing the Arthurian poems that would come together in his widely read *Idylls of the King* (1859). What could be more transgressive in a middle-class world devoted to industry and progress than finding life models among the knights of the Round Table? Whatever your class background, you could have a moral ancestry that stretched back to the Round Table, and under your sober black broadcloth wear the gleaming armor of the righteous warrior.

General chivalric values could be derived from almost any of the Arthurian knights. But the prime figures of the nineteenth-century revival were not usually Arthur, Lancelot, or other more seasoned warriors. Instead, it was often the youthful and virginal Galahad and the impetuous Gawain, whose beardless faces graced innumerable paintings, wall hangings, and lithographs. Their quests were less for warrior fame than for the Grail, an appropriate symbol for a nationalism validated by the Christian imagery of innocence, sin, and redemption. Like the Christian quest that authorized warrior violence in the Crusades, this invocation of the chivalric in both England and America canonized the great military leader as also the perfect Christian gentleman. Not only could military aggression and conquest be justified by religion as well as nationalism, but there was also the extra piquancy that the Grail quest and indeed the history of the Round Table itself could be interpreted as a lost cause, like the life of Christ, the hero who dies on earth but is celebrated in heaven.

For the post–Civil War South this chivalric myth led to the virtual cult of Robert E. Lee, and in later versions stood behind such popular (if unlikely) Cold War images as George Washington praying at Valley Forge. In the post–Civil War United States as well, the aura of knighthood gave the gloss of eternal values, whether it was to an early workers' organization (the Knights of Labor, founded in 1869) or to a Catholic lay group (the Knights of Columbus, founded in 1882). Frederick Engels mocked all of this as medieval foofaraw, but his more interesting point was how much the new man of the nineteenth century called upon old symbols of manly innocence to buttress his cause. The use of chivalric imagery by the propagandists of both sides during World War I indicates that the imagery of either religious or chivalric sanction is hardly the possession of one nation or another. The Lost Cause in essence has no necessary politics other than wounded honor and the desire for revenge. Even today in Germany, where Civil War reenactments have become almost as popular as they are in the United States, the Confederate battle flag may often stand in as an emblem for neo-Nazis prevented by law from flying the swastika.

# BARBARIC ENERGY AND CIVILIZED MANNERS

> Each man calls barbarism whatever is not his own practice. . . . And yet for all that, the savor and delicacy of some uncultivated fruits of those countries is quite as excellent, even to our taste, as that of our own. . . . So we may well call these people barbarous, in respect to the rules of reason, but not in respect to ourselves, who surpass them in every kind of barbarity. Their warfare is wholly noble and generous, and as excusable and beautiful as this human disease can be; its only basis among them is their rivalry in valor.
>
> —Montaigne, "Of Cannibals" (1578–80)

> Clean linen too is a luxury which a civilized man, without any imputations upon his soldierly qualities, may in moderation desire to enjoy.
>
> —Sir John Kaye, *Lives of Indian Officers* (1869)

What justifies war in a civilized society? To a great extent the nineteenth-century European answer was the need to keep barbarism from the gates. Drill in the early seventeenth century had given a cohesion and purpose to a military group that was meant to embody national purpose. Now the opposition of civilization and barbarism similarly strengthened a sense of national identity. In the very century when military technology took a leap forward unparalleled since the introduction of gunpowder, the rhetoric of honor, gentlemanliness, and European racial superiority became a comforting justification for both imperial conquest and obliterating the enemy with the products of a rapidly mutating industrial weapons economy.

But "barbarism" historically has no fixed definition—sometimes, when it is "savage," it might be negative; at others, when it is "primitive," it might be positive. One you deplore; the other you could admire. As a moral judgment about weaponry, it can mean the most primitive or the most sophisticated. Attila the Hun with his heap of human skulls was barbaric to medieval Europe, as was the A-bomb to Japan. It all depends on how war itself is defined and especially where the honor in warfare is located. But is barbaric war the absence of honor or a different and perhaps older form of it? In the charges leveled against George III in the Declaration of Independence, Thomas Jefferson focused on three actions that smack of the "barbarous": first, the use of mercenaries; second, the fomenting of domestic revolt; and third, the enlistment of "the merciless Indian Savages, whose known rule of warfare, is an undistinguished destruction of all ages, sexes, and conditions."

But the more usual attitude is ambivalence, and the quantity of talk about "civilization" in the nineteenth century suggests a deep uncertainty along with a need for reassurance about not only the barbarian outside the gates but the barbarian within. As we have seen, the figure of the berserker, or those dark forest shadows that the Middle Ages called "wild men," aroused mixed feelings. On the one hand, they were barbarians, either from the outside or homegrown, flush with impassioned emotions, devoid of self-control, against which a precarious civilization could define itself. On the other, they represented an instinctual, "natural" power that was alluring, at least in image. Throughout the Middle Ages, wild men appeared on shields and escutcheons, and they were frequently the bogeyman of choice in court masquerades, including the notorious occasion in thirteenth-century France when several young aristocrats were burned alive when their pitch-coated "wild man" costumes caught fire. By the nineteenth century, for Englishmen, contemplating the attacks on women and children by the Sepoy mutineers or for Americans horrified by Indian massacres, barbarism signified a lower, dishonorable form of masculinity that should be rejected entirely or that needed Christian teaching to improve.

The nineteenth-century expansion of European colonial power thus also registered in intriguingly warped ways the impact of other cultures and their sense of what it means to be a man. One widely accepted view of the western European nations attributes their new power in the world to a characteristic interaction between technology and innovation that relegated more conservative nations like the Ottoman Turks—let alone the tribes and countries of Africa and Asia—to the military and therefore the political backwaters. But that interpretation leaves out the eager imitation of some primitive and even barbaric virtues because they promised to help scrape away the corruptions of the civilization whose military technology had ensured their defeat. It was a tradition with some history.

Under the impact of Renaissance exploration, there had been a renewed admiration for the primitive warrior in the seventeenth century—the "noble savage," a term coined by John Dryden in the 1670s, and popularized as an idea by Jean-Jacques Rousseau a century later. But the admiration was practical as well. In the forests of the French and Indian War, for example, the individualistic fighting style of the Indians was often more than a match, both literally and figuratively, for the well-drilled English armies. Certainly in the United States, it is hardly a surprise to find James Fenimore Cooper in the early decades of the nineteenth century describing his wilderness-wise hero Natty Bumppo as having "little of civilization but its highest principles as exhibited in the uneducated; and all of savagery not incompatible with those great rules of conduct" (7).

In Europe, the increasing number of wars against older but less technologically advanced warrior cultures (both inside and outside the European tradition) thus helped establish a pattern of defeating the enemy through "civilization" and weaponry, while longing for his "barbaric" forms of direct combat and instinctual power. These paradoxes of the state machine of war and the individual combatant, of the moral claims of civilization and the energies of barbarism, of the rational orders of strategy and tactics and the irrational compulsions of heroism, of the reliance on ever newer weapons technology and the need for more and more fallible, predominantly male, bodies—must therefore be recognized as an increasingly central part of the whole business of waging modern war. Just as the individualist heroes of the early seventeenth century solaced the passage into a modern world of sieges and armies, the theater of empire in the nineteenth century became the site where a personal honor debilitated by the modern world could be recharged with nationalist fire against a "barbaric" enemy.

Such double-mindedness began early in the century. Napoleon's campaign in Egypt (1798–1800), for example, had a mixed heritage of nationalistic *raison d'état* and metaphoric warrior need. It was politically justified as a way to control east-west trade routes and force the British out of India. But it also allowed a confrontation with a heroic past, the country that both Alexander and Caesar had subjugated, and whose conquest would make Napoleon and his armies the self-conscious heirs of the ages. Thus the motley cultural residue of that campaign: the discovery of the Rosetta Stone, which unlocked the mystery of hieroglyphics, at the same time that French troops were using the Sphinx for target practice.

Napoleon's opponents in Egypt were the Mamluks, the warrior caste of Turkish slaves who had pushed the Crusaders out of the Latin East in the thirteenth century and become sultans of Egypt. In the sixteenth century they were defeated by the Ottoman Turks, but for the most part they retained their power and wealth in Egypt. Allied to the tradition of nomadic warrior cavalry like that of Mughal India, the khans of China, and Tamerlane, the Mamluks' preferred method of warfare was as mounted archers using a special composite curved bow, and they played polo as military training. Fetishizing archery just as the French knights fetishized the horse and the sword, they dressed for battle in what for western Europeans was medieval armament, including even a spiked mace, straight out of the tournament lists. Accordingly, their idea of conquest was a multitude of individual combats.

Wedded to this ritualized and individualistic battle, they were no match for the orderly tactics and pounding artillery of the French. After Napoleon defeated the Mamluks in 1798 at the Battle of the Pyramids, only the destruction of his fleet by Admiral Nelson a few months later thwarted his political plans for Egypt. But culturally the overthrow of the Mamluks was of a piece with Napoleon's defeat or suppression of other traditional warrior elites. Just as the French National Assembly took goods and property away from the Knights Hospitaler in 1792, he suppressed the Santo Stefano order in Italy, which had been founded in the sixteenth century as part of the Catholic Counter-Reformation. Later, he confiscated all the land of the Teutonic Knights of Prussia (1809), the ancient order at the head of whose table Chaucer's Knight had sat.

The Teutonic Knights had in fact not been a warrior power since the sixteenth century, but Napoleon's eagerness to eradicate whatever remained of their medieval presence strengthens the impression that his campaign in Egypt was another kind of crusade, one with secular goals, using gunpowder and all the forces of an advanced "civilization" to fight a medieval enemy. At the same time, however, the fruits of victory appeared to include an incorporation of the purer honor of that conquered warrior virtue. After the downfall of the Mamluk army, Napoleon gained his own personal Mamluk, an imposing warrior named Roustan who stayed in close attendance, domesticated, perhaps, but still fearsome. In some deep sense Napoleon, although his weapons and armies had defeated the Mamluks, had also bought into their idea of warrior honor.

Lawrence Keeley, in *War Before Civilization*, points out that even in early tribal battles, the more "civilized" tribes tended to adopt primitive tactics, but were superior in logistics. A similar situation occurred in the sixteenth century, when the Spanish and Portuguese invaded South and Central America and faced indigenous tribal civilizations more accustomed to heavily ritualized (although often still brutal) warfare and mowed them down with gunpowder weapons (and the help of European diseases to which the native peoples had no immunity). Then even the relatively inefficient smoothbore harquebuses easily overmatched spears and swords, although on a man-to-man level battles frequently became single combats. But in the course of the nineteenth century, the size of European armies and the firepower they could muster virtually guaranteed the final, if not always the immediate, defeat of any warrior tribal groups they faced. European and American scientific innovation would help defeat numerous traditional tribes and cultures around the world, either because their enemies did not have the technology or because they eschewed its use. Against rifles and, later, machine guns, the massed shock tactics of African and Middle Eastern tribal warriors—along with their cultural expectation that battles were often ways of making slaves of the enemy rather than exterminating them—were finally useless.

With armies becoming more complex in both technology and organization, arms races played a greater and greater role in political warfare, monarchs disappeared entirely from the battlefield, generals tended to direct action from a distance, and new heroes emerged more often from the combat with primitive but honorable barbarians than with industrialized equals. Until World War I, the main targets of gatling and machine guns were not Europeans but the warriors of tribal honor societies, particularly in Africa. Instead of marking the death of honor, the new weapons thus became its handmaiden. Europeans are more technologically advanced, therefore they have been singled out by destiny: the chosen people deserve the ultimate weapon. Of course, the flaw in the argument is that weapons don't care who holds them. When the machine gun comes back to Europe in World War I, especially in the hands of the Germans, the racial superiority it was supposed to imply had already begun to rot from within, beginning the twentieth-century dispersal of empires.

As a society's aggressive or defensive face to the world, the army thus could morally justify an ever-accelerating arms race. To describe the enemy in imperialist warfare as "barbaric" helped consolidate the illusion that it was really honor, training, and racial superiority that was winning, rather than guns, bullets, and explosives. Across Europe, more and more military men were celebrated in the popular press, as well as in official ceremonies. In Germany, Moltke's leadership of the general staff made him a hero of strategy, responsible militarily for Prussia's reemergence as a great power, although he was rarely on the battlefield himself. Others were heroes for their fight against the "barbarians." In the 1860s Charles George Gordon led a Chinese army to help the Manchus repress a rebellion. He died at Khartoum in the Sudan in 1885 after attempting against orders to defeat the army of the Mahdi, a Muslim religious leader who led the revolt against Anglo-Egyptian military rule. It was another lost cause that needed to be avenged. Horatio Herbert Kitchener had been part of the unsuccessful attempt to relieve Gordon at Khartoum. He succeeded in reoccupying the Sudan in 1898 at the battle of Omdurman, then served decisively in the Boer War, commanded British troops in India, became consul general of Egypt, and finally was named secretary of state for war at the beginning of World War I. It was his mustachioed face that looked out of World War I British recruiting posters and his accusatory pointing finger that urged men to enlist.

Both Gordon and Kitchener were darlings of British public opinion at a time when the fantasies of a general European conflict were also being heated by the embryonic science fiction genre's images of future wars. The bare statistics of these encounters between "civilization" and "barbarism" are overwhelming. At Omdurman, for instance, British and Egyptian soldiers under Kitchener were attacked by Mahdist dervishes. When the day was over, more than ten thousand dervishes had been killed, with losses of about five hundred in Kitchener's army, and Kitchener went on to become the model of British generalship and wartime sacrifice, even though it was less his strategy and fortitude than his twenty machine guns that made the decisive difference. Kitchener nevertheless became a popular hero, his prowess enthroned on a mountain of the slain. Something of the values he embodied appears in *The Four Feathers*, the widely popular 1902 novel by A. E. W. Mason, in which the hero, Harry Feversham, son of a general, redeems his unwillingness to fight with his regiment by disguising himself as a native and then saving the lives of the men who, along with his fiancée, had given him the white feather emblems of cowardice. The 1939 film ups the ante on this saga of individual honor by having Harry distinguish himself at the Battle of Omdurman, where the real-life young Winston Churchill was part of the last cavalry charge. In some peculiar but familiar form of cultural guilt, then, technological advances that made individuals less important fed the need for more individual heroes—just as after World War II the presence of the atom bomb hovered over a golden age of American westerns that featured conflicts solved in dusty streets by two men carrying six-shooters.*

In *The Four Feathers* honor and class are united: the symbolism of the white feathers that his friends and fiancée gave the hero to signify his unmanly behavior comes from the belief that to find them in the tail of a game bird means that the bird is not purebred. Heroes, however, did not always have to be upper class. In revolutionary France, the older forms of honor and glory were now open to all, at least in theory. But after the brief surge of revolutionary democratic fervor and the institution of the Legion of Honor in 1802 as an imperial substitute for the suppression of French knighthood, there was a narrowing of French military honor in the eighteenth and nineteenth centuries, for which Napoleon's cynical remark that "troops are made to get killed" might be considered a portent. In England before the nineteenth century, common soldiers were generally considered to have no honor worth mentioning and could not be awarded any decorations. It was not until 1856 that the British government, at the insistence of the queen, created the Victoria Cross—made of bronze from captured Crimean cannons—for heroic actions by junior officers and those of other ranks, who previously had no recognition at all for acts of valor, heroism, or gallantry. Such rituals constituted a widening of the definition of a chivalric military order to include any man whose actions had merited the praise of the state and its people. The process differed from country to country. In some, like Germany, although the idolization of military men was remarkably high, the government was still so wedded to a class-oriented view of true warriorship that the ability of middle-class men to become officers, let alone receive medals and recognition, was severely limited.

In part, this expansion of the field of state-sanctioned honor in England meant that the working-class soldier could potentially be as celebrated as the upper-class officer. But it also signaled the way that war was becoming more deeply embedded in "normal" society. The presence of military men in eighteenth-century British plays and novels was usually restricted to army officers based in nearby quarters, naval officers on leave, and such local figures as recruiting sergeants. With the exception of these soldiers and officers who were part of a professional system, the

* The nineteenth-century imperial battles against primitive tribes, with their aura of strange mystic powers, were visually mirrored in the late twentieth century by movie battles against hordes of extraterrestrials (*Starship Troopers*) or monsters (*The Mummy Returns*).

father and husband at war was a minuscule part of the soldier image until the nineteenth century.

But with the enlisting or impressment of large portions of the population, the image of the soldier as unacceptably sexual and undomestic started to change, and his other sources of identity—husband, father, brother, son, provider, citizen, worker, and even sportsman—became a public issue. As a soldier, he was expected to leave domesticity behind him, but as a member of society, like Hippolyta, the queen of the Amazons, who marries Theseus, the ruler of Athens, after being defeated by him in battle, he was also expected to allay his military masculinity with marriage. Until the advent of mass armies, it had been traditional for soldiers in ranks and even officers to be either prohibited from marrying or, in more permissive armies like the British, to need permission from their superiors, who might charge a fee.* Even as the status of the soldier rose, however, the number of such permissions, especially for the rank and file, was severely limited. By 1867 in the British army, for example, it was one in ten, a percentage that even dropped toward the end of the century, despite a rise in the illegitimacy rate that might have encouraged a more lenient attitude. In all countries there were some military theorists who believed in the need for a celibate army, just as many sports coaches still believe in a celibate team. It wasn't until midcentury that the British term of enlistment was reduced from twenty-one years to twelve; in the tsarist army, by contrast, it remained twenty-five years. But even with such commitments marriage became more possible as an adjunct of military identity that connected it even more directly to the moral standards of the state it served, and the introduction in England of a six-year short-term enlistment option in 1870 allowed an even more flexible relation between men at war and men in peace.

Of course, there were and would continue to be military groups that resisted the presence of women. Many English soldiers stationed in India, as well as later historians, saw the advent of the memsahib, when Englishwomen were allowed to join their officer husbands, as the end of an empire designed, advertently or not, for male honor, creativity, and sexual freedom. Similarly, the French Foreign Legion maintained the romance of a military world in which "unranked men" were not allowed to marry, and an individual's past, his nation, and even his identity could be obliterated, supplanting civilian dishonor with military honor.

* Until 1942 the company commander's permission was required for marriage in the U.S. Army.

But within less isolated armies, regimental loyalty—for officers in particular—began to be built up on the model of a family, not only through comradeship but also through the presence of wives and children, which created overlapping emotional affinities. As this ethos spread to the ordinary soldier, it also helped minimize desertion by creating a focus of loyalty closer to home than the distant national state. Thus the short life of the individual soldier could be gathered up into the immortality of the regiment—the 7th Cavalry, the Gordon Highlanders. In the nineteenth century the appeal of this regimental family for both single and married officers was strong. Almost all of George Armstrong Custer's male family either served with him or accompanied his troops to where they were stationed. His brothers Tom and Boston, as well as his nephew Autie Reed, died with him at the Little Big Horn, and his widow Elizabeth's first book about their life together was called *Following the Guidon*, the regimental flag.

Without undermining aggressiveness, this concern with the domestic side of the soldier's character indicates a new solicitude about the relation of military masculinity to its home nation—in England the relation of empire to the "home counties." The army was not just the metaphoric shield of the nation but an essential part of its self-definition; the alliance of family and nation afforded a moral sanction in the name of the woman celebrated as "The Girl I Left Behind Me." According to some theories the origin of the tune is Elizabethan. But from the late eighteenth century it was traditionally played when soldiers left a place of safety for a place of battle, perhaps most memorably when Custer led the 7th Cavalry out of Fort Lincoln in search of hostile tribes in the basin of the Little Big Horn.

In many European countries, the ideal family in this vision might have been Christian. But despite the imagery of medieval chivalry, pulse-pumping anthems like "Onward! Christian Soldiers," and a frequently non-Christian foe, religion was not always the central element in the imagination of empire. While Kitchener was a poster boy for the evangelicals, other empire builders like Gordon and Cecil Rhodes were decidedly anti- or nonreligious, often in reaction against a strict religious upbringing. Rhodes, whose legacy included a country in southern Africa named after him, particularly longed for an Anglo-Saxon union that would include a restored United States, an idealized warrior league reflected in Stoker's *Dracula* (1897), where the young men who band together to track the vampire to Transylvania include an American, "a moral Viking." Rhodes died in 1902, and the Rhodes scholarships he established in his will at first made awards to citizens of Great Britain and its colonies, the United States, and Germany (which was excluded with the coming of World War I).

These dreams of national destiny did not need a religious sanction in any institutional sense. The invocation of warrior roots seemed to be enough, especially when such dreams were stirred up further by spectacles like Buffalo Bill Cody's Wild West Show, which extensively toured England and Europe from 1883 on.* Another hero of empire, Robert Baden-Powell, who founded the Boy Scouts, similarly favored a nonreligious sense of national destiny (and was a great fan of both Cody and Frederic Remington's illustrations for Owen Wister's western stories). In the first edition of his book *Scouting for Boys,* he likened what he was trying to achieve to the code of honor that underlay the samurai warrior, the medieval knight, the American Indian, and the Zulu.

In the 1890s, Cody added "and Congress of the Rough Riders of the World" to the show's name and featured an extravaganza including cowboys, gauchos, vaqueros, and samurai along with hussars and other European cavalrymen. The name "rough riders" would later be adopted by Theodore Roosevelt for the troop of frontiersmen, Ivy League graduates, working-class city dwellers, cowboys, and Park Avenue scions he had recruited as irregulars in the Spanish-American War. More recently, it has become the name of a condom distinguished by surface abrasiveness.

For all the publicity and presence of war, however, in Europe itself, from the Battle of Waterloo in 1815 until the beginning of World War I in 1914, the number of wars shrank enormously from its seventeenth-century high point. For Great Britain, the only major conflict of note was the Crimean War of 1854–56, while the Austro-Prussian War of 1866 (called the Six Weeks' War) and the Franco-Prussian War of 1870–71 were both over quickly and failed to pull any other states into their orbit. Similarly, despite the efforts of both North and South to attract European support, the Civil War, with its tremendous casualties, still stayed within its own national sphere.

So far as nineteenth-century European manhood was concerned, then, the soldier may have been an admirable figure, but his world of operations was far from civil society. "Civilized" warfare thus aimed to preserve prosperity and unity at home by focusing aggression outward, pushing

* During Buffalo Bill's 1891 European tour, the German army paid close attention to his logistical use of transportation and supplies.

full-scale war to the periphery of a civilization increasingly defined as European. Only France, during the Commune (1871), when Paris fought against the provinces, had any midcentury experience comparable to the U.S. Civil War or to the time of the revolutions when every male citizen was potentially or actually a soldier. For the most part the wars fought by European states were less against one another than within their expanding overseas empires, in combat with the often tribal inhabitants of countries ripe for economic exploitation. Only with World War I did war come decisively back to Europe, no longer through the surrogate battles of empire but now animated by the need to prove national honor on home ground.

The telegraph and the railroad in the late nineteenth century were already bringing the home front and the battlefield closer, although not as close as they would be in World War I, when people in the south of England could hear the artillery blasting away on the Somme, Parisian taxicabs were requisitioned to take troops to the Marne front, and Mom (or Mütter) could send a cake to her son in the trenches with the reasonable expectation that it would arrive in a few days, icing intact. The close juxtaposition of home front and battlefront lay in the European future, along with both the civilian bombing and the antiwar movements that would seem its natural corollaries. As twentieth-century media brought the place of war and the place of peace closer and closer together, war has become both a more immediate experience, because we see it, and a more detached experience, because of the way we see it. With the increased domestication of the soldier's home-front life as well as the perception that war happens somewhere else, it is no wonder that, until the attacks on the World Trade Center and the Pentagon made the threats immediate, some American enlistees during the Gulf and Bosnian Wars often seemed irritated that they were being asked to fight and might be wounded or even die in battle.

# THE BOY GENERAL

> Talk about the "Thin Red Line" of the English. Here was a thick Red line of Sioux and growing thicker every moment. Out of the clouds of dust, anxious to be in at the death, came hundreds of others, shouting and racing toward the soldiers, most of whom were seeing their first battle, and many, of whom I was one, had never fired a shot from a horse's back.
>
> —Private William O. Taylor, describing the Indian response to Major Marcus Reno's first charge on the village at the Little Big Horn, 1876

Perhaps nowhere was this line between the civilization that was to be defended and the barbarism that promised a new energy more deeply uncertain than in the American West. In Europe the wild man of the Middle Ages had disappeared into the realms of myth and the barbaric Other was far away; but America was the Other's natural home. In the post-Napoleonic period, many European aristocrats left civilized Europe behind to venture into the West as part of a self-conscious effort to infuse their own depleted values with primordial virility. Eighteenth-century Americans in Europe had often played into "noble savage" expectations: Benjamin Franklin appeared in the French court dressed in buckskin, and Benjamin West, when he was shown the recently unearthed Apollo Belvedere in Rome, exclaimed that the statue resembled a Mohawk warrior. In America, the savage or the barbaric world that was a past greatness from which Europe had fallen was a present reality.

In the late eighteenth and early nineteenth centuries, French aristocrats, whose values had been so definitively rejected by their own countrymen, in particular were drawn to this New World resurrection of warrior honor. The first thorough ethnography of Indian tribes was done by a nineteenth-century French visitor. The Germans came somewhat later, but the English were also enticed. Depending on your point of view, you could admire the Indians for their social organization (as the Iroquois were admired in the eighteenth century), for their fortitude in the face of dispossession (the Seminoles after Andrew Jackson's expulsion orders), or for their closeness to the primitive state of human nature. A trip to the West, no matter how luxurious your baggage, was an anointing at the wellsprings of aboriginal masculinity, where, as Byron wrote of Daniel Boone's children:

> *Tall, and strong, and swift of foot were they,*
> *Beyond the dwarfing city's pale abortions,*
> *Because their thought had never been the prey*
> *Of care or gain: the green woods were their portions. . . .* (260)

To experience that world, Sir William Drummond Stewart, a veteran of Waterloo, made a trip in 1837 from the Missouri frontier to western Wyoming for an annual meeting of fur traders, trappers, and scouts. There, Stewart met and so admired Jim Bridger, the famous scout and mountain man, that he gave him a full suit of armor, which Bridger later wore on special occasions.

For many Americans, brought up in a masculine tradition of frontier hardiness, the lure of the West was even more compelling. After the Civil War, the frontier army, now shrunken to a fraction of its wartime size, was filled not with citizens rising to defend their homes and ideals but with a ragtag complement of a few Civil War officers, young men from the East looking for work, and immigrants, especially German and Irish, looking to become Americans. Poorly paid, living in substandard housing, forced to endure extremes of temperature and weather, the army of the West oddly resembled the Indians themselves, pushed out of their native lands as unfit for "civilization." The army's mission was to prove itself against this enemy—there had to be an enemy—in order to be heroes back home rather than just outcasts. In England, the public generally ignored colonial wars, except when there was a heroic spectacle, as with Gordon and Kitchener. But the West was much closer for Americans, and when they paid attention, the newspapers and public opinion of the East considered what was happening on the frontier to be a gigantic morality play in which (depending on your point of view) either the defenders of civilization aimed to domesticate the "savages," or the murderous army was in the process of eradicating the culture and livelihood of a noble people. Custer himself said frequently—in a series of articles he wrote for a New York magazine between 1872 and 1874—that he was moved to write because of the misinterpretations in other parts of the country of what actually went on in the West.

Savage warrior energy was celebrated, but it had to be defeated. For the most extreme antagonists, the depictions of Indian life in Cooper's Leatherstocking novels, especially *The Last of the Mohicans,* were the cause of a misguided humanitarian belief in the nobility of the Indian warrior. Like the identification of Christianity with a European civilization that often validated imperialist expansion into Africa and Asia, the wars of the plains were a kind of holy war that either drew on religious terms like "heathen" or "red devils" to stigmatize the enemy or sought to Christianize and thereby civilize him. As many historians have pointed out, these two points of view were also institutionalized in the conflicting authority of the Department of the Army and the Department of the Interior. But even while the Indians were excoriated as cruel and bloodthirsty barbarians by military men and settlers alike, there was also a hardly disguised admiration for their ability as horsemen and fighters. From the regular army point of view they were incapable of or unwilling to conduct "civilized warfare," although Custer himself qualified that phrase with the aside "if the solecism be allowed." What was so civilized about warfare in any case, and why should the Indians have to measure up to arbitrary white standards?

In fact, Custer, like many army officers who had to change their Civil War assumptions about how to fight, felt the need to think and even be like an Indian in order to have any chance of defeating them. In *My Life on the Plains,* the collected version of his articles about General Winfield Scott Hancock's 1867 expedition against the Cheyenne to protect the surveyors and builders of the Union Pacific Railroad, he summarized his sense of the combat:

> Here in battle array, facing each other, were the representatives of civilized and barbarous warfare. The one, with but few modifications, stood clothed in the same rude style of dress, bearing the same patterned shield and weapon that his ancestors had borne centuries before; the other confronted

> him in the dress and supplied with the implements of war which the most advanced stage of civilization had pronounced the most perfect. Was the comparative superiority of these two classes to be subjected to the mere test of war here? Such seemed the prevailing impression on both sides. (47)

Indians were Custer's enemies, but Indians were also his scouts, and he was especially pleased with the Crows, who came from one of the most militarily structured societies on the plains, on whose lands the Little Big Horn battlefield stands: "I now have some Crow scouts with me as they are familiar with the country. They are magnificent looking men, so much handsomer and Indian like than any we have ever seen, and so jolly and sportive; nothing of the gloomy, silent redman about them" (*Boots and Saddles*, 274–75).

What a host of complexities are reduced and ignored in the word "Indian"! But Custer looks for affinity as much as hostility. Custer's own prestige, based on his leadership of one of the few effective cavalry charges of the Civil War, had a touch of the antique about it, and the Indian warrior style was similarly reminiscent of an older time and older conflicts. The greatest honor for many plains tribes was based on "counting coup," getting close enough to an enemy to touch him with a coup stick without wounding him. Counting coup stressed individual honor over group discipline, and the Native Americans were also noted for their lack of interest in pitched battle in regular rows under the authority of an acknowledged leader. Like the British battles against the tribes of the frontier of Northwest India, the battles against the Native Americans in the West promised real hand-to-hand fighting that could restore the sense of individual combat in a world of mass armies and high-powered weapons. *My Life on the Plains,* for example, is filled with admiring depictions of the western "characters" Custer encountered, both Indians and white men (including Wild Bill Hickok). The warriors of a tribe might thus seem close to an ideal that the army could only approximate—men in a world of freedom outside the confines of the state, where honor, physical prowess, and military insight were the measures of manliness. Certainly there was a large complement of inveterate Indian haters on the plains. But for anyone of some reflection the empathy was there as well. As William O. Taylor, a soldier with the 7th Cavalry, who was among Major Marcus Reno's group who first attacked the village, wrote almost forty years later about a warrior who died trying to assault his position:

> Never had I seen a more perfect specimen of physical manhood, he must have been about thirty years old, nearly if not quite six feet in height and of splendid proportions. He looked like a bronze statue that had been thrown to the ground. . . . I could not help a feeling of sorrow as I stood gazing upon him. He was within a few hundred rods of his home and family which we had attempted to destroy and he had died to defend. The home of his slayer was perhaps a thousand miles away. (62–63)

The roots of such an attitude, which was hardly atypical even for a soldier, lay in an awareness of the difference between fighting for an army and fighting for a home, between the professional soldier and the man forced into warfare. Both were part of the mythic legacy of the American Revolution—the militias versus the regular army—and they gathered strength from the unconventional warfare waged by other guerrillas, like that of the Spanish against the Napoleonic occupation, where bravery and sacrifice were always stressed more than foresight and by-the-book tactics, heroic individualism more than drill and order. In Taylor's view, the slain warrior was the ideal embodiment of the military in the service of the domestic, fighting for his homeland, his strength as well as his physical beauty a sharp contrast to "the pale abortions of the city," his death a rebuke to the civilization out to destroy him.

Why was a world that had witnessed the immense slaughter of the Civil War—24,000 casualties at Antietam, 44,000 at Gettysburg—so fascinated by the Battle of the Little Big Horn, in which a little over 210 men died (the numbers vary) in the space of about half an hour? Like the charge of the Light Brigade (157 deaths in twenty minutes), it became more important as a symbol, a touchstone for conceptions of honor and bravery, and, not incidentally, ambivalence about the act of battle itself. Between the Lincoln assassination and the Kennedy assassination, no single event in American history provoked so much commentary and analysis, and it began almost immediately. President Ulysses S. Grant swiftly condemned Custer and called the defeat "an unnecessary sacrifice" caused ultimately by the greed of miners who had invaded the Indian territory of the Black Hills after an expedition led by Custer himself had announced the discovery of gold. That Grant, General Phil Sheridan, and members of Grant's cabinet had already secretly planned to support the settlers with an attack on the tribes made the "sacrifice" somewhat ironically a justification for further war. Little of this was known at the time. Yet the fascination with Custer only grew, fed quickly by Frederick Whittaker's 1876 biography, approved by Custer's widow, which included severe attacks on Grant's behavior toward Custer and his complicity in the disaster.

Custer fought not much more than a week's train and boat journey from the East Coast. Only a few weeks before setting out from Fort Lincoln, he had been in Washington, where, much to Grant's upset, he had testified to a congressional committee about corruption in supplying the reservation Indians. Grant was a Republican and Custer had recently become a Democrat. This was the Centennial Summer, "the Year of the Hundred Years" as Longfellow called it, and while in the East, Custer had stopped off in Philadelphia to see the celebratory exhibitions. Were his ambitions political as well? The Democratic convention was about to open; some thought his name should be put forward for president.

But why should the mystery of Custer's defeat retain its grip even now in a post-Holocaust world? In the last decade of the twentieth century alone, I counted dozens of books about it still in print and being published, including two major biographies in the last ten years. If Gettysburg represents the quintessential battle between North and South, and its battlefield the most imposing collection of monuments, Little Big Horn symbolizes all that is complicated and unsettled in the combat between Indians and whites, the savage warrior and the thin blue line—a lightning rod for ambiguity. The triumphal arches, obelisks, and engraved plinths of Gettysburg have a Roman feel to them: this is still a world connected to Europe and its ways of memorializing wars—the grand gesture, the clash of regiments, the plan of battle. But the scattered tombstones of the Little Big Horn evoke the shadows of hundreds of individual moments, each a puzzle of shifting meaning: Indian truth, army truth, but Custer replacing them all. For Custer haters and Custer lovers alike, the preoccupation with what happened represses the larger meaning of the clash and turns it into a search for verifiable facts.

In trying to explain the continuing fascination of Custer's defeat at the Battle of the Little Big Horn, many recent writers have plausibly cited the essentially racist refusal to believe that white civilization, as exemplified by the dashing young hero (who was thirty-six when he died), could be defeated by the forces of barbarism. But in terms of the paradoxical forces I have been tracing in Europe as well as America, the disquiet with late-nineteenth-century American civilization—what Mark Twain and Charles Dudley Warner called the Gilded Age—itself also plays a role.

Custer, like other military men on the frontier, thought that the fountainhead of conflict between Indians and whites was white greed. But as a soldier he had his orders and, as the youngest general in the Union army and a spectacularly successful commander of cavalry, he had his own dashing legend to live up to; he was as sensitive to the nuances of reputation as were his warrior foes. In his most familiar photograph, he appears with flowing hair and mustache, personalized uniform, hollow cheeks, and leather gauntlets crossed over his chest—a picture of assertive compliance, the rebel in uniform. Compared to the narrow world of medieval knighthood, the growing technological, industrial, and information-gathering society in which Custer made his mark immeasurably widened the audience of any public career, while increasing both the scrutiny and the mythmaking. To his admirers he may have been the "Boy General" and a "cavalier in buckskins"—a symbol of American renewal and refreshment for ancient military heroism. His hostile testimony to Congress about profiteering merchants only enhanced the way the Battle of the Little Big Horn became the emblematic conflict between two definitions of honor, American military braggadocio and Indian stoic display: one rooted in a mythic European past but already warped by concerns of self-image and debased by commerce; the other in much closer touch with the sources of archaic honor but now fighting to retain some small portion of cultural autonomy. Historians and history buffs who try to explain the defeat at the Little Big Horn have focused on Custer's decision to leave behind Gatling guns that could have turned the tide despite the overwhelming odds he faced. The usual reason given is that the guns were too awkward to drag along through the rolling folds and dips of that part of the country. But they were made to be disassembled. Given Custer's theatrical sense of his own warrior honor, it is not implausible that he may have also thought they undermined the purity of his quest for a direct hand-to-hand confrontation.*

The Indian victory at the Little Big Horn was the last before their general defeat, and in some sense the continued fascination with the battle and with Custer is a kind of compensation. Local defeat makes general victory romantic, erasing the guilt and essential dishonor of a clean sweep: if we could not have been defeated, if there were no real contest, what is the glory in winning? The surge of "manifest destiny" that in the

* Generals Crook and Miles believed this, as, possibly, did Sherman. Elizabeth Custer didn't like the statue put up at West Point because, she said, it depicted Custer in buckskin and there were too many mere stage performers—was she thinking of Buffalo Bill?—who looked that way.

late nineteenth century pushed the United States across the continent and beyond had often been called "triumphalism" as if it were only unrelieved success. But this strain of defeat enshrined in the Little Big Horn seems necessary as well, giving the lie to the braggart side of American myths about itself, finding in the boy general's own combination of traits—youth, energy, ambition, self-centered recklessness—the death's head at the banquet. So Custer became a poster-hero focus of meaning for some, an empty center for others, such as Julia Face, an Oglala Lakota interviewed in 1909:

> Q. Was Long Yellow Hair [Custer] recognized in the fight or among the dead on the day of battle?
> A. No one recognized Custer. It was thought he was some cowboy. (Hardorff, 190)

# THE STATISTICS OF HUMAN NATURE: NORMS AND THE ABNORMAL

Custer, Crazy Horse, and Sitting Bull were heroes, men of war whose images have only grown since their deaths. But their battles existed in a world that was increasingly preoccupied with what was normal rather than what was eccentric or outsized in human nature. One of the distinctive contributions of the nineteenth century was the effort to establish methods of quantifying all sorts of behavior and then to extract numerical norms that quickly became morally normative as well. At one level, the material for making such generalizations was gathered from more accurate counting and record keeping. The memoirs of Grant and Sherman, for example, condense the minute tracing of battle movements and casualty rates from the numerous reports that had become an essential part of an officer's responsibility. Such statistics made the quantification of war more possible than ever before and helped convey an illusion of ex post facto control over the risks of warfare.

The same was true for the embryonic social sciences, whose data were deployed to define appropriate behavior within the state's degree of tolerance. Although "statistics" later became a general word for any collection of numerical facts, its first use in the late eighteenth century emphasized the relevance of its enumerations to the improvement of political society. In Belgium, Adolphe Quetelet, who began his career as an insurance actuary, was made supervisor of statistics in 1830. From his experience as director of the census, he first developed his concept of the "average man" in *A Treatise on Man* (1835) and later methodized it in the peremptorily titled *On the Social System and the Laws That Regulate It*. Another important figure somewhat later in the century was Sir Francis Galton, cousin of Charles Darwin and the inventor of a system of fingerprinting still in use. In the 1880s, he coined the term "eugenics" to describe how society could improve or eradicate those elements of human physiology and psychology that he felt would be detrimental to future generations. Indeed, both Quetelet and Galton professed that the goal of establishing statistical norms was to help refine the human race and thereby expunge social sins like war. Eugenics translated the methods of industrial and scientific progress into the social realm by discovering what was normal, that is, where the greatest number of people gathered on any curve of statistical distribution, from intelligence to weight to manual dexterity.

But the most immediate use of norms was to identify who was outside the pale of society and who was inside. Such numbers were never very neutral. There was an innate tendency toward moralism in the idea of the average, hardly contradicted by the observation that many early statisticians and sociologists were, like Thomas Malthus, clergymen. While some reformers used statistics to fight for improvements, others found in them a social fatalism: if a group can be statistically shown to be a certain way, it must innately be that way. Poverty, in other words, was a preexisting condition, and the abnormal easily merged with the outlandish, the illegal, and the antisocial.

The effect of the idea of the norm on the perception of human character, individual and collective, cannot be exaggerated. The physiognomic fascination with reading human faces, which had existed since antiquity, was revived with the publication of Johann Kaspar Lavater's four volumes of *Physiognomic Fragments* (1775–78). Lavater's book was replete with engravings, often of works by noted artists. Its widespread popularity and quick translation from Lavater's German into many European languages reflected a Romantic desire to find a method by which to read the lineaments of the mind and emotions in those of the face. In the seventeenth century, the fascination with human nature had usually been confined—for the amateur—to composing a character in writing. But Lavater's book showed how important sight had become as a way of penetrating the mystery of another nature. It virtually ached for the appearance, some fifty years later, of photography to eliminate the aspect of "art" in physiognomy and turn it into a "science."

Here again norms and categorization came into play. Within the world of social acceptability, individuals used photography to create images of themselves with *cartes de visite* that were designed to be left behind on the mantel during social calls. In the scientific world, doctors beginning to theorize the nature of the abnormal used photographs to show the faces of the criminal and the insane. The French doctor G. B. Duchenne, for instance, published in 1862 a book of photographs of the mentally ill having their muscles shocked by electrical charges into recognizable expressions, in order to prove that such expressions were involuntary and thus rooted in physiology. More intriguingly, Hugh Welsh Diamond, a Scottish alienist (the early term for psychiatrist) in the 1850s, tried to cure his patients by showing them photographs of themselves, on the assumption that once they saw themselves from the outside, they would regain the social self that was the basis of all normality.

Particularly widespread was the urge to identify basic criminal types—what we might call the norm of the aberrant. The French criminologist Alphonse Bertillon, who would later play an absurd role as a handwriting expert in the Dreyfus trials, and the Italian Cesare Lombroso (author of *The White Man and the Man of Color*, 1871, and *The Criminal Man*, 1876) proposed systems for analyzing the physical traits by which to classify criminals and those with criminal "tendencies." Photography and scientific measurement became the prime methods of validating moral judgments about difference. Physical anthropologists like the Frenchman Paul Broca and the Swiss Carl Vogt revised the pseudoscience of phrenology into a full-scale consideration of cranial differences between races as well as between the designated normal and the criminal, while Galton invented a camera that allowed him to superimpose photographs in order to extract the essential elements of race and crime.

Such norms allowed a new kind of policing that tried to discern crime before it happened, to tell who was the most likely criminal after a crime occurred, and to make crime into a permanent social problem rather than a series of isolated human acts. In fingerprinting, phrenology, cranial measurement, physiognomy, even the study of such telltale criminal indicators as the shapes of ears, science and pseudoscience mixed together to establish the degrees and variations of human difference that would cut across classes and nationalities. Intellectually as well as socially, this fascination with the norm created an odd but perhaps companionable combination of tyranny and freedom. Tyranny was the assumption that the norm was the only way to be, from which there could not or should not be any deviation; freedom was the substitution of a wide array of human possibilities for absolute distinctions between the normal and the abnormal, the acceptable and the eccentric, the standard and the freakish. Historians of the social sciences have pointed out that the idea of the norm forces people into molds. But without the distribution curve, say, would we have that distinctively modern sense, rooted in the nineteenth century, that the normal can shade easily into the monstrous, that Jekyll might become Hyde, not because they are two but because they are one?

As that last analogy implies, two mythic figures of the nineteenth century gathered strength and definition from the preoccupation with the norm. The somewhat earlier birth is that of the monster, whose business from the eighteenth century onward is often as either a spectral revenger from the grave or a dire warning of what is to come. The monster may be a ghost, a demon, a manufactured creature, or another self, a doppelgänger, as it was called in German Romanticism. But its genesis combines a fear and a fascination with the animal and barbaric—the tangled past, often, as in *Frankenstein* (1818), on the verge of a seemingly boundless future.

In a complementary way, the urge toward classification and order stands behind another mythic figure, the detective, whose preeminent version is that child of the late 1880s, Sherlock Holmes, a keen observer of details missed by others who then shapes them into a rational explanation. Without norms where would the nineteenth-century detective—Poe's Dupin, Conan Doyle's Holmes—be? Crucially, both Holmes and Dupin have no official positions. Like the duelist, the freelance detective takes control back from the expanding bureaucratic state and makes both identity and honor individual once again. Even though by fighting crime his solutions ultimately benefit the state, he also makes his own moral judgments—Holmes will let people go whose guilt he does not believe should be punished by official law.

Neither the detective nor the monster can be assimilated into the normal social order: the detective as amateur and outsider, solving crimes that baffle the police; the monster customarily destroyed by the end of his story, but always ready to reemerge in a sequel. The continued presence of the monster in particular—Frankenstein, Mr. Hyde, Dracula—shows how the desire for rational and statistically controlled norms masks a profound anxiety about the potential for the uncontrollable to burst through the thin veneer of the civilized exterior. As Van Helsing says in *Dracula*, "What science cannot measure it presumes does not exist."

The imagination of the monstrous thus hides clues to the reasons for the obsession with the organically intertwined identities of men and nations toward the end of the nineteenth century. If this is the abnormal, what then is the normal? Monstrous doubles, as in Robert Louis Stevenson's *The Strange Case of Dr. Jekyll and Mr. Hyde* (1886), particularly express a deep-seated doubt over what is civilized and what is savage in masculine makeup. The essential issue in Stevenson's novel is self-control, and he even uses military metaphors to characterize the conflict of selves within Jekyll as part of his growing awareness of "the perennial war among my members." The drug he has devised to separate the two selves, he fears, will be powerful enough to shake "the very fortress of identity." Like an autoeugenicist, Jekyll wants to release his primitive self so that he might soar away from it to an even greater perfection. But Hyde grows more and more powerful, and he won't go away.

The Jekyll-and-Hyde story is a timeless myth of the inability to escape the savage past with its violence and energies, but it is also a specifically nineteenth-century tale of the incompatibilities of class within the supposedly harmonious nation. Unlike the soldier, who might be Christianized and domesticated, or the working-class rebels who might be enticed into fighting an external enemy, Hyde remains an unalloyed spirit of perpetual disruption, who can be gotten rid of only by killing his respectable host. In its later incarnations, especially when transferred to the visual medium of theater or film, the Jekyll-and-Hyde story can be invoked to explore the submerged feminine in men, or the submerged masculine in women. But its essence is always the lure and seduction of whatever is repressed, the secrets behind walls, the parts hidden under clothes, the warring members for the moment pushed to one side but always ready to rise again.

This desire to bring the barbaric self out into the open and thereby to separate the good from the evil—doomed in Stevenson's novel—is oddly parallel to the moral excuses for imperial warfare against the uncivilized. It reflects as well the constant journalistic preoccupation of the time with the numbers of immigrants coming from eastern Europe—as Dracula comes to invade London—and from the outposts of empire in Africa and Asia. Just at the historical moment, then, when the sense of national destiny and racial purity were becoming most acute, a rising anxiety shuddered at all those forces presumably bent on polluting the spotless nation. Capitals and major cities like London, Paris, and New York were losing whatever they had retained of their ethnic homogeneity to floods of immigration, building an overwhelming pressure on a supposedly stable national identity that existed primarily in either past nostalgia or present propaganda. For the fearful, the unbearable fluidity of national identity was symbolized in London by the gin shops, slop shops (cheap clothing stores), and other "dregs of the docks" down by the waterfront. There the specter of the new immigrants was as gruesome as the monsters in top hats who wandered their narrow streets, both fictional, like Mr. Hyde, and based on fact but turned into myth, like Jack the Ripper.*

One of Conan Doyle's early Sherlock Holmes stories gives an intriguing angle on this split between the world of respectability and the world of crime. "The Man with the Twisted Lip" begins with Watson leaving his "armchair and cheery sitting-room" and his wife behind to go on a mission to London's East End to search an opium den for the husband of his wife's friend. As he passes one of the wiped-out customers, he hears a whispered command to meet him outside. It turns out to be Holmes, of course, disguised as a degenerate opium smoker, and on a case. The case involves a respectable young man named Neville St. Clair, who lives in the countryside with his wife and children and commutes every day to London. On a trip into the city, his wife was shocked to see her husband's face at the second-floor window of a disreputable building that backed onto the river. When she tried to run upstairs, a villainous-looking East Indian sailor stopped her. The police arrived and forced their way in, but St. Clair was nowhere to be found. Evidence of foul play was everywhere, including St. Clair's coat weighed down with coins on a mud bank outside the window. The police arrested "the man with the twisted lip" whom they found in the room, a "crippled wretch of hideous aspect" named Hugh Boone, and charged him with murder.

There are many other convoluted turns in the story, including Holmes's first mistaken deductions. But at the final revelation "The Man with the Twisted Lip" turns out to be a benevolent, demonsterized version of the

* The Ripper's murders of prostitutes in the late 1880s exemplify a complex relation in the public mind between monstrous crime and the urge to purify, since two of the most popular suspects were an Orthodox Jewish ritual butcher driven mad by the corruption of the East End and a black sheep member of the royal family.

Jekyll and Hyde story: Neville St. Clair and Hugh Boone are the same person. Like Holmes himself at the beginning of the story, St. Clair has learned to disguise himself. By chance he discovered that he could make much more money as a strange beggar on the streets of London than he could in any respectable job. The sailor is actually his friend, who has rented him the room where every morning, after taking his train in from the nineteenth-century equivalent of suburbia, he dons his makeup and ragged clothes. But his greatest fear—and the reason that he is willing to be put in jail as Boone until Holmes reveals his secret—is reputation. The proper Victorian husband has the capacity to transform himself into the fascinating but disgusting beggar—and make a fine living doing it—but, caught in the double image of himself as an acceptable or an unseemly version of nineteenth-century masculinity, triumphing in disguise although depleted in actuality, he doesn't want anyone to know. At the end of the story, it is unclear whether he will ever tell his wife.

# THE SPECTER OF DEGENERACY

> The physician, especially if he has devoted himself to the special study of nervous and mental maladies, recognizes at a glance, in the *fin-de-siècle* disposition, in the tendencies of contemporary art and poetry . . . the confluence of two well-defined conditions of disease, with which he is quite familiar, viz. degeneration (degeneracy) and hysteria, of which the minor stages are designated as neurasthenia.
>
> —Max Nordau, *Degeneration* (1893)

In the nineteenth century, then, both the idea of the soldier (along with actual soldiers) and the idea of nationality (along with actual nations) became more explicitly related to the general concept of masculinity than they had been since Rome and the Teutonic tribes. From the earliest times, tribes and other geographically delimited and socially defined groups had attempted to distinguish themselves from others, the most obvious markers being skin color, language, and customs. The Greek word that gives us "barbarian" comes from the perception that such persons spoke a language that sounded like the nonsense syllables "barbar" to the Greek listener. So, too, the ancient myths of many groups define their origins, the unique favor of their deities, and how they live. Some brown-skinned groups considered themselves the happy mean between white and black; some Asians and some blacks considered whites to be denatured "ghosts"; and some whites associated purity with themselves and deficiency with all others.

National identity had been talked of in the seventeenth century, and caricatured national differences had been part of European folklore since at least the Hundred Years' War. But there was little overarching sense of national destiny or all-enveloping propaganda about the superiority of one nation over another until the nineteenth century, when loyalty to the nation and its manhood became a shibboleth compounded of race, language, and an often partially manufactured national history. A few centuries of burgeoning state building and political consolidation had thus produced a self-centered effort among Europeans to understand how they had achieved what they believed to be the highest form of civilization: what were the patterns of history that had put them at the top of the heap, and what were the deficiencies that condemned others to the lower levels of human nature? Racial distinctions were central to those deficiencies, but so were distinctions of class (and wealth), intelligence, and morality. Theories of historical progress were adduced to answer the question, as were the new resources of experimental science, for a vital European advantage was assumed to be cognitive preemptiveness: I can write about and analyze you; therefore I am better than you.*

Yet, just while concepts of linear development, causal progress, and norms of physiology, psychology, and behavior were being established, the craving for the barbaric, the alinear, the fundamental, and the expressive revived as well. For every aspiring Jekyll, there was a sinking Hyde. Some theorists looked outward to declare the superiority of their own group; others looked inward with more apprehension. Social unrest had been a keynote of the first decades of the nineteenth century. For the working-class agitators in England known as Chartists, as well as the middle-class European revolutionaries of 1848, the enemies were political passivity, authoritarian repression, and even, in more liberal societies, the narcotic effect of civilization itself. As John Stuart Mill wrote in "On Civilization" (1836), "There has crept over the refined classes, over the whole class of gentlemen in England, a moral effeminacy, an inaptitude for every kind of struggle." In effect, the savage was the prime energetic individual, while civilization for all its benefits fostered only enervation. The only answer to what Mill perceives as "a natural consequence of the progress of civilization" is the vague formulation of "a system of culti-

* The Renaissance made fashionable the idea that human greatness had moved steadily westward, first from Greece to Rome, and later to England, which took up the scepter. In the mid–nineteenth century, the organizers of Abraham Lincoln's presidential campaign made their own revision: "Westward the course of empire takes its way./The girls link on to Lincoln, their mothers were for Clay."

vation adapted to counteract it" (442–43). For an antebellum generation of young upper-class New Englanders, that same sense of desuetude and enfeeblement, what George Fredrickson has called "the inner Civil War," could be purged by joining the abolitionist movement and by welcoming the first years of conflict with the South. In a similar impulse, rather than support abolition and look eagerly toward the Civil War, the sickly Francis Parkman packed up for the West to write *The Oregon Trail.* Mill would have recognized both alternatives as responses to a feeling of uselessness and a desire to replace a stultified "civilized" tradition with energetic immediacy.

Instead of being simply triumphal, the masculinity that was the personal equivalent of this by-product of expanding empires therefore often seems remarkably fragile, beset from all sides by alternatives and differences, constantly in danger of collapse if its norms are not met and its purities are allowed to become corrupted. In medieval cosmology, the earth was the center of the universe, and man was the center of the earth. Seventeenth- and eighteenth-century science may have displaced man from the center of creation, but much intellectual and political energy was bent toward the definition of "man" in various spheres: how does man behave economically, politically, socially, militarily? Now Darwin's argument that there is a discernible process through which human beings evolved from lower animals brought the seemingly more civilized nineteenth century much closer to the barbaric past and in the process undermined the central importance of man on earth as well.

It is always intriguing to discover a language of the past that people took for granted as much as the air they breathed, but which now seems almost totally arbitrary and for the most part has vanished (and perhaps we might wonder what our own language of assumed truth is and when it will seem just as arbitrary and absurd). Cutting across the nineteenth-century fascination with codifying norms of behavior, celebrating national character and destiny while also establishing more rigid boundaries between male and female, was an overriding fear of national degeneration. It permeates writing and thinking throughout Europe, in politics, in academia, and in popular journalism. Most exemplified in the proliferation of cities, social degeneration was a miasma from which no person or nation could escape. Looking at the lower classes and their "poverty, insanity, and crime" is one aspect of the plaint; the upper classes being "*too* civilized" is the other.

One set of social implications of evolution theory, summarized in Herbert Spencer's phrase "survival of the fittest," implied that if individuals and nations weren't on the way up, they were on the way down. Such reductive ideas of evolution thus became closely connected to theories of racial improvement or degeneration. It may seem as if evolution was a beacon in the darkness, promising a fit future for the species if not for the individual. But many writers could speak about evolution (for the few) and degeneracy (for the many) in the same breath, and the determinism of the degenerationist point of view also suggested the deep pessimism of much racialist theory in the nineteenth century, with its belief in innate characteristics and its fatalism about human development. From that perspective, little in human life is functional or evolving—all is degradation, beginning with the Fall; progress does not exist.

Theorists of colonialism have focused on the eastward-looking aspect of this anxious national masculinity. Edward Said in *Orientalism*, for example, traces the beginnings of the combined fascination and horror in the manufactured European vision of the Arabic "East" back to Napoleon's invasion of Egypt. Certainly there was hostility between Europe and Islam before the nineteenth century. In its later form, however, it does not focus so specifically on the political and religious conflict between Christianity and Islam (as in the time of the Crusades) but on a more secular combat of the European sense of nationalism with a threateningly different social and sexual culture—not how it actually was, but how it was imagined.

Degeneration was thus not just an infection from the outside that could be fought and destroyed; it was also an innate potential that perhaps could never be mastered. It stigmatized the "primitive" enemy, but it also underlay the veneer of civilization in every man. Buttressed by ever more pages of medical and demographic statistics, it cast a jaundiced eye over the meaning of nationalism itself, as disparities within populations became apparent: Were southern Italians really as Italian as northerners? Were Midlands industrial workers and London bankers equally English? The revival of the medieval had created a model for national cultures that was ideally whole and unalloyed, but it also brought with it the gothic horror of the barbaric and the uncontrollable. As sociologists and statisticians and doctors looked around at their societies, alloys and impurities were everywhere.

In its milder forms the perception of degeneration could be a call to regeneration. In 1848, there were nationalist revolutions against dynastic rule in Austria-Hungary, France, Italy, and Germany, some partially successful, some repressed. This was the so-called springtime of peoples, the fruit of the literary nationalism of the Napoleonic period: a pervasive sense of national uniqueness and thus the need for special treatment and respect by other powers. In arguments that supplied liberal nationalists with ideals until World War I, they found political energy by identifying nationalism with ethnicity rather than with monarchical traditions.

But even with such optimism, there was a pervasive despair. Any historian looking back on the late nineteenth century can tick off numerous advances in medicine and public health: Louis Pasteur's germ theory and development of vaccines, Joseph Lister's antiseptic surgery, and Rudolf Virchow's systematizing of cell pathology, as well as advances against malaria, yellow fever, diphtheria, anthrax, cholera, and tuberculosis. But for many at the time, the only direction for "civilization" was downhill. Everything from declining birthrates to alcoholism to increased spectatorship at ball games was adduced as evidence that the nation, any nation, was neither uniform without nor pure within. Looking back on what he saw as a century of degeneration, Max Nordau focused on the increased pace of modern life:

> Even the little shocks of railway travelling, not perceived by consciousness, the perpetual noises, and the various sights in the streets of a large town, our suspense pending the sequel of passing events, the constant expectation of the newspaper, of the postman, of visitors, cost our brains wear and tear. (39)

Nordau was hardly original in his condemnations, but in his preoccupation with the growing prevalence of the "ephebe" (feminized man) and the "gynander" (masculinized woman), he did echo and summarize decades of anxious sentiment. The American physician George Beard, for instance, had written in 1881 that nervousness—for which he coined the word "neurasthenia"—was the hallmark of his century, and he too had cited railroads and the rapid chaos of modern life as one of the reasons, along with the "mental activity" of women. Civilization, in other words, had induced desires that were against nature.

Beard was much more positive than Nordau about neurasthenics as carriers of art and culture, but he still sought to cure them with medical means: science would find a way out of this crisis. Others argued against women's education on the grounds that it would be physically destructive to their bodies, especially their reproductive systems, as well as their social roles. In England, the 1850s and 1860s had seen widespread worry about what was thought to be the high number of single women, for which male emigration was blamed. In essence, the future of society and culture was to be tied directly to procreation. "Race suicide" or its equivalent was the phrase in both journalism and pseudoscience for what was perceived to be happening across Europe.

The other side of the hearty self-congratulation about the superiority of the European male was a fear that many men were not fit to reproduce. During the Boer War at the end of the nineteenth century, it was reported with horror that only two-thirds of British volunteers were considered even vaguely fit while only 10 percent had no problems at all. In the industrial city of Manchester, matters were even worse, with three-quarters of the prospective soldiers considered physically unacceptable. In 1900, according to statistics, there were five times as many potential soldiers under five-foot-six as there were in 1845. Looking back, we might question whether this was due to some sweeping degeneration of the British race or in fact was the stunted fruit of the Industrial Revolution. But the disquiet was real enough. In 1904 the British government established the Committee on Physical Deterioration to deal with the problem, just as several decades later John F. Kennedy, after complaining about the number of American males rejected from the service for physical disability, established the President's Council on Physical Fitness.

Through a whole panoply of scientific language, physiological investigation, and encounters with "primitive" tribes, each country took its turn on the issue. In midcentury England, for example, the growing dismay over national debility focused heavily on venereal disease, especially the health of the imperial soldier and what inadvertent bounties he might be bringing back to the home country. In an explicit bit of political imagery, the Contagious Diseases Acts tried to stem the tide of venereal corruption that advocates believed was rolling in from the East. Unlike the battlefield diseases that Florence Nightingale and Clara Barton brought to public notice, these were the diseases of fraternization and sexual license that produced high infection rates in the colonies despite strenuous efforts to police them.

One criticism of the Contagious Diseases Acts was that they focused almost exclusively on women as the carriers. Another response to the crisis was the establishment of the various local and national "Purity Committees" that campaigned for male restraint and against prostitution in the 1880s. Much of what goes under the name of "Victorian"—for example, the belief that lack of sexual response in women is normal—was

Purity Committee doctrine. Like the eugenic theories of Francis Galton, the activities of the Purity Committees was aimed at promoting better "stock" and wiping out the widely perceived degeneration of the English male body. Its sexual prohibitions were equally against upper-class promiscuity and lower-class licentiousness. In 1870s England there were widespread fears of national catastrophe if birth control were not stopped and if the "better classes" didn't propagate freely. Picking up the cudgels, eugenicists later complained that these "aware classes" (unlike the "race apart" of the British poor or the "dangerous classes" of France) were not reproducing enough and recommended the commercial production of condoms for the masses in order to restore the balance. "Marry and propagate within your own race" was the message. Only then could the civilizing mission of the superior race be justified—the marriage of eugenics and imperialism.

In France the empire of Napoleon III at midcentury similarly called for a revival of the masculine spirit. But its defeat in the Franco-Prussian War helped foster a dread of national decline that was supported by an impressive array of medical evidence about inherited alcoholism, impotence, and insanity—reflected in Emile Zola's novels of the "hereditary taint" of the ill-starred Rougon-Macquart family and in many of the stories of Guy de Maupassant. Drinking was a serious problem in France, which had the highest per capita consumption rate of alcoholic beverages in Europe. Toward the end of the century, the number of establishments selling alcohol had increased enormously, as had the population of insane asylums and the number of people suffering from venereal disease. No wonder that the French government, now republican after Napoleon III's fall, publicly ascribed the plummeting French birthrate—below the mortality rate in some years—and the poor physical condition of army recruits to a civilization in need of reinvigoration.

As a newly unified and militarily victorious nation, the Germans may have had fewer doubts about their own national vitality, but there were enough expressions of fears of sexual and racial degeneration, including movements against pornography, to indicate that such worries were part of general European (and, as we shall see, American) miasma. Wilhelm II, emperor of Germany and king of Prussia from 1888 to the end of World War I, was a great believer in military display; he constantly tinkered with uniforms and ceremonies. Like a caricature of Frederick the Great—the foppish and Frenchified young man who grew up to be the military genius of eighteenth-century Europe—Kaiser Wilhelm demanded a rigid and monolithic public masculinity for himself that corresponded uncertainly with his short stature, physical fragility, nervousness, and withered left arm. Whatever the roots in his own psyche, such absolute standards coming from the top induced in German society a theatrical hypermasculinity to ward off fears of both personal inadequacy and national degeneracy. In fact, the most popular book detailing the cultural sinkhole into which Europe seemed to have fallen was written by a German, Nordau's *Degeneration*, which was quickly translated into both English and French.

The idea of culture invoked by Nordau as the ideal was not that of the eighteenth-century international wise man—like Benjamin Franklin, David Hume, Voltaire, Rousseau, or Goethe—or that of the Romantic artist, whose sensibility was beyond national particularities. Instead, nation was identified with race, and degeneracy was not just an unfortunate by-product of excessive civilization; there were actual villains. Nordau himself was a Zionist Jew. But the response to the fear of national degeneration had spawned more extreme theories of the need for racial purity, like those of Count Joseph Gobineau, the diplomat and Orientalist whose *Essay on the Inequality of the Races* (1853–55) would later influence Adolf Hitler, with its argument that the Aryan race had degenerated because of contamination by the "lower orders." All of Europe, wrote Gobineau, had become a degenerate hybrid through racial mixing. But however extreme Gobineau's pseudoscientific formulations of racial difference were, they only mirrored images of difference that were, in watered-down versions, voiced by many in the nineteenth century. Such theories extended a simple nationalism of self-interest into a definition of national genius and national character so strong (and so precarious) that it could not brook the presence of outsiders or alien blood.

Once again there is ample precedent for such ideas in dynastic decisions as the expulsion of the Jews from Spain in 1492 or the laws harassing Huguenots in France after 1685. But the resistance to the idea of a purified nationality has roots as well. More than a century before, Daniel Defoe, in his poem "The True-Born Englishman" (1701), had mocked pretensions to national purity by recounting the numerous groups that had overrun England:

> *We have been Europe's sink, the jakes [toilet] where she*
> *Voids all her offal outcast progeny.*

To define a pure Englishman is therefore an impossibility:

*A true-born Englishman's a contradiction,*
*In speech an irony, in fact a fiction. . . .*
*A metaphor invented to express*
*A man akin to all the universe.*

In this comparatively early phase of English nationalism, Defoe was already trying to define honor not by national or class identity but by "personal virtue." But like the invocation of *"sang impur"* in *"La Marseillaise"* to accompany a surge of national self-consciousness, nineteenth-century movements toward national self-definition closely equated national character with racial traits and supposedly inherent virtues that excluded the alien and the different.

With the ethnocentric national revolutions of 1848, the migrations caused by the Irish potato famine in the 1840s, the immigration of Chinese to build the U.S. transcontinental railroad, antisemitic pogroms in Russia—displacements voluntary and involuntary—the nineteenth century created outsiders in vast numbers. These outsiders were almost entirely men, in motion from their ancient homelands to some other place, fleeing disaster or allured by the prospect of some small prosperity. In the United States, after economic depressions beginning in 1873 began to burst the bubble of expectation aroused by the gold rush, the surge of immigrants provoked new racial barriers. The Chinese Exclusion Act (1882) was directed against the working class, while accepting middle-class merchants and professionals, but anti-Chinese riots in the 1880s showed how such legal niceties paled next to the invocation of a fearful racial difference. In the same decade, the Ku Klux Klan (destined to rise again during World War I) helped instigate an enormous increase in the number of lynchings of African Americans, often for supposed sexual crimes. White manhood, in short, despite its seeming power, saw itself as desperately embattled, and the first line of defense was a purified nation.

What accounts for this reassertion of a simplified, even simplistic, masculine identity in the later nineteenth century? Does the sense of embattledness come from a feeling of being overwhelmed by the growth of the state, economic uncertainty, and the ancient demand "to be a man" in the face of increasingly obvious technological dehumanization? Much of the discussion of individual and nation in the nineteenth century was buttressed by organic theories that stressed their mutual relation. Theories of degeneration therefore drew freely on works that claimed direct analogies between physical, mental, and social degeneration, like Bénédict Morel's *Treatise of Physical, Mental, and Moral Degeneracies of the Human Species and the Causes That Produce These Morbid Changes* (1857), which heavily influenced Nordau and such criminologists as Lombroso, who aimed to codify the "criminal type" using an array of physical features. In such physiologically inclined theories, society is the individual writ large, a gigantic form of the individual body—which is almost invariably male. Accordingly, individual corruption and national decadence went hand in hand. Like people, societies could sicken and die. Social pathology was no mere metaphor; it actually existed. Whether the cause was the personal immorality of specific individuals or the imagined depravity of entire alien groups, metaphors of disease and the need to purify in order to achieve racial and national health abounded: the body was depleted, disorders had to be rooted out, diseased limbs (individuals and groups) should be amputated if they couldn't be cured.

In essence, the theory of national degeneracy drew upon the same uneasy awareness of the relative virtues of barbarism and civilization. Morel, for example, defined degeneracy as a morbid deviation from an original type, comparing the debility of the present with the force and purity of the past. By reinforcing the relation between individual male vitality and the soundness of political and cultural institutions, such ideas created a fertile setting for war, which Lenin called "the health of the state." Expressed as national virtue and honor, war in these terms furnishes the ideal cohesion that unites divergent social groups and cures any crisis in masculinity, allowing national masculine character to exhibit its prowess on an international stage, validated by the eyes of others, no longer a cliché but the heart of the performance.

# MASCULINE, FEMININE, EFFEMINATE: SEX AMONG THE CIVILIZED

> Man puts himself at once on a level with the beast if he seeks to gratify lust alone, but he elevates his superior position when by curbing the animal desire he combines with the sexual functions ideas of morality, of the sublime, and the beautiful.
>
> —Richard von Krafft-Ebing, *Psychopathia Sexualis* (1886)

The society afraid of its own tendencies to degeneracy had two kinds of enemies: those that undermined its strength and those whose energies could be co-opted to restore an ebbing masculinity. Generally, the latter were the ferocious enemies—the Zulus of Africa, the Pathans of the Indian northwest frontier, the Lakotas of the American West. But the former were embedded in nineteenth-century society itself. As John Stuart Mill's invocation of "moral effeminacy" indicates, the prime agents of the deleterious effects of civilization were often dressed in metaphors of inadequate masculinity. He specifically defined effeminacy as the avoidance of any suffering—"the spectacle, and even the very idea, of pain"—which had been delegated to certain social groups like the soldier, the policeman, and the judge, so that it could be ignored by everyone else, especially the men of those classes with money and power who might have been expected to be the natural sources of a nation's vitality. But "effeminacy" cast a wide net. In the eighteenth century, it was used by Edward Gibbon in *The Decline and Fall of the Roman Empire* (1776–88) to refer to what he considered to be the tyrannical and sybaritic nature of Oriental society, with its lack of British freedom and masculine vigor. By contrast, John Brown's *Estimate of Manners and Principles of the Times* (1757) had stigmatized a mercantile society that lacked the warrior energy of the past. This was a change that Gibbon, for one, welcomed, since he believed that trade reduced conflict between nations. But for Brown it sapped the national strength. His charge of "effeminacy" attacked an incipient bourgeois culture, where few aspired to be like dueling aristocrats, quick to take offense and defend "honor." Similarly, when William Hazlitt wrote about the "effeminacy" of John Keats's poetry or Charles Kingsley attacked the Anglo-Catholic "effeminacy" of John Henry Newman in the name of a more "muscular Christianity," they were referring to a taste for luxury rather than for other men.

But with nineteenth-century theories of degeneracy, the sapping of masculine national strength was blamed on women, Jews, immigrants, and other out-groups as the carriers of racial impurity. The way such phenomena are generally discussed today is to say the out-group has been "feminized" by the in-group and cast as the source of weakness and passivity. Certainly the tradition of allying weakness with women and strength with men is a long one. But a new term is needed to discuss what happened in the nineteenth century because the process of defensive purification begins not so much with women as with members of marginalized racial groups. Women may often be included in this category, but they also occupy a privileged place as an alternate source of national moral strength. Although not part of the male war system, they are part of society. No matter how much women in general are the target of an often virulent misogyny, the "good woman"—usually defined as minimally sexual, pliant, supportive, and subordinate—comes in for praise. Both Charles Darwin and Herbert Spencer, for example, considered women to be as evolved as male children, while Baudelaire looked upon them as the essence of "savagery within civilization" and therefore a source of both fascination and disgust.*

To a marked extent, "woman" in this formulation was sexual woman, an intriguing turnaround from the seventeenth- and eighteenth-century

* For a similar double bind, compare the nineteenth-century view of menstruation as a wound: either women overcome it and are therefore greater than men, or women are depleted by it and therefore become bloodthirsty vampires.

characterization of "woman" in libertine philosophy. Then Rousseau, for one, assigned man to the realm of nature (with its potential for purification and freedom) and woman to the realm of society (with all its corruptions and artifices). But in the wake of the French Revolution, the historians Jules Michelet and Hippolyte Taine connected women to beastly violence and social upheaval—not always negatively. Like the bare-breasted Marianne leading the forces of the revolution in Delacroix's painting, such a view of women emphasized their connection to primordial power and freedom rather than to the social niceties and backstairs licentiousness of the ancien régime. It was a somewhat disdainful attitude toward the sexual side of female identity that many nineteenth-century feminists shared in their efforts to gain women greater political power. Emancipation was equated with consciousness and consciousness with the power of rationality. For those who valued that form of "civilization," the loss of conscious control in sexuality was an indication of its inhuman degradation. The sex drive, in short, was inimical to the progress of civilization, and even the most progressive reformers generally kept far away from supporting sexual freedom as part of their program. As the banners of suffragette Christabel Pankhurst read before World War I, "Votes for women and chastity for men."

For men of a different bent, however, female sexuality and particularly the prostitute represented the mysterious and alluring world of the city, the barbaric core of modernity. In public the distance between respectable and unrespectable for women was often very narrow. As Charles Bernheimer points out, a woman on the street in nineteenth-century France could be put outside the law merely because a police official detected what he considered to be a provocative look or salacious gesture. Whether it was Victorian London or seemingly more libertine Paris, the need was to seek that animal self in the dark alleys and winding streets of the city—in Stevenson's Mr. Hyde or Zola's Nana. Like the male monster with his uncontrollable desires, the prostitute, whose open and available sexuality ensured the stability of monogamous marriage, was simultaneously outside the pale and a safety valve necessary for social stability.

Which aspect of the barbaric and the uncivilized seemed most impatient, and which was branded "male" or "female," depended on what was being praised and what was being attacked. In another mood, say, Baudelaire could pair the savage with the dandy as twin antisocial figures, and therefore to be admired. The taste for exotic adventure that sent David Livingstone to Africa or Paul Gauguin to Tahiti is the distorted mirror image of American newspaper denunciations of immigrants on Manhattan's Lower East Side that likened them to the savage Indians of the frontier. Such attitudes were always grounded in the specifics of their own settings, but the imagery was the same: the diseased urban world, the degenerating nation, had to be cured. The extremity of the response varied from country to country. But whether the cure was an extra helping of Nature (as in Thoreau) or of Art (as in Baudelaire), material conquest or an imperialism of the spirit, the cautionary figure was whatever was not civilized man—woman, savage, Jew—all the ambiguous agents of potential weakness and reckless fascination.

Why do the masculine and the feminine become so separated during the nineteenth century? Religious injunctions, in medieval Christianity or among contemporary fundamentalist Christian and Islamic groups, have always played a role in distinguishing the sexes. But beginning with the nineteenth century, the innate differences often postulated by religion were supported by a modern scientific and medical language. The preoccupation with discerning norms and the normal in all sorts of behavior and action, especially the line between the social and the antisocial, thus appears in discussions of masculinity and femininity as well.

In periods of war, dating back to tribal times, the collective male heart beats in rhythm and the collective psyche travels a single path. With the coming of mass communications, mass armies, and the increasingly entwined relation of citizen to state, those beats seem, at least in propaganda and often in actuality, to be even more in unison and that path even narrower. But when war is not present or in the offing, the pressure diminishes for a univocal definition of both masculine identity and the national purpose. New paths, new feelings, new experiments can spring up. Wartime yields what could be called a centripetal masculinity, focusing consciousness on a narrowly limited number of traits; the masculinity of peacetime would then be centrifugal, spinning off new possibilities as well as dead ends.

But centrifugal and centripetal often exist as aspects of each other, like the fast-moving wheels of the new locomotives that seemed to be going backward even as they plunged forward. The relative lack of European wars from 1815 to 1914 left a space within which other forms of masculinity could flourish, even as it heightened the traditional contrast between the social functions of the sexes. In newly democratic nations, citizenship was gendered more explicitly than ever before. Women could not vote in England until 1918, in the United States until 1920, and in

France, under the Code Napoléon's ceding of all power to husbands and fathers, until after World War II.

This bifurcated male/female power corresponded to differences in dress as well. Whereas in previous centuries, there was usually an equal lavishness or austerity in male and female dress, with the nineteenth century the foppery and bright colors of the previous centuries was replaced by that sine qua non of male dress, the black suit. For a time, women could still be spectacles, often in vivid colors. But the look of men was reserved and ascetic, so much so that even at the time, commentators wondered why the male European costume of choice made it seem as if every man were going to or coming from a funeral. Only the soldier was as vividly dressed as women in the period, and by midcentury the lavish panoply of the Napoleonic Wars was giving way to more muted tones, except for dress uniforms. Soldiers may have been the heirs of a past filled with scary warriors, but they themselves were "civilized."

With such a contrast between male and female visible in every home, public place, and even street corner, it is difficult not to read the self-conscious preoccupation of nineteenth-century men with dressing in black as a visible emblem of a self-consciousness of maleness itself, expressing an inchoate but widespread desire to embody a masculine essence. Even in the United States, which had seen the advent of women's pants popularized by (and named for) Amelia Bloomer since the 1850s, "overemphasized sex dress" was considered to be one of the great barriers to equality. As Mary Austin wrote in 1919 in an essay entitled "Woman and Her War Loot," one of the benefits of the war just ended was not merely an increase of women in new occupations, which had been growing even before the war, but that "even in conservative Great Britain it has been clearly established that woman is two-legged, and that when she is engaged upon two-legged business there is no impropriety in saying so" (179).

Austin wrote from California, where norms of gender distinction taken for granted in England and on the East Coast of the United States may have already been undermined in the later nineteenth century. But it remains an open question whether earlier desires to enforce visual as well as physical segregation of the sexes springs from an assumption of male power or is an expression of male anxiety. In the seventeenth century, the Spanish upper classes, noted both for their black clothes and for their devotion to the *pundonor*, were subjects of a monarchy in steep political and military decline. John Harvey calls the nineteenth-century equivalent "a resolute assertion of power within a period of political anxiety" (196). But if we consider as well the obsession with Arthurian legend even down to World War I, many of these men dressed in funereal black must have imagined themselves in glittering armor with nimbuses of light around their heads.

Were real men, then, the inheritors of a unique masculine destiny or—as the writings of Marx, Darwin, and Freud were arguing—the products of complex social, evolutionary, and psychological forces? The Romantic theme of the double, that other self that undermined and even sought to destroy the image of social propriety and control, became even more attractive as the nineteenth century wore on and the gap grew between the confines of the civilized and the energies of the barbaric, both within the urban world and on the frontiers of empire.

Since the nineteenth century was also a time when attitudes toward knowledge took on a certain nationalist tinge (with, for instance, French and German psychologists having very different views of what constituted sexual norms), the pervasive stigmatizing of the feminine differs from country to country. But we must look for the atmosphere of ideas as much as for their specificity—what binds together nations and cultures that are often so intent on stressing their differences.

Nowhere do those differences show so much as in sexual attitudes. Every age's and every culture's sense of the difference between male and female is built up not merely from biology and past history but also from immediate images and events. The supposed facts of biology were seized upon, especially in popular journalism, as the most important way to describe the essential differences because they were quantifiable and the phenomena they represented seemed more controllable. But war and the threat of war bring less tangible but even simpler forms of masculinity and femininity to the fore. The search for the eternal masculine and the eternal feminine that heated up so much in the half century before World War I therefore might have been formulated by different writers in different ways, but the impulse is the same. In response to the low birthrates and perceived physical degeneration, many argued that absolute sexual differentiation was the key to a vigorous civilization because it ensured a proper and ample supply of children. Similarly, a lack of female interest in sex was considered by many writers to be one of the proofs that civilization had finally advanced beyond the instincts of brute nature and was focused on social good rather than personal pleasure. As William James remarked in *Principles of Psychology* (1890), chastity, the control of the animal self, was the difference between civilization and barbarism.

Like the love/hate relation with the barbaric, the common view that women were unsuited for either public life or war carried with it the elevation of that difference from men into a belief in either the saintly or the diabolic roots of female power. The male longing for the spiritual, submissive woman was shown in innumerable paintings and drawings of women languid, sleeping, and even dying, each in her way a confession of the need for solace in a cutthroat commercial and political world—another aspect of civilization not so readily or easily criticized. Alternately, there were depictions of ferocious women, ravening, torturing, commandeering men, even women as vampires intent on sucking men's blood and vital essences out of them, while literary pornography featured a wide array of sexually devouring women, including an extraordinary number with clitorises large enough to function as penises. Along with these fantasies of the ferocious, self-motivated woman came efforts at compensation as well, with paintings that evoked the past or exotic cultures—in ancient Rome or in Turkish harems—as times and places when men and women had distinct social roles, with the man, of course, in complete charge.

So much nineteenth-century art and fiction prefers the frail, retiring woman, even on the verge of death, to the active and therefore threatening woman. (In fact, the number of women in art and life who died young may be evidence of the influence of cultural expectation on the human body, helped along by a medical establishment that also believed in the exemplary virtue of female physical frailty.) Such pure women helped men to escape their innate bestiality into a kind of transcendence, while the "other sort" of woman exemplified the bestiality. Once again, a precarious masculinity was the central focus: woman either helped direct the male urge away from the body and toward the realm of the spirit or else she actively hindered it.

With the national paranoias stoked by the push for bigger and better battleships rising higher and higher, the need to fashion a masculinity that would be able to meet the challenges of military competition became more acute until its manic fruition in the 1890s. In France, for example, almost a century-long preoccupation with sexuality as an essential part of male identity, as well as the medically attested problems of a fallible male body, had spawned by the 1890s what Charles Bernheimer has called "an obsessive fear of becoming female" (260)—or perhaps an excessive stimulation by the possibility. Two desperate expressions of this fear were a cult of dueling among young men and government efforts to foster larger families. In popular Anglo-American slang, the word "sissy" made its first appearance as a derogatory term for a man or boy, rather than an affectionate term for a woman. On a seemingly more intellectual level, the medical obsession with perversions, which cut across many industrialized countries in both Europe and America, also seems to have responded to the same underlying agitations. Richard von Krafft-Ebing's *Psychopathia Sexualis* was a compendium of perverse possibility that, I can testify, was still fascinating male teenagers in the 1950s (in an edition printed in 1945). The idea of perversion, of course, necessarily invokes a norm, and Krafft-Ebing had an especially strong urge to create new categories and taxonomies for the deviations he was documenting, coining "sadism"—and not incidentally drawing his cases from a degenerate middle class, which he frequently contrasted with the robust peasantry.

The extreme and often desperate we/they split between male and female in the later nineteenth century, the gradual hardening of the differences between men's and women's social roles, thus metamorphosed into both fascination with and hostility toward sexual perversions, the most disturbing of which mocked those boundaries: the mannish, sexually avid woman, and the effeminate male—both poised to pollute and undermine masculinity by their appeal to male weakness.

As we have noted, the word "effeminacy" for most of its history referred particularly to the behavior of men who were too enamored of women and thereby made soft and unmanly. By the late nineteenth century, there was a widespread preoccupation with distinguishing some essence of the "manly" from what undermined or seemed to resemble it. To supplement the adjective "masculine," the more abstract noun "masculinity" had been imported from French in the mid–eighteenth century, while "manly," depending on the source, now seemed to imply domestic responsibility, self-control, and a competitiveness without rancor. In a characteristic usage, Anthony Trollope in *The Prime Minister* (1876) spends several paragraphs separating mere behavior and "deportment" from the true inner manliness he admires, which has a tender side that doesn't always have to express itself in duels or military activity. But whatever its characteristics, such masculinity had little to do directly with women. The prevalence of male-only institutions with their protective camaraderie, keeping women and also the wrong sort of man out, was another aspect of this preoccupation, as well as such fictional comrades as the misogynist Sherlock Holmes (who only really approved of one woman, Irene Adler) and the married Dr. Watson, who was always ready to leave his wife behind for an adventure in detection.

At the same time, "homosexual" expanded from an adjective characterizing particular physical acts to a noun designating a character type. For some polemicists "the homosexual" was a third possibility for human nature, beyond the polarities of male and female, an alternate form of masculinity rather than a deficiency. For most, however, the newly created category reflected the taxonomic language of perversion and degeneration, fatally defining the criminal instead of describing the crime. Nineteenth-century French medicine, for example, defined homosexual activity not as a drive in itself but as a weakened heterosexuality; an enfeebling of the masculine, not a category opposed to it. As the French sexologist Edouard Toulouse wrote in 1918, the homosexuality that the French considered to be rife in the German army would not infect French soldiers because Frenchwomen were more attractive than German women (Nye, 95). Toulouse's guarantee oddly harkened back to laws in Renaissance Venice promoting prostitution in order to combat homosexuality. But this time the assumption was hastened by the authority of a century's seemingly scientific data on "inversion" and "abnormality." Like masturbation or the perversions enumerated by Krafft-Ebing, homosexuality was deemed a disease of the imagination, unhealthily nurtured by the aimless nervous energy of the city.*

The belief that homosexuality was a deficient or unachieved form of heterosexuality bears the imprint of a crude Darwinism that considered evolution to proceed only in a straight line, like technological progress. Alan Sinfield in *The Wilde Century* also argues that the trial and conviction of Oscar Wilde (1895) marks the beginning of a widespread cultural identification between the effeminate and the homosexual that did not exist before, when effeminacy had been a recognized, although often deplored, characteristic, but not one that implied actual sexual activity. Thomas Wentworth Higginson in 1882 referred to Wilde's work as "unmanly manhood" not because it was the work of a homosexual but because it appealed too much to women. Higginson is an interesting example of the earlier attitude because his own politics seem relatively open to groups stigmatized by the larger society: he had been one of the secret supporters of John Brown and led a black regiment during the war. After the war, he crusaded for equal rights for blacks as well as for women's suffrage, and is noted in literary history for encouraging Emily Dickinson to continue to write poetry. But still he was made uneasy by Wilde's writing, as he was by Whitman's.

Many of Britain's most famous soldiers and empire builders—like

* The introduction of "homosexual," this oddly half-Greek, half-Latin term, is ascribed to the writer Karoly Maria Benkert in 1869. Two other new coinages—"uranian" or "urning," after Urania, the name for Aphrodite in the *Symposium*—never achieved the same popularity.

Gordon, Kitchener, Rhodes, and Baden-Powell—were noted for the retinues of young men that collected around them. This same-sex passion rarely had any stigma attached to it in what was considered to be a normal military situation, and therefore physically chaste. But the sense that habitual and immutable criminal inclinations were rooted in certain personality types, along with the anticipation of defending national character in wars that needed to be fought by "real men," helped create the urge to legally distinguish an outlaw from an acceptable man. Male homosexuality was thus added to prostitution and venereal disease as proper concerns of the state. France had decriminalized homosexual behavior early in the century, and England had abolished the death penalty for sodomy in 1861. But in 1885, as part of a bill dealing with prostitution, the British Parliament passed an amendment to outlaw private sexual relations between men under the name of "gross indecency." It was proposed—some argue, to ridicule the entire bill—by Henry Labouchère, a sometime friend of Oscar Wilde. Whatever Labouchère's motivation, the bill passed, making England the only European country with such a law. In the 1880s and 1890s, similar laws were passed in most of the United States.*

Like the masturbation cited by so many writers as the first step toward personal and social degeneration, physical homosexuality was seen as a rejection of the overriding need to continue civilization in general and national power in particular. Wilde was specifically prosecuted for his relations with working-class young men—the so-called rent boys. By an easy extension that many newspaper editorials and commentators continued to make loudly, he was a degenerate upper-class man bent on destroying the moral fiber of the nation's youth, like some depleted Dracula come to feed on their energy. Other homosexual scandals, like the Cleveland Street Affair (1889) in England, which featured a male brothel in the West End visited by members of the circle of the son of the Prince of Wales, and the Eulenberg scandals in Germany a decade later—which implicated confidants of Kaiser Wilhelm—further raised the apparition of a suspect masculinity in the seats of power. In Prussia, as in many countries, homosexuality was considered to be potentially antinational and almost innately disloyal for the way it diverted men from the heterosexual domesticity that was considered to be the heart of social order. Kaiser Wilhelm II himself, like many Germans of the military

* The notion that prostitution, venereal disease, and homosexuality were major social concerns had generally not crossed the bureaucratic or political mind of the eighteenth-century state.

classes, had considered the British aristocracy to be effeminate for its dandyism and general lack of interest in such warrior pursuits as dueling. Who knows how much his heated-up war rhetoric amid a looming arms race may have been compensation for the presence of "unmanly" scandal, just as in the United States of the 1950s executive orders banning homosexuals from federal employment were necessary to prove that the American government was not "soft" on communism.

# SPORTS AND THE MANLY IDEAL

> Periods of martial exaltation are essentially uranian [homosexual] periods, just as we see the belligerent peoples particularly inclined to homosexuality.
>
> —André Gide, *Corydon* (1924)

Effeminacy, luxury, and leisure were all part of the late-nineteenth-century constellation of unmanliness that sapped a nation's vitality. To its critics, effeminacy drew upon the most repellent qualities of the feminine to create neither a good male nor a good female. To be manly, in this shorthand, was not to be homosexual. The presence of the effeminate made a mockery of both male and female, and in the process helped to define them as more essentially separate. Like the fear of an aggressive female sexuality (or the belief that female sexuality did not exist or was quiescent), the attack on effeminacy was rooted in the belief that the collapse of sexual differentiation would hamper procreation, and thereby enfeeble the national future. Unlike the "real" man or woman, but kin to the sexually ravenous vampire woman, the homosexual was believed to be unable to repress sexual desire. So by the end of the century the stigma of effeminacy shaded easily into homosexuality in general, just as the fantasies of female sexual avariciousness contaminated the image of the "New Woman" of the 1890s, whose major sins otherwise would seem to have been having a job, riding a bicycle, and, as Mary Austin noted, all too obviously having two legs.

True, women's sports were beginning to flourish despite those, including some women, who thought that the "limited energy" of the female reproductive system would be destroyed as surely by cricket and basketball as by algebra and economics. But women, from being primarily spectators of male sports, as they had been in medieval tournaments, were becoming active participants in sports of their own. The stereotype of the frail Victorian woman had begun its terminal decline. Firm gender distinctions may have been symbolically essential to nineteenth-century nationalism, but there was a practical side as well. Women's sports, it could be argued, helped strengthen bodies that would bear the future inheritors of empire. As in the film *Westward the Women* (1951), the mail-order brides could fight their way undaunted through hostile Indians, poisoned waterholes, and a thousand other disasters, so long as just before they met their future husbands they dropped their rifles and put on their makeup and best dresses.*

As fears of national degeneracy grew throughout the century, the link between sports and national vitality, first promoted at the time of the French Revolution and the Napoleonic Wars, became even more important. Throughout the nineteenth century sports had been the particular realm of an energetic male fellowship and purified physicality that, while excluding women, at least professed to have no sexual implications. Before this time, of course, soldiers were trained in physically demanding drill techniques that fostered camaraderie as well as efficiency. But increasingly sports and athletic games in the industrialized nations were emphasized as both a physical and moral preparation for war.

Begun in the late eighteenth century in Germany and Sweden but popularized during the Napoleonic Wars by a Berlin high school teacher named Friedrich Ludwig Jahn, gymnastic societies quickly became nationalist centers as well, nurturing what Jahn referred to in *The German Art of Gymnastics* (1816) as "love of fatherland through gymnastics." (The Nazis would later invoke Jahn, like Wagner, as one of their honored forerunners.) Jahn, who was later called *"Turnvater"* (grand old man of

* Many writers believed that women were not equal to men either physically or mentally, but that women shouldn't be entirely weak and torpid either. Patricia Vertinsky cites Herbert Spencer, *Principles of Education* (1859), as a precursor of the idea that women need physical training to ensure the vitality of the race. But until the 1960s, women's basketball was a half-court game because it was feared that women would be injured if they played on a full court.

gymnastics) as if that were his name, sought particularly to revive Greek and Roman gymnastics as a way of responding to the depressing defeats of Prussian manhood by Napoleon's armies.

The perfected male body that was the goal of Jahn's exercises was formed in opposition to middle-class leisure and materialism, stressing instead physical energy, nationalist roots, and, often, a working-class perspective. It also owed a powerful debt to the late-eighteenth-century rediscovery of Greek civilization spearheaded by Johann Winckelmann. Winckelmann's scientific work was fundamental for the modern shape of archaeology, but he also believed that the classical world embodied a purity of form from which his own civilization had fallen. For the most part, the quintessence of that purity was the figure of the athlete, for Winckelmann's ancient world was an essentially womanless space—with the exception of such cautionary figures as Socrates's shrewish wife Xantippe and the seductive Cleopatra—where the most important relations were between men. The central importance of Greek and Latin literature in nineteenth-century higher education further emphasized the argument that manliness involved a distinct element of male camaraderie, even passion. This cult of the classical thereby joined hands with the cult of the medieval, which also highlighted the beauty and spirituality of the virgin boy, the Galahad whose purity, asceticism, and self-sacrifice would be a tonic for the nation.

One might think, then, that the effeminate male was as much the enemy to a robust homoeroticism as he was to the norms of both masculinity and femininity; this is certainly the force behind Gide's later association of homosexuality with the military in *Corydon*. For some, no doubt, there was a justification of physical homosexuality in this evocation of that classical past, but at least in theory the idea was wholly ascetic, without any sexual element to tarnish it. Juvenal's *mens sana in corpore sano* (a sound mind in a sound body) was the endlessly repeated motto of the movement, and it quickly spread to England and America, never quite getting as strong a foothold in southern Europe as it did in the north, until the advent of Mussolini.

Underlying the gymnastic exercises was the familiar organic metaphor identifying the health of the male body with the health of the national body. In the formulation of Thomas Arnold, headmaster of Rugby from 1828 to 1842, the goal was "the body of a Greek and the soul of a Christian knight"—a manliness that would reinvigorate the depleted national moral stock. Historians have doubted whether Arnold was as interested in sport as Thomas Hughes makes out in his massively popular boy's book *Tom Brown's School Days* (1857). But Hellenism, medievalism, and muscular Christianity nevertheless drank from many of the same springs, as the title of Hughes's later book, *The Manliness of Christ* (1880), indicates. While in the often-invoked world of Plato's *Symposium* the progress of masculine love went from the physical up the ladder of Eros to the love of pure Being, the nineteenth-century Platonists added the state as a top rung, retailoring the homoerotic ideal to include whatever nationalism was their own. The physical body was an image of inner spiritual life: the beautiful body implied the beautiful soul; the ugly body, the ugly soul. Members of darker races, who could never be sculpted in pure white marble, were therefore by definition ugly on both accounts and necessarily marked by physical flaws.

It is easy enough to dismiss the excesses of this urge to physical purity, but it had a democratizing element as well, if you happened to be white. The amalgam of spirit and flesh was not the unique property of a monarch or an upper class, like the medieval contrast between the king's mortal body natural and his immortal body politic. It was meant instead to be a general truth, a definition of manliness that purported to ignore class, family, and wealth, interweaving the destiny of the new mass state with the physical condition of its male members.

Team sports made the metaphoric relation between the well-trained individual body and national vitality even more explicit. Arnold's Rugby was the home of the game that Americans later turned into football, and other team sports such as cricket and soccer began to gather large audiences outside the school to make the public spectacle of male sports an important part of leisure activities by the middle of the century. By the 1870s and 1880s, personal fitness, team sports, and patriotism formed a virtually unquestioned triad of male definition, from which women were as barred as they were from voting.

Crucial to the development of sports was, first, the model of military discipline, the rhythms of male bodies working together. But even more essential was the increasing moralization of sports, the way in which individuals subordinated themselves and their ambition to the needs of the group and the code of fair play. Like the regimental family, sports fostered a collective identity into which individual competitiveness could be comfortably folded. At the same time, the insistence on games and rules allowed young men to associate physically with one another without fear of arousing "unnatural" sexual instincts. Thus, as sports developed in the nineteenth century, it supplied a model of manly and moral friendship without the taint of effeminacy, in which the commingled sense of duty, patriotism, and moral (if not always religious) fervor was authenticated by focusing on and, later, sacrificing the physical body. In the first conscriptions of World War I, whole British football teams would go to war together, banded in the same regiment. The war that finally came was in some way thought to resemble a game, a version perhaps of the "great game" of empire. Until the power of German machine guns was fully understood, charges might even begin with the gruesomely insufficient spectacle of an officer kicking a soccer ball into no-man's-land.

Like the medieval tournament, sports developed from a *mêlée* of men, each trying to win for himself, into a system of rules, with clearly marked sides and boundaries. For authorities fearful of lower-class crowds getting out of control, rules protected sports from the chaotic barbarism from below at the same time that they preserved the image of properly masculine prowess on the field. In the 1860s, for example, while the North and South were preoccupied by the Civil War, the newly organized baseball organizations of New York took the time to argue with Southern groups over the fly ball: should it be an out if caught on a bounce, as had been the previous rule, or did it need to be caught in the air? The no-bounce side won; it was not "manly," they argued, to catch the ball after it had already hit the ground.*

Many subsequent efforts were made to diminish unnecessary brutality in sports. The Marquess of Queensberry's rules, first published in 1867, sought to bring some order to what had been bare-knuckled boxing (use of gloves, three-minute rounds, ten-second recovery from a knockdown, and so on) and thereby create a "manly art of self-defense" that combined physical brutality with a respect for propriety. Some innovations, however, like Walter Camp's promotion of tackling below the waist in U.S. football, actually increased the number of injuries. Camp had been one of the founders of the Intercollegiate Football Association in 1876 (the year of the Little Big Horn and the American Centennial) and was instrumental in shaping the American form of the game that had been known as rugby football. In 1889 he helped to create the concept of the All-American team. Although some of Camp's innovations, like the eleven-man squad and the concept of down yardage, made football a less chaotic game than it had been, the image of national combat seemed never far from his mind. He considered the critical difference between American

* The connection between the Civil War and baseball is not just fortuitous. A legend later grew up that Abner Doubleday, the supposed inventor of baseball, had fired the first gun at Fort Sumter.

football and other forms to be the concept of interference. At a White-House conference called by Teddy Roosevelt in 1905 to deal with the already severe problem of deaths from football violence, Camp opposed the introduction of the forward pass, and even his most original contribution, the line of scrimmage (1880), took its lead from the language of combat. Custer uses the word in his memoirs, and the officers of the British Empire used it to describe their Asian and African wars. The school song of my high school, Central of Philadelphia, written by three members of the class of 1907, makes the equation even more explicit:

*On ballfield or in life,*
*In peace or deadly strife,*
*For thee thy sons will labor,*
*For thee, oh dear old High.*

In many ways the athlete is both a fraudulent and a paradigmatic version of the warrior, with all the pure moves of combat but little of the fear, chaos, and death. Sports and athletic contests had always had a symbiotic relation to war in classical times, as evidenced in the games that play a central role in epics such as the *Iliad*, the *Aeneid*, and *Beowulf*, as well as the well-known cessation of hostilities during the Olympic Games in ancient Greece. Whatever its claims, then, to being an alternative to war (and not all sportsmen cared to make such claims), nineteenth-century sports in all its forms also prepared men to be citizen soldiers, physically for the players and psychologically for the spectators. The duke of Wellington's oft-repeated aphorism that "the battle of Waterloo was won on the playing fields of Eton" became even more a guiding precept as the century wore on. Even though Wellington had almost certainly meant that the bloody, rough-and-tumble sports of the pre-Arnold era had been the appropriate preparation for the confusion and chaos of battle, his lines instead became a mantra for fair play, the sacrifice of the individual for the group, and, once again, the stiff upper lip. In the face of fears of racial degeneracy, amid the new burdens of empire, sports could be the energizer and the purifier, creating the right sort of man, but also the right sort of soldier-imperialist, bringing civilized order and fair play to the frontier, along with rituals of initiation, physical pain, and manly stoicism that were not unlike those undergone by the more barbarous foe.

· · ·

By the turn of the century, then, men of all classes were expected to be able to play sports as part of a complete masculine identity. For those with more money or ambition, foreign exploration and combats with nature were yet another way to restore manly challenge to an excessively civilized world. So Witold Rybczynski describes the impact of Yosemite on Frederick Law Olmsted in 1865. Less than a decade before, Olmsted had designed Central Park in New York as a "people's park" to reinvigorate those otherwise unable to leave the city. But in Yosemite he grasped as well that "the experience of scenery, whether man-made or natural, could be a powerful *civilizing* force" (258), and perhaps a way to reform civilization itself. Similarly, European aristocrats had traveled to America, English missionaries to Africa, and Americans to Hawaii and the Pacific, all in search of an exotic experience that would test their mettle. Here, the subjugation of geographic space was an intriguing psychic equivalent of political imperialism, not just the pragmatic expansion of markets or the urge to vanquish "inferior races," but a combat with nature itself. Romantic heroes in fiction had often been depicted high up in mountainous crags, and the challenge of mountain climbing became a metaphor of transcendence. Mont Blanc had been conquered in 1786, the Jungfrau in 1811, and the Matterhorn in 1865. Thereafter the goals of this competition to go the highest and the deepest and the farthest were outside Europe, but the sense of testing man against nature was the same. In the years before World War I, the North Pole was reached by the American Robert E. Peary in 1909, and the South Pole by the Norwegian Roald Amundsen in 1911. It hardly seems a coincidence then that on the day World War I began, Sir Ernest Shackleton headed out to travel by ship and dogsled some two thousand miles across the Antarctic. Robert F. Scott and his team had died in their return from the South Pole in 1912 after discovering that they had been beaten to the prize by Amundsen. But in the amateur ethic, hardihood could be as important as being first. Shackleton's ship, later crushed by ice floes, was called the *Endurance,* and the end titles of *South* (1919), the film made by Frank Hurley, the expedition photographer, feature these inspiring words:

> Thus ends the story of the Shackleton Expedition to the Antarctic—a story of British heroism, valor and self-sacrifice in the name and cause of a country's honor. The doings of these men will be written in history as a glorious epic of the great icefields of the South, and will be remembered as long as our Empire exists.

Like the building of battleships, such ventures into the undiscovered and the untracked had unavoidable political implications, even though the stress was usually on the individual competition with nature, as in the Everest climber George Leigh-Mallory's famous answer to the question "Why do you climb?": "Because it's there." Such exploring contrasted individual daring and risk with the regimentation of military drill. But by the time of Sir Edmund Hillary's successful climb in 1953, with seven and a half tons of equipment, the relative weight of individual accomplishment and technological support had changed, just as it had in warfare. Hillary and Tenzing Norgay's triumph may be grand, but its connection to the politics of the time—the coronation of Elizabeth II and the revival of postwar England—also seemed more obvious.

The lure of such adventure was not just for the specially trained. At the age of twenty-three, for example, Theodore Roosevelt climbed the Matterhorn, sixteen years after Edward Whymper made it to the top. The imitation of Whymper's Matterhorn climb by Roosevelt and numerous others indicates how much in the decades before World War I the experience of accepting the challenge of nature was the individual equivalent to the group experience of sports for young men. In both, the male body was being tested physically and, by implication, morally in the civilized version of an initiation ceremony. Were men able to match the majesty of mountains, like those Albert Bierstadt painted of the western United States in the 1860s and 1870s, whose grandeur threatened to overwhelm the few puny humans below their enormous sides? It was a challenge not unlike those posed to the young men of Native American or African or Asian tribes, but now presented to "civilized" men: what challenges are you willing to face in order to grow up?

Answers to these questions about the developmental cycle of masculinity were beginning to come in part from the new academic discipline of anthropology. Anthropology had begun to make its way on the intellectual scene of Europe and America in the first half of the nineteenth century, with a primary focus on comparative anatomy (from which spring many of the works on racial difference) and on customs and ethnography. Reporting the strange behavior and odd look of "savages" gave a seemingly scientific basis for invidious distinctions between races and nations. The encounters with primitive tribes due to the expansion of empires afforded a wealth of material, although only gradually did anthropologists appear who tried to systematize and understand tribal cultures, instead of merely collecting as many details as possible. Ethnographic societies appeared in Paris (1839) and in London (1842). In 1886 the Royal

Ethnological Museum was founded in Berlin with a clear mandate to learn everything there was to know about these cultures so that they could be better ruled.

By its constant if often implicit contrast between the "savage" being studied and the presumably civilized observer, anthropology became a prime way of perceiving and defining not only what was different about other cultures (and therefore what the reader was not), but also what was alluring (and therefore what the reader might want to be). Whatever the imperialist uses of much early anthropological study, in its increasingly popular form, especially as interest shifted to comparative mythology in the late nineteenth century, it emphasized efforts to explain contemporary religion, marriage customs, war, and other social activities in terms of primitive forebears. Responding to eighteenth-century ideas that it was the use of tools that distinguished barbarism from savagery and drawing on his own extensive studies of Native American kinship systems, the American anthropologist Lewis Morgan in *Ancient Society* (1877) proposed a theory of cultural evolution that proceeded from hunter-gatherer savagery to the settled agriculture of barbarism and finally to the urban society and advanced agriculture of civilization. Similarly, he argued that sexuality progressed toward monogamy from promiscuity, just as religion went from polytheism to monotheism.

In these and later discussions, masculinity took a central place, particularly its grounding in rituals of initiation that marked the passage from boyhood to manhood, that established kingship and authority, and that regulated warfare—trial by ordeal, and the overcoming of pain to guarantee acceptance into the tribe. For modern man, then, the depiction of the primitive in anthropology represented a lower, earlier form of the life that led up to modern civilization, as well as an antidote to its ills. Historians who wanted to explain the often enigmatic practices of the classical world as analogous to those of contemporary primitive tribes were often indistinguishable from those who believed that the classical world was the perfection from which their civilization had fallen. To a believer in "the strenuous life" like Teddy Roosevelt, the encounter with nature, the rediscovery of mastery through initiation, could counteract the neurasthenia that George Beard said was the hallmark of his century. Beard had wanted to accomplish the cure by medical means, but anthropology implied that a healthy dose of physical trial in the midst of nature, a harkening back to our precivilized ancestors, could serve as well. To create a better man and, by extension, a better nation, masculinity itself had to be reritualized, to recapture its more authentic past.

What might be learned *from* the primitive, as opposed to what could be learned *about* the primitive to better manipulate him, became much more central to anthropological study with the late-nineteenth-century arrival of Franz Boas. His approach questioned the belief that "savages" were an imperfect form of European civilization, and proposed instead that their cultures were different enough to be not fully understandable by European analogies. In the 1880s and 1890s, when imperialism and preparations for war were heating up, Boasian anthropology was beginning to introduce an implicit critique of the moral justifications of imperial policy. It undermined the assumption that race was a static concept, as well as the belief that there was a continuum between savagery and civilization in which some races and groups were obviously inferior and others obviously superior.*

From origins that implied an iron hierarchy of civilizations, anthropology had begun to perceive something like human unity in the diversity of cultures. It was an ideal not unlike the one that animated Pierre de Coubertin, who spearheaded the refounding of the Olympic Games in 1896. Coubertin's goal was not militaristic but international, patriotic without favoring any particular country, seeking through sports to promote connections among nations rather than the differences between them—another effort to revive the ideals of the classical past to reinvigorate the depleted present. The games were to be nonprofessional and nonmaterialistic—the antidote to all the ills of nineteenth-century civilization.

Coubertin's vision of amateur sportsmen competing for the good of the world had been inspired in 1883 by a pilgrimage to the tomb of Thomas Arnold at Rugby. But his idealistic effort to reconstitute a politically purified masculinity quickly took on darker colors during the decade of war anxiety that gave birth to the Olympic movement. The five-ringed Olympic logo memorializes the fact that there were five Olympic Games before World War I prevented a sixth, which was to have been held in Berlin. Only later was it decided that the five rings represented the five sources of Olympic contestants (Africa, the Americas, Asia, Australia, and Europe). Even the founding myth, that the Olympic truce stopped wars, was not quite true, although it did guarantee safe passage to athletes and spectators. But Coubertin's hope that peaceful sports

* By 1930 neither "savage" nor "barbarian" was used in mainstream Anglo-American anthropology. "Savage" was revived by Claude Levi-Strauss in *The Savage Mind* (1962), which argued for the complexity of the thought processes of primitive peoples.

competition would replace war has yet to be vindicated. Like the ancient Olympics themselves, which were plagued with military violations and individual corruption, the modern Olympics are inescapably politicized. How could it be otherwise, when they were founded during an era when national cults of manliness focused directly on sports competitions?

Modern sports festivals have strayed little from those nineteenth-century roots. There is always a core of self-worship for the audience that watches and cheers, whether in a hometown arena or in the national arena of television. Even today, in a supposedly more international world, there are so many events going on at once in the Olympics that television coverage from whatever country must construct a coherent narrative, invariably a nationalist story stressing its own athletes, with perhaps a few vignettes of others who embody recognizably kindred values.

# THE CRUCIBLE OF THE 1890s

> Who is there who would not like to be thought a gentleman? Yet what has that name been built on but the soldier's choice of honor rather than life? . . . In the midst of doubt, in the collapse of creeds, there is one thing I do not doubt, that no man who lives in the same world with most of us can doubt, and that is the faith is true and adorable which leads a soldier to throw away his life in obedience to a blindly accepted duty, in a cause which he little understands, in a plan of campaign of which he has little notion, under tactics of which he does not see the use.
>
> —Oliver Wendell Holmes, Jr., "A Soldier's Faith" (1895), Memorial Day speech to the graduating class of Harvard College

In what situations does masculinity revive and reshape itself into a more militant form? The sharp gender distinctions of the late nineteenth century, as well as the propaganda of European empire, emphasized man as the creator of a history that was made up primarily of other men. Men conquered nations, migrating to the outposts of empire and across the frontier, bringing a national culture with them in which women had only peripheral importance.

As we look back over the relation of warfare to society since the advent of gunpowder and the centralized state in Europe, it is tempting to theorize that times of war anxiety create a cultural urge to assert the absolute difference of male and female. Certainly the pervasive threat of war in late-nineteenth-century Europe raises the ante: men should be men and women should be women, it seemed to many, and nowhere more than in wartime, when the nation needed to call upon the virtues of both genders—albeit in their proper and separate spheres. Women were beginning to move out of the home into work, sport, and even politics. But when the governments were eager for newer and more elaborate armaments, and a daily press continually heralded the apocalyptic battle to come, a clash developed between changing sexual attitudes and the approaching shadow of a war that would test the nation. For in the battle to come, any competitor must be defined as truly masculine.

This need to polarize male and female did not occur only in anticipation of conflict. Some of the most marked simplification of masculine norms occurred in reaction to defeat. But the underlying principle was the same: war required a masculinity as purified and as streamlined as a spear; deviation meant defeat.

The combat of masculinities in 1890s Europe was thus between a heterosexual physical lineage (threatened by alcoholism and other less specifiable forms of "degeneration") and a homosocial cultural continuity, defined primarily by a nationalism that itself was threatened by "lesser" forms of masculinity. The ghosts of those eighteenth-century writers who thought that true masculine honor had been lost with the coming of commercial society must have been pleased. Against those who argued that more trade relations between countries led to a more united world, they had said the result would be a precipitous drop in manliness. Even those who supported the arts of peace worried, John Stuart Mill talking of effeminacy and Alexis de Tocqueville remarking on the "tremendous lassitude" that enveloped France after the Napoleonic Wars.

The result in many countries was an effort to find outlets, both public and private, that would strengthen the national self-image. The emotional embrace of barbarism and the celebration of the heroic, previously associated with the aristocracy, were adopted as a basic masculine style even among the commercial classes themselves. In 1870, for example, France under Napoleon III had sought a war with Prussia out of motives that the emperor phrased explicitly in terms of both national honor and manliness. The loss of that war not only gave rise to foreign policy based on revenge; it also sparked an era in which dueling once again became the most frequent way to settle disagreements. After the Napoleonic Wars, demobilized officers could be found challenging everyone in sight on minute points of honor. But now dueling was in vogue not just among the upper classes and the military, but among tradesmen and poets as well. In republican societies like France, in societies sensitive to the nuances of hierarchy like the American South, as much as in the militaristic nations like Prussia, a general definition of manliness had begun to absorb the older aristocratic urge to duel. Noblemen and gentlemen dueled, but so did students. Men with obvious physical prowess dueled, but so too did fops and dandies. In a world of citizens and laws, dueling both announced a special male status and avoided, through ritual, a demeaning brutality.

The increase in dueling is only one example of the many nineteenth-century efforts to conjure up an older, more chivalric tradition of male self-assertion in response to the mercantile preoccupation with money, as well as to political democracy, with its leveling of prominence and its undermining of the opportunities for distinction. In the United States, the cause of abolition and the Civil War had been eagerly greeted by the otherwise bored and aimless young men of antebellum New England, who believed that the energies of the revolution had entirely dissipated and a growing materialism was corroding both the national character and their own. Similar fears of civilized deficiency helped send young British aristocrats to India to revitalize their sense of class duty, and in Dickens's *A Tale of Two Cities* (1859)—set during the French Revolution but speaking directly to current concerns—the foppish and disengaged wastrel Sydney Carton saves his soul and discovers a new integrity by sacrificing himself on the guillotine.

Dueling in France generally concerned private citizens, while in the more militarily organized Germany it was a privilege that set men who dueled apart from the ruck of civilians and often included savage saber scars on the cheeks as a visible mark of that difference. In England, where the standing army was identified with royal privilege and oppression, the duel had been mocked by Addison and Steele as far back as the early eighteenth century, and so combatants often went to the Continent to settle their differences. In the more precarious society of the United States, by contrast, dueling had much firmer footing. The famous 1804 duel between Alexander Hamilton and Aaron Burr was only one of many, and the duel of honor was particularly prevalent in the South as part of the chivalric tradition. Later in the century, in Henry James's *The American* (1877), it is considered to be primarily a European custom, although James's hero shows an odd craving for it as an explicit test of honor. In his 1895 Memorial Day address, Oliver Wendell Holmes, Jr., two years James's senior, confirmed the allure:

> The students at Heidelberg, with their sword-slashed faces, inspire me with sincere respect. I gaze with delight upon our

> polo players. If once in a while in our rough riding a neck is broken, I regard it, not as a waste, but as a price well paid for the breeding of a race fit for headship and command. (92)

Was this increase in the frequency of dueling in France, this celebration of Theodore Roosevelt's "strenuous life" in America, evidence of a growing militarism or a reaction against the democratic leveling of modern life? In Germany, as Holmes indicates, it was part of a military tradition, while in the United States it connected with a national sense of frontier hardiness and a revived revolutionary militancy. In the South particularly, where Northern commercial superiority had been blamed as the ignoble cause of the Confederacy's defeat in the Civil War, dueling flourished, with all the chivalric Sir Walter Scott trappings that Mark Twain mocked in the feud between the Shepherdsons and the Grangerfords in *Huckleberry Finn*. The deaths of Pushkin (1837) and Lermontov (1841) in duels suggest that the lack of chivalric traditions in Russia similarly made the duel a necessity for asserting masculine honor among an aristocracy and upper middle class that deeply admired French culture.

The variations in the duel from country to country depended largely on the differing role of the army in national identity. In early-nineteenth-century France, the army had to a great extent been identified first with the revolution and then with Napoleon's conquests and national *gloire*. But when aristocratic officers reassumed their prominence, the feeling that the army equaled France dissipated, especially among the laboring classes, whose strikes were often repressed by military force, and in the countryside, where conscription took its toll of able family-farm workers. Even though in theory the French army was under civilian control, the Bonapartist tradition of the strong military-political leader remained a constant thread in French public life from the military coup of Louis Napoleon that brought on the Second Empire in 1852 to the threat to the Third Republic posed by General Boulanger in 1889. The Dreyfus case in the 1890s revealed a basic conflict between French military tradition and republican ideals. But even then the fact remained that any identification of the army with the essence of France had itself been revived only twenty years before, by the "nation in arms" propaganda of the Franco-Prussian War, a war that the French had, of course, lost.*

* Like the Minuteman of the American Revolution, who left his plow to go to war, the "nation in arms" was the French version of a myth of civilians ready to go to war when needed.

In France, then, while the immediate issues may have been personal, the overarching national loss of honor in the Franco-Prussian War created an atmosphere in which those conflicts needed to be settled in a duel, if not to the death, at least until the requisite number of shots were fired or blows and parries exchanged to make certain that both participants could leave with their honor intact. In the seventeenth century, Hobbes had argued in *Leviathan* that honor was only the expression of power, but in post-1870 France its assertion through the duel also served as self-justification by those either powerless or positionless—an odd egalitarianism. To be challenged, even to have the capacity to fight, meant to be respected. The duel, especially in France and Germany, let the trappings of bourgeois civilization fall away to reveal the pure warrior mettle beneath. There were duels over women, over politics, and over a wide variety of personal insults. The spirit was pervasive, and what to our eyes seem to be the most unlikely people were involved: Karl Marx was an avid fencer, dueled as a student, and considered challenging a rival later in life; Marcel Proust fought a duel with someone who accused him of being a homosexual. In 1896, Edouard Drumont fought a duel with Bernard Lazare. Lazare was a Jewish supporter of Alfred Dreyfus, Drumont a journalist and author of the antisemitic tract *La France juive*, which voiced fears that Jews were in control of the French army as well as the rest of French society. It was a noteworthy duel (Lazare won), but only one of many between Jews and antisemites who, even though they may have believed that Jews were alien to French society and national honor, nevertheless could not refuse a challenge that in effect validated the status of their enemies.

The thread that connects these national variations is the way the duel purports to muster an ideal warrior energy to help reinvigorate a defunct or deficient civil sphere. This defensive fin de siècle masculinity thus indicates how deeply embedded was the idea that the public social world furnished an arena in which male honor was either gained or lost, and how much the willingness of individual men to defend that honor was considered direct evidence of the vitality of society itself. Whether parodied or embraced, the display of masculine violence idealized in the duel aimed to revive a *pugnatores* heritage, restoring warrior masculinity as a national ideal.

The prime difference between these duels and those of centuries past was that it could no longer be assumed that men of equally exalted rank were settling their differences on the field of combat. Instead of being the emanation of an already developed aristocratic sense of personal and family honor, dueling in the late nineteenth century tended to be the validation of that honor, whether the duelists were gentlemen by birth or not. Dueling had thus become a style of personal masculine validation that extended even into the less lethal world of fencing. After World War I, in such countries as Austria, Germany, France, and Hungary, there were a marked number of Jewish fencers, many even representing their countries in the Olympics.

Intriguingly, this immediate recourse to "pistols [or swords or sabers] at dawn" was particularly widespread among late-nineteenth-century French journalists, a relatively new class of men who had assumed the role of criticizing public figures and nominating themselves as the chief audience for honor. At a time when nationalism had become the accepted faith of both the secular and the religious in Europe and America, the arguments over what styles of personal masculine behavior enhanced and what degraded national character became central as well. Journalists and politicians insisted that the classes with money and status needed a taste of war to reinstill a sense of duty toward their country. Then as now, the whole question of heroes and exemplary heroic action was directly related to an uncertainty about the national character, and each incident was examined in detail for traces of decline or continuity. We no longer have the institution of the duel (except in *mano-a-mano* political debates), but our own journalists have similarly scrutinized every possible instance of "heroic" behavior with just as much interest in the temperature of our national honor, so much so that a new populist trope of the policeman or paramedic or plain citizen caught in the spotlight is to say, "I don't consider myself a hero"—a denial that of course makes him or her seem even more heroic.

Such attitudes heated up considerably with the prospect of actual war on the horizon. The need to purge the national body of those who were perceived as less than men, or as men of the wrong kind, picked up speed and urgency in the 1890s and as the century turned. Pervading the atmosphere was a greater hostility to whatever was different and a more explicit sense of racial entitlement. Among the emblematic targets were the bisexual writer Oscar Wilde in England and the Jewish army officer Alfred Dreyfus in France. The impulse seems remarkably similar: these were men whose presence offended the nation's idea of what a man was and how he ought to behave.

The Wilde and Dreyfus cases resemble "civilized" versions of tribal initiations, with the difference being that the trial was to determine whom to expel from the tribe, who was not a man, rather than to accept the youth who had become one—exclusion rather than inclusion. Why this first emerges as an attack upon the sexually different in England and upon the religiously or ethnically different in France is unclear, although trials of prominent homosexuals took place in both France and Germany in the years following Wilde's.*

The Dreyfus affair explicitly involves a fear of growing German military power. In conservative army circles, Jews had always been suspect. Could Jews really ride horses? it was asked, forerunner of the question asked of the Tuskegee airmen in World War II: could blacks fly planes? But beyond such supposed equestrian deficiencies, Dreyfus, said his accusers, was selling secrets to the Germans. Jews were crypto-Germans in any case. Even worse, they were like Freemasons, without national allegiance and bent upon bringing on a war between Germany and a France weakened by the loss of her military secrets. Thus the symbol of national degeneracy was also connected directly to the loss of technological military superiority.

At heart the Dreyfus case raised the question of who would succeed in defining France. Even for many who might admit that Dreyfus had been framed, the issue was still national allegiance—why save an outsider and destroy confidence in the army?—while for Dreyfusards like Emile Zola the issue was the superiority of civilian authority over the military, the greater importance of the republic than of the army.†

In the ominous atmosphere at the end of the nineteenth century, people looked for a war that would purge the feeble strains of masculinity and conjure up the ancient strengths. The United States, which until then had shown little enthusiasm for foreign adventure (as opposed to defeating and domesticating the Native Americans at home), turned the manifest destiny bandwagon toward a war against Spain in Cuba and the Philippines. The great spokesman for this national reinfusion of warrior energy was that Matterhorn climber, sportsman, and proponent of the strenuous life, Theodore Roosevelt.

* Perhaps the most interesting of these trials was that of Kaiser Wilhelm's close friend and advisor Philipp Prince zu Eulenberg-Hertefeld. Eulenberg, although married with children, accompanied the kaiser (who liked to be depicted as the paterfamilias of Germany) on his frequent all-male excursions and as a diplomat attempted to mitigate the kaiser's more bellicose policies, thus becoming a target for homophobic journalists and militaristic politicians alike.

† This conflict in French society over who truly represents the state—the Parisian politicians or the army—resurfaced with the Algerian crisis in the 1960s, when the head of state, Charles de Gaulle, was himself an army officer who had been head of the Free French army during World War II.

Roosevelt's views hardly came out of nowhere. His own sickly childhood and adolescence propelled him into challenge after challenge. Roosevelt had spent time on a ranch in the Dakota Territory after the deaths of his wife and his mother in 1884. In response he decided to become a different kind of man from the Harvard fop he had been. Another sickly New Englander who went west to cure his ailments both physical and mental was Owen Wister, whose picture of 1880s Wyoming in *The Virginian* (1902) helped set the pattern for the heroic westerner: strong, silent, shy with women, and with a code of behavior moral, masculine, and entirely admirable.

Wister had attended Harvard with Roosevelt, who had become president in 1901 after the assassination of William McKinley, and Wister dedicates the novel to him and his apostleship of the strenuous life. It was, he said in the preface, "a vanished world," in which the cowboy was already a nostalgic figure—his position on the frontier, astride what Frederick Jackson Turner in 1893 called "the meeting point between savagery and civilization," already vanishing, his cattle drives across the plains doomed by barbed wire, his separation from the cities of the East cut by the coming of the railroad. Nevertheless, the cowboy was to Wister and to so many others a figure whose values could supply a manly substance to correct the emptiness of the present:

> This handsome, ungrammatical son of the soil had set between us the bar of his cold and perfect civility. . . . The creature we call a *gentleman* lies deep in the hearts of thousands that are born without chance to muster the outward graces of the type. (13)

The Virginian's name is never given, but his geographic origin implies that he is another Lost Cause figure, whose personal honor has survived the wreck of the Confederacy. Seemingly the man of the vanished past, he is also the model for the future. So far as the narrator is concerned, the enemy in the Virginian's world is not the Indians but the foul world of the ugly western towns, along with the distorted values of the eastern settlers who were beginning to pour into them. In awe of the heroic stature of the cowboys and the beauty of the landscape, the narrator asks: "Does this same planet hold Fifth Avenue?" (31)

Like the group of men Roosevelt collected for his Rough Riders from among factory workers, cowboys, and East Coast aristocrats, the Virginian represents a restoration of masculinity from the roots of nature. He is the result of what Turner described as the "Americanization" that occurred on the frontier:

> It takes him from the railroad car and puts him in the birch canoe. It strips off the garments of civilization and arrays him in the hunting shirt and the moccasin. . . . Before long he has gone to planting Indian corn and plowing with a sharp stick; he shouts the war cry and takes the scalp in orthodox Indian fashion. (33)

This embrace of the natural world as the arena for masculine renewal wound its way through the numerous tales of heroes and villains of the post–Civil War West, the period from about 1865 to 1890 that saw a full flood of dime novels and in which virtually every American western movie is set. Unlike the complexity of the city, the West depicted there is a place of directness and simplicity, with knife-edge distinctions between good and bad, life and death, law and anarchy, that served to reinitiate the men who understood its message into their masculine birthright. The barbaric could be a threat to the highest forms of civilization; it could also be a sanctification, and thereby a threat to civilization at its most superficial.

It was a seductive message of individual possibility, akin to but not quite the same as the European imperialist message of heroism in the name of the Christian state. In American style, Roosevelt's message was that of the solitude of the individual knight-errant rather than the hierarchical chivalry of a military order. Unlike, say, the British boys' adventure novels that stressed honor and the group along with individual resourcefulness, American dime novels often celebrated outlaws, whose crimes could be portrayed as part of a rebellion against illegitimate authority, even while other boys' books, like the Horatio Alger series, promoted more quiescent and conservative values.

Similarly, while British boys were reading the imperial adventure stories of novelists like G. A. Henty, which stressed the civilizing mission, German boys read Karl May, first-person tales of a German in the American Southwest. Writing during the vogue of Buffalo Bill's Wild West Show in Europe and inspired by the novels of James Fenimore Cooper, May was a pacifist who saw the West as a primitive crucible of heroism. Strikingly, his German characters are much more moral and much more sympathetic to basic Indian nobility than are the Americans, who share the British mercantile urge and see the Indians only as enemies or as customers to be exploited. May died in 1912, but his books continued to sell.

Clearly, something in the combination of cowboys, Indians, and the scene of frontier society appealed deeply across class, political, and national spectrums as an imaginative way to resolve the paradoxes of civilization and barbarism. May's novels, like the American and British adventure stories, helped supply a purer inner life for their readers, where the individual in the midst of nature could make common cause with the noble savage. Perhaps inevitably, Hitler was also a fan, and May's popularity hardly ended with the Third Reich. Between 1945 and 1990, his tales of the Indian Winnetou and the scout Old Shatterhand were selling a million copies annually in Germany, and a series of West German westerns, starring the American Tarzan star Lex Barker, were based on them. By the late 1990s there were 500 cowboy and 150 Indian societies in Germany. As the owner of the largest western saddle and tack store in Germany remarked, "There's something about the cowboy that's very special—he lived by a code of honor instead of law." It was a sentiment close to what May had written, close to the justifications of dueling, and close to the creed of Wister's Virginian: "It is only the great mediocrity that goes to law in these personal matters" (281).

The 1890s were a fertile time for such visions, both in fiction and in fact. Stephen Crane's *Red Badge of Courage* (1895), the story of the initiation of a young man into the first days of battle, sought to create a model of the change from boy to man. Roosevelt at first admired the book until he experienced actual battle in Cuba, where Crane himself had gone as a war correspondent to see, as he said to Joseph Conrad, if *Red Badge* was "accurate." Roosevelt apparently didn't think so; Crane's characters, he decided, thought too much.

> I did not see any sign among the fighting men, whether wounded or unwounded, of the very complicated emotions assigned to their kind by some of the realistic modern novelists who have written about battles. At the front everyone behaved quite simply and took things as they came, in a matter-of-course way: but there was doubtless, as is always the case, a good deal of panic and confusion in the rear where the wounded, the stragglers, a few of the packers, or two or three newspaper correspondents were. (Freidel, 112)

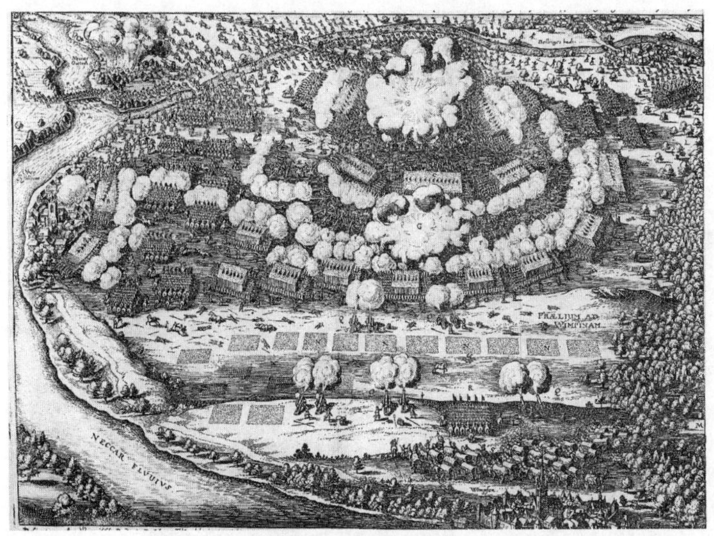


THE BATTLE OF WIMPFEN, 1622

(Matthäus Merian) By the time of the Thirty Years' War (1618–48), handbooks of military strategy and tactics flourished, along with an exhaustive use of etchings to depict famous battles. Here, in one of many such illustrations to the *Historische Chronica* of Johann Gottfried, the victory of Catholic over Protestant forces near Heidelberg is presented in meticulous detail.

THE HANGING

(Jacques Callot) Callot's book *Les Misères et malheurs de la guerre* was published in 1633, in the midst of the Thirty Years' War and at about the same time that the countryside around his hometown of Nancy was being devastated by irregulars from a variety of armies. In seventeen plates he shows how endemic war had turned soldiers into rapists, thieves, and murderers. Here some marauding irregulars are being punished in a mass hanging.

THE CHILDREN OF COUNT KARL GUSTAV WRANGEL

(David Klöcker Ehrenstahl, 1651) An early image of children playing with war toys. Wrangel was commander in chief of the Swedish army in Germany during the Thirty Years' War.

MORIZUMI BEING BLOWN UP BY A LANDMINE

(Utagawa Kuniyoshi, 1848–49) The Takeda warrior Masakiyo Morizumi, at the fourth battle of Kawanakajima (1556), appears to commit ritual suicide with his followers. Like England celebrating Arthurian warriors in the nineteenth century, Japan, on the verge of abolishing the samurai class, witnessed a flowering of nostalgia for the warriors of the medieval past, particularly the Warring States period of the sixteenth century. Here the dishonorable war of powder and explosions is contrasted with the samurai honor of noble defeat.

EARLOBES

(Salvatore Ottolengi) Reflecting the widespread late-nineteenth-century belief that national ideals of masculinity were being polluted by both "degenerate" races and the pressures of modern society, Ottolenghi, in his *Trattato di Polizia Scientifica* (1910), attempted to codify in elaborate detail the Darwinesque idea that criminals were the vestiges of earlier evolutionary stages and could be recognized by physical characteristics.

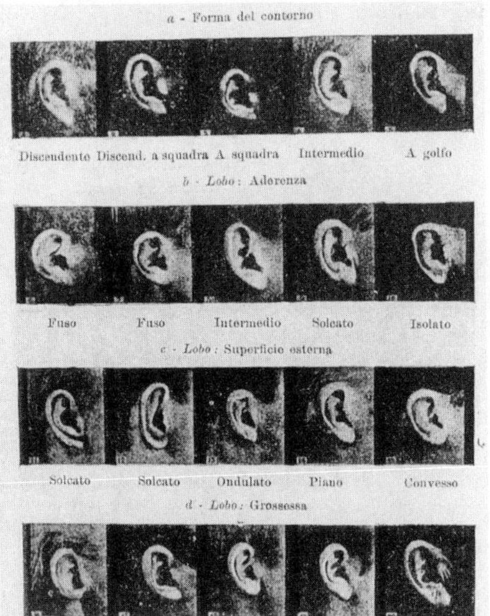

GEORGE ARMSTRONG CUSTER AND COMRADES

(D. F. Barry, 1874) At Fort Abraham Lincoln in 1874, two years before his last stand, Custer poses with officers, their wives, and friends—the American version of the regimental family so central to nineteenth-century armies. Custer is third from the left.

LORD OF THE RING

The more general fears that national racial degeneration would spell defeat in war had their counterpart in the individual's effort to control the involuntary (and unfruitful) release of sperm. J. L. Milton's book *On the Pathology and Treatment of Gonorrhea and Spermatorrhea* (1887) includes several helpful mechanisms to prevent nocturnal emissions, including this "four-pointed urethral ring," dressed up with a charming bow.

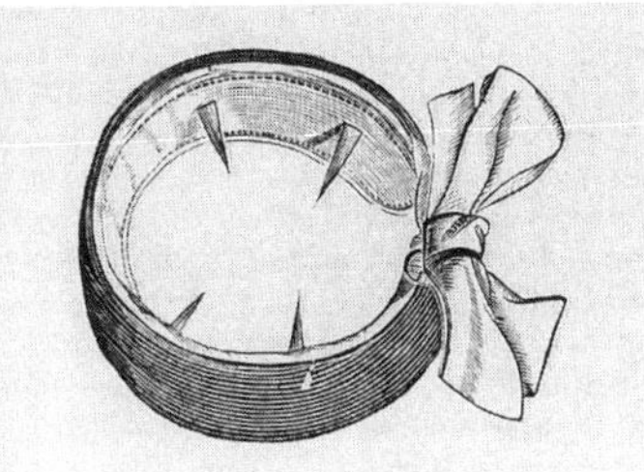

Early Training

Some time near the end of the nineteenth century, this little boy in a pinafore posed with what may have been his first gun, a small toy rifle.

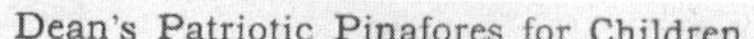

Patriotic Pinafores, 1911

Unfortunately the family of the little boy in the previous picture didn't have the wherewithal to get him one of these, complete with fake medals and a dashing belt. It would take World War I to undermine, for a time, such dreams of heroism.

COVER OF A CHILDREN'S PAINTING BOOK (C. 1917)

War preparedness infiltrated even the world of children, although the setting is bucolic, without a hint of the bloody conflict outside.

DESTROY THIS MAD BRUTE

(H. R. Hopps, U.S.A., c. 1917) In World War I, propaganda on all sides, but especially from the Allies, stressed the combat of civilization with an inhuman barbarism. Germany is shown here as a giant beast threatening the world.

JOAN OF ARC SAVED FRANCE

(Haskell Coffin, U.S.A., 1918) Like the knight, this armored and heroic woman of the Middle Ages could also become an inspiration, here for women to lend their own form of support to the war.

The Barricades

(Otto Dix, from *Death and Resurrection*, 1922) In less strident ways, artists responded to the devastation of World War I. The nightmarish atmosphere of trench warfare was experienced by both sides during the war, as was the sense of constant companionship with dead comrades.

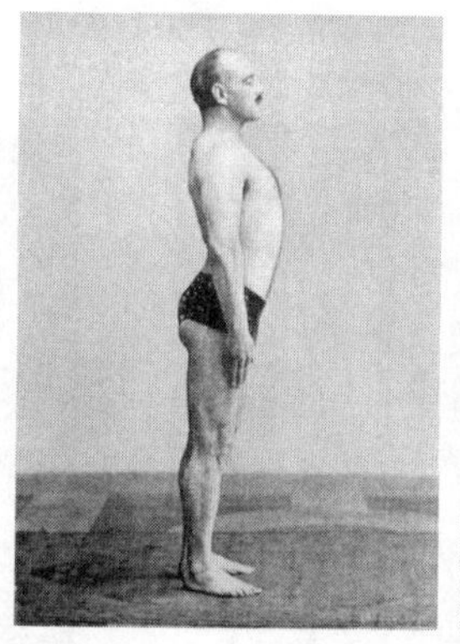

Comparison of a European Soldier and a Polynesian Warrior

In his book *The Culture of the Abdomen* (1927), F. A. Hornibrook argues that cancer is a civilized disease of "the bodily sewage system," a "chronic poisoning" curable only by exercise and correct posture. Here the European soldier at attention is an example of artificiality in contrast with the "freedom" of the native warrior, whose bodily organs are all "in correct relation to each other and to their containing walls."

COLONEL T. E. LAWRENCE

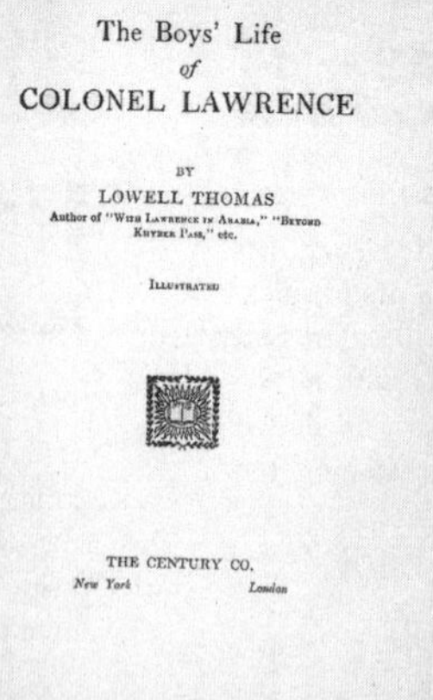

The Boys' Life
*of*
COLONEL LAWRENCE

BY
LOWELL THOMAS
Author of "With Lawrence in Arabia," "Beyond Khyber Pass," etc.

Illustrated

THE CENTURY CO.
*New York* *London*

Lawrence of Arabia

Lowell Thomas called T. E. Lawrence's exploits in World War I "the most romantic career of modern times." This portrait adorns the title page of one of the many editions of *The Boys' Life of Colonel Lawrence*. As in the nineteenth century, barbaric and non-European models of masculinity could be a source of new energy, especially when a certified "one of ours" like Lawrence was the hero.

Soldier Holding Shovel with Banner

(Igawa Sengai, 1937) The heroic Japanese officer is not only deflecting gunfire with his shovel-banner, but is also defeating his faceless Chinese opponent with a saber thrust that remarkably resembles anal intercourse.

Temptation

C. D. Batchelor won the 1937 Pulitzer Prize for this cartoon depicting the lure of war as a prostitute enticing a young man. The original title, "Any European Youth," in some later versions read "Any Youth."

By His Deeds Measure Yours

(John Falter) A 1943 advertisement in *Life* placed by the Magazine Publishers of America sought to inspire the home front by comparing the soldier to the martyred Christ.

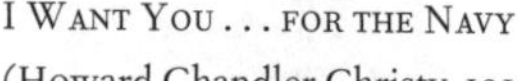

I WANT YOU . . . FOR THE NAVY

(Howard Chandler Christy, 1917) A winsome dark-eyed girl in Navy drag makes an ambiguous promise to those who would join up in World War I.

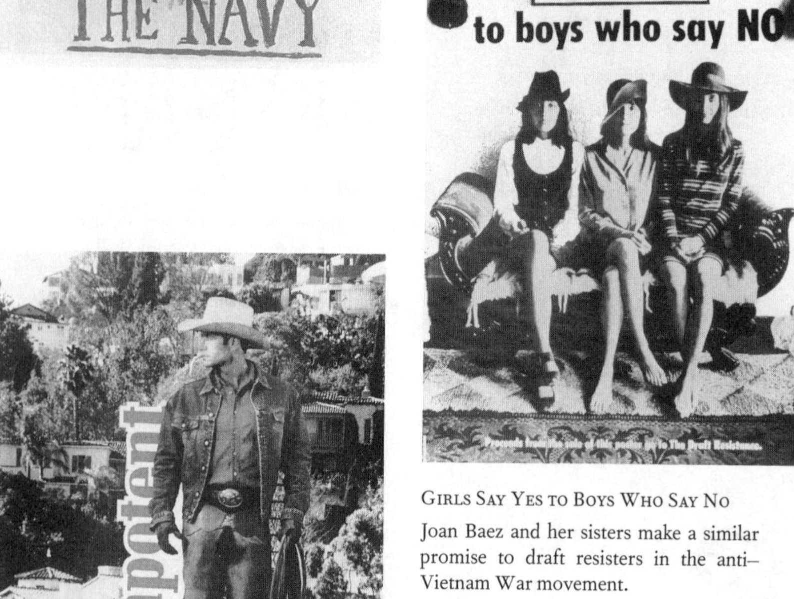


GIRLS SAY YES TO BOYS WHO SAY NO

Joan Baez and her sisters make a similar promise to draft resisters in the anti–Vietnam War movement.

IMPOTENT

In another upending of traditional imagery, the California Department of Health used the imagery of the Marlboro cowboy and the macho westerner to push an anti-tobacco campaign in 2001.

Roosevelt's sarcasm at the expense of the less than courageous underlines the two impulses that drove forward with a new intensity in the decades before World War I as part of the purification of society for battle: one to purge the alien, the weak, and the unmanly within; the other to defeat the primitive enemy without and take on his strength. Despite the heavily technological terms of the late-nineteenth-century arms race, the cry was still for "men" who would fight to the death for the state and its goals. But not all men qualified to be "men" for this purpose. Wilde and Dreyfus were attacked in Europe as emblematic members of unmanly groups; in the United States, numerous African Americans were lynched in the South by vigilantes, while even more of those who had been emancipated during the Civil War and given economic and political clout by Reconstruction were symbolically emasculated by the coming of Jim Crow laws.*

In this era as well, native peoples were being more actively repressed than ever before. On the American frontier, the prophet Wovoka had revived the millenarian Ghost Dance religion, with its belief in the coming of a messiah who would defeat the whites. Since the tribes had in effect been militarily defeated since the 1880s, the Ghost Dance had the aspect of a mystic response to a collective breakdown in a warrior culture that could no longer depend on its traditional skills. Instead of submitting to those who had defeated them, they restored their sense of manliness by cloaking themselves with a belief in absolute invulnerability. So assumed the young Lakota warriors who were massacred by the 7th Cavalry at Wounded Knee (1890) with the machine guns the army had lacked at the Little Big Horn fourteen years before.

But intriguingly enough, the disenfranchisement of African Americans by poll taxes and literacy tests, as well as new segregation laws, gathered strength at just the same time that, in the aftermath of their military defeat, some Native Americans not only got the vote, but were also being heralded as the "first Americans"—true progenitors of those settlers now taking over their lands. In the kind of preening that would inspire self-congratulatory slogans like that of the marines in the late twentieth century—"We're looking for a few good men"—a nostalgia for the old warrior Indian and his culture, always just beneath the surface, had decisively reemerged.

In a particularly comical form of the new warrior nostalgia, Rodman

* In another such example, Australian aborigines were disenfranchised in 1902, in an act of what Philippa Levine has called the "whitening" of the British Empire.

Wanamaker, the department store heir and activist for Native American rights and citizenship, sponsored expeditions in 1908 and 1909 to gather as many tribes as possible in a Declaration of Allegiance to the federal government and, not incidentally, to find out who killed Custer. It was a question that had little resonance for the tribal warriors. Not only did no one know who killed Custer, but also, according to laboriously collected testimony, many if not most had not even known he was there. He had cut off his long blond curls sometime before and in any case the word "Custer" was used freely by Indians to mean any officer or even the army itself. But the white myths of the "last stand" were not to be dismissed so lightly. Hadn't Buffalo Bill, hardly three weeks after the Little Big Horn, scalped an Indian, appropriately named Yellow Hair, in revenge for Custer? Wanamaker insisted, and so the aging former enemies nominated one of their own, Brave Bear, as Custer's killer, expecting that he would now be killed himself to put an end to the cycle of revenge. Instead he was given a prize.

The asymmetry between the way African Americans and Native Americans were treated is appropriate to the times, if not to the professed moral standards of a democracy. Until the Thirteenth, Fourteenth, and Fifteenth Amendments, the Constitution, in the midst of defining the duties of citizens, made it clear that an African American was to be counted not as a whole man, but as three-fifths of a man. The formula was designed specifically for purposes of taxation, but the implications for a whole cultural attitude toward black men could hardly be ignored. No one who knew the past of black slaves, warrior or otherwise, was there to argue their claims. The contributions of black soldiers to the American Revolution and the Civil War had been forgotten or reviled, and the militancy of Nat Turner or Denmark Vesey was more to be feared than celebrated. In the time of a widespread national desire to act on the world stage, the need was to reenergize American masculinity from its natural roots, and those roots, it was clear, were red rather than black. Even though actual Indians were as badly off on their reservations as blacks were in the ghettos, the "Red Man," now militarily defeated, was in the process of becoming a symbol of warrior pride.

Similarly, in *The Virginian*, published four years after the Rough Riders made their famous charge in the Battle of Santiago, the East is depleted and in need of an infusion of the West to restore its masculine energy. But the potential for living that life, for Wister at least, did not extend much beyond men who resembled him racially. In the introduction to a portfolio of prints of the West by Frederic Remington, Wister's bland emphasis on the need for the truly heroic man to be racially pure (i.e., Anglo-Saxon white) is shocking. The new celebration of the Indian as the "first American" has not entirely eluded him, but he reserves the greater part of his contempt for the "half-breed" and his "skulking" look. The enemies of masculinity are once again the feminine, the mixed, and the sophisticated—all part of a society and order that has corrupted true men and must be purged or left behind. Similarly, in one of Wister's short stories, "The Evolution of the Cow-Puncher" (1895)—first published in *Harper's Weekly,* which then called itself "the magazine of civilization"—an upper-class Englishman comes to Texas and immediately discovers the medieval knight beneath the dross of so-called process:

> Directly the English nobleman smelled Texas, the slumbering untamed Saxon arose in him, and mindful of the tournament, mindful of the hunting-field, galloped howling after wild cattle. . . . (*Owen Wister's West,* 37)

One more generous form taken by these assumptions about the renewing power of nature is the preservation of natural spaces and resources through the establishment of a park system, which Theodore Roosevelt helped expand extensively during his presidency. More invidious versions focused on the distinction between the African American and the Native American. Mainstream American manhood thus emerged from the nineteenth century flanked by the repression, even murder, of black men on one side (who had so recently received their freedom and the vote) and the symbolic celebration on the other of the Indian warrior (who had been decisively defeated and relegated to reservations).

The essence of racism is to mistake historically bounded phenomena for innate, to believe that the supposed characteristics of a particular group at the moment defines its entire condition. Roosevelt himself, after at first praising the contribution of black troops to the victory at San Juan Hill, later generally ignored or minimized what they had done. Although racism is aimed at all members of these groups, it is particularly directed against the males, for it says in effect that they are not men, therefore they are of no account, and can even be killed with impunity. Inheriting the theory of racial difference that so pervaded the late nineteenth century, Wister was hardly alone in his assumptions, even at a time when anthropology was beginning to explore a more open idea of "culture." In 1896 Roosevelt wrote to Stephen Crane about his story of the killing of a frontier sheepherder by Mexicans:

> Some day I want you to write another story of the frontiersman and the Mexican Greaser in which the frontiersman shall come out on top; it is more normal that way!*

Not that the celebration of warrior roots was any more altruistic. From their earliest years, many sports teams proudly bore names like Indians, Braves, and Redskins. In the 1980s and 1990s, with the coming of Native American protest against these names, defenders claimed that they were merely traditional and even honorific. But the donning of these barbaric verbal uniforms, especially in the wake of the final military action against the tribes at Wounded Knee in 1890, emphasizes how little innocence there was in that honor.

* Davis, 161. By contrast, John J. Pershing, then a lieutenant, was so impressed at San Juan Hill by the solidarity of white and black, northerners and southerners, regulars and Rough Riders, "unmindful of race or color," that he was later scornfully nicknamed "Black Jack" for his support of his troops.

# BE PREPARED

If the frontier was the mythic and literal place where rejuvenation could occur, what remedy was there for the cities? The divide between the effort to preserve a natural landscape and the desire that this landscape be purged of any impure forms of masculinity is mirrored in the frequent distinction made by historians between imperialists who saw an empire as a "sacred trust" in which local groups had a degree of autonomy, and those for whom the prime impulse was the God-given destiny to rule the globe, exploit its resources, and annihilate all who objected. The sacred-trust imperialists began to separate from the God-given-destiny imperialists in England with the Boer War, and in the United States with the Spanish-American War. The commitment to the ideals of Scouting was one of the distinguishing factors. In these terms, Sir Robert Baden-Powell, the founder of the Boy Scouts, was a sacred-trust imperialist rather than a commercial or political imperialist. His social idealism about the army is easily criticized, but was nevertheless heartfelt. In the otherwise ignoble war between Britain and South Africa, where 450,000 British troops were finally mustered to defeat 40,000 Boers, Baden-Powell became a public symbol of British fortitude for withstanding seven months of Boer attacks on his stronghold at Mafeking (1899–1900). Early British defeats in the war had shocked the nation, and Baden-Powell (who may have been disobeying orders by even taking his troops to Mafeking) not only defended the town but also arranged cricket matches and other social events for the diversion of soldiers and civilians alike.

The Boy Scouts were a central part of an early-twentieth-century focus on the "boy" that brought earlier preoccupations with national degeneration into a pragmatic scheme of moral, physical, and intellectual training that might undo its worst effects. Baden-Powell was especially worried not only about the needs of empire but also about the development of young men—of all nations, he insisted—who needed to have the kind of physical and mental training in masculinity that so many adult men lacked. Boys would be the future, and how they became men should be the riveting concern of nations. In the United States, G. Stanley Hall published *Adolescence* (1904), the first extended study of the male teenager (before the word was invented) as a developmental stage, focusing much of his attention on the problem of masturbation and the subsequent inward turning of the mind, which Hall argued needed to be brought out into the larger world through sports and other physical activities. At the same time, the immensely popular *Peter Pan* (1904) by James M. Barrie carried—through its invariable casting of an actress to play Peter—the implicit message that a boy who doesn't want to grow up is a girl.

Baden-Powell, however, with his desire to retain the best traits of the boy in the man, might have approved. He married late himself, was generally uncomfortable around women, and was later to call his best scoutmasters "boy-men"—hardly anything sinister at the time, but something to remember now that the American Boy Scout movement has so misunderstood its past as to reject homosexuals as both scouts and scoutmasters.

On the more martial and adventurous side, an immense outpouring of boys' literature from the 1860s onward stressed the sporting side of military battle and intrigue. In these books war and empire were celebrated as the crucible of manhood, while their moral message was about playing the game and not letting down the side. One of the earliest was *Under Two Flags* (1867) by Ouida (Louise de la Ramée). But the most prolific

British author of such books was G. A. Henty, a former war correspondent in the Crimea and in Europe, Africa, and India, whose novels placed young characters in dramatic war and crisis situations that mirrored those of history. Such works, together with the journalistic celebration of war heroes like Gordon, Kitchener, and Baden-Powell himself, pointed the imaginations of young men in Britain toward visions of adventure, self-sacrifice, and moral transcendence through situations of physical jeopardy, while the tales of Karl May and others did the same for young men in Germany. The specific setting could be the European past, as in Baroness Orczy's *Scarlet Pimpernel* (play, 1903; novel, 1905), which featured a seemingly effeminate fop who is actually a daring adventurer—Orczy's version of *A Tale of Two Cities.* Hewing even closer to the English past were Conan Doyle's *The White Company* (1891) and *The Adventures of Brigadier Gerard* (1896), set during the Hundred Years' War and written at the same time as the Sherlock Holmes stories. Sometimes the protagonist of these works was a boy himself—as in Robert Louis Stevenson's *Treasure Island* (1883), an exotic tale of pirates and desert islands written a few years before *Dr. Jekyll and Mr. Hyde*—or else there was a boy close by to observe the hero and learn from him.* As in such schoolboy novels as *Tom Brown's School Days,* the emphasis was always on the process by which boys did—or did not—become men, whether in the comparative safety of the playing field and dormitory, or dodging bullets and bombs, poisonous snakes and pirate cutlasses. As Antonia Fraser points out in her *History of Toys,* the invention of a new process in the casting of lead soldiers in the 1890s made them cheaper and more available, and, for the first time in the nineteenth century, they replaced trains as the favored toy for young boys.

Baden-Powell absorbed all these influences and more into his conception of the Boy Scouts. At a time when the new anthropological study of initiation and other tribal rituals had begun to seep into the popular consciousness, he looked especially at how boys were trained in both historical and contemporary warrior cultures around the world, and explicitly wrote that the Boy Scout tests were the "toned down equivalent of tribal initiation rites." Like Ernest Thompson Seton's Woodcraft Indians in the United States, which directly emulated the training of an Indian brave in the ways of the natural world and how to read them, or Dan Beard's Sons

* In works like Mark Twain's *Huckleberry Finn* (1884) and Rudyard Kipling's *Kim* (1901) (on which Baden-Powell based the Cub Scouts), the title characters are orphans as well, the better to explore a wider social canvas.

of Daniel Boone, Baden-Powell's Scout was also to be a combination of Robinson Crusoe and Sherlock Holmes, steeped in the practical knowledge necessary for survival in a complicated world as well as able by observation and analysis to penetrate its secrets.

The Boy Scouts were officially founded in 1908 and the Girl Guides in 1912. Its female auxiliary notwithstanding, the essence of the Scouts was pride in and development of the resources of the male self. From the first, Baden-Powell had been inspired to remedy what he considered to be the lack of knowledge and initiative in the young soldiers under his command. Although preparation for war was not explicitly mentioned—and the peacetime uses of Scout training were even emphasized—the traits to be developed in the Scout clearly would have such application. Technology would not be as important as individual character, adherence to a chivalric moral code, and knowledge of the natural world.

The Boy Scouts, like similar American and German prewar youth movements, was explicitly conceived as an effort to renovate society. The movement's stress on morality and self-sufficiency was part of the general attack on materialism in the 1890s, and the soldier or the pseudo-soldier was the vehicle of its nostalgia for a civilization that would properly honor masculine nature. The romanticizing of war was certainly a potential in such movements, and not incidentally their members usually banded together in groups and had a distinctive uniform. To apply a distinction made by Alfred Vagts in *A History of Militarism* (1937), the movement's panoply and rituals, although they had a military aspect, were not necessarily militaristic: they did not assume, as would later fascist youth groups, that the military point of view was central to all of society's workings.*

Wearing a uniform as a boy, even a sailor suit, certainly has a proto-military aspect, looking forward to the man the boy will become, even while sugarcoating its warrior potential. It also sets him apart from the civilian world. As Hemingway's hero, Frederic Henry, remarks in *A Farewell to Arms*, "In civilian clothes I felt a masquerader. I had been in uniform a long time and I missed the feeling of being held by your clothes" (243). But to say that from the start the motive of such training was to teach young men to take orders and be subservient to authority is to take one direction into which the movement went and make it stand for the whole. Certainly, there were those who considered Scouting to

* Martin Ceadel in *Thinking About Peace and War* defines militarism as believing that "war is necessary to human development and is a positive good" (3).

be directly connected to basic training. When I was a Scout in the 1950s, we always started our meetings with close-order drill, so that we would know "dress-right-dress" and "about face" in preparation for being drafted into the next war. But Baden-Powell's motives were more complicated. In essence, he was attempting to unite an ideal of manly behavior (to which boys could aspire) with the military sanction of uniforms and organizational loyalty. Although his motto was "country first, self second" and the sports and exercise often had an explicit national purpose that went beyond the local group and the local allegiance, Scouting also directly appealed to the spirit of wanderlust and adventure, which could turn out to be purely personal and even antiauthoritarian.

It was just this ambiguity that gave the Boy Scout movement its wide appeal and great success. It sought to turn boys into men, and the specifics of class, race, and nationality, in theory at least, had little part in it. "Muscular Christianity," for example, may have been embraced by large parts of the middle classes, but it did not always appeal to the working class. Scouting did. To be like an Indian after the actual Indians had been decisively defeated; to be a woodsman, even though living in a city; to belong to a comradely group while learning the skills to survive in a welter of potentially death-defying or at least challenging situations; to be, in short, the moral knight-errant while adhering to a code of conduct that the rest of the world had forgotten—these were the goals. Baden-Powell, himself one of the media heroes of empire, in the Scout *Handbook* stressed the heroic possibilities of ordinary people. As with the gradual opening up of military honors to soldiers in the ranks, the implication was that the imperial hero was not a lofty being from a higher class but the normal person writ large, and the Scout was the designated emissary of that heroism to ordinary life. In Saki's "it can happen here" novel of 1913, *When William Came*, it is the younger generation of Scouts who make the first gesture of resistance against the conquering Germans by refusing to march in their triumphant parade.

Rather than either a militarist machine (as youth groups would become under fascism) or a happy place for boys to flourish outside of society (as Ernest Thompson Seton and Dan Beard had envisioned), Baden-Powell's Boy Scouts were designed to appeal to a variety of intentions and motives, some benevolent, others more nationalist and extreme. Despite his professed openness to all nations and races, Baden-Powell himself had difficulties with including Scouts who were not white, especially in India and South Africa. By the same token, he at first welcomed the *Hitlerjugend* as an outgrowth of the German Scout movement and was only persuaded after some time by his associates to denounce it as a perversion of Scouting ideals. Perhaps one of the worst charges of racism against him was leveled by Michael Rosenthal in *The Character Factory,* citing lines from Baden-Powell's *The Downfall of Prempeh* (1896), his account of the defeat of the Ashantis: "The stupid inertness of the puzzled negro is duller than that of an ox; a dog would grasp your meaning in one-half the time. Men and brothers! They may be brothers, but they are certainly not men" (256). Vile this passage certainly is, and in accord with the worst racist caricatures of the time. But in Baden-Powell's distinction between brothers and men, it also reflects his deep-seated view that being a man, let alone a gentleman, is a construction that requires self-control and hard work. In this universe of social Darwinism, blacks, like women, were as children who might not possess the capacity to be anything more, but boys, even white English boys, had to prove their mettle.

One important difference that influenced national responses to the crusade to turn boys into men was the role of voluntary organizations in each nation. American voluntary organizations in particular had flourished as part of the frontier, and they continued to be strong into the late nineteenth and early twentieth centuries, from the YMCA to the Ku Klux Klan. In the British Empire, by contrast, all such groups were organized by the state and its army; the nonmilitary figures were primarily missionaries. In France, voluntary organizations had been abolished by the revolution on the grounds that they were no longer needed because the state would supply all that was necessary. (It is one of Tocqueville's central distinctions between the United States and France in *Democracy in America.*) But Britain at home also maintained a deep ambivalence. Wars and empire may be ennobling, but armies, especially professional armies, were a potential threat to the mother country. At the beginning of World War I, when Germany, Austria, and even France had had compulsory service in place for years, which allowed for quickly mobilized armies numbering in the millions (France and Austria about four million, Germany about five), the British had a professional army of some 700,000 troops under arms, with no plans for conscription, and so had to rely for the first two years of the war on volunteers, of which there were some two and a half million.

According to Lord Kitchener, the minister of war, this was just as it should be. The morale of the volunteers in his New Army would be guaranteed by their enlistment as a group of friends, who had played together and now would go to war together. This would be a national army for a people with a deep suspicion of the professional soldier, a people more used to being protected and nurtured by sea power than by armies on land. So the units had names like the Chums and the Pals to supply what Kitchener called "a pre-formed fabric of friendships and allegiances," representing the young male core of innumerable villages and neighborhoods now tied directly to the national purpose. In its numbers and its weaponry, modern war may have promised to be unprecedented, but the effort to root the strength and morale of a unit in preexisting affinity reached back into the localism of feudal warfare.

Licensed by war, then, a male camaraderie that had become either suspect or exaggeratedly hearty and heterosexual after the Wilde trials underwent a resurgence in the name of national unity and defense. Even the subterranean prewar homoeroticism was validated, through images of the beautiful young men gone off to war, to honor, and to their deaths, modern-day Galahads. How many of these young men had been Boy Scouts, I have been unable to discover. But the amateur ethos, the emphasis on a personal code of moral behavior, and the connection between battle and sports imply that there were many, and their attitudes were reflected in the higher echelons. In the first year of the war, parachutes and helmets, for example, were forbidden as unsporting, and steel helmets were only brought in as standard at the time of the Battle of the Somme (1916). To heighten the atmosphere of war as a kind of elaborate schoolboy game, General Douglas Haig disparaged the machine gun as a threat (even as it was mowing down men charging across no-man's-land) and spoke about battles in the language of cricket. But at the Somme, whatever the rhetoric, the guns and the mud swallowed up these friends and acquaintances in shocking numbers. By 1917, the original battalions of Pals and Chums were almost gone, decimated by wounds and death. The Great War continued, but the game war, the war of sportsmen and Scouts, had long been over.

*Part VII*

# THE TWENTIETH CENTURY: WEAPONS OF MASS DESTRUCTION AND THE WARRIOR SPIRIT

# HONOR IN NO-MAN'S-LAND

They can play a bugle call like you never heard before
So natural that you want to go to war
—Irving Berlin, "Alexander's Ragtime Band" (1911)

Now, God be thanked Who has matched us with His hour,
And caught our youth, and wakened us from sleeping . . .
Glad from a world grown old and cold and weary,
Leave the sick hearts that honour could not move,
And half-men, and their dirty songs and dreary,
And all the little emptiness of love! . . .
Honour has come back, as a king, on earth,
And paid his subjects with a royal wage;
And Nobleness walks in our ways again;
And we have come into our heritage.
—Rupert Brooke, "1914"

Even with the uprisings of 1848, the nineteenth century was a time of relative stability in the European state system, the fruit of the balance of power created at the Congress of Vienna in 1815. The coming together of Italy and the creation of a political Germany under the sway of Prussia threatened change, but Europe still dominated most of the world financially, militarily, and politically. Meanwhile, the far-away battles of empire against a technologically primitive foe, the celebrity of a few hero-soldiers, and the relatively untraumatic aftermath of the few European wars after Napoleon had led to an enthusiasm for war coupled with increasingly abstract idea of what war was and what a soldier did.

The 1890s and early 1900s were thus rife with the belief that war would supremely distill masculine identity in ways impossible in a peacetime world. Modern society had lost the explicit rituals of masculinity familiar in a tribal setting. Boys had to find out for themselves how to be men.

Scouting would help remedy that, while adult males would learn there was no automatic physiological right to manhood that being biologically a man did not imply that one was necessarily a "real man."

All the talk of degeneracy, of purging the "unmanly," of restoring the purity of national bloodlines, was thus part of a public retribalizing across Europe and America that stressed the invention or the renewal of rituals of masculinity. Among those rituals war was the ultimate ordeal. In the words of numerous commentators, it would replace the petty traps and evasions of normal society with the absolutes of life and death, honor and cowardice, individual interest and the welfare of the group. Long after purging blood had faded away as a medical practice, it still seemed right for the body politic. War would be not just a cleansing of bad social blood; it would affirm national vitality and individual honor. Many writers expected that war would rescue the nation from moral decay and bring men back to the basic truths from which they had wandered, resolving the conflicts between degeneration and progress, spirituality and materialism, under a new banner of purity.

Who defined that purity and who wanted to sustain it was open to question. Every country had its own view. The past was not only prologue to the present but pretext as well, either to avenge ancient wrongs or assert new aspirations. Warring states were not just fighting to assure dynastic power, or to gain territory, raw materials, and markets. They were defending abstractions like national honor and their goals were likewise abstract: to humble the other side, to save civilization from their barbaric opponents. In every country there were high enlistment rates among the middle and professional classes, intent on defending their personal honor and their vision of their nation, headpieces stuffed with images of medieval knights. As in the U.S. Civil War and the Franco-Prussian War, both sides claimed to be protecting basic values and each considered the other to be bent on destroying those values. To the English, the Germans were a race of barbarians who had emerged into statehood just in time to create a technology aimed only at slaughter; to the Germans, the English were a race of shopkeeping materialists whose greed and hypocrisy had almost annihilated the human urge to spiritual transcendence.

Historians can argue about who was more wrong or more deluded. But each side felt justified. The British view was summarized by Douglas Haig, former commander in chief of the British Expeditionary Force, in an address to the undergraduates of St. Andrew's University in 1919. The Allies had fought for

> a world ideal in which God was with us. We were doing battle for a higher form of civilization, in which man's duty to his neighbour finds a place more important than his duty to himself, against an Empire built up and made great by the sword, efficient indeed, but with an efficiency unredeemed by any sense of chivalry or of moral responsibility towards the weak. (Ecksteins, 191)

But whatever the high-flown rhetoric on both sides, the incredible incommensurability remained between the pretext for war and how the war itself unfolded, as if no one had any idea that there should be some balance between war aims and what had to be done to achieve them.

In normal life, individual death may gather meaning for the survivors in a variety of ways—a record of accomplishment, a tragic accident, a life cut off too soon, or, most often, simply someone who was loved. But only war, especially war carried on for a cause, purports to give meaning to collective death. A war carried on by a volunteer or conscripted army of ordinary citizens carries the expectation of an even greater meaning. An insult to my country is an insult to me; my country's weakness undermines my masculinity; beyond what is needed or prudent, my masculinity requires a strong military face in the world to be whole. Unlike professional soldiers or volunteers who have enlisted to better their peacetime circumstances, citizens who leave home and hearth are galvanized to an ideal, or at least some serious and believable cause for which to fight.

World War I therefore marks a more, intense stage in the definition of national honor, one in which war must be extolled as a testing ground for every citizen: the men to fight, the women to support them. Some women, like the British members of the White Feather movement, publicly mocked noncombatant males by handing them white feathers on the street. A. E. W. Mason's novel *Four Feathers* was filmed twice during the war, while other films featured Boy Scouts galvanized into action by the threat.

To buttress these ideals, World War I was suffused with the imagery of the chivalric—in posters, in poetry, and in propaganda. But these ironclad heroes of the imagination quickly collided with the brute force of the new military technology and the mud-soaked impersonality of the trenches. There were camaraderie and individual valor aplenty, but all was subsumed in the gigantic movements of men and matériel, the enormous casualty figures, and the prodigious production of weapons.

Personal honor, entwined with national purpose, was expressed in each warring country as a newly energized masculinity. Manliness embodied all that was best and most definitive of national pride and identity. The language of the national cause stressed a moral justification independent of any material goal, as if, like the hosts of heaven in *Paradise Lost*, soldiers could throw off their armor in the battle with Satan and win by character alone.

But gradually honor, which had seemed to be an objective social standard to which all men must aspire, began to take on a more psychological cast. Instead of being a cultural value, it was coming to refer also to a sense of personal integrity, a shapeliness of character, that was always in danger of being breached. By the same token, the codes of behavior that had sustained it appeared not as invariable truths but as magical incantations against psychic disintegration. In the presubjective world of the Middle Ages, the soul was inside and honor was the boundary between oneself and another. In the world of psychology and Freud, the ability of honor to sustain a sense of wholeness was severely in jeopardy.

Propaganda therefore linked personal honor to national interest. When religious difference is no longer a professed motivation for European war, war justifies itself almost exclusively as a means of serving national interests. So seventeenth- and eighteenth-century war, although sometimes decked out with a few religious curlicues, was fought with little need to defend it as "just." The political language of liberty or order emerged as a kind of collateral explanation in the nineteenth century. But it was in the twentieth century that the need to justify war was most elaborately presented in the form of propaganda.

No longer was the soldier "scum," as he had been in the wars against Napoleon; now he was the ideal representative of the nation, more in line with the earlier celebration of the sailor and the fleet. In the United Kingdom, for example, after the political dissension of the first third of the century when armies could be called out to repress working-class agitation, there emerged a concept of the all-embracing "destiny of the British race." Honor, integrity, patriotism, and a rough-hewn wisdom were now the core of the soldier's public image. In England, from 1815 onward, the name Thomas Atkins, like John Doe in law, became the generic example used in army forms. Decades before Kipling gave it his imprimatur in "Barrack-Room Ballads" (1892), whenever you wanted to refer to the common soldier, the backbone of the army and the nation, it was Tommy Atkins you invoked.* The requirements of an expanding military bureau-

* The forms were used for privates in the cavalry and infantry. Tommy was also the general name for a male servant (as Betty was for a female).

cracy to make its paperwork run more smoothly had brought into being an icon of the new status of the soldier.

The soldier's self-respect also rose, as conditions of service were improved and corporal punishments like flogging either lightened or banned. A rising public literacy and an expanded role for public opinion in government also played their roles. For some an expectation arose that when the working-class Tommys and the upper-class Nigels fought together for England there would be social egalitarianism as well. Despite differences in class, ethnicity, and background, the comradeship of a volunteer army engaged in the great cause of national honor would create an almost utopian social world, or so the hopes went.

War propaganda came into being when there was an audience to be convinced that war, along with its human and economic sacrifices, must be fought. As Richard Aldington wrote bitterly in his novel *Death of a Hero* (1929),

> "Our splendid troops" were to come home—oh, very soon—purged and ennobled by slaughter and lice, were to beget a race of even nobler fellows to go and do likewise. We were to have a great revival in religion, for peoples' thoughts were now turned from frivolities to great and serious themes. We were to have a new and greater literature . . . but really I lack the courage to continue. Let those who are curious in human imbecility consult the newspaper-files of those days. . . . (206)

For the most part, until the Napoleonic Wars, the prime audience was elite, and so the apparatus of war propaganda was rudimentary. With democratic war, or any war that requires volunteers or conscripts to fight it, as well as taxpayers to fund it, propaganda becomes much more important.

The jingoism of the newspaper magnates of the 1870s and later had sold smaller wars against less well prepared enemies. But they had also never ceased to announce the coming of a larger, more all-embracing European war. So the techniques developed in the sensationalist press would be used extensively by all sides in World War I because this was a war that needed to be sold. In the early years of the war, Europe was still a world of states in which monarchs called the tune and often dressed in military uniforms. At first, then, it was they who personalized a conflict that would turn out to be described more accurately through the numbers of artillery shells and corpses than through deeds of individual honor.

Although the prewar system of European alliances that was meant to stabilize politics and prevent conflict had actually contributed to the war's expansion, its immediate cause was almost banally individual: the assassination of Archduke Francis Ferdinand of Austria by the Serbian nationalist Gavrilo Princip in Sarajevo. The war would hasten the collapse of the Austro-Hungarian monarchy, but at the outset the assassination was an insult to the dynastic succession, and thus an insult to the country that could not be resolved diplomatically. But mass war was just over the horizon, and mass war needs mass inspiration.

An essential part of the push toward war on all sides was thus to emphasize the role that everyone must play in the great conflict. In the diffuseness of peacetime, different masculinities might be indulged, but in war military masculinity was the core of national cohesiveness, and, not coincidentally, the essence of defining *us* against *them*. With mass communications, then, normative images of masculinity and femininity permeated society and potentially touched every person within it as a necessary building block of their sense of self.

Each country had its own casus belli. In Britain it was Empire and Empire was identified with the nation. In a message dated August 9, 1914, five days after war was declared, King George thanked enlistees and professional soldiers for "leaving home to fight for the safety and honour of my Empire." In retrospect, the invocation of "my Empire" sounds a tinny note as any inducement to a mass war. But the propaganda emphasis on "our" came quickly. Posters appeared everywhere that encouraged enlistment and turned the war into a normal part of life. In one of the most famous, Lord Kitchener points directly at the viewer and says he "needs you." Women were needed as well, in the war as nurses but also at home. "Women of Britain Say—Go!" emphasizes one poster with an image of a woman watching soldiers from a house window, and in a sexier come-on than Kitchener's, another has an attractive woman looking out at the viewer and saying "I Want You—for THE NAVY." Later, documentary films like *The Battle of the Somme* would be produced and taken around to various parts of the country to whip up enthusiasm among the local population.

The new medium of film also offered a way to galvanize national opinion somewhat more obliquely by inspiring invocations of the warrior past. The Italian film *Cabiria* (1914), directed by Giovanni Pastrone with intertitles by Gabriele D'Annunzio, argued for Italy's entry into the war under the guise of an epic story of the wars between Italy and Carthage.

Its cinematic sweep influenced D. W. Griffith in *Birth of a Nation*, and *Birth of a Nation* in its turn would influence Veit Harlan's *Kolberg* (1945), in which a German city refuses to capitulate to Napoleon's army. Film would be a long-lived resource. In the USSR, communist doctrine usually looked toward the end of history and avoided bringing up the tsars of yore. But with war threatening, the Soviets turned to Sergei Eisenstein's film *Alexander Nevsky* (1938) for a hero who had defeated the Teutonic Knights in the thirteenth century. The soldiers of the present would be the direct descendants of an heroic past. In Germany, the Iron Cross, which was first awarded in 1813 and then reinstituted in 1870 to mark the Franco-Prussian War, in 1914 was permitted to adorn soldiers of non-German origin as well. It would be revived again by Hitler in 1939.

The propaganda of World War I thus repetitively hammered home the pervasively interwoven issues of masculinity and war, and by implication the ambivalence about them. When armies were run by warrior aristocrats and manned by the lower orders, knighthood and its style of warrior masculinity had been essentially a discussion among the upper classes, sometimes including, as in Henry V's England, their view of lower-class men—the sturdy yeoman archer—or, as in Germany, the ferocious *landknecht*. But the mass armies of World War I marked a definitive middle-classing of war and an expansion of war consciousness. What had been a primarily upper-class discussion of these issues became through the new presence of the mass media a national discussion, reviving to a certain extent the French revolutionary idea of the nation in arms, but far beyond the nineteenth-century celebration of a few exemplary military heroes. Whereas before, masculine ideals had been influenced by both religion and nationalism, now it was the *image* of the soldier, as repeated innumerable times in the ear and the eye, that became the standard.

Images of warrior masculinity therefore drifted closer to the waking and dreaming life of the ordinary European and American man in the twentieth century than they ever had before, due both to the unprecedented scale of war and to its unprecedented publicity. Both self-consciously and unconsciously a warrior masculinity seemed more incumbent on men in general than it ever did before in the world of professional soldiers, or even in the glory days of the revolutionary nation in arms. At first, there was no new fabric of ideas about masculinity and femininity, or masculinity and nationalism, but war propaganda combined with the new mass communications brought about a tremendous repetition and reaffirmation of late-nineteenth-century attitudes. Previous changes and modulations of male and female images had taken centuries; now the close tracking of immediate events engendered a quicker oscillation between different models of masculinity. This was especially true in democratic societies, where opinion could not be mobilized as single-mindedly as it would be by totalitarian dictators, especially under fascism and Nazism, where rituals connecting individual to state virility, present events to past heroism, became widespread.

The optimistic assumption fostered by media and government propaganda during World War I was that themes of chivalric masculinity and national self-justification from all previous wars had coalesced into that conflict. But the paradox of World War I was that this occasion of renewed honor turned out to undermine and even, for a time, demolish it. Expecting a short war, every country involved was to some degree economically and politically unprepared for the long war that came, with its need for the state takeover of industries, communications, commerce, and transportation. Men going to war with the pumped-up expectation of plucking a renewed masculine honor from every firefight, and serving one's country in the bargain—not to mention the cause of all civilization—were met instead with the ghastly realities of the Western Front. There, honor was swallowed up along with everything else, creating a chasm of ideals and disillusionment, a discontinuity between the rush toward war of the nineteenth century and what this new war actually involved. Nineteenth-century popular and elite culture had often conferred a grandeur on military masculinity by its invocation of a spiritual Arthurian ideal. But the image turned out to be just an image. Whatever inner armor was supplied by medieval ideals was not enough to withstand concussion grenades, artillery shells weighing hundreds of pounds, and poison gas. The warrior honor of the nineteenth century, which in the images of the Arthurian quest for the Holy Grail promised a purification that transcended the body, had to face the din, dirt, death, and annihilation of the trenches.

Fired by images of a civilized honor that would make modern man equal to his primitive predecessors in personal honor and superior in national purpose, the soldiers of World War I were thrown into a war that quickly demonstrated the absence of any easy analogy with the rites of primitive tribes. Modern initiation into mass, industrialized war, it turned out, did not reaffirm the tribe through one man's spiritual quest. Instead it introduced him to the emptiness of values and all the words used to describe them. As Hemingway's wounded hero Frederic Henry thinks in *A Farewell to Arms:*

> I did not say anything. I was always embarrassed by the words sacred, glorious, and sacrifice and the expression in vain. We had heard them, sometimes standing in the rain almost out of earshot, so that only the shouted words came through, and had read them, on proclamations that were slapped up by billposters over other proclamations, now for a long time, and I had seen nothing sacred, and the things that were glorious had no glory and the sacrifices were like the stockyards at Chicago if nothing was done with the meat except to bury it. There were many words that you could not stand to hear and finally only the names of places had dignity. . . . Abstract words such as glory, honor, courage, or hallow were obscene beside the concrete names of villages, the numbers of roads, the names of rivers, the numbers of regiments and the dates. (184–85)

These were sentiments reflected by many writers on all sides of the conflict. There would still be medals and there would still be courageous acts. But words like "honor" took on an inevitable tinge of irony. The age-old myths of military heroism and the more recent projections of national pride had collided with the bare face of war as technology and industrialization. The desire for a new, more robust identity propagandized through adventure tales, sports, and political exhortation found in the trenches the emptiness of the language of both religious sacrifice and warrior fame.

The honor that had disappeared or imploded was specifically the honor defined by public language and given meaning by public utterance. It was the state's co-optation of that language for the last few centuries that was being dismissed, rather than honor itself. In the immediacy of war, only personal honor seemed suitable to the situation. Honor was not an abstraction; if it existed, it was what happened or, more often, did not happen right in front of you. National honor was another matter. "Blighty," which had been the early-twentieth-century nickname for England (from the Urdu meaning "foreigner" or "European"), became the name for the wound that would allow one to go home.

At home, however, where generalizations about male courage were useful for rallying public opinion, they still retained some credibility, often to the surprise of combatants on leave. As the casualties mounted, the public need to emphasize an accrued honor rose as well. In many countries, as part of the memorializing of the war dead—many of whom could not even be found, let alone identified—the idea was born to designate a central focusing image for all those unnamed and lost. On Armistice Day 1920, two years after the war ended, the grave of the Unknown Warrior was dedicated in Westminster Abbey. Proposed by David Railton, who had been a chaplain in the trenches, it remains the only floor grave in the abbey that can't be walked over. One year later, a similar grave for the American Unknown Soldier was dedicated in Arlington Cemetery. Although there had been a mass burial in 1866 of unidentified bodies from the battles of Bull Run, and the remains of one-third of those who died in Civil War battles were unidentified, this was the first time that an emblematic "unknown" soldier was designated to try to bridge the unbridgeable gap between the individual experience of war and the massive numbers of the dead. The nineteenth century had been filled with memorials to officers and occasionally their men, but the Unknown Soldier introduced an era of the celebration of the emblematic soldier, a necessary image for a world of mass war.*

"Warrior" had more resonance for the British than "soldier," bathing the myriad anonymous deaths in the light of medieval traditions of chivalry and Christianity that had inspired so many. The cleansing uplift of such language has had a long life. In the 1990s, during the planning for a BBC series on the Great War, the American historian Jay Winter had long arguments with the producers over the sequence dealing with the Battle of the Somme: he wanted to call it "slaughter"; they wanted to call it "sacrifice." The so-called Christmas Truce in 1914—when soldiers on both sides of no-man's-land spontaneously shared food, drink, and songs—had raised the possibility that even in war there was a Christian fraternity between nations. Officers on both sides ordered that the situation was never to be repeated. But, almost a century later, the medieval language of Christian redemption and warrior honor was still being invoked to gloss the world of blood, filth, and futility.

* Who should be remembered and how still remains controversial, as the conflicts over the Vietnam Veterans Memorial indicate, where the sheer multitude of the names, with all their individual specificity, peers across the Mall at the sculpted forms of three emblematic combatants.

# DEATH AT A DISTANCE

> Anyone who thinks he is coming out here to wander over the stricken field . . . protected from harm by the mystical light of heroism playing about his hyacinthine locks, had better stay home.
>
> —Richard Norton, founder of the American Volunteer Motor-Ambulance Corps (1916)

> Perhaps wars weren't won anymore. Maybe they went on forever. Maybe it was another Hundred Years' War.
>
> —Ernest Hemingway, *A Farewell to Arms* (1929)

A few years ago, my family and I were spending two summer weeks in a farmhouse on the grounds of a vineyard called Lilliano in Tuscany, some twelve miles from Siena, about midway up a long slope that rises from the Val d'Elsa to the ridge where the town of Castellina in Chianti perches. Lilliano was both the vineyard and the town, although it didn't seem like much of a town, just a few houses that abutted the large main building and a church, always closed as far as we could tell, with a small park in front of it, complete with one park bench and a phone booth. There was no phone in our farmhouse and so we would go down to that booth occasionally to call a restaurant or change a plane reservation. On the wall of the church was a stone plaque, the only bit of architectural variety in its otherwise gloomy closed facade, and on the plaque were the names of sixteen young men from this tiny, hardly postage-stamp-sized town who had died in World War I. I had seen many grand memorials, from a great number of wars. I had read the statistics of casualties and wondered at the impact of so many deaths. But nothing really brought home to me the utter devastation that a war could bring until I looked at this memorial plaque in the middle of a virtually deserted town, almost eighty years after the guns of that war had stopped. How many had lived in this town then; what percentage of the men of fighting age were these sixteen? I didn't know, but the precise numbers hardly seemed to matter.

On German or British posters Frederick Barbarossa or Henry V looked down from the glorious past on the battlefields of Ypres and Passchendaele. But in the trenches they were among the missing. Even though psychically armored with nostalgia for heroes past, the soldiers of the mass armies of World War I were for the first time experiencing the pulverizing power of industrialized war, marking the beginning of a general awareness that it was not the idea of honor that was gone so much as it was the belief that to die honorably in battle was an enhancement of identity. Modern war, with its monstrous destructiveness, turned out to obliterate more than to uplift masculine nature. Instead of the rapid war and direct conflict envisioned by military planners, the new technology—especially in artillery—and the mass army had brought about not a dynamic war of movement but the static trench warfare and enormous casualties that characterized the Western Front and remains as the common memory of World War I. The culmination of this new style of war would come with the development of the atomic and hydrogen bombs, with their ability to vaporize whole populations.

One of many men who eagerly anticipated the war was Cyril Holland, Oscar Wilde's elder son. For him, battle was the crucial way to wipe out the stain on his family's name (which had been changed after Wilde's conviction and jailing). As he wrote to his younger brother Vyvyan in June 1914:

> Gradually, I became obsessed with the idea that I must retrieve what had been lost. . . . The more I thought of this, the more convinced I became that, first and foremost, I must be a *man*. There was to be no cry of decadent artist, of effeminate aesthete, of weak-kneed degenerate. . . . I live by thought, not by emotion. I ask nothing better than to end in honourable battle for my King and Country. (140)

This was the traditional way to be remembered, the nature of true fame, dating back to the Indo-European tribes at the dawn of written language. By the same token, in the samurai code, death in battle, or death by suicide in a righteous cause (like that of the forty-seven *ronin* in the seventeenth century), was a statement of essential moral identity. Even when the hero is found wanting, there might still be some saving grace, and so there is a monument to Benedict Arnold's leg to commemorate his wound at the Battle of Saratoga—the only honorable part of him, implies the inscription.

On May 9, 1915, at a time when many still thought the war would be over shortly and dreams of vindicated honor might still flourish, Cyril Holland né Wilde was killed in what his brother generously said "amounted to a duel with a German sniper." But such "duels" and the honorable combat they implied were becoming much less frequent. Despite the effort to romanticize Tommy Atkins, or the French *poilu*, or the German *frontschwein*, on such a battlefield, the soldier was less a modern version of a chivalric knight than a military version of a factory worker, doing his coglike part in the military machine. As John Keegan has written, the World War I soldier had been decisively "deskilled." He had learned drill, but there was little instruction otherwise. Guns were easier to use and you just had to aim them, although in the trenches and when you went over the top, there was little time or opportunity to do even that. The infantry, the bulk of the armies, were there to follow the artillery barrage that was meant to soften up the enemy and prepare for the ultimate cavalry breakthrough that never came. Orders were to be followed or, in the case of officers, relayed to others. Personal initiative was not an issue.

In the basic equation of traditional warfare, honor was indirectly proportional to distance. From the Native American or Pacific Islander counting coup, to the knight with his broadsword, to the soldier with his bayonet, the closer you were to the enemy, the more honor might be garnered. In *Paradise Lost* Milton echoes a long tradition when he says that the cannon was invented by Satan, the debased epic hero. In the same way, the crossbow, the mortar, and the rifle were the hallmarks of a crippled or blunted sense of military honor; for some, they were equivalent to dishonor.

In the beginning of the war, all sides believed in the power of the offensive. What David Lloyd George called the "knock-out blow," the German General Staff owed to their interpretation of Clausewitz, and the French army stressed as part of the all-out attack cult of the bayonet. Later military historians agreed that it was absurd for the general staffs of the Allied and Central Powers to ignore the lessons of the Crimean War, the U.S. Civil War, and the Boer War—especially those that involved long-drawn-out strategic situations. But at the time expectations rested instead on theories of immediate and overwhelming victory, which had evolved from analyzing what Napoleon had done. The model nearest to hand was the Franco-Prussian War, a conflict between equally civilized combatants that was over in a comparatively short time. But the anticipation of such quick, decisive battles was fostered as well by innumerable victories over poorly armed primitive tribesmen in the colonies (defeats were ignored). There, direct attack was not only a strategic byword; it was also predicated on the cavalry-based assumption that a charge into the ranks of the enemy was the most honorable way to wage war.

Undertaken for coolly rational strategic reasons, these theories of decisive battle also bore an unmistakable relation to more extreme views of the absolute division between what was male (and aggressive) and what was female (and yielding): penetrate and destroy. *Birth of a Nation*, released just six months after the war began, similarly falsified the strategic situations of the U.S. Civil War with battle scenes of cavalry charges overwhelming enemy positions. Like the French and British general staffs, D. W. Griffith had not learned the lessons of the Civil War in one way (the role of firepower and defense) and had learned it too well in another (the revival of cavalry). As Richard Schickel points out:

> He seems not to have recognized, even after firsthand inspection, that World War I was, singularly and tragically, exactly the opposite—a war of stalemate and attrition. Curiously, the war he "fought" on screen was the war many of the generals on both sides of the real thing kept fantasizing, and trying to position themselves for, a war in which a dramatic breakthrough, some bold and dashing stroke, would put an end to agony and waste. (353)

As at Crécy and Agincourt, dubious definitions of military honor overrode issues of strategy; the supposed soul of war was at odds with its new techniques. In place of the expected regular rows of advancing soldiers, the trenches with their labyrinthine patterns furnished a dark parody of the logic of the chessboard.

So the gap widened between military discipline and what might actually win battles. It was the dead end of the tactical practices instituted by Maurice of Nassau. To prepare, armies were still doing much the same kind of close-order drill that had undermined Braddock at Fort Duquesne—which quickly proved useless in the trenches, like the bayonet practice for the hand-to-hand fighting that hardly ever happened. Neither technology nor plans for battle uncritically inherited from Napoleon were decisive, as masses of men were sacrificed to gain a temporary advantage. Somewhat before the British and the French, the Germans showed a willingness to dig in and accept both trench warfare and the machine gun as part of the new reality. But the others soon followed suit, and the statistics tallying the highest number of deaths in battle since the U.S. Civil War are all too familiar. The seventeenth-century idea of fighting to the last man and the last *sou* had returned a hundred- and a thousandfold: in two weeks in August 1914, France lost over 200,000 men; in 1915 Russia lost approximately two million men; in one week in June 1916 the Austro-Hungarian Empire lost some 280,000 men; and on the first day of the Battle of the Somme, July 1, 1916, almost 60,000 members of the British army were killed.

Whether on the level of both a soldier's individual motivation or a general's strategic perspective, World War I thus splits between the ideal vision of the war as source of honor, masculinity, and national pride—and war as a pragmatic, bloody reality. So much of the incidental panoply of previous warfare disappeared forever with World War I. The battlefields of the past, crowded with masses of men engaging one another in smoke- and flame-filled scenes, had been replaced with the emptiness of no-man's-land. Paintings of the U.S. Civil War or the Franco-Prussian War still look like the grand operations of old. But World War I marks the end not only of the illusion of noble war but also of the static pictorialism of war painting, its ghastly parade of dead and dying men in boldly colored uniforms. Helmets were now meant more for protection than for theatrical intimidation. For uniforms, the British army had officially adopted khaki (from the Hindustani word for "dust") at the time of the Boer War, and the Americans followed suit in 1902. The French infantry had blue coats and red trousers at the beginning of World War I, but changed the next year, while the Germans were in green or gray. With long-range weapons, the strategic need was to cut down the visibility of soldiers rather than to enhance it. Although the Italians often stuck to their own red pants and other armies retained some vestige of their former plumage, on the whole, uniforms had become more drab, and the endless mud made them even drabber.

Trench warfare was almost by definition inglorious. It notoriously featured not grand charges with bayonets fixed or sabers raised, but either static defenses or tedious but deadly fights over a few feet of land—at first holding the line, then falling back and advancing again in a strange dance that lasted years. The supposedly supreme test of warrior resolve, hand-to-hand combat, was hardly ever possible. Instead of direct contact, much of the battle that was happening on the Western Front, like the enemy himself, was invisible, until it happened to fall directly on you. Death came at a distance—through bombardment, machine guns, flame-throwers, poison gas—and was more terrifying for that.

Paradoxically, in some ways the battlefields of Belgium and northern France were clearer than ever before, as can be seen from old newsreels featuring soldiers moving across empty plains punctuated by bursts of bombs and mortars. The Napoleonic situation in which a soldier could quickly be enveloped in the smoke from his own gun had been eliminated by the new technology. In 1901, smokeless powder, with its greater propellant velocity, had been introduced. The Napoleonic gun had a range of perhaps a hundred yards, the World War I rifle a mile or even two, and with smokeless powder and the new telescopic sights the soldier had a much better chance of seeing what he was shooting at, but little chance at all of seeing who was shooting at him.

All these improvements had hardly made the battlefield less chaotic than the smoke-filled scene of Waterloo. There may have been no smoke from the guns, but there was smoke from heavy artillery bombardments, along with clouds of dust, dirt, and debris in the air. Not only that, these shells ranged in size up to almost a ton, compared to the sixty- to seventy-pound shells of the Franco-Prussian War. In addition to the confusion Clausewitz called typical of battle, or the uncertainty of Byron's Don Juan or Stendhal's Fabrizio at Waterloo, the entrenched World War I soldier also felt helpless, supported only by his equally helpless comrades, his view of his world confined to a glimpse of sky until the command came to go over the top. The noise from the long-range artillery was almost ceaseless, and although the battlefield itself may have been more visible, the enemy was now more invisible. Any dream that the war would be direct, like ten thousand duels multiplied, was lost in the shell craters of no-man's-land, where the barbed wire invented to divide the American West crisscrossed the ground, fencing in not cattle but men.

Yet, as Max Plowman wrote, there was often more of a feeling of camaraderie with those invisible fellows on the other side than with the folks at home, as well as a dislike of the officers who were insisting on a bloodthirsty attitude:

> In this sunshine it seems impossible to believe that at any minute we in this trench, and they in that, may be blown to bits

> by shells fired from guns at invisible distances by hearty fellows who would be quite ready to stand you a drink if you met them face to face. (Fussell, 164)

Their affinity was to share a nightmarish experience that others could never appreciate. As Robert Graves observes in *Goodbye to All That*, his 1929 autobiography, returning soldiers were often taken aback by the contrast between the belligerence of the home-front war and the trench feeling of connection to the men on the other side of no-man's-land. When they ventured to voice any opinion that the war was not a crusade of honor, they were often vilified or even sent to madhouses.

In the Musée de la Grande Armée in Paris, amid exhibits of armor, guns, and other artifacts of the panoply and self-congratulatory side of war, one glass case catches my eye. There lies entombed a mud-streaked greatcoat once owned by an artillery lieutenant who died in 1915. It is a relic of the Battle of Verdun, a literal *nostalgie de la boue*, memory of the mud—its dirt dry and flaking now almost ninety years later, its cloth beginning to rot, but in itself a reminder not of *la gloire* but what actual human beings had to suffer. Near Verdun, not far from the fort of Douaumont that was the scene of tumultuous fighting, there is a wide field covered with crosses marking the graves of 50,000 known dead. Behind them, in an ossuary that resembles a cathedral are the bones of 300,000 more, the unknown. As you walk on the battlefield of Verdun, small signs marked "*village détruit*" point you down leafy paths to crumbling blocks of masonry and metal that mark what is left of destroyed villages that had been taken and retaken ten times or more. When the war receded from Verdun, there was no vegetation left. An average of a ton of explosives had fallen on every square meter of the battlefield. After the war, in addition to the memorials, the French government also created a massive reforestation project, so that what was a blasted landscape now resembles a pleasant forest. Until, that is, you see the tombstones, the plaques, and the remnants of trenches and barbed wire, and until you notice the ground. For the reforestation has worked, but under the trees the ground for the most part remains poisoned and looks oddly bare. Botanists say that it will probably never be entirely safe, and bomb squads still dig out live shells almost a century later.*

* Hundreds of tons of unexploded shells continue to be found every year at Verdun.

# REASON IN MADNESS

In both Europe and the United States, war had been hailed as a panacea to cure the problems of peace—civil unrest, degeneration, loss of national will, as well as psychological depression, feelings of unworthiness, listlessness, and all the general feelings of aimlessness that were called *accedie* in the Middle Ages. The pioneering sociologist Emile Durkheim in *Suicide* (1897) dubbed it "anomie"—a word literally meaning "without the law," but broadly referring to a state of being in which one lacks any sense of social standards for behavior, which could lead to suicide, crime, or the death-in-life of decadence. Durkheim didn't specifically recommend war as the cure for anomie. But in the popular imagination of the last decade of the nineteenth century and the first decade of the twentieth, war was promoted as the universal tonic. It would bring back order and instill both national and personal pride, reconnecting the disaffected to their societies and strengthening the commitment of the socially engaged.

But when the promised restorative of war did arrive, it turned out to be less than benevolent, causing—in addition to physical maiming and death—a wide array of psychological ailments that were at first collected under the general term of "shell shock." The attempt to define shell shock marks a crucial landmark in the history of warfare because it was a much greater challenge to the assumed relation of war and masculinity than even the highest casualty report. With the recognition that more and more men were depleted rather than energized by war, shell shock directly brought into question the conception of war as the arena of honor.

Mental illnesses connected to war had been noticed before, but never in such numbers or such excruciating detail. There are observations of conditions resembling battle fatigue as far back as the seventeenth century, and some writers claim that it was noticed even in the classical world. But it was the era of the citizen soldier and the mass army that brought the problem of war's effect on the mind to center stage. Early attempts to isolate and define the mental effect of war were fitful. Before "nostalgia" was used generally to describe any longing for a past time, it referred specifically to a mournful psychological longing for home. Akin to what we would call separation anxiety, this nostalgia was conspicuous especially in military men, and noted by physicians in the Napoleonic Wars (as *nostalgie*), the U.S. Civil War, and later.*

Not long before World War I, psychiatric casualties were also widespread in the Russo-Japanese War, where the remarkable decrease in deaths caused by infectious diseases may have made mental diseases more visible. In World War I, the newly widespread condition was first dubbed "shell shock" because most psychiatrists and psychologists charged with treating the afflicted soldiers thought it was due to the noise and physical disruption of incessant bombardment. For their part, many military men considered the symptoms to be a deceitful way of shirking one's duty, an attitude that still persisted in World War II, when General George Patton slapped a soldier for what he considered malingering and thus caused a minor scandal. But in World War I, the growing number of cases soon forced armies to drop that interpretation officially and encourage treatment for affected soldiers. For the most part the bulk of the therapies—both those that involved inflicting pain like electric shock, and those that were more analytic—were less concerned with the individual's well-being

* The French army in Vietnam referred to it as *"la cafard"*—the blues, tedium, but the same word is also used to refer to a sanctimonious person, a hypocrite.

than with restoring his proper relation to authority. In effect, their primary goal was to return the soldier to active duty: Don't let down the side. Act with honor.

Much of the medical as well as the military resistance to psychological explanations for shell shock and their desire for a material cause—the actual sound and earthshaking power of artillery shells—came from the belief that an hysteric reaction, which might include paralysis and convulsions, was not truly masculine. Although few at the time made the equation explicit, the male hysteria that appeared during combat was strikingly similar to what women experienced during peacetime. Both sexes exhibited feelings of victimization and passivity, and a similar, often physical, inability to act.*

How could men who were soldiers at war, often on the front lines, exhibit forms of mental illness associated either with women or with effeminate, neurasthenic men? Either the theory or the facts had to go. As the number of those afflicted grew, shell shock therefore helped to undermine previous theories of psychopathology that ascribed mental problems to hereditary racial degeneration and inborn disposition. Gradually it became clear that an hysteric response to war could not be predicted either by the strength of the bombardment or the "character" of the individual.

Although the belief in a physical predisposition to mental breakdown was still strong in traditional psychiatry, many were beginning to consider circumstantial causes like the actual situation of the military group along with a psychoanalytic stress on early childhood experiences as factors. Shell shock, it turned out, was not confined to one nation's army or one social class within an army. War neuroses were as prevalent among officers as they were among the ordinary soldiers, the difference being that in the generally middle- and upper-class officers the symptoms came out psychologically, while in the working-class soldiers they generally took physical form: paralysis, mutism, blindness. Therapists like W. H. R. Rivers in England, who worked both as a psychologist and an anthropologist, began to make connections between an ethnological view of the pressures upon behavior within an entire society and a psychological focus on the individual.

As some psychologists began to observe, shell shock came from a clash

* For those few soldiers who were able to fight but refused to, there was also a peculiar symmetry between their refusal and the New Woman's rejection of domesticity. Doctors and laymen alike often considered both to be against nature.

between war technology, cultural expectations of proper behavior, and a soldier's individual will. The technology was so overwhelming that the will became paralyzed and the tormented soldier could neither help his fellows nor act in accordance with the sense of honor he had been taught. After propaganda that brought men into war by emphasizing the entwining of duty to country and fraternal obligation to "chums" and "pals," tremendous guilt was the usual result. The nineteenth-century regimental group, with its high eternal banners of courage and manliness for comrades of the same stripe, had helped support the individual with a sense of history and camaraderie. But in the bloodbath of the trenches, where all insignia were equally covered with mud, it created instead an internalized sense of failure to live up to its impossible standards. The link with the past was shattered again and again. The proud names and numbers became a mere bureaucratic shell whose members at the end of the war bore little resemblance to the group at the beginning.

Historically, the successful treatment of shell shock made mental health professions like psychiatric social work respectable, opened the previously hostile medical profession to the possibility of psychoanalytic (especially Freudian) explanation, and introduced the general public to a view of war in which injuries could be mental as well as physical. Despite the belief of scoffers that the number of shell-shock cases would drop precipitately once the armistice was signed, they only grew, peaking in England, for example, at more than 100,000 in 1922, four years after the cease-fire—a figure that did not take into account the numerous unhospitalized neurasthenics, of whom Robert Graves counted himself as one. There were also almost 100,000 American cases by 1919, and the War Department would spend upward of a billion dollars in their treatment over the years.

In fact, the British public and British newspapers tended to accept the psychoanalytic view of shell shock some time before medical or military people did (although they also believed in the persistence of patriotic morale long after it had vanished from the front). The reason may be that they were sympathetic to the abnormal stress of war and what it could do because they were feeling some of it themselves: from the sound of Western Front guns audible in London, the aerial bombardments, the sunken commercial ships, the sight of disabled servicemen on the street. After the giddy days of 1914 and 1915, when it seemed that the war would be a brief astringent for a depleted civilization, the loss of trust in war's "normality" may have also undermined the analogous belief that the kind of masculinity that can wage war is normal and can stay that way without grave difficulty. In Germany, Freud's associate Sandor Ferenczi noted widespread impotence in frontline soldiers. The wartime situation, he concluded, forced a withdrawal of sexual energy from the outside world because it was needed to solace a desperately weakened sense of self. But the only result was a vicious circle: the more need there was for solace, the more withdrawal, the more impotence, and therefore the need for more solace. The "combat fatigue" of World War II, the "brainwashing" of Korea, and the "post-traumatic stress syndrome" of Vietnam were still in the future, but with shell shock the psychological side of war, its impact on the mental health of the individual solider—and civilian—caught in its clutches, had become a major issue.

# PRIMITIVE BODY AND MACHINE BODY

Siegfried [Sassoon] said that we must "keep up the good reputation of the poets"—as men of courage, he meant.
—Robert Graves, *Goodbye to All That* (1929)

The sudden awareness that madness, or at least neurasthenia, could cut across all classes of men went hand in hand with the war-fostered discovery of the frailty of the male body. The worries about the physical degeneracy of the male population of Europe in the decades before World War I had encouraged local, national, and even international movements to expand gymnastics and sports. Coubertin's Olympics movement had made athletic contests a key to the ideal interaction of nations, and in 1905 he dedicated *Le gymnastique utilitaire,* his book on the need for gymnastic training, to Teddy Roosevelt, the recognized world advocate of the strenuous life. In popular entertainment the male body was featured as well—not only the trick riding and feats of prowess in Buffalo Bill's Wild West Show and Congress of All Nations, but also the flexibility of Harry Houdini escaping from any confinement, and the image of male physical power created by the Prussian strongman Eugen Sandow, who appeared virtually naked to show off his sculpted conditioning. Among his frequent props were the fluted columns and even the fig leaf that signaled the acceptable nudity of Greek and Roman art. Two of the many books he wrote to publicize his bodybuilding techniques were *Sandow on Physical Training: A Study in the Perfect Type of the Human Form* (1894) and *Body-building; or, Man in the Making* (1904), fully illustrated with photographs of Sandow, his family, and his students flexing their muscles. In a word first coined in the early nineteenth century that entered more popular usage around this time, Sandow was a "he-man."* Such theatricalizing of male physicality reinforced its emblematic position as the image of a strong state as well as a strong psyche. Not coincidentally, this was also the period in which Sir Francis Galton, after years of preaching the principles of eugenics, founded the Eugenics Society (1904) to advance the perfection of the British race.

By the same token, as the Wilde trial in England had made clear, the physicality of the artistic male was considered particularly suspect. Being cultured was just a step away from being effeminate. Poets, painters, and writers thus often went out of their way to prove their robustness, fighting duels in France or appearing in the United States as a group who stressed their blunt style and their connection to the outdoors—Frank Norris, Stephen Crane, Jack London, Ernest Hemingway, and beyond—all in revolt against the "genteel" tradition.

Recasting the artistic male as an emblem of potency and power took many forms. For poets like Rupert Brooke or Rainer Maria Rilke, war would be a chance to awaken from a honorless sleep (as in Brooke's "1914") or, in Rilke's phrase, to have an aimless life "invigorated with death." Both Brooke and Rilke were part of a large group of writers who tried to bring older literary forms to bear on the experience of war. As Paul Fussell argues in *The Great War and Modern Memory*, much of the writing of English poets of the war pressed older poetic traditions into service as ways to make the war comprehensible and in some way subordinate to traditional literary understanding and traditional poetic forms, even when they were used ironically. Ravel's *Le Tombeau de Couperin* (1917) is an intriguingly similar example from music. Written during the war, which Ravel himself could not fight, as a tribute to the fallen French soldiers, the composition associates itself with an older French baroque musical style even while it attempts to bring in under its wing the ghastly realities of the present.

* "He-man" is a word of American origin. The first citation is from 1832, just about the same time that machinists were distinguishing between male and female screws.

But so many memoirs published during and after World War I expressed the realization that the literary and artistic language of the past needed to be either discarded or recharged with new content. A crucial scene in many of these works is the encounter with the "first corpse," the abrupt realization of mortality and the frailty of the male body in the splintering obliterations of the battlefield. An emblem of lost innocence for the soldier who sees it, the First Corpse foretells what will happen again and again but never so vividly, that individual, personalized shock rapidly diminishing in the face of multiple deaths and gory wounds.

In contrast to Fussell, Samuel Hynes in *A War Imagined* emphasizes the other side of the war's radical effect on traditional literary language, accompanied by an urge toward experimentation, a search for new forms fit to express this new human experience. A passage in Robert Graves's *Goodbye to All That* encapsulates one version of the tug-of-war between refabricating old forms and searching for new. Graves meets Sassoon near the front lines and shows him some of his war poems:

> He frowned and said that war should not be written about in such a realistic way. In return, he showed me some of his poems. One of them began: "return to me, colours that were my joy,/Not in the woeful crimson of men slain. . . ." Siegfried had not yet been in the trenches. I told him, in my old-soldier manner, that he would soon change his style. (146)

Graves delights in the paradox of the man with the medieval warrior surname of Siegfried who is inexperienced in the ways of modern war. But continuity and discontinuity were both happening at once. Ravel's effort to preserve a musical tradition might be set beside Stravinsky's to emphasize disruption and change, while in painting, Pablo Picasso and Diego Rivera responded to World War I by a classicizing style aimed at containing disorder at the same time that such movements as Dadaism and Surrealism luxuriated in the insights of disorder itself.

For literature in particular, one aesthetic result of the bankruptcy of the grandiose abstractions of public honor was a stripped-down style of directness, an effort to be frank about the horrors of war that ran the gamut from straightforward reporting to an almost absurd hyperreality. In early works like Brooke's "1914," personal honor and national glory were invoked as a means of rising above the all-too-vulnerable male body. But as the war wore on, a reindividualizing literature of first-person witness became more common, continuing after the war in novels and memoirs of disillusionment, whose emphasis on wounds and wounding seemed set on bringing that body back into perspective and in the process reinstating something of its human nature.

Henri Barbusse's *Under Fire* appeared in 1916, Ernst Jünger's *Storm of Steel* in 1920, John Dos Passos's *Three Soldiers* in 1921, Jünger's memoir-essay *Copse 125* in 1925, and Hemingway's *A Farewell to Arms* and Erich Maria Remarque's *All Quiet on the Western Front* both in 1929. They were only the most prominent in a great flood of poems, novels, memoirs, and recollections written by participants in the war—the first war in history to be so voluminously documented, in part because it was the first war to draw so heavily upon a literate, self-conscious male community. Since the heroic battles of classical and Renaissance epics, there had been few works in European literature that took war as their basic setting, unless, as in Shakespeare's history plays, their story was of kings. By contrast, in novels such as Henry Fielding's *Tom Jones* and Laurence Sterne's *Tristram Shandy* in the eighteenth century, or Stendhal's *Charterhouse of Parma*, Thackeray's *Vanity Fair*, and even Tolstoy's *War and Peace* in the nineteenth, war was more important as scene and setting than as central issue.

But in the twentieth century war again became an event that imaginative fiction tried to comprehend, not just in its tumult but in its tedium—the drifting, uncertain time of terror between boredom and battle. Here, too, the scene had changed: rather than the wanderer in the midst of the chaos of the Napoleonic battlefield, the focus was more often the social microcosm of the patrol, as it would continue to be in novels of World War II like Norman Mailer's *The Naked and the Dead*. In a fictional mirror of the increasing importance in twentieth-century war of small-unit tactics, Barbusse, Jünger, Hemingway, and Remarque all wrote from a gritty eye-level view of the war that eschewed the "big picture" and "the great game" to focus on the activities of a group of men together. Rather than the honor that in idealized figures like Galahad represented a purification of the physical body, here the body, along with its wounds, messes, and decay, was made the center of attention. Usually the male group in question was the infantry patrol, slogging through the mud of no-man's-land rather than soaring above it—a presaging of the emphasis on the multiethnic squad in American novels and films of World War II.*

* The subtitle of Barbusse's *Under Fire* (*Le Feu*) is *Journal d'une escouade* (*Journal of a Squad*).

Unlike Barbusse or Frederic Manning in *The Middle Parts of Fortune*, Graves doesn't describe many blown-apart bodies or other forms of dispiriting death in *Goodbye to All That*. But there is a chilling matter-of-factness about death that permeates his memoir; a friend or acquaintance will be described and then let go with a "that was the last I ever saw of him." Graves is similarly matter-of-fact about his youthful homosexual desires, his virginity, his wounds, and other bodily features that in a memoir before the war would not have been considered relevant or proper for understanding his character.

Although Jünger, like many of his fellow memoirists in other countries, celebrated the frontline soldier and often mocked the obtuseness of commanders, his slant was somewhat different. Instead of grimness, he faced the corpse-ridden landscape with what might almost be called gaiety. Unlike Barbusse, Graves, and Hemingway, and the even more explicitly antiwar viewpoint in Jaroslav Hašek's *Good Soldier Schweik* (1920–23) and Remarque's *All Quiet on the Western Front*, Jünger still believed that war could be the crucible of both personal and national character, no matter how degraded the process of this particular war might be. *The Storm of Steel*, published just after the war, depicts, among other gruesome scenes, Jünger's contemplation of the layering of bodies and dirt in a trench as an archaeological dig through which he can discover the shapes of past battles. But in *Copse 125*, five years later, he looks above the muck and blood to admire aviators as an image of war's visionary possibilities:

> Only in the realm of air is the duel still possible to-day, and with it the chivalry that here below has to die out from the days of the great armies, since it is always only the quality of the few. In their case, when one of them has to land owing to a wound or engine trouble, he is received by the enemy as a friend and honoured as a man. (69–70)

This undisguised hankering after the chivalric indicates Jünger's underlying belief in the necessity of war as salvation:

> Those who seek to abolish war by civilized means are just as ridiculous as those ascetics who preach against propagation in order to usher in the millennium. . . . Wherever they are left undisturbed at their work, there civilization emits its first scent of decay. (56–57)

· · ·

Disillusionment may be a basic theme of post–World War I literature. Hašek, who had been drafted into the Austro-Hungarian army and then captured by the Russians, created in *Schweik* a twentieth-century analogue to Grimmelshausen's character Simplicissimus in the Thirty Years' War—a wandering soldier whose adventures illustrate the futility of war and the venality of all authority. Remarque, a soldier who was wounded twice in the war and later became a journalist, similarly saw war as the product of a world in which old men and civilians let the young fight and die for them. But for Jünger, though World War I did not live up to his expectations, war in general still maintained its allure.

Many artists as well, while not necessarily sanctioning war, often used its imagery to energize their own desire for aesthetic change. At one extreme were prewar aesthetic cults of violence that mirrored the political advocacy of direct action in such works as Georges Sorel's *Reflexions sur le violence* (1908), which argued that it was the only weapon the working class had against the repressive tactics of the capitalist class. As part of his manifesto, Sorel specifically stressed the need to invoke past myths of heroic battle to galvanize the workers. Such a belief in the cleansing virtues of violence was hardly confined to the left or to the anarchists who claimed credit for many assassinations across Europe in the years before World War I. Stravinsky for one welcomed the war because it would mean the victory of the strong over the weak. Like other modernists, as well as Richard Wagner a half century before, Stravinsky looked to reenergize an outmoded artistic language with an exploration of the barbaric and the exotic. The old "civilized" language of transcendent value had been exploded by the eruptions of the present. Its outworn ideas would be jettisoned and ancient myths discovered anew.

With similar goals of both artistic and national regeneration, Gabriele d'Annunzio created for himself a post-Wildean image as both aesthete and man of action, plunging from one tempestuous heterosexual affair into another, celebrating Italian nationalism and masculine energy in a way that presaged the propaganda of Mussolini's fascist movement in the 1920s. D'Annunzio came from a humble and, to his biographers, an ambiguous background. His father had changed his name from the more plebeian Rapagnetta, and the son continued the process of self-making and self-inflation. The heroes of his poetry and fiction were dashing adventurers, as he was and wished to be, making love and war with equal vigor. In his 1909 novel *Forse che si, forse che no* (*Maybe Yes, Maybe No*), the aviator hero says that he doesn't know which pleases him most—"to spill sperm or to spill blood" (Rhodes, 175). D'Annunzio was particularly intent on arousing the Latin races to band together against the barbarians (in this case, the Germans) and seize lands that were rightfully Italy's. He agitated for Italy's entry into the war on the side of the Allies, and during the war his contributions to the Italian effort included dropping bombs and poems from his plane onto enemy soldiers, primarily Austrians. With the war over, he took it upon himself to gather a band of followers and seize the port of Fiume, then part of Yugoslavia. The Italian government refused to support him, the Treaty of Rapallo declared Fiume independent, d'Annunzio declared war on Italy, and he, together with his company, was finally forced to leave Fiume by Italian bombs.

D'Annunzio's comic-opera flamboyance was reflected somewhat more soberly by a variety of artists and movements intent on making a great noise in the world. In fact, the period just before the onset of World War I was a fertile time for artistic manifestos of all sorts that aimed to overthrow the canons and style of older literature and art, and not coincidentally the image of man they embodied. It was the beginning of an aggressive and self-conscious avant-garde—a word that itself came from the terminology of war, that announced its aspirations as manly and world-changing rather than effete and precious.

The advent of war seemed to justify both the desire for primal truth and the embrace of technology, the primitive and the modern. The modern was the renewed barbarism ahead of us, just as the primitive was the barbarism behind. Some artists in search both of a new image of art and of their calling plunged into the mythic, or embraced the new, while others mirrored the influence of both efforts in order to upend the past. Picasso, for example, absorbed whatever was in the air: the primitive through the influence of African mask forms on *Les Demoiselles d'Avignon* (1907), the speed and disruption in his experiments with Cubism.

The first tendency, as exemplified in the music of Stravinsky, sought to reenergize overly sophisticated artistic forms with an increased, almost ethnographic, awareness of the basic myths that drove human nature, as in *Le Sacre du printemps* (1913). Like the Expressionism of painters like Edvard Munch and even earlier Vincent Van Gogh, this urge emphasized the connection between the mythic, the spiritual, and the psychological—outside of supposedly civilized institutions.

The other searched for inspiration in what was considered to be the heart of contemporary life. There speed, movement, and geometric design, together with a disheveled point of view, were considered quintessentially modern, as opposed to the calm unities and unruffled certainties of the past. In his Futurist manifesto, published in the French newspaper *Le Figaro* in 1909, Filippo Tomasso Marinetti made his artistic standard the "new technology of the automobile" and the rapid changes made possible by motion pictures. It was the beginning of an artistic romance with the airplane, the car, and the motorcycle that would last through the twentieth century. Outworn cultural traditions were to be replaced by the gleaming new technology, the imperturbable eye of authority by the rapid shifts of focus necessary to penetrate the modern scene. The racing car, said Marinetti, was more beautiful than that prized possession of the Louvre, the Winged Victory of Samothrace, and the Winged Victory was not just chosen as an arbitrary representative of classical art, but for its embodiment of a heroic past that would now be superseded. Like d'Annunzio before and Jünger later, Marinetti considered himself to be a synthesis of aesthete and war maker. In 1915, as Italians debated whether or not to join the fight, he published a book of poems called *Guerra sola igiene del mondo* (War, the Only Hygiene for the Earth).

The association of the machine with a new individualism may seem perverse if we consider the dehumanizing technology that fights the war and runs the factories. Was the machine hostile to the human or a grandiose extension of it? In 1748, Julien de la Mettrie's *The Man-Machine* had asserted the mechanical nature of the human body in order to free human identity from the soul and assert its primarily secular and physical basis. On the eve of World War I, according to Marinetti's visionary "metalization of the human body," man would by his own machine inventions become outfitted for the modern world with an even more powerful and vital body. Philosophers of the 1890s as disparate as Henri Bergson and Nietzsche had linked a new cultural energy and life force with the release of inhibition that the modern world was bringing, although both to varying degrees attacked the mechanization of daily life. But the war brought a positive view of the mechanical. The highly tooled and dynamic machine self was also apparent in the experimental work of artists in Russia before the revolution. The Constructivism proclaimed by El Lissitzky, Alexander Rodchenko, and Naum Gabo in 1913 similarly embraced technology and the machine, stressing the purities of geometry as the way to bring clarity to the new view of the world. Technology would not undermine either war or masculinity but enhance and perfect them. As Ernst Jünger phrased it, the best men would be matched with the best machines, "for the two were inseparable."*

In essence, the machine self in whatever form was the self that could survive the cataclysms of the new world of violence. Marinetti and d'Annunzio had elaborated the idea of a new man that was being assembled with large parts of appended machinery, and Jünger agreed:

> I see in old Europe a new and commanding breed rising up, fearless and fabulous, unsparing of blood and sparing of pity, inured to suffering the worst and to inflicting it and ready to stake all to attain their ends—a race that builds machines and trusts to machines, to whom machines are not soulless iron, but engines of might which it controls with cold reason and hot blood. (*Copse 125*, 79)

This machine world would be man-made, technological and barbaric at once, opposed to the blandness of nineteenth-century progress, the stifling of a nurturing femininity, and all the excesses of a dying bourgeois civilization. Jünger wanted his new breed to grow in the millions and looked to demobilization to create a new society based on ex-soldiers. But he was very opposed to drill and regularity as inhibitions in war where "there is no rule but the exception." He rejected the Prussian military idea that the ideal soldier was *kadavergehorsamkeit,* listening like a corpse in utter submission. Taking his own initiative as the norm, Jünger the officer could escape the corpse-soldier alternative of a demoralizing mechanization. Rather than the factory model and repetitive machine self, his ideal was the individualist machine of the aviators he admired, the mixture of hero and machine that Charles Lindbergh in his autobiography called "We."

Throughout the Nazi period, Jünger tried to maintain his distance, but millions of other former soldiers were more attracted to mass movements. In one version, then, the new masculine machine body that had emerged from World War I was a quintessence of heroic individualism; in another, however, it would resemble the unthinking mass man imagined by Carel Kapek in *R.U.R.* (*Rossom's Universal Robots*) in 1921, whose satire of a technological world introduced the word "robot" (Polish for "compulsory laborer") into English.

* Marinetti's manifesto on the 1935–36 war between Ethiopia and Italy was entitled *War Is Beautiful.*

# T. E. LAWRENCE: THE RESURRECTION OF ADVENTURE

Like the poets who tried to adapt traditional forms to wartime experiences, some voices tried to encompass the unprecedented scale of World War I by claiming it echoed the wars of old. In his book on the Battle of Gallipoli, published in 1918, John Masefield, for example, who was to become British poet laureate in 1930, prefaces each chapter with a quotation from *The Song of Roland*. But being pinned down in the trenches of the Western Front or on the beaches at Gallipoli seemed to have little to do with the renewed sense of daring and adventure that had been promised as the benison of war. That required space, not the claustrophobia of the dugouts, and light, not the gloom of the battlefield of dreadful night. The European soldier, who previously had asserted his superior civilization over primitive peoples both morally and technologically, in this war seemed to become primitive and barbaric himself. The trenches were the dark subterranean image of the war, men dug into the ground, tanks rumbling over the blasted ground above, sappers digging tunnels far below the surface in order to blow up the enemy from beneath. Its ideal counterpart, as Jünger and others wrote, was the war in the sky, where the surge to light and space had helped create the cult of the pilot and the chivalric behavior possible only in the air, the only place where words like "honor" might actually have some meaning. After the war it helped set the scene for the phenomenon of Lindbergh, who dared to do what no one had done before—cross the Atlantic alone in a plane. Like George Leigh-Mallory and Andrew Irvine climbing Everest, Lindbergh helped both to resurrect and to validate a vocabulary of masculine courage that the war seemed to have tarnished irredeemably.

On another ground, far from Europe, an ideal war did seem to exist, where light and space and adventure and the old ways of war appeared to be alive still, where the stasis of the trenches might be redeemed by dashing adventure, and where some shred of chivalric glory might be salvaged from the general inferno. This was the war in the East, the war against Turkey in Arabia, Palestine, and Egypt. There, while fighters galloped across the desert, battle could seem like a true heroic crusade, rather than the messy business it was on the Western Front. When this war was over in December 1917, Edmund Allenby had captured Jerusalem, as Richard the Lion-Hearted could not. But the overriding hero was not the commanding general Allenby. It was Captain, later Colonel, T. E. Lawrence. The soldier as ideal defender of the nation may have superseded the soldier as scum and cannon fodder, but the slaughter of World War I tarnished that glory with its blood-soaked anonymity. Lawrence, like Lindbergh, rose out of that mass slaughter as a new kind of hero who might somehow make sense of the paradox that World War I had made so acute: war as both a meaningless bloodbath and the noblest pursuit of men.

There were innumerable people in the aftermath of World War I who managed to put their hands on the levers of the new media fame and make themselves notorious. If that were all there were to T. E. Lawrence, he would remain a figure of his time. But something in his image attracted admirers and critics then and attracts them now. In essence, Lawrence's quite self-consciously created career brought together a whole array of contradictions in Anglo-American attitudes toward war and masculinity that had a larger European resonance as well. Hypersensitive to what in *The Seven Pillars of Wisdom* he calls "civilisation-disease," Lawrence was a romantic medievalist whose head was filled with stories of knights and conquests, a kind of modern Don Quixote. But unlike Quixote, he actually led or helped lead a guerrilla army of sword-wielding horsemen, warriors who seemed to Lawrence to be brothers across the centuries to medieval knights.

A literary and artistic aesthete interested in medieval artifacts, rubbed brasses, heraldry, and medieval weapons, Lawrence was also a man of action. In his own nature and his military career he helped knit together for an admiring British and American public the masculine relation between soldier and artist that seemed forever broken after the trials of Oscar Wilde. The literary men of World War I who had tried to somehow fuse their own experience with the language they had inherited had made similar steps, as had the enlistees who came to the front directly from their upper-class backgrounds and prep schools, like many of Roosevelt's Rough Riders. But Lawrence also added to the mix the exoticism of a Victorian eccentric like Sir Richard Francis Burton, who had gone disguised to Mecca and Medina, as well as the male camaraderie of a Gordon, a Kitchener, and a Baden-Powell.

At five-foot-four Lawrence was hardly much taller than the recruits whose size had so horrified the army brass at the time of the Boer War. The illegitimate son of the Irish peer Sir Thomas Chapman, he had gone to Oxford, where he became fascinated with all things medieval, especially military architecture, and wrote a thesis on Crusader castles that won him an honors degree in history (1910). While he was researching in the Near East, he made observations of Turkish armaments and installations that would prove useful in World War I. Joining several archaeological expeditions to the area, he gained the familiarity with local languages and customs that during the war brought him to the intelligence office of the British War Department and later to more active service in Egypt, where he convinced his superiors to support the Arab revolt against the Turks as a way of diverting a German ally. As political and military liaison to the Arabs, Lawrence submerged himself in their culture, dressing in Bedouin robes and gaining the nickname of "El Aurens"—with its English connotation, the Golden One—and "Amir Dynamite" for his skill in coordinating guerrilla attacks on crucial Turkish train routes. But his vision of Arab nationhood was scuttled by the Versailles conference and Lawrence, disillusioned with politics if not with war, publicly refused the medals for distinguished valor and national service that his admirers were poised to shower upon him.

Although Lawrence's exploits occurred during the war, his fame, like that of Lindbergh, was a postwar phenomenon, stirred up primarily by the American correspondent and lecturer Lowell Thomas, who in 1917 had his firm Thomas Travelogues accredited by the American government to make documentaries that might serve as propaganda for American intervention. After the war was over, Thomas stayed and began to develop a lecture with film clips about the war in the East. To a world whose view of battle was still mired in the trenches of the Western Front (where two of Lawrence's brothers had died), the Lawrence of Thomas's lecture restored the heroic ideal. Instead of the black clothes of the Victorian middle class or the mud-soaked khaki of the modern soldier, he wore flowing white robes, tying his image to nineteenth-century dreams of the Orient as well as to Winckelmann and Pater's view of the white purity of the classical world.

Fashioning a lecture called "With Allenby in Palestine and Lawrence in Arabia," which increasingly focused on Lawrence, Thomas cast the story of the British effort in the Middle East in terms of an American western—the aloneness of the desert frontier, the mounted men sweeping down on a lonely town—as well as a more European dream of chivalry reborn. Thomas's lecture was tremendously successful, despite its length—more than two hours—and he gave it five times a week for months to capacity crowds. Joel C. Hodson, who has written about Thomas's role in the creation of Lawrence's legend, estimates that it was given some four thousand times to audiences that totaled about four million. In addition there were thousands of articles in the 1920s and into the 1930s about Lawrence and his exploits.

The medieval knight, the frontier cowboy, and the modern soldier all came together in the "Holy Land" portrayed by Thomas, who called the war against the Turks there "the last crusade," the title of his lecture in England, in which he stressed specific geographic parallels. But instead of a Christian Holy Land, it was a spiritual arena for masculinity to refind itself, without the need to bow to any particular god. Now the Muslim Arab rebels were the Crusaders, led by Lawrence against the Turks, who were also Muslim. Lawrence's own religious views were minimal, even actively hostile, and, unlike Havelock and Kitchener, he refused to become an idealized Christian soldier for the evangelicals. His interest in the medieval world was less Christian than Arthurian, and his celebrity, and perhaps his view of himself, was that of a secular, almost atheist, saint. As he wrote, "Easily was a man made an infidel, but hardly might he be converted to another faith." At least in Thomas's account, his faith is heroic war. "If there were gods," Lawrence wrote to Charlotte Shaw, "there might be men" (*Seven Pillars of Wisdom*, 32; letter, 16.VI.27).

As an advisor to the Arab rebels and therefore outside an immediate command structure of his own, Lawrence also brought back to war the treasured idea of the gifted amateur. Like the Olympic ideal of the amateur athlete, the pose had something of the strayed aristocrat about it. Lawrence went so far as to say that even armor was an unfair advantage in warfare. Attracted by the physical endurance of the desert Arabs and what he conceived to be their freedom from the ills of modern civilization, Lawrence saw himself not as a professional soldier, but as a volunteer, enthusiastic only for his nation's honor and his own. For Lawrence personally, it also helped him evade the stigma of being in authority or subject to it—another way to maintain the purity of his motives.

Lawrence's celebrity, again like Lindbergh's, announces a new democratization of the idea of masculinity. Whereas nineteenth-century definitions of the "gentleman" tended to be middle-class imitations of aristocratic values, the agitations of the prewar decades tried as well to strip from those values the aristocratic vices of frivolity, dandyism, and effeminacy. Ideals that were first tailored for a particular class were now cut off from their class origins and applied generally. To use "manly" or, say, the German *mensch* in this context became a way to attack the shreds of looming aristocratic allusion in the term "gentleman," for it implied that neither birth nor wealth nor command of technology was as important as some masculine moral essence, as in Robert Burns's phrase "A man's a man for a' that."

Lawrence accomplished all of this in his own way. Throughout his life he was attracted by heroic display and masquerade. But he was also dogged with a sense of fraudulence that was rooted in both his own psychological history and the legacy of a century's worth of British imperial ambiguity about "going native"—the lure of the exotic Other and the hostility toward it. Lawrence's particular version of these attitudes involved seeing the urge toward celebrity to be part of a lower, rootedly "vulgar" and "public" self that must be punished:

> The hearing other people praised made me despair jealously of myself, for I took it at its face value; whereas, had they spoken ten times as well of me, I would have discounted it to nothing. I was a standing court martial on myself, inevitably, because to me the inner springs of action were bare with the knowledge of exploited chance. . . . Indeed, the truth was I did not

> like the "myself" I could see and hear. (*Seven Pillars of Wisdom*, 565–66)

As the adventure novels of G. A. Henty and the poems and novels of Kipling suggested, to masquerade was to be in power. Dressed in his pure white Bedouin costume, his dagger and other accessories close to hand, Lawrence presented an image of the metamorphic English hero of the new age, able to command the respect of warrior tribes while retaining in his pale blondness the essence of his own race.

After the war, Lowell Thomas's celebration of Lawrence had the double effect of inciting Lawrence to tell his own version of his story as a public writer at the same time that he attempted to withdraw from the public eye by enlisting under the name of John Hume Ross as a low-ranking aircraftman in the newly formed Royal Air Force. But he was soon discovered by Fleet Street journalists and left the service to avoid embarrassing his superiors and himself.

A long draft of the manuscript of his memoir of the Arab revolt, *The Seven Pillars of Wisdom*, had been completed before his enlistment in the RAF. Unable to return to that branch of the service, Lawrence once again went the paradoxical route of getting a friend in a position of power to help him enlist in an even less prestigious branch of the military, the Tank Corps, which he joined in 1923 under the name of T. E. Shaw. Meanwhile, he was hard at work pruning *The Seven Pillars of Wisdom* with the advice of George Bernard Shaw, Thomas Hardy, Winston Churchill, Robert Graves, and other distinguished literary friends. In 1926 the book was published in a lavish limited edition, and an abridgment, *Revolt in the Desert*, came out in 1927. But the full trade edition did not appear until after his death in a motorcycle accident in 1935.

In his letters Lawrence perpetually criticized *Seven Pillars*, writing to Edward Garnett in 1922, for instance, that "artistically it has no shape: and morally I detest its intimacy." But the book was also an effort to purge the recognition he both longed for and detested, the monolithic "Lawrence of Arabia" that, with Thomas, he at first helped to promote: "Indeed I don't know for whom I wrote it, unless it was for myself" (*Selected Letters*, 201). What attracted him to the Arab cause, Lawrence said, was a desire to ally himself with people committed to an overriding idea and so help quiet his own sense of inner distractedness: "Even I, the godless Fraud, inspiring an alien nationality, felt a delivery from the hatred and eternal questionings of self in my imitation of their bondage to the idea; and this despite the lack of instinct in my own performance" (*Seven Pillars*, 548).*

This need to discipline, this search to enforce boundaries of behavior on a self that otherwise claimed to be without boundaries, took the form it did in part because of immediate history—Lawrence's own life and World War I. But it boasted as well a cultural ancestry made up of Lady Hester Stanhope, Sir Richard Francis Burton, Robert Louis Stevenson, Gauguin, Flaubert, and a host of European painters from Delacroix on down through the century, all of whom were fascinated by the barbaric and exotic. Often an individual response to the industry, commerce, and oppressive sexual customs of Victorian urban gloom, it was a desire also given shape, as Edward Said has argued, by the cultural assumptions collectible under the name "Orientalism"—a longing for a mystery neither Catholic nor Protestant, a pastoral rebirth in the desert.

Like some darker figures of the twentieth century, including Hitler and Mussolini, but also Churchill, Lawrence brought together in his aspirations the military hero and the artist. But Lawrence's particular sense of the emptiness of his fame was also evidence of a radical cleavage between the body that was looked at by others and the inner self that was ashamed of the gaze after which it lusted. By writing he turned himself into a third person in order to punish the derelictions of the first person, just as in *Seven Pillars* he tried to harmonize his anomalous roles as individualist adventurer and agent of British imperial power, the varying elements of superiority and submission that were so deeply a part of Lawrence's personal psychological makeup. Writing allowed an identity that was neither the ostentatious and theatricalized fame of Lawrence of Arabia nor the submerged and secretive T. E. Shaw, but an amalgam of both.

At the heart of *Seven Pillars*, as at the heart of all war memoirs, whether grim or celebratory, is the fragile male body, in this case, Lawrence's own. Robert Graves in *Goodbye to All That* notes that Lawrence was terrified of being touched, and his letters often speak of his disgust for the bodily. One of the crucial passages in the book describes the events at Der'a when Lawrence, dressed in Arab robes and out to spy on the Turkish defenses, is captured and then subjected to anal rape, which manages to accomplish what months of deprivation and physical hardship as a guerrilla fighter have not—to break down his carefully constructed sense of self: "That night the citadel of my integrity had been

* Eric Kennington quotes Lawrence in 1922 as saying, "It is an evil work. . . . It can never be published. I could not live if it was loosed abroad" (A. W. Lawrence, 243).

irrevocably lost." As he wrote later to Charlotte Shaw, George Bernard Shaw's wife, while showing her this chapter:

> I want to dirty myself outwardly, so that my person may properly reflect the dirtiness which it conceals . . . and I shrink from dirtying the outside, while I've eaten, avidly eaten, every filthy morsel which chance threw my way. (*Selected Letters*, 290)

Intriguingly, Lawrence uses the same image of the citadel, with its echoes of medieval architecture, when he writes in another letter about the "inviolate citadel" that has been assaulted by his celebrity, his "eagerness to overhear and oversee myself."*

The violence of Lawrence's depiction of his rape in *Seven Pillars* sits in odd contrast to the often idealized and sentimentalized male/male love of World War I poetry and literature. The combination of heroics with traumatic reaction (and obsessive restaging) in the incident at Der'a therefore seems analogous to the "I'm not that way" motivation that helped send Cyril Holland to his death in World War I. Later in his life, Lawrence actually hired young servicemen to whip him severely and periodically until he ejaculated, supposedly at the request of a certain "Old Man," who would otherwise prosecute him for some petty theft and reveal his illegitimacy. His need to be whipped thus seems to be a penance for the desires he discovered in himself. Only though writing, it seems, could Lawrence for a brief time subdue his incredibly baroque inability to accept himself as he was. Yet, that something was "irrevocably lost" at Der'a implies that speaking of it could never be solace enough, no matter how much Lawrence wrote.

Lawrence may seem like an odd case from which to speculate on general ideas of masculinity in the period that encircles World War I. But the resonance that his story had with a wide audience points to a newly articulated need to prove manhood explicitly, a more intensified version of Samuel Johnson's belief that all men think meanly of themselves for not having been soldiers. What made him, and has continued to make him, an intriguing figure is not so much his difference as his heightened typicality, his intensified exhibition of some basic contradictions and anomalies in masculine nature, vintage late nineteenth and early twentieth century, but in some ways still current.

Lawrence's childhood submersion in legends of chivalry, his aspira-

* Compare the "fortress of identity" so under siege in Stevenson's *Jekyll and Hyde*.

tions to heroic greatness, even his desire to be a man among men while fearing to be a man attracted to men, are all part of the general cultural baggage of his time, not just in England but across Europe and America as well. In response to the revelations about the ritual whippings, some of Lawrence's biographers, noting his general inability to connect emotionally with any women who were not either older or inaccessible, have defended him against charges of homosexuality by saying that passionate friendships between men were "of the period." But such a justification is too much of our own period, when nothing can be read innocently. It surely misses the way in which so much of the literature of the war itself is preoccupied with the distinction between the homosocial, the homoerotic, and the homosexual. What the Wilde trials underlined—surely something Lawrence was aware of—was the actual continuum between them, the fear that one could shade too easily into the others.

But even more threatening was the belief that physical homosexuality, in Britain and elsewhere, was associated directly with treason. In April 1916, Sir Roger Casement, an Irish nationalist who was negotiating with the Germans for aid in the cause of Irish independence, was arrested for gunrunning. After he was stripped of his knighthood and sentenced to death, intelligence officials in the British government circulated to journalists pages from his "black" diaries, which detailed a crowded life of homosexual encounters. In the circumstances it has been argued that this was a strategy to forestall sympathy, especially in the United States, with the Irish cause. But the general implication was much wider. Later in World War I a secret list was distributed in British government circles naming homosexuals, usually the most obviously effeminate and often those connected to the aristocracy, who were considered to be potential subversives susceptible to blackmail by the German General Staff. In France what was widely known to be an actual homosexual relation between the French and German spies in the Dreyfus case never became an important issue. But in England and the United States the association between sexual deviation and political unreliability continued to be a preoccupation—down to the absurdities of the McCarthy period in the United States after World War II, when right-wing homosexuals like Roy Cohn persecuted left-wing homosexuals to prove their own loyalty, just as right-wing Jews attacked left-wing Jews like the Rosenbergs to do the same.

But whatever the specifics of Lawrence's personal torments, there were images and styles of being that offered some shelter, and so Lawrence too, after making his legend as a hand-to-hand warrior in the primitive mode, turned, like so many others, to the machine. Throughout his life after Arabia, Lawrence had specially built fast motorcycles on which he would ride across the countryside, seeking and mastering the risk by his own combination of body and machine, the centaurlike combination of man and motorcycle. As he wrote to Lionel Curtis in 1923:

> Everything bodily is now hateful to me (and in my case hateful is the same as impossible). . . . I eat breakfast only, and refuse every possible distraction and employment and exercise. When my mood gets too hot and I find myself wandering beyond control I pull out my motor-bike and hurl it top-speed through these unfit roads for hour after hour. (*Selected Letters*, 236–37)

Anyone noting the similarities between Lawrence and Jünger, not to mention other apostles of the machine man of the future like Marinetti, d'Annunzio, and Lindbergh, might be forgiven if he concludes that, like theirs, Lawrence's psychology overlapped considerably with attitudes that are often associated with fascism. In fact, toward the end of his life, Lawrence was contacted by the embryonic fascist movement in England headed by Sir Oswald Mosley. Although he repeatedly rebuffed their advances, the notion of kinship persisted, especially in those areas where the cult of Lawrence's style of heroism fed into the cult of the fascist leader. But Lawrence himself was no longer that kind of hero, and perhaps he never was. Less a leader than a solitary, after the war he wanted to lose himself in the machine rather than be its driver, more like Charlie Chaplin in *Modern Times* than Chaplin in *The Great Dictator*. Joining first the RAF and then the Tank Corps after World War I, he sought to return from his noxious and solitary celebrity to an anonymity within the ranks. Like Ernst Jünger, who recoiled from the corruption of Weimar society after the war to reassert his solidarity with the *frontschwein*, Lawrence looked for a new cohesion with soldiers like himself. Writing to Robert Graves in 1935, he made the equation explicit:

> I went into the R.A.F. to serve a mechanical purpose, not as a leader but as a cog of the machine. The key-word, I think, is machine. . . . One of the benefits of being part of the machine is that one learns one does not matter! . . . There is no woman

> in the machines, in any machine. . . . You can understand a mechanic serving his bits and pieces, whereas she could not. (*Selected Letters*, 522)

Like Jünger's praise of the chivalric airmen when there was no chivalry left on the ground, Lawrence too not only tried to obliterate his public identity into the RAF-machine, but also embraced the motorcycle as the idealized self-machine. For others, however, the image of the machine body and the perpetuation of wartime camaraderie into the postwar world had a much more explicitly political purpose.

# FRONT LINE AT HOME: PACIFISM AND PARAMILITARY VIOLENCE

> The machine-gun settled down to business, grinding out metal like the busy little death factory it was.
>
> —Dashiell Hammett, *Red Harvest* (1929)

As the nineteenth century neared its end, the talk of war had been a tonic to energize bourgeois passivity and a protest against the safety of mercantile culture. To many Europeans who would fight in World War I, war at first promised an idealistic experience like that fondly associated with the Civil War in the United States: an escape from complacency into action, from self-involvement into comradeship in a great common cause, from materialism into selflessness. But what they discovered was an anonymous mass war that had little to do with the sonorous abstractions of propaganda or heroic poetry, a war in which human will, whether that of a general or a soldier, was severely limited.

Simultaneously the end product of nineteenth-century material progress and the revolt against it, World War I also paradoxically marked a refurbishing of the warrior image of masculinity even as its technological advances and mass wars destabilized it. In its wake three directions for masculinity became central to the interwar period—or if you prefer, the lull in the Thirty-one Years' War. The first was a spreading antiwar discussion that in some forms was strictly pacifist, and in others would come to terms with war, but in all raised the possibility that war was not the only way to deal with conflicts between nations. The second was the reconstitution of wartime camaraderie in veterans' organizations, which in the rising totalitarian states of Germany and Italy became the first support for fascism and Nazism. The third was the effort, as Hemingway dubbed it in *A Farewell to Arms*, to declare a "separate peace," that is, an individual refusal to join the mass movements of nations. The first trend, although it generated social and political action of its own, was more philosophic, raising the general question of the social (and, after World War II, the male) need for war. The second helped build support for a renewal of the war and an expansion, in Hitler's Germany and Mussolini's Italy, of war aims. The third gathered most of its life from fictions of individualism and arcs of personal biography. Sometimes this separate peace, as in the popular stories of vigilante heroes, amounted to a separate war as well. But through the powerful imagery of figures like the hard-boiled detective after World War I or the gunfighter after World War II, it stressed a need to restore energy not through the group but through isolation, where masculinity might regain its integrity through private virtue.

The impact of the war at home thus went far beyond news stories and the sounds of barrages in the distance. Both during and especially after the war its signs were evident to anyone who could see. Mathew Brady and his associates in the Civil War had helped pioneer the photographic spectacle of wounding and death—sometimes the serenity of the dead sharpshooter in Devil's Den (who was actually put in place by the photographer), sometimes the more disturbing piles of bones being shoveled into mass graves, in black-and-white or hand-colored images. Anthropology might celebrate the wound as warrior initiation, and the newspapers might print the names of the honored dead. But despite the efforts of World War I governments to keep such pictures out of the news, it could not censor the mutilated, maimed, and broken who walked every street.

Discussions of what constitutes a just war go at least as far back as Augustine's *City of God* in the fourth century, and by their nature hardly question war per se. Early modern efforts to establish international laws for war, like that of Hugo Grotius in the seventeenth century, often invoked the Roman distinction between an enemy state (*hostis*) and a private enemy (*inimicus*) to mark the line separating what was acceptable behavior toward soldiers and what toward civilians. Like virtually everyone else up to his time and for some time thereafter, Grotius assumed that war was an innate human necessity. But he also stressed that international relations should not be just scattershot efforts dependent on the goodwill of the belligerents but part of a codified diplomatic system.

With the seventeenth and eighteenth centuries, diplomacy thrived, but it was not until the middle of the nineteenth century that there were organized efforts to limit war, including several meetings of the Universal Peace Congress, the creation of the Nobel Peace Prize (1897, first awarded 1901), and in 1899 the first Hague conference. The agenda for these conferences, along with the Geneva conferences sponsored by the Red Cross, at first focused on a court of arbitration to settle international disputes, the banning of specific weapons, and treatment of the wounded and sick, prisoners of war, and the civilian population.

Any humanitarian effort to mitigate the horrors of war could easily imply that war was inevitable. But with the twentieth century for the first time came widespread questioning of the belief that war was an elemental part of political, economic, and social life. Natural arguments for war, with their Darwinian roots in the idea of the primitive and the instinctual, would resurface after World War II in works by such writers as Konrad Lorenz and Robert Ardrey. But at the beginning of the century they were beginning to get strong competition from those who stressed moral and practical objections to war as national policy.

"Pacifism" itself was a French-coined word first used in the 1890s and then in 1901 adopted by the Universal Peace Congress in Glasgow. To account for some significant variations in its meaning, Martin Ceadel has elaborated a suggestion from the historian A. J. P. Taylor that "pacifism" be reserved for the absolute belief that wars are always wrong, while "pacificism" designates those many ideas and groups that concede that some wars may be necessary, even while they stress the need for peaceful arbitration before that point is reached. Drawing support from the tradition of the just war and interested more in reform than in abolition, pacificists may not be antiwar and may not even be nonviolent.

The word may be cumbersome, but the distinction is real. Not quite pacifist, but opposed to war as an instrument of a capitalist economy, socialist parties across Europe had before the guns of August all pledged not to participate; when war came, they joined in, virtually to a man. During World War I, there were individual pacifists and conscientious objectors who cited religious objections, but they were often treated harshly by their own governments as akin to traitors. In Britain, where religious objections to war, like those of the Quakers, were familiar, pacifists were acceptable to military authorities only if they had a demonstrable religious background; even then, they only exempted the protester from directly combatant service. Other objectors, like the philosopher Bertrand Russell and the critic Lytton Strachey, who refused to do any war-related work, risked jail.*

In the United States, which perhaps had more war resisters than any European country as well as large segments of the population that wanted to remain neutral, the fledgling movie business took both sides in the controversy. Some films characterized the pacifist as either a woman who changes to a militant patriot when shown the error of her ways, an unmanly American afraid of getting shot at, or an actual traitor, secretly working for the Germans. *The Battle Cry of Peace* (1915), for example, cast its pacifist as a secret enemy agent bent on undermining American preparedness. Other films tried to make the case for a responsible antiwar position. Thomas Ince's *Civilization* and Herbert Brenon's *War Brides,* both released in 1916 and both set in imaginary monarchies, argued for disarmament and against the inevitability of war. On the prowar side, *The Fall of a Nation* (1916), written and directed by Thomas A. Dixon, the author of *The Clansman,* on which *Birth of a Nation* was based, takes an even harsher tone: its villain is an American millionaire profiteer backed by the Germans to arm immigrants and overthrow the government. The revolt succeeds, Germany takes over, and it is only defeated when the millionaire's supposed sweetheart, a former peace activist, organizes a group of women who first flirt with enemy soldiers and then kill them.

The respectability of an antiwar position, whether pacifist or pacificist, grew with the disgust over World War I, which inspired the efforts of some nations and individuals in the 1920s and 1930s to limit war. Before the war, the economist Norman Angell's *The Great Illusion* (1910), from which Jean Renoir may have taken his film's title, argued on political and economic grounds that modern war could not be won, while Phillip Gibbs's *Realities of War,* published soon after the war, candidly appraised the horrors he witnessed as one of the few reporters allowed near the field. Angell won the Nobel Peace Prize in 1933. As a result of his work

* When Russell refused to pay a fine of £100, the government confiscated his library, sold it, and later imprisoned him for six months.

and that of others, an antiwar movement explicitly based on a secular rather than a religious or absolutely pacifist view of warfare was one of the major effects of World War I.

As the antiwar movement developed, particularly in England and France but elsewhere in Europe as well, it stressed the destructive pattern of old men sending young men out to die. No longer, it was asserted, would there be an unquestioning train of men following the call of their leaders (and fathers) to battle. Tales of the incompetence of generals became a major theme: their willingness to sacrifice bodies to gain a few feet of ground, their elitist stress on cavalry at the expense of infantry. After World War I the British army had sharply reduced its numbers and recruiting was much more difficult in the face of a general revulsion, even among many professional soldiers, over the casualty count in the war, as well as a political attack from the left against defense spending (which happened in France as well). In 1933, the Oxford Union debated and passed a motion that "this House will in no circumstances fight for its King and Country," and in 1936, in a widely noted gesture, 120,000 young Englishmen signed a pledge to renounce war. A new version of masculinity, disentangled from an automatic relation to both nationalism and war, was being fashioned to oppose the machine-self of the acquiescent soldier.

The pacificist message that new wars would be fought with even more devastating technology also seemed to influence the victors in World War I to try to limit war through political means, since the desire not to have war, it could easily be argued, required military strength to back it up. Until the Versailles treaty no victor in war had ever attempted such a massive demilitarization of the vanquished. The Locarno conference (1925) followed Versailles with the creation of a system of treaties aimed at mutual security, and aggressive war was renounced in the Kellogg-Briand Pact (1928), although without any provision of legal sanctions for violations. The World Anti-War Congress (1932) tried without much success to bring together pacifist and antiwar groups from many countries.

The motives of many of those participants varied from the ethical to the religious to the political to the practical, and could be easily impugned by those looking for self-interest. Many of those who signed the Oxford Peace Pledge were specifically protesting against a war in defense of the British Empire. Henri Barbusse, the war novelist and one of the organizers of the World Anti-War Congress, had joined the Communist Party; his antiwar activities helped protect a militarily weak and still politically isolated Russia. The arguments of other antiwar activists had more than a slight racist aspect, either in actuality or in effect. The noted ichthyologist and first president of Stanford University, David Starr Jordan, for example, took the eugenic point of view that war, by killing off "the most virile," leads to racial destruction and the domination of the "unfit" (Dijkstra, 399). Like those who believed that war would invigorate the race, Jordan had the same assumptions but arrived at the opposite conclusion. Other critics derived their attitudes toward war from antisemitism. Henry Ford thought that World War I was begun solely for profit and in 1915 he outfitted a "peace ship" to spread his message in Europe, although once the United States had entered the war he was in the forefront of military production. In the 1920s, his *Dearborn Independent* newspaper published a series of articles blaming all that was wrong with European civilization on the "international Jew: the world's foremost problem." Later isolationists in the United States during the 1930s similarly argued against fomenting war against the Nazis merely to save the Jews. Whatever the motives of antiwar arguments, selfless, self-serving, or some mixture of both, none was enough to prevent World War II or later wars. But the arsenal of the antiwar movement's arguments grew during the century, as did its basic belief that neither war nor aggressive behavior between nations was an inevitable consequence of being human.

*We fought in 1917 . . .*
*And drove the tyrant from the scene . . .*
*We're in a bigger, better war*
*For your patriotic pastime.*
*We don't know what we're fighting for—*
*But we didn't know the last time!*

—Ira Gershwin, "Strike Up the Band" (1927)

Antiwar arguments between the wars had to face an atmosphere in which the European left and right, soldiers and artists, were also continuing to stress the need to flaunt virility and force in order to transform what all considered to be a dying culture. The specific political argument may have been over what leader or what party would reenergize this burnt-out world, but much of it was stated in the same images of violence and change that animated the first supporters of World War I.

The central issue, as before, was the recovery of honor, both personal and national. Although new weapons technologies fed war, the history of twentieth-century war—with the greatest technological advances in history—illustrated repeatedly how the impulse to war could also be hostile to technology and industry, evoking instead a world of masculine privilege whose sway over battle was otherwise becoming less and less apparent.

Men at war are always superstitious. Amulets, clothing, and potions to support a belief in invulnerability are only the most obvious manifestations. When the scale of violence increases, and the likelihood of escaping unscathed plunges, the invocation of mythic protection becomes even more elaborate. Sightings of ghostly armies or divine figures like the Angel of Amiens were as much part of World War I as the massive artillery barrages that delivered thousands of pounds of munitions to every square yard of ground. As empires fell, new forms of authority came forward to fill the gap.

It had been a feature of popular war since the seventeenth century that the participants wanted to carry their cause into civil life, whether it was Cromwell's army in effect ruling England once they had defeated the king or the French revolutionaries trying to reform every aspect of society. During the American Revolution, the comradeship of soldiers was considered the bulwark of freedom, a voluntary association that stood against the arbitrary power of social hierarchy—one reason, perhaps, why the militia became a more significant war myth afterward than it had ever been at the time. The French especially were explicit in linking liberty and equality to fraternity, hardly a step away from the mythic camaraderie of the front line.

In much of the postwar fiction of the twentieth century, the returning soldier finds himself alone among civilians who cannot understand and can only vaguely sympathize with his experience. The experience of past soldiers suddenly adrift in a world without trenches and guns thus prompted the development of reentry rituals both to celebrate their achievements and to insulate their governments from their resentments. Fifth Avenue in New York became the American place for marching veterans to parade, like the Champs Elysées in Paris, Trafalgar Square in London, and Unter den Linden in Berlin. As in the Roman triumph, the troops were to be both celebrated and ritually cleansed before they would be welcomed back into civilian society. In the United States, this ceremony began to be accompanied with a ticker-tape parade, the highest tribute peacetime society could give: to turn away for a moment from making money.

For many veterans, however, the experience of World War I continued to define their relation to the state, but now their purpose was to correct rather than to serve. Instead of assimilating and resuming their former identities, groups of old soldiers sprang up who felt that the camaraderie of the front should be the model for peacetime society, their codes of solidarity a protest against the technology and urbanization that had made warrior masculinity seem irrelevant and unappreciated by the civilian world. The idealized comradeship of the trenches would be the model on which the revitalized nation was built. The war had been the greatest experience of their lives and now, like a certain former Austrian corporal living precariously in Munich and failing to make a living from his painting, they felt rejected and ignored by the society they had sacrificed to defend.

Even in the United States, which had hardly suffered as much as the European nations, or committed as many troops, the resentments were widespread. The Depression saw a "Bonus Army" of between twelve and fifteen thousand men and their families come to Washington in the spring of 1932 to demand compensation for wartime service. Their agitation was harshly repressed and their shanty dwellings burnt by a professional army headed by Douglas MacArthur. Even Broadway musicals and the movies were subfused with disillusionment and cynicism about wartime patriotism. Ira Gershwin's sardonic lyrics for the title song in *Strike Up the Band* praise a war between the United States and Switzerland drummed up by a cheese company president who doesn't want the competition. Similarly, although the frothy Hollywood backstage musical *Gold Diggers of 1933* begins with "We're in the Money," a paean to the acquisitive 1920s and the hope of a return to prosperity after the Depression, it ends with an enormous production number built around the song "Remember My Forgotten Man." At the start, after a down-and-out man picks up a butt from the sidewalk, a young woman gives him a whole cigarette, but he is too wiped out even to respond to her kindness. Then she sings:

*Remember my forgotten man.*
*You put a rifle in his hand,*
*You sent him far away,*
*You shouted "Hip Hooray,"*
*But look at him today.*

Other women sing with her from nearby windows and a man sitting on a sidewalk is rousted by a cop until the young woman shows the cop the Medal of Honor inside the man's seedy jacket. As the music continues, marching soldiers are cheered as they go to war. Then they march in the rain toward the battlefield, while from the opposite direction the weary and wounded return. These lines become the lines of men waiting for a handout at a soup kitchen with looks of despair on their faces. The ending returns to spectacle: with the silhouettes of marching soldiers making patterns behind them, other men march forward toward the audience singing with an unmistakable air of menace:

*We are the real forgotten men.*
*You have to bring us back again. . . .*
*For glory was our pride,*
*But somehow glory died.*

A grim message for a supposedly "escapist" entertainment that may not have been lost on Hitler, who always considered art to be a branch of politics and was a fan of American musicals. Much has been written about the influence of Wagner on Nazi ideas of spectacle, but more than a word or two should be said about the influence of Busby Berkeley.*

Whatever fraternal energies the war had nurtured in the United States quickly dissolved into isolationism under the pressures of the Depression. In Germany and Italy, they led to an overwhelming militarization of society itself. The essence of the response in what would become the totalitarian countries was to stress the primacy of will. Whereas in democratic countries, political pressure groups contended for recognition by the state as legitimate entities and ways of being, in fascist Italy and Nazi Germany individual identity was to be defined primarily and even solely through the state.

In the seventeenth century Descartes had founded a cohesive personal identity on the ability to think, and the monarch in the centralized state had furnished a kindred political image. But that coherence, in both the individual and the state, had begun to decompose with the breakdown of monarchical society itself, first with the democratic revolutions of the late eighteenth century, and then with the collapse of so many empires in World War I. Earlier revolutions had substituted "the people" for the monarch as the core of the state. But the nineteenth century brought with it powerful new ideas that cast the individual not as the driver of creation

* The influence of Fritz Lang's *Metropolis* (1926) on Berkeley should be noted as well. In the final script of *Gold Diggers*, this number is in the middle of the film. By the time of release, it had been moved to the finale and several lines had been added, including some of those I've quoted—sharpening the contrast with the "We're in the Money" number that begins the film.

but as the toy of larger forces either outside or within: Darwin's evolution, Marx's capital, Freud's unconscious. Not only Descartes's human monarch of thought and perception, but Kant's individual moral consciousness as well was swept aside by the movement toward a collective future. In the pervasive paradox, to be gathered up in the national cause was to lose the sense of powerlessness and inadequacy that mass events and impersonal forces had otherwise enforced. Despite Marx's effort to argue that class consciousness was a way out of the narrowness of state-defined political welfare, a preoccupation with national interests was true of the Soviet state as well, although it was much more successful than its rivals in persuading people in other countries that it had at heart the interests of the human race in general.

Between the wars, fascist movements in many countries took the themes of masculinity and virility and turned them into an explicit politics of nationalism. Unlike similar tendencies in the late nineteenth century, the interwar movements, in both democratic and totalitarian countries, were populist, restoring national self-respect by putting people back to work amid the heady atmosphere of a revived national greatness. Especially among the defeated, the atmosphere of the Lost Cause hung heavily. Austria-Hungary and Turkey had lost World War I, and Russia had withdrawn from the war after the October Revolution, their multinational empires fragmenting in a newly nationalistic world. But it was especially in the newest European states—Italy and Germany, barely two generations after each had been unified—that wartime humiliation seemed to create an overriding need to reassert actual and metaphoric virility for the nation and regain the "respect" lost by the war. Before the war, both countries had been host to cults of military virility, much like their later Axis partner, Japan. Germany had, of course, lost the war, while Italy, although on the winning side, received few of the spoils and was more noted for its defeats than for any marked military successes. In Europe after World War I, then, it was the defeated and the wounded who tried to fill the vacuum of masculine national power, while the victorious Allies generally withdrew from war and preparedness.

Mussolini's Italian fascist party had been the first, in the 1920s, to parlay the discontents of the postwar period into political power. During the 1920s Mussolini was admired in both Europe and America as a "modern" political figure leading his country to new greatness. Rising to power in Germany a decade later, the ex-corporal Hitler, much to Mussolini's irritation, followed in his footsteps, making similar promises to renovate society from the inside out, under the sponsorship of a glorious warrior past. Like the Ghost Dancers who tried with ritual and superstition to restore the power of a defeated warrior culture, large portions of European manhood after World War I, whether the victors or the defeated, were disillusioned and in various ways sought to restore or replace their illusions. The dreams of heroism and national revival with which they had entered the war, instead of sparking the energy and dominating spirit of nineteenth-century nationalism, had revealed their hollowness.

In the quest to fill this void, the male group was crucial, and the nostalgia for frontline comradeship was a longing for those moments of elation when there was no difference between individual and group interest, when all hearts beat as one. In England, it took the form of the dream of war as the breaking down of class barriers—a prime corollary to twentieth-century mass war, although it hardly happened in an instant—and a commitment to social change through the muddy utopia of the squad. In postwar Germany it appeared as the *Männerbund*, the company of men, that would form the basis of the *Männerstaat*, the state based on men connected to one another.

Political philosophers have argued over the similarities and differences between Nazi, fascist, and Soviet forms of the totalitarian state, which sought to erase any difference between who you were yourself and who you were as a citizen of the new state. But the similarities are also striking. Stepping into the political void created by the collapse or impotence of older dynasties, all three states made much of the claim to an immortality that stretched unbroken into the future. But neither Nazi Germany nor fascist Italy survived the death of its leader. The Soviet experience was somewhat different. The USSR certainly began to change decisively with the death of Stalin, but communism still retains adherents around the world, in a variety of forms that Marx and Lenin might not recognize.

From the 1920s to the 1950s, then, a battle raged between competing views of Western manhood, the most organized being the Nazi and fascist efforts to restore what was conceived of as the old warrior purity. Central to their programs were the extreme lengths to which they went to identify their states as warrior societies in which military masculinity was the necessary form of identity. Here would be the way to rectify the greatest "civilized" impurity of all: the growing presence of masculinized women and feminized men of all sorts. War would once again be the crucible of the truly masculine.

Paramilitary organizations in fascist Italy, Nazi Germany, and ultranationalist Japan thus were suffused, in their uniforms, rituals, and politics, with a nostalgia for the heroes that were gone—the Roman past for Mussolini's followers, the German tribal past for Hitler's, and the samurai for the Japanese. Germany especially made the *frontgemeinschaft* of 1914–18 into a pervasive myth, but Italy, England, and France had their own versions, a romanticizing of the soldiers on the ground that paralleled the wartime celebration of the individual chivalry of the air.*

Both Hitler and Mussolini agreed that only a state premised on making perpetual war could be the context for a reborn masculinity. War would defeat poverty, restore productiveness, stamp out malaria—the list was endless. Pacifists and anyone else who questioned either a particular war or the idea of war were outside the pale. The primary loyalty of the individual was to the German state, which was identified with the Nazi Party. To build this unitary political world, every aspect of cultural life was grist. As Joseph Goebbels once told the journalist Bella Fromm about her coverage of a fashion show, all that she wrote should "have a sufficiently Germanic focus" (Dippel, 131).

Throughout interwar Europe, the language of war infected a variety of cultural activities, from sports to politics. War weapons had come home as well. In the United States the gangs of the 1920s and their governmental adversaries both adopted machine guns as a primary weapon, now in a handheld version named after its inventor, John Taliaferro Thompson—the tommy gun, which he had originally called the Trench Broom. The "war" against organized crime in the United States, along with the use of troops (as in the nineteenth century) to break strikes, definitely gave a military cast to events in the 1920s and 1930s. But it was first in Italy and then in Germany that political society itself became militarized after World War I, not in the style of the old order of an elite aristocracy but as a new order that embraced all classes.†

As a political theory, fascism represented a revolt against a nineteenth-century Europe defined by capitalism economically, the middle class socially, and "civilization" culturally—all of which were perceived as sources of depletion of national energies. Ernst Jünger remarks in his

* Many fascist groups took their imaginative inspiration from different eras of military history: some might be monarchists (like the French Camelots du Roi), rebels, counterrevolutionaries, or guerrillas. In France, Colonel de la Rocque's Croix de Feu acted as a political action group, picketing such films as Jean Renoir's *La Grande Illusion* and *The Rules of the Game.*

† The tommy gun was not in production until 1919, when it was sold primarily to police. It was adopted by the marines in 1928 and became a general-issue military weapon in World War II.

memoirs of World War I that if the Germans had been half as barbaric as they were painted to be, they would have done a lot better. Nazism sought to remedy that deficiency. Reflecting the title of Hitler's autobiography, the fascist state defined itself through conflict and struggle—*kampf*—which absorbed the individual into the national will. Such ideas reflected the same pseudo-Darwinian fervor that animated Nietzsche's belief that growth comes only from struggle or Theodore Roosevelt's praise of the strenuous life as the key to manhood and growth. But the fascist difference was the institutionalization of them in the form of military masculinity. At the root of all social organization were the army and the comradeship in arms against the enemy that was its prime duty. Either move forward in dynamic struggle or die trying.

Ideally, thought the philosophers of fascism, the organic state would undermine the materialistic and Darwinian competition for position and power, characteristic of men in peacetime, and substitute the higher goal of the reinvigorated nation—the *volk* and the *vaterland*, which could be guaranteed only by those who had fought for it. To restore those energies, it was necessary to return to the heroic past and embrace brutal struggle and savagery as the essential nature of man. For popular consumption much of this warrior *volkgeist* was thrown together with large helpings of Wagner on the ancient Teutonic myths, Nietzsche on the repulsive placidity of Christian life and the need for a warrior revival, regional poetry celebrating the German countryside, and such Romantic heroes as the tribal leader Arminius (Hermann), who had defeated the Romans in the Teutoburg forest in A.D. 9. It was a disparate package of myths, philosophy, and history, necessarily inflated for a country that had been unified for barely two generations. But it stuck in the imaginations of men who had suffered defeat, first by the war and then by the Depression, and wondered why.

The propaganda was that every soldier would be the reincarnation of a medieval German knight. But more often the mixture of technology and barbarism in Nazi warfare, along with Hitler's invariable order of no retreat, invoked instead the pure war spirit of the berserker, now somehow merged with the machine soldier of the future. According to Nazism, struggle, battle, and war were the primary crucibles of the only national and the only male identity worth having. They were the real meaning of Germany, the virile barbarian in contrast with whom the enemy was either subhuman or so depleted as to be incapable of true military courage.

The original berserkers were shock troops that came in at a crucial point in the battle to add a note of mania. But Hitler was the berserker in power and simultaneously the most public example of war neurosis: nervous, irritable, perhaps impotent but preoccupied with sexual purity, and in search of power to compensate for real and fancied injuries, he struck a chord in others seeking to restore a lost personal and national self-esteem. It is striking how the deficiencies of the berserker hero, the frequently sociopathic individual who yet in a wartime situation may win medals, describe Hitler as well. As one American psychiatrist wrote:

> Because they are able to express hostility for a time without fear or anxiety, they are able to carry on for a long period, apparently unaware of the danger. They prove somewhat troublesome to their leaders because of their bad judgment, their intolerance of long periods of waiting without action, and their unwillingness to retreat. They have a tendency to regard retreat as a sign of weakness on the part of their officers, which it is their duty to counteract. Such misplaced enthusiasm may prove dangerous for the group as a whole. (Grinker and Spiegel, 45)

In the classical tradition only pastoral retreat was an appropriate alternative to the normal competitiveness of political, military, or mercantile society—Cincinnatus at his plow or General Thomas Fairfax in his gardens at Nun Appleton. But in fascist and Nazi ideology, the paramilitary organization took the place of that solitary, meditative man in the midst of a cultivated nature. Perpetual war was necessary to revive national honor, and political parties deployed violence in peacetime situations to make the world whole again. Hitler may have ridden to power by manipulating superannuated generals like Hindenburg and Ludendorff. But his more substantial inspiration was the Freikorps, the paramilitary group that even the civilian Weimar government had called in to help crush the Communist Spartacist rebellion in 1919 and murder its leaders, Rosa Luxemburg and Karl Liebknecht. Yet Nazi propaganda rarely evoked war heroes as such; more important was the idea of war, comradeship, and the spirit of the front line that had to be replicated at home, in opposition to the legitimate government. As Ernst von Salomon wrote in 1929:

> They were the *Landsknechte* [ferocious sixteenth-century mercenaries]—but where was the land they served? . . . Where

> was Germany? In Weimar? In Berlin? Once it had been on the front line, but the front fell apart. Then it was supposed to be at home, but home deceived. (Kaes, 24–25)

The marauding bands of the Freikorps were hardly the first example of demobilized soldiers who were difficult, if not impossible, to reabsorb into the civilian population and subordinate to civilian authority. The condottieri of the Hundred Years' War and the highwaymen of seventeenth-century England, along with pirates and bandits of all sorts, were often soldiers whose war-making skills and war-shaped views of the world put them in opposition to peacetime life. But the Freikorps and paramilitary groups like them in Germany, Italy, France, and other European countries between the wars were out to reshape the state itself. In a world where traditional values had collapsed, the army, the only pure group to emerge from the war, would be the model on which the new world would be based.

In Italy such groups were called *squadristi* in tribute to their war origins, and the theory that they should be the core of the new state was *squadrismo*. Similarly, the ex-soldiers of Weimar whose free-floating negativity had been galvanized into groups like the Freikorps identified their enemies as Jews, Bolsheviks, and capitalists, in roughly that order—all the Others whom they felt were destroying the fatherland. Germany hadn't really lost the war; its generals had been "stabbed in the back" by cowardly politicians. The crippling inflation of the 1920s, in which wheelbarrows full of marks were needed to buy basic necessities, was another example of the work of the fiendish manipulative cabal that needed to be destroyed.

The pervasive sense of the emptiness of traditional values was hardly confined to the new fascist parties, and even the tendency to identify oneself as a man of the left or the right marked a new political era where us/them was even more pronounced than before the war. But behind both the fascist and the Nazi appeals was a vision of regenerating those values by going back to a primitive purity in which the only unquestioned value was the honor of the soldier, the warrior who linked past and present greatness, not the stiff and bemedaled Prussian officer but the mud-caked frontline grunt. Jünger, for example, always distinguished the soldiers he praised from the "Prussianism" of officers he mocked for their rigidity and elitism.

The nineteenth-century military was for the most part under the aegis of the dynasts. But with the rise of the fascist dictatorships, popular nationalism wore military dress, and armies became associated with fascism because fascism made the army so central to its view of society. The enemy was any international perspective. Cosmopolitanism committed the worst sin: it was without national roots. As Oliver Wendell Holmes, Jr., had told the Harvard senior class of 1895 in a somewhat more innocent time:

> There are many, poor and rich, who think that love of country is an old wife's tale, to be replaced by interest in a labor union, or, under the name of cosmopolitanism, by a rootless self-seeking search for a place where the most enjoyment may be had at the least cost. (Posner, 88)

It was not a very encouraging message for those who would be in their mid-forties when the Versailles treaty and the League of Nations were up for approval by Congress. And so the Senate refused to ratify them, at a historical moment when there were many who thought any policy that favored international relations and a cosmopolitan view of world problems was an insult to national self-containment, thwarting the warrior desire to settle differences and accrue honor by war.

Although Leon Trotsky in Bolshevik Russia also invoked the army analogy to describe his vision of the Soviet economy and Jünger in the title of a 1930 work referred to "total mobilization," it was fascism especially that presented itself—through imagery, rituals, and social structure—as the quintessential identification of the military virility of the male individual with the control, power, and honor of the newly reborn state. Weimar had already fostered a cult of nature that included a Romantic emphasis on mountain climbing and physical fitness, which the Nazis only expanded. Women could participate, but it was the male body that was to be perfected, and especially the body of the farmer and worker that was the Aryan ideal—the real man, as Hitler wrote in *Mein Kampf*, the source of all creativity. This Nazi vision of the purified masculine body marked the reemergence of barbarian virility as the way to political renewal. In the late-nineteenth-century preoccupation with racial degeneration, the focus had been the corrupt national society. But Hitler postulated that once the new Germany became the beacon of purity, it would be the rest of the world that would need cleansing.

The language and attitudes of war pervaded the 1920s, nowhere more than in sports. Physical fitness became a craze in the countries of both the Allies and the former Central Powers. Even in France, where the nineteenth-century gymnastics movement had never quite taken hold, spectator and participatory sports became more widespread in the 1930s, while in England "keep fit" was a pervasive motto. Like "be prepared," "keep fit" was a phrase that implied a goal, and as in Turnvater Jahn's original post-Napoleonic impulse to organize gymnastics, the possibility of war always lurked behind any encouragement of young men to participate in sports.

The prewar emphasis on fostering a new generation of boys who would become the backbone of the new world and be ready to fight its battles began in the creation of the Boy Scouts, the aesthete-heroes of d'Annunzio and Marinetti, and the superman of Nietzsche. In the 1920s it was put directly in the service of enhancing the manly image of the nation. The fascist national anthem focused directly on youth, *"la giovinezza,"* and one of the earliest Nazi programs reorganized the youth programs of the Weimar Republic into party organizations, the most famous being the *Hitlerjugend*, which was explicitly charged with providing protomilitary training for youth between the ages of fourteen and eighteen. Enhancing the image of his own vitality, Mussolini decreed that there be no public references to his birthday in order to foster an image of agelessness; he cavorted on staged occasions with compliant lions and tigers, posed bare-chested with harvesting peasants, and dreamed of having his ministers jump through hoops of fire. Although much less physically active, Hitler similarly tried to project images of power and immortality; he was depicted by photographers like Leni Riefenstahl from angles that enhanced his stature, and he adopted vegetarianism in part because, as he said, having a potbelly would totally undermine what he wanted to accomplish.

Thus it was not just the invocation of masculinity that characterized the fascist state. It was also its display. Along with the effort to effect a total coordination of civil and military society, individuals and institutions, came a distinctive array of visual imagery as well. Fascism, although it came to power closely connected to past institutions—the monarchy in Italy, the army in Germany—would nevertheless create a new race of men. In this renewal, sports and the physical body played a crucial role. The enormous expansion of spectator sports in the interwar years suggests another way in which the male body was becoming more theatricalized as well as increasing its position as the focus of larger political rivalries. The trend continues today: as war has become less hand-to-hand combat, contact sports, with their direct collision of bodies (especially in boxing, football, soccer, and hockey), have become a more pervasive public ritual. Since World War II, the emphasis has come to be on professional sports. But in the 1920s and 1930s it was on amateur sports. In the United States, for instance, the interest in football was in intercollegiate rivalries (Army-Navy, Yale-Harvard) rather than professional ones, and the great names in the sport were almost always those of college players or coaches. In accord with Coubertin's Olympic dream, the amateur athlete was morally purer than the professional—an emanation of the national spirit rather than a self-conscious performer.

Fascism in general and Nazism in particular represent an extreme version of the interdependence of politics and biology. Their enemies were all physically deficient and their supporters were models of perfect masculinity. The perfect Aryan body, as depicted by filmmakers like Riefenstahl and sculptors like Arno Breker in all its muscled transcendence, was to be the image of the perfect Nazi state. In the irony or synchronicity of history, not twenty-five years after Teddy Roosevelt's obsession with manliness, the United States was led by his distant cousin Franklin Roosevelt, whose crippling disability from polio was often mocked by Hitler as the image of what he took to be America's weak warrior will.

The 1936 Berlin Olympics was thus to be the showplace for the Nazi vision of Aryan physical perfection, and Hitler's famous refusal to congratulate Jesse Owens, the black American track and field winner, showed the extent to which national rivalries and ideological clashes were centered on sports. Similarly, when Max Schmeling defeated Joe Louis in twelve rounds in 1936, Nazi newspapers cheered, and when Louis knocked Schmeling out in the first round of a rematch in 1938, it was America's turn.

In Soviet Russia, there was a similar fascination with the effort to renovate society by producing a new man. Obviously there are a multitude of differences between fascism and communism as political systems. But in the history of twentieth-century masculinity it is striking how similar their efforts were to both collectivize and idealize male identity, and how central a role the dictator himself played in the creation of those ideals. In the face of the disillusionment and the desire for an individual "separate peace" that characterized the response to World War I in the more democratic nations, the Soviet Union, Nazi Germany, and fascist Italy in their different ways rekindled individual male honor and identity through the rituals of the state.

Even more than under fascism, work and physical activity under communism became a crucial form of male identity. In their different ways, fascist man and Soviet man were both machines, highly tooled to face the modern world. The Industrial Revolution had defined work as a central element of self-conscious male identity among the working classes. In the nineteenth century, work had separated men from their families and thereby often split families themselves apart. Labor was alienated, according to Marx, from both the product of its hands and the support of others, both at home and at work. In the Soviet system, this alienation was to be eliminated by organizing individual workers into groups subordinated primarily to the proletarian state and connected secondarily to working classes in other countries. Marx had written that when the state withers away, everyone would become artists, but with the state still firmly in place, it was the exemplary worker who was celebrated. In the USSR this figure was particularly embodied in Aleksey Grigorevich Stakhanov, the miner whose name and idealized image (and sevenfold increase in the average production norm) was constantly invoked as the model for all.*

In fascism especially the display of masculinity was epitomized by the uniform and the display of massed individual bodies responding as one—succinctly captured by Leni Riefenstahl's film *The Triumph of the Will* (1935), in which Hitler arrives like Lindbergh from the skies, the triumphant will wearing the garb of an airman, the plane that encases him a more perfect form of his own body. The fascist aestheticizing of the military man recalls Marinetti's prewar threnodies to war's cleansing power as well as Jünger's celebration of the machine body, the quintessence of the airman. Many of these fascist uniforms—in Germany, Italy, and Spain—were black and featured the insignia of death's heads—yet another stage in the history of the effort to make the soldier terrifying and to emphasize his embrace with death on the road to Valhalla. The comic-opera grandiosity of the uniforms of the defunct Austro-Hungarian Empire adorned (and in some forms still do) collegiate marching bands in the United States. But in fascist Europe the skulls and darkness were the talismans of both a closeness to death and a transcendence of it. As Jünger had written in *Fire and Blood* (1925), "It is the meaning of the soldier to be frightful" (Leed, 11). That the uniform might be empty, the shining surface without anything beneath it, the fascination gaudy but insubstantial, would be shown only by combat itself. But even now, the emblems of Nazism still allure the disenchanted. After the numberless

* Many historians now link Japanese and German militarism to each country's need to make an abrupt transition from an agrarian to an industrial society—a phase occurring in the Soviet Union as well.

murders in the name of purity, Nazism's primary legacy is a bunch of trappings.

Political scientists have delved into the institutional and structural differences between the various forms of fascism that arose in Europe during the interwar period. But from the angle of the relation of war to masculinity, each one partook of certain basic phenomena: a ceaseless celebration of the heroes of the past, a preoccupation with death in battle as the prime test of masculinity, a love of the machined body and the mechanized army as images of purity and indomitability, and a cult of the leader as model man. Some of these attributes contradicted one another (the simultaneous glorification of the warrior past and the technological present), and some varied with the country (the greater importance of the death cult in Germany and Spain than in Italy). But all were linked in the overriding effort to define a national ideal of manhood in the face of the political disillusionment and personal disintegration fostered by World War I and the Depression.

# THE THIRTY-ONE YEARS' WAR: THE SUPREME LEADER AND THE SOLITARY CHAMPION

> He had burned several times to enlist. Tales of great movements shook the land. They may not be distinctly Homeric, but there seemed to be much glory in them. He had read of marches, sieges, conflicts, and he longed to see it all.
>
> —Stephen Crane, *The Red Badge of Courage* (1895)

> [I] revelled in the fantasies which the earlier stories of Rudyard Kipling had taught me to regard as appropriate to a subaltern in a line regiment.
>
> —Charles Carrington, *Soldier from the Wars Returning,* on his World War I experiences

Perhaps the most deep-seated frustration of modern warfare is the gap between anticipation—to be more than one can be in civilian life, to find honor, to serve country—and the emptiness that is discovered, the death, the maiming, and the anonymity. So many of those who analyze what came to be called the "disillusionment" of the war generation, the "lost generation," tend to gloss over the enormous expectations fed by the appeal to warrior traditions, and attribute the disillusionment entirely to the war itself. The disparity could be felt by soldier and civilian alike—those who lost friends and loved ones, of course, but also those who were swept up in the national crusade. As Charles Carrington, who fought in both world wars, remarks, the civilians "who had indulged their fancies in the romance of war" were often more disillusioned than the soldiers who had actually experienced it.

Powerfully permeating European and American culture as a whole, in forms that grew from native roots but shared similar atmospheres and nurturing, World War I therefore brought with it a crisis of male individuality, in which the assumed connections of masculine identity with a national political or religious cause had been severely undermined. This uncertainty would be exacerbated in the late 1920s by the onset of worldwide economic depression, yet another indication that whatever the propaganda of a new warrior status, the scope of individual masculine will was at the whim of invisible global forces. In the discrepancy between effort and economic reward, the Depression was equivalent to the psychological depersonalization of the war, and its advent may have helped engender the spate of new war memoirs in 1929–31, as well as the re-publication of old ones, as a way to reassert the value of individual experience.

As military technology in the twentieth century moved inexorably toward the atomic bomb and beyond, and the role of men in war became more and more attenuated compared to their weapons and their support systems, the assertion of individual or collective heroism tried to fill the breach. Into the widening gap between the experience of World War I—in the trenches and at home—and the ideas available to understand it, marched a variety of imaginative constructions to carry on the war by other means. In popular literature it was a loose cohort of lone vigilantes, and in politics the *führerprinzip*, the principle of the single dynamic leader who claimed to surmount those invisible forces and bend them to his will. For fascism the individual was less important than the state, and so individual and national honor were united in the figure of the leader. Instead of the lone avenger, this was the quest of the group.

As the term implies, the *führerprinzip* arose primarily in the dictatorships, with its idea that there was only one person who could revitalize the lost honor of the country, one who could merge modernity with barbaric masculine roots and remake the state. Like some warped avatar of the venerated Unknown Warrior, such a figure necessarily came out of the war, and from those on the front lines. In both Italy and Germany, with lesser versions appearing in other European countries, it was the heroic personality, the leader as exemplary man, embodiment of ultimate manhood, that was needed to bring both the country and its men back to their proper stature.

Drawing upon the utopian expectations of a renewed male brotherhood based on the squad of soldiers, fascism also promised a quieting of class and social conflict in the name of the resurgent nation, much as states like England, Germany, and France allayed internal conflict by imperial expansion in the nineteenth century—or as the violence of the individual knight became chivalric when swept up in the Crusades. Mass war had seemed to stamp out warrior individualism and honor to create instead an industrialized identity for the soldier. But with totalitarianism, that worker identity is fused with a wartime commitment to the group and the leader to create a sense of belonging to something higher, as if the leader were only the emanation of the ruling ideology.

There were many messianic figures whose myths drew fans and followers during and after World War I—d'Annunzio, T. E. Lawrence, Charles Lindbergh, Mussolini, Hitler, Roosevelt, Churchill, Stalin—along with such fictional creations as the detective, the benevolent alien Superman, and Batman, the socially conscious and defanged version of Dracula. But, although there were fascist movements in countries like France and England, often with leaders who aspired to quasi-divine status, the more characteristic democratic response to postwar disillusionment was skepticism about national calls to action. The national rituals of masculinity characteristic of totalitarian regimes contrast intriguingly with more individualist fantasy figures like the detective and the cowboy. They also correspond to the two visions of chivalry: the solitary champions Gawain and Don Quixote, knights-errant sallying forth to correct the world, and the Crusaders or the samurai obeying an overriding authority.

We may reasonably prefer the lone avengers to the murderous dictators, but all—whether fictional characters or real people with programs and policies—were fantasy figures whose presence salved the sense of individual failure and inadequacy. Essential to both was the idea of a code based in some way upon the soldier's experience of the war: for the totalitarians, a code modeled on a frontline camaraderie that excluded any who had not taken part; for the democrats, an internalized code of individual morality. Both variants were part of a pervasive interwar testing of the masculine self in extreme situations, real and fictional, on the tops of mountains and in the depths of cities. In each the otherwise uncertain male body and the ego it contained sought strength through facing an almost perpetual crisis. Hemingway's formula of courage as grace under pressure stressed the individualist side of the trial—what George Fredrickson in his account of young New Englanders before the Civil War called "the dominant American belief that the individual could find fulfillment outside of institutions" (22)—while the growing militarist and fascist movements exulted in the need for group struggle and the creation of an organic state.

The most intriguing of the individualist fantasy figures was the American creation usually known as the hard-boiled detective. In a debased peacetime world, where the uncomplicated standards of wartime masculinity no longer seemed applicable, the detective's profession offered the only remaining scope for heroism. Oddly like the medieval knight, who began as an employee of the local lord until that lord began to associate himself with the knight's chivalric values, the detective was a professional sleuth and gun for hire who was socially below his generally middle-class audience but willing to put his life in jeopardy to protect its interests. He got beaten up more than his readers did and he probably made less money. Instead of coming to terms with the peacetime world, he turned Hemingway's separate peace into his own personal war.

The main character of nineteenth-century adventure literature was the normal man—or, more often, boy—thrown into nature or war or some testing jeopardy, and forced to discover the resources necessary for survival. In essence, the format had been the same since *Robinson Crusoe.* In the 1920s boys' literature was retooled for an older male audience, compensating with adventurous individualism for a growing male insecurity. The new detective thus had few vestiges of the aristocratic amateur who occupied 221b Baker Street. No longer in deerstalker hat and greatcoat like Holmes, and first appearing in the low-cost pulp magazines of the postwar period, in stories often written by men who, like Dashiell Hammett, had served in World War I, this new detective resembled a strayed soldier more than he did the amused dilettantes of the past. He had returned to the pleasures of peace to discover instead a postwar world of deception and corruption, greed and self-indulgence, within which he can only take revenge for his lost comrades, who otherwise would have died for nothing, like Hammett's Sam Spade in *The Maltese Falcon* (1930) choosing justice for the dead partner he disliked over commitment to a woman he loved.

Although both the detective and the fascist partake of a general atmosphere of masculine redefinition in the 1920s and 1930s, clearly the impulses and images that in some countries and in some people led to state fascism, in others engendered its opposite. Particularly in the United States, an enlarged popular-culture world of individualism arrived after World War I—adventurers, detectives, and cowboys, whose exploits filled the mass-market pulp magazines. They drew upon earlier models, but their stories were more brutal and more explicit tests for the presence of a manliness that owed less to group values than to some inner sense of the need for new standards. The detective especially took center stage and kept it for several decades. He shared some characteristics with forebears like Poe's Dupin and Conan Doyle's Sherlock Holmes: he was a connoisseur of detail and a discoverer of pattern, with a disdain for the restrictions of the official police and a commitment to his own code of behavior. Also like Holmes, he was a kind of lone guerrilla warrior, waging an unconventional, nonprofessional war, like the irregulars and raiders of the American Revolution and the Civil War. As solitary as Wister's cowboy, his private code of behavior made him as stoic, self-contained, and complete as any knight-errant, the only remnant of the nineteenth-century American ranter his sardonic wit. But unlike the cowboy hero, who had the vastness of the plains within which to build a new world, the detective struggled amid the debris of the old.

The detective was especially the product of the Allied countries of the United States, England, and France. The underlying archetype of his story was the quest, to make the world whole by his ability to explain the presence of crime and thereby to purge it at least for the duration of the story. In this single-minded search for an assurance that only he can give about the underlying patterns of reality, the popular literature detective of the 1920s and 1930s is akin to more rarefied figures in high modernism, like James Joyce in *Ulysses* or T. S. Eliot in *The Waste Land* (both 1922)—writers who draw upon ancient myths, previous literature, and the new variety of modern voices to reconstruct a splintered world. "These are the fragments," writes Eliot at the end of his poem, "that I have shored against my ruin," and he says explicitly that he was influenced by Jessie L. Weston's *From Ritual to Romance*, with its account of the pattern of Arthurian quest (50). The chivalric buttress of nationalism may have been discredited, but the chivalric loner, whether hero-character or hero-writer/artist, might yet redeem him.

The war had also brought with it the spy adventurer. Between 1915 and 1919 John Buchan, who was director of information in the British Foreign Office, wrote five novels featuring Richard Hannay as a spy-hunting hero, while Somerset Maugham in *Ashenden* (1928) took the type further along the way to Ian Fleming's James Bond. In 1920 the pseudonymous "Sapper" (Cyril McNeile) published the first of several novels featuring Bulldog Drummond, an ex–army officer who turned his abilities against crime; he was, as the subtitle to the first installment of his adventures put it, "a demobilized officer who found peace dull." On the nostalgic side, P. C. Wren's immensely popular *Beau Geste* (1924) celebrated the romance of nineteenth-century warfare and the cohort of honor-stricken heroes of the French Foreign Legion. Even Sherlock Holmes, in one of Conan Doyle's later stories, could be found disguised and nosing around the Foreign Office. Not very many years later, in films made during World War II, he would be transported from Victorian London to track down Nazi spies.

As a hero, the cool American detective represented a somewhat different kind of nationalism, keeping his counsel as part of an effort to reestablish honor on an individual basis—after the failure of national honor in World War I. His taciturnity, as well as his willingness to use shady means to gain his ends, was another aspect of the revulsion against "big words" like honor and heroism. He solved cases, but not usually in the manner of Holmes finding the crucial clue whose place in the puzzle only he understands. Instead, the new detective drew even more than his predecessors on an empathy with the criminal mind. This detective's personal masculinity was also a much more explicit issue than it was in British versions of the figure, where bravery, nationalism, and contempt for lesser races still often went hand in hand.

The American version instead was "hard-boiled," covered only by a fragile shell as he fights villains who tend to be either sexually manipulative women or homosexual men. Politically, he might be a figure of the left or the right, in line with two of the founding fathers of the American species, the radical Hammett, whose Sam Spade saw the decay under official society, and the nativist Carroll John Daley, whose Race Williams lived up to his name with racist and xenophobic remarks. In *The Maltese Falcon*, Spade is an antihero, a "blond Satan" enmeshed in a story of the greed-driven search for the golden falcon, the prize demanded from Charles V by crusading knights interested only in loot. The supposed high ideals of the medieval past are revealed to be just as venal as the cheap betrayals of the present. There is little transcendence left of any sort, the quest is a sham, and even the priceless falcon turns out to be a fake. Toward the end of the 1930s Raymond Chandler again stresses the knightly side of the detective's character, revealing the hard-boiled detective's cynicism as a mask over his moral quest. As Chandler describes the detective in "The Simple Art of Murder," "down these mean streets a man must go who is not himself mean, who is neither tarnished nor afraid. . . . He must be, to use a rather weathered phrase, a man of honor, by instinct, by inevitability, without thought of it, and certainly without saying it" (*Later Novels*, 991–92). But even Chandler's hero Philip Marlowe can't avoid succumbing in some way to the corruption of the present. As he says at the end of *The Big Sleep* (1939), "I was part of the nastiness now" (230).

Wayward knights and sentimental cynics have had a long fictional life and it is difficult to think of twentieth-century literature without them. The detective's distinction was his status as a middleman between official and unofficial society. Like Hammett's Continental Op in *Red Harvest* (1929), he egged on the opposing gangs until they destroyed each other. It was a self-selected separateness that even now still retains a good deal of its imaginative allure.

In French films of the late 1930s these doomed heroes were often played by Jean Gabin—not as a detective, who at least pretends to believe in the power of his own will to thwart whatever forces conspire against him, but as an individual struggling against an indifferent universe. Julien Duvivier's *Pépé le Moko* (1937) and Marcel Carné's *Quai des Brumes* (1938) and *Le Jour se lève* (1939) help establish Gabin's image. Jean Renoir's antiwar film of 1937, *La Grande Illusion,* particularly uses the context of World War I to portray the change from the chivalric aristocrat to this kind of everyman antihero. The characters are all cavalry officers, now airmen, imprisoned in a castle governed by another airman, Count von Rauffenstein. Rauffenstein believes in an international brotherhood of class, to which both he and the fresh-faced, aristocratic young hero Boeldieu, played by Pierre Fresnay, belong. But by attempting an escape Boeldieu aligns himself with a French nationalism that embraces all classes and ethnic groups, sacrificing himself for Maréchal (played by Gabin), the man of the people, and for the Jew Rosenthal.* In a mythic sense, it is another defeat of Ares by Hephaistos, the aristocratic warrior tradition by the democracy of earth and labor. Aristocratic bravado, with its sense of class entitlement, is no longer the cynosure of male heroism; instead, the model is the ability to struggle with universal fatalism, to lose but not to be beaten. As Hemingway's idea of the "separate peace" implied, only individual honor was a possibility, whether fighting with human or archetypal foes.

The implications of these changing male images in French popular culture received a philosophic foundation during World War II in Jean-Paul Sartre's existentialism and Albert Camus's idea of the absurd, both of which emphasize action over any idealized or essentialized definition of personal nature. The Gabin character in this way is an existentialist

* The name Maréchal simultaneously recalls the grand medieval warrior William Marshal and a contemporary stableman.

*avant la lettre,* a mysterious melancholy-enveloped hero: What has he seen to set him apart from other men? Is he thinking of his experiences in the war? Whatever it may be, it is a solitary insight.

In his films there are actual forces after the Gabin character—enemies, police—but the more salient pressure comes from the indifferent world itself. Once again, the paranoia about the mysterious people who really run the world—which manifested in grand Hitlerian prototypes like Fritz Lang's Dr. Mabuse—comes from the German cinema most of all. It was brought by German expatriate directors and cameramen fleeing Hitler to the United States, where they helped establish the style called "film noir." Film noir is, of course, a French term, coined in 1947 to describe American films, then reexported self-consciously to the United States in the 1960s with the New Wave to influence films made by young directors of the 1970s such as Francis Ford Coppola, Martin Scorsese, and William Friedkin. Originally developed in German films of the 1920s to depict a world in which people had little choice or will, and were often manipulated by all-powerful totalitarian figures, this style of heavily shadowed rooms, wet pavements, and oblique camera angles was used after World War II to depict ordinary people caught in a whirlpool of fate. Film noir merged with and reenergized the more individualist American hard-boiled detective style by focusing on heroes who struggle, desperately but often futilely, against phantasmagoric, all-powerful enemies who seem to emerge from the dark fabric of the world itself. Fatalistic and heroic at the same time, these dark tales harken back to the world view of Chaucer's Knight, adrift in a landscape where only action and violence have meaning, doomed to war incessantly against the powers that he can never finally defeat.

# THE THREAT OF IMPURITY: RACISM AND MISOGYNY

Meat vs. Rice
American Manhood against Asiatic Coolieism
Which Shall Survive?
—American Federation of Labor pamphlet (1902)

As the talk of the utopia of the trenches in World War I indicates, one idealized characteristic of mass war is its potential embrace of otherwise excluded or marginal ethnic, religious, and class groups. The sociologist and political leader W. E. B. Du Bois encouraged his fellow African Americans to enlist because he believed that participation in the war would finally make them full citizens. The Fourteenth Amendment had declared that black males had voting rights, but, despite service in the American Revolution, the Civil War, and the Spanish-American War, they were still viewed psychologically as if each were something less than a man. Their war service, argued Dubois, would change that. Jews had similarly served in the German and Austrian armies, a few becoming officers and many receiving medals. In Germany and England, the war was also seen by many as the unifier of a disparate nation, in France as healing the trauma of the Dreyfus affair. Not only for African Americans but also for many immigrant groups, the political issue of equal rights as citizens is thus strangely distorted by its early association with warfare and manliness. Death in battle, it goes without saying, is a high price to pay for social acceptance, but for many who grasped this opportunity to demonstrate their patriotism, it seemed worth it.

After World War II, some of this utopian promise was on the way to being realized. But after World War I, the desire to purify and exclude seemed to grow in intensity, and not just in the racial theories of Nazism. In the United States, a wave of xenophobia swept across the country, directed against immigrants, political radicals, and—Du Bois to the contrary—returning black servicemen, who in the years immediately following World War I were a prime target for lynchings. In 1931 the German director G. W. Pabst had made a film called *Kamerad-schaft,* in which German and French miners lay aside their national hostilities to work together. But as the following decades would show, rather than a hand across national boundaries, comradeship would turn out to be for many a weapon against all who were different.

The strong element of national nostalgia that pervaded many political movements from the end of the nineteenth through the twentieth century, down even to the theocratic revolutions of today, not only looks back to a heroic utopian past, but also uses that imagined past as a standard by which to purge the impurities of the present. One utopia, therefore, looked toward a future in which the differences between people were celebrated and supported. But in other utopias, all would be forced to be the same. Racism, misogyny, homophobia, and hatred of nonbelievers were linked in the idea of a purity that had to be defended at all costs, which was especially associated with war, where impurity would lead to defeat. Camaraderie bound men together, but only certain men and hardly any women could apply. In Germany, World War I field marshal Hindenburg, who was president of the Weimar Republic from 1925 to 1934, had managed to get Jewish veterans exempted from many anti-semitic laws. But one of the first laws the Nazis passed was to ban Jews from joining the army. Still, some nationalistic Jewish veterans tried to make common cause with the Nazis, but they were finally thwarted by a decree of September 1935 that purged Jews from all the military services.

Nevertheless, there had been some attempt in the United States particularly to portray mass patriotic war as a way to bind together a variety of national groups. One World War I poster captioned "Americans All" featured an American flag draped on the left and in front a female figure perhaps representing Liberty touching the laurel wreath atop an honor roll with these names engraved on it: Du Bois, Smith, O'Brien, Cejka, Hauke, Pappandrikopolos, Andrassi, Villotto, Levy, Turovich, Kowalski, Chriczanevicz, Knutson, and Gonzalez. This multiethnic view of the American military presaged the virtually clichéd roll call of the squad in World War II films. But when it was produced, it was optimistically far ahead of its time. The louder voices, like those in the American Legion (founded in 1919), tried to translate uniforms into uniformity for fear that the country would continue to be contaminated by the waves of immigration. Any deviation from the norm—which was often being defined on the spot—needed to be rooted out as dangerous. The Legion was particularly disturbed by communists, pacifists, suffragettes, and temperance preachers, and launched a campaign for "100% Americanism" to attack any group whose view of the world seemed to threaten their narrow view of the glory of the warrior dead.

The fear of radical influences, whether from immigrants or homegrown abnormality, was hardly confined to the Legion. On the eve of World War I, with the growing immigration of eastern European Jews, antisemitism had begun to grow again in the United States, just as at the same time the increasing northward migration of southern blacks would be marked in D. W. Griffith's *Birth of a Nation* by a newly intensified racism. Hardly a year after the war Woodrow Wilson proposed new peacetime sedition legislation to extend that already passed during the war. His target was particularly what he considered to be the divided loyalties of "hyphenated Americans." Echoing Teddy Roosevelt before him, Wilson argued for "compliant" and "passive" citizenship: "Any man who carries a hyphen about with him carries a dagger that he is ready to plunge into the vitals of the Republic" (Kennedy, 87).

Although Congress declined to follow through with Wilson's plans, war, it seemed, was not yet a collective experience that reached out to all who fought; it was an elite one, predetermined and controlled by national, racial, and ethnic groups fearful of losing their traditional power. In ways that oddly reflect the hostility to difference that characterized later totalitarian movements, as well as looked back to nineteenth-century "purity" committees, America after World War I endured a rampant urge to repress as many manifestations of moral and political laxity as possible: the 1917 closing of Storyville, the New Orleans red-light district; the outlawing of alcohol with Prohibition in 1919; the 1920 Palmer raids rounding up and expelling foreign radicals; the harsh restriction of immigrants from southern and eastern Europe and the entire exclusion of those from Asia through the National Origins Act of 1924. In such an atmosphere, even pacifists like Jane Addams were considered to be subversives, and there was little return to the prewar interest in solving social problems until the election of Franklin Roosevelt in 1932.

With a particular twentieth-century vehemence, war in the popular imagination thus continued to be a ritual used to say who we were and who we were not. The more war was carried on by mass conscripted armies and the more home-front support was necessary to keep the war going, the more it seemed the enemy had to be demonized and the common soldier turned into a hero. The mercenary and professional armies hardly needed as much propaganda-generated hostility to do their jobs, although it certainly helped when the practical necessities of warfare needed to be energized by a thirst for blood and revenge.

One of the most powerful incitements to revenge in the propaganda of modern war has been stories of rape. When civilian populations have been involved, rape has always been a component of warfare. In tribal situations, it may take the form of acquiring slaves as well as preempting the enemy's line of inheritance. But the propaganda image of the enemy as a rapist out to despoil "our" women owes much of its power to nineteenth-century racial theory that characterized the enemy as sexually predatory—simultaneously seductive, all-powerful, and an inhuman beast—who had to be destroyed. Accordingly, many lynchings featured the victim with pants pulled down and castrated—a graphic image of the sexual torture and humiliation his alleged acts supposedly deserved. The racist stereotype of the hypersexual African American man echoes the one of Jews in the nineteenth-century images so elaborately propagated by the Nazis, as well as the World War II Allied propaganda that portrayed Japanese men as sexual predators (the "rape of Nanking") and Germans as brutes. The point is not that there was no evidence of such behavior, but the way in which the attack was expressed, linking masculinity, sexuality, and national identity in one indissoluble bond.

In the long view of history, nationalism and ethnicity were beginning to separate. The United States, as the most obvious product of waves of immigration, may have moved in this direction first. But racist attitudes, especially in wartime, persisted there as well, as the forced relocation of Japanese citizens during World War II illustrates, along with the segregation of African American and Japanese American military units. There had been anti-German hostility, even some lynching, during World War I in both the United States and England, enough to make some prominent citizens change their names, including the British royal family, who abruptly shifted to Windsor from Saxe-Coburg-Gotha. But during World War II, the brunt of American racism was directed against the Japanese, while the Germans—perhaps in reaction to the propaganda excesses of World War I—were rarely so totally stigmatized as a people, even though the United States was actually more in danger (and suffered more) from German sabotage.

But nowhere was the atmosphere of purity more prevalent than in Germany, whose laws linked ethnicity and citizenship so firmly that it was not until 2000 that they were separated and anyone born in Germany was considered German. The constant Nazi invocation of the *Volk* and its tribal heroes identified national identity and ethnic identity even more closely, stigmatizing non-Aryan races as unmanly. But even though Aryan males were inside the ring of acceptability, they still had to prove themselves, since the only lasting identity was that forged in battle for the state.

The effort to purge all difference was only one of the ways both Nazi and fascist totalitarianism resembled a kind of neotribalism, treating all outsiders as potential or actual enemies. Economically, the system was called autarky, a bid for total economic, social, and political self-sufficiency. As the corporation was Mussolini's basis for the reorganization of the Italian economy, the model for society would be a single human (masculine) body. Like the fantasies of the solitary hero, these autarkic nationalisms were beholden to no one, alone against all the rest. In the face of a fragmented world, they offered a distorted version of the national self-determination preached by Wilson's Fourteen Points, just as the fascist subordination of the individual to the state oddly mirrored one of Wilson's four war aims in World War I: "national morality to be like individual morality."

Essential to this self-enclosure was its racial purity, defined against an array of the impure whose elimination was single-mindedly promoted by the Nazis, to whom Mussolini gave his more lukewarm support with his own antisemitic laws in 1938. A symbolic and cleansed masculinity was to be the counterpoise and complement to both the advance of technology and the decadence of an expanding international civilization. Jews especially were the prime enemy because they represented an international order of connection and self-definition that undermined the celebration of the intertwined nation and race. Like Louis XIV ejecting the Huguenots from France, Hitler did not realize or care that removing Jews from national life would undermine German technological and artistic advance in the name of national purity. The Nazi prohibitions embraced everything that Jews had created, including "Jewish science." The goal was decontamination of the national body from the polluting threat, whatever its source. Aristocrats were similarly suspect. Compared to the Aryan masculinity and femininity on which the regime's propaganda was built, they too had dubious connections elsewhere.

In fact, if antisemitism had not been central to Hitler's nationalism, Germany might have won World War II, or at least negotiated favorable peace terms. But despite a pressing need to push war production forward, trains were commandeered and both men and matériel were diverted to implement the Final Solution. At a time when manpower was desperately needed, slave laborers were worked to death to implement the belief that ethnic cleansing and genocide could disinfect the world. Without those diversions of resources, Hitler might possibly have triumphed. But then he would not have been Hitler.

Hitler's racism was an impediment to his war effort not just because it lost him the services of innumerable "undesirable" scientists, engineers, and inventors, but also because it led him to emphasize "willpower, resolve, endurance" rather than weapons as the way that the war would be won. With opinions formed by nineteenth-century theories of the connection between cultural and physical degeneracy, he considered national self-definition and honor to be synonymous with racism. The German people were also well prepared to hear the message. *Signal,* the glossy propaganda magazine produced in all the European languages, was especially sarcastic about the way France drew upon their colonies for troops of color. The barely hidden message was the unspeakable dishonor of being killed by a black soldier. But on the surface was a derisive sarcasm about the mongrel inadequacy of France as a nation. If these were her soldiers, what did it mean to be French?

Following the pseudoscientific ideas of the late nineteenth century, the fascist regimes also asserted that the enemies of this struggle for a purified identity were not only "inferior" races but also any women who did not fulfill the supportive roles dictated by male political power. The tendency in many countries after World War I to institutionalize a more rigid distinction between male and female seems to follow directly from wartime separation. Richard Aldington in *Death of a Hero* (1929) considered that this "widening gulf which was separating the men of that generation from the women" (234) was due to the resentment of the soldiers that only men had to die in the war and their inability to express to the women who were at home the enormity of their experience. As a result was born "a new, curious race of men, the masculine men" (265), who separated themselves almost entirely from a world of women either ignorant of their sacrifice or out to swallow them up.

The cultural position of women in the early twentieth century obviously varied greatly, from the agitation for voting rights in England before the war and the suffrage granted by the Nineteenth Amendment in 1920 in the United States to the good-wife view promoted by fascism and the fellow worker of Soviet communism. But in all cases, war or the threat of war helped occasion the demand to make such distinctions and formulate such policies overtly. The split between male and female roles thus mirrored the split between master and inferior races. In his immensely popular *Sex and Character* (1903), Otto Weininger had made the equation even more explicit than usual. Drawing upon nineteenth-century physiology and psychology, Weininger argued that women were never genuine because they had "no existence and no essence" (286). Unlike men, they lacked both rationality and morality, being nothing but "man's expression and projection of his own sexuality" (300). Even so they were preferable to Jews: "The true conception of the State is foreign to the Jew, because he, like the woman, is wanting in personality" (307), and a well-run state needed to purge any evidence of their influences.

Weininger committed suicide shortly after his book was published, but his ideas, like those of other racist/misogynists, were widely influential, especially in Germany and his native Austria. Complexity was to be banished; only the clarity of completely opposed male and female traits could sustain male honor and national security. Honor for women, by contrast, consisted primarily in procreation: *Kinder, Küche, Kirche* (children, kitchen, church) was the slogan that had been current since the days of the kaiser; or, in Mussolini's formulation, *"La guerra sta all'uomo come la maternità alla donna"* (War is to men what maternity is to women).

Here, in effect, is a language of psychological compensation employed to reassert a national manhood in the face of military failure. As homosociability and sometimes explicitly encouraged homosexual behavior had been important to many warrior cultures, it also seems to hold true that in modern warfare homophobia was downplayed or kept at arm's length because of the overwhelming need for male solidarity and tenderness. Women were always perceived as a more threatening force than other men, and aggressiveness toward women became a way to overcome the fear of being unmanned.

The whole history of male honor hangs heavily over the interwar period, as the relations between men and women, between men and their identities as citizens, and between men and their own masculinity became explicit issues in unprecedented ways. Fascism particularly polarized gender as part of its sharper honing of masculine identity. Women might bring forth the children required to fight future wars, but in history and culture they had little or no part. The nation, it seems, had been born by male parthenogenesis. This need to repress the feminine in order to exalt the masculine in a reborn warrior culture suggests that the Taliban effort, for example, was not so much a part of Islamic culture as it was a stage in nationalism.

In Europe and America between the wars, science also took a hand. The experiments in the late 1920s and early 1930s that led to the isolation of testosterone in 1935 and progesterone in 1936 won the 1939 Nobel Prize in Chemistry for the German Adolf Butenandt and helped establish a biochemical shorthand for sexual difference that remains popular today. In the same decade, behavioral psychologists were also trying to codify male/female difference. The Americans Lewis Terman and Catherine Miles in 1936 published *Sex and Personality* in an explicit effort to make "masculine" and "feminine" measurable: "Alleged differences between the sexes must give way to experimentally established differences" (3). Their studies had begun in the early 1920s as an investigation of gifted children and, although they specifically rejected such terms as "normal" and "invert," there remains a eugenic air to their work. Once these differences were established, then "defects of personality can be compensated for and to some extent corrected" (468).*

More outlandish claims to improve gender "inadequacy" had been made after World War I by the Frenchman Alexis Carrel, who had won the 1912 Nobel Prize in Physiology or Medicine for his organ transplant discoveries. Later, in an effort to restore a national virility lost in the war, Carrel experimented with transplanting testicles from sheep, goats, chimps, and monkeys to men. Serge Voronoff made even more news

* During World War I, Terman pioneered intelligence testing among American troops.

in the 1930s with his transplanting of monkey glands into male scrotums, and numerous legitimate physicians and quacks took up the calling, performing not only transplants but also vasectomies and other operations that would supposedly increase hormone production and restore masculinity.

Surrounding this scientific effort to establish a quantifiable definition of male and female in the 1920s was an atmosphere of hedonism in which both men and women participated. The New Woman of the 1890s had metamorphosed into the woman of the 1920s, who dressed more provocatively, smoked in public, and joined men at the bar in the freemasonry of the speakeasy. New social perspectives were emerging as well. Before and after the war, psychologists like G. Stanley Hall, Arnold Gesell, John B. Watson, and Myrtle McGraw were focusing on human development from a variety of perspectives that combined the influence of Freud and Darwin. Their views were often opposed to one another's, especially when it came to deciding whether it was "nature" or "nurture" that mattered the most. But all had decisively moved away from the cranial determinism of the nineteenth century. Sexuality especially was being talked and written about more freely. With the work of Freud and others, the awareness of sexuality as a cultural force was increasing in the intellectual world, while popular entertainment itself dabbled more freely in the sexually explicit and illicit, especially the erosion of the double standard. A more complex view of sexual identity was reaching the public agenda. Magnus Hirschfeld, a German doctor, had started a homosexual rights movement in 1897, and from 1921 to 1935 he sponsored meetings of the World League of Sexual Reform. In 1937 he published *The Sexual History of the World War,* a title, and an approach to a historical event, that would have been virtually unimaginable before.

As anti-immigrant movements and such aspirations to perfection as Prohibition indicate, however, there was a strongly puritanical element as well, in American culture particularly, that both decried and was fascinated by what it considered to be sin. The stage and especially the fledgling film industry seemed destined for the depiction of this ambivalence. There the dark side of female emancipation was embodied in the predatory woman—the vamp—whose sexual power depleted and degraded masculinity, just as the sexual reticence of the "good" woman represented its salvation. The trend had begun only a few years after audience demand had induced film companies to identify performers, and its avatar was Theda Bara, born in Cincinnati as Theodosia Goodman, whose stage name, it was whispered in the film magazines and gossip columns, was an anagram for "Arab Death." Her first starring role and defining film was *A Fool There Was* (1915), based on a play with the same title that was derived from Kipling's 1897 poem "The Vampire":

> *A fool there was and he made his prayer*
> *(Even as you and I!)*
> *To a rag and a bone and a hank of hair*
> *(We called her the woman who did not care)*
> *But the fool he called her his lady fair—*
> *(Even as you and I!).* (220)

In the film a successful businessman is hopelessly entangled by the vamp's heartless charms, loses his family and career, and, unable to break away from her, dies a miserable wreck. In the process he has become a drug and alcohol addict, but the true unspoken addiction is to the sex that his pure wife cannot or will not give him. He craves it and the vamp dispenses it, but—and here is her essence—although she is the sole object of his desire, she herself needs no particular man for sexual satisfaction. Released a few months after the war began, the film struck a nerve and was quickly followed by many like it. Sometimes the vamp, as in *A Fool There Was,* devoured her victims without a qualm; sometimes, as in *The Vampire* (1915), she was more sinned against than sinning. But always, like Louise Brooks's Lulu in G. W. Pabst's shrewdly titled *Pandora's Box* (1929), she had the power to bring men to their knees.* As Salomes each dancing for the head of John the Baptist, their special victims were men of spiritual aspiration.

The image of female sexual insatiability was certainly familiar to past European cultures; it was founded on the apparent physiological fact that women can always have more sex, while men, even though they may desire to continue indefinitely, cannot. "*Toujours plus*" the Marquis de Sade called it, and, if we assume a perfect symmetry between physiology and culture, we would conclude that women have always had the capacity for more sexual enjoyment than did men. That is certainly the import of the Greek myth of Tiresias, who had been both man and woman, and was punished by Hera for revealing that women enjoy sex nine times more than men.

* To enhance the image of the barbaric in less predatory women, nail polish was introduced in the mid-1920s, at first exclusively in shades of red.

Whether the Tiresias story is a male myth or a female myth or some combination of the two can only be sorted out through an historical perspective. The belief that women enjoy sex voraciously can be a male fantasy when we consider striptease, prostitution, and other male-client, female-merchant situations. Classical scholars speculate that in the Eleusinian mysteries in ancient Greece, a sacred woman ritually exhibited her forbidden places and engorged a consecrated phallus. In its modern form such a ritual might involve a performer professing to enjoy the act precisely because of the presence of the paying audience. What may have originally been a display of matriarchal autonomy, to which the male audience was subordinate, is thus transformed into a display of patriarchal obedience. So too, in different eras, the urge of some women to keep their sexual pleasure a secret may imply a desire to retain control in the face of an otherwise overwhelming patriarchy. Even now "earth mother" is popularly used to imply not insatiability but a wide and capacious embrace.

The male version of the vamp was the sheik, another exotic import, whose sexual aggressiveness and erotic refinement (rarely without a whip in his hand) was belied by his smooth features. His less insinuating counterpart was the grinning athletic adventurer, like Douglas Fairbanks. In *The Mark of Zorro* (1920), for example, Fairbanks plays both the rich young wastrel Don Diego as well as the masked hero in a Californio version of *The Scarlet Pimpernel* (1905). But where *Pimpernel*'s and *Zorro*'s great forerunner, Dickens's *A Tale of Two Cities,* kept the two characters separate, film allowed them to be presented as aspects of the same individual—the steely hero beneath the effete exterior.

Fairbanks's screen image was another aspect of the boy culture of the 1920s. Innocent yet fearless, he got the girl and defeated the villain through no seductive wiles of his own, just his own physical bravado and moral straightforwardness. Like the mountain-climbing films popular in the Weimar Republic, as well as the vogue for big-game hunting that peaked in the 1920s and 1930s, such images of youthful adventure tried to contradict the pre- and postwar fears of men like Theodore Roosevelt that young men were growing up in "slothful ease."

In contrast to this healthy open-air atmosphere, the mythology of the vamp, with its simultaneous fear of and fascination with the sexually voracious woman, was set in more enclosed spaces. It also owed some of its renewed energy to the early-twentieth-century medical discovery of the differences between syphilis and gonorrhea, the development of some effective treatments, and the (erroneous) image of women as the main disease-spreading vectors. Moralistic warnings against the sexual power of women and fears of strange diseases being brought back from the more sexually exotic outposts of empire had taken on a pseudoscientific tinge. Although it was not until World War II that full-scale bureaucratic organization of sexual hygiene was attempted, Paul Ehrlich's discovery of the Salvarsan treatment for syphilis in 1909 made it a military issue in World War I as well, and brothels near the front lines and in rest areas were often policed, as they had been in urban France since before the war. A Pulitzer Prize–winning cartoon drawn by C. D. Batchelor in 1936 neatly brings the two strains together: a scantily draped prostitute with a skeleton's face stands on a stairway in a run-down neighborhood. Her cleavage bears the word "war," and she entices a young man labeled "Any European Youth." "Come on in," she says. "I'll treat you right. I used to know your daddy."

The disease-producing effect of sexuality was only the most obvious side of a general condemnation of the kind of promiscuity embodied in the figure of the vamp. From the eighteenth century onward, there had also been a litany of moralists decrying the debilitating effect of fashion on what should be a virile culture. This fear of cultural feminization gathered momentum in the expanding world of late-nineteenth-century commerce and consumption; the threat of an oncoming war that demanded "real men" then contributed the shadow of demonization. Women not only weakened men, but also had a diabolic power. Dracula's most susceptible victims are women and weak men; he is defeated only by Mina Harker, a strong woman—"She has man's brains," says the vampire expert van Helsing—and her strong but somewhat bumbling male companions. This woman warrior, a kind of Athena, was also invoked by the Austrian Secessionist artists as an emblem for themselves. In Gustav Klimt's *Hope I* (1903), for example, she appears as a pregnant woman, pushing away male forms of darkness and evil in an image similar to that of Dürer's *Knight, Death, and the Devil* almost three hundred years before.

Rare enough before World War I, these images of a strong woman with affinities to men were submerged by postwar images of women whose strength, sexual and otherwise, undermined male power and authority, even while many nonfictional women had to give up their jobs to returning soldiers. The battleground of the war had in peacetime been translated into a battle of the sexes to restore lost masculine power. As Henry Miller writes of a sexual encounter in *Tropic of Capricorn*, published in

1939 but detailing his life in the 1920s, "somebody had to pay for making me walk around in the rain grubbing a dime. Somebody had to pay for the ecstasy produced by the germination of all those unwritten books inside me" (220). In these terms, aggression against women was also aggression against the bourgeois world of commerce and competition. The continuing polarizing of male/female difference thus gathered practical justification from the experience of class war. At the same time, to increase the fear and defensiveness in the susceptible, new political and social roles and a new leniency about sex were opening up possibilities for women. Women's suffrage, which had become law in very few countries before World War I, was pushed forward by the war, so that by 1939 it existed in more than thirty countries, including the United States, Great Britain, the Soviet Union, and Germany, but it did not reach France and Italy until after World War II—although there were few other changes in social policy to accompany the opening up of sexual attitudes.

The less voracious twin of the vamp in the public imagination after World War I was the flapper. "Flapper" had been used in England since the 1880s to refer to a young prostitute and by extension any young girl, often with her hair in a plait or pigtail to denote her freedom from a conventional feminine look. It became the term for the young independent woman of the postwar period, with close-cropped hair, often wearing trousers or short dresses, smoking, drinking, dancing, and, by implication at least, having sex freely. In Germany the same style was characteristic of the so-called *backfisch* (fried fish), or teenage girl. With their short hair, flappers also had a boyish look, like the *gamine* in France, that blurred the absolute visual division between male and female. When they weren't dressed in short skirts, they might be wearing trousers—another fad with a military precedent, where trousers and slacks (as the name implies) were considered to be off-duty wear, i.e., not breeches or kilts. In England after the war, dresses for men had been promoted in a short-lived fad, but trousers for women remained, along with the implication that someone else was now wearing the pants, or at least sharing them. The connection between sex and politics was not lost on contemporaries: in 1928, the first election after suffrage for women twenty-one and over had been legalized in England was referred to as the "flapper vote."

Robert Graves and Alan Hodge in *The Long Week End*, a book on English life between the wars, considered the boyish look of the flapper to be a compromise between heterosexuality and pederasty for men whose ideal of camaraderie had been founded on an ethos that excluded women as pals and was suspicious of them as sexual partners. Despite such dark imaginings, mere trendiness certainly played an important role in the dissemination of the fad. But whatever the reason, the 1920s, along with the puritanical effort to reestablish a stricter male/female difference, showed a growing playfulness about the boundaries of male and female that may in its turn have incited the new purity movements, just as the Nazi emphasis on manhood was a reaction against what was considered to be the sexual license of the Weimar Republic, which preceded Hitler's takeover. Female impersonation had been a comic staple of the vaudeville stage, but a Mack Sennett film of 1919 called *Yankee Doodle in Berlin* takes it into foreign affairs. An American aviator named Bob White, played by the female impersonator Bothwell Browne, disguises himself as a woman in order to fool the kaiser and steal military secrets. Then, as the *American Film Institute Catalogue* describes the plot:

> Bob flirts with the Kaiser, Hindenburg, and the Crown Prince, and each becomes jealous of the others. Bob lures the Kaiser to his downfall with an Oriental dance. Hindenburg tells the Kaiser's wife that her husband is visiting a woman in her chambers, and the results prove disastrous for all three men. Bob manages to gain the military secrets and the enemy is defeated in time. (Hanson, 1072)

Unlike the usual distinction between the purity of the Allied spies (like Edith Cavell) and the impurity of the Axis spies (like Mata Hari), here it seems that being a vamp is fine so long as it's a man pretending to be a woman rather than a real woman.

The patriotic motive as a way of excusing what would otherwise be considered to be aberrant behavior appears as well in the notorious novel by Radclyffe Hall, *The Well of Loneliness* (1928), which was published at the same time as the spate of war memoirs. In it Stephen Gordon, a woman who has been rejected by her mother for her lesbianism and banished from her house, seeks to prove herself to her motherland if not her mother by becoming an ambulance driver during the war. The urge to go to war to prove a courage and worth—not to mention citizenship—unrelated to sexual orientation seems parallel to Siegfried Sassoon's remarks about the need for poets to enlist, as well as to W. E. B. Du Bois's prewar injunctions to young black men. But Hall's novel was ruled an "obscene libel" in Britain and banned until 1943.

# TARGETING CIVILIANS

Every single man, woman, and child is a partner in the most tremendous undertaking in our American history.
—Franklin Roosevelt,
December 9, 1941, radio broadcast

The mass mobilization of World War I had gone far beyond the transformation of millions of men into uniformed soldiers. Noncombatants like the poet e. e. cummings and the heroine of *The Well of Loneliness* became ambulance drivers. But beyond these battlefield participants, to a degree that had no precedent in modern European history, both male and female civilians became part of the war effort as well, employed in war industries, suffering deprivation and death from the bombing of cities and towns. The easy nineteenth-century distinction between the home population and the soldiers who were somewhere else was no longer much solace, nor was the admiration for far-off heroism now so simple or so safe. Depending on where you were, the front could be geographically nearby or distant, but it was never far away psychologically. Newspaper sales skyrocketed with the desire for news about fighting that seemed nearer every day, and the phrase "home front" began to enter the language.

Civilians have always suffered in wars. It has been estimated, for example, that twice as many civilians as soldiers died in the Napoleonic Wars, and if death from disease were added, the total would be even larger. But civilian casualties in the twentieth century went far beyond what happened to those who stood in the way of forage or battle. Nor did they substantially resemble the effect of the Spartan allies burning crops around Athens in the Peloponnesian War, or the armies hauling off livestock and burning villages in the Thirty Years' War, or even, more recently, Sherman's march through Georgia in the Civil War—all tactical efforts to neutralize or destroy the ability of civilians to aid their own armies. In the twentieth century, by contrast, the attack on civilians became a matter of policy.

As the technology of distant attack improved and the role of public opinion became more central, the sphere of war enlarged immensely, until it reached even sheltered civilian populations, who in the past had heard the news only at a distance. Improvements in communications had made the increasing connection between home front and battlefront part of the nature of twentieth-century war. For the most part the closeness was rarely more enlightening than the previous distance had been, since journalistic coverage, along with the new breed of combat photographers, was heavily restricted and censored by all sides in both world wars and even since. The coverage of Vietnam that turned it into "the living-room war" was a partial exception. But the detailed briefings of the Gulf War and the "embedded" journalists of the Iraq War once again returned control of the flow of information almost entirely to the military.

Targeting civilian population centers turned into a new strategy, with both material and psychological dimensions. In World War I, German U-boats preyed on British shipping, and British ships set up blockades against German suppliers. The results of this new symbiosis could be terrifying or grimly ironic. The Germans dropped bombs on London from dirigibles and for four and a half months in 1918 shelled Paris with long-range artillery launching thousand-pound missiles.

With the expansion of the air war beyond the battlefield, ever larger civilian populations became vulnerable or believed they were. In the United States in the 1920s, General Billy Mitchell argued for strategic bombing of civilians, implying that a strong air force was all that was necessary to win future wars. Aviator heroes were thick on the ground between the wars—Lindbergh for the United States, Göring for the Nazis, Italo Balbo for Mussolini's government. The 1937 Japanese bombing of cities and the Franco government attack on Guérnica may have been decried in the United States and elsewhere among the soon-to-be Allies. But both strategic and carpet bombing became standard practice in World War II, and the Nazi propaganda machine was happy to point the finger at General Sherman to exonerate their own scorched-earth policies.

The modern blurring of any sharp distinction between civilian and soldier had long enough historical roots. The nation in arms of the French Revolution had helped revive the tribal assumption that every male citizen was ipso facto a soldier. With mass war, soldiers, instead of being recruited or impressed from a population of otherwise unemployed young men, were drawn from the general community. Like their forebears in the Greek city-state, they would presumably return to that community once the war was over. Similarly, in the millennia since Athens and Sparta, advances in war technology had made the overlap of civilian and soldier a practical issue as well. As Charles Carrington notes, the emphasis on airpower and bombing in World War II ensured that the "load was shared" more equitably between soldiers and civilians. In addition, the intersection of industry and war began in the Industrial Revolution, when the military was first in line for improvements in cloth and food manufacture. With advanced technology playing a greater and greater role in warfare, the strategy of attacking the enemy's industrial base (and civilian workforce) became at least as important as attacking his soldiers.

In fact, the language for distinguishing a civilian from a soldier was itself not much more than a century old. The philosophical and political recognition of the neutrality of all those not in arms dates from the late eighteenth century, and "civilian" as a word specifically meaning "noncombatant" doesn't arrive in English until the middle of the nineteenth century. In English, it originally had the specialized meaning of someone who was professionally involved in civil law (in contrast with canon or common law). By the end of the eighteenth century, it could also refer to a covenanted employee of the British East India Company not engaged in any military capacity. This was a promising forerunner to our own usage, although in the 1830s the essayist Thomas De Quincey, hardly a linguistic purist, stated in print his irritation with the expanded meaning. But De Quincey was swimming against the tide. The military in particular had picked up the word to apply to those they were not. As the London *Daily Telegraph* noted in 1864, "All over the world military men view any civilian interference with dislike."

The question of who exactly was a civilian and who a soldier was far from settled. With the dawn of organized guerrilla warfare, the distinction between soldier and civilian became even more difficult to enforce with any precision. The Spanish resistance to Napoleon's army during the Peninsular War of 1808–14, immortalized by Goya's *Disasters of War*, was only one of the most prominent of a number of late-eighteenth- and early-nineteenth-century efforts by members of a nominally civilian population to repel an invader or occupying power, including a Corsican rebellion during Napoleon's youth. Goya's etchings particularly depict the atrocities committed by men in uniform (the French) against men in civilian clothes (the Spanish), and this seemingly legalistic detail became one of the crucial factors in the response of armies to such unofficial warfare. So far as many professional soldiers were concerned, guerrilla warfare undermined traditional military ideas of honor because it implied that any defense of the mother/fatherland is right, including sabotage and murder. In World War I, the German army was particularly self-righteous about civilian warfare against itself, justifying the execution of civilians and the destruction of cities like Louvain by invoking rules of war governing "proper" noncombatant behavior. The crucial question was who should be considered a "lawful belligerent" and who not. Those who were not would be protected as civilians under international law—unless they were fighting as guerrillas, in which case they would not be protected either as noncombatants or as official combatants and so could be slaughtered at will. *The Great Escape*, the film version of an actual escape of Allied officers imprisoned by the Nazis during World War II, grimly underlines the punctilious emphasis on the uniform. The British officers, who have recut and dyed their uniforms into civilian clothes, are executed as spies, while the American, caught trying to cross the border, even though seemingly out of uniform, flashes his captain's bars and is returned alive to the prison camp as an official combatant.

The changing relation between soldiers and civilians, or, more precisely, the militarizing of the civilian population, was most obvious in the totalitarian states. But as FDR's post–Pearl Harbor speech implied, in times of war the blending of civilian and soldier could pervade the democracies as well. Bringing home front and battlefront ever closer was propaganda aimed at shaping civilian opinion, armed with a whole new array of tools as formidable for its purposes as machine guns, tanks, and poison gas were for war: cheaper newsprint, faster presses, color printing, telegraphy, radio, motion pictures. Each nation at war used all of these new processes to demonize the enemy and to bring a celebration of its soldiers and their heroism to every eye and ear back home. For mass war and the citizen soldier also encouraged revenge as an explicit political motive—national hatreds, whipped up by propaganda that made whole countries into conglomerate monsters, in which all were equally guilty.

Is the need to describe the enemy as subhuman or different an essential part of war? In the embryonic phase of their nationalism during the Hundred Years' War, the English considered the French to be effeminate and the French thought the English hopeless drunks. But that hardly seems commensurable with the hatred the Nazis had for Jews and Slavs as races that could be treated like vermin.

This propaganda of the absolute iniquity of the enemy, so elaborately fostered in World War I, aimed to create the climate of emotional opinion believed necessary to strengthen civilian will. Among the Allies especially, the imagery of the bloodthirsty Hun became pervasive, while the Germans, with their submarine warfare and their policy of severely punishing civilian populations for guerrilla attacks, did little to contradict it. The Allied blockade of German cities, the German sinkings of commercial vessels in both wars, the aerial bombing of London, Paris, Berlin, and numerous other cities—all ran roughshod over whatever line may have existed between combatants in uniform and noncombatants in civilian clothes. With World War II the sense that there was no distinction between the home front and the war front became even keener. Perhaps necessarily, then, the period from 1939 to 1945 witnessed the most widespread guerrilla activity since the Napoleonic Wars.

Total war had arrived, and along with it came the renewal of a rhetoric of absolute difference between combatants that would extend past the war into the us/them polarities of the Cold War. When war becomes so pervasive, everyone is a combatant and anyone without a uniform may be suspect until proven loyal. In the world of dynasties and monarchs, treason had been treason to the ruler; now, it was treason to the idea of the state as embodied in the leader. Whether defined by class under Soviet communism or by race under Nazism, the enemy was a lethal obstacle on the way to a triumphant future. Once again, Hitler took this idea further than anyone else. The enemy was not only despised racial outsiders like Jews or Slavs, but could also potentially include one's own men. During the war, the number of German soldiers executed for treason (which could mean anything from desertion to self-inflicted wounds and defeatism) soared higher than in any other army. In the French armed forces one hundred were executed; in the British forces, forty; in the American army, only one. But in Germany the figure was between thirteen thousand and fifteen thousand. Perhaps these figures mean that the German army was less than enthusiastic about Hitler's plans for world domination, but more likely they were the result of a belief that any hesitancy, any minor flaw, meant that the facade of total group unanimity would collapse and therefore it had to be immediately expunged.*

Thus the increased attacks against civilians in both world wars seem analogous to the efforts of totalitarian countries to purge both the racial and the class enemy from their own population, the less-than-human elements whose annihilation would ensure victory. While the Allies tried to mask the errors, inaccuracies, and even premeditations in their bombing technology that caused destruction to civilian centers, many on the German General Staff believed in both wars that ruthlessness to civilian populations was something to brag about in order to undermine resistance and encourage acceptance of the new regime.†

In reservist societies like Germany, where every man was legally a potential soldier and the army and the nation had been merging since the Napoleonic Wars, there was a normal sense of continuity, even identification, between the military and the political, only briefly put to the side by the Weimar Republic. In France, by contrast, where the suspicions raised by the Dreyfus case extended into the twentieth century, that connection existed primarily for royalists and military partisans, as it did in England, where hostility to a standing army was deep-seated. But even in Nazi Germany, where the line separating civilian and soldier was perhaps the murkiest, political realities enforced certain distinctions. Until 1944, for example, Hitler tried to shield the German civilian population German civilian population from the pains of war by keeping up the production of consumer goods. Already, of course, the public life of the individual citizen had been gathered up into the national party and its rituals of willpower and self-assertion, and within that one party there was only one way to be a citizen. *Ein Volk*, *ein Reich*, *ein Führer* was the Nazi slogan—one people, one state, one leader. With the appointment of Goebbels as "plenipotentiary general for total war" and the creation of the Volkssturm, the people's army for which every man from sixteen to sixty-five was eligible, the male German citizen became absorbed almost entirely into the soldier.

* The one American soldier executed for treason in World War II was Private Edward Slovik. In World War I, the figures were 48 for Germany, 346 for Britain, and 650 for France. Even in 2000 the British government was still unwilling to pardon those executed after courts-martial in World War I.

† There was also a practical opposition in Germany to this view, which argued that atrocities made it harder to deal with those same civilians.

Every citizen was a pure German and every civilian a potential or actual soldier. This recipe for victory was not a Nazi invention. It had been an article of faith among the leaders of the German navy from the time of Kaiser Wilhelm II that the United States would make an easy target because of the mongrel mélange of lower-class social groups that made up its armies and navies. It was only a short step to Hitler's view that the United States since the Civil War had been a society in decay—a "conglomeration of disparate elements" (Herwig, 182) directed by Jews and therefore unable to fight a war against a pure warrior culture like Germany's—although he did admire American football and was inspired to imitate American marching bands in the plans and paraphernalia of his party rallies.

In 1941, an American horror film briefly opened a somewhat different perspective. This was *The Wolf Man,* written by Curt Siodmak, a refugee from Nazi Germany, who drew upon north German myths to create a plot in which a mild-mannered American, tyrannized by his English father, discovers through the intervention of an old Gypsy woman that he becomes a murderous beast at the full moon. Hardly anyone would consider *The Wolf Man* a war film. But as an allegory of the awakened America that would fight, despite Hitler's belief (like the father's in the film) that the democracies were too weak, it sounds an intriguing cautionary note, phrased in a language of myth oddly analogous to the Nazi belief in warrior sufficiency.

*The Wolf Man* may have been an unnoticed contribution of popular culture to the whole question of preparedness and fighting will. But on the supposedly more reasonable level of political and military decision making, the German and Japanese military on the eve of World War II, like the South viewing the North in the U.S. Civil War, generally believed that American (and British) superiority was material, not spiritual, and would be inevitably defeated by warrior pride. The General Staff, whose autonomy had in the nineteenth century been encouraged under Helmuth von Moltke, was now subject to Hitler's micromanaging control to prevent what he considered to be their cowardice in considering strategic options. As Hitler remarked to General Franz Halder, as he dismissed him before the Battle of Stalingrad, "We need National Socialist ardor now, not professional ability" (Friedrich, 359).

The American soldier in particular, as the product of a decadent society, was not a warrior; instead, according to Nazi (and Japanese) propaganda, he was either a murderous gangster or a coward wary of hand-to-hand fighting. Even after such defeats as the Battle of the Bulge, in which German soldiers were overpowered in direct ground battles, the Nazis continued to believe in their warrior superiority. On the verge of the final Nazi collapse, propaganda still foretold of an underground Werewolf organization that would carry on the war against the occupying forces—a backhanded tribute to *The Wolf Man* but a threat that never materialized. Like Nazi racial theories, the Werewolf fantasy was based on magical thinking: as the real situation becomes more desperate, the need to purge imagined impurity overtakes every other motive. The maniacal preoccupation with details in the administration of the death camps similarly makes the irrational seem rational, just another set of instructions in the sacred quest to maintain order and national honor.

Nazi racism especially represents a dead-end entwining of medieval traditions of the warrior elite and the nineteenth-century image of national purity as achieved through the perfected male body. But it also participates in more general movements to which even the victors in World War II were not immune. World War I had confirmed the precedent that, as technology opened the way to more and more absolute weapons and war itself became more total, there was a correspondingly greater need to see the enemy as both subhuman and obdurate enough to justify its use. At the same time, the emphasis on the national purity and self-sufficiency necessitated by ideology—the belief in the warrior nature and all that follows from it—often took attention away from the material preparations for war and sometimes encouraged decisions that were made more for distorted ideas of honor and symbolism than for practical strategy. Until Pearl Harbor, both American and British tacticians generally considered the Japanese military to be inferior, incapable of mounting a serious threat. Japanese naval planners, for their part, were preoccupied with constructing a battle fleet that reflected symbolic stature as much as real effectiveness.

Practical-minded skeptics might laugh at the idea of Freudian war, in which the phallic power of greater weaponry gets deployed against an obdurate enemy. These are mere weapons—rockets, artillery, and even airplanes—whose shapes are a convenience of design and aerodynamics. But fantasy has a deep role in war preparations, and nowhere is it more significant than in the twentieth century, when it is merged with the explicit image of a masculinized and virile state, or, in the case of the bombings of the World Trade Center in 1993 and 2001, when the attack is made in the name of an exclusionary masculine culture against what it considers to be, as did the fascists, an emasculated mercantile culture.

The central role of an ideology of masculinity in the interwar period is thus crucial: a vision of right behavior deeply indebted to nostalgia, for which all of reality constituted only new examples of preexisting truths. In yet another example of the way ideology overrode practicality, while in the United States thousands of Rosie the Riveters were aiding American industry and the comic book character Wonder Woman was introduced to inspire young readers, in Nazi Germany, in the midst of an enormous labor shortage, women were not employed in munitions factories because Hitler believed it was "biologically harmful for the race" and would undermine the propaganda of *Kinder, Küche, Kirche* (Milward, 46).

# NO RETREAT AND UNCONDITIONAL SURRENDER

Like the governments of fascist Italy and Nazi Germany, Japanese nationalists invoked their own warrior fantasies to support a policy of expansion. While the empires of Europe in Asia began to collapse in the wake of World War I, in Japan samurai and *ronin* traditions were being revived by army officers as an attack on the "corruption" of the modern world and a revival of national power.

As in the history of chivalry in the West, the samurai ethos had been codified just at the moment that samurai were actually losing their identity as a warrior class. For Japan this was the seventeenth century, when internal war virtually ceased to exist under the Tokugawa military rule. Bereft of most of their military function, samurai were becoming schoolmasters and government bureaucrats, although they still retained their privilege of having last names and carrying both a long and a short sword. Two hundred years later, after Japan had been forcibly opened to trade with the West by British and American gunships, imperial rule was restored. The period of seclusion, when Japan turned almost entirely inward, was over. With the abolition of feudal rights in 1871, the samurai class was in effect abolished as well, along with its political dominance over the government.

But even as rebellions by discontented samurai were defeated by the new national army, the samurai spirit, cut loose from its class tether, began to infuse the nation as a middle-class and working-class masculine ideal. The average Japanese might be a bureaucrat or a "salaryman" working for a corporation, but underneath his westernized clothing could beat the heart of a medieval warrior. In the early twentieth century, when Europeans and Americans were preoccupied with reasserting their own warrior past, the samurai code was also being publicized as a tonic that could restore health to civilized society. In 1905, Inazo Nitobe, a professor, diplomat, and self-described "bridge" between Japan and the West, published *Bushido: The Soul of Japan* (1905), a book that specifically linked nostalgia for chivalry with nostalgia for the great days of the samurai. Praising what he (or his translator) called the samurai's "ultra-Spartan system of 'drilling the nerves,' " Nitobe detailed all that he considered to be best in the samurai "code," including the honor of *seppuku*, even as he condemned its excesses. Bushido, he concluded, was "as leaven among the masses, furnishing a moral standard for the whole people" that would otherwise succumb to Western materialism and utilitarianism (32–33, 163).

As we have seen, this view of Bushido was an attractive image for westerners as well. Before World War I, many in Europe viewed Japan as a warrior society unadulterated by either commerce or the control of civilian politicians, with its aristocratic military class still intact. During the Russo-Japanese War, both the Germans and the British sent them military aid, and the popular presses of both nations echoed with praise of the warlike spirit of the Japanese. Similarly, Robert Baden-Powell had included Bushido as an ideal code of honor in his exhortation to the Boy Scouts, paramilitary groups like the Action Française invoked the samurai as a kindred spirit, and writers on war preparedness held up the samurai ethos of the Japanese army as a model to follow. Nitobe himself was a Quaker for whom Christianity could blunt the harsher edges of Bushido in the same way that it did medieval knighthood. He died in 1933 without divining how, in Japan itself, the revived samurai spirit would furnish a moral justification for ultranationalists intent on Japan's version of American manifest destiny: their divine right to rule Asia through what they called the Japanese East Asia Co-Prosperity Sphere.

Like the nineteenth-century soldiers of the British Empire who believed that being white and Christian implied they should rule the world, the Japanese government sought to convince the Koreans, the Chinese, the Indonesians, and many others that they had come as liberators. World War I had begun to end the European domination of the world, and the Japanese moved into the places where European colonialism had weakened, especially Southeast Asia. As John W. Dower points out, the Japanese had also taken over the pseudoscientific racism of the West and reframed it as moral superiority. At the outbreak of World War II, numbers of Japanese writers and artists, like so many of their European fellows at the beginning of World War I, felt a new "clarity of purpose" in this battle to cleanse the world for their own "purer" civilization. Like the Germans in both world wars, Japanese also argued that the Americans and British were too effete and mercantile to support a war. Echoing similar Nazi ideas, such symbolic assumptions had practical effects: antisubmarine defense was minimized because Japanese naval commanders believed that Americans were too soft for submarine duty. Certainly the Japanese tried to create and maintain as much of a military buildup as possible, but the material weaponry often seemed secondary and in thrall to a blindered view of racial and national difference. They stressed instead their own crusade for true honor and the realm of the spirit against the materialism and tyranny of the West. It was a message that resonated among many Asians, who took a degree of satisfaction at the Japanese defeat of the Western nations—until they discovered that as rulers the Japanese were just as bad as or worse than what they replaced.

Other differences between national warrior traditions had their own effects. In the chivalric world of the West there was always at least an ideal possibility for the solitary knight-errant to be unbeholden to any order outside himself and his sense of honor. But the samurai was almost entirely subject to others: during the rise of the samurai class this was his local lord; in the twentieth-century diffusion of the samurai ideal, it was the divinely descended emperor. Instead of a myth of origin like that of the United States, which specifically invoked the Founding Fathers as men who created it on purpose, Japanese emperor-worship emphasized the priority of the state and the Yamato throne over the individual, any individual. With war approaching and the homeland to be defended, military service combined the obligation to both emperor and nation, and that loyalty, as it was for the samurai, was absolute, in effect making the civilian and the military nations one.

On the level of strategy, Allied war-making problems were often due to lack of coordination between British and American planners, as well as competition among the military services. Thanks to the institution of the General Staff, the Nazis had comparatively good coordination. But they were undone by inflexible goals, the inability to improvise, and a lack of delegation—all the results of Hitler's immovable role as central authority and his basic tactic of maintaining power by pitting different governmental and military groups against one another.

In a conundrum whose long trail winds from the beginnings of gunpowder weapons, the greater the belief in the indomitable national warrior tradition, the more technological innovation seemed to be a spurious, dishonorable interposition of the modern world. Through premeditation, ineptness, or lack of interest, totalitarian leaders in Europe encouraged competition and duplication of function among their underlings because it gave them absolute and final power. Mussolini, for example, was the self-appointed war, navy, and air minister from 1933 to 1943. In Japan there was a lack of coordination and an interservice rivalry that went far beyond similar tensions among the Allies, especially because there was no unquestioned central authority except the emperor. Metaphors of indomitability still guided these nostalgic warrior cultures, and the centralization of military decision making in the hands of Hitler or Mussolini hardly helped. Victory was to be expected, and planned for primarily by envisioning lightning strikes rather than the less glamorous mapping out of logistics and small-scale tactics.

All three of the Axis powers relied heavily on the import of strategic raw materials to fuel their war effort. No more was mule hunting in the U.S. Southwest a basic chore of supply officers. The embryonic internal combustion engine, which was comparatively rare in World War I, had come into its own and oil was a primary need. But whatever resources each country possessed at the beginning of World War II soon began to run out, through both use and embargo, as the war continued. Throughout the war territorial expansion moved in the direction of more resources, toward the Grozny and Baku oil fields of southern Russia for Hitler or into Southeast Asia for the Japanese, where there were supplies of tin and rubber.

Mussolini's Italy was particularly unprepared in economic growth as well as scientific and technological production to back up Il Duce's aggressive rhetoric. Its only military success had been the defeat of the Ethiopians in 1935–36, in a technologically one-sided war that resembled a playback of nineteenth-century colonial battles between automatic weapons and wooden assegais. Nazi Germany did much better than Italy in preparing itself for war, but still began to run out of steam after two years of overwhelming success on the battlefield. The Nazis had adopted a conception of decisive battles that annihilated the enemy, putatively derived from Napoleonic practice and Clausewitzian theory by the savants of the German General Staff, but owing as much if not more to Hitler's absolutist ideas about national survival. Like Napoleon, Hitler wanted to win quickly enough that precious supplies would not be exhausted, and, like Napoleon, he met his match in the invasion of Russia, where decisiveness turned out to be less important than endurance.

In the clash between the assumption of one's own innate superiority and the enemy's equally innate weakness, blitzkreig imploded. The contrast between nostalgic traditions and modern weaponry, along with the overheated nationalism both imply, would become a significant feature of many conflicts in the post–Cold War world. Nationalist rebels might use more primitive weapons (down even to the stones of the *intifada*) as evidence of their sincerity and trust in their cause, while nations with actual military power were often loath to use it for fear of offending world opinion and recalling images of fascist planes bombing a medieval Ethiopian army.

The twentieth century thus marks a new stage in European war. From the end of the Middle Ages, wars in Europe had arguably been fought as often for heroic nostalgia and revenge for past defeats as they had for territory or defense. Those motives still pervaded the propaganda and much of the policy of war making: Hitler insisted after Germany defeated France that the treaty had to be signed in the same railway coach near Compiègne where the treaty ending World War I had been signed, and his army propaganda magazine *Signal* followed up the victory with a long article juxtaposing then and now photographs (including images of the German entry into Paris during the Franco-Prussian War).

Not that technology was ignored by the warrior states. Germany, especially early in the war, had equipment more advanced than its foes. But the development of military technology always existed in an uneasy tension with the berserker belief that the struggle of pure warrior honor should be enough to prevail. Although the ideologues of perpetual war-readiness had concertedly pushed forward early rearmament, the speed of twentieth-century technological change often ensured an equally quick obsolescence for new developments. When countries such as Great Britain, the United States, and Russia, which were more ambivalent about entering the war, finally brought their industrial and inventive capacities up to wartime levels, they surged ahead. While the Nazi economy failed to maintain production at the prewar level, the Allies increased not only the number but also the quality of their military necessities in all areas. The image of a state totally committed to the Führer and to the war effort was more true in propaganda and in the pervasive presence of the secret police than it was in economic organization.

This tendency to let the populace-arousing talk of military greatness run ahead of the actual ability to win wars saturated both Nazi Germany and fascist Italy, as it did Japan in the 1930s and 1940s. Simply stated, the official line and deep-seated belief was that weaker states would fall before the image and actuality of resurgent warriorhood. Training was not neglected, especially in Germany and Japan, but the assumption of the superior spiritual warriorhood of their soldiers and the inferiority of their enemies gradually took its toll. Such propaganda would have been a cynical manipulation of nationalist pride, had it not been either believed or assented to all the way to the top. It served entrenched myths as well as particular political interests, like the German army view that they had never surrendered in World War I, but had been "stabbed in the back" by politicians. War would be waged not on the eighteenth-century model of negotiation but entirely *a l'outrance*, to the limit. Hitler's orders of no retreat on both Eastern and Western Fronts confirmed that this was not a war for territory but for a conception of the world. As he told Albert Speer and others after 1944, and tried to put into practice, if Germany could not win the war, it should be destroyed, for the German people would have proven themselves unworthy of his dreams.

To a certain extent, the insistence that there be no retreat emanates from a totalitarian view of warfare in which only triumph or death exist. Stalin as well often demanded the same of his commanders. But Hitler's orders also inescapably invoke the images of national and personal warrior honor on which he and Goebbels built their regime.

Absolutes invite absolute responses. Stalin's no-surrender order before the Battle of Stalingrad invoked both the carrot of patriotism and the stick of imprisonment or execution for malingerers. But long before Stalin's order it had become clear that not only was there a Nazi policy of exterminating Jewish civilians but also a concerted plan to kill off Soviet prisoners of war as members of the "subhuman" Slavic race. The SS may have spearheaded the attack on the Jews, but the German army, with some honorable exceptions, acquiesced. Where race was concerned, the new shape of warfare had further erased the line between combatant and noncombatant, soldier and civilian, as well as totally undermining the pretense that there were standards of military honor and professionalism that would never be breached.

To the war of absolute annihilation the Allies responded with a demand for unconditional surrender in both Europe and the Pacific. But it was in the Pacific war that the opposition was more unyielding. The strategy of unconditional surrender in Europe carried with it the memory of World War I, in which German civilian leaders surrendered and the German military could claim it had never been defeated. That would not be allowed to happen in World War II. Political awareness of what it meant to defeat Nazism was not high in the American army, except among those few soldiers who understood the underlying issues. As far as the German enemy was concerned, American soldiers rated him higher as a fighter than they did, say, their nominal allies the French and the Russians. Only the sight of the concentration camps shook the general view that this was a traditional war against a worthy foe.

The antagonisms that fueled the Pacific war were very different. For the United States, a country that had not been invaded by a foreign power since the War of 1812, World War II in Europe was still war at a distance. The ancient urges to expand or protect territory did not seem to apply. But at Pearl Harbor the United States had been attacked by surprise on "a day that would live in infamy," while representatives of the Japanese government were negotiating for peace in Washington. Revenge therefore became the hallmark of the war with Japan, and it engendered a widespread hatred of the enemy among American soldiers, stoked by the racial difference that was for the most part absent in the European war. On the home front, *Life* magazine played up the role of race by running an article called "How to Tell Your Friends [i.e., the Chinese] from the Japs," while army censors refused to pass for publication a photo of American soldiers helping wounded Japanese soldiers for fear that the show of compassion would hurt morale. No wonder that in the Pacific itself, Charles Lindbergh, observing the action, was shocked at the contempt that GIs had for the enemy, to the extent of pulling gold teeth out of corpses. Even language played a role. As John W. Dower has pointed out, whereas a distinction could be made in English between Nazis and Germans, in the Pacific it was all "Japs" (69).

For their part, a significant proportion of the Japanese military harbored their own racist ideas, not just about the Allies but also about the various Asian races over whom they believed it was their destiny to rule. The result was what Dower has called a "war without mercy." While the

Nazi conception of absolute war still allowed for some comparatively humane treatment of military prisoners, especially officers, the Japanese were much harsher. In ten months of average confinement, 1 percent of GIs in German hands died, while in thirty-eight months of average confinement by the Japanese, 35 percent died. Akin to the tradition of ritual suicide that accompanied their refusal to surrender (and their disdain for those who did), many within the samurai-suffused military believed that to be taken prisoner was a humiliating loss of honor, without which they were not even men, let alone soldiers. Among many Japanese civilians as well, this long samurai tradition of honorable death even (or especially) when facing defeat inspired mass suicides when the Allies took Saipan. As the Allies advanced across the Pacific, there were desperate suicide attacks by soldiers with inadequate weapons, *seppuku* committed by commanders, and the deaths of civilians at the hands of their own soldiers in places close to the home islands, like Okinawa—all to preserve the honor of the lost cause and to prevent Japanese citizens from falling into the hands of the dishonorable foe.

Dower argues that the Japanese people in general were not necessarily so absolute in their view, but that this was certainly the way the ultranationalists and militarists in power wanted them to be seen. In their turn, Allied propagandists embraced this unbending myth of fanatic Japanese uniformity to reinforce the need for absolute victory in the Pacific. Unlike in Europe, there were also no-surrender orders issued by the Allies in specific Pacific battles, and the stories of atrocities in Japanese camps (and the Japanese propaganda depicting American soldiers as thugs and murderers) made it unlikely that soldiers on either side would surrender.

Of such absolute gestures the most famous were the kamikaze raids by pilots attacking American warships moving toward Japan. The word "kamikaze" itself, which means sacred wind, or evidence of the direct action of the gods, itself harkens back to a storm that in the late thirteenth century wrecked a Mongol fleet attacking Japan. Furnished with a samurai short sword and with a *hachimaki* cloth tied around their heads in honor of the Shinto god of war, these pilots, knowing that they would probably never come back, flew off to die in samurai glory in the clearest modern equivalent of hand-to-hand warriorhood against a greater technology. Many Japanese commanders objected to the kamikaze. But even its military supporters did not argue that it would be a winning strategy, only an "honorable" response to Allied seapower.

Modern mass armies, because they need to make effective soldiers out of citizens drafted from "normal" life, tread a line between the discomfort of the front lines (to incite effective aggression against the enemy) and their comfort (to stem excessive hostility to one's own officer corps and rear echelons). Roughly speaking, the more dictatorial and militarized a society, the less attention is given to the comfort side of the equation. Soviet lack of logistic support during World War II, for example, might even be interpreted as a policy to push soldiers forward against the enemy with no excuse or opportunity for relaxation, while the relative comfort of German trenches and emplacements in Normandy, say, seems to have fostered a dangerous complacency.

Both the Germans and the Japanese, in fact, stressed combat and operations over organization and supply, the strong suits of the Allies. In the European war, the Allies had about 25 percent more logistic support than the Germans, even though the Germans were much closer to home. In the Pacific war, the difference was even wider, with something like a dozen rear-echelon supporters for every American fighting soldier compared to at most two for every Japanese. For the warrior culture, it was primarily the front line that counted, and, even in a world of long-range bombers and aircraft carriers, tanks and bazookas, and battles like the Coral Sea in which the enemy fleets were never in plain sight of each other, that belief carried on a tradition of disdain for any weaponry beyond the sword and the bayonet.

The heroic ideal was hand-to-hand combat. But the reality was death at a distance. Instead of the mutual respect that single combat always implied, mass war and an annihilating technology increasingly dictated an absolute difference between our side and the enemy, whoever we or they might be. However humane the motives might be for some, to justify unconditional surrender, extermination, or a no-retreat policy, the enemy had to some extent to be characterized as not human. His face was the face of an animal, an insect, a monster, or the devil. With that image in mind, launching suicide attacks or dropping bombs on radar blips became a good deal easier.*

* The invocation of testosterone as a catchall explanation for male aggressiveness bears a close affinity with these ideas. For the revival after World War II of the effort to trace war to basic human (i.e., male) nature, now shorn of fascist politics, see below, pp. 501–18.

# SHADOWS ON THE WALL AND THE COMMON MAN

> Probably, we will never be able to determine the psychic havoc of the concentration camps and the atom bomb upon the unconscious mind of almost everyone alive in these years . . . that we might . . . be doomed to die as a cipher in some vast statistical operation in which our teeth would be counted, and our hair would be saved, but our death itself would be unknown. . . .
>
> —Norman Mailer, *The White Negro* (1957)

The two world wars, or the single Thirty-one Years' War of the twentieth century, had for the first time in history helped establish a world context for both war and the military masculinity that fueled it. Different and distant cultures had always created their own traditions of both war and masculinity, even though, as with Europe and Japan in the Middle Ages, there often seemed to be some significant analogies in rituals and self-conceptions. But now those traditions were forced to face the test of the battlefield together. The fascist states had banked on a self-enclosed neowarriorism to buttress their goal of an economic self-sufficiency in which the rest of the world would serve their interests. Now, both materially and psychologically, there was a renewed recognition of an interdependent system of states more all-embracing than the European balance of power produced in the beginning of the nineteenth century at the Congress of Vienna.

By greeting World War I with such enthusiasm, the European custodians of empire tried to ignore or repress the incipient national self-consciousness in Asia. But after World War II and the appearance on the world stage of powers of different ethnicities, the European white male himself was transformed from the presumed norm of nineteenth-century colonialism into an ethnic himself, subject to external challenges and internal doubts. Asians, for example, even while they might have hated Japanese despotism in their own countries, were inspired in their struggles by the ability of Japan to fight on an equal footing with Europe and the West.

Advances in technology and expenditures of manpower thus decisively made World War II the end of an era in European military masculinity as it had been shaped from the late Middle Ages onward. With World War II even the Germans, who had been fed a steady diet about the thousand-year reich and the triumphant future, were generally grim about what lay ahead. Despite the propaganda of the totalitarian governments, there was only a limited popular sense that men would be made and nations would regain their virility this time. In the United States, World War II also had little of the enthusiastic militarism of the previous war; its songs were more likely to be about separation and longing to be home with loved ones—"We'll Meet Again," "Now Is the Hour"—than the noisy patriotism of "Over There." As Lee Kennett remarks in *G.I.: The American Soldier in World War II*, there was "little taste for discussions on the justness of the American cause" and a decided "aversion to flagwaving and heroics" (89).

The development of the atomic bomb had also ended gunpowder's exclusive place in armaments. Less obviously, both the absolute annihilation possible with the nuclear bomb and the racial extermination policies embodied in the death camps heralded the effective end of Europe's central importance in world history as well as the end, or at least extreme modification, of the dominant European idea of masculinity. The widespread enthusiasm that had greeted World War I as a tonic for European civilization, the beliefs of Hitler and Mussolini that another war would help them inaugurate a glorious future, succeeded primarily in weakening European power in the world, bringing most of the colonial system to an end, and visiting a devastation on Europe itself unparalleled since the Thirty Years' War of the seventeenth century. After four years of World War I, there were twenty million dead; after six years of World War II, the count was fifty million. But nearly half the war dead in World War II were civilians as compared to about one in twenty in World War I.

The numbers of those whose homes were destroyed and who were forced to become refugees were in the millions more.

The destruction of civilian populations and targets in total war had been variously exemplified in the Falangist attack on Guérnica, the massacre and destruction of Lidice, the V-2s dropping on London, and the firebombing of Dresden and Tokyo. But its decisive image became the atomic bombs dropped on Hiroshima and three days later on Nagasaki. This was more than a battle situation being visited on an entire population; this was literal annihilation. Along with the Nazi death camps, it became one of the basic images of the war and what world war meant—the reduction of individuals to ciphers, to numbers, to shadows on a wall. Philippe Berthelot, who was a diplomat in World War I and later became a French counselor of state who tried to promote friendly relations with both Germany and England, remarked after World War I, "When a man dies, I suffer; when a million and a half die, that's statistics" (Roeder, 93). Since he himself died in 1934, he could hardly have foreseen how the numbers that seemed so overwhelming to him would be dwarfed by those of World War II.

Even though A-bombs dropped by American forces ended the war, the vapor from the blasts, like some psychological gas attack, drifted back across the United States and the rest of the world, creating in many a more intensified sense of individual despair at being caught in the web of larger forces. As weapons became more all-destroying, the claims to technological specificity grew as well, from the World War II Norden bombsight to the Gulf War Scud missiles. But atomic weapons were of a different scale altogether, and all the previous ironies of blow-back weaponry came together in "the Bomb": the gas of World War I turned by the wind against whoever was firing it; the long-range artillery falling on one's own troops; even the U.S. hydrogen bomb testing during the Cold War that, it turned out, gave the Soviets all the information they needed to make their own bombs. All these images, of the difficulty of reining in a destructive technology, persist even in the era of "surgical strikes."

Yet in the basic paradox of modern warfare, as the brandishing of weapons of mass destruction increased, so also did the emphasis on the individual soldier, the ordinary hero. In the United States particularly, even though the American Revolution and the Civil War had been popular wars, and groups like the Rough Riders and the Harlem Hellfighters of World War I had been briefly celebrated, it was World War II that decisively altered the low civilian opinion of the soldier. Writing just after the Napoleonic Wars, Byron in *Don Juan* had mocked the desire of his heroes to get their names mentioned in dispatches, and World War I propaganda on both sides had stressed the heroic knight sallying forth against the foe. But for World War II the common man was the center of the story. Ernie Pyle's "Joe Blow" stories celebrated the challenges faced by soldiers whose hometowns were a map of America. From Aaron Copland's *Fanfare for the Common Man,* which became one of the most played pieces of music in the world, to Bill Mauldin's immensely popular Willie and Joe cartoons for *Stars and Stripes* during the war, the focus was not on the hero or the officer, but on the lowly dogface who fought, bitched, and often died. As Mauldin wrote in *Up Front:*

> I don't make the infantryman look noble, because he couldn't look noble even if he tried. Still there is a certain nobility and dignity in combat soldiers and medical aid men with dirt in their ears. They are rough and their language gets coarse because they live a life stripped of convention and niceties. Their nobility and dignity come from the way they live unselfishly and risk their lives to help each other. They are normal people who have been put where they are, and whose actions and feelings have been molded by circumstances. (14–15)

The soldiers celebrated by Pyle and Mauldin rarely if ever achieved any spectacular John Wayne–like heroics. Although they often chafed under the army's rules, they were not antiaristocratic or antiofficer figures like the British Tommy Atkins. Instead, they were GI Joes doing their jobs. By their indomitable ordinariness their stories linked the local world to the national effort—the uncommon common man called from his home to fight for his country.

Two ideas of the soldier were thus in uneasy relation in the twentieth century. One was the older view that the ordinary foot soldier was scum or cannon fodder, frequently a mercenary, who had no particular claim to citizenship and its rights and privileges merely because of his military service. The other view was born in the popular revolutions when fighting for one's country became the primary criterion for being a citizen, as it was in the early years of the French Revolution. Then, *only* soldiers could be citizens, and women as well as minorities considered less than manly need not apply. The difference in World War II was that all its mass armies had been built on the assumption of the citizen soldier, whether fascist or democrat. In the United States particularly, GI Joe was a citizen before he became a soldier, and the two identities were often in conflict, especially when it came to the ordinary soldier's hostility to the army's rigid hierarchy, its almost fascist preoccupation with uniformity, and what was perceived as its "chickenshit" attention to triviality in the name of an unquestioned discipline that had previously been called the stiff upper lip.*

Such attitudes were attested in voluminous detail by sociological teams and opinion polls commissioned by the army itself to discover the inner workings of volunteer and conscripted soldiers compared to a professional military. Psychologically and practically, the United States, for all the "big stick" belligerence of the era of Teddy Roosevelt and the accompanying desire to acquire an empire of its own, was comparatively unmilitarized next to the European powers. The political scientist and historian Paul Kennedy refers to the "negligible army" of the United States before World War II. While often eager for flashy adventuring, from San Juan Hill to Grenada, the American public and the military itself seemed much less interested in subjugating, occupying, and administering large stretches of foreign territory. The model of the soldier was therefore less the goose-stepping professional or the uniformed reservist than Teddy Roosevelt's band of intrepid amateurs, and the resentment of authority for its own sake was high.

How then to balance discipline with the need to bitch and complain? Even the term "GI" itself (for "government issue"), like Mauldin's grubby Willie and Joe, Dave Breger's "G.I. Joe," and George Baker's "Sad Sack," testified to the self-mocking humor of the foot soldier. While the armed services controlled information about the war in a way incompatible with the ideals of a democratic society, Mauldin's cartoons were only censored when they inadvertently showed secret equipment. On the other hand, there was also little depiction of the dead and dismembered, unlike Mathew Brady's battlefields of bones in the Civil War. The first image of a dead American soldier did not appear until 1943 in *Life* magazine, and John Huston's graphic documentary *The Battle of San Pietro,* which was made for the Signal Corps, was not released until long after the war in Europe was over.

This war-fostered stress on the common man and an expanded idea

* Paul Fussell has a particularly eloquent chapter on this in *Wartime*. Hostility toward the service was generally a phenomenon of the army rather than of the more upper-class navy or the gung-ho marines.

of full citizenship had peacetime effects as well. Many had gone into World War I expecting the onset of a social utopia in which class differences would disappear. But to the extent that the old class structure was modified in Germany, France, England, and the United States, those changes were often underwritten by an intensified racism. In a world not yet ready for a more inclusive social amalgamation, somebody, it appeared, had to be left out so that others could be let in. But after the xenophobia of the 1920s in the United States, a reborn urge to a new social contract had been tentatively begun under the New Deal and was confirmed, a bit less tentatively, by World War II. The war was particularly crucial in paving the way for an expansion of the idea of American citizenship. As the GI Bill of Rights confirmed, compulsory service was to be matched by the government's obligation to the soldier, in both benefits and equal rights.*

Racial and national stereotypes encourage the transfer to any individual the hatred mustered for the group in general. The propaganda that nurtures such stereotypes thus diffuses personal responsibility for hatred ("It's in the national interest") while it dehumanizes the enemy. In the United States of the 1950s the need to purge the Other, usually defined as a Communist, was still powerfully present. But the urge to inclusion turned out to be even more powerful and more long-lived. Though the democratizing effect of the propaganda of World War II scarcely meant that the place of Jews, African Americans, Japanese Americans, and innumerable other ethnic groups in the American consensus was assured, it was inexorably growing, and with that recognition of other traditions, the idea of a single masculinity was necessarily challenged. After World War II, there was a war to be fought in peacetime as well, what many black leaders and newspapers referred to as "the double V"—victory abroad and at home. For some that war was only against the Red Menace; for others it was against antisemitism and racism, to test the democratic assumptions that had been so trumpeted in the war against Hitler.

The cause of American inclusiveness thus gained ground even in the shadow of the Cold War. Sometimes the effect of a growing white awareness of black dissatisfaction was comically transparent, as when the government minted half-dollars with the profiles of George Washington Carver and Booker T. Washington on them—along with the slogan

* In 1971, under the pressure of the war in Vietnam, the voting age was dropped from twenty-one to eighteen to ensure that all those who fought for their country could also vote for their leaders.

"Americanism**Freedom and Opportunity For All"—to help make sure that black Americans would not be lured away by foreign creeds. But despite the Japanese internment camps and despite the segregated armed forces, the war had helped plant the seeds of a larger idea of being an American: a man who fights America's enemies.

Racism had hardly disappeared. But the war expanded the promise of racial unity, if only because more manpower was needed to run the armament plants. And how could postwar discrimination retain any official status so long as the enemy had been Hitler's own explicit antisemitism and racism? Surmounting continued segregation in the armed forces and the isolationism that had called a war against Hitler "the Jews' war," the national propaganda effort, in such products of the Office of War Information as the "Why We Fight" series of films, downplayed both race and class to portray an America pulling together against the enemy. "Who can comprehend it, the vast tableland of America?" wrote Norman Mailer in *The Naked and the Dead* (1948), the first and most successful of the many postwar novels about the war. Instead of the metallic hull of the phalanx, within which every soldier became facelessly similar, or the "thin red line of heroes" in uniform, the multiethnic, multireligious, and multigeographic squad of World War II books and movies embodied a mixed and more individualized social ideal, with all its tensions and possibilities.

In this change in the attitude toward the soldier, the military itself was at first reluctant to lead. So far as black-white integration was concerned, in the early days of the war there were protests against any changes on the grounds that the army was not a "sociological laboratory." But the idea that government should use its power for social change had been part of a national discussion that began with the Depression and continued under the New Deal. The deep penetration of the war effort into American civilian life—down even to my own exertions as a four-year-old to collect flattened tin cans and bacon grease—helped set the stage for an argument not about whether a good society could be created but to what extent the government should have a hand in bringing it into being.

Instead of the homogeneity of the tribe, it was the heterogeneity of the nation that was at issue. As war went on, the army was more willing to assert a national standard of integration despite local laws and customs. Certainly riots and protests occurred, but under the pressure of war—and not a little because we were supposedly fighting against antidemocratic forces—policies were changing. The success of black combat units in the Pacific, Italy, and the Battle of the Bulge had begun to undermine racist arguments about a drop in morale and efficiency if blacks did anything more than work in supply and artillery. In 1944 a general order integrated all base facilities. Once again, all bases, especially in the South, did not fully comply, but the armed forces as a whole had accepted the principle, the navy and the newly independent air force somewhat before the army. By the 1950s, concludes Neil A. Wynn in *The Afro-American and the Second World War,* the armed forces had become the least segregated national institution in the country.

In the civilian economy there were similar changes. Under pressure from black leaders, Franklin Roosevelt's Executive Order 8802 ended discrimination in defense industries, although there was still hostility to the changes from employers and many white workers, especially those who, like the blacks, had migrated from the South to seek jobs. But the industrialization necessitated by the war was leading inexorably to greater urbanization and a job market that was widening, if only temporarily, for both black and rural migrants.

For the one million African Americans who served, the white strikes against black hiring in defense plants, along with the de facto segregation of much of the army, was deeply disillusioning. But many black veterans later became important figures in the postwar civil rights movements that rallied to transform policies and laws into political and social realities. Racism undeniably still existed, even in institutionalized forms, but its pseudoscientific theory of superiority had been forever tarnished by the Nazi death camps. Now the most familiar face of racism became, like governors Orval Faubus and George Wallace, local, individual, and thus easier to supersede as generations supplanted one another. More decisively and broadly than World War I, World War II had begun a reorganizing of America in terms of race, class, and geography that would become central to the politics of the last half of the twentieth century.

# BRAINWASHING AND THE WAR WITHIN

On the Government side, in the party militias, the shouting of propaganda to undermine the enemy morale had been developed into a regular technique. . . . Of course such a proceeding does not fit in with the English conception of war. I admit I was amazed and scandalized when I first saw it done. The idea of trying to convince your enemy instead of shooting him!

—George Orwell, *Homage to Catalonia* (1938)

Without exonerating the Allies for their own racism and their efforts to spread war to the civilian populations of the enemy, it is still clear that the concentration camps of the Nazis and the activities of the *Einsatzkommandos,* who murdered civilians in Eastern Europe, as well as the brutality of the Japanese to both civilians and prisoners of war, were matters of governmental policy, rather than local or isolated incidents. The war crimes trials, especially at Nuremberg, for the first time in history not only asserted the right of the victors to judge the wartime behavior of the vanquished (which, it could be argued, had happened before, if not so explicitly), but also established the precedent that the individual soldier or military bureaucrat, was required to exercise an independent moral judgment about the commands of his superior. The chain of command and the greater good of the group, in other words, were no final excuse for acting upon orders that were by some general criterion "crimes against humanity." There may be "rules of war" that prohibit certain kinds of behavior, but there was now also a legal entity called "humanity" whose standards of behavior overruled the views of both particular nations and particular leaders—and the individual, especially the individual at war, was bound to follow its ideals.*

The wars between democracy and monarchy at the end of the eighteenth century had resembled the religious wars of the post-Reformation period in the role of belief, whether religious or political, in their propaganda. But no matter how heartfelt the religious convictions of a monarch and his generals were—and religion was often an excuse for dynastic expansionism—a good proportion, usually a majority, of their soldiers were mercenaries with no stake in the cause other than a day's pay. By contrast, the French revolutionary armies were fighting for an explicitly revolutionary ideology, the Americans somewhat less so. But even in the late eighteenth century, there would have been little point for a French interrogator to try to convince a Prussian soldier that his destiny lay with revolutionary ideals, or for a Prussian to try to win a revolutionary soldier over to a preference for hereditary monarchy.

In sharp contrast, the twentieth-century wars between the various brands of fascism and the Allied democracies and Soviet Russia drew extensively on a desire to prove, assert, and force both individuals and peoples to believe that one system was better than another. With very different figures like Napoleon and George Washington, the popular leader had taken over symbolic as well as actual power from the monarch as the embodiment of the state. In turn, the symbolic leaders of the twentieth century, aided by the new media of film and radio, identified themselves with all-embracing value systems. The old nineteenth-century and World War I propaganda of the battle between barbarism and civilization had not disappeared, and was often invoked. But the more pervasive rhetoric summoned up whole systems of belief: liberal humanism versus totalitarian fascism, godless communism versus a capitalist democracy supposedly inseparable from Christianity.

Since Nazi belief was tied directly to Aryan masculinity, murder often took the place of indoctrination. But what kind of man did the democracies believe in and attempt to create? Much of World War II propaganda,

* The legal basis for the Nuremberg trials was the Locarno Pact of 1925, which guaranteed the borders of Belgium, France, and Germany, and mandated arbitration as the only way to change borders in the East. Signed by Germany and the other powers, it was denounced and abrogated by Hitler in 1936 when he militarized the Rhineland.

both military and political, was aimed at reinforcing myths of war, not for territory or treasure but for an ideology of innate national virtue. At the same time, as *Homage to Catalonia*, George Orwell's account of his participation in the Spanish Civil War, illustrates, there were issues of specific political belief just below the surface, especially when Spaniards on one side tried to persuade Spaniards on the other to desert.

Orwell mockingly calls these efforts to persuade not in accord with "the English conception of war," which presumably is just to fight and assume God is on your side. In the United States, this belief in the innate virtue of national ideals was even more extreme. Although in World War I American posters had been as elaborate as anything produced by the Central Powers, there still remained a widespread belief that the difference between Americans and the rest of the world was that we happily lacked an explicit national creed. Ideologies were what other countries had. The American hero, like the Virginian or Teddy Roosevelt, was plainspoken, straightforward, and innocent. Although a vast proportion of the draftees came from urban areas, the popular image of the soldier was Alvin York, the World War I hero from backwoods Tennessee celebrated in *Sergeant York* (1941), who was raised a pacifist (although a dead shot) and was drafted unwillingly into war when his country called, but learned the importance of fighting our enemies.

Certainly World War II propaganda carried its heavy share of dramatized differences between dictatorship and democracy, coercion and freedom. But the American assumption remained that our ideals were natural and effortless, while theirs were repressive and inhuman. The news coverage of the Moscow show trials of the 1930s, in which one after another stalwart of the Russian Revolution confessed to treason against the Soviet state, as well as fictionalized accounts like Arthur Koestler's *Darkness at Noon* (1940), fixed the nightmarish image of a totalitarian system that could, through torture or other forms of mind alteration, force a person to betray his loved ones and himself. Psychological warfare in particular, although familiar in World War II from Axis Sally and Tokyo Rose, whose broadcasts aimed at undermining the morale of American troops, was thus an activity of our enemies, not our own Office of War Information, which was only proclaiming the truth.

In fact, even during the war, it turned out that indoctrination was not just the corrupt activity of degenerate nations but an American thing to do as well. We may not have imitated the coercive manner of the Japanese thought police sometimes caricatured in army training films, but we did use our own form of friendly persuasion. As Ron Robin details in

*The Barbed-Wire College*, almost 400,000 German POWs were sent to American reeducation camps where they were shown movies like *Young Mr. Lincoln* and *The Story of G.I. Joe*, took classes on the Constitution, and read books like *For Whom the Bell Tolls* and *The Song of Bernadette*. Meanwhile, in more far-fetched projects, government scientists, like their counterparts in Germany, experimented with LSD and marijuana as ways to get information and turn spies into double agents.

What these forms of indoctrination and the later fears about brainwashing implied was that beliefs were not innate and could be changed, that there was no necessary link between being a citizen of a particular country and believing in the publicly professed ideals of that country. In Europe, familiar with the changes in political ideas and political parties, this was not much of a revelation. But in the United States, where national identity was rooted in the idea of a natural innocence, it could have a devastating effect. On the one hand, all the win-the-war propaganda against the evil Nazis, fascists, and Japanese stressed the moral crusade, while at the same time the monolithic ideologies of the enemy were contrasted unfavorably with American pluralism. But one man's monolithic mass is another's nation committed to a common goal. Unlike the automaton view of the Axis armies, in the United States Army the common effort sometimes clashed and sometimes fruitfully entwined with the point of view of individuals and groups left out of the social consensus. Mailer's *Naked and the Dead* fictionally expresses this characteristic World War II symbiosis by interweaving the individual stories of the lives of his characters before they went to war with the joint mission they are asked to undertake and their own ethnic and religious hostilities. In the wartime American army, still segregated, there was widespread hostility both to the army and to officers, but it rarely extended to any criticism of America itself. While the evidence gathered from extensive studies of soldiers' attitudes implied that the notion of an apocalyptic moral combat made a much greater impression on the home front than on the average dogface, the postwar welcome home, especially the GI Bill of Rights, did seem to deliver on the promise of a changed world, in which the privilege of higher education, previously restricted to the upper classes, would be open to all citizen soldiers.

With the end of World War II, the defeat of the Axis Powers had also succeeded in stigmatizing the fascist forms of extreme nationalism and the sense of male identity that went with them. But the Cold War world that followed the war still pitted Communist Man and Capitalist Man against each other as embodiments of an absolute ideological difference.

Until the emergence of the Third World, every political issue was either/or, us/them. In 1946 Churchill called the border between the Soviet Union and the West an "iron curtain." Just a year later, President Harry Truman announced the Truman Doctrine, specifically aid to Greece and Turkey and other countries "resisting attempted subjugation by armed minorities or outside pressures." And in the early 1950s President Dwight Eisenhower helped cement the apocalyptic rhetoric that was to permeate American foreign policy for so many years: "Forces of good and evil are massed and armed and opposed as rarely before in history. Freedom is pitted against slavery, lightness against dark" (Podell and Anzovin, 540; Dallek, 170).

After the military consolidation of Western Europe under NATO and the Sino-Soviet alliance of 1950 fostered a global view of political blocs poised against each other, in both the United States and the USSR conformism at home and xenophobia abroad became national policies. Yet, as B. H. Liddell Hart had predicted in 1947, what ensued was not a direct confrontation, but "camouflaged war"—fought through diplomacy and by surrogate and client states. Virtually every local war or political division could be translated into the, for the moment, eternal conflict between the Communist and the non-Communist world, and otherwise national conflicts (as in Korea or Vietnam) took on the coloration of the international power struggle by proxy.

The us/them paranoia of the Cold War had been heightened still further a few years after World War II with the fears that the Russians too would get the Bomb. But it was primarily in reaction to the Korean conflict that an explicit American effort arose to define what we were versus what they were, as men and as societies. Instead of propaganda furnishing the justification for war, as it had in World Wars I and II, war was now the corollary of propaganda. With anticommunism in the United States a leading road to electoral victory, domestic politics became preoccupied with ideological battles whose main staging place was far away. In such an atmosphere, pride and paranoia were fused: small towns staged mock–Communist takeovers of their governments to show what defeat would be like, while others shivered in self-important terror that they would be the prime targets for Russian atomic missiles.

What vision of masculinity suited this new bipolar world, so suffused with the overhanging Armageddon to come? In a sense, the imagery of the Cold War had come full circle to that of the Middle Ages: believers versus heathens in combat for the soul of civilization. What was civilian and what military, what in the sphere of public behavior and what private, in a world where state-sponsored paranoia encouraged a constant search for the "subversives" among us (or them)? Naturally, there are wide differences in degree here, but if we are taking the temperature of an era, the similarities are striking between the psychic atmospheres of the two surviving great powers. In the Soviet bloc the secret police was the arm of the state responsible for deaths, deportations, and imprisonment for all those considered to undermine the national will. In the United States the pervasive atmosphere gave rise to the investigations of Communist subversion by a variety of governmental groups, both local and national—including that of Hollywood by the House Un-American Activities Committee—as well as articles in national magazines like that by Herbert Philbrick in the *Saturday Review of Literature*. Philbrick, the noted author of *I Led Three Lives*, informed his readers about the sure ways to be able to tell whether your friends and family were Communists.

To the uncertain identities battered by the threat of the Bomb and the memory of the concentration camps, Cold War anticommunism thus added the possibility of the self-subversive: you could be a Communist and not even know it yourself. In 1940s films, the person driven mad was often the inconvenient wife of an oppressive husband, whose weakness he plays upon; in the 1950s that weak inner self assumed a political dimension, often more male than female—the weak son, the untrustworthy father. Caught in the general paranoia, anyone might turn out to be an alien, especially the most loyal and the most beloved. When science fiction took its turn at the same themes, the threat of the monstrous erupted into normal life, as in *Invasion of the Body Snatchers* and *The Thing*. In terms of an expression of general fears of a weak and fearful sense of identity, there was little difference between *I Married a Communist* (1950) and *I Married a Monster from Outer Space* (1958), *I Was a Communist for the FBI* (1951) and, with more self-conscious mockery, *I Was a Teenage Frankenstein* (1957).

The defiant localism and frequent lack of interest in foreign or even national domestic issues in the United States did have a positive side because, compared to countries with more extreme nationalist urges, it implied that politics does not have to infuse all of life, contrary to the insistence of the dictators and their minions. But there was also a countertrend, in which the uncomplicated and directly physical (and courageous) masculine response to battle was becoming more and more muddled by the less quantifiable traits of the male mind. Although there were still World War II generals, like George Patton, who believed that anyone claiming a psychological problem or diagnosed that way was a coward or malingerer, the general attitude had changed decisively from the old days of shell shock. The *Saturday Evening Post,* known for its patriotic covers by Norman Rockwell celebrating American values, featured an article on returning veterans in April 1945 entitled "They Won't All Be Psychoneurotics." *Ladies' Home Journal* did a multipart series on how to treat men back from the wars, and the 1946 Oscars for best picture, direction, screenplay, editing, and two acting awards went to the ironically titled *The Best Years of Our Lives,* whose story followed the often difficult adjustments to peacetime life of a sailor, a soldier, and a pilot.

The process of accepting and even sympathizing with the psychological impact of war on the men who fight it had begun in earnest with the initial recognition of the therapeutic usefulness of the psychiatric point of view during World War I; this perspective had now prevailed to the point that one-third of all casualties were considered to be psychological. Faced with wounds that could not be tied directly to a bomb or a bullet, psychotherapy furnished a language that could articulate what was taken to be a soldier's inner landscape. The social standards of integrity and honor that the state had taken over from the language of the chivalric and military class were inadequate to illuminate or judge this more internal and tangled place. Instead of using theories of racial degeneracy or tainted heredity to explain individual behavior on the battlefield, American military psychotherapists in World War II generally arrived at the conclusion that there was no clear-cut distinction between the weak and the strong, the "honorable" and the "dishonorable." As the psychologist Eli Ginzberg and his colleagues put it, "Every man has his breaking point" (24).* Unlike the Nazis' post-Darwinian emphasis on the need for endless struggle, such therapists took up the Freudian idea that civilization meant inhibiting hostility. In drafting a citizen for war, the state was essentially asking him to release that hostility, do something that was "uncivilized," for which there was no possible peacetime preparation except perhaps gang warfare and sports. The need to draft men brought up not to take violence too far, if they were allowed to express it at all, and send them off to kill other men thus required indoctrination—not just the basic training and drill that would make actions virtually automatic but also the invocation of a larger cause for which the fighting and the killing were

* Despite this more enlightened view, the military was still hesitant about letting civilians in on the problem of war-related mental illness. Even John Huston's generally optimistic *Let There Be Light* (1946), a Signal Corps documentary dealing with the treatment and recovery of veterans, was not declassified until the 1980s.

being done. To buttress that demand to kill the enemy, the enemy needed to be presented as eminently killable and so propaganda became even more important as a way of morally justifying behavior in the soldier that the citizen had been taught to reject or disguise. But for all the "Why We Fight" propaganda in the United States, it turned out that the main fighting motive of American soldiers in World War II was to go home. The larger cause for which they were fighting, as it had often been in previous wars, was the respect of their fellow soldiers, and what kept them going was camaraderie rather than the formulas of national virtue.

In retrospect, there seems to be an effortless progression from the expanding use of public propaganda to the increased psychologizing of the war experience, to the fascination with brainwashing and indoctrination. Manipulation of the mind, weakening of willpower, fragmentation of the personality—all were in the air in the postwar period. They acquire a nightmarish image in the Thought Police of *1984* (1949), George Orwell's novel of the totalitarian future, in which there was hardly any way to steal a private moment from the all-seeing gaze of Big Brother, and people could be erased from history, become "unpersons," by being dropped down the memory hole. Such manipulations form part of the pleasures of capitalism themselves in Vance Packard's *The Hidden Persuaders* (1957), which detailed how hidden messages in advertising manipulated buying habits as part of consumer society. If it were true, as Hannah Arendt argued in *Origins of Totalitarianism*, that true totalitarian control comes from within, it seemed that all of mass industrial society, whatever its nominal politics, was in some sense totalitarian. Into this cultural atmosphere, where the very substance of a stable individual identity was threatened by the presence of the atomic bomb, by the Nazi extermination camps, and by mysterious methods of altering your mind and sense of who you were, came the "brainwashing" of the Korean War. Just four days after United Nations ground forces attacked North Korea, a captured American army officer publicly confessed to war crimes.

I put brainwashing in quotation marks because the army never used that word, but preferred to make a distinction between brainwashing, which alters basic character, and indoctrination, which alters beliefs. But still the word persisted. In fact, the most remarkable aspect of the whole brainwashing issue was how obsessive it became culturally—how widespread and resonant the fear was among all classes of people—while how very small was the number of men to whom any such deep indoctrination had actually happened. Yet the threat to the mind pervades the popular culture of the United States in the 1940s and 1950s. John Lundy, a scientist at the Mayo Clinic, who in the mid-1930s first popularized the use of thiopental sodium to reduce "voluntary inhibition," helped furnish some scientific basis for the preoccupation. After the 1950s the drug was replaced by quick-acting benzodiazepines, which facilitated natural sleep. But Hollywood scriptwriters and popular novelists had so built "truth serum" into their stories that it became an all-purpose designation for any drug that could supposedly remove *both* voluntary and involuntary inhibitions, tap directly into the unconscious, and render the victim a pliable tool in the hands of his captors. In Richard Condon's novel *The Manchurian Candidate* (1959), made into a film by John Frankenheimer (1962), a whole group of American soldiers are made to believe that things had happened that had not, and made to forget things that had—all in the service of making one of their number, a decorated American hero, the instrument of a covert Chinese Communist takeover of the United States through the agency of a supposedly anticommunist senator.

Although there never was a "Manchurian candidate" and, according to most psychologists and neuroscientists, there never could be, audiences embraced the possibility as part of a general paranoia about the ability of the enemy to gain control of their minds. It was a fear compounded by fantasies of the mysterious East, fiendish fictional characters like Dr. Fu Manchu, topped off with dread of atomic war. But unlike bombs, this threat would come from within, in the guise of the seemingly most heroic and most patriotic American of all.

The reality was simultaneously simpler and more complex. Brought up on a war that in public pronouncements was cast in the same terms of barbarism and civilization that were laid down in World War I, American soldiers in Korea faced not a war but a "police action" under the banner of the United Nations. The United States supplied the bulk of the soldiers, but for the home front as well as for those fighting, the goals of the action were poorly spelled out. To use a later phrase, what were our "vital interests" in Korea? Five years after World War II ended, even after almost a tripling of army manpower since the reinstitution of the draft in 1948, there was yet no American propaganda office and little national mobilization. As a result, the visual images of the war reaching the home front were less censored than those of World War II, leading to even more questions about our presence. In 1951 President Truman replaced General MacArthur over conflicts in strategy, and in 1952 Eisenhower was elected president, in part on a platform criticizing the conduct of the war.

If political and military leaders could be so divided, what about the ordinary soldier? Prepared by World War II films built on stereotypes of

American purity and the enemy's venality, in which the hero faced either glorious death or the brutalities of capture, prisoners of war were unprepared for indoctrination techniques that featured a kindly, welcoming interrogator who offered them a cigarette, asked after their health, and then proceeded to present evidence that American motives for being in Korea were decidedly impure and ambiguous. Many of the same themes would resurface in Vietnam more than a decade later: the problem of an ideological war waged on nationalistic lines in an Asian country where no one had attacked us and we had no obvious stake beyond the general Cold War imperative of halting the spread of communism wherever it appeared.

Time after time in Korea, American prisoners of war were faced with challenges to their sense of themselves *as Americans* that threatened to crack the armor of moral superiority like an eggshell, and often succeeded. All too often, American cultural insularity, as expressed in the inability or unwillingness to eat unfamiliar food, led to death from malnutrition. But in the Chinese Communist effort to win over or mold minds, the indoctrination of prisoners of war in Korea was helped tremendously by the political ignorance of most GIs—and by their interrogators' deep knowledge of American culture. Instead of having relative assurance about a clear adversary, as in World War II, soldiers in Korea were left adrift, wondering who we were fighting for and why, how American interests, let alone American values, were being threatened.

With an average ninth-grade education, remarks Eugene Kinkead, "Not only did the prisoners not know much about the history of Communism, they didn't know much about that of the U.S. either" (105). Unable to understand how our system could be criticized, young enlisted men were vulnerable to criticisms that took cherished ideals like freedom and self-determination and argued that it was the United States, not the North Koreans or the Chinese, that was guilty of violating the basic political beliefs outlined in the Declaration of Independence. Just following orders was a difficult response to make after Nuremberg. Instead of fighters for freedom, pressed their interrogators, American soldiers were pawns in an undeclared war.

In the end only 11 soldiers were actually convicted of collaboration, of some 415 accused or investigated, and all those had their sentences reduced by boards of review, sensitive to the general public sympathy for their ordeal. But in the national tailspin the only thing that mattered was that the soldier's brain was in jeopardy and, if anticommunist and science fiction novels and films were to be believed, we were all in danger of becoming puppets. In 1953, for the first time, repatriated prisoners of war were given psychiatric exams, and in 1955 the army, based on what was discovered about collaboration in Korea, created for the first time a code of conduct for American soldiers that stressed the sustaining power of both religion—Christian services were depicted in the army training film—and the chain of command. Totalitarianism had built its power on the isolation of the individual within the social system: you either belonged or were an unredeemable outsider. Similar techniques of isolation were used in brainwashing and indoctrination. Instead of camaraderie, or the resources of both religion and the chain of command emphasized by the Army Code of Conduct, there was only the prisoner and the interrogator.

Beneath the fear, what brainwashing seemed to confirm was that implicit and rarely articulated national ideas had run thin as both a reason for fighting and a buttress for a soldier's own identity. Teddy Roosevelt's call to the strenuous life as reinvigoration of the blood of the nation's young men echoed hollowly as well. Accordingly, the postwar period was tangled in a simultaneous effort to fend off the Communist threat while at the same time feverishly trying to fashion more explicitly American ideals. The Pledge of Allegiance, which had originally appeared in a juvenile magazine called *The Youth's Companion* in 1892, had been officially adopted by the government in 1942, and the phrase "under God" added in 1954. Meanwhile, Flag Day became a national holiday in 1949, while Edward R. Murrow's series *This I Believe* sought to expand the definition of belief beyond a narrow sectarian patriotism into a larger sense of what it meant to be an American. As Murrow's liberal version indicates, however, the central term in the efforts of both right and left to project "America" was *belief*, whether religious or secular. To make up for the unfortunate lack of an ideological education, images such as Norman Rockwell's painting of George Washington praying at Valley Forge were widely circulated. Despite the slim historical evidence for such an act, it dovetailed perfectly with the idea of a religion of American patriotism. As Richard Nixon proclaimed in a *Saturday Review of Literature* essay on Whittaker Chambers's *Witness*, a best-selling anticommunist memoir, "America was a political reading of the Bible."

# THE SOLITUDE OF THE WESTERNER

Hitler should beware the fury of an aroused democracy.
—Dwight Eisenhower to Milton Eisenhower,
September 1, 1939

You speakin' to me?
—Alan Ladd, *Shane* (1953)

Because the propaganda of World War II and the revelations after the war of Nazi racial extermination so emphasized the absolute difference between the Allies and the Axis, one crucial influence on postwar attitudes toward masculinity, especially in the United States, was the combined effect of fighting fascism abroad in the "good war" while experiencing the army itself as a semifascist organization without the freedoms and rights associated with civilian life. The jackbooted Germans in particular were the exemplars of a masculinity many wanted to reject, along with the discipline and group-mindedness associated with the fascist personality. At the same time, the devastation promised by a nuclear arms race and the cold-blooded "efficiency" of the Nazi death camps made science and technology themselves suspect. Lindbergh, for example, who had previously felt that advances in science "would automatically benefit mankind," contemplated Hiroshima and concluded that "it was now obvious that through shortsighted leadership airpower might destroy the civilization that created it" (178).

Who would be the heroes of a mass age, when generals directed battle from far behind the lines, or when having the idea to weld a cowcatcher apparatus to a Sherman tank was more important than heroic behind-the-lines adventures in conquering the hedgerows of Normandy? Here was a central problem of democratic war: the disparity between the public image needed to inspire the troops—and the civilians at home—gets further and further separated from what is needed to win.

Certainly small-unit tactics were important in twentieth-century war, and the image of the squad and the patrol resonate in both war literature and war history. Yet in the popular culture of the postwar world, it was the lonely hero—especially the cowboy and the detective—who furnished an image of stolid male heroism to counteract the fears of both anonymous atomic destruction and submersion in the totalitarian mass. In the face of an advancing technology and urbanization, postwar American popular culture reaffirmed and extended masculine codes of camaraderie and aloneness for an audience of moviegoers and paperback readers heavily made up of veterans, their families, and friends.

If the willingness and the ability to make war is a crucial index of masculinity, what is the effect of losing a war? Ian Buruma has described how Japanese art after World War II connected losing the war with a pervasive male impotence. But in modern war the winners hardly escape similar fears. Despite the victories in both Europe and the Pacific, despite the postwar boom economy, 1950s America is riddled with images of both personal and national weakness. One form of solace for that sense of frailty was the re-creation of heroes from the warrior tradition.

Crucially distinguishing the knightly from the samurai visions of the world is that there was nothing in the samurai ethic to encourage the defense of the weak against the strong. In reality, the medieval knight may have usually been a member of an armed band, but the medieval *idea* of the knight—and perhaps the idea of many knights about themselves—was as a solitary defender of individual righs against arbitrary power. The samurai code, by contrast, emphasized clan loyalty (as in *Chushingura*, the seventeenth-century story of the forty-seven *ronin* who avenged their lord and then committed *seppuku*); and the individual samurai had the right to kill anyone of a lower class who happened to annoy him by such lèse-majesté as daring to speak. The rights of the weak were virtually nonexistent in medieval Japan, the rights of the strong pervasive. But in wartime it was the samurai ethic of honorable sacrifice that was emphasized, for example, in Kenzo Mizoguchi's epic film version (*The Forty-seven Ronin,* Part I, 1941; Part II, 1942), which met the wholehearted approval of the military government. After the war, the occupation government at first repressed all samurai films as part of a general ban on period films for their supposedly militaristic and feudal perspective. By the 1960s, with occupation censorship long gone, period films were back, including new versions of the story of the forty-seven *ronin,* like Hiroshi Inagaki's *Chushingura* (1962). But the loyal, self-sacrificing retainer was no longer the only view of the samurai.

Akira Kurosawa's *Seven Samurai* (1954) had already decisively revised the prewar faithful samurai, whose honor consists in his allegiance to his class and his lord. Instead, Kurosawa's film focuses on a group of individual wandering samurai who have joined together to help a farming village against bandits. Inspired as well by Kurosawa's admiration for American westerns, especially those of John Ford, *Seven Samurai* is set at a time when clan loyalties have disintegrated and samurai virtues, like those of the western gunfighter, have become more individual. Like the roles later played by Toshiro Mifune in *Yojimbo* (1961) and *Sanjuro* (1962), the main characters are wandering masterless men who must make their own moral choices. In this world of drifting individuals, the significant first act of the oldest samurai in *Seven Samurai* is to cut off his topknot in order to disguise himself as a priest and rescue a kidnapped child—obscuring his class status to emphasize his moral status. It was a style of heroism that harkened back to warrior knights like Saint George, who began life as a farmer, and it had many imitators in the postwar period, including the Man with No Name in *A Fistful of Dollars* (1964), a *Yojimbo* imitation that launched Italian spaghetti westerns.

In Japan, the axis between the masculinity of the present and the masculinity of the past is especially central to Kurosawa's use of Toshiro Mifune, who embodies in his roles not only the offhand omnicompetent samurai but also the drained modern man. In *Stray Dog* (1949), for example, he plays a detective whose gun has been stolen and who must search through all Tokyo for it, even while he hunts down a criminal. Playing comparable roles in American film at the same time is Gregory Peck, who in *Gentleman's Agreement* (1947) is a journalist fighting antisemitism in the "war at home," as well as the aging gunslinger in *The Gunfighter* (1950), who is trying to get rid of both his gun and his reputation, but is constantly being challenged by young men who want to take his place. This western story line of the old gunman unable to step down surfaces so often in the plots and subplots of the postwar years that in one, *The Fastest Gun Alive* (1956), the gunfighter-turned-shopkeeper finally has to stage his own death to be free of the burden of reputation.

But so long as he still carries a gun or his samurai swords, the essence of this solitary figure is his ability to withstand the taunts of the villains until the right moment. The macho image of the western hero or the samurai after World War II is often not outwardly aggressive (usually the characteristic of the villain) but a judicious mixture of the aggressive with the stoic. It was a formula for righteous action reflected in Eisenhower's prewar letter to his brother and expressed in the postwar western by the reticence of Alan Ladd in *Shane* and by numerous other western heroes. Like Sergeant York, the pacifist turned war hero, they embody the fury of the patient man pushed beyond his self-imposed limits.* The message of this pattern of calm before the storm is not so much of repressed violence that must emerge as it is of an individual capacity for moral outrage that is uncorked only after severe provocation. Whether through Ladd's taciturnity in *Shane,* John Wayne's drawn-out speaking style, Robert Mitchum's drawl, or, in other genres, Humphrey Bogart's world-weariness, the style of this hero announces not belligerence so much as power in reserve. Ironically or appropriately, one of the first cultural imports into the victorious United States from the defeated Japan was martial arts. Karate came first, brought back by American servicemen as well as emigrating Japanese nationals. Zen Buddhism, the samurai religion, often came along as part of the package, but instead of being a support for militarism and emperor-worship, it was reconstituted, like the samurai himself, for peace and self-containment.

From the beginning of American film, the conventional western had fashioned a myth of men facing moral decisions on the ragged edge of a civilization, where only guns spoke decisively. But in the postwar period the western moved from its more usual second-class status in the Hollywood ranking to center stage. The westerner once again became the symbolic core of masculinity because his struggle with the forces arrayed against him was so direct and so personal. From 1946 to 1951, 20 percent of all U.S. movies made were westerns, and eight of the top ten television shows were too; of the top fifty grossing films between 1949 and 1952, twenty-five were westerns. One hundred years after the Civil War, the

* One of the earliest formulations of this stance is in John Dryden's lines about Charles II in his poem "Absalom and Achitophel" (1682): "Beware the Fury of a Patient Man."

postwar western, so often set in the period from 1865 to 1880, reasserted a genealogy of heroes that mended the split between nation and maleness through a new unity in the solitary heroic individual. Held on to for too long, that new image would become a trap itself and lead to the disillusionment of Vietnam. But at the time, after the wartime emphasis on the group and the vast collaborative effort, the western hero was a significant part of a redefinition of masculinity away from authority, big ideas, and large institutional structures. Intriguingly enough, along with its American and Japanese versions, it also struck a chord in Europe, especially in the former belligerents Italy (the westerns of Sergio Leone and others) and Germany (the films based on Karl May stories). Just as in the Middle Ages, knighthood had mutated from a term of social class to one of generalized male honor, the idea of the warrior-soldier again detaching itself from its connection to an institution to become a quality of the self. Even the hired gun might become a moral force, as Shane or Kurosawa's samurais decide to support the embattled farmers, or as Paladin, the hero of *Have Gun Will Travel,* one of the most watched shows in 1950s television, applied his skills in personal violence to defend the innocent and bring down the guilty. On his calling card was the image of a white knight, while his name invoked the twelve legendary champions who attended Charlemagne.

The western hero turned his talent for violence into a solitary virtue tapped only when absolutely necessary. But in the real postwar world the image of the veteran was usually much less commanding. In *The Best Years of Our Lives* all three of the returning veterans have problems reentering peacetime society and all three must be helped by the strong women in their lives. They may have won the war, but now they face the more daunting battle of the bedroom and peacetime domesticity. As in the case histories recorded by army psychiatrists, all three have difficulty handling the penchant for violence instilled by their war experience, although, again typically, while the sailor and the pilot act theirs out more tangibly, the most upper-class vet, a bank official who had been a dog soldier, has the fewest sexual problems and turns instead to drinking to quiet his rage.

In a pattern particularly familiar in twentieth-century war, peacetime society in much of early 1950s popular culture means women, just as war in so many war novels means their absence. World War I had helped polarize the difference between men and women, turning difference into hostility; World War II further increased the distance that had to be bridged once the war was over. In essence, the situation was another form of the basic wartime and Cold War division of us versus them; not only humans versus aliens, or Americans versus Russians, but also men versus women. Immediately after the war, for example, realistic film stories of returning veterans stressed the problem of reentry into a world (primarily of women) that has gotten along quite well without them. In another more mythic and cartoonish aspect of this cultural preoccupation with what to do with the returning veteran, soldiers without guns in real life read about dicks with guns in detective novels, intent on seeking revenge on an uncaring or hostile world for their murdered friends, their lost values, and their own wounds.

The equation between masculine fragility and sexual violence had been virtually taken for granted in wartime fiction. In the ambience of male/female separatism that increases in power after World War II, sexual and personal disappointment are often turned against women to make up for impotence in the world. In *The Naked and the Dead,* for instance, Mailer writes of the ferocious lovemaking between General Cummings and his wife early in their marriage:

> Margaret is kindled by it, exalted for a time, sees it as passion, glows and becomes rounded, but only for a time. After a year it is completely naked, apparent to her, that he is alone, that he fights out battles with himself upon her body, and something withers in her. (416)

A few years later, Philip Wylie gave this war-born divide a more global, science fiction tinge in *The Disappearance* (1951), in which all of the women in the world disappear from all the men, and vice versa. Occupying alternate universes, each sex has to deal with the postwar period in its own way.

In such a sexually polarized and threatening world, the most acceptable sort of woman is often the woman not as sexual partner but as pal, like the detective's loyal secretary, partaking of the same camaraderie and living by the same code. This separation between woman as friend, woman as sexual partner, and woman as wife—already foreshadowed in the earliest detective fiction—continued to be a major motif of the detective novel, given even sharper outline by the experience of war. The detective was a one-man army fighting a personal battle against crime, and he needed to be imagined and to imagine himself as a man unbeholden to women.

Intent upon his spiritual and physical rearmoring, he is like a throwback to the celibacy of the medieval warrior classes, the monkish Crusaders, whose misogyny ensured that their gene pool would not be passed on.

In *I, the Jury* (1947), Mickey Spillane's first Mike Hammer novel and one of the great best-sellers in American history, the woman he falls in love with is a psychiatrist named Charlotte Manning, who turns out to be the criminal mastermind. Just before he kills her in revenge for her murder of his wartime buddy, Hammer explains her motivation:

> How many times have you gone into the frailty of men and seen their weaknesses? It made you afraid. You no longer had the social instinct of a woman—that of being dependent upon a man. You were afraid, so you found a way to increase your bank account and charge it to business. (167)

As he talks, the vamp-psychiatrist undresses to seduce him, but he shoots her anyway. Fearful of having almost been her victim, he becomes her executioner, wreaking fantasy retribution for his reader and fellow victim, the veteran who has come home to discover that the world has changed in unfathomable ways. Rather than patriotism or chivalry or salvation, Hammer's quest is nakedly for revenge.

# POSTWAR MALE SEXUALITY AND THE KINSEY REPORTS

With his helmet's final doff
Soldier lifts his power off.
Soldier bare and chilly then
Wants his power back again . . .
Hunts a further fervor now
Shudders for his impotence . . .
Stiffens: yellows: wonders how
Woman fits for recompense.
—Gwendolyn Brooks, Annie Allen (1949)

Woman—the incomplete sex—and what does she need to complete her—a man.
—A. I. Bezzerides, *Kiss Me Deadly* (1956)

In disgust at an encroaching technological and urbanized civilization, the westerner looked back to national roots, while the detective relied on his own hypermasculinity to fight against the tide of complacency and corruption. Those were the outsized images of fictional individualism that occupied a large space in the popular mind of the 1950s. But an even more pervasive question about masculinity preoccupied the public discussions of the postwar period, a question that focused on the male body. This was no mere heroic tale, but a combined scientific and social inquiry. Had that male body—and therefore masculinity itself—always been the same, with only an overlay of historical change that obscured its essential features? Or was it a product of its times? One central theme of the postwar period in America is the constant tug-of-war between the category of the natural and the category of the social. Which really controlled behavior? Was it history or was it innate biological characteristics?

In the 1960s, writers like Konrad Lorenz and Robert Ardrey, looking at what seemed to be analogies between animals and human beings, would argue that aggression was written into male genes and that war, like aggression, was inevitable. But an earlier postwar approach to the male body had an opposite conclusion, because it sought to focus on actual sexual behavior. The primary author of these studies was a zoologist, a student of wasps named Alfred C. Kinsey. The Kinsey reports on sexual behavior in men (1948) and women (1953) actually arrived on the scene almost a decade before the popular books of Lorenz and Ardrey (although some of Lorenz's work had been published earlier). But in the atmosphere of the 1950s and 1960s, the Kinsey reports and the aggression theories present contrasting attitudes toward a seemingly universal masculinity that had been simultaneously exalted and depleted by World War II. Whereas one could read Ardrey or Lorenz and emerge depressed about the entrapment of human nature by biology, Kinsey used sexuality not to confine but to enhance personal nature. Whereas Lorenz and Ardrey would write in the shadow of a deepening Cold War and the nuclear arms race, Kinsey's studies were carried out as part of a utopian project, fostered by wartime hopes and fears, of a more open American attitude toward sexuality, both male and female. By gathering the testimony of thousands of interviewees and invoking the wide breadth of sexual expression in the animal world, Kinsey sought to define what was natural in sexual activity rather than what was morally enjoined. Like that of French existentialism, a philosophy popular after the war, his criterion of value was human action rather than any abstract essence of maleness or femaleness.

In the same way that World War I had led to the openness of the Jazz Age, the disruptions of World War II encouraged a greater frankness in both sexual behavior and language. War novels like Mailer's *The Naked and the Dead* and James Jones's *From Here to Eternity* (1951) spoke frankly of sexuality in a manner far beyond even the plain speaking of the novelists after World War I. In that atmosphere, the Kinsey reports helped create a new consciousness of the varieties of sexuality within the supposedly monolithic categories of male and female. Sexual crusaders from the time before and after World War I like Havelock Ellis, Margaret Sanger, and Eustache Chesser had addressed themselves to issues of sexual technique and sexual behavior and were often censored and arrested for their presumption to flout public moral standards. But Kinsey took the sex manual and birth control advice several steps further by making sex a topic susceptible to analysis and quantification. Not only could you read about a wide variety of techniques and behaviors in Kinsey, you could also find out what percentage of your fellow citizens were interested practitioners of each. Like the analyses of the attitudes of American soldiers in World War II, the Kinsey reports used the techniques of sociology to consider beliefs and behavior in a social context rather than as elements in a premeditated moral system.

Part of the way to this new frankness had already been prepared by anthropologists like Franz Boas, Bronislaw Malinowski, and Margaret Mead, who tried to step outside Western judgmental categories by considering sexual behavior in the context of varied tribal cultures. Kinsey turned that same lens upon the United States, explicitly attacking the idea that sexuality was an absolute of personal nature and exploring instead its various permutations and combinations in a widespread population. The result was one of the most extensive dethronings of older ideas of the "normal" sexuality since the nineteenth century and the substitution of a range of sexual activities—Kinsey's seven-point sliding scale—rather than a strict bifurcation. In a popular culture where devouring vamps like Spillane's Charlotte Manning preyed on "the weakness of men," where women were encouraged to be homemakers and wives even though the number of women in the workforce was constantly increasing, and where movie actresses like Marilyn Monroe, Jane Russell, Diana Dors, and Brigitte Bardot emphasized their voluptuous compliance with the fantasies of men, Kinsey's emphasis on the differences *within* male and female had a subtly subversive effect.

But at the same time, in a defiantly rearguard action against what was an actual flux in traditional gender roles, many loud public voices after the war were more intent upon emphasizing the absolute difference between male and female, and especially the undermining effect of women on male authority and vision. Philip Wylie's *Generation of Vipers* (1942) had in the midst of the war begun the attack in a jeremiad condemning the American mother whose overbearing attachment to her sons made it so difficult to create a generation of warrior males.

> Our land, subjectively mapped, would have more silver cords and apron springs crisscrossing it than railroads and telephone wires. Mom is everywhere and everything and damned near everybody, and from her depends all the rest of the U.S. Disguised as good old mom, dear old mom, sweet old mom, your loving mom, and so on, she is the bride at every funeral and the corpse at every wedding. . . . The mealy look of men today

> is the result of momism and so is the pinched and baffled fury in the eyes of womankind. . . . I give you mom. I give you the destroying mother. I give you her justice—from which we have never removed the eye bandage. I give you the angel—and point to the sword in her hand. (185, 197, 203)

Continuing the diatribe in the year before Kinsey's report on male sexuality came out, the journalist Ferdinand Lundberg and the clinical psychiatrist Marynia F. Farnham published *Modern Woman: The Lost Sex,* in which they argued "that contemporary women in very large numbers are psychologically disordered and that their disorder is having terrible social and personal effects involving men in all departments of their lives as women" (v). Lundberg and Farnham tend to stay away from Wylie's inflamed rhetoric. But they are similarly in debt to a simple-minded version of Freud's formulation of the Oedipus complex as an overriding explanation for male passivity and female aggressiveness. Indicting both Victorian sentimentality and the feminist effort to be like men, which have led to mothers who "reject, overprotect, dominate or overfondle" their children, they approvingly quote a psychiatric consultant to the army and navy surgeons general who "in a recent speech held mothers responsible for the great number of psychoneurotic rejects by the Selective Service Administration" (318).

Lundberg and Farnham may speak generally about the way mothers have been derelict in raising their children. But, like Wylie, it is boys that they really worry about, since the penis envy of their careless moms has raised a generation of weak-willed men unwilling to take on their proper adult male patriarchal roles as "stalwart men." The truly "feminine mother," they write—in words oddly reminiscent of Mike Hammer in *I, the Jury* that same year—

> knows that she is dependent on a man. There is no fantasy in her mind about being an "independent woman," a contradiction in terms. She knows that she is dependent on the phallus for sexual enjoyment, which, as she is genitalized, she is in need of. Having children is the most natural thing possible, and it would never occur to her to have any doubts about it. (319)

This is the same mother, according to Wylie, from whom we must "take back our dreams which, without the perfidious materialism of mom, were shaping up a new and braver world" (203). Wylie finishes his book with a resounding paean to democracy and a vision of the new dawn at the end of the war. Lundberg and Farnham, more intent on practical social policy, conclude that America is a "sick culture" that needs more governmental support to foster a new mental health that insures "the primacy of the home" (376).

With due allowance for the passage of about a half century and two world wars, the tone of these books resembles that of Max Nordau's 1893 European bestseller *Degeneration*. Even though we had fought and won the most extensive war in human history, even though the men who fought it would be lionized fifty years later as the "greatest generation" and a "band of brothers" who left civilian life to defeat the most militarized societies in the world, on the eve of the Cold War, according to writers like these, American society was going down the psychological tubes. They were hardly alone in their fears, which stretched across the political spectrum. Wylie, Lundberg, and Farnham were closer to the liberal side of the argument. Influenced by Freudian thought, they focused in part on the crucial importance of a healthy sexuality. Because Mom by contrast was a controlling puritan, a more open expression of sexuality, of course within social norms, promised a way to individual and perhaps cultural cure. As George Orwell in *1984* implied, the sexual and emotional relations between individuals was the nexus of human freedom, the essence of what totalitarianism was out to destroy.

Meanwhile, the conservative reaction to the war, as well as to the Kinsey reports, emphasized the threat of sexuality to what was usually referred to as the nation's moral fiber, or, in a veiled allusion to masturbation, the sapping of the nation's moral strength. These fragile structures had already been under siege by the returning veterans, whose European experience especially had made them unsuitable supports for the national strength needed to fight the Cold War—a fear of European sexuality only strengthened in 1952 when a young American soldier named George Jorgensen returned from Denmark renamed Christine, outfitted with breasts and a vagina and eager to talk about her transformation. The formerly firm biological difference between male and female seemed in just as much jeopardy as the corresponding social roles.

Although Kinsey's reports expanded the sphere of what was considered natural in sexuality, the lure of the natural as a mode of explanation continued to lead to a stigmatizing of the unnatural. And there was enough fear of a debilitated or excessive masculinity emerging from the war to make the stigma as general as possible. In one of the most popular attacks on the postwar world, the newspaper columnists Jack Lait and Lee Mortimer began publishing a series of "confidential" books (*Washington Confidential, New York Confidential, U.S.A. Confidential*) that claimed to rip the lid off respectability and show the actual festering corruption underneath. Wylie, Lundberg, and Farnham were concerned with a general social and psychological malaise, and in their different ways sought to find some principles for a cure. But Lait and Mortimer saw the United States as engaged in a cultural war between the healthy and the degenerate, among whom they counted most New Deal Democrats, independent women, schoolteachers, and homosexuals. In such a wholesale condemnation, all sexuality not sanctioned by marriage was somehow suspect: "None but the blind or those who don't want to see can fail to be aware of the diseased state of the nation's sex life." Lait and Mortimer's deepest fears closely mirror Nordau's preoccupation with feminized men and masculinized woman, but instead of using his highbrow terminology, they called them faggots and queers:

> The entire nation is going queer! . . . The masculinization of women, which had its counterpart in the feminization of men, is obvious wherever one travels in this nation, in all the forty-eight states and the territories. It is as pitiful a menace as the nation faces. (42, 45)

The broken thread that connects these various efforts to take the measure of American society—and find it wanting—is masculinity. As at the end of every war, and unlikely to change until women become an equal part of the military, with the end of World War II a culturally agreed-upon story defining and even guaranteeing masculinity had abruptly vanished. All the problems, disturbances, and other anomalies of masculinity previously swept up and plastered over by the single-minded male war role were then free to re-emerge in more baroque forms.

We had won the war and now who were we? After the loss of the war's unifying national vision, a spectrum of possibilities arose, from a neo-military effort to retain wartime control to more fragmentary efforts to redefine the image of masculinity—which would not bear fruit until the 1960s and later. Before the war, the public vocabulary of business had generally been that of service, going back to Andrew Carnegie's praise of the "stewardship of wealth." But as the new masters of a booming postwar world, business leaders like Robert McNamara at Ford began to take on a military vocabulary of strategy and decisive battle. In the lower echelons of corporations, one image that became familiar to postwar audiences was the organization man, who had given up his life to the company that employed him and was as ready to do its every bidding as his wife was to join him, pulling up stakes and moving with their family to whatever part of the country the company required. The model for such loyalty was, of course, the life of military service that most of these men and some of the women had only recently left behind. War had brought with it a larger sense of the entire nation as a unit. But for many all that seemed to remain of that wider perspective was the uniformity and the need not to deviate from the norm, as in the notorious appendix to William H. Whyte, Jr.'s *The Organization Man* (1956), "How to Cheat on Personality Tests," where the reader was instructed on how to hide the unappetizing shreds of character that were useless in the modern corporation.*

In another guise, the unsteady definition of masculinity in a peacetime world promoted a movement toward macho assertion, even when, as in Spillane's Mike Hammer or the hero's response to the femme fatale in film noir, it seemed a thin veil for an underlying weakness and doubt. With the Cold War in the air, the almost immediate possibility of battle overhung every activity. As my Scout troop was told by our scoutmaster when we asked why we had to spend the first half hour of our meetings doing close-order drill, "You're going to need to know it when the next war comes, so you might as well have a head start." This was a world of young male fashion that imitated the soldier style from khaki pants to crew cuts—one of the few times in history when short rather than long hair signified the warrior.

*Life* was a particularly sedulous bearer of the spotlight on the men of the new era. Already in 1946, it was telling its readers that an otherwise obscure and difficult New York painter named Jackson Pollack might be America's greatest artist. In 1953 it celebrated Hemingway as America's greatest writer by putting him on the cover and all of *The Old Man and the Sea* inside. In Pollack's broad-shouldered physique and lumberjack shirt or Hemingway's grizzled face and Norfolk sweater, the message was clear: the prime American artist was a real man. Even for writers and artists who were actually gay, the obligatory style of masculinity was shirtsleeved, dungaree-clad, and stoic. At the same time that *Life* was

* In the film of *The Man in the Gray Flannel Suit* (1955) the hero, wondering whether to sell out his ideals, thinks back to the more clear-cut moral decisions and tumultuous romance of wartime, while his wife makes dinner in their suburban kitchen and his children watch westerns on television.

celebrating macho artists, it wasn't hesitant about stigmatizing other, less appropriate forms of young manhood, telling its teenage readers (or more probably their parents) why they shouldn't become beatniks and discussing whether or not going steady was acceptable, even while it clued their parents in on what arcane terms like "square" and "cool" meant.*

Along with the need to brandish a rough-hewn image as the mark of manhood came a sometimes blatant, sometimes subtle, effort to stigmatize homosexuality, or at least its more affectedly fashion-conscious display, as less than truly masculine. With the licensed male bonding of wartime gone, homophobia thus takes on a crucial importance in the definition of masculinity. In *Coming Out Under Fire,* Alan Bérubé has amply documented that during the war there was a high degree of tolerance for gay men in the services. While the official policy was hostile, on the local level, with some exceptions, there was either acceptance or lack of interest in prosecution, a situation that became more prevalent when Section Eight (i.e., unfit but still honorable) discharges were expanded to include homosexuality. As many historians have argued, World War II changed the terms of homosexual life in America in a variety of ways. Army psychiatrists were beginning to move gradually away from the assumption that homosexual behavior was "deviant" and to undermine the stereotype of the effeminate homosexual that persisted for so many decades after the Wilde trial. Meanwhile, the increased opportunities for men to mingle socially and intimately brought by the war not only helped create a national gay community but also engendered more sympathy and understanding among their heterosexual male friends and buddies.

Yet there was fear and apprehension as well. Intense emotional relations between men in wartime, with the physical aspect rejected or relegated to the realm of ambiguity, remained central to war literature and art down to the Vietnam films of the 1970s and beyond. In the camaraderie culture fostered by the war, such male star duos as Bob Hope and Bing Crosby, Bud Abbott and Lou Costello, and, slightly later, Dean Martin and Jerry Lewis showed up regularly on the list of top box-office stars. (Three of Martin and Lewis's first four starring roles were in armed service comedies like 1950's *At War with the Army.*) Unlike the more innocent and less self-conscious relationship of, say, Laurel and Hardy in the 1930s, when the team could even dance together, these were close

* See Emile d'Antonio's film *Painters Painting* (1972) for some excellent examples of this tough-guy artistic pose.

buddy relationships that often had a competitive edge, especially Hope and Crosby when Dorothy Lamour was around. They were pals but not *so* close. The common World War II phrase "asshole buddy" as a term of endearment between soldiers is another instance of the combination of a wartime desire for close male friendship with a cautious mockery—just in case anyone took it too literally.*

Since the birth rate was actually up after the war and into the 1950s, it was hard to maintain national degeneracy arguments with the same force that they had had at the end of the nineteenth century. But homosexuality and "the homosexual" made easy targets in an era that emphasized the virtually patriotic need for a clear difference between male and female. As usual, wartime had reaffirmed that need, but the popular culture of the 1950s was particularly avid about making the point. With the constant threat of nuclear war, or at least low-level skirmishes between American and Soviet power around the globe, men should be men and women women. It was never too young to begin. For three hundred years, infant boys and girls had dressed alike. After the turn of the twentieth century, trousers and dresses began to distinguish them. At the time of World War I, the colors associated with those clothes began to be codified, not at first what we have come to expect—boys wore pink and girls wore blue, which was considered to be delicate and dainty because it is the color of the day. But with World War II, pink for girls and blue for boys became the infant standard, although pink and black was also high fashion for fifties teenagers.

With the advent of the Cold War, although the army itself had never asserted any political reason why homosexuals could not serve, sexual and political subversion became intertwined. Looking back through the lens of nostalgia on what appeared to be the clarity and simplicity of wartime masculinity, some men, most loudly those in public life, transformed it into peacetime posturing and belligerence, rooting out all those they considered to be weak and disloyal. In a virtual repetition of the fears that surfaced in England at the time of World War I, in 1950 there were not only Senator Joseph McCarthy's charges that there were hundreds of Communists at the State Department but also the revelation that dozens of employees had been fired for homosexual activity. As a Senate report later that year concluded, "One homosexual can pollute a Government office" (D'Emilio and Freedman, 293). The professed argument

* In December 1945, *Esquire* ("the magazine for men") had published an article entitled "Farewell Noël Coward," stressing the need to be *real men* in the wake of the war.

was that because homosexuality was socially stigmatized and morally enfeebling, homosexuals could be easily blackmailed into becoming traitors. The 1951 flight to Russia of Guy Burgess and Donald Maclean, two acknowledged homosexuals and spies, seemed to confirm the identification of sexual and political "tendencies" (to use a word of the period)—even though homosexuality was a criminal offense in Russia as well. Finally, newly elected President Eisenhower in 1953 issued an executive order defining "sexual perversion" as sufficient reason either to fire or not to hire a federal employee and authorizing full field investigations to supply the evidence.

It is difficult not to conclude that the wholesale stigmatizing of any group as innately tending toward disloyalty was, like the internment of the Japanese during World War II, more the result of inchoate fears than of actual knowledge. But the significant difference is that during the war it was a group that seemed to mirror the far-off enemy, while after the war it was a group whose existence threatened the assumption of a "normal" family-oriented heterosexual masculinity. A 1959 congressional report that connected pornography to political subversion bears out the suspicion that the long shadow of nineteenth-century ideas of masturbatory degeneracy still threatened the nation—at about the same time (1953) that the first issue of *Playboy* appeared.

As McCarthy's later charges that the army itself was rife with Communist subversion indicated, the basic issue was less communism than it was masculinity. If a bastion of masculinity like the army could be suspect, who was safe? The comparative absurdity of the 1954 army-McCarthy hearings effectively ended McCarthy's career, but his views continued to have supporters then and now. And the suspicion of the homosexual as less than a real man continued, even for those who would otherwise have deplored both McCarthy and his tactics. Underneath the fears and the absurdities, the issue was still the characteristic twentieth-century tug-of-war between the male camaraderie fostered by battle and the peacetime fear of male closeness as the sign of homosexuality. Just as the easy promiscuity of wartime heterosexuality had been countered in the 1950s with paeans to marriage and domestic life, the fear of being thought to have a suspect masculinity spread far beyond the homosexual community. Holden Caulfield, the teenage hero of *Catcher in the Rye* (1951), worries that when his teacher Mr. Antolini patted his head, he was being "flitty," even though he was married. After all, Holden's friend Luce had told him that

> half the married guys in the world were flits and didn't even know it. He said you could turn into one practically overnight, if you had the traits and all. He used to scare the hell out of us. I kept waiting to turn into a flit or something. (143)

In part this new view of the incomplete masculinity of the homosexual came under the sponsorship of Freudian theory. In a step away from the consensus of his time, Freud had redefined male homosexuality not as either an innate deficiency, a moral emptiness, or a crime but as a stage in masculine development on the way to full heterosexuality, a developmental modification of the underlying bisexuality of all men and women. Focusing narrowly on the cases that came into their offices, many orthodox Freudians in the 1950s, bent on curing specific homosexuals, nevertheless felt free to pronounce on homosexuality in general. Kinsey in particular came into the cross fire for his attack on psychoanalysis as the source of what Kenneth Lewes in *The Psychoanalytic Theory of Male Homosexuality* calls "unrealistic norms of health and 'naturalness' " (125). Edmund Bergler, one of the most prolific writers on these issues, stated flatly that there are "no happy homosexuals," and few such opinions were changed by Kinsey's statistics. Was it Freud or was it the fifties? In his detailed study of the controversy, Lewes argues that rigidified psychoanalytic theory, in contrast with Freud's own willingness to rethink the issue, along with the effort of many émigré analysts to prove their loyalty to the American consensus, helped foster "a closed, propagandistic set of social norms" among a community that should have been on the side of a more expansive and less judgmental view of human nature. Lewes also says that the male-centered origins of psychoanalysis, with its emphasis on phallic potency and female insufficiency (penis envy), played a role as well. Some defenders of the idea of the "incomplete" homosexual today still maintain an increasingly empty bastion, even though the American Psychiatric Association removed homosexuality from its Diagnostic and Statistical Manual of Psychiatric Disorders (DSM) in 1973, and in 1975 the American Psychological Association did likewise. Hysteria, however, that traditional pseudomedical catchall for anything wrong with women, had been dropped in 1952.

# NO BODY'S PERFECT

> The human body was really a very frail, defenseless organism C-for-Charlie suddenly realized.
>
> —James Jones, *The Thin Red Line* (1962)

Amid the general anxieties about male and female social roles in the 1950s, academic disputes over dry tomes like the Kinsey reports made front-page news in a world more saturated with media than ever before. Of course, a primary social function of popular media is to dispense etiquette in the guise of information. But the codes of behavior celebrated in *Life* or *Cosmopolitan* or *Redbook* sold themselves as an etiquette of not just social success but also of personal nature—a sort of advice whose goals were less controllable than what to wear to the prom or how to behave at the office. Character could be the armature of subversive change as well as official acceptance. For every reader who shuddered at *Life*'s picture of the beatnik pad, another found it mysterious and intriguing.

The title of this chapter—with a little shift in its spelling—invokes the famous last line from that comic epic of gender transformation, Billy Wilder's *Some Like It Hot* (1959) because it so succinctly summarizes the place of the body, particularly the acting body in 1950s culture. By "acting" I mean the body in action as well as the body in performance. In the language of Method acting, especially as developed in the Actors Studio, this is often called the "instrument" or physical-emotional body of the performer. But the Method language and preoccupation with the body extends to other arts as well: the gestural emphasis of action painters (like Jackson Pollack or Helen Frankenthaler); the celebration of bodily and emotional memory that animated so much of the fiction of Jack Kerouac, the incantatory poetry of Allen Ginsberg, and the confessional poetry of Robert Lowell, Theodore Roethke, and Sylvia Plath. This emphasis on patterning a movie, a play, a painting, a novel, or a poem on the energy and agency of the performer's, the artist's, the author's, or the subject's physical presence constitutes a linking metaphor by which we might know some crucial elements of the fifties more clearly.

Even more than in the 1920s and 1930s, the expansion of entertainment in the postwar period situated magazines, television, and movies as the mediators of one's experience of the world and of oneself, especially through their images of masculinity and femininity. The star system of the 1920s and 1930s encouraged both worship and stylistic imitation. But the 1940s and 1950s ushered in a preoccupation with film actors as social symbols, Rorschach tests by which individuals could connect their dreams across the American landscape. This search for emblematic stars, for admiration and for psychic support, became central to postwar culture, and it was hardly confined to the movies.

What were the characteristics of these new models? According to that noted theater critic Holden Caulfield, they were the opposite of what he called "phoneys":

> In the first place, I hate actors. They never act like people. They just think they do. Some of the good ones do, in a slight way, but not in a way that's fun to watch. And if any actor's really good, you can always tell he *knows* he's good, and that spoils it. (119)

Self-congratulation drives Holden crazy, and he sees it everywhere, especially in American performers in the Anglophile tradition, like Alfred Lunt and Lynn Fontanne: "They didn't act like people and they didn't act like actors. It's hard to explain. They acted more like they knew they were celebrities and all. I mean they were good, but they were *too* good" (126). What Holden instinctively dislikes—and the major acting style of the 1950s, the Method, defines itself against—is a performance that apes some buttoned-up, usually English, style of official selfdom, especially when tarted up with noblesse oblige. As he says about Olivier's Hamlet, "He was too much like a goddam general, instead of a sad, screwed-up type guy" (117). Since no body's perfect, it's even worse to pretend to be.

Self-conscious artistry, obvious skill, and a condescending professionalism are the heart of the problem for Holden. Like many of the emotionally tangled characters in fifties films, Holden is not looking for perfect performances but for models of being, especially models of growing up. His disgust with performers and his railing against the movies indicate how much the search for models of social behavior in postwar America focused, as it never had before, on the examples the movies furnished.

Holden is much clearer about what he's against than what he's for. But the most culturally pervasive response to the postwar vacuum of masculinity was the rise of new male stars, whose images often explicitly challenged older forms of masculinity, even while defining a new kind of masculine beauty and assertiveness. Montgomery Clift, for example, in his second film, *The Search* (1948), plays a soldier who adopts a young German war orphan. In his first, *Red River* (also released in 1948), he had played cattleman John Wayne's adopted son, who challenges Wayne's aggressive authoritarian ways with his own more humane and sensitive—but still sharpshooting—brand of leadership. Another new young actor, Marlon Brando, scored a tremendous success on Broadway as Stanley Kowalski, the bare-chested "gaudy seed-bearer" of *A Streetcar Named Desire* (1947), who can still break down and weep from his need for his wife, Stella. Brando then began his Hollywood career playing a war-wounded paraplegic in *The Men* (1950), for which he prepared by living with injured veterans while confined to a wheelchair himself.

The fabled rebelliousness of Clift, Brando, and, later, James Dean—along with that of the characters they played—defined itself against a generation of missing or failed fathers, who were either overpowering or impotent. So many films of the period focused on a young man, wounded physically or psychologically, who has to learn to grow up. He may be a loner, like Dean in *Rebel Without a Cause* (1955), or he may be a member of a gang from which he has to separate, like Brando in *On the Waterfront* (1954). But the catalyst of his maturing is usually a woman. In nineteenth-century adventure fiction, the same pattern was often present, but there was little conflict in those stories between the values of the group and the love of the good woman. In postwar films, however, love for a woman frequently separates the hero from the male group as both an earlier stage of masculine development and a potential homoerotic all-male world.*

Like most of the members of the Beat Generation, and unlike the organization men whose conformity helped define the beat rebellion, the young actors of this period had never been in the war. In friendship they found their own camaraderie and in the family their arena of combat, but most often without any larger public purpose. For a brief period at the end of the war, Hollywood delved into issues of racism, antisemitism, and other social ills, but always in terms of the hostile relationships within the family. There, the object of the personal search for meaning is often a father, literally or figuratively absent, like Old Dean Moriarty in Kerouac's *On the Road*, "the father we never found" (307). It is striking, in fact, how Oedipal conflicts pervade so much narrative drama and fiction of the 1950s. Even young heroines have more problems with fathers than with mothers, like Natalie Wood's Judy in *Rebel Without a Cause* or Esther Greenwood in Sylvia Plath's novel *The Bell Jar* (1963).

The answer is usually to give up the search for an adequate father and become a man, or a woman, on your own. In *On the Road*, the quest for the lost father is only a pretext for Kerouac's unending mission to capture on paper Neal Cassady, the real person on whom Dean Moriarty is based. Through him, Kerouac focuses the desire for a family of choice rather than one dictated by necessity and inheritance. What urges their journey of personal discovery forward is the effort to find the lost father, however disreputable and inadequate, so that he must finally be rejected.

In contrast with Anglo-mimics like the Lunts, whose acting style projected a refined and orderly self that was to be contemplated as a product, these newly celebrated images of character implied that depths of feeling could be found in everyone, not just in the inner life of the sensible classes. More protean in both their class and their sexuality, they helped establish an art based on the armature of the body. It was a text of the antitext, a return to flesh and feeling, the magnification of a vulnerability that denied traditional forms with their more detached commitment to order.

Intensifying this emphasis on emotion, the most characteristic plots of serious American drama in the 1950s therefore focused on the character vulnerable to contradictions and irresolution rather than either the stock types of 1930s social realism or the archetypal figures of romance or agit-

* Much of the Allied propaganda during the war had identified both Nazi and Japanese militarists as a kind of adolescent gang that had to be disciplined by their elders.

prop. These were often characters with unfinished, unresolved business in their pasts. Dramatic structures thus frequently built toward an explosion of the past into the present, in which some unmentionable event or feeling had to be unveiled, a primal scene—the revelation of parental sin, a homosexual act, a betrayal usually associated with illicit sexuality—that required exposure and confession for absolution, a public revelation of the wounds of private feeling.

That much of the personal experience to be mined was inner, psychological, and tinged with traits conducive to alienation and rejection corresponded to the outsider position of many of the artists who created such works—outside by religion, by sexual orientation, by politics, by birth, by class, by language. For them, an emphasis on the self was not ahistorical and quietist. Instead, it took a definite attitude toward history and authority, usually one of contempt and resistance, if not outright rebellion.

In the process of forging that social marginality into a cultural centrality, a layered self was created, whose interleaved areas of conventionality and rebellion have often been reduced or dismissed. Yet there was something more at stake in, say, the plays of Tennessee Williams, the novels of Jack Kerouac, and the poetry of Robert Lowell than a simple Freudian contrast between repression and sublimation or a Marxist contempt for the diversion of political energy into fruitless emotional self-involvement. Instead, it was the interplay, the tension between these seeming opposites, that energized such works and gave them a permeability and an inconclusiveness that characterized Method acting as well.

Reflecting its fascination with the divided character, a characteristic fifties strategy on the level of story was to face up to and contain its contradictions, instead of reconciling and thereby subduing them in the mirror relation of social order and dramatic closure. The implication, for both actor and character, underlined the choice between social assimilation (and subduing one's personal nature) or trying to bring some aspect of inner psychology and past with you, and making explicit and unmistakable the cost of what was left behind. The search in the fifties for the new text and the new character thus proceeded particularly by investigating and invigorating what was difficult, if not impossible, to assimilate: the individual, the inarticulate, the mad.

The result in actual performance was a kind of Jekyll-and-Hyde conception of character, what some Method teachers formulated as the difference between the part in you and the you in the part. In this emphasis on the performer's ability to tap into his or her emotions and past, the

Method also took a position at least implicitly wary of language as a tool of reason and articulation, and more than one critic has remarked on how suspiciously Lee Strasberg and other Actors Studio stalwarts viewed the actual words of a play or script. This suspicion had its roots in Stanislavsky's own mystical side, but was particularly strengthened in the fifties by the interest in the antitheater theories of Artaud, the plays of Alfred Jarry and Eugene Ionesco, and the cultural emphasis on the artist as prophet-guru that enveloped figures as different as Hemingway, Kerouac, and Salinger. Reflecting its ambiguous attitude toward the written text or even language itself, the Method motto, if it could be said to have one, was "acting between the lines."

The public imagery of the fifties repeatedly parodied the Method actor as a raw nerve mumbling and scratching himself. Yet such characters also clearly appealed to an audience as interested in recalling and renovating their emotional lives as were the actors, and equally attracted to family dramas as the context of self-discovery. Rather than the polished social surface of character and situations, the new style of acting dramatized the extraordinariness of ordinary private nature. Like the endless personal and social etiquettes of the mass-market magazines, these more confused and contradictory personalities engaged their audiences through a relation to the American self-help tradition. The raw materials of the old self were to be shaped to make a new one through a process of endless work—much as Strasberg and other acting teachers developed techniques for actors to make their personal experience "usable" by tapping the unconscious for what Strasberg called "affective memory."

In short, practices and people that were considered marginal by normal society became defined as central by a significant proportion of fifties artists in all fields. In literary terms, for example, Hemingway's sense of the honed (and thereby external) professional craft of the writer was to be replaced by the standard of the internal self. Kerouac particularly sought to revive a literature of feeling, affect, melodrama, and even sentimentality to do battle with the lords of literary discipline. He became very upset, for example, when Allen Ginsberg sent him the manuscript of *Howl* because there were words crossed out and emendations made. For Kerouac that was already a compromise. As he noted in a series of aphorisms printed as "Belief and Technique for Modern Prose," "Something that you feel will find its own form." The better way was to write automatically. Like the automatic writing that lay behind Yeats's *A Vision*, Kerouac's also sought to look into the inner workings of personal time: "Like Proust be an old teahead of time" ("Belief," 159–60). The fabled roll of Teletype paper on which he wrote the first draft of *On the Road* is an apt metaphor for the redefinition of both news and novel that he sought. Kerouac's goal was to connect artistic work to real, immediate autobiography and memory, so much so that Ginsberg dubbed him "Memory Babe." Once again, this memory was not ahistorical. But the history sought by Kerouac, Ginsberg, and even Burroughs—along with poets such as Lowell, Plath, and Roethke—was a personal history that would correct and replace the bankrupt history of public events.

In the most noteworthy fifties films, then, as in fifties popular culture generally, there was more pressure than ever before on stars to act out the audience's fantasy life, especially interwoven fantasies of impotence and rebellion. The implicit questions were: Is masculinity exclusively identifiable with individualism? What is growing up? What is gained and what lost in the connection to adult society and traditional forms? In the 1950s the male teenager in both Hollywood films and the popular press became a frequent target of both criticism and praise. But the questions raised were relevant for others as well. At the core of this exploration was an emphasis on the performer—not as a vehicle for words so much as an artist of the self, who used his or her own life and feelings to reinvigorate outmoded forms.

Despite many theories to the contrary, I think we can never quite be sure what is conformist and what is subversive in the artifacts of popular culture, of high culture, or of any cultural level. Because of the central importance to the culture of the 1950s of the conflicts I have been describing, there are quite different heroic messages available in films such as *Viva Zapata*, *On the Waterfront*, *Blackboard Jungle*, and *Rebel Without a Cause:* official messages of assimilation as well as subversive messages of resistance and even rebellion. To young men returning from battle, to young men wondering how to grow up in a Cold War world, postwar American culture explored strategies of dealing with issues of ambition, realism, and the never-ending conflict of individual and communal desires that is rooted in American culture. At the center of that exploration was no longer the indomitable soldier of myth but the often frail masculine body. "No body's perfect" is its mantra because each is different, escaping generalization, never completely a subject, but also not merely an object either.

# WAR WITHOUT A FRONT: VIETNAM AND THE END OF THE COLD WAR

One of the most tenacious problems to overcome in writing a book of this kind, which in a small compass tries to look at the relationship between war and masculinity over almost a millennium, is to try to find some general truths while at the same time avoiding the air of detached omniscience. My point of view is historical, not eternal, and I have tried at least to sketch the many factors that help create historical moments. At various times I have been more personal for a moment when it seemed to be appropriate. But now, as I write these final chapters, I am only a few days from the terrorist destruction of the World Trade Center in New York and the attack on the Pentagon. So I must contemplate as well what has brought us to this moment and what it portends for the future.

Final chapters are always difficult. The urge to look into the past to help understand the present has itself come up to the present, and what has been learned? The threads are there to be pulled together, but unlike books, history goes on. I started this book by downplaying the seemingly invariable facts of male biology and emphasizing instead how the shaping effect of social change and historical context have created a constantly shifting idea of masculinity. I end it in a time of economic globalization that implicitly claims to put an end to tribal rivalries and create a world that is organized by a rational assessment of needs and goals. I began it as a study of large patterns connecting ideas of masculinity with the history of war in the West since the Middle Ages. I approach its end to find many of these issues part of current events. As the war in Kosovo, the continuing conflict in Israel, and the events of September 11, 2001, and after forcefully remind us, rivalries still exist, ancient battles are still invoked to justify present politics, and different ways of being a man are either celebrated or stigmatized across whole cultures. So it seems even more appropriate to rebalance the equation and point not to biological necessities but to mythic patterns of nostalgia for "real" masculinity that remain to be disentangled from sources of identity like the physical body, religion, and nationalism. The rationality of multinational corporations is as fragile an absolute as the facts of the body.

Part of my aim in writing this book has been to explore how certain ideas of what is natural or normal, particularly conceptions of masculinity and manhood, are in fact tremendously plastic and malleable, influenced by a variety of historical factors, some obvious, like war and its panoply, some not so obvious, like political changes in citizenship and cultural changes in attitudes toward human nature, especially sexuality. Enveloping all these ideas is the increasing role of propaganda and the widespread availability of art, information, and hearsay around the world, through newspapers, radio, television, films, and now the Internet. The ability to know (or think we know) what is going on in all its corners is hardly an insignificant factor in a world that is more interconnected in a variety of economic and political ways than ever before.

But for all this "knowledge," whether in ancient societies or our own, stereotyped beliefs about what is masculine or feminine survive long after the original need or reason for them has gone because they purport to be fundamental and unchanging, the bedrock of history rather than an expression of it. Although World War I, for instance, witnessed the disappearance or disintegration of several empires, a continued popular imperialism through films such as *Gunga Din* and *Beau Geste* (both 1939) promoted, like the American western, a nostalgic view of a past when men were men. Much of modern war has been kept alive by racism and romance, nostalgia and the memory of conflicts fed and even half invented by modern authors. The details may change, but the spirit remains. So nineteenth-century tales of empire were recycled to inspire the twentieth century: British soldiers in World War II still read G. A. Henty's nineteenth-century boys' novels written a century before; images of a John Wayne style of heroism permeated the minds of American soldiers in Vietnam just as Homeric heroism filled the thoughts of Henry Fleming in *The Red Badge of Courage*. Nor was the need to instill a personal picture of individual bravado confined to the rank and file. When Douglas MacArthur was supreme commander in occupied Japan, he often spent his evenings watching American westerns; John F. Kennedy would curl up with a James Bond novel, and Richard Nixon repeatedly screened *Patton*, the film biography of one of the most obstreperous and self-aggrandizing American generals of World War II. In this milder ritual of brainwashing, such heroic images allayed any hesitancy about plunging into a firefight and shored up the conviction of righteous violence. Without the imaginative persuasiveness of these images, a technologically advanced style of war might not long endure, and therefore, increasingly in the twentieth century, states and leaders created a propaganda of male honor to inspire individuals to sacrifice their lives for causes.

Which then comes first—war or masculinity? Without the invocation of masculine honor, would any more than a small proportion of the population be willing to fight as soldiers? Would war, aggressive if not defensive, become outmoded as the definition of masculinity expanded, or would it become the occupation solely of professionals? Historians and political scientists have long argued that aggressive war and the so-called Great Power system are independent of each other, and that it is markedly uneven economic and political development that causes war. But that analysis, aside from basing its conclusions on a European historical model, leaves out the question of motivation for war on the individual level of both soldier and citizen. Without that correlation, why not just accept that your nation is now down rather than up, as Sweden and Spain did after the early eighteenth century? Why fight the rhythms of history? Fantasies of honor, belief in political and religious ideologies, and nostalgia for the past all play a crucial role. Wars consume resources, but they also consume men, and they feed especially on the idea that men naturally go to war—an idea that enshrines a masculine heroism that will inspire men to go to future wars.

One characteristic of the period from World War II to the present that the "war against terrorism" or the "jihad against the West" only underlines is how much more obvious the paradoxes of modern masculinity have become, how much sharper the edge between traditional and more contemporary views. Real people have already been killed and no doubt more will be in this latest conflict. But its essence seems often more exclusively symbolic than the wars of the past, built on a series of simple oppositions familiar in European thought since the eighteenth century: female and effeminate versus masculine and virile, mercantile and commercial versus self-sufficient and autarkic, secular and inclusive versus religious and separatist. Along with these conceptual contraries come similarly opposed emblems: the cave versus the skyscraper, the rock versus the rifle, the true believer versus the secular citizen.

But much of what strikes Americans as new and unprecedented has been commonplace in Europe and the rest of the world for some time. Unlike the wars of the past, which for all their propaganda about national honor could be described as efforts to either expand possessions or resist expansion, the most recent attacks seek a different sort of triumph. There is little desire to actually conquer another country except metaphysically, no occupation force, no system of government. In essence, after some five hundred years of wars between political units called nations, a new tribalism has emerged on the world stage that is both dubious about the secular state as a way of organizing peoples and either incapable or unwilling to implement its institutions. Appropriately, the network of bin Laden associates called Al Qaeda allied itself with and sought shelter in Afghanistan, which was run by a group uninterested in forming a state by any European definition. There, under Taliban rule, all the usual state functions of social service assumed and promoted by Mussolini, Hitler, Stalin, and other despots of the twentieth century were ignored or undermined, and the only interest of the government appeared to be enforcing its own version of the Islamic moral code, using their ostentatious hair and beards to maintain a sharp contrast between their own masculinity and the cloistered femininity and hidden flesh of women in their all-engulfing chadors.

Yet however strange this eruption of the tribal and the fundamentalist seemed to be in a supposedly modern world, it did reflect, if distortedly, changes occurring in the European idea of both war and masculinity. After World War II, the coming of the United Nations, the North Atlantic Treaty Organization, the Warsaw Pact, and other international war-making and peacekeeping coalitions, conquest began to decline as a crucial issue for the major European and Asian powers. Although it remained significant in other parts of the world—as the continuing tensions between China and Taiwan, India and Pakistan, the Palestinians and the Israelis, or in the Balkans make clear—in Europe itself, where towns and rivers and forests could echo battles going back through the centuries, the casus belli of land seemed to vanish.

Without the demand for territory, except in the metaphysical sense of wanting to convert the entire world to Islam, there is no front, no direct confrontation with the enemy, no decisive battles as they have been known. Even when there are issues of resources, as in the Persian Gulf War, all the power of the United States could not then persuade its allies that Iraq should be invaded and Saddam Hussein toppled. The objectives remained limited—liberate Kuwait—and the desire for a full-scale conclusion, or unconditional surrender, thwarted.

Napoleon had inaugurated a century or more of military strategists looking for decisive victories. But at the end of the Cold War, the prime characteristic of present and future wars seemed to be their indecisiveness. Since World War II and especially since the collapse of the Soviet Union, this has been the major pattern of warfare—the ambiguous side of a world increasingly interconnected, in which the borders of nations have become more permeable as the need to make common cause increased. Professedly fought on behalf of smaller states, and thereby resembling both World War I (Belgium) and World War II (Poland), the Gulf War mirrored other postatomic wars in having circumscribed goals with little potential for worldwide expansion.

The end of the Cold War for the most part also curtailed wars that were displaced confrontations between the United States and the Soviet Union. Certainly there would still be conflicts that bore the marks of jockeying for position between one and another of the Great Powers. But a conspicuous characteristic of the period from the 1980s onward was the number of wars that were either being fought by industrial powers in their own backyards (like Russia in Afghanistan and Chechnya), undeclared wars with separatist elements (like Spain in the Basque country), civil wars (as in Rwanda), or wars between neighboring countries far from the European cockpit (between Iran and Iraq, or between India and Pakistan). With the notable exception of the artificially unified (under Tito's communism) and then disintegrating Balkans, after the establishment of, first, the European Economic Union in 1957 and then the European Union in 1991, war was effectively banished to the borders of Europe and beyond by a mercantile and secular organization that resembled medieval Catholicism in its Europe-wide reach.

After the devastation of World War II in Europe, the Soviet Union, and Japan, state-sponsored war in the last half century has thus generally remained peripheral to the populations of industrial countries, especially the virtually untouched United States. For the most part, such countries were willing to spend money and send professionals to fight wars, but rarely to draft or conscript the general male population. The citizen in arms had been the standard from the eighteenth-century revolutions until World War II, but even in the Cold War, whatever the U.S. or Soviet propaganda of a final Armageddon, the actuality was smaller wars, often fought by technologically advanced professional armies against primitive, cause-oriented nationalisms. Although these fighters were themselves armed by the technical expertise of the industrial countries, their true coin was their willingness to sacrifice numbers of men to win. Especially since Vietnam, conscript armies no longer seem to be the basic resource of war for the industrialized countries. In both the Gulf War and Kosovo, the United States tried to fight while committing relatively few ground troops—attracting the scorn of Saddam Hussein, who, like Hitler before him, mocked the West as a collection of degenerate societies unwilling to sacrifice the men and face the body count that warrior societies like his own took for granted as the badge of honor. It was a battle style reminiscent of European trench warfare in World War I, but no longer part of European or American strategy. The need for the support of a democratic electorate gradually narrowed the possibilities for directly engaging large numbers of that electorate on the front lines. The propaganda of technological superiority had backfired: if we are so advanced, why can't we win without committing more of "our boys" to the battle—whatever that battle must be.

Most of those battles were in what had come to be called the Third World—a term that began as a metaphoric nod to those countries left outside the bipolar power structure of the Cold War and now connotes technological backwardness and economic hardship. With the policies of John Foster Dulles as secretary of state under Eisenhower and the election of Kennedy as president in 1960, the world had been divided into either Communist or anticommunist, with a still devastated Europe in between. But in fact neither the United States nor the USSR was particularly successful at permanently wooing Third World loyalty despite the all-embracing claims of their political and economic ideologies. The multinational makeup of the United Nations also shifted attention from exclusively European preoccupations to the problems of the rest of the world. As Paul Kennedy remarks, "local circumstances, indigenous cultural strengths, and differing stages of economic development" helped undermine universalist claims (397). The many smaller nations of the UN did not have the power and sway of the five permanent members of the Security Council (China, France, Russia, the United Kingdom, and the United States), but they had numbers and in the General Assembly (51 members originally, now 191) they had a forum for grievances and perspectives that had never before been so widely heard.

Just as the arena of war shifted away from the European mainland to become a feature of developing countries, European political and cultural thought was being forced by the rise of the Third World to confront conceptions of nationalism and masculinity that varied widely from their own traditional norms. Ideas of nationhood founded on either dynastic continuity or racial exclusivity (or both) had to be reconciled with events like the Nisei fighting for the United States and the different races, so scorned by the Nazis, fighting for France. So, too, there arose a powerful postwar assertion of a nonwhite, non-European perspective in books like Frantz Fanon's *Peau noire, masques blancs* (*Black Skin, White Masks,* 1952) and *Les damnés de la terre* (*The Wretched of the Earth,* 1961), which gave a general theoretical framework to many of the new national movements in Africa and Asia that were provoking growing conflicts between their European and their non-European populations. Fanon especially focused on the social context of neurosis, psychologizing the colonial relationship of white empire and subjects of color.

Characteristic of the half century and more between the end of World War II and the terrorist bombing of the World Trade Center and the Pentagon are thus often seemingly contradictory urges in both politics and culture. On the one hand, the founding of the United Nations stressed an idea of world citizenship that was meant to allay, if not extinguish, the competition between nations. On the other, Wilsonian ideas of self-determination urged forward a whole array of African and Asian wars bent on establishing national sovereignty in the wake of imperial, if not yet colonial, collapse. As a somewhat belated fruit of the global context for war, a more all-embracing definition of human nature was also struggling to be born. In the United States, *Family of Man,* the 1956 Museum of Modern Art photography show, emphasized the commonalities between all people in thematic areas focusing on birth, courtship, marriage, and death. But to other writers, critics, and politicians, an ideal of tolerance that did not respect difference as well as similarity was merely another effort to expunge minority culture.*

* In another gesture in this direction, an antigenocide convention was passed by the United Nations in 1948, although never signed by the United States.

The United States was the only major power to emerge from World War II without widespread devastation to its infrastructure and economy. The plans of Hitler and the Japanese militarists for world domination were in ruins, and, as in World War I, the empires of the victors had eroded as well. Yet, although the British Empire gave way to the self-governing nations of the commonwealth, and the hold of France in North Africa and Southeast Asia loosened considerably, both countries after World War II tried to keep up the facade of a European Great Power by bluster and assertion, as well as overextended expenditures and commitments, to make up for the loss of worldwide mastery. Accordingly, the great hero of British popular fiction was Ian Fleming's James Bond, the civil servant with "a license to kill," who handily defeats the megalomaniacs and sexual deviants out to rule the world while maintaining his British stiff upper lip and dry wit.

A somewhat different but allied response to the feared loss of national power in a world dominated by the United States and Russia came from Charles de Gaulle, the wartime leader of the Free French who returned from private life to become president of France in 1958. Hitler had fought his war for a purified definition of the German race and the German nation. But de Gaulle capitalized on the French (or at least Parisian) reputation for hospitality to a variety of the world's races in order to attempt to position France as the leader of the Third World. As the leader of the Free French, de Gaulle could make plausible his effort to reject the overhanging shadow of the collaborationist Vichy government and reestablish France not as the nation that had been defeated by the Nazis and that had promulgated its own antisemitic laws and concentration camps, but as a group of resistance fighters who had saved *la patrie* from the enemy. The rhetoric of grandeur and *gloire* (a favorite word of both de Gaulle and Louis XIV) became an essential part of his diplomatic effort to stand outside and above the U.S.-USSR conflict that shaped the Cold War, a key element in his campaign being the effort to bring France into the nuclear club and dispute American hegemony in the West with its *force de frappe*.

After briefly leading a provisional government in 1946, de Gaulle had kept himself aloof from party politics, in somewhat the way of Eisenhower, the leader of the European invasion, who was courted by both political parties until he finally accepted the Republicans and became president of the United States from 1952 to 1960. Both represent a postwar impulse to see the ideal soldier-leader as a figure untainted by political infighting, but with some larger sense of the nation. Intriguingly also, neither was seen in the mold of the ostentatious military man given to theatrical gestures: de Gaulle preferred a grand detachment, Ike a folksy straightforwardness. Next to the eccentric British commander Bernard Montgomery and the irascible American George S. Patton, Eisenhower seemed to be the soul of measure and judiciousness, while de Gaulle, despite his famous prickliness, never had the self-aggrandizing flair of either Napoleon or General Boulanger (who had almost succeeded in a coup against the government at the time of the Dreyfus case).

For those who had lost or were losing empires and those who aspired to at least imperial status, the whole question seemed to be found in styles of national self-assertion that involved military sway. The effort of the French, for example, to maintain a hold on Vietnam ended in the defeat at Dien Bien Phu in 1954. But the generals there seemed not to have learned the lesson, especially Raoul Salan, who was part of the military coup in Algeria in 1958 that helped bring de Gaulle back to power as president of the Fifth Republic, and a few years later, after de Gaulle moved toward accepting Algerian self-determination, supported the secret army terrorist organization (OAS) that plotted to invade France itself in 1961.

With the old soldier de Gaulle as head of state overseeing the arrest and trial of the officers involved in the plot, any assumed or automatic relation between the French army and the good of the nation received as shattering a blow as had been dealt by the Dreyfus case. By contrast, the citizen vs. soldier showdown in American politics had occurred a few years before, when President Truman fired General MacArthur for insubordination during the Korean War. Already under Truman, the War Department, which had existed since the first days of the United States, had in 1947 become the Department of the Army. Along with the Department of the Navy and the new Department of the Air Force, it had been reshaped into the Department of Defense, which thenceforth held the only cabinet seat. Perhaps such a change in nomenclature is a thin reed on which to rest a large change in the American attitude toward making war. But the fact remains that now there was only one cabinet secretary speaking specifically for the armed forces. Under President Kennedy, that voice belonged to Robert McNamara, who brought to Vietnam the managerial techniques that had worked so well at Ford and that themselves had been influenced by the organizational strategies that won World War II. Statistics sprung up everywhere, along with action memos studded with bullet points. As Stanley Karnow remarks, "No conflict in history was studied in such detail as it was being waged" (271).

One intriguing effect of the new bureaucratizing of army strategy and logistics, foreshadowed by MacArthur's firing, was the end of a long tradition of showboat generals. Not that the showboat spirit was gone, just that the army no longer tolerated it as much. Civilian politicians were another matter. As William Manchester points out, Kennedy was a great admirer of MacArthur: "He was Kennedy's kind of hero: valiant, a patrician, proud of his machismo, and a lover of glory" (696). Perhaps it is no wonder then that in his memoir of the early years of the Vietnam War, *A Rumor of War*, Philip Caputo indicts equally both the glory-hunting cowboy politics of Kennedy and the briefcase-general abstraction of William Westmoreland, who in a war with few pitched battles determined victory primarily by counting bodies—like the toting of scalps or the piles of heads collected in primitive warfare.

Kennedy's own role in the furthering or slowing down of the Vietnam War has been much debated. But his efforts, like those of Lyndon Johnson after him, not to be "soft" (the metaphor is again fitting) on communism or hesitant about matters of war wind rhetorically through his foreign policy. In the face of name-calling about unmanliness and cowardice, the underlying urge was to make sure the United States did not lose a war. As Richard Russell, a senator from Georgia who had previously been dubious, said after the Tonkin Gulf incident, "Our national honor is at stake. We cannot and we will not shrink from defending it" (Karnow, 391). The effort to maintain national masculine honor by military assertion in the face of a world becoming increasingly more varied indelibly marked the Cold War world. Much sarcasm was spent on mocking the Asian preoccupation with not losing face, but the Western powers had their own version. More troops would continue to be sent to Vietnam in an effort not to lose face in a war that had no front. Without direct confrontation, where was the honor?

The Vietnam War, for both the French and the Americans, diverged fundamentally from the basic European model of battle, as well as from the nineteenth-century confrontations between natives and the forces of colonial power. The Battle of Dien Bien Phu in 1954 did resemble a traditional Napoleonic decisive confrontation: the forces of General Giap defeated the French and the French withdrew. But combat in Vietnam was rarely so directly confrontational. The American army had a taste of this kind of war before in the jungles of the Philippines, but MacArthur's island-hopping strategy and the grand naval confrontations of the Pacific war maintained the assumed equation between military power and military success. Korea and its 38th parallel also seemed to promise a familiar clarity in war aims, on the level of geography if not of policy. So long as the Cold War was hot, the contrast between East and West, communism and capitalism, seemed clear.

But in Vietnam the American army, American politicians, and the American public were introduced to war without rows of armed men facing one another to contest occupied ground, without a visible front line marked easily on a map, and with little tangible way to decide what winning meant. The American and European prejudice, fostered by studying nineteenth-century war, along with the theories of Clausewitz and others, was for decisive battle and unconditional surrender—historical precedents that World War II seemed to confirm. But the war in Vietnam, like most wars with a strong guerrilla component, was a war of attrition, ill-suited to generate news that would satisfy a public at home that was being told that the nation's honor was at stake.*

Although the North Vietnamese and their southern guerrillas, the Vietcong, were fighting to unify the country, the difference between the territory they held and that held by the American army was constantly shifting, a patchwork of villages and trails and jungle. For the Americans, the enemy could be anywhere, a characteristic of guerrilla warfare since the eighteenth century, when native soldiers fought against an occupying army. It was what the French had faced earlier in Vietnam and in Algeria as well, what the British faced in Palestine and Ireland, what the Israelis face in Israel.

For the soldier in Vietnam, fighting a war without a front meant being in constant jeopardy. Tours of duty were shorter in Vietnam, little more than a year before one was rotated back to the States. But being in harm's way was much more constant. Fighting for the South Vietnamese and against the North Vietnamese and the Vietcong meant not being able to quite bring into play the simple racial distinctions of World War II in the Pacific. In fact, like the cavalryman at the Little Big Horn who wrote of the dead Indian defending his home and family, the typical American soldier in Vietnam respected the Vietcong shooting at him, but had contempt for the soldiers of the Republic of Vietnam nominally fighting by his side. Racially, the enemy and the friend looked the same, and guerrilla warfare in the south, which even penetrated the supposedly safe areas of the rear echelons and cities, made no place completely secure. Placid villages could be just what they seemed or hide deadly enemies. And when fear took over, as it did so often, the deadly racial equation took its toll: any dead Vietnamese became ipso facto a dead enemy.

* The lack of a front line and clear distinctions between friend and enemy in Vietnam is also reflected in the number of friendly-fire incidents and the widespread "fragging," or shooting of officers by their own men.

Although more bombs were dropped on North Vietnam than in all of World War II, despite strategic hamlets, pacification, Vietnamization, and other efforts to win the hearts and minds of the Vietnamese, the enemy remained elusive. Gliding through the jungles of his homeland, he was difficult to tag metaphorically as well. Who could represent him? Not "Uncle" Ho Chi Minh, who looked more like the harmless Asian elders attacked by the Japanese in World War II newsreels than a redoubtable enemy, and who to boot had prominently said in 1945 that he was basing his plea for the independence of Vietnam from France directly on the American Declaration of Independence. Meanwhile, our allies, like Prime Minister Ngo Dinh Diem, resembled caricatures of fat-cat politicians; his sister-in-law, the relentless Madame Nhu, was the Dragon Lady familiar from Milton Caniff's comic strip *Terry and the Pirates;* and the South Vietnamese Air Force commander and later premier, Nguyen Cao Ky, admiringly associated himself with Hitler.

As in Korea, there was little national mobilization of a persuasive visual imagery for Vietnam. In fact, visual propaganda was more often in the hands of the antiwar movement than the government. The kinds of doubts that had surfaced in the national agitation over brainwashing became intensified as the war dragged on with little news that could give any promise of a quick resolution. The United States had been unsympathetic to French designs on Vietnam (with Eisenhower refusing aid at Dien Bien Phu). So why were we so engaged now? The government line was the Cold War assumption that world communism was a monolith and the Cold War assurance that we were preventing its victory in Asia, which would otherwise fall like a succession of dominoes. But instead of unambiguously boosting the national sense of honor, Vietnam had the effect on America of stimulating widespread questioning of the American role in the postwar world, as well as disillusion with our foreign policy in general. Appropriately enough, along with that questioning came a parallel alienation from much of the received notion of American masculinity.

# MAKE LOVE, NOT WAR: THEORIES OF INNATE AGGRESSION AND THE ANTIWAR MOVEMENT

Girls say yes to boys who say no.

—Vietnam draft resistance slogan

In retrospect, the American involvement in Vietnam carried with it something of the uncertain macho residue of the 1950s: the triumphant emergence from World War II intermingled with the seesaw progress of the Cold War, the boom economy coupled with the paranoia about the Soviet possession of atomic weapons. As a result, manpower and high technology were thrown into the battle before anything like a national consensus was achieved, and the result was a full-fledged antiwar movement that escaped its former habitats in the radical left and the isolationist right to permeate a good portion of the fabled middle of the road.

Born to challenge a foreign policy that seemed based on a heedless invocation of national honor, the civilian movement against the Vietnam War in the United States strikingly combined political protest against the war with a protest against the style and substance of traditional norms of masculinity. At the same time, the time-honored control of American politics by an East Coast elite was being eroded on the local and national level by the rise of ethnic and racial political issues that went beyond the pork barrel needs of the past.

In the 1960s and 1970s, then, the changing face of American society ran head-on into the warrior fantasy of a monolithic "American" point of view. The American army in Vietnam was itself perhaps the most ethnically and racially diverse in American history, as well as largely blue collar in origin, in contrast with the more middle-class army of World War II. Almost nine million served, less than four and a half million in the army, with deaths in battle of 31,000 (about 47,000 for all branches of service). But the draft ended in 1973, and in later engagements the United States has moved toward an exclusively professional armed forces. The disillusionment with the knee-jerk warrior culture that seemed responsible for the foreign policy decisions that led us into Vietnam may not have totally reorganized our priorities in relation to the rest of the world, but it made an indelible impact on the role of the military. When asked twenty years later what the army had learned from Vietnam, General Norman Schwarzkopf, who commanded the troops in the Gulf War, said in effect that the armed forces should never fight a war without making sure they had support back home.

By the same token, in this new world of limited wars with hopefully specific goals, Vietnam may have witnessed the last literary war as well, because in order to inspire widely accessible fiction or poetry, wars must be fought by men and women who are not professional soldiers. Certainly there will be memoirs and perhaps the occasional work of fiction, but compared to World Wars I and II, there will be little literature. The experience of war, which was central to the writing of the twentieth century, has receded to a smaller place in the spectrum of human experience, as has the kindred idea, powerful in Western culture since the *Iliad* and the *Aeneid*, that, once the resources of art focus on war, something essential will be learned about human nature.

The combat deaths in Vietnam represented less than a sixth of the deaths in World War II, but with news of the war pouring daily into American homes, and the antiwar movement itself fostering alternate sources of information along with an alternate view of the war, they resonated even more than Ernie Pyle's hometown stories of soldiers in a war the country generally supported. This disillusionment with the terminology of national honor as well as with national styles of masculinity was similar in its way to the disillusionment that pervaded literature and art after World War I. The difference, of course, was that in the Vietnam era, because of enhanced communication, it occurred during the war itself. Perhaps the last literary war, Vietnam was also the first full-scale media war, saturating the home-front audience through radio, television, and movies. Not only could civilians at home see footage of what had happened recently, or events like the self-immolation of Buddhist monks protesting the war, but also soldiers in the field could tune in to popular culture back home, with its frequent antiwar bent, especially in popular songs.

Much of the antiwar movement, like the draft resistance, took its language of protest from the resistance movements of World War II and the "national liberation" movements of the postwar period. Part of its politics was an identification with peoples fighting to be free of colonial oppression, thereby creating a sympathy with the North Vietnamese as well as the guerrillas in the south. At the same time, the protesters upended the Cold War connection between perversion and subversion, and the 1950s television model of the happy suburban family was mocked as a distortion of real American values. An emblematic event in this way was the appearance of Jerry Rubin in a Revolutionary War soldier's uniform, along with the frank testimony of Dagmar Wilson of the Women Strike for Peace, at a hearing of the House Un-American Activities Committee in August 1966. Throughout the 1950s, HUAC, along with the Senate Internal Security Committee, once chaired by McCarthy, had been the source of heated denunciation and praise for its efforts to define "true Americanism" against the Cold War enemy. Not alone but certainly with a uniquely high degree of publicity, it had monitored, cited for contempt, and destroyed the careers of numerous Communists, ex-Communists, suspected Communists, and fellow travelers, all in the name of a one-sided definition of patriotism and national honor. Both the serious antiwar movement, represented by Wilson, and Rubin's mockery undermined the committee's (and the government's) claim to an exclusive lock on the definition of Americanism. As Martin Luther King, Jr., was to argue, the way to save national honor was by stopping the war, not continuing it.*

King's paradox reflects the prevalent turnabout in the late 1960s and early 1970s of traditional wisdom about both war and sexuality. I have referred to what was happening in the United States because it was the

* The HUAC interrogators had previously been able to stigmatize left and liberal groups by pointing out that they would accept Communists but not Nazis as members. Wilson said she would accept anyone who was against the Vietnam War. It was this all-inclusive aspect of the antiwar movement that helped undermine the old divisions of left and right on which HUAC and other subversion-hunters depended.

United States that was fighting the Vietnam War. But youth movements in Europe, like the protests in France against the Algerian war, were also challenging sexual and political conventions in forms that were to emerge more fully in the feminist movements of the 1960s and 1970s and the gay liberation movements that followed in their wake. Long hair and beards, previously the inheritance of the hirsute soldier, became the emblem of the antiwar movement, in contrast with the military crew cut. Freaks resembling the berserkers waded into combat, but this time they were crusading against the idea of battle instead of revitalizing it. In one slogan of the time, the personal was identified with the political rather than opposed to it, and freedom was an individual as well as a national issue. In such an atmosphere of revision, oppression was considered to have many forms, as in the 1977 San Francisco Gay Pride parade that juxtaposed images of Hitler, a Ku Klux Klan cross burning, the Ugandan dictator Idi Amin, and the antihomosexual activist Anita Bryant.

For all the male and female stereotypes that were perpetuated even in the counterculture, the antiwar side of its politics made a crucial distinction: without war, the absolute difference between male and female may collapse of its own weight, deprived of a crucial support. Instead of the time-honored "men are Y and women X" formulas, the sexually freer world of World War II, along with Kinsey's books on sexual behavior, had helped bring the private world of sexuality into public discussion, sometimes to be censured or deplored, but more often as part of a quest for knowledge: What was sexuality beyond the monoliths of male and female? What were sexual norms—if there were any? It is striking that even in the supposedly repressive American 1950s, while political dissent was often policed, there was a growing openness in sexual reference in both popular and high culture, from the willingness of studios to release films without the Production Code seal of approval (like Otto Preminger's *The Moon Is Blue*, 1953) to the greater availability of previously censored texts like D. H. Lawrence's *Lady Chatterley's Lover*, James Joyce's *Ulysses*, and Vladimir Nabokov's *Lolita*. Similarly, in postwar Japan one of the biggest best-sellers was Theodore Van de Velde's 1926 how-to book *Ideal Marriage*, for the first time translated without censorship.*

* The Supreme Court in 1952 had declared movies protected speech under the Constitution. In 1966, three Supreme Court justices reversed a lower court's decision against the printing of John Cleland's eighteenth-century novel *Fanny Hill* and defined pornography as any work "utterly without redeeming social value." This was the cue for the revamping of the Production Code and the institution in 1968 of a rating system.

Even before the image of men and masculinity began to change due to the antiwar movement, the received wisdom about the nature of women had been challenged even more deeply. In France, where women had finally gotten the vote in the aftermath of World War II, Simone de Beauvoir published *The Second Sex* in 1949, a full-scale attack on the "innate" theories of women's nature that animated books like Lundberg and Farnham's *Modern Woman: The Lost Sex,* with its message that women must return to the home and hearth from which they had so disastrously strayed. Instead, de Beauvoir, like a latter-day Christine de Pizan, argued that the idea of woman was constructed by the circumstances of different historical periods as well as by perceived physical differences in strength: "We must view the facts of biology in the light of an ontological, economic, social, and psychological context" (33). In the United States, a similar emphasis on the effects of social pressure on female identity appeared in Betty Friedan's *The Feminine Mystique* (1963), and both her work and de Beauvoir's become founding texts of a revived feminist movement.

Not only were the relative social, economic, and political positions of men and women being opened up for discussion, but so was the sufficiency or gender bias of their bodies. Kinsey had focused almost exclusively on the orgasm as the indicator of sexual preference, and, reflecting Kinsey's own hostility to psychological categories as being overly based upon conservative social mores, feminists attacked the gender bias of Freud's postulation of the vaginal orgasm as the ultimate in female pleasure and extolled the clitoral orgasm instead. No longer would orgasm be the virtually exclusive property of men. At the same time, postwar research into endocrinology had led to the development of a contraceptive pill that could be taken by women. With this scientific innovation, some control of the results of sexual behavior passed into women's hands, engendering a greater degree of sexual equality between men and women: the fear of unwanted pregnancy could be removed, and the erotic side of sexuality distinguished decisively from the procreative. Like Rochester's courtiers watching women embrace Signior Dildo, nervous men of the period feared that they would no longer be needed; once there was sexual autonomy for women, what would their role be?

But so many of the sexual manuals of the 1950s and 1960s stressed a virtual cult of orgasm as the prime indicator of sexual success that, even as men and women were beginning to become more equal in the bedroom and in the marketplace, the emphasis was on a goal-oriented sexuality that itself seemed stereotypically male. If cultures might be sorted out in accordance with how they value different aspects of sexual intercourse, we might distinguish, in addition to this orgasm culture, perhaps four others: a flirtation/foreplay/courtship culture in which what happens later is only a consummatory afterthought and may not be necessary at all; a penetration/penetrated culture that values the intersection of bodies more than anything that leads up to or away from it; a *karezza* or *coitus reservatus* culture that stresses not penetration or being penetrated so much as the sexual play possible after that step; and a postcoital culture in which aftermath is all. This perhaps whimsical but also plausible taxonomy gives some grounding to the images of a masculinity out to prove itself that suffuse so many American foreign policy pronouncements into the 1970s; the orgasm culture of the postwar years leading up to Vietnam oddly resembles the newfound urge of the United States to use its power in parts of the world that had previously never awakened its interest.

De Beauvoir's assertion that women are made, not born, marks the beginning of a concerted movement to undermine the centuries-old effort to cast women in the role of the natural being, while men were considered social. Of course, as I have noted along the way, there were moments in European history when the reverse assumption was in effect, and women, usually the upper-class women of the court, represented the social world, while men, like the libertines of Rochester or the noble savages of Rousseau, were closer to nature. For the most part, however, the trend had been in the opposite direction. But a crucial tenet of the feminist movement of the postwar period was to reject any biological determinism of the role of women. How odd, or appropriate, then, that at the same time others were arguing the instinctually violent nature of man. As the concept of women and femininity began to be understood as more of a variable historical phenomenon than an innate biological one, men were cast as the "natural" sex, usually to their discredit.*

Part of the prelude to these changes in sexual and political attitudes—accompanied into being by opposition to the Vietnam War and a general distaste for the inequities of American culture—was therefore a growing fascination, which continues to this day, with explanations of male behavior that relied on supposedly innate characteristics going back to either biological imperatives or the hypothetical behavior of cavemen. The fascination is understandable. Faced with a world in which it seemed

* Echoing feminists such as Charlotte Perkins Gilman before World War I, the feminism of the 1960s and 1970s often invoked a monolithic patriarchy, which manipulated both men and women, to define itself against.

that some of civilization's highest technological achievements were on the verge of destroying the human race that had created them, the retreat to essences—"That's the way men/human beings are and have always been"—had a certain degree of explanatory comfort about it.

Both fascism and communism had considered the essence of life to be struggle, and the new theories of innate aggressiveness inadvertently bought directly into those metaphors of the basic primitiveness of male motivation underneath the civilized facade. One of the most influential of these writers was Konrad Lorenz, whose *On Aggression* (1963) became a best-seller in Europe and America in the 1960s. Lorenz's book was translated into English in 1966, the same year that the playwright Robert Ardrey published *African Genesis,* which he subtitled "A Personal Investigation into the Animal Origins and Nature of Man"—a more popular version of the ideas of Lorenz and others. Although Lorenz writes under the shadow of World War II and the atomic bomb makes several guest appearances, Ardrey's book makes much more explicit connections between the behavior of animals, birds, and primitive humans on the one hand and the arms race, the Cold War, and the Hungarian Revolution of 1956 on the other.

Lorenz, who was to receive the Nobel Prize for Physiology or Medicine in 1973, had studied at Munich in the 1930s and taught in Austria and Germany. His work with birds in particular helped modernize the effort to find the evolutionary roots of behavior through comparative studies. Reframing his own empirical studies in the light of Freud's post–World War I postulation of a death wish, Lorenz in *On Aggression* assumed a universal aggressive instinct that "in natural conditions . . . helps as much as any other to ensure the survival of the individual and the species" (x–xi).

Thus, for Lorenz aggression was an essence that underlies all human and animal nature, from a punch in the nose to an atomic bomb, from irritation at someone you don't like to wars for territory and resources. Like all instincts, Lorenz argued, aggression is spontaneous and arises periodically even in the absence of explicit aggression from another being. As a biologist, he was well aware of how complicated was "the working structure of the instinctive and culturally acquired patterns of behavior which make up the social life of man," but his interest was in finding the "few causal connections" in those patterns. Those connections were, he argued, deeply rooted in basic human and animal nature—"hardwired" as we would say now.

Until the biochemical basis of gender differentiation was discovered, behavior and gender were equivalent. If men or women didn't behave according to norms, customs, and social expectations, then they were deficient and could be considered sick or criminal or even inhuman. Kinsey therefore extensively used animal analogies to provide a natural context for human sexual behavior. He linked animal and human sexuality in order both to detach the sexual body from tribal and religious prohibitions and to support his argument against a socially repressive concept of sexual abnormality, i.e., that diverse forms of sexual behavior were not the result of civilized corruption but recognizable variations in nature. Lorenz, by contrast, rooted the natural in the instinctual, and verged on making the instinctual the necessary; i.e., it is difficult if not impossible to act differently.*

At the end of his book, after an elaborate study of parallels between different forms of animal behaviors, Lorenz proposes some ways of getting out of what might seem to be the fatal bind of humans trying to live in peace with instincts created for war. For both Lorenz and Ardrey, the basic image of instinct in general and aggression in particular is hydraulic: if you don't give the inner pressure some outlet, the whole system will explode. Lorenz thus rejects any effort to remove all aggressive stimuli, or to morally condemn aggression, or to breed aggression out of human nature by eugenic methods. Taking any of these measures "would be about as judicious as trying to counteract the increasing pressure in a continuously heated boiler by screwing down the safety valve more tightly" (277). Instead, Lorenz recommends a cathartic method, redirecting aggression toward some other object, and he gives as examples ritualized behaviors such as sports and especially the Olympic Games, the beneficial effects of friendship, the commitment to causes that benefit all humankind, the cultivation of the arts, and the ability of humor to let us stand back and laugh at ourselves, thus undermining the self-deceptions of pride.

Drawing heavily upon the work of Lorenz and other ethologists, Ardrey particularly emphasized the primordial history of the human race, especially the role of hunting and the aggressive need to enlarge one's territory, what he called "the consequences of our total animal legacy." His style is more melodramatic than Lorenz's and he presses the

* With both Kinsey's and Lorenz's emphasis on the continuities between the human and the animal, we have come 180 degrees from the exertions of the ancient Greeks to contrast their civilization with both the animal and feminine, as well as early Christianity's effort to distinguish the human, male as well as female, from the animal.

human analogies almost to absurdity. Here, for example, he retells a scene of dominance from one of Lorenz's observations, in which a newly arrived top bird has to choose a mate from the female "leftovers":

> A female [jackdaw], we recall, takes the rank of her male. All in a happy hour the scrubby little female had become the President's wife. All in a happy hour the unwanted spinster from the wrong end of the pecking order had taken her place at the head. The glass slipper fitted; the pumpkin coach arrived. (93)

Lorenz's formulas for the diversion of aggression can hardly be criticized, but his book forcefully underlines the tremendous uphill battle we have to fight against what he defined as our aggressive instincts. Ardrey, in his more explicit and histrionic way, called his last chapter "The Children of Cain." In general, his outlook for the human future is gloomier: "We were born of risen apes, not fallen angels, and the apes were armed killers" (348). The only hope, if hope there is, lies in our awareness of this basic animal nature.

In the twentieth century, major wars generally correlated with efforts to understand what were assumed to be the roots of male aggression. Whereas nineteenth-century social Darwinists considered aggression to be a natural masculine trait that should be enhanced to combat an effete civilization, the discovery of testosterone in the 1920s encouraged a focus on men and male aggression as the problem. Whether the ultimate goal was to encourage or condemn aggression, both nineteenth- and twentieth-century efforts to find its source exhibited a parallel search for a simple-switch causality. For hard-liners like Ardrey, innateness led to inevitability: saying that aggression was an essential part of human, i.e., male, nature implied that little could be done about the basic urge. For meliorists like Lorenz, new understanding might accomplish something: find the switch, turn it in another direction, and war will cease.*

I have discussed the role of biological and ethnological explanation elsewhere in this book and there's no need now to argue again with those who believe that the needs of primitive tribes, basic instincts, and/or

* At almost the same time, new research in neurobiology seemed to give further ammunition to the hard-liners, like the discovery in the 1960s that certain men with lowered intelligence and high aggressiveness had an extra Y chromosome. But, although this idea had enough anecdotal circulation to inspire the movie *Alien 3* (1992) almost thirty years later, its applicability to a general masculine population had been long since debunked by neurobiologists and anthropologists alike.

brain chemistry fully determine all that occurs in contemporary life. My point here instead is that ideas about an innate aggressive instinct—like all ideas—bear the distinctive imprint of their own time, here the rise of fascism and World War II. We are also entitled to be suspicious of newer efforts to explain all human behavior by recourse to basic biology and neurology because so many arguments in the past two hundred and more years have been dressed up with supposedly hard biological facts—that criminals had peculiarly shaped ears, that Jews were effeminate, that Africans had lesser intelligence and were therefore born to be slaves, that masturbation caused insanity. For a thousand years and more, it was believed that women were ruled by passion while men strived for reason. The nineteenth century turned that around into the male's lust and the female's moral conscience, which was uninterested in sex. Now biochemical determinism, theories of innate aggression, and ritual invocations of testosterone lead comedians and commentators to assume that men are ruled more by their bodies than are women, and so the wheel turns.

As most scientists now agree, the biological is a potential shaper of personal nature, not a compulsion, and neurobiologists have shown that testosterone can decrease aggression as well as increase it. Perhaps at some time in the distant past, human instinct and action were as closely related as those of the jackdaw, but that relation has changed so much over the course of millennia that the appeal to instinctual simplicity is almost meaningless. The basic fallacy is the assumption that biological or neurological knowledge will simplify our understanding of the causes of behavior, reducing complex phenomena to a handful of chemicals. But as research into DNA and the genetic code has shown, the more we get down to the essential details in sequencing, the more complex causal relations become, not less. The crucial interpretive problem, therefore, is that even if Lorenz's postulation of an aggressive instinct were true, how do the biological facts relate to the actions of an individual in different circumstances, and how then do those individual actions translate into social and cultural kinds of aggression? Too often, the invocation of a biological causality results in a kind of genetic fallacy that shows the distant origins but spends little time on how those origins have been modified in the course of centuries. Theories of innate aggressive instincts and hunter-gatherer forefathers rarely help us know more about either the past or the present. They are of little use in comprehending the difference between World War II in Europe and World War II in the Pacific, or why brainwashing became a national concern in the Korean War, or the antiwar response to Vietnam, or the rise of feminism. Lorenz talks about purging the spontaneous eruptions of the aggressive instinct by, in his example, pummeling a boxing bag. But what is the equivalent action for a nation? What should its cathartic displacement be?

As we have seen so often in history, war is a complex institution, characterized by planning and organization, and depending on a whole variety of social, economic, and psychological factors. It is as often fought for abstract ideas and symbols as it is for tangible gain, and especially in modern war those abstractions are particularly important for inspiring soldiers to battle. This is the prime function of propaganda, which awakens personal concepts of honor and attempts to tie them to the larger structures of nation and ideology. But as nations become more ethnically varied, the causal line from biology to instinct to individual behavior to social action to global concerns becomes more and more complex, if it can be said to exist at all. Like racialist theories of blood nationalism that aim to maintain the cohesion of the in-group through hostility to the out-group, theories of innate human nature seem doomed to vanish in a more pluralistic world. Like Hitler's assumption that an ethnically pure Germany would easily defeat the "mongrel" United States and its immigrant armies, they presume to explain everything by a few basic principles, and end up explaining not very much at all.

# PARTING WORDS: TERRORISM AS A GENDER WAR

As a history comes closer and closer to the present, the broad outlines of many trends become more confused and various. The events of September 11, 2001, and the subsequent war in Afghanistan against the Taliban and Al Qaeda thus cast an intriguing light on many of the issues considered in these pages.

One central issue has been the many threats to the legitimacy of the nation-state, especially as it was defined in Europe over the last few hundred years to be the unquestioned summum bonum of human political organization. The United Nations and whatever submission of national sovereignty to the world good it implies is one kind of threat; religiously based terrorism and its hostility to secular societies is another. Since its birth in the sixteenth century, the European nation-state had stepped into the gap between individual male values and their military embodiment by taking to itself the awarding of honor and the waging of war. But by the end of the twentieth century the state was losing that function, or at least its mythic connections, especially in the industrialized world. Nations might have armies, but armies were often no longer the sole or even primary repository of "real men."

Yet even with global economic, cultural, and political connections increasing, the state persists as a prime form of human organization. Globalism has modified, and will continue to modify, some of its structures but will hardly usher it out of existence. Despite the claims of British critics who say that joining the European Union and adopting the euro will destroy "England," the likelihood is strong that connection to Europe will emphasize the specifics of British culture and history even more strongly. When the interstate highway system was begun in the United States in the 1950s, critics said that it would destroy local culture, but in many cases, it led highways around towns and allowed them a chance to foster their own traditions. The future of human organization thus seems to be a balance between a core local existence and shifting boundaries. Oppression, along with racial and ethnic hatreds, will not disappear, but, looking back over the centuries, some signs of improvement are apparent. The sway of the centralized culture typical of the modern state is still being challenged by separatist groups like the Basques and the Occitanians, while in areas like the former Yugoslavia, negotiations for multiethnic governing coalitions continue. But the racist ideas that so dominated European political discourse in the nineteenth and early twentieth centuries have lost their general appeal and been pushed into the program of particular parties, like those of Le Pen in France and Haider in Austria.

Within Europe, then, major wars may be hard to come by in the future, unless there is a generally perceived common enemy. Terrorism thus appears (or reappears) at an appropriate moment in the history of both politics and masculinity. Modern terrorism first came onto the world stage as the political aggression of the disenfranchised, either in the name of alternate nationalisms (as in Algeria, Northern Ireland, and Israel), or in the attacks against world capitalism made by radical groups in Europe and Japan in the 1960s and 1970s. It was preeminently a politics of individuals and small groups, and as it developed, it came to represent the dark side of global interconnections, relying for its capital on a system of worldwide finance that also protected the finances of multinational corporations from scrutiny, taking advantage of an increasing permeability of national borders to immigrants, and exploiting the mobility available to individuals in a democratizing world.

Like the guerrilla warfare of the past, which usually focused on attacks by natives against the foreign occupiers of their country, early terrorism was the weapon of small cultures fighting for autonomy and, above all, for publicity on the world stage. Since it first came to worldwide notice with the attacks on Israeli athletes at the 1972 Olympics, terrorism, even more than guerrilla warfare, has been primarily symbolic and propagandistic: the weapon of the weak against the strong, meant to galvanize opinion, focus energies, and create solidarity for one's side rather than win decisively in any Clausewitzian sense. In the waning years of the Cold War, Ronald Reagan spoke the language of Armageddon, the final conflict between the forces of light and the forces of darkness, but was politician enough to accommodate and bend when it was pragmatic to do so. By contrast, guerrilla tactics of harassment, sabotage, and, above all, avoidance of pitched battle emphasize a war of attrition, and the need for technologically superior professional forces to climb down out of their electronic control rooms and fight on the ground, or else to leave.

Terrorist tactics in general try to imply that all the high technology in the world cannot stop a determined enemy, even one armed only with primitive weapons, especially if it is psychologically bent on self-sacrifice. But the tactics of suicide bombers oddly resemble the changes in other more conventional national armies in that they rely on small professional forces, in which semi-independent groups are the most effective combatants. The soldier is no longer a member of an actual army but of, at most, a small group, prepared carefully by his recruiters for certain death, binding a ritual cloth around his head and looking to a transcendent afterlife as his reward. All war has in effect become a suicide mission.

The September 11 attacks, however, show how the previously nationalistic and quasi-political goals of terrorism have changed into something more apocalyptic, summoning the imagery of Armaggedon if not the actuality and making those groups, even the most militant Palestinians, who are actually fighting for a state with its own sovereignty, seem by contrast rational and part of the world community.

Commentators have often been puzzled by the new fundamentalisms in the world, Christian, Jewish, Islamic, Hindu—in virtually all traditional religions. But I would say that this is a neglected aspect of the general drift of the world toward more global structures of relationship and away from the nation-states that have dominated political life since the Renaissance. Not all globalization can be comprehended in the rise of multinational corporations, the appearance of American fast-food companies on the street corners of Asia and Africa, or the ability to recognize the face of Muhammad Ali or Michael Jackson.

The challenge of Osama bin Laden and Islamic fundamentalism, more palpably than other fundamentalisms, is that they want to establish a global definition of both civilization and masculinity based on their particular beliefs and even their biochemistry. Other fundamentalisms are still working within the nationalistic framework. However much they might want to change their own country into a holier place, it is still their country that they are changing. But Islam, unlike Christianity, developed without a military, imperialist Rome to play its own beliefs against. As a result, in some versions it has retained a more male and warrior-oriented aspect than has Christianity, which even in its most militant periods has had an alternate, even pacifist tradition that could be appealed to.*

Faced with a movement that dispensed with national boundaries, the United States turned the terrorist attack against New York and Washington into a conventional war by targeting the nation-state most clearly associated with those who launched the attacks. But terrorism of the bin Laden sort seeks no battle so keenly as the battle of the spirit. Suicide fighters of the past, like the kamikaze pilots of World War II, represented one strategy (a last-ditch one at that) among many. They also drew upon many of the same emotions that recruiters excited in the suicide bombers: the commitment to religion along with the promise of glory, although in Japan at least this did not involve anything quite like the hedonistic Islamic afterlife or the Valhalla of the German tribes.

In a sense, then, modern terrorism resembles assassination more than it does war. Focusing upon individuals and symbolic places, what could its tangible gains be? The Brigada Rossa terrorist wanted to bring down the Italian government, the Algerian terrorist to free his country from France, the Stern Gang terrorist to get the British out of Palestine, the Palestinian terrorist to win recognition for a Palestinian state. What gains were expected if the attacks of September 11 were "successful" in any long-range sense? Perhaps there was an illusory belief that, as Charles Manson predicted of his murders in the 1960s, a race war would be provoked that would bring down the United States. But what would happen tangibly? Most of the political demands Osama bin Laden outlined before September 11, like the withdrawal of U.S. troops from Saudi Arabia, call for America to pull back from its intervention in the rest of the world, just as Japanese military planners sought to get the United States

* Christianity also absorbed more of the matriarchal traditions that preceded it. There is no equivalent in Islam to the figure of Mary, and therefore little alternative to male clerical authority.

not to interfere in Japan's expansion into East Asia and the Pacific. Here is another analogy between Pearl Harbor and September 11: both seem to have been meant to warn the United States away from an area of the world, to make American politicians realize that they didn't want to risk soldiers in such battles—but both succeeded only in provoking further military commitment.

So far as political goals go, then, the Al Qaeda network is hardly interested in defeating the United States and taking over the country. They want instead to frighten Americans away from Muslim countries and convince audiences that Al Qaeda should have political power there, not in the United States. They seek to bring down the great Satan, capitalism, America, whiteness, Christianity, the West—whatever it is—and thereby enhance themselves. The attacks are not about nationhood but about masculine tribal self-esteem.

The paradox of the attacks is thus that, whatever the devastation and loss of life they wreak, they ultimately fail as warfare on other than the psychological level. Just as before the September 11 attacks, American military power, along with the support it can summon especially from its European allies, is unprecedented in world history. Even more importantly, as the war in Afghanistan demonstrated, lessons about the relation between bombing and ground troops, trying to win hearts and minds as well as defeat the enemy, and quitting while you are ahead instead of seeking absolute victory have begun to be learned, however falteringly and inconsistently. After some gross missteps (like George W. Bush's use of the word "crusade"), the American government tried to present an ecumenical image to the world, responding with a message of inclusiveness to bin Laden's insistence on the rhetoric of absolute difference. Bush in his early statements presented himself as more like Shane, the patient man pushed beyond all endurance, than like John Wayne, the berserker plunging into the heat of battle. It was later, after what appeared to be American victories, that the more bellicose rhetoric took over, including the effort to expand the war to the "axis of evil"—an obvious attempt to apply the language and the emotional associations of World War II to the perceived new threat.

Is it possible to separate the rhetoric of heroism, honor, and masculinity from the specific arena of warfare and weapons? The idea of the military hero as the man on whom all other men must pattern themselves infects the tangled nexus of war, masculine honor, and sexuality as well. As we have seen, cultural beliefs do have life cycles. Some move forward; others are rooted in the past until they become outmoded, even though some individuals might cling to them for their own reasons: the belief that the past was better, that an absolute truth exists somewhere on earth, that there are firm boundaries, not just physical or genetic but also psychological and social, between the sexes.

The United States and Europe, the villains in the fundamentalist equation, are also the places where over the last century the definition of masculinity has most separated from its military embodiment. Here is where the psychological attack especially comes into play, for the enemies of western technological and cultural power are also the enemies of a Western idea of gender that has slowly but perceptibly over the last century changed from the assumption that male and female are polarities to the belief that they are a continuum. As it was for the neowarrior societies of Nazi Germany and militarist Japan, the result for the radical Islamic world represented by bin Laden is that American men are no better than women, that secularism is debilitating, and that diversity means weakness. As bin Laden said in an interview in 1998:

> Our brothers who fought in Somalia saw wonders about the weakness, feebleness, and cowardliness of the U.S. soldier. . . . We believe that we are men, Muslim men who have the honor of defending [Mecca]. We do not want American women soldiers defending [it]. . . . The rulers in that region have been deprived of their manhood. And they think that the people are women. By God, Muslim women refuse to be defended by these American and Jewish prostitutes. (Judt, 4)

Such comments point out how paradoxical is the combat between the "pure" (and masculine) warrior society and the "impure" (and feminine) commercial society. Although the warrior group reaches back to tribal roots and professes to emphasize the brotherhood of the group, it actually fosters a frequently maniacal separatism and localism, while the mercantile culture of the West with its individualist ethic actually cultivates an affinity with the group, out of patriotism, practicality, or some combination of both. The crucial question is how the group is defined: in its exclusive connections with one another against the rest of the world with a Führer or holy warrior at its head, or as an inclusive, ever-expanding camaraderie where authority is, at least in principle, constantly open to challenge.

The possibility that male and female may be connected rather than eternally separate is a special threat to traditional societies that are still emerging from an agricultural into an industrial world, where a strict division of male versus female work seems necessary to the stability of life itself. Given the high ratio of men to women and the difficulties of subsisting on the family farm, there are large numbers of young men for whom domestic life is a dim possibility. In medieval Europe, they might have gone either to war or into the church. With bin Laden's brand of Islamic fundamentalism, they can do both.

In such societies, the seamless identification of the warrior image with general masculinity thus preserves a sense of male uniqueness, as does polygamous marriage and the requirement that women show virtually nothing of their bodies or faces. The result is an overcompensation familiar in warrior societies, where the combined fear of women (as weakeners of male sexuality) and disdain for them (as representing the softer virtues of domestic life) results in the need for a sexual subordination that reestablishes male honor at the top of the ladder of being.

None of these attitudes or customs are unfamiliar in Western history. They are based on a polarized idea of male and female that simultaneously asserts masculine power even as it covertly admits that the male sense of honor and selfhood is so flimsy that the slightest exposure of the female body may shatter it. The remarkable irony of history is that just at the time that, in the wake of World War II, such attitudes have been open to the most widespread criticism, at a time when women have achieved more structural equality than ever before, when homosexual behavior is no longer so officially stigmatized, the West is faced with an enemy emerging from the ancient lands of the Aryan warriors, whose own canons of sexuality attempt to reestablish a past from which the West has been distancing itself.

Instead of the monolithic states of interwar fascism, the world has in the last half century moved toward a greater number of multicultural states, whose diverse makeup reflects the new waves of immigration for economic interests that followed World War II. More than ever before, the populations of the industrialized countries represent not racial purity but a rainbow of the rest of the world, and the conflict is not so much between nations as it is between the forces of commonality and the forces of exclusion. But this diversity, which has nurtured the acceptance of racial, religious, and ethnic difference, has become the enemy for the most militant groups. In a changing world, not changing becomes the mark of virtue. Rigid styles of masculinity that have evolved for cultural situations that no longer exist and for reasons that are no longer functional are brought back as the ideological core of a refusal to engage with the present. Arising from tribal pockets, such essentially local masculinities now take the world stage because of the availability of weapons, the ease of transportation, and the permeability of borders, putting an advanced technology intended to bring people together into the hands of those who want to avoid the future at any cost. Thus, whatever bin Laden's specific complaints about American foreign policy, the energy of his attacks on the West comes instead from a much more fundamental response to the modern world, including its Islamic nations.

Once again, this is a phenomenon that has its parallels in the West. The fundamentalist branches of other religions, as well as less institutionalized spiritual practices, have grown over the past few decades in part because of a shared sense that they have been both exploited and left behind by an increasingly commercialized and mercantile world. But whatever the affinities of their critique of modernity, few have scapegoated the West as thoroughly as militant Islam, which bases its nostalgia for a past religious purity so firmly on a particular style of warrior masculinity.

In secular societies, the culprit is more likely to be the state itself. With the end of the Cold War and the forging of more intricate global connections, the implicit analogy between man and state, individual and national honor, seems more fragile than ever before. Except when facing a threat from the outside, nationalism is a quiescent force, although still a powerful element of personal identity. Yet the professed ideal of democratic states is that the citizen is an autonomous being who submits to the state's laws but is not totally defined by them. The militia and "freemen" movements of the 1990s in the United States, which culminated finally in Timothy McVeigh's bombing of the Oklahoma City federal building, is a homegrown example of the refusal to accept the legitimacy of the national government, let alone any international order. Like the Al Qaeda network, but with a more individualist American tinge, the roots of these movements are primarily local, their politics an aggrieved sense of disenfranchisement, and their religion an appeal to the support of past patriarchal values. In defeat or victory, the atmosphere of the Lost Cause hangs over their actions. Summoning up the Mamluks and the samurai and all the other warriors who have fallen, they represent themselves as heroes for an insecure generation, armed with both the most up-to-date technology and the ideas of their antitechnological forebears. Appropriately enough, their strength is not in the cities but in the countryside, where an intense private honor system that embraces family and friends but rejects all others cultivates both the sense of injustice and the feeling that national values have no connection to them. Like some of the Islamic terrorists, they may represent the last stand of agricultural societies that desperately want to preserve their own systems of connection and laws in opposition to all that industrial and postindustrial society have wrought. But their revolt is not in the name of religion but to fulfill the desire to restore the nation to what they imagine to be its earliest form, when men were men.

Whatever the questions of global economy, technological advance, and weapons delivery, the language of war, of getting people to fight against a real or imagined enemy, is often still individual. The heroicizing of the aggressive warrior in militia movements, along with the justification of violence in the name of the unborn among some antiabortion activists and other vigilante groups, reflects how since the 1980s the United States itself has gone through similar spasms of wondering what the role of traditional masculinity is in the modern world. Little of this uncertainty has found its way into literature except for the fictions of survivalism and racial superiority. But it has become the matter of popular films. As so many action movies of the past two decades show, at a time when technology lets any nondescript, physically uninspiring person have the power to annihilate many, there is some nostalgic satisfaction in seeing a correlation between body and violence, action and personal will, where the hero—Sylvester Stallone, Arnold Schwarzenegger, Jean Claude Van Damme—has access to both the most advanced technology and his own cuirasslike bare chest and muscled arms. Like paintball wars, extreme sports, and battlefield reenactments, their stories are filled with artificially pumped-up excitement and jeopardy. Many of these films are mythic efforts to synthesize technology and personal physical prowess in the same spirit as the army's 2001 advertising campaign: "An Army of One."

Since the end of the Vietnam War, American films have been filled with characters in whom the line between the human and the technological is ambiguous. *RoboCop* represents one sort, the remanufactured man; the androids of films like *Blade Runner* and *Aliens* another, apparent human beings who are actually robots. Indirectly commenting on the use of overwhelming firepower in Vietnam and later wars, such characters raise the question of whether superweaponry is enough. Despite all the "smart bombs," the answer seems to be no. Some recourse to the individual and the primitive is necessary in order to ground the otherwise abstract technology: Rambo emerges from the swamp with his bow and arrows to defeat his enemies, like the Indians triumphing over Braddock at Fort Duquesne. Although sometimes cloaked in Cold War politics, action films are at root about questions of personal honor—the violence of righteous revenge that is beyond the law, like the justifications of dueling that began in the sixteenth century, when the state was assuming the monopoly of violence. The difference now is that the honor dramatized in most action films is not aristocratic but democratic, heroes without family name, whose only resource is themselves. Ironically enough, with September 11, at a time when the United States was indulging in widespread nostalgia about World War II and its citizen soldiers, a full-fledged enemy appears who targets civilians and makes heroes of the policemen and firemen who protect them. At least for the moment, the heroic on the Western side, in the images of the World Trade Center, is defined by the normal person doing his or her job.

Films may still rely on the solitary hero, but the political propaganda of the warrior who will set the corrupt world right by violence now no longer comes out of either official Europe or official Japan but from thwarted and marginalized small groups around the world. Most prominently in the Middle East, it is the revenge of the nomad against the settled, or of the religion of the desert against the values of the city. These recent events underline the relativity of the European view of masculinity and how it has been shaped by the idea of the nation and citizenship. But the resurgent focus on tribal loyalties in the Islamic world also shares some structural resemblances with the conflicts in Bosnia after the death of Tito, the Hutu/Tutsi conflict in Rwanda, and other responses to the end of imperial rule that enforced rather than cultivated cooperation. That civilians are the primary target of many of these attacks further underscores the fact that they mean to destroy morale much more than infrastructure. But in fact, to bring civilians so forcefully into jeopardy in effect often reknits an industrial and mercantile world otherwise more likely to savor its freedoms without paying their preservation too much attention.

Is the most recent form of terrorism thus the last gasp of a militant warrior personality type that has survived the centuries? What, if anything, is valuable in the warrior tradition? What is worth saving, and what has led us into the horrors of the twentieth and twenty-first centuries? In the 1990s the United States saw a brief efflorescence of a mythic and pseudopoetic men's movement, heralded by Robert Bly's *Iron John*, which drew upon the Jungian idea that each man had in him four archetypes—the King, the Magician, the Lover, and the Warrior—and the Warrior was especially in need of nurturance. Like William James's moral equivalent of war, this was the warrior who did not need to kill to prove his prowess, but whose energy and traits of integrity and assertiveness could be turned in more socially useful directions. Here, too, the perceived problem was that the warrior self had either been commercialized, feminized, and technologized into impotence or had been exaggerated and darkened into death and violence. At its best, this movement asked whether the need to rearmor or "rewarrior" oneself was a spiritual battle rather than a physical battle (like the original meaning of jihad), and whether it required a different sort of transformative adventure than war. At its worst, it was a self-indulgent audience of men listening to laments about male vulnerability, unwilling to give up the undeniable historical structures of male privilege but able to play the victim because others resented and caricatured that privilege, instead of just silently assuming it. Either way, the various movements found it hard to resist a suffocating air of self-congratulation, most egregiously in the chant of the Promise Keepers: "Thank God I'm a man!"

The problem with such an effort to renovate positive warrior traits—honor, integrity, self-sacrifice, camaraderie, openness—while purging negative ones is that it continues to be built on a polarized masculinity and femininity, in which any individual woman is considered to be Woman unless proven otherwise, while any individual man is constantly being tested to see whether he is Man or not. Although men may wield social power as Men, individual men have to continue striving and being tested, while each woman can unproblematically claim that identity. Masculinity, in other words, may be pure, but any man needs to constantly prove it by himself and distinguish it from ersatz forms. Once again, we are back in the realm of warriors and the initiation of war.

The questions thus remain: Are there any masculine myths suitable for a settled or global world, or are men doomed to feel insufficient in the face of modernity, women's rights, globalization, technology—whatever you prefer as the prime villain? After a millennium and more of metamorphosis, are the old myths on the verge of a final collapse as men struggle toward some new synthesis? Which myths and traditions and nostalgias actually strengthen masculinity; which undermine it?

My tentative sense is that Europe and the United States in particular are in the aftermath of a period in the histories of both war and masculinity, and that we have moved decisively toward seeing human nature as a larger and more complex whole, in which judgments about individuals need not be based on their sexuality, their religion, or their race. Part of that change, it must be said, is in the weakening of the bonds of nationalism if not nationality. When the warrior tradition becomes imbued with nationalism, it has often been at its worst—self-important and intolerant of others—although the individual warrior tradition also has its faults, when personal integrity turns into solipsism.

But if there has been any positive result from the bloodiest century in history, it has been the visible changes in the definition of being human, particularly in extending it to all races and to women as well as men. We have not reached the egalitarian Utopia, but large portions of the world have certainly changed. Has this been the result of the annihilating violence of twentieth-century war? Will the coming of a worldwide spectrum of political possibility parallel an opening up of a spectrum of sexual possibility? Before the "axis of evil" came onto the scene, the Bush administration had put enormous effort into reassuring both American Muslims and the Islamic world that the American battle was not with them but with a few specific "evil ones." The language of good and evil was invoked time and time again, but the religious and triumphalist tinge it so often had in the past was downplayed. "Unpatriotic," which had previously been the sole criterion of judgment during wartime, now had to be balanced with "insensitive" as a criticism of policy. The negotiation between groups of widely differing backgrounds and agendas that has become a mainstay of national and local politics had international implications as well. There was no repetition of the Japanese deportations and internments of World War II. Muslim men were questioned by the FBI, and there were many reported instances of injustice and mistreatment. But the government also had to be publicly responsive to charges of racial and ethnic profiling.

One of the frequent immediate reactions to the September 11 bombings was to look disdainfully at the American media culture with its incessant gossip about the trivial details of the life of the famous, its breathless hankering after scandal and personal exposure, and say that the attacks had evoked a new seriousness in the United States, as Lloyd George and others thought World War I would bring. Soon enough, though, the media gossip mill was back in full swing, and with its resurgence it might be difficult not to think that the old warrior ethic of austere self-sacrifice and loyalty has in fact been defeated by commercialism and the profit motive.

The truth may be more complex. Certainly, the attack, literally and symbolically, was directly against the commercial moneymaking side of

American culture. Reflecting the Taliban destruction of the Buddha statues in Afghanistan, the Al Qaeda bombers deployed iconoclasm to bring spiritual defeat to a mercantile culture. But gossip and aimless consumerism are on the fringes of a larger battle. Perhaps, as the dour critics of the eighteenth century thought, commerce actually is antiwar in effect. As connections with other nations balance and subdue international hostilities, the imperatives of a consumer society foster an unwillingness to allow death or deprivation for too long. To the warrior society, commerce is without any moral dimension; it is purely about getting and spending. But commerce also fosters a network of interconnections that might supersede national honor with principles that apply to the world.

At home and abroad, the United States is often mocked for trying to be the world's policeman. Yet this urge, however imperfectly, ignorantly, and sometimes cynically it may often be carried out (Rwanda being a prime example), coincides with the United Nations Charter reaffirmation of the Kellogg-Briand pact's outlawing of aggressive war. Military action that is undertaken to implement a world honor, a moral point of view that transcends national boundaries, like human rights, is always subject to often justifiable accusations that it merely protects the interests of the powerful. But in the history of both war and humanity, the invocation of a language of ethical responsibility rather than of national honor or material gain is itself a milestone, of aspiration if not of achievement.

It sounds utopian and foolish to say that we are at the end of a cycle in European history, one that began in the Middle Ages and that defined masculinity, femininity, and society by what they excluded. But the conjunction of a fundamentalist warrior-oriented terrorism and an industrialized world willing to accept a wider spectrum of both male and female possibilities may not be a coincidence at all. Perhaps it is a necessary step in the emancipation of the human race from its own mind-forged manacles.

Certainly there will still be subgroups, gangs of all sorts, that identify themselves more by their enemies and their willingness to fight than by who they are in themselves. But the question remains whether the national states that defined themselves by what they were not might be changing into more comprehensive places, and the restrictive idea of masculinity that went along with that politics of exclusion might be changing as well. The twentieth century began with much talk of the clash between civilization and barbarism. But civilization in that limited sense may be a worn-out and discredited concept that needs to be replaced with something at once more all-embracing and more sensitive to individual difference. Everyone is not only the product of cultural influences but also an exception to them, and a rebuke to their overpowering generality.

Whether the newly globalized world will usher in multiple masculinities as well, and what effect those varieties will have on traditional forms, remains to be seen. Whatever happens, the real need is to feel the currents of old belief in ourselves, like underground streams—not streams that have been there from eternity but those that were laid down a century or more ago in response to circumstances and ideas that have otherwise vanished. We still feel them, and the only way to be free of them is to recognize their existence, to be able to stand back and see how they developed in the course of history rather than as part of some chimerical innate human nature.

# *Bibliography: Notes and Sources*

*From Chivalry to Terrorism* is a work of synthesis. Readers looking for new research will probably not find it here. What they will find, I hope, are fresh and provocative juxtapositions of subjects usually thought to be unrelated and new interpretations of old assumptions about the relation of men to war.

This book has its origins in my curiosity about a tangle of cultural connections that coalesce around the words "man" and "war," and curiosity has guided my research. To write a book like this is to be perpetually indebted, and I'm sorry if a desire to keep the story flowing has not allowed me to pay full enough tribute to the work of so many without whose scholarship and insight this could never have been written. Along the way I have read many outstanding works of scholarship that focus on a multitude of moments in human history, books that pursue these arguments with more subtlety and detail than I can do here. Reading these works, I am constantly in awe of the archival work and scholarly interpretation that have been done—and this book could not have been completed or even contemplated without them.

I am also well aware that in my effort to show broad movements and changes in cultural attitudes about those two one-syllable, three-letter words, I have missed many more. Even as I sit here writing this preface, virtually at the end of my work on the book, I have a pile of ten or twenty more books I'd like to read that deal with one or another of these subjects or eras—and every day word comes of the publication of more. A book on war and masculinity might be finished, but it will never be completed.

The bibliography that follows, then, is hardly meant to be exhaustive, nor does it even refer to every book that contributed to the making of this one. It represents a preliminary foray into an in-depth knowledge of any of these periods or movements or ideas. Out of the numerous books that have been written on the various subjects covered in *From Chivalry to Terrorism*, I include here those that I have found particularly useful in formulating my own ideas and those where interested readers can pursue a special topic in more detail.

As any reader of history knows, there are innumerable controversies lurking behind almost every fact and interpretation. To launch on a book like this is to encounter huge continents of research, seas of detail, and the occasional scholarly storm about the actual lay of the land. But here I choose for the most part to focus on the general terrain and do not delve into the skirmishes unless (like the controversy over the "military revolution" of the sixteenth and seventeenth centuries) it is an important issue in itself.

In what follows I have organized the sources according to the sections in which their impact appears most prominently. When a book is drawn upon in more than one place, the first reference suffices unless absolutely necessary for clarity. Generally I have cited primary sources from the most easily available version or translation. In the case of poems and plays, I have given page number rather than line numbers, so as not to needlessly clutter the page; most specific citations can be readily found in book- or Web-based concordances. In the case of the epigraphs, I have mentioned the source if it is not obvious from the main citation.

Finally, I want to acknowledge my debt to some of those writers who have written generally about the history of warfare, especially Hans Delbrück, Michael Howard, and John Keegan, as well as the compilers of such overviews as the *Cambridge History of Warfare*, the various *Oxford Companions*, and other reference works that have made the twentieth and twenty-first centuries such a fruitful time for historical scholarship.

## GENERAL WORKS

Chambers, John Whiteclay, II, ed. *The Oxford Companion to American Military History*. New York: Oxford University Press, 1999.

Dupy, R. Ernest, and Trevor N. Dupuy. *The Encyclopedia of Military History from 3500 B.C. to the Present*. New York: Harper, 1970.

Gottesman, Ronald, ed. *Violence in America*, 3 vols. New York: Scribner's, 1999.

Hogg, Ian V. *The Complete Handgun, 1300 to the Present*. London: Phoebus, 1979.

———. *The Complete Illustrated Encyclopedia of the World's Firearms*. New York: A&W, 1978.

Holmes, Richard. *Acts of War: The Behavior of Men in Battle*. New York: Free Press, 1985.

Howard, Michael. *The Causes of Wars and Other Essays*. London: T. Smith, 1983.

———. *War in European History*. New York: Oxford University Press, 1976.

———, ed. *Theory and Practice of War*. Bloomington: Indiana University Press, 1975.

Keegan, John. *The Face of Battle*. New York: Viking, 1976.

———. *A History of Warfare*. New York: Knopf, 1993.

———. *The Mask of Command*. New York: Viking, 1987.

Keegan, John, and Richard Holmes. *Soldiers: A History of Men in Battle*. New York: Viking, 1985.

Macdonald, John. *Great Battlefields of the World*. London: Marshall Editions, 1984.

Paret, Peter, ed. *Makers of Modern Strategy: From Machiavelli to the Nuclear Age*. Princeton: Princeton University Press, 1986.

Parker, Geoffrey, ed. *Cambridge Illustrated History of Warfare*. Cambridge, England: Cambridge University Press, 1995.

## INTRODUCTION: ARMS AND MEN

### *Works Cited*

Blomberg, Catharina. *The Heart of the Warrior: Origins and Religious Background of the Samurai System in Feudal Japan*. Sandgate, England: Japan Library, 1994.

Dover, K. J. *Greek Homosexuality*. London: Duckworth, 1978

Homer. *The Iliad*, tr. Robert Fitzgerald. Garden City, N.Y.: Anchor Press, 1974.

Watanabe, Tsuneo, and Jun'ichi Iwata. *The Love of the Samurai: A Thousand Years of Japanese Homosexuality*, tr. D. R. Roberts. London: GMP, 1989.

## PART I: MEN AND MASCULINITY

### *Works Cited*

Badinter, Elisabeth. *XY: On Masculine Identity*, tr. Lydia Davis. New York: Columbia University Press, 1995.

Benveniste, Emile. *Indo-European Language and Society*, tr. Elizabeth Palmer. Coral Gables, Fla.: University of Miami Press, 1973.

Brothers, Leslie. *Friday's Footprint: How Society Shapes the Human Mind*. New York: Oxford University Press, 1997.

Duby, Georges. *The Chivalrous Society*, tr. Cynthia Postan. Berkeley: University of California Press, 1977.

Marshall, S. L. A. *Men Against Fire: The Problem of Battle Command in Future War*. New York: Morrow, 1947.

van Gennep, Arnold. *The Rites of Passage*, tr. Monika B. Vizedom and Gabrielle L. Caffee. Chicago: University of Chicago Press, 1960.

*On Etymology*

Ammer, Christine. *Fighting Words: From War, Rebellion, and Other Combative Capers*. New York: Paragon, 1989.

Buck, Carl Darling. *A Dictionary of Selected Synonyms in the Principal Indo-European Languages*. Chicago: University of Chicago Press, 1949.

Hollyman, K.-J. *Le Développement du Vocabulaire Féodal en France pendant le Haut Moyen Age*. Genève: Droz, 1957.

Pokorny, Julius. *Indogermanisches Etymologisches Wörterbuch*, 2 band. Bern and Munich: Francke, 1959.

*Other Useful Works*

Angier, Natalie. *Woman: An Intimate Geography*. New York: Houghton Mifflin, 1999.

Centlivres, Pierre, and Jacques Hainard. *Les Rites du Passage Aujourd'hui*. Lausanne: L'Age d'Homme, 1986.

Eliade, Mircea. *Shamanism: Archaic Techniques of Ecstasy*, tr. Willard Trask. Princeton, N.J.: Princeton University Press, 1964.

Fausto-Sterling, Anne. *Myths of Gender: Biological Theories About Women and Men*. New York: Basic, 1985.

Gilmore, David D. *Manhood in the Making: Cultural Concepts of Masculinity*. New Haven, Conn.: Yale University Press, 1990.

Godelier, Maurice, and Marilyn Strathern, eds. *Big Men and Great Men: Personifications of Power in Melanesia*. Cambridge, England: Cambridge University Press, 1991.

Gosden, Roger. *Cheating Time: Science, Sex, and Aging*. New York: W. H. Freeman, 1996.

Guttentag, Marcia, and Paul F. Secord. *Too Many Women? The Sex Ratio Question*. Beverly Hills, Calif.: Sage, 1983.

Herdt, Gilbert H., ed. *Ritualized Homosexuality in Melanesia*. Berkeley: University of California Press, 1984.

———. *Sambia Sexual Culture: Essays from the Field*. Chicago: University of Chicago Press, 1999.

Marcus, Ivan C. *Rituals of Childhood: Jewish Acculturation in Medieval Europe*. New Haven, Conn.: Yale University Press, 1996.

Nicholson, John. *Men and Women: How Different Are They?*, 2nd ed. Oxford, England: Oxford University Press, 1993.

Sergent, Bernard. *Homosexuality in Greek Myth*, tr. Arthur Goldhammer, pref. Georges Dumézil. Boston: Beacon Press, 1986.

Smith, John Maynard. *The Evolution of Sex*. Cambridge, England: Cambridge University Press, 1978.

## PART II: ARMS AND HONOR

The Lloyd George epigraph is quoted from Martin Gilbert, *The First World War: A Complete History* (New York: Henry Holt, 1994), p. 83.

The Urban II epigraph can be found in Edward Peters, ed., *The First Crusade*, 2nd ed. (Philadelphia: University of Pennsylvania Press, 1998), p. 53. See also Fulcher of Chartres, *A History of the Expedition to Jerusalem, 1095–1127*, tr. Frances Rita Ryan, ed. Harold S. Fink (Knoxville: University of Tennessee Press, 1969).

### *Works Cited*

Aytoun, Andrew. *Knights and Warhorses: Military Service and the English Aristocracy Under Edward III.* Woodbridge, England: Boydell, 1994.

Bloch, Marc. *Feudal Society*, 2 vols., tr. L. A. Manyon. Chicago: University of Chicago Press, 1961.

Chaucer, Geoffrey. *The Canterbury Tales.* In *Works*, 2nd ed., ed. F. N. Robinson. Boston: Houghton Mifflin, 1957.

Chrétien de Troyes. *Les Romans. II. Erec et Enide; IV. Le Chevalier au Lion (Yvain).* Paris: Honoré Champion, 1973, 1971.

———. *The Complete Romances*, tr. David Staines. Bloomington: Indiana University Press, 1990.

Christine de Pizan. *The Book of the City of Ladies*, tr. Earl Jeffrey Richards. New York: Persea, 1982.

Clover, Carol J. "Hildigunnr's Lament." In *Structure and Meaning in Old Norse Literature*, ed. John Lidnow, Lars Lonnroth, and Gerd Wolfgang Weber. New York: Oxford University Press, 1986, pp. 141–83.

Contamine, Philippe. *War in the Middle Ages*, tr. Michael Jones. Oxford: Blackwell, 1984.

Dane, Joseph A. "The Three Estates and Other Medieval Trinities." *Florilegium* 3 (1981): 283–309.

Dickins, Bruce, and Alan S. C. Ross, eds. *The Dream of the Rood.* London: Methuen, 1934.

Duby, Georges. *The Chivalrous Society.* Berkeley: University of California Press, 1977.

———. *William Marshal: The Flower of Chivalry*, tr. Richard Howard. New York: Pantheon, 1985.

Dumézil, Georges. *The Destiny of the Warrior*, tr. Alf Hiltebeitel. Chicago: University of Chicago Press, 1970.

———. *Horace et les Curaces.* New York: Arno, 1978.

———. *The Stakes of the Warrior*, tr. David Weeks. Berkeley: University of California Press, 1983.

*Egil's Saga*, tr. Hermann Pálsson and Paul Edwards. New York: Penguin, 1976.

Froissart, Jean. *Chronicles*, tr. Geoffrey Brereton. New York: Penguin, 1968.

Holt, J. C., *Robin Hood.* New York: Thames and Hudson, 1982.

Huizinga, Johann. *The Waning of the Middle Ages.* Garden City, N.Y.: Doubleday, 1954.

Jones, Terry, *Chaucer's Knight: The Portrait of a Medieval Mercenary.* Baton Rouge: Louisiana State University Press, 1980.

Kagan, Donald. *On the Origins of War and the Preservation of Peace.* New York: Doubleday, 1995.

Keegan, John. *The Face of Battle.* New York: Viking, 1976.

Keeley, Lawrence H. *War Before Civilization: The Myth of the Peaceful Savage.* Oxford University Press, 1996.

Keen, Maurice. *Chivalry.* New Haven, Conn.: Yale University Press, 1984.

Lavie, Peretz. *The Enchanted World of Sleep.* New Haven, Conn.: Yale University Press, 1995.

Malory, Sir Thomas. *Le Morte d'Arthur,* 2 vols. New York: Penguin, 1969.

Marie de France. *Lais,* tr. Robert W. Hanning and Joan Ferrante. New York: Dutton, 1978.

Morris, Ivan. *The Nobility of Failure: Tragic Heroes in the History of Japan.* New York: Holt, 1995.

*The Nibelungenlied,* tr. A. T. Hatto. New York: Penguin, 1965.

*Njal's Saga,* tr. Magnus Magnusson and Hermann Pálsson. New York: Penguin, 1960.

Peristiany, J. G., ed. *Honour and Shame: The Values of Mediterranean Society.* Chicago: University of Chicago Press, 1966.

Peristiany, J. G., and Julian Pitt-Rivers, eds. *Honour and Grace in Anthropology.* Cambridge: Cambridge University Press, 1992.

Plato. *Laches and Charmides,* tr. Rosamund Kent Sprague. New York: Bobbs-Merrill, 1973.

———. *Symposium,* tr. Benjamin Jowett. New York: Bobbs-Merrill, 1948.

*The Poem of the Cid,* tr. W. S. Merwin. London: Dent, 1959.

Scammell, Jean. "The Formation of the English Social Structure: Freedom, Knights, and Gentry, 1066–1300." *Speculum* 68 (1993): 591–618.

Shay, Jonathan. *Achilles in Vietnam: Combat Trauma and the Undoing of Character.* New York: Atheneum, 1994.

Strayer, Joseph, ed. *Dictionary of the Middle Ages.* New York: Scribner's, 1982.

Strickland, Matthew, ed. *Anglo-Norman Warfare: Studies in Late Anglo-Saxon and Anglo-Norman Military Organization and Warfare.* Rochester, N.Y.: Boydell, 1992.

Sturluson, Snorri. *The Prose Edda,* tr. Jean I. Young. Berkeley: University of California Press, 1964.

Sun Tzu. *The Art of War,* tr. Lionel Giles. Harrisburg Pa.: Military Services Publishing, 1944.

Tacitus. *The Agricola and the Germania,* tr. H. Mattingly and S. A. Handford. New York: Penguin, 1970.

Thucydides. *Complete Writing,* tr. Richard Crawley. New York: Modern Library, 1951.

Upton-Ward, J. M. *The Rule of the Templars.* Woodbridge, Suffolk, England: Boydell, 1992.

West, Martin L., tr. and intro. *Greek Lyric Poetry.* Oxford, England: Clarendon, 1993.

### *On the Classical Background*

Brown, Peter. "Bodies and Minds: Sexuality and Renunciation in Early Christianity." In David M. Halperin, et al., eds., *Before Sexuality,* pp. 480–93.

Davidson, James N. *Courtesans and Fishcakes: The Consuming Passions of Classical Athens.* New York: St. Martin's, 1998.

DuBois, Page. "Eros and the Woman," *Ramus* 21 (1992): 97–116.

———. *Sowing the Body: Psychoanalysis and Ancient Representations of Women.* Chicago: University of Chicago Press, 1988.

Finley, M. I. "War and Empire." In *Ancient History: Evidence and Models.* New York: Viking, 1986.

Fraser, Antonia. *The Warrior Queens.* New York: Knopf, 1989.

Halperin, David M. "Why Is Diotima a Woman? Platonic Eros and the Figuration of Gender." In Halperin, et al., eds., *Before Sexuality,* pp. 257–308.

Halperin, David M., John J. Winkler, and Froma I. Zeitlin, eds. *Before Sexuality: The Construction of Erotic Experience in the Ancient Greek World.* Princeton, N.J.: Princeton University Press, 1990.

Hanson, Victor Davis. *The Western Way of War: Infantry Battle in Classical Greece,* 2nd ed. Berkeley: University of California Press, 2000.

Keuls, Eva. *The Reign of the Phallus: Sexual Politics in Ancient Athens.* New York: Harper, 1985.

Knox, Bernard. "Introduction to the *Iliad,*" tr. Robert Fagles. New York: Viking, 1990.

Rawson, Elizabeth. *The Spartan Tradition in European Thought.* Oxford, England: Clarendon, 1969.

Rich, John, and Graham Shipley, eds. *War and Society in the Greek World.* New York: Routledge, 1993.

———. *War and Society in the Roman World.* New York: Routledge, 1993.

Richlin, Amy. *The Garden of Priapus: Sexuality and Aggression in Roman Humor,* rev. ed. New York: Oxford University Press, 1992.

———, ed. *Pornography and Representation in Greece and Rome.* New York: Oxford University Press, 1993.

Simmons, Joe. *Vision and Spirit: An Essay on Plato's Warrior Class.* Lanham, Md.: University Press of America, 1988.

Spence, I. G. *The Cavalry of Classical Greece: A Social and Military History with Particular Reference to Athens.* Oxford, England: Clarendon, 1993.

Strutynski, Udo. "Ares: A Reflex of the Indo-European War God?" *Arethusa* 13 (1980): 217–31.

Tacitus. *Germania,* tr. J. B. Rives. Oxford, England: Clarendon, 1999.

Vernant, Jean-Pierre. "One . . . Two . . . Three: Eros." In David M. Halperin, et al., eds., *Before Sexuality,* 465–78.

———. *Problèmes de la guerre en Grèce ancienne.* Paris: Mouton, 1968.

Williams, Bernard. *Shame and Necessity.* Berkeley: University of California Press, 1993.

*On the Medieval Background*

Alvarez, Manuel Fernández. *Charles V: Elected Emperor and Hereditary Ruler.* London: Thames and Hudson, 1975.

Anderson, Theodore M., and William Ian Miller. *Law and Literature in Medieval Iceland: Ljósvetninga saga and Valla-Ljóts sagas.* Stanford, Calif.: Stanford University Press, 1989.

Baldwin, John W. *The Language of Sex: Five Voices from Northern France Around 1200.* Chicago: University of Chicago Press, 1994.

Barber, Malcolm. *The New Knighthood: A History of the Order of the Temple.* Cambridge, England: Cambridge University Press, 1994.

Barber, Richard, and Juliet Barker. *Tournaments: Jousts, Chivalry, and Pageants in the Middle Ages.* Woodbridge, England: Boydell, 1989.

Barnie, John. *War in Medieval English Society: Social Values in the Hundred Years War, 1337–99.* Ithaca, N.Y.: Cornell University Press, 1974.

Benson, Larry D., and John Leyerle, eds. *Chivalric Literature: Essays on Relations Between Literature and Life in the Later Middle Ages.* Toronto: University of Toronto Press, 1980.

Bernstein, David J. *The Mystery of the Bayeux Tapestry.* Chicago: University of Chicago Press, 1986.

Bloch, R. Howard. *Medieval Misogyny and the Invention of Western Romantic Love.* Chicago: University of Chicago Press, 1991.

Boswell, John. *Christianity, Social Tolerance, and Homosexuality: Gay People in Western Europe from the Beginning of the Christian Era to the Fourteenth Century.* Chicago: University of Chicago Press, 1980.

———. *The Kindness of Strangers: The Abandonment of Children in Western Europe from Late Antiquity to the Renaissance.* New York: Pantheon, 1988.

Cantor, Norman. *The Civilization of the Middle Ages.* New York: HarperCollins, 1993.

Chastellain, Georges. *Histoire du bon chevalier Iacques de LaLain, Frère et Compagnon de l'Order de la Toison D'or.* Brussels, 1634.

Chickering, Howell, and Thomas Seiler. *The Study of Chivalry: Resources and Approaches.* Kalamazoo, Mich.: Medieval Institute Publications, 1988.

Christine de Pizan. *Le Livre des faits et bonnes moeurs du sage roi Charles V.* MM. Michaud, ed., *Nouvelle Collection des mémoires relatifs à l'histoire de France depuis le XIIIe siècle jusqu' á la fin du XVIIIe siècle.* Paris: Didier, 1854.

Clover, Carol J. "Maiden Warriors and Other Sons." *JEGP* 85 (1986): 35–49.

———. "The Politics of Scarcity: Notes on the Sex Ratio in Early Scandinavia." In *New Readings on Women in Old English Literature,* eds. Helen Damico and Alexandra Hennessey Olsen. Bloomington: Indiana University Press, 1990, pp. 100–34.

———. "Regardless of Sex: Men, Women, and Power in Early Northern Europe." *Representations* 44 (Fall 1993): 1–28.

Crouch, David. *William Marshal: Court, Career, and Chivalry in the Angevin Empire, 1147–1219.* London: Longmans, 1990.

Davis, Natalie Zemon. *Society and Culture in Early Modern France.* Stanford, Calif.: Stanford University, 1975.

Denholm-Young, N. *Collected Papers: Cultural, Textual and Biographical Essays on Medieval Topics.* Cardiff: University of Wales, 1979.

Dickeman, Mildred. "Demographic Consequences of Infanticide in Man." *Annual Review of Ecology and Systematics* 6 (1975): 107–37.

Du Boulay, F. R. H. *An Age of Ambition: English Society in the Late Middle Ages.* London: Nelson, 1970.

Duby, Georges. *The Knight, the Lady, and the Priest.* New York: Pantheon, 1983.

Ellis, John. *Cavalry: The History of Mounted Warfare.* New York: Putnam, 1978.

Ferguson, Arthur B. *The Indian Summer of English Chivalry.* Durham, N.C.: Duke University Press, 1960.

Fletcher, Richard. *The Quest for El Cid.* New York: Knopf, 1990.

Gabrieli, Francesco. *Arab Historians of the Crusades,* tr. E. J. Costello. London: Routledge, 1969.

Gillingham, John, and J. C. Holt, eds. *War and Government in the Middle Ages.* Totowa, N.J.: Barnes and Noble, 1984.

Halperin, David M. "Sex Before Sexuality: Pederasty, Politics, and Power in Classical Athens." In *Hidden from History: Reclaiming the Gay and Lesbian Past,* ed. Martin Bauml Duberman, Martha Vicinus, and George Chauncey, Jr. New York: New American Library, 1989, pp. 37–53.

Hawks, Sonia Chadwick, ed. *Weapons and Warfare in Anglo-Saxon England.* Oxford University Committee for Archaeology Monograph 21 (1989).

Herlihy, David. "Life Expectancies for Women in Medieval Society." In *The Role of Women in the Middle Ages,* ed. Rosemarie Thee Morewedge. Albany, N.Y.: SUNY Press, 1975, pp. 1–22.

Hibbert, Christopher. *Agincourt*. New York: Dorset, 1978.

Husband, Timothy, with Gloria Gilmore-House. *The Wild Man: Medieval Myth and Symbolism*. New York: Metropolitan Museum, 1980.

Kaeuper, Richard W. *War, Justice, and Public Order: England and France in the Later Middle Ages*. Oxford, England: Clarendon, 1988.

Keen, Maurice H. "Chaucer's Knight, the English Aristocracy, and the Crusade." In *English Court Culture in the Later Middle Ages*, ed. V. J. Scattergood and J. W. Sherborne. New York: St. Martin's, 1983, pp. 45–62.

———. *Laws of War in the Late Middle Ages*. London: Routledge, 1965.

———. *Nobles, Knights, and Men-at-Arms in the Middle Ages*. London: Hambledon, 1996.

Knight, Stephen. *Arthurian Literature and Society*. New York: St. Martin's, 1983.

Kolve, V. A. *Chaucer and the Imagery of Narrative: The First Five Canterbury Tales*. Stanford, Calif.: Stanford University Press, 1984.

MacCana, Proinsias. *Celtic Mythology*. New York: Peter Bedrick, 1985.

Mathew, Gervase. *The Court of Richard II*. London: Murray, 1968.

Meun, Jean de. *L'Art de Chevalerie* [1284?], ed. Ulysse Robert. Paris: Firmin Didot, 1897. [Translation of Vegetius, *De Re Militari*.]

Miller, William Ian. *Humiliation and Other Essays on Honor, Social Discomfort, and Violence*. Ithaca, N.Y.: Cornell University Press, 1993.

Murray, Jacqueline, and Konrad Eisenbichler. *Desire and Discipline: Sex and Sexuality in the Premodern West*. Toronto: University of Toronto Press, 1996.

Onians, Richard Broxton. *The Origins of European Thought About the Body, the Mind, the Soul, the World, Time, and Fate*. Cambridge, England: Cambridge University Press, 1951.

Painter, Sidney. *French Chivalry*. Baltimore: Johns Hopkins University Press, 1940.

Partner, Peter. *God of Battles: Holy Wars of Christianity and Islam*. Princeton, N.J.: Princeton University Press, 1997.

Patterson, Lee. *Chaucer and the Subject of History*. Madison: University of Wisconsin Press, 1991.

Poly, Jean-Pierre, and Eric Bournazel. *The Feudal Transformation, 900–1200*, tr. Caroline Higgitt. New York: Holmes & Meier, 1991.

Prestwich, Michael. *Armies and Warfare in the Middle Ages: The English Experience*. New Haven, Conn.: Yale University Press, 1996.

Purdom, Liam O., and Cindy L. Vito, eds.. *The Rusted Hauberk: Feudal Ideas of Order and Their Decline*. Gainesville: University Press of Florida, 1994.

Radding, Charles M. *A World Made by Men: Cognition and Society, 400–1200*. Chapel Hill: University of North Carolina Press, 1985.

Rossiaud, Jacques. *Medieval Prostitution*, tr. Lydia G. Cochrane. Oxford, England: Blackwell, 1988.

Scaglione, Aldo. *Knights at Court: Courtliness, Chivalry, and Courtesy from Ottonian Germany to the Italian Renaissance*. Berkeley: University of California Press, 1991.

Seward, Desmond. *The Hundred Years War: The English in France, 1337–1453*. New York: Atheneum, 1978. Illustrated edition, London: Constable, 1996.

Seymour, William. *Battles in Britain and Their Political Background*, 2 vols. in 1: I: 1066–1547; II: 1642–1746. London: Sidgwick & Jackson, 1975.

Strickland, Matthew, ed. *Anglo-Norman Warfare: Studies in Late Anglo-Saxon and Anglo-Norman Military Organization and Warfare*. Rochester, N.Y.: Boydell, 1992.

Trease, Geoffrey. *The Condottieri: Soldiers of Fortune*. London: Thames and Hudson, 1970.

Vane, Malcolm. *War and Chivalry*. London: Duckworth, 1981.

Wright, Thomas. *The Political Songs of England, from the Reign of John to That of Edward II*. New York: AMS, 1968.

### *On the Japanese Warrior*

Berry, Mary Elizabeth. *Hideyoshi*. Cambridge: Harvard University Press, 1982.

Blomberg, Catharina. *The Heart of the Warrior: Origins and Religious Background of the Samurai System in Feudal Japan*. Sandgate, England: Japan Library, 1994.

Friday, Karl F. *Hired Swords: The Rise of Private Warrior Power in Early Japan*. Stanford, Calif.: Stanford University Press, 1992.

Perrin, Noel. *Giving Up the Gun: Japan's Reversion to the Sword, 1543–1879*. Boston: Godine, 1979.

Watanabe, Tsuneo, and Jun'ichi Iwata. *The Love of the Samurai: A Thousand Years of Japanese Homosexuality*, tr. D. R. Roberts. London: GMP, 1989.

## PART III: FROM ARMOR TO PERSONALITY

### *Works Cited*

Abbott, W. C., ed. *Writings and Speeches of Oliver Cromwell*, 4 vols. Cambridge: Harvard University Press, 1937–47.

Baroja, Julio Caro. "A Historical Account of Several Conflicts." In J. G. Peristiany, ed. *Honour and Shame: The Values of Mediterranean Society*. Chicago: University of Chicago Press, 1966.

Beckett, J. V. *The Aristocracy in England, 1660–1914*. Oxford, England: Blackwell, 1986.

Billaçois, François. *The Duel: Its Rise and Fall in Early Modern France*, tr. Trista Selous. New Haven, Conn.: Yale University Press, 1990.

Boyle, Roger. *A Treatise of the Art of War*. London: Herringman, 1677.

Burg, B. R. *Sodomy and the Perception of Evil: English Sea Rovers in the Seventeenth-Century Caribbean*. New York: New York University Press, 1983.

Castiglione, Baldesar. *The Book of the Courtier*, tr. George Bull. New York: Penguin, 1976.

Cervantes, Miguel de. *Don Quixote*, tr. Samuel Putnam. New York: Viking, 1968.

Davenant, Sir William. *The Author's Preface to His Much Honoured Friend Mr. Hobbes*. In *Seventeenth-Century Poetry and Prose*, ed. Helen C. White, Ruth Wallerstein, and Ricardo Quintana, 2 vols. New York: Macmillan, 1951–52, II, pp. 243–46.

Delbrück, Hans. *History of the Art of War* [*Within the Framework of Political History*], tr. Walter J. Renfroe, Jr. 4 vols. Lincoln: University of Nebraska Press, 1982.

Dewald, Jonathan. *Aristocratic Experience and the Origins of Modern Culture: France, 1570–1715*. Berkeley: University of California Press, 1993.

Donne, John. *Poetry and Prose*, ed. Frank J. Warnke. New York: Modern Library, 1967.

Dryden, John. *Poems and Fables*, ed. James Kinsley. New York: Oxford University Press, 1962.

Elias, Norbert. *The Civilizing Process: The History of Manners*, tr. Edmund Jephcott. New York: Pantheon, 1982.

Elliott, John H. *The Count-Duke of Olivares: The Statesman in an Age of Decline*. New Haven, Conn.: Yale University Press, 1986.

Grimmelshausen, Hans Jakob Christoffel von. *The Adventures of Simplicius Simplicissimus,* tr. George Schulz-Behrend. Columbia, S.C.: Camden House, 1993.

Grotius, Hugo. *The Law of War and Peace,* tr. Louise R. Loomis. New York: W. J. Black, 1949.

Hobsbawm, Eric. *Primitive Rebels: Studies in Archaic Forms of Social Movement in the Nineteenth and Twentieth Centuries.* New York: Norton, 1965.

Hobbes, Thomas. "The Answer of Mr Hobbes to Sir Will. D'Avenant's Preface Before *Gondibert.*" In *Seventeenth-Century Poetry and Prose,* ed. Helen C. White, Ruth Wallerstein, and Ricardo Quintana, 2 vols. New York: Macmillan, 1951–52, II, pp. 224–30.

Jomini, Antoine-Henri. *The Art of War,* tr. G. H. Mendell and W. P. Craighill. Westport, Conn.: Greenwood Press, 1971.

La Rochefoucauld, François de. *Maximes,* ed. Dominique Secretan. Geneva: Droz, 1967.

Machiavelli, Niccolò. *The Art of War,* tr. Neal Wood. New York: Da Capo, 1990.

Marvell, Andrew. *Complete Poems,* ed. Elizabeth Donno. New York: Penguin, 1985.

McNeill, William H. *Keeping Together in Time: Dance and Drill in Human History.* Cambridge: Harvard University Press, 1995.

Milton, John. *Paradise Lost,* ed. Merritt Y. Hughes. Indianapolis, Ind.: Odyssey, 1962.

Montaigne, Michel de. *Complete Essays,* tr. Donald M. Frame. Stanford, Calif.: Stanford University Press, 1957.

Parker, Geoffrey. *The Military Revolution: Military Innovation and the Rise of the West, 1500–1800.* Cambridge, England: Cambridge University Press, 1988.

Roberts, Michael. *The Military Revolution, 1650–1660.* Belfast: Queen's University of Belfast, 1956.

Rochester, John Wilmot, Earl of. *Complete Poems,* ed. David M. Vieth. New Haven, Conn.: Yale University Press, 1968.

Russell, Jeffrey Burton. *The Devil: Perceptions of Evil from Antiquity to Primitive Christianity.* Ithaca, N.Y.: Cornell University Press, 1977.

Shakespeare, William. *The Complete Works.* Baltimore: Penguin, 1969.

Stone, Lawrence. *The Crisis of the Aristocracy, 1558–1641.* Oxford, England: Clarendon, 1965.

Tallett, Frank. *War and Society in Early Modern Europe, 1495–1715.* London: Routledge, 1992.

Watt, Ian. *Myths of Modern Individualism: Faust, Don Quixote, Don Juan, Robinson Crusoe.* Cambridge, England: Cambridge University Press, 1996.

### *On the "Military Revolution"*

Barker, Thomas M. *The Military Intellectual and Battle: Raimondo Montecuccoli and the Thirty Years War.* Albany: State University of New York Press, 1975.

Black, Jeremy. *European Warfare, 1660–1815.* New Haven: Yale University Press, 1994.

———. *A Military Revolution? Military Change and European Society, 1550–1800.* Atlantic Highlands, N.J.: Humanities Press International, 1991.

———, ed. *The Origins of War in Early Modern Europe.* Edinburgh: John Donald, 1987.

Levy, Jack S. *War in the Modern Great Power System, 1495–1975.* Lexington: University Press of Kentucky, 1983.

### *Other Useful Works*

Baumgartner, Frederic J. *France in the Sixteenth Century.* New York: St. Martin's, 1995.

Coole, Diana. *Women in Political Theory: From Ancient Misogyny to Contemporary Feminism,* 2d ed. Boulder, Colo.: Rienner, 1993.

Cordingly, David. *Under the Black Flag: The Romance and the Reality of Life Among the Pirates.* New York: Random House, 1995.

Creighton, Margaret S., and Lisa Nordling, eds. *Iron Men, Wooden Women: Gender and Seafaring in the Atlantic World, 1700–1920.* Baltimore: Johns Hopkins University Press, 1999.

Diamond, Jared. *Guns, Germs, and Steel: The Fates of Human Societies.* New York: Norton, 1999.

Frevert, Ute. *Men of Honour: A Social and Cultural History of the Duel,* tr. Anthony Williams. Cambridge, England: Polity, 1995.

Gaukroger, Stephen. *Descartes: An Intellectual Biography.* Oxford, England: Clarendon, 1995.

Gentles, Ian. *The New Model Army in England, Ireland, and Scotland, 1645–1653.* Oxford, England: Blackwell, 1992.

Hale, John R. *The Art of War and Renaissance England.* Washington, D.C.: Folger, 1961.

Hobbes, Thomas. *Leviathan,* ed. C. B. Macpherson. New York: Penguin, 1968.

Kennedy, Paul. *The Rise and Fall of the Great Powers: Economic Change and Military Conflict from 1500 to 2000.* New York: Random House, 1987.

Kiernan, V. G. *The Duel in European History: Honour and the Reign of Aristocracy.* New York: Oxford University Press, 1988.

Koenigsberger, H. G., and G. L. Mosse. *Europe in the Sixteenth Century.* New York: Holt, Rinehart & Winston, 1968.

Langer, Herbert. *Thirty Years' War,* tr. C. S. V. Salt. New York: Hippocrene, 1980.

Lee, Stephen J. *The Thirty Years War.* London: Routledge, 1991.

Ranum, Orest. *The Fronde: A French Revolution.* New York: Norton, 1995.

Rediker, Marcus. *Between the Devil and the Deep Blue Sea: Merchant Seamen, Pirates, and the Anglo-American Maritime World, 1700–1750.* Cambridge, England: Cambridge University Press, 1987.

Scarry, Elaine. *The Body in Pain.* New York: Oxford University Press, 1985.

Van Creveld, Martin. *The Rise and Decline of the State.* Cambridge, England: Cambridge University Press, 1999.

## PART IV: THE BATTLE AND THE SEXES

### *Works Cited*

Addison, Joseph, Richard Steele, and others. *The Spectator,* 5 vols., ed. Donald F. Bond. Oxford, England: Clarendon Press, 1965.

Berger, John. *G.: A Novel.* New York: Pantheon, 1972.

Brown, Peter. "Bodies and Minds: Sexuality and Renunciation in Early Christianity." In David M. Halperin, et al., eds. *Before Sexuality.*

Burton, Robert. *Anatomy of Melancholy,* 5 vols., ed. Thomas C. Faulkner et al. New York: Oxford University Press, 1989–2000.

Congreve, William. *The Way of the World,* ed. Brian Gibbons. New York: Norton, 1994.

Dawkins, Richard. *The Selfish Gene.* New York: Oxford University Press, 1989.

Elias, Norbert. *The Court Society,* tr. Edmund Jephcott. New York: Pantheon, 1983.

Etherege, Sir George. *Poems,* ed. James Thorpe. Princeton, N.J.: Princeton University Press, 1963.

Ford, Ford Madox. *No More Parades.* New York: A. & C. Boni, 1925.

Foucault, Michel. *The History of Sexuality.* Vol. I: *An Introduction;* Vol. II: *The Use of Pleasure,* tr. Robert Hurley. New York: Random House, 1978, 1985.

Hull, Isabel V. *Sexuality, State, and Civil Society in Germany, 1700–1815*. Ithaca, N.Y.: Cornell University Press, 1996.

Konner, Melvin. "Why We Do What We Do: The Secrets of Human Nature." *Bottom Line* (March 15, 1992).

Laqueur, Thomas. *Making Sex: Body and Gender from the Greeks to Freud*. Cambridge: Harvard University Press, 1990.

Lawner, Lynn, ed. and tr. *I Modi: The Sixteen Pleasures*. Evanston, Ill.: Northwestern University Press, 1988.

Leys, Simon. Review of Jean François Billeter, *The Chinese Art of Writing. New York Review of Books* (April 18, 1996).

Nashe, Thomas. *The Unfortunate Traveller*. In *Shorter Novels: Elizabethan*. New York: Dutton, 1930.

*Old English Coffee Houses*. London: Rodale, 1954.

Orgel, Stephen. *Impersonations: The Performance of Gender in Shakespeare's England*. Cambridge, England: Cambridge University Press, 1996.

Snyder, Louis L., ed. *Frederick the Great*. Englewood Cliffs, N.J.: Prentice-Hall, 1971.

*The Song of Roland*, tr. Patricia Terry. New York: Macmillan, 1992.

### *Other Useful Works*

Ackroyd, Peter. *Dressing Up, Transvestism and Drag: The History of an Obsession*. New York: Simon & Schuster, 1979.

Bernstein, David J. *The Mystery of the Bayeux Tapestry*. Chicago: University of Chicago Press, 1986.

Brumberg, Joan Jacobs. " 'Something Happens to Girls': Menarche and the Emergence of the Modern American Hygienic Imperative." *Journal of the History of Sexuality* 4 (1993): 99–127.

Bullough, Vern. "Age at Menarche: A Misunderstanding." *Science* (1981): 365–66.

Bullough, Vern, and James Brundage. *Sexual Practices and the Medieval Church*. Buffalo, N.Y.: Prometheus, 1982.

———, eds. *Handbook of Medieval Sexuality*. New York: Garland, 1996.

Cantarella, Eva. *Bisexuality in the Ancient World*, tr. Cormac O Cuilleanain. New Haven, Conn.: Yale University Press, 1992.

Cohen, Michèle. *Fashioning Masculinity: National Identity and Language in the Eighteenth Century*. New York: Routledge, 1996.

Darmon, Pierre. *Trial by Impotence: Virility and Marriage in Pre-Revolutionary France*, tr. Paul Keegan. London: Chatto & Windus, 1985 [Le Tribunal de l'Impuissance, 1979].

Dover, K. J. *Greek Homosexuality*. London: Duckworth, 1978.

———. *Greek Popular Morality in the Time of Plato and Aristotle*. Berkeley: University of California Press, 1974.

Dugaw, Dianne. *Warrior Women and Popular Balladry, 1650–1850*. Cambridge, England: Cambridge University Press, 1989.

Gilman, Sander L. *Difference and Pathology: Stereotypes of Sexuality, Race, and Madness*. Ithaca, N.Y.: Cornell University Press, 1985.

Henderson, Jeffrey. *The Maculate Muse: Obscene Language in Attic Comedy*. New York: Oxford University Press, 1991.

Kon, Igor S. *The Sexual Revolution in Russia: From the Age of the Czars to Today*, tr. James Riordan. New York: Free Press, 1995.

Lynn, John A., ed. *Tools of War: Instruments, Ideas, and Institutions of Warfare, 1445–1971*. Urbana: University of Illinois Press, 1990.

Marsh, Margaret, and Wanda Ronner. *The Empty Cradle: Infertility in America from Colonial Times to the Present*. Baltimore: Johns Hopkins University Press, 1996.

McCormick, Ian, ed. *Secret Sexualities: A Sourcebook of Seventeenth and Eighteenth Century Writing*. New York: Routledge, 1997.

McNeil, David. *The Grotesque Depiction of War and the Military in Eighteenth-Century Fiction*. Newark: University of Delaware Press, 1990.

Miller, William Ian. *Humiliation and Other Essays on Honor, Social Discomfort, and Violence*. Ithaca, N.Y.: Cornell University Press, 1993.

Robinson, E. F. *The Early History of Coffee Houses in England*. Christchurch, N.Z.: Dolphin, 1972.

Roper, Lyndal. *Oedipus and the Devil: Witchcraft, Sexuality, and Religion in Early Modern Europe*. New York: Routledge, 1994.

Rutkow, Ira M. *Surgery: An Illustrated History*. St. Louis: Mosby–Year Book, 1993.

Sedgwick, Eve Kosofsky. *Between Men: English Literature and Male Homosocial Desire*. New York: Columbia University Press, 1985.

Stanton, Domna C. *The Aristocrat as Art: A Study of the Honnête Homme and the Dandy in Seventeenth- and Nineteenth-Century French Literature*. New York: Columbia University Press, 1980.

Steinberg, Leo. *The Sexuality of Christ in Renaissance Art and in Modern Oblivion*, 2d ed. Chicago: University of Chicago Press, 1996.

Symons, Donald. *The Evolution of Human Sexuality*. New York: Oxford University Press, 1979.

Webb, Stephen Saunders. *Lord Churchill's Coup: The Anglo-American Empire and the Glorious Revolution Reconsidered*. New York: Knopf, 1995.

## PART V: HEROES FROM BELOW

### *Works Cited*

Black, Jeremy. *A Military Revolution? Military Change and European Society, 1550–1800*. Atlantic Highlands, N.J.: Humanities Press International, 1991.

Boswell, James. *Life of Samuel Johnson*. London: Oxford University Press, 1953.

Byron. *Don Juan*, ed. Leslie A. Marchand. Cambridge, Mass.: Houghton Mifflin, 1958.

Clausewitz, Carl von. *On War*, ed. Anatol Rapoport. New York: Penguin, 1968.

Fortescue, Sir John. *A History of the British Army*. London: Macmillan, 1910–30.

Fraser, Antonia. *A History of Toys*. London: Spring Books, 1966.

Goldsmith, Oliver. "On Public Rejoicings for Victory." In Oliver Goldsmith, *Miscellaneous Works*, 4 vols. London: Rivington, 1820.

Grant, U. S. *Personal Memoirs*. New York: Viking, 1990.

Lord, George deF., ed. *Poems on Affairs of State*, vol. 1 (1660–1678). New Haven, Conn.: Yale University Press, 1963.

Luvaas, Jay, ed. *Frederick the Great on the Art of War*. New York: Free Press, 1966.

Marvell, Andrew. "The Last Instructions to a Painter." In Lord, George deF.

———. "The Second Advice to a Painter." In Lord, George deF.

Sherman, W. T. *Memoirs*. New York: Viking, 1990.

Sterne, Laurence. *Tristram Shandy*, ed. Ian Watt. Boston: Houghton Mifflin, 1965.

Sun Tzu II. *The New Art of War*, tr. Thomas Cleary. San Francisco: Harper San Francisco, 1996.

Swift, Jonathan. *Gulliver's Travels*, ed. Louis A. Landa. Boston: Houghton Mifflin, 1960.

Vagts, Alfred. *A History of Militarism,* rev. ed. New York: Meridian, 1959.

Waller, Edmund. "Instructions to a Painter." In Lord, George deF.

*Other Useful Works*

Connelly, Owen. *Blundering to Glory: Napoleon's Military Campaigns.* Wilmington, Del.: Scholarly Resources, 1987.

Doyle, William. *Oxford History of the French Revolution.* New York: Oxford University Press, 1989.

Duffy, Christopher. *The Military Life of Frederick the Great.* New York: Atheneum, 1986.

Fehrenbacher, Don E. *Slavery, Law, and Politics: The Dred Scott Case in Historical Perspective.* New York: Oxford University Press, 1981.

Freeman, Joanne B. *Affairs of Honor: National Politics in the New Republic.* New Haven, Conn.: Yale University Press, 2001.

Herman, Barbara. "Could It Be Worth Thinking About Kant on Sex and Marriage?" In *A Mind of One's Own: Feminist Essays on Reason and Objectivity,* ed. Louise M. Anthony and Charlote Witt. Boulder, Colo.: Westview Press, 1993, pp. 49–67.

Higginbotham, Don. *George Washington and the American Military Tradition.* Athens: University of Georgia Press, 1985.

Howarth, David. *Waterloo: Day of Battle.* New York: Atheneum, 1968.

Johnson, Samuel. "The Bravery of the English Common Soldiers." In *Political Writings,* ed. Donald Greene. New Haven, Conn.: Yale University Press, 1977.

Lewis, Thomas A. *For King and Country: The Maturing of George Washington, 1748–1760.* New York: HarperCollins, 1993.

Mitford, Nancy. *Frederick the Great.* New York: Harper, 1970.

Nosworthy, Brent. *With Musket, Cannon and Sword: Battle Tactics of Napoleon and His Enemies.* New York: Sarpedon, 1996.

Pocock, J. G. A. *The Machiavellian Moment: Florentine Political Thought and the Atlantic Republican Tradition.* Princeton, N.J.: Princeton University Press, 1975.

Richardson, Frank M. *Mars Without Venus: A Study of Some Homosexual Generals.* Edinburgh: Blackwood, 1981.

Shy, John. *A People Numerous and Armed: Reflections on the Military Struggle for American Independence,* rev. ed. Ann Arbor: University of Michigan Press, 1990.

Stuckenberg, J. H. W. *The Life of Immanuel Kant,* pref. by Rolf George. New York: University Press of America, 1986.

Taylor, Peter K. *Indentured to Liberty: Peasant Life and the Hessian Military State, 1688–1815.* Ithaca, N.Y.: Cornell University Press, 1994.

## PART VI: THE NINETEENTH CENTURY: WAR AND NATIONAL IDENTITY

### Technological Progress and the Lost Cause

*Works Cited*

Baudelaire, Charles. *"Mon coeur mis à nu."* In *Oeuvres Complètes,* ed. Claude Pichois. Paris: Gallimard, 1975.

Carlyle, Thomas. *On Heroes, Hero-Worship, and the Heroic in History.* London, 1870.

Clarke, I. F., ed. *The Tale of the Next Great War, 1871–1914: Fictions of Future Warfare and of Battles Still-to-Come.* Syracuse, N.Y.: Syracuse University Press, 1995.

———. *Voices Prophesying War: Future Wars, 1763–3749.* New York: Oxford University Press, 1992.

Friedrich, Otto. *Blood and Iron: From Bismarck to Hitler, the von Moltke Family's Impact on German History.* New York: HarperCollins, 1995.

Griffith, Paddy. *Forward into Battle: Fighting Tactics from Waterloo to Vietnam.* Chichester, England: Anthony Bird, 1981.

Hobsbawm, Eric, and Terence Ranger, eds. *The Invention of Tradition.* New York: Cambridge University Press, 1983.

Howard, Michael. *The Franco-Prussian War: The German Invasion of France, 1870–1871.* New York: Macmillan, 1962.

James, William. *The Moral Equivalent of War.* Boston: Atlantic Monthly, 1910.

Mahan, Alfred Thayer. *The Influence of Sea Power upon History, 1660–1783.* Boston: Little, Brown, 1890.

McPherson, James M. *Battle Cry of Freedom: The Civil War Era.* New York: Oxford University Press, 1988.

Marx, Karl, and Friedrich Engels. *The German Ideology.* Amherst, N.Y.: Prometheus, 1998.

Mason, A. E. W. *The Four Feathers.* New York: Pocket Books, 2002.

Moorehead, Caroline. *Dunant's Dream: War, Switzerland, and the History of the Red Cross.* New York: Carroll & Graf, 1998.

Twain, Mark. *A Connecticut Yankee in King Arthur's Court*, ed. Allison R. Ensor. New York: Norton, 1987.

Wells, H. G. *First and Last Things.* New York: Putnam, 1908.

*Other Useful Works*

Adas, Michael. *Machines as the Measure of Men: Science, Technology, and Ideologies of Western Dominance.* Ithaca, N.Y.: Cornell University Press, 1989.

Asprey, Robert B. *War in the Shadows: The Guerrilla in History.* New York: Morrow, 1994.

Best, Geoffrey. *Humanity in Warfare: The Modern History of the International Law of Armed Conflicts.* London: Weidenfeld and Nicolson, 1980.

Bond, Brian. *War and Society in Europe, 1870–1970.* New York: St. Martin's, 1983.

Cannadine, David. *Aspects of Aristocracy: Grandeur and Decline in Modern Britain.* New Haven, Conn.: Yale University Press, 1994.

Chapman, Mary, and Glenn Hendler, eds. *Sentimental Men: Masculinity and the Politics of Affect in American Culture.* Berkeley: University of California Press, 1999.

Craig, Gordon A. *The Battle of Königgratz: Prussia's Victory over Austria, 1866.* Philadelphia: Lippincott, 1964.

Daumas, Maurice, ed. *A History of Technology and Invention*, vol. III: *The Expansion of Mechanization, 1725–1860*, tr. Eileen B. Hennessy. New York: Crown, 1979.

Ellis, John. *The Social History of the Machine Gun.* New York: Pantheon, 1975.

Franklin, H. Bruce. *War Stars: The Superweapon and the American Imagination.* New York: Oxford University Press, 1988.

Haycock, Ronald, and Keith Neilson, eds. *Men, Machines, and War.* Waterloo, Canada: Wilfrid Laurier University Press, 1988.

Headrick, Daniel R. *The Tools of Empire: Technology and European Imperialism in the Nineteenth Century.* New York: Oxford University Press, 1981.

James, Lawrence. *1854–56 Crimea: The War with Russia from Contemporary Photographs.* New York: Van Nostrand, 1981.

———. *The Rise and Fall of the British Empire.* New York: St. Martin's, 1994.

Jones, E. L. *The European Miracle: Environments, Economics, and Geopolitics in the History of Europe and Asia.* Cambridge, England: Cambridge University Press, 1981.

Lynn, John A., ed. *Tools of War: Instruments, Ideas, and Institutions of Warfare, 1445–1871.* Urbana: University of Illinois Press, 1990.

McNeill, William H. *The Pursuit of Power: Technology, Armed Force, and Society Since* A.D. *1000.* Chicago: University of Chicago Press, 1982.

McWhiney, Grady, and Perry D. Jamieson. *Attack and Die: Civil War Military Tactics and the Southern Heritage.* University: University of Alabama Press, 1982.

Schott, Linda. "Jane Addams and William James on Alternatives to War." *Journal of the History of Ideas* (1993): 241–54.

Showalter, Dennis E. *Railroads and Rifles: Soldiers, Technology, and the Unification of Germany.* Hamden, Conn.: Archon, 1976.

Van Creveld, Martin. *Supplying War: Logistics from Wallenstein to Patton.* Cambridge, England: Cambridge University Press, 1977.

———. *Technology and War: From 2000* B.C. *to the Present.* New York: Free Press, 1989.

## Barbaric Energy and Civilized Manners

Sir John Kaye is quoted in Byron Farwell, *Queen Victoria's Little Wars* (New York: Harper, 1972).

### *Works Cited*

Cooper, James Fenimore. "Preface to the Leather-Stocking Tales." In *The Deerslayer.* New York: Appleton, 1873.

Keeley, Lawrence H. *War Before Civilization: The Myth of the Peaceful Savage.* New York: Oxford, 1996.

### *Other Useful Works*

Appleby, Joyce. *Inheriting the Revolution: The First Generation of Americans.* Cambridge: Harvard University Press, 2000.

Clark, Anna. *The Struggle for the Breeches: Gender and the Making of the British Working Class.* Berkeley: University of California Press, 1995.

Edgerton, Robert B. *Death or Glory: The Legacy of the Crimean War.* Boulder, Colo.: Westview Press, 1999.

Flint, John. *Cecil Rhodes.* Boston: Little, Brown, 1974.

Green, Martin. *The Adventrous Male: Chapters in the History of the White Male Mind.* University Park: Pennsylvania State University Press, 1993.

Greenberg, Kenneth S. *Honor and Slavery.* Princeton, N.J.: Princeton University Press, 1996.

Horwitz, Tony. *Confederates in the Attic: Dispatches from the Unfinished Civil War.* New York: Pantheon, 1998.

Hull, Isabel V. *The Entourage of Kaiser Wilhelm II, 1888–1918.* Cambridge, England: Cambridge University Press, 1982.

Hyam, Ronald. *Empire and Sexuality: The British Experience.* Manchester, England: Manchester University Press, 1990.

Jenkyns, Richard. *The Victorians and Ancient Greece.* Cambridge: Harvard University Press, 1980.

Kanitz, Walter. *The White Kepi: A Casual History of the French Foreign Legion.* Chicago: Regnery, 1956.

Kimmel, Michael. *Manhood in America: A Cultural History.* New York: Free Press, 1996.

Kostyal, K. M. *Field of Battle: The Civil War Letters of Major Thomas J. Halsey*. Washington, D.C.: National Geographic Society, 1996.

Leslie, Edward E. *The Devil Knows How to Rule: The True Story of William Clarke Quantrill and His Confederate Raiders*. New York: Random House, 1996.

Levinson, Sanford. *Written in Stone: Public Monuments in Changing Societies*. Durham, N.C.: Duke University Press, 1998.

Liebersohn, Harry. *Aristocratic Encounters: European Travelers and North American Indians*. Cambridge: Cambridge University Press, 1998.

Mackenzie, John M. *Popular Imperialism and the Military, 1850–1950*. Manchester, England: Manchester University Press, 1992.

———, ed. *Propaganda and Empire: The Manipulation of British Public Opinion, 1880–1960*. Manchester, England: Manchester University Press, 1984.

Miller, Charles. *Khyber, British India's North West Frontier: The Story of an Imperial Migraine*. New York: Macmillan, 1977.

Millin, Sarah Gertrude. *Rhodes*. London: Chatto & Windus, 1937.

Milner, Clyde A., II, Carol A. O'Connor, Martha A. Sandweiss, eds. *The Oxford History of the American West*. New York: Oxford University Press, 1994.

Mosse, George L. *The Image of Man: the Creation of Modern Masculinity*. New York: Oxford University Press, 1996.

———. *The Nationalization of the Masses: Political Symbolism and Mass Movements in Germany from the Napoleonic Wars Through the Third Reich*. Ithaca, N.Y.: Cornell University Press, 1975.

Nutting, Anthony. *Gordon of Khartoum: Martyr and Misfit*. New York: Clarkson Potter, 1966.

Porter, Andrew. *European Imperialism, 1860–1914*. London: Macmillan, 1994.

Procter, Ben. *William Randolph Hearst: The Early Years, 1863–1910*. New York: Oxford University Press, 1998.

Silver, Alain. *The Samurai Film*. New York: A. S. Barnes, 1977.

Sobieszek, Robert A. *Ghost in the Shell: Photography and the Human Soul, 1850–2000*. Cambridge: MIT Press, 1999.

Strobel, Margaret. *European Women and the Second British Empire*. Bloomington: Indiana University Press, 1991.

Thorp, Raymond W., and Robert Bunker. *Crow Killer: The Saga of Liver-Eating Johnson*. Bloomington: Indiana University Press, 1958.

Trollope, Joanna. *Britannia's Daughters: Women of the British Empire*. London: Hutchinson, 1983. Esp. pp. 118–28, on "memsahib."

Trustram, Myna. *Women of the Regiment: Marriage and the Victorian Army*. Cambridge: Cambridge University Press, 1984.

Wachtel, Andrew Baruch. *Making a Nation, Breaking a Nation: Literature and Cultural Politics in Yugoslavia*. Stanford, Calif.: Stanford University Press, 1998.

Weber, Eugen. *Peasants into Frenchmen: The Modernization of Rural France, 1870–1914*. Stanford, Calif.: Stanford University Press, 1976.

## The Boy General

### *Works Cited*

Custer, Elizabeth B. *Boots and Saddles: or, Life in Dakota with General Custer*. Norman: University of Oklahoma Press, 1976.

Custer, George A. *My Life on the Plains*, ed. Milo Milton Quaife. Lincoln: University of Nebraska Press, 1952.

Hardorff, Richard G., ed. *Lakota Recollections of the Custer Fight: New Sources of Indian Military History*. Lincoln: University of Nebraska Press, 1997.

Taylor, William O. *With Custer on the Little Bighorn: A Newly Discovered First-Person Account*. New York: Viking, 1996.

Whittaker, Frederick. *A Complete Life of General George Armstrong Custer*. New York: Sheldon, 1876.

*Other Works of Interest*

Barnett, Louise. *Touched by Fire: The Life, Death, and Mythic Afterlife of George Armstrong Custer*. New York: Holt, 1996.

Connell, Evan S. *Son of the Morning Star: Custer and the Little Bighorn*. San Francisco: North Point, 1984.

Dixon, Joseph Kossuth. *The Vanishing Race: The Last Great Indian Council*. Garden City, N.Y.: Doubleday, 1914.

Hofling, Charles K. *Custer and the Little Big Horn: A Psychobiographical Inquiry*. Detroit: Wayne State University Press, 1981.

Lowie, Robert H. *The Crow Indians*. Lincoln: University of Nebraska Press, 1983.

Miller, David Humphreys. *Custer's Fall: The Indian Side of the Story*. Lincoln: University of Nebraska Press, 1957.

Utley, Robert. *Cavalier in Buckskins: George Armstrong Custer and the Western Military Frontier*. Norman: University of Oklahoma Press, 1988.

Welch, James, with Paul Stekler. *Killing Custer: The Battle of the Little Bighorn and the Fate of the Plains Indians*. New York: Norton, 1994.

## The Statistics of Human Nature

*Works Cited*

Conan Doyle, Arthur. *The Adventures of Sherlock Holmes*. New York: Penguin, 1981.

Stevenson, Robert Louis. *The Strange Case of Dr. Jekyll and Mr. Hyde*. New York: Signet, 1978.

Stoker, Bram. *Dracula*. New York: Signet, 1978.

*Other Useful Works*

Abrams, Philip. *The Origins of British Sociology, 1834–1914*. Chicago: University of Chicago Press, 1968.

McDonald, Lynn. *The Early Origins of the Social Sciences*. Montreal: McGill–Queen's University Press, 1993.

## The Specter of Degeneracy

*Works Cited*

Defoe, Daniel. "The True-Born Englishman." In George deF. Lord, ed. *Poems on Affairs of State*.

Fredrickson, George M. *The Inner Civil War: Northern Intellectuals and the Crisis of the Union*. New York: Harper & Row, 1965.

Lutz, Tom. *American Nervousness, 1903: An Anecdotal History*. Ithaca, N.Y.: Cornell University Press, 1991.

Mill, John Stuart. "On Civilization." In *John Stuart Mill: A Selection*, ed. John M. Robson. Indianapolis, Ind.: Odyssey, 1966.

Nordau, Max. *Degeneration*, intro. George L. Mosse. Lincoln: University of Nebraska Press, 1993.

Said, Edward W. *Orientalism*. New York: Vintage, 1978.

*Other Useful Works*

Barkan, Elazar, and Ron Bush, eds. *Prehistories of the Future: The Primitivist Project and the Culture of Modernism*. Stanford, Calif.: Stanford University Press, 1995.

Chamberlain, J. Edward, and Sander L. Gilman, eds. *Degeneration: The Dark Side of Progress*. New York: Columbia University Press, 1985.

Dijkstra, Bram. *Idols of Perversity: Fantasies of Feminine Evil in Fin-de-Siécle Culture*. New York: Oxford University Press, 1986.

Pick, Daniel. *Faces of Degeneration: A European Disorder, c. 1848–c. 1918*. Cambridge, England: Cambridge University Press, 1989.

## Masculine, Feminine, Effeminate

*Works Cited*

Austin, Mary. "Woman and Her War Loot." In *The Early Sunset Magazine, 1898–1928*, ed. Paul C. Johnson. San Francisco: California Historical Society, 1973.

Bernheimer, Charles. *Figures of Ill Repute: Representing Prostitution in Nineteenth-Century France*. Cambridge: Harvard University Press, 1989.

Harvey, John. *Men in Black*. Chicago: University of Chicago Press, 1995.

Higginson, Thomas Wentworth. *Army Life in a Black Regiment and Other Writings*. New York: Penguin, 1997.

James, William. *The Principles of Psychology*. Chicago: Encyclopedia Brittanica, 1990.

Krafft-Ebing, Richard. *Psychopathia Sexualis*. New York: Putnam, 1965.

Nye, Robert A. *Crime, Madness, and Politics in Modern France: The Medical Concept of National Decline*. Princeton, N.J.: Princeton University Press, 1984.

Sinfield, Alan. *The Wilde Century: Effeminacy, Oscar Wilde and the Queer Moment*. New York: Columbia University Press, 1994.

Trollope, Anthony. *The Prime Minister*. New York: Oxford University Press, 1983.

*Other Useful Works*

Adams, James Eli. *Dandies and Desert Saints: Styles of Victorian Manhood*. Ithaca, N.Y.: Cornell University Press, 1995.

Allen, Peter Lewis. *The Wages of Sin: Sex and Disease, Past and Present*. Chicago: University of Chicago Press, 2000.

Anderson, Patricia. *When Passion Reigned: Sex and the Victorians*. New York: Basic, 1995.

Ardener, Shirley, ed. *Perceiving Women*. New York: Wiley, 1975.

Birkett, Jennifer. *The Sins of the Fathers: Decadence in France, 1870–1914*. New York: Quartet, 1986.

Bristow, Joseph. *Effeminate England: Homoerotic Writing After 1885*. New York: Columbia University Press, 1995.

Bullough, Vern L. *Science in the Bedroom: A History of Sex Research*. New York: Basic, 1994.

Faber, Geoffrey. *Oxford Apostles: A Character Study of the Oxford Movement*. London: Faber and Faber, 1933.

Gosden, Roger. *Cheating Time: Science, Sex, and Aging.* New York: W. H. Freeman, 1996.
Greenberg, David F. *The Construction of Homosexuality.* Chicago: University of Chicago Press, 1988.
Hanson, Ellis. *Decadence and Catholicism.* Cambridge: Harvard University Press, 1997.
Holland, Vyvyan. *Son of Oscar Wilde,* rev. ed. New York: Carroll & Graf, 1999.
Maines, Rachel P. *The Technology of Orgasm: "Hysteria," the Vibrator, and Women's Sexual Satisfaction.* Baltimore: Johns Hopkins University Press, 1999.
Mason, Michael. *The Making of Victorian Sexuality.* New York: Oxford University Press, 1994.
Mosse, George L. *Nationalism and Sexuality: Respectability and Abnormal Sexuality in Modern Europe.* New York: Howard Fertig, 1985.
Porter, Roy, and Lesley Hall. *The Facts of Life: The Creation of Sexual Knowledge in Britain, 1650–1950.* New Haven, Conn.: Yale University Press, 1995.
Rosario, Vernon A. *The Erotic Imagination: French Histories of Perversity.* New York: Oxford University Press, 1997.
Showalter, Elaine, and English Showalter. "Victorian Women and Menstruation." *Victorian Studies* (September 1970): 83–89.
Simpson, Colin, Lewis Chester, and David Leitch. *The Cleveland Street Affair.* Boston: Little, Brown, 1976.
Slotkin, Richard. *Regeneration Through Violence: The Mythology of the American Frontier, 1600–1860.* Middletown, Conn.: Wesleyan University Press, 1973.
Smith-Rosenberg, Carroll. *Disorderly Conduct: Visions of Gender in Victorian America.* New York: Knopf, 1985.
Spencer, Colin. *Homosexuality in History.* New York: Harcourt Brace, 1995.

## Sports and the Manly Ideal

### *Works Cited*

Gide, André. *Corydon,* tr. Richard Howard. New York: Farrar, Straus & Giroux, 1983.
Rybczynski, Witold. *A Clearing in the Distance: Frederick Law Olmsted and America in the Nineteenth Century.* New York: Scribner, 1999.
Van Dalen, Deobold B., Elmer D. Mitchell, and Bruce L. Bennett. *A World History of Physical Education: Cultural, Philosophical, Comparative.* Englewood Cliffs, N.J.: Prentice-Hall, 1953.
Vertinsky, Patricia. *The Eternally Wounded Woman: Women, Doctors and Exercise in the Late Nineteenth Century.* Manchester, England: Manchester University Press, 1990.

### *Other Useful Works*

Early, Gerald. *The Culture of Bruising: Essays on Prizefighting, Literature, and Modern American Culture.* Hopewell, N.J.: Ecco, 1994.
Goldstein, Warren. *Playing for Keeps: A History of Early Baseball.* Ithaca, N.Y.: Cornell University Press, 1989.
Guttmann, Allen. *A Whole New Ball Game: An Interpretation of American Sports.* Chapel Hill: University of North Carolina Press, 1988.
Hoberman, John M. *Sport and Political Ideology.* Austin: University of Texas Press, 1984.
MacAloon, John J. *This Great Symbol: Pierre de Coubertin and the Origin of the Modern Olympic Games.* Chicago: University of Chicago Press, 1981.
Mangan, J. A., ed. *Sport in Europe: Politics, Class, Gender,* vol. 1. London: Frank Cass, 1999.

McCrone, Kathleen E. *Playing the Game: Sport and the Physical Emancipation of Women, 1870–1914*. Lexington: University Press of Kentucky, 1988.

Oriard, Michael. *Reading Football: How the Popular Press Created an American Spectacle*. Chapel Hill: University of North Carolina Press, 1993.

White, C. Edward. *Creating the National Pastime: Baseball Transforms Itself, 1903–1953*. Princeton, N.J.: Princeton University Press, 1996.

The Crucible of the 1890s

*Works Cited*

Davis, Linda H. *Badge of Courage: The Life of Stephen Crane*. New York: Houghton Mifflin, 1998.

Freidel, Frank Burt. *The Splendid Little War*. Boston: Little, Brown, 1958.

Holmes, Oliver Wendell, Jr. "A Soldier's Faith" (1895), Memorial Day speech. In *The Essential Holmes*, ed. Richard A. Posner. Chicago: University of Chicago Press, 1992.

Levine, Philippa. *Prostitution, Race, and Politics: Policing Venereal Disease in the British Empire*. New York: Routledge, 2003.

Roosevelt, Theodore. "The Strenuous Life." In *Essays and Addresses*. New York: Century, 1900.

Turner, Frederick Jackson. *Rereading*, ed. John Mack Faragher. New York: Holt, 1994.

Wister, Owen. *Owen Wister's West: Selected Articles*, ed. Robert Murray Davis. Albuquerque: University of New Mexico Press, 1987.

———. *The Virginian: A Horseman of the Plains*, ed. Philip Durham. Boston: Houghton Mifflin, 1968.

*On the Early History of Anthropology*

Harris, Marvin. *The Rise of Anthropological Theory: A History of Theories of Culture*. New York: Crowell, 1968.

Koepping, Klaus-Peter. *Adolf Bastian and the Psychic Unity of Mankind: The Foundations of Anthropology in Nineteenth-Century Germany*. London: University of Queensland Press, 1983.

Niethammer, Carolyn. *Daughters of the Earth: The Lives and Legends of American Indian Women*. New York: Simon & Schuster, 1977.

Rivers, W. H. R. *Psychology and Ethnology*, ed. G. Elliot Smith. London: Routledge, 1999.

Stocking, George W., Jr. *After Tylor: British Social Anthropology, 1888–1951*. Madison: University of Wisconsin Press, 1995.

———. *Victorian Anthropology*. New York: Free Press, 1987.

Vincent, Joan. *Anthropology and Politics: Visions, Traditions, and Trends*. Tucson: University of Arizona Press, 1990.

*On Dreyfus*

Birnbaum, Pierre. *Anti-Semitism in France: A Political History from Léon Blum to the Present*, tr. Miriam Kochan. Oxford, England: Blackwell, 1992.

Bredin, Jean-Denis. *The Affair: The Case of Alfred Dreyfus*, tr. Jeffrey Mehlman. New York: Braziller, 1986.

Burns, Michael. *France and the Dreyfus Affair: A Documentary History*. Boston: Bedford/St. Martin's, 1999.

Cahm, Eric. *The Dreyfus Affair in French Society and Politics*. London: Longmans, 1996.

Johnson, Martin P. *The Dreyfus Affair*. New York: St. Martin's, 1999.

Liddell Hart, Basil. "French Military Ideas Before the First World War." In Martin Gilbert, *A Century of Conflict, 1850–1950*. New York: Atheneum, 1967.

Nye, Robert. *Masculinity and Male Codes of Honor in France*. New York: Oxford University Press, 1993.

Zola, Emile. *The Dreyfus Affair: J'Accuse and Other Writings*, ed. Alain Pagés, tr. Eleanor Levieux. New Haven, Conn.: Yale University Press, 1996.

## Be Prepared

### *Works Cited*

Ceadel, Martin. *Thinking About Peace and War*. New York: Oxford, 1987.

Hall, G. Stanley. *Adolescence*, 2 vols. New York: Appleton, 1904.

Hemingway, Ernest. *A Farewell to Arms* [1929]. New York: Simon & Schuster, 1995.

Rosenthal, Michael. *The Character Factory: Baden-Powell and the Origins of the Boy Scout Movement*. New York: Pantheon, 1986.

Vagts, Alfred. *A History of Militarism*, rev. ed. New York: Meridian, 1959.

### *On Youth Movements*

Jeal, Tim. *The Boy-Man: The Life of Lord Baden-Powell*. New York: Morrow, 1990.

Laqueur, Walter. *Young Germany: A History of the German Youth Movement*. London: Routledge, 1962.

MacDonald, Robert H. *Sons of the Empire: The Frontier and the Boy Scout Movement, 1890–1918*. Toronto: University of Toronto Press, 1993.

Mosse, George L. *The Nationalization of the Masses: Political Symbolism and Mass Movements in Germany from the Napoleonic Wars Through the Third Reich*. Ithaca, N.Y.: Cornell University Press, 1975.

### *Other Useful Works*

Benfey, Christopher. *The Double Life of Stephen Crane*. New York: Knopf, 1992.

Brown, Bertram Wyatt. *Southern Honor: Ethics and Behavior in the Old South*. New York: Oxford University Press, 1982.

Davis, David Brion. *From Homicide to Slavery: Studies in American Culture*. New York: Oxford University Press, 1986.

Dawson, Graham. *Soldier Heroes: British Adventure, Empire, and the Imagining of Masculinities*. New York: Routledge, 1994.

Estleman, Loren D. *The Wister Trace: Classic Novels of the American Frontier*. Ottawa, Ill.: Jameson, 1987.

Harris, Ruth. *Murders and Madness: Medicine, Law, and Society in the Fin de Siécle*. Oxford, England: Clarendon, 1989.

Horsham, Reginald. *Race and Manifest Destiny: The Origins of American Racial Anglo-Saxonism*. Cambridge, Mass.: Harvard University Press, 1981.

Kann, Mark E. *On the Man Question: Gender and Civic Virtue in America*. Philadelphia: Temple University Press, 1991.

Leach, William. *Land of Desire: Merchants, Power, and the Rise of a New American Culture*. New York: Pantheon, 1993.

Moeller, Susan D. *Shooting War: Photography and the American Experience of Combat*. New York: Basic Books, 1989.

Nelson, Claudia. *Boys Will Be Girls: The Feminine Ethic and British Children's Fiction, 1857–1917*. New Brunswick, N.J.: Rutgers University Press, 1991.

Price, Richard. *An Imperial War and the British Working Class: Working-Class Attitudes and Reactions to the Boer War, 1899–1902*. London: Routledge, 1972.

Remington, Frederic. *Frederic Remington's Own West*, ed. Harold McCracken. New York: Dial Press, 1960.

Rivers, J. E. *Proust and the Art of Love: The Aesthetics of Sexuality in the Life, Times, and Art of Marcel Proust*. New York: Columbia University Press, 1980.

Roper, Michael, and John Tosh, eds. *Manful Assertions: Masculinities in Britain Since 1800*. New York: Routledge, 1991.

Street, Brian V. *The Savage in Literature: Representations of "Primitive" Society in English Fiction, 1858–1920*. London: Routledge, 1975.

Townsend, Kim. *Manhood at Harvard: William James and Others*. New York: Norton, 1996.

Weber, Eugen. *France: Fin de Siècle*. Cambridge, Mass.: Harvard University Press, 1986.

White, G. Edward. *The Eastern Establishment and the Western Experience: The West of Frederic Remington, Theodore Roosevelt, and Owen Wister*. New Haven, Conn.: Yale University Press, 1968.

Wister, Owen. *Salvation Gap and Other Western Classics*. Lincoln: University of Nebraska Press, 1999.

## PART VII. THE TWENTIETH CENTURY: WEAPONS OF MASS DESTRUCTION AND THE WARRIOR SPIRIT

### Honor in No-Man's-Land

Irving Berlin is quoted in Robert Gottlieb and Robert Kimball, eds. *Reading Lyrics*. New York: Pantheon, 2000.

#### *Works Cited*

Aldington, Richard. *Death of a Hero*. New York: Covici Friede, 1929.

Brooke, Rupert. *1914 & Other Poems*. London: Sidgwick & Jackson, 1931.

Ecksteins, Modris. *Rites of Spring: The Great War and the Birth of the Modern Age*. New York: Houghton Mifflin, 1989.

#### *Other Useful Works*

Buruma, Ian. *Anglomania: A European Love Affair*. New York: Random House, 1998.

Gilman, Charlote Perkins. *The Man-Made World, or, Our Androcentric Culture*. [1911]. New York: Source, 1970.

Horne, John and Alan Kramer. *German Atrocities, 1914: A History of Denial*. New Haven: Yale, 2001.

Hynes, Samuel. The *Edwardian Turn of Mind*. Princeton, N.J.: Princeton University, 1958.

———. *The Soldier's Tale: Bearing Witness to Modern War*. New York: Penguin, 1997.

Janney, William, Jr. *The Lions of July: Preludes to War, 1914*. Novato, Calif: Presidio, 1995.

Owen, Wilfrid. *The Poems of Wilfred Owen*, ed. Jon Stallworthy. New York: Norton, 1985.

Paret, Peter, Beth Irwin Lewis, and Paul Paret. *Persuasive Images: Posters of War and Revolution from the Hoover Institution Archives*. Princeton, N.J.: Princeton University, 1992.

Silkin, Jon, ed. *The Penguin Book of First World War Poetry*. New York: Penguin, 1979.

Stallworthy, Jon, ed. *The Oxford Book of War Poetry*. New York: Oxford, 1984.

## Death at a Distance

### *Works Cited*

Richard Norton is quoted in Arlen J. Hansen, *Gentleman Volunteers*. New York: Arcade, 1995.

Fussell, Paul. *The Great War and Modern Memory*. New York: Oxford, 1975.
Graves, Robert. *Goodbye to All That*. Harmondsworth: Penguin, 1950.
Holland, Vyvyan. *Son of Oscar Wilde*. New York: Carroll and Graf, 1999.
Keegan, John. *The Face of Battle*. New York: Viking, 1975.
Schickel, Richard. *D. W. Griffith: An American Life*. New York: Simon & Schuster, 1984.

### *Other Useful Works*

Berghahn, Volker R. *Militarism: The History of an International Debate, 1861–1979*. New York: St. Martin's, 1982.
Bourke, Joanna. *An Intimate History of Killing: Face-to-Face Killing in Twentieth-Century Warfare*. New York: Basic, 1999.
———. *Dismembering the Male: Men's Bodies, Britain, and the Great War*. Chicago: University of Chicago, 1995.
Brownlow, Kevin. *The War, The West, and the Wilderness*. New York: Knopf, 1979.
Carrington, Charles [Charles Edmonds]. *A Subaltern's War*. London: Davies, 1929.
Cobb, Richard. *French and Germans, Germans and French: A Personal Interpretation of France Under Two Occupations, 1914–1918, 1940–1944*. Hanover, N.H.: University Press of New England, 1983.
Gilbert, Martin. *The First World War: A Complete History*. New York: Henry Holt, 1994.
Herrman, David G. *The Arming of Europe and the Making of the First World War*. Princeton, N.J.: Princeton University, 1995.
Middlebrook, Martin. *The First Day on the Somme*. New York: Norton, 1972.
Terraine, John. *The Smoke and the Fire: Myths and Anti-Myths of War, 1861–1945*. London: Sidgwick and Jackson, 1980.
Webster, Donovan. *Aftermath: The Remnants of War*. New York: Pantheon, 1995.

## Reason in Madness

### *Works Cited*

Durkheim, Emile. *Suicide: A Study in Sociology*, tr. John A. Spaulding and George Simpson. New York: Free Press, 1951.

### *Other Useful Works*

Call, Annie Payson. *Nerves and the War*. Boston: Little, Brown, 1918.
Hall, Herbert. *War-Time Nerves*. Boston: Houghton Mifflin, 1918.
Hall, Nathan G., Jr. *The Rise and Crisis of Psychoanalysis in the United States: Freud and the Americans, 1917–1985*. New York: Oxford, 1995.
Higonnet, Margaret Randolph, Jane Jenson, Sonya Michel, and Margaret Collins Weitz, eds. *Behind the Lines: Gender and the Two World Wars*. New Haven, Conn.: Yale, 1987.
Levine, Murray. *The History and Politics of Community Mental Health*. New York: Oxford, 1981.
——— and Adeline Levine. *A Social History of Helping Services: Clinic, Court, School, and Community*. New York: Appleton–Century Crofts, 1970.

Showalter, Elaine. *Hysteries: Hysterical Epidemics and Modern Culture*. New York: Columbia, 1997.

———. *The Female Malady: Women, Madness and English Culture, 1830–1980*. New York: Pantheon, 1985.

Stone, Martin. "Shellshock and the Psychologists," in *Anatomy of Madness*, eds. W. F. Bynum, Roy Porter, Michael Shepherd, 3 vols. London: Tavistock, 1985 vol. 2, pp. 242–71.

Winter, J. M. "Military Fitness and Civilian Health in Britain during the First world War," *Journal of Contemporary History* 15, 2 (April 1980), pp. 211–44.

———. *Sites of Memory, Sites of Mourning: The Great War in European Cultural History*. Cambridge, England: Cambridge University, 1995.

———, ed. *Shell-shock and the Cultural History of the Great War*. *Journal of Contemporary History* 35, 1 (2000).

## Primitive Body and Machine Body

### *Works Cited*

Barbusse, Henri. *Under Fire: The Story of a Squad* (*Le Feu*). New York: Dutton, 1917.

Dos Passos, John. *Three Soldiers*. New York: Penguin, 1997.

Hynes, Samuel. *A War Imagined: The First World War and English Culture*. New York: Atheneum, 1991.

Hašek, Jaroslav. *The Good Soldier Schweik*, tr. Paul Selver. New York: New American Library, 1953.

Jünger, Ernst. *The Storm of Steel*. New York: Fertig, 1995.

———. *Copse 125*. London: Chatto & Windus, 1930.

[Manning, Frederic.] *The Middle Parts of Fortune: Somme & Ancre, 1996*, 2 vols. London: Peter Davies, The Piazza Press, 1929 (published expurgated as *Her Privates We*, written by "Private 19022").

Remarque, Erich Maria. *All Quiet on the Western Front*. Boston: Little, Brown, 1929.

Rhodes, Anthony. *D'Annunzio: The Poet as Superman*. New York: McDowell, Obolensky, 1959.

Sorel, Georges. *Reflections on Violence*, tr. T. E. Hulme and J. Roth. London: Collier, 1951.

### *Other Useful Works*

Hewitt, Andrew. *Fascist Modernism: Aesthetics, Politics, and the Avant-Garde*. Stanford, Calif.: Stanford University Press, 1993.

Humphreys, Richard. *Futurism*. New York: Cambridge University Press, 1999.

Joll, James. *Three Intellectuals in Politics*. New York: Pantheon, 1950.

Neaman, Elliot Y. *A Dubious Past: Ernst Jünger and the Politics of Literature after Nazism*. Berkeley, Calif.: University of California, 1999.

Nevin, Thomas. *Ernst Jünger and Germany: Into the Abyss, 1914–1945*. Durham, N.C.: Duke University, 1995.

Stern, J. P. *Ernst Jünger*. New Haven, Conn.: Yale, 1953.

## T. E. Lawrence: The Resurrection of Adventure

### *Works Cited*

Hodson, Joel C. *Lawrence of Arabia and American Culture: The Making of a Transatlantic Legend*. Westport, Conn.: Greenwood Press, 1995.

Lawrence, A. W., ed. *T. E. Lawrence by His Friends*. London: Jonathan Cape, 1937.
Lawrence, T. E. *Selected Letters*, ed. Malcom Brown. New York: Norton, 1989.
———. *Seven Pillars Of Wisdom*. Garden City, N.Y.: Doubleday, 1938.

*Other Useful Works*

Adams, James Eli. *Dandies and Desert Saints: Styles of Victorian Manhood*. Ithaca, N.Y.: Cornell, 1995.
Allen, M. D. *The Medievalism of Lawrence of Arabia*. University Park, Pa.: Pennsylvania State University, 1981.
Crawford, Fred D. *Richard Aldington and Lawrence of Arabia: A Cautionary Tale*. Carbondale, Ill.: Southern Illinois Press, 1998.
Dawson, Graham. *Soldier Heroes: British Adventure, Empire and the Imaginings of Masculinities*. London: Routledge, 1994.
Kennedy, Kieran, Jr. "Who Framed Roger Casement?" *Lingua Franca* 10, 8 (November 2000): 44–53.
O'Donnell, Thomas J. *The Confessions of T. E. Lawrence: The Romanic Hero's Presentation of Self*. Athens, Ohio: Ohio University Press, 1979.
Richelson, Jeffrey T. *A Century of Spies: Intelligence in the Twentieth Century*. New York: Oxford, 1995.

## Front Line at Home

*Works Cited*

Ceadel, Martin. *The Origins of War Prevention: The British Peace Movement and International Relations, 1730–1854*. Oxford, England: Clarendon, 1996.
*Dearborn Independent*. "The International Jew." In *The Fear of Conspiracy: Images of Un-American Subversion from the Revolution to the Present*, ed. David Brion Davis. Ithaca, N.Y.: Cornell University Press, 1971, pp. 228–40.
Dijkstra, Bram. *Evil Sisters: The Threat of Female Sexuality and the Cult of Manhood*. New York: Knopf, 1996.
Dippel, John V. H. *Bound upon a Wheel of Fire: Why So Many German Jews Made the Tragic Decision to Remain in Nazi Germany*. New York: Basic. 1996.
Gottlieb, Robert, and Robert Kimball, eds. *Reading Lyrics*. New York: Pantheon, 2000.
Grinker, Roy R., and John P. Spiegel. *War Neuroses*. Philadelphia: Blakiston, 1945.
Hammett, Dashiell. *Red Harvest*. New York: Knopf, 1929.
Holmes, Oliver Wendell, Jr. "A Soldier's Faith." In *The Essential Holmes*, ed. Richard A. Posner. Chicago: University of Chicago Press, 1992.
Hove, Arthur, ed. *Gold Diggers of 1933*. Madison, Wisc.: University of Wisconsin Press, 1980.
Kaes, Anton, Martin Jay, and Edward Dimendberg, eds. *The Weimar Republic Sourcebook*. Berkeley: University of California, 1994.
Leed, Eric J. *No Man's Land: Combat and Identity in World War I*. Cambridge, England: Cambridge University Press, 1979.

*Other Useful Works*

Brock, Peter. *Freedom from Violence: Sectarian Nonresistance from the Middle Ages to the Great War*. Toronto: University of Toronto Press, 1991.
———. *Pacifism in the United States from the Colonial Period to the First World War*. Princeton, N.J.: Princeton University Press, 1968.

———. *The Quaker Peace Testimony, 1660 to 1914*. Syracuse, N.Y.: Syracuse University Press, 1990.

Ceadel, Martin. *The Origins of War Prevention: The British Peace Movement and International Relations, 1730–1854*. Oxford, England: Clarendon, 1996.

———. *Pacifism in Britain, 1914–1945: The Defining of a Faith*. Oxford, England: Clarendon, 1980.

———. *Thinking About Peace and War*. New York: Oxford University Press, 1987.

Cooper, Sandi E. *Patriotic Pacifism: Waging War on War in Europe, 1815–1914*. Oxford: Oxford University Press, 1991.

Diggins, John P. *Mussolini and Fascism: The View from America*. Princeton, N.J.: Princeton University Press, 1972.

Fischer, Klaus P. *Nazi Germany: A New History*. New York: Continuum, 1995.

Hess, Stephen, and Sandy Northrop. *Drawn and Quartered: The History of American Political Cartoons*. Montgomery, Ala.: Elliott & Clark, 1996.

Ingram, Norman. *The Politics of Dissent: Pacifism in France, 1919–1939*. Oxford, England: Clarendon, 1991.

Jay, Martin. *Marxism and Totality: The Adventures of a Concept from Lukács to Habermas*. Berkeley: University of California Press, 1984.

Kaplan, Carla. "Undesirable Desire: Citizenship and Romance in Modern American Fiction." *Modern Fiction Studies* 43 (spring 1997): 144–69.

Keen, Sam. *Faces of the Enemy: Reflections of the Hostile Imagination*. San Francisco: Harper & Row, 1986.

Lyttelton, Adrian, ed. and intro. *Italian Fascisms from Pareto to Gentile*. New York: Harper, 1973.

Mack Smith, Dennis. *Mussolini*. New York: Knopf, 1982.

Pencak, William. *For God and Country: The American Legion, 1919–1941*. Boston: Northeastern University Press, 1989.

Ridley, Jasper. *Mussolini*. New York: St. Martin's, 1997.

Spackman, Barbara. *Fascist Virilities: Rhetoric, Ideology, and Social Fantasy in Italy*. Minneapolis, Minn.: University of Minnesota Press, 1996.

Stern, Fritz. *The Politics of Cultural Despair: A Study in the Rise of the Germanic Ideology*. Berkeley: University of California Press, 1961.

Weber, Eugen. *Varieties of Fascism*. Princeton, N.J.: Van Nostrand, 1964.

## The Thirty-one Years' War

### *Works Cited*

Carrington, Charles. *Soldier from the Wars Returning*. New York: McKay, 1965.

Chandler, Raymond. *The Big Sleep*. New York: Random House, 1992.

———. *Later Novels and Other Writings*. New York: Library of America, 1995.

Crane, Stephen. *The Red Badge of Courage: Great Short Works*. New York: Harper, 1965.

Eliot, T. S. *Complete Poems and Plays, 1909–1950*. New York: Harcourt Brace, 1952.

Fredrickson, George M. *The Inner Civil War: Northern Intellectuals and the Crisis of the Union*. New York: Harper & Row, 1965.

Hammett, Dashiell. *The Maltese Falcon*. New York: Random House, 1992.

### *Other Useful Works*

Bond, Brian. *Liddell Hart: A Study of Military Thought*. New Brunswick, N.J.: Rutgers University Press, 1977.

Watt, Donald Cameron. *Too Serious a Business: European Armed Forces and the Approach to the Second World War.* Berkeley: University of California Press, 1975.

Weber, Eugen. *The Hollow Years: France in the 1930s.* New York: Norton, 1994.

## The Threat of Impurity

### *Works Cited*

Aldington, Richard. *Death of a Hero.* New York: Covici Friede, 1929.

Graves, Robert, and Alan Hodge. *The Long Week End: A Social History of Great Britain, 1918–1939.* New York: Macmillan, 1941.

Hanson, Patricia King, ed. *The American Film Institute Catalogue: Feature Films, 1911–1920.* Berkeley: University of California Press, 1988.

Hirschfeld, Magnus. *The Sexual History of the World War.* New York: Falstaff, 1937.

Kennedy, David M. *Over Here: The First World War and American Society.* New York: Oxford University Press, 1980.

Kipling, Rudyard. *Complete Verse.* New York: Doubleday, 1940.

Miller, Henry. *Tropic of Capricorn.* Paris: Obelisk, 1957.

Terman, Lewis Madison, and Catherine Cox Miles. *Sex and Personality: Studies in Masculinity and Femininity.* New York: McGraw-Hill, 1936.

Weininger, Otto. *Sex and Character,* authorized translation from the 6th German ed. New York: Putnam, 1906.

### *Other Useful Works*

Sengoopta, Chandak. *Otto Weininger: Sex, Science, and Self in Imperial Vienna.* Chicago: University of Chicago Press, 2000.

Studlar, Gaylyn. *This Mad Masquerade: Stardom and Masculinity in the Jazz Age.* New York: Columbia University Press, 1996.

Theweleit, Klaus. *Male Fantasies,* tr. Stephen Conway, 2 vols. Minneapolis, Minn.: University of Minnesota Press, 1987.

Tuana, Nancy. *The Less Noble Sex: Scientific, Religious, and Philosophical Conceptions of Woman's Nature.* Bloomington, Ind.: Indiana University Press, 1993.

## Targeting Civilians

### *Works Cited*

Friedrich, Otto. *Blood and Iron: From Bismarck to Hitler, the von Moltke Family's Impact on German History.* New York: HarperCollins, 1995.

Herwig, Holger H. *Politics of Frustration: The United States in German Naval Planning, 1889–1941.* Boston: Little, Brown, 1976.

Milward, Alan S. *The German Economy at War.* London: Athlone Press, 1965.

### *Other Useful Works*

Burrin, Philippe. *France Under the Germans,* tr. Janet Lloyd. New York: New Press, 1996.

Cobb, Richard. *French and Germans, Germans and French: A Personal Interpretation of France Under Two Occupations, 1914–1918, 1940–1944.* Hanover, N.H.: University Press of New England, 1983.

Gleason, Abbot. *Totalitarianism: The Inner History of the Cold War.* New York: Oxford University Press, 1995.

Harper, Phillip Brian. *Are We Not Men? Masculine Anxiety and African-American Identity.* New York: Oxford University Press, 1996.

Kee, Robert. *1939: In the Shadow of War.* Boston: Little, Brown, 1984.

———. *1945: The World We Fought For.* Boston: Little, Brown, 1985.

## No Retreat and Unconditional Surrender

### *Works Cited*

Dower, John W. *War Without Mercy: Race and Power in the Pacific War.* New York: Pantheon, 1986.

Mayer, S. L., ed. *Signal: Hitler's Wartime Picture Magazine.* Englewood Cliffs, N.J.: Prentice-Hall, 1976.

———. *Signal: Years of Triumph, 1940–42.* Englewood Cliffs, N.J.: Prentice-Hall, 1978.

Nitobe, Inazo. *Bushido: The Soul of Japan,* tr. William Elliot Griffin. Rutland, Vt.: Tuttle, 1969.

### *Other Useful Works*

Ambrose, Stephen E. *Band of Brothers: E Company, 506th Regiment, 101st Airborne from Normandy to Hitler's Eagle's Nest.* New York: Simon & Schuster, 1992.

Dear, I. C. B., and M. R. D. Foot, eds. *The Oxford Companion to World War II.* New York: Oxford University Press, 1995.

Hoopes, Roy. *When the Stars Went to War: Hollywood and World War II.* New York: Random House, 1994.

King, Winston. *Zen and the Way of the Sword: Arming the Samurai Psyche.* New York: Oxford University Press, 1993.

O'Neill, Richard. *Suicide Squads: Axis and Allied Special Attack Weapons of World War II: Their Development and Their Missions.* London: Salamander, 1981.

Overy, Richard. *Why the Allies Won.* New York: Norton, 1996.

Watt, Donald Cameron. *Too Serious a Business: European Armed Forces and the Approach to the Second World War.* Berkeley: University of California Press, 1975.

Weinberg, Gerhard L. *A World at Arms: A Global History of World War II.* Cambridge, England: Cambridge University Press, 1994.

## Shadows on the Wall and the Common Man

### *Works Cited*

Fussell, Paul. *Wartime: Understanding and Behavior in the Second World War.* New York: Oxford University Press, 1989.

Kennedy, Paul. *The Rise and Fall of the Great Powers: Economic Change and Military Conflict from 1500 to 2000.* New York: Random House, 1987.

Kennett, Lee. *G.I.: The American Soldier in World War II.* Norman, Okla.: University of Oklahoma Press, 1997.

Mailer, Norman. *The Naked and the Dead.* New York: Rinehart, 1948.

———. *The White Negro.* San Francisco: City Lights, 1957.

Mauldin, Bill. *Up Front.* New York: Henry Holt, 1945.

Roeder, George H., Jr. *The Censored War: American Visual Experience During World War Two.* New Haven, Conn.: Yale University Press, 1993.

Wynn, Neil A. *The Afro-American and the Second World War,* rev. ed. New York: Holmes and Meier, 1993.

*Other Useful Works*

Aichinger, Peter. *The American Soldier in Fiction, 1880–1963: A History of Attitudes Toward Warfare and the Military Establishment.* Ames, Iowa: Iowa State University Press, 1975.

Barnett, Corelli. *The Audit of War: The Illusion and Reality of Britain as a Great Nation.* London: Macmillan, 1986.

———. *The Lost Victory: British Dreams, British Realities, 1945–1950.* London: Macmillan, 1995.

Bix, Herbert P. *Hirohito and the Making of Modern Japan.* New York: HarperCollins, 2000.

Dower, John W. *Embracing Defeat: Japan in the Wake of World War II.* New York: Norton, 1999.

Keegan, John. *The Battle for History: Re-fighting World War II.* New York: Vintage, 1995.

Lee, Irvin H. *Negro Medal of Honor Men.* New York: Dodd, Mead, 1968.

Lee, Ulysses. *The Employment of Negro Troops.* Washington, D.C.: Center of Military History, 1963.

Stouffer, Samuel A., et al. *The American Soldier,* 4 vols. Princeton, N.J.: Princeton University Press, 1949–50. Vol. 1, *Adjustment During Army Life;* vol. 2, *Combat and Its Aftermath;* vol. 3, *Experiments on Mass Communication;* vol. 4, *Measurement and Prediction.*

Winkler, Allan M. *The Politics of Propaganda: The Office of War Information, 1942–1945.* New Haven, Conn.: Yale University Press, 1978.

## Brainwashing and the War Within

*Works Cited*

Arendt, Hannah. *The Origins of Totalitarianism.* New York: Harcourt, 1973.

Dallek, Robert. *The American Style of Foreign Policy: Cultural Politics and Foreign Affairs.* New York: Oxford University Press, 1983.

Ginzberg, Eli, John L. Herma, and Sol W. Ginsburg. *Psychiatry and Military Manpower: A Reappraisal of the Experience in World War II.* New York: King's Crown, 1953.

Kinkead, Eugene. *In Every War but One.* New York: Norton, 1959.

Liddell Hart, B. H. *The Revolution in Warfare.* New Haven, Conn.: Yale University Press, 1947.

Orwell, George. *Homage to Catalonia.* New York: Harcourt, 1952.

———. *1984.* New York: Harcourt, 1949.

Packard, Vance. *The Hidden Persuaders.* New York: McKay, 1957.

Philbrick, Herbert A. "Can an American Be Trusted?" *Saturday Review of Literature,* April 5, 1952, 20–21.

———. *I Led Three Lives: Citizen, "Communist," Counterspy.* New York: Grosset & Dunlap, 1952.

Podell, Janet, and Steven Anzovin. *Speeches of the American Presidents.* New York: Wilson, 1988.

Robin, Ron. *The Barbed-Wire College: Reeducating German POWs in the United States During World War II.* Princeton, N.J.: Princeton University Press, 1995.

*Other Useful Works*

Garrett, Richard. *P.O.W.* London: David & Charles, 1981.

Kedward, Roderick, and Roger Austin, eds. *Vichy France and the Resistance: Culture and Ideology.* Totowa, N.J.: Barnes & Noble, 1985.

Lifton, Robert J. *Thought Reform and the Psychology of Totalism: A Study of "Brainwashing" in China*. New York: Norton, 1961.

Marks, John. *The Search for the "Manchurian Candidate": The CIA and Mind Control*. New York: Times Books, 1979.

Wainstock, Dennis D. *Truman, MacArthur, and the Korean War*. Westport, Conn.: Greenwood, 1999.

## The Solitude of the Westerner

### *Works Cited*

Dwight Eisenhower is quoted by Stephen Ambrose in *Citizen Soldiers: The U.S. Army from the Normandy Beaches to the Bulge to the Surrender of Germany, June 7, 1944–May 7, 1945*. New York: Simon & Schuster, 1997.

Buruma, Ian. *Behind the Mask: On Sexual Demons, Sacred Mothers, Transvestites, Gangsters, Drifters and Other Japanese Cultural Heroes*. New York: Pantheon, 1984.

Lindbergh, Charles A. *Autobiography of Values*. New York: Harcourt Brace Jovanovich, 1978.

Spillane, Mickey. *I, the Jury*. New York: Signet, 1947.

### *Other Useful Works*

Braudy, Leo. *The World in a Frame: What We See in Films*, 25th anniversary ed. Chicago, Ill.: University of Chicago Press, 2002.

Buscombe, Edward, ed. *The BFI Companion to the Western*. New York: Da Capo, 1988.

Cawelti, John G. *The Six-Gun Mystique*. Bowling Green, Ohio: Bowling Green University Press, 1971.

Wright, Will. *Sixguns and Society*. Berkeley: University of California Press, 1975.

## Postwar Male Sexuality and the Kinsey Reports

### *Works Cited*

Bérubé, Allan. *Coming Out Under Fire*. New York: Free Press, 1990.

Brooks, Gwendolyn. *Annie Allen*. New York: Harper, 1949.

D'Emilio, John, and Estelle B. Freedman. *Intimate Matters: A History of Sexuality in America*, 2d ed. Chicago: University of Chicago Press, 1997.

Kinsey, Alfred C., Wardell B. Pomeroy, and Clyde E. Martin. *Sexual Behavior in the Human Female*. Philadelphia: W. B. Saunders, 1953.

———. *Sexual Behavior in the Human Male*. Philadelphia: W. B. Saunders, 1948.

Lait, Jack, and Lee Mortimer. *U.S.A. Confidential*. New York: Crown, 1952.

Lewes, Kenneth. *The Psychoanalytic Theory of Male Homosexuality*. New York: Penguin, 1988.

Lundberg, Ferdinand, and Marynia Farnham. *Modern Woman: The Lost Sex*. New York: Harper, 1947.

Salinger, J. D. *The Catcher in the Rye*. New York: Bantam, 1964.

Whyte, William H., Jr. *The Organization Man*. Garden City, N.Y.: Doubleday, 1956.

Wylie, Philip. *The Disappearance*. New York: Rinehart, 1951.

———. *Generation of Vipers*. New York: Rinehart, 1942.

### *Other Useful Works*

Brecher, Edward M. *The Sex Researchers*. Boston: Little, Brown, 1969.

Ehrenreich, Barbara. *The Hearts of Men: American Dreams and the Flight from Commitment*. Garden City, N.Y.: Doubleday, 1983.

Gathorne-Hardy, Jonathan. *Sex the Measure of All Things: A Life of Alfred C. Kinsey.* Bloomington, Ind.: Indiana University Press, 2000.

Kidwell, Claudia Brush, and Valerie Steele, eds. *Men and Women: Dressing the Part.* Washington, D.C.: Smithsonian Institution Press, 1989.

Robinson, Paul. *The Modernization of Sex: Havelock Ellis, Alfred Kinsey, William Masters, and Virginia Johnson.* New York: Harper & Row, 1976.

Weeks, Jeffrey. *Coming Out: Homosexual Politics in Britain from the Nineteenth Century to the Present.* London: Quartet, 1977.

### No Body's Perfect

#### *Works Cited*

Jones, James. *The Thin Red Line.* New York: Scribner, 1962.

Kerouac, Jack. "Belief and Technique for Modern Prose." *Evergreen Review* 2, 8 (1959): 159–60.

———. *On the Road* [1957]. New York: Penguin, 1976.

Plath, Sylvia. *The Bell Jar* [1966]. New York: Bantam, 1972.

#### *Other Useful Works*

Keen, Sam. *Fire in the Belly: On Being a Man.* New York: Bantam, 1991.

Richie, Donald. *Some Aspects of Japanese Popular Culture.* Tokyo: n.p., 1981.

### War Without a Front

#### *Works Cited*

Caputo, Philip. *A Rumor of War.* New York: Holt, Rinehart & Winston, 1977.

Fanon, Frantz. *Black Skin, White Masks,* tr. Charles Lam Markmann. New York: Grove, 1967.

———. *The Wretched of the Earth,* tr. Constance Farrington. New York: Grove, 1963.

Karnow, Stanley. *Vietnam: A History.* New York: Penguin, 1983.

Manchester, William. *American Caesar: Douglas MacArthur, 1880–1964.* Boston: Little, Brown, 1978.

#### *Other Useful Works*

Addington, Larry H. *America's War in Vietnam: A Short Narrative History.* Bloomington, Ind.: Indiana University Press, 2000.

Crozier, Brian. *De Gaulle.* New York: Scribner, 1973.

Donovan, Colonel James A. *Militarism, U.S.A.,* foreword by General David M. Shoup. New York: Scribner, 1970.

Drucker, Peter F. *Concept of the Corporation,* with new intro. by the author. New Brunswick, N.J.: Transaction, 1983.

Gabriel, Richard A., and Paul L. Savage. *Crisis in Command: Mismanagement in the Army.* New York: Hill and Wang, 1978.

Hackworth, David H., and Julie Sherman. *About Face: The Odyssey of an American Warrior.* New York: Simon & Schuster, 1989.

Herr, Michael. *Dispatches.* New York: Knopf, 1977.

Horne, Alistair. *The French Army and Politics, 1870–1970.* New York: Peter Bedrick, 1984.

Jamieson, Neil L. *Understanding Vietnam.* Berkeley: University of California Press, 1993.

Jeffords, Susan. *The Remasculinization of America: Gender and the Vietnam War.* Bloomington, Ind.: Indiana University Press, 1989.

Kolodziej, Edward A. *French International Policy Under De Gaulle and Pompidou: The Politics of Grandeur.* Ithaca, N.Y.: Cornell University Press, 1974.

Lacouture, Jean. *De Gaulle,* tr. Frances K. Price. New York: New American Library, 1966.

Langguth, A. J. *Our Vietnam: The War, 1954–1975.* New York: Simon & Schuster, 2000.

Lembcke, Jerry. *The Spitting Image: Myth, Memory, and the Legacy of Vietnam.* New York: New York University Press, 1998.

Shay, Jonathan. *Achilles in Vietnam: Combat Trauma and the Undoing of Character.* New York: Atheneum, 1994.

## Make Love, Not War

### *Works Cited*

Ardrey, Robert. *African Genesis: A Personal Investigation into the Animal Origins and Nature of Man.* New York: Atheneum, 1966.

De Beauvoir, Simone. *The Second Sex,* tr. H. M. Parshley. New York: Bantam, 1961.

Friedan, Betty. *The Feminine Mystique.* New York: Norton, 1963.

Lorenz, Konrad. *On Aggression,* tr. Marjorie Kerr Wilson. New York: Harcourt, Brace, 1966.

### *Other Useful Works*

Berkowitz, Leonard. *Aggression: A Social Psychological Analysis.* New York: McGraw-Hill, 1962.

———. *Aggression: Its Causes, Consequences, and Control.* Philadelphia: Temple University Press, 1993.

Davis, Kingsley. "Wives and Work: The Sex Role Revolution and Its Consequences." *Population and Development Review* 10, 3 (1984): 397–417.

Ehrenreich, Barbara. *Blood Rites: Origins and History of the Passions of War.* New York: Metropolitan, 1997.

Feshbach, Seymour, and Jolanta Zagrodzka, eds. *Aggression: Biological, Developmental, and Social Perspectives.* New York: Plenum, 1997.

Kemper, Theodore D. *Social Structure and Testosterone.* New Brunswick, N.J.: Rutgers University Press, 1990.

Martin, Paul, and Patrick Bateson. *Measuring Behaviour: An Introductory Guide,* 2d ed. Cambridge, England: Cambridge University Press, 1993.

## Parting Words

### *Works Cited*

Bly, Robert. *Iron John: A Book About Men.* Reading, Mass.: Addison-Wesley, 1990.

Judt, Tony. "America and the War." *New York Review of Books,* November 15, 2001, 4–6.

### *Other Useful Works*

Brod, Harry, ed. *The Making of Maculinities: The New Men's Studies.* Boston: Allen & Unwin, 1987.

Brogan, Patrick. *World Conflicts: A Comprehensive Guide to World Strife Since 1945.* Lanham, Md.: Scarecrow, 1998.

Faludi, Susan. *Stiffed: The Betrayal of the American Man.* New York: William Morrow, 1999.

Lewis, Bernard. *The Middle East: A Brief History of the Last 2,000 Years.* New York: Scribner, 1995.

Marwick, Arthur. *War and Social Change in the Twentieth Century.* New York: St. Martin's, 1974.

———, ed. *Total War and Social Change.* New York: St. Martin's, 1988.

Rashid, Ahmed. *Taliban: Militant Islam, Oil, and Fundamentalism in Central Asia.* New Haven, Conn.: Yale University Press, 2000.

Riesebrodt, Martin. *Pious Passion: The Emergence of Modern Fundamentalism in the United States and Iran,* tr. Don Reneau. Berkeley: University of California Press, 1993.

Simons, Anna. *The Company They Keep: Life Inside the U.S. Army Special Forces.* New York: Free Press, 1997.

Speir, Hans. *Social Order and the Risks of War.* New York: George W. Stewart, 1952.

# *Acknowledgments*

In the seven and more years this book has traveled from its beginnings to this final form, I have depended heavily on many different sources of information, immense amounts of the learning of others, hints and happenstances of conversations, comments, criticism, and challenges.

I am deeply indebted in particular to those who have read sections and in some cases the entire manuscript to give me the benefit of their perspective and knowledge: Joyce Appleby, Dorothy Braudy, Carol Clover, Marc Cooper, Joseph Dane, Jim Kincaid, Del Kolve, Ian Mitroff, James Penner, Dana Polan, Eugen Weber, and Jay Winter.

Two people deserve special thanks: Sandy Dijkstra, my agent, who was in on the project from the beginning and was unflagging in her energy and enthusiasm for it, and Jon Segal, my editor at Knopf, whose careful attention to the flow of what I was trying to say as well as to the many details of my argument has improved the book immeasurably.

Ken Evans, Dave Tomkins, and Frank Mabee helped track down many of the more elusive facts. Others have added important details, directed me to crucial sources, and in a variety of ways improved what I was trying to accomplish here: Ramona Bajema, Adam Bellow, Warren Bennis, Joe Boone, Alex Capron, Erwin Chemerinsky, Susan Faludi, Tuck Finch, Judith Jackson Fossett, Grace Gabe, Edward Gregg, Tim Gustafson, Cliff Irwin, Bruce Jackson, Marsha Kinder, Joyce Kozloff, Max Kozloff, Julie Kwan, Philippa Levine, Vincent Malle, Peter Nosco, Geoff Nunberg, Robert Nye, Jack Peradotto, Bob Putnam, Russ Rhymer, Ben Schwarz, Giles Slade, Kevin Starr, Stephen Toulmin, Alan Trachtenberg, Treva Tucker, Kenny Turan, Stephen Saunders Webb, and a special nod to Dorothy Gallagher, whose commitment to fatalistic biological theories forced me to come up with better arguments for my point of view.

By publishing two articles, on the widely disparate subjects of seventeenth-century premature ejaculation poetry and 1950s Method acting, Larry Goldstein at the *Michigan Quarterly Review* encouraged my own interest in this subject before I knew it was a subject. Early on as well, attending a series of discussions on masculinity headed by Sam Keen made me aware of how one incisive but sympathetic mind might frame and then explore some of these issues. Talking with Glenn Foy in the years of the genesis of this project especially helped develop my own ability to voyage in those waters. I want to thank as well those who invited me to speak about these interests and in the process helped me shape my ideas, especially Bruce Jackson at SUNY-Buffalo and my friends and colleagues at the Los Angeles Institute of the Humanities.

My search for appropriate illustrations was aided by the kindness and expertise of Ken Brown; Tom Crow and the incredibly helpful staff at the Getty Research Institute; Jane Handel, finder of strange photographs extraordinaire; Selma Holo and Jennifer Jaskowiak at the Fisher Gallery of the University of Southern California; Alan Jutzi at the Huntington Library; Barbara Plante of the Springfield Museum of Fine Arts; David Rodes and Claudine P. Dixon of the Grunwald Center, Armand Hammer Museum; and Carol Wells and Michele Urton at the Center for the Study of Political Graphics.

Finally, I want to thank my wife, Dorothy, the finest first reader a writer could hope for, sympathetic, critical, quick to spot the false notes and eager to praise the harmonious ones. I miss our cat Frank, who spent so many hours on my lap curled up while I read and wrote. Thanks as well to the otherwise egregious Colonel Griffith J. Griffith, who despite his many sins managed to leave the city of Los Angeles the land that became Griffith Park, along whose wandering paths I tried to sort out a good portion of the ideas and history explored here.

# Index

## *Illustration Credits*

Column of Marcus Aurelius: Scala/Art Resource, New York
Bayeux Tapestry (the Battle of Hastings): courtesy of the town of Bayeux, France
The duke of Anhalt: Universitätbibliothek, Heidelberg, Codex Manesse (Cod. Pal. Germ. 848)
Trench warfare: courtesy of the Robert Hunt Library, London
Mars and Venus: Alinari/Art Resource, New York
Bayeux Tapestry (cleric striking a woman): courtesy of the town of Bayeux, France
*Venus and Mars Surprised by Vulcan* (Goltzius): The J. Paul Getty Museum, Los Angeles. © The J. Paul Getty Museum
*Venus and Mars Surprised by Vulcan* (Boucher): by kind permission of the Trustees of the Wallace Collection, London
Ulrich von Liechtenstein: Universitätbibliothek, Heidelberg, Codex Manesse (Cod. Pal. Germ. 848)
Saint Demetrius: by permission of the Metropolitan Museum of Art, The Cloisters
Saint Michael: courtesy of the Pinacoteca Nazionale di Siena
Saint Sebastian: courtesy of the National Gallery of Art, London
*Knight, Death, and the Devil* (Dürer): Henry E. Huntington Library and Art Gallery
*Portrait of a Halberdier* (Pontormo): The J. Paul Getty Museum, Los Angeles. © The J. Paul Getty Museum
*Captain Thomas Lee* (Gheerarts): Tate Gallery, London/Art Resource, New York
*Jim Bridger, in a Suit of English Armor* (Miller): Joslyn Museum, Omaha, Nebraska
*Prince Albert at Age Twenty-Four* (Thornton): Royal Collection, copyright reserved to Her Majesty Queen Elizabeth II
Parliamentary Recruiting Committee poster: Henry E. Huntington Library and Art Gallery
*The Battle of Wimpfen* (Merian): Henry E. Huntington Library and Art Gallery
*The Hanging* (Callot): courtesy of the Grunwald Collection of Graphic Art, UCLA
*The Children of Count Karl Gustav Wrangel* (Ehrenstahl): © Skokloster Castle Archives, Stockholm
*Morizumi Being Blown Up by a Landmine* (Kuniyoshi): Springfield (Mass.) Museum of Fine Arts
General Custer, Officers and Ladies (Barry): Denver Public Library, Western History Collection

Earlobes: from Salvatore Ottolengi, *Trattato di Polizia Scientifica*
Four-pointed urethral ring: from J. L. Milton, *On the Pathology and Treatment of Gonorrhea and Spermatorrhea*
Boy with toy rifle: collection of the author
Patriotic pinafores: courtesy of the Weidenfeld and Nicolson archives
Child's painting book: Henry E. Huntington Library and Art Gallery
*Destroy This Mad Brute* (Hopps): courtesy of the Hoover Institution Archives
*Joan of Arc Saved France* (Coffin): Henry E. Huntington Library and Art Gallery
*The Barricades* (Dix): Grunwald Center for the Graphic Arts, UCLA. Gift of Mr. and Mrs. Stanley I. Talpis. © 2003 Artists Rights Society (ARS), New York/VG Bild-Kunst, Bonn
European soldier and Polynesian warrior: from F. A. Hornibrook, *The Culture of the Abdomen* (1927)
T. E. Lawrence: Henry E. Huntington Library and Art Gallery
*Soldier Holding Shovel with Banner* (Sengai): anonymous private collection
Batchelor cartoon: © *New York Daily News*, L. P., reprinted with permission
*By His Deeds Measure Yours* (Falter): courtesy of Magazine Publishers of America
*I Want You . . . for the Navy* (Christy): collection of the author
Draft Resistance poster: image courtesy of Center for the Study of Political Graphics
*Impotent:* collection of the author

## ALSO BY LEO BRAUDY

*"Rich in original insights . . . a marvelously provocative study."* —The New York Times Book Review

### THE FRENZY OF RENOWN

*Fame and Its History*

For Alexander the Great, fame meant accomplishing what no mortal had ever accomplished before. For Julius Caesar, personal glory was indistinguishable from that of Rome. The early Christians devalued public recognition, believing that the only true audience was God. And Marilyn Monroe owed much of her fame to the fragility that led to self-destruction. These are only some of the dozens of figures that populate Leo Braudy's panoramic history of fame, a book that tells us as much about vast cultural changes as it does about the men and women who at different times captured their societies' regard.

Spanning thousands of years and fields ranging from politics to literature and mass media, *The Frenzy of Renown* explores the unfolding relationship between the famous and their audiences, between fame and the representations that make it possible. Hailed as a landmark, here is a major work that provides our celebrity-obsessed, post-historical society with a usable past.

History/Cultural Studies/0-679-77630-3